D0164799

Marketing Across Cultures

Fifth edition

Marketing Across Cultures

Jean-Claude Usunier

Julie Anne Lee

 Prentice Hall
FINANCIAL TIMES

An imprint of **Pearson Education**
Harlow, England • London • New York • Boston • San Francisco • Toronto
Sydney • Tokyo • Singapore • Hong Kong • Seoul • Taipei • New Delhi
Cape Town • Madrid • Mexico City • Amsterdam • Munich • Paris • Milan

Pearson Education Limited

Edinburgh Gate
Harlow
Essex CM20 2JE
England

and Associated Companies throughout the world

Visit us on the World Wide Web at:
www.pearsoned.co.uk

First published 1992
Second edition published 1996
Third edition published 2000
Fourth edition published 2005
Fifth edition published 2009

© Prentice Hall Europe 1992, 1996
© Pearson Education Limited 2000, 2005, 2009

The rights of Jean-Claude Usunier and Julie Anne Lee to be identified as author(s)
of this work have been asserted by them in accordance with the Copyright, Designs
and Patents Act 1988.

All rights reserved. No part of this publication may be reproduced, stored in a retrieval
system, or transmitted in any form or by any means, electronic, mechanical, photocopying,
recording or otherwise, without either the prior written permission of the publisher or
a licence permitting restricted copying in the United Kingdom issued by the Copyright
Licensing Agency Ltd, Saffron House, 6–10 Kirby Street, London EC1N 8TS.

All trademarks used herein are the property of their respective owners. The use of any
trademark in this text does not vest in the author or publisher any trademark ownership
rights in such trademarks, nor does the use of such trademarks imply any affiliation
with or endorsement of this book by such owners.

ISBN: 978-0-273-71391-3

British Library Cataloguing-in-Publication Data
A catalogue record for this book is available from the British Library

Library of Congress Cataloging-in-Publication Data
Usunier, Jean-Claude.
    Marketing across cultures / Jean-Claude Usunier, Julie Anne Lee. – 5th ed.
      p. cm.
    Includes bibliographical references and index.
    ISBN 978-0-273-71391-3
    1. Export marketing–Social aspects. 2. International business enterprises–
Social aspects. 3. Intercultural communication. I. Lee, Julie, 1948– II. Title.
  HF1416.U85 2009
  658.8′4–dc22

                                    2008038953

10 9 8 7 6 5 4 3 2
11 10 09

Typeset in 10/12pt Minion by 35
Printed by Ashford Colour Press Ltd, Gosport

The publisher's policy is to use paper manufactured from sustainable forests.

Brief contents

Contents

14 Intercultural marketing communications 2: personal selling, networking and public relations   423

Introduction
Marketing in the global villages

Classical consumer marketing textbooks generally emphasize world markets and are often cross-border extensions of American marketing thought, blatantly ignoring people, languages and cultures and implicitly arguing in favour of uniformity. Whereas large multinational companies, such as Mars, Pepsi-Cola, L'Oréal or Nestlé, in fact do not follow traditional textbook recipes: their practice is always much more adaptive to and respectful of local contexts. This text offers a different approach to global marketing, based on the recognition of diversity in world markets and on local consumer knowledge and marketing practices. We invite the reader to undertake an exercise in de-centring. We try to break out of our 'Francocentric' and 'Aussie-centric' boxes, in much the same way as Gorn[1] invites us to break out of 'North American boxes'. Understanding international diversity[a] in consumer behaviour, advertising, sales and marketing management becomes the central teaching objective for an international marketing textbook.

This text adopts a cultural approach to international marketing, which has two main dimensions:

1. A cross-cultural approach, which begins by *comparing* national marketing systems and local commercial customs in various countries. It aims to emphasize what is country specific and what is universal. Such an approach is essential for the preparation and implementation of marketing strategies in different national contexts.
2. An intercultural approach, which is centred on the study of *interaction* between business people, buyers and sellers (and their companies) who have different national/cultural backgrounds. This intercultural view also extends to the interaction between products (their physical and symbolic attributes, as well as the messages surrounding them) from a definite nation-culture and consumers from a different nation-culture. Thus, interaction is meant in a broad sense: not only between people, but also between people and messages, and people and products. In this book, commerce is emphasized as much as marketing. When the word *commerce* is used in this text, it refers to the complex dimensions of business relationships entwined with interpersonal relations.

The basic assumption behind this book is that culture penetrates our inner being subconsciously and at a deep level. World cultures share many common features. Nevertheless, when common elements are combined they all display a unique style, *vis-à-vis* kinship patterns, education systems, valuation of the individual and the group, emphasis on economic activities, friendship patterns, time-related organization patterns, the criteria for aesthetic appreciation, and so on. The examples that are used in this book are by their very nature eclectic. We have chosen examples that seem to be the most striking and pertinent.

This book does not try to describe cultures exhaustively, or from an insider's point of view. What we have attempted to provide for the reader is *a method for dealing with intercultural situations in international marketing*. The underlying postulate of this book is that international marketing relationships have to be built on solid foundations. Transaction costs in international trade are high: only a stable and firmly established link between business people can enable them to overcome disagreements and conflicts of interest. In international marketing it is advisable to be very methodical and long-term oriented, to select a limited number of partners and opportunities, and to develop them to their fullest extent.

Changes in the fifth edition

The fifth edition has been extensively rewritten, and a numerical referencing system incorporated into the text, to improve the readability and flow of ideas. The dramatic increase in the number of cross cultural and international marketing studies published in the last few years has seen many of the original research findings extended to other cultures, other contexts and integrated with other theories and ideas. Rather than include details of each study, we have summarized the results to present a more cohesive picture (where possible) and referenced examples of the research in the area. Full reference lists, including the most current articles are available on the following website: **www.pearsoned.co.uk/usunier**.

This edition has been refocused on the marketing discipline. Marketing related examples have been added throughout to stimulate the readers application of cross cultural ideas to this discipline. Several less relevant sections and chapters were removed, including those dealing with the regionalization of country environments and the negotiation chapters.

Finally, interesting facts and ideas that can be found on the Internet have been added to web boxes throughout the text. Hot links to further information about these facts and ideas can be found on the following website **www.pearsoned.co.uk/usunier**. We would like to encourage readers to access these links and explore the many interesting paths to which these links lead. We invite readers to visit this website, to use it jointly with the book, and to give us feedback, suggestions, and information which they think might increasing the site's relevance and exhaustiveness.

Target audience

This book is designed for instructors and students who consider global diversity as an asset and an opportunity, rather than a liability or a threat, and who find pleasure in discovering new ways of life and experiencing the challenge of cultural differences in world markets. *Marketing Across Cultures* is particularly useful and relevant in the case of multicultural, multilingual, and multinational classes, institutions and/or countries. This book is to be proposed as a primary textbook for those instructors who want to emphasize culture, sales, negotiations, and a cross-cultural approach to consumer behaviour and market research, and as a secondary text for other IM instructors who want to follow a more traditional approach to international marketing.

The fifth edition has been written for:

- senior undergraduate students who already have studied a marketing management course;
- postgraduate students (MBA in particular) for a cross-cultural/international marketing elective course;
- research students who have a in-depth interest in cultural and comparative aspects of International Business and Global Marketing; and
- senior executives for developing culturally-sensitive approaches to global marketing strategy.

For instructors

All cases mentioned in the book are freely accessible in their electronic version to instructors using the book. For accessing other cases on the *Marketing Across Culture*'s Site, contact **npjcu@hotmail.com** (please sign your mail with your institutional signature, indicate the URL of your personal webpage on your institution's site and attach your course outline).

Additional references per chapter and large bibliographies on some particular issues (country-of-origin, cross-cultural advertising, international business negotiations, and so on) are available to instructors on: **www.hec.unil.ch/jusunier/teaching/references/index.htm**.

An instructor's manual with suggested answers for end-of-chapter questions, teaching notes for cases, slides, and additional learning resources is available at **www.pearsoned.co.uk/usunier**.

Outline

Part 1, comprising the first three chapters, is devoted to the cultural variable. These chapters try to define it, to delineate the components of culture, and finally to emphasize its dynamic nature. Part 2 deals with the globalization of markets, which is *the* central issue in international marketing; Chapters 4 and 5 examine consumer behaviour, taking both a local and a global perspective, while Chapter 6 deals with local and regional marketing environments. Part 3 presents the general impact of globalization on international marketing strategies (Chapter 7), with special emphasis on a key issue for product policy, namely, the dilemma between adaptation and standardization (Chapter 8). Chapter 9 deals with the complex management of meanings related to brand names for international markets and to country of origin images. In Chapters 10 and 11, which concern price policies and the choice of distribution channels, emphasis has been deliberately placed on the culture-based approaches to such decisions. That is why, for instance, we accentuate bargaining (with its cultural variations) in Chapter 10, and the Japanese *keiretsu* distribution system, in Chapter 11.

Part 4 presents marketing communications in an intercultural environment. It starts with a general overview (Chapter 12) of language, culture and communication issues, which are applied in the next two chapters to advertising issues, personal selling, public relations and bribery and ethical issues in international marketing. Table I.1 presents a summary of the basic contents of Chapters 4 to 14, linking culture to marketing issues.

This book is written from both a European and an Australasian viewpoint with many examples relating to these two areas of the world. As with all international marketing texts, this one is not universal. It may be percieved as being less pragmatically written and less issue-oriented than most. Statements may sometimes be classed as value judgements, since they are not always supported by empirical evidence, as is the case in American textbooks. Therefore this book may sometimes seem unusual to native English-speaking readers. We regard this approach as part of the message of the book: it is a more contextual, and therefore less explicit.

Each chapter concludes with questions and is followed by an appendix comprising some or all of the following: cases, exercises and critical incidents. In addition, many interesting links, cases and exercises have been included on the book's website (**www.hec.unil.ch/jusunier/teaching/index.htm**) and in the instructor's manual. Since different national versions of this book have been published (Dutch, English, French and German), it may be used in cross-cultural training settings.

Acknowledgements

We wish to acknowledge the help of the academic institutions that have provided us with the opportunity to teach and research international marketing

Table I.1 The impact of cultural differences on selected aspects of marketing

Area of marketing	Cultural differences influence . . .	Chapter
Consumer behaviour	Cross-cultural consumer attitudes and decision making	4
	Local consumers and global consumption	5
Market research	Equivalence and methods in cross-national market surveys	6
Overall marketing strategy	Global versus locally customized marketing strategies	7
Targeting market segments	Cross-border vs. country clustering	7
Product policy	Adaptation or standardization of product attributes	8
Brand image	Brand and country-of-origin evaluations by consumers	9
Price policy	Bargaining rituals/Price-quality evaluations/Price strategies towards consumers, competitors and suppliers	10
Distribution channels	Channel style and service, producer–distributor relationships	11
Communication	World-views (through language) and communication styles	12
Advertising	Tailoring messages to local audiences' cultural traits	13
Personal selling	Selling styles, sales force management, networking and public relations, bribery and ethical issues in an international context	14

over the last ten years. We are also indebted to many colleagues for their ideas and assistance and for encouraging us to put more and more emphasis on the cultural dimension of international marketing. We would also like to thank senior editor Thomas Sigel for his support and Peter Hooper, Aylene Rogers and Colin Reed at Pearson Education who have been instrumental in the production of this book, as well as Saskia Faulk for her great contribution in writing new cases. We accept responsibility for any errors and shortcomings.

Note

a. Here, diversity is not meant in its American sense with a strong anti-discrimination stance (reported for instance by Litvin[2]), but rather in its simplest meaning of 'state or quality of being different or varied', with no value judgement about whether 'diversity' is good or bad. In fact it is neither good nor bad, as shown by Lian and Oneal[3] through a cross-national study linking cultural diversity to economic development for 98 countries over the 1960–1985 period.

References

1. Gorn, Gerald J. (1997), 'Breaking out of the North American box', in Merrie Brucks and Debbie McInnis (eds), *Advances in Consumer Research*, vol. 24, Association for Consumer Research: Provo, UT, pp. 6–7.
2. Lian, Brad and John R. Oneal (1997), 'Cultural diversity and economic development: a cross-national study of 98 countries, 1960–1985', *Economic Development and Cultural Change*, vol. 46, no. 1, pp. 61–77.
3. Litvin, Deborah R. (1997), 'The discourse of diversity: from biology to management', *Organization*, vol. 4, no. 2, pp. 187–209.

Acknowledgements

We are grateful to the following for permission to reproduce copyright material:

Figure 3.1 from Hofstede, G., 'Motivation, leadership and organization: do American theories apply abroad?', *Organizational Dynamics*, 9(1), pp. 42–63, copyright 1980, with permission from Elsevier; Table 3.4 from *Culture's Consequences*, 2nd edn, Sage Publications Inc. Books (Hofstede, G., 2001), with kind permission of Professor Hofstede; Table A4.1 from Solomon, Michael R., *Consumer Behavior: Buying, Having, & Being*, 4th edn, © 1999, reproduced by permission of Pearson Education, Inc., Upper Saddle River, NJ; Table 1 in A4.3: adapted table, based on figures excerpted from the European Commission's 'Progress Report on the Single European Electronic Communications Market 2007' (13th Report), COMN(2008) 153 final/[SEC(2008) 356]; Table 2 A4.3 reprinted with permission from *Innovation* (Summer 2002), the Quarterly of the Industrial Designers Society of America, p: 703.707.6000; f: 703.787.8501, e: **idsa@idsa.org**, w: **www.idsa.org**; Table 6.1 from *Consumer Behavior*, 4th edn, Samuel, Craig C. and Douglas, Susan P., 2001, © John Wiley & Sons Limited, reprinted with permission; Table 6.3 © March 1978 by ESOMAR® The World Association of Research Professionals (this article first appeared in *European Research*, published by ESOMAR); Table 8.3 from Lange, André and Newman-Baudais, Susan (2003), 'World Film Market Trends, Focus 2003', Marché du Film, European Audiovisual Observatory, May 2003 (**www.obs.coe.int**); Table 8.4 IMES Research (2002) 'The Food Service Market in Saudi Arabia', IMES Consulting Ltd, 2002; Table 12.1 from *Ethnologue*, 12th edn, Languages of the World, SIL International (1992); Table 12.2 from *Nielsen Net Ratings*, 2003, published by Nielsen/Net Ratings, Oxford; Figure 13.2 from 'Coordinating international advertising' in *Journal of Marketing*, 42(1), January, pp. 28–34, American Marketing Association (Peebles, D.M., Ryans, J.K. Jr and Vernon, I.R., 1978); Table 13.1 from 'Branding new and improved wars' in *FAIR*, Solomon, Norman, October 2002, reprinted with permission, and also from 'The art of naming operations' in *Parameters*, pp. 81–98, Seiminiski, Gregory C.I. (1995), reprinted with permission.

We are grateful to the following for permission to reproduce the following texts:

Extracts in A2.1 and A3.2: A2.1 from Ferraro, Gary, *Cultural Dimensions of International Business,* 5th edn © 2006, reproduced by permission of Pearson Education, Inc., Upper Saddle River, NJ; extracts in A2.2, A2.3 and A3.2 from *Intercultural Interactions: A Practical Guide* by Brislin, Richard W., Cushner, Kenneth, Cherrie, Craig and Young, Mahealani, copyright 1986 by Sage Publications Inc. Books, reproduced with permission of Sage Publications Inc. Books in the format Textbook via Copyright Clearance Center; extract in A2.4 from Usunier, J.-C. and Napoleon-Biguma, C., 'Gestion culturelle du temps: Le cas Bantou', in *Management Interculturel: Modes et Modeles*, Economica (Gauthey, F. and Xardel, D., eds, 1991), pp. 95–114; extract in Box 3.2 from Hofstede, G., *Cultures and Organizations: Software of the Mind*, McGraw-Hill, (Hofstede, G., 1991), with kind permission of Professor Hofstede; extract on p. 39 from *Male and Female: A Study of the Sexes in a Changing World*, pp. 7–8, William Morrow (Mead, M., 1948), copyright © 1949 Margaret Mead, reprinted by permission of HarperCollins Publishers, William Morrow; extract on p. 49 from *Culture's Consequence*, 2nd edn, Sage Publications Inc. Books, (Hofstede, G., 2001), by kind permission of Professor Hofstede; extract on p. 78 from *Journal of Consumer Satisfaction, Dissatisfaction and Complaining Behavior*,

Blodgett, Jeffrey, Hill, Donna and Bakir, Aysen, copyright 2006 by *Journal of Consumer Satisfaction, Dissatisfaction and Complaining Behavior*, reproduced with permission of *Journal of Consumer Satisfaction, Dissatisfaction and Complaining Behavior* via Copyright Clearance Center; extract in Box 4.4 from *Le Systeme des objets*, Gallimard (Baudrillard, J., 1968), by kind permission of Verso; extract in A4.1 from Solomon, Michael R., *Consumer Behavior: Buying, Having and Being*, 4th edn © 1999, reprinted by permission of Pearson Education, Inc., Upper Saddle River, NJ; extracts from cases in A4.3, A5.1, A5.2, A5.3, A7.1, A7.2, A8.1, A8.2, A11.2, A12.3, A13.1 and A13.5 from Faulk, Saskia and Usunier, Jean-Claude, The Institute of Research in Management of the University of Lausanne (IRM); extract in Box 5.2 from *Advances in Consumer Research*, Doran, Kathleen Brewer, copyright 1997 by Association for Consumer Research, reproduced with permission of Association for Consumer Research via Copyright Clearance Center; extract in Box 5.5 *Business of Europe: Managing Change* by Steele, Murray, copyright 1991 by Sage Publications Inc. Books, reproduced with permission of Sage Publications Inc. Books in the format Textbook via Copyright Clearance Center; extract in Box 6.4 from 'Qualitative research in developing countries', *Journal of Market Research Society*, 24(2), pp. 90–1, (Goodyear, M., 1982); extract in Box 7.3 Deher, Odile

(1986) 'Quelques facteurs de succès ou la politique de produits de l'entreprise exportatrice: les liens entre marketing et production', *Recherche et Applications en Marketing*, PUG. 1986; extract in A7.4 from *Dangerous Enchantment*, pp. 82–92, Harlequin Books S.A. (Mather, A., 1996); extracts in A9.2 and A9.3 from Cundiff, E.W. and Hilger, M.T., *Marketing in the International Environment*, 2nd edn, © 1988, reproduced by permission of Pearson Education, Inc., Upper Saddle River, NJ; extracts in A10.1 and A12.4 from *International Marketing and Export Management*, pp. 85–7 and 310, Addison Wesley (Albaum, G., Strandskov, J., Duerr E. and Dowd, L., eds), (Duerr, M.S. 1989) permission granted by Pearson Education; extract in Box 12.1 from 'The silent language in overseas business', *Harvard Business Review* (May–June), pp. 87–96 (Hall, Edward T., 1960); extract in Box 13.1 from *International Marketing Review* by Luqmani, Musshtaq, Yavas, Ugur and Quraeshi, Zahir, copyright 1989 by Emerald Group Publishing Limited, reproduced with permission of Emerald Group Publishing Limited via Copyright Clearance Center; extract in Box 14.4 from *L'argent Noir*, by Péan, P., © Librairie Arthème Fayard 1988.

In some instances we have been unable to trace the owners of copyright material, and we would appreciate any information that would enable us to do so.

Part 1 The cultural variable in international marketing

© Getty Images

Introduction to Part 1

In an increasingly interdependent world where barriers to trade and international exchange constantly diminish, cultural differences remain the single most enduring factor to influence marketing strategies. Part 1 of this book introduces key concepts in cultural studies that influence our understanding of local markets and the design of international marketing strategies.

Chapter 1 presents the basic elements of culture and international marketing. It provides a discussion of seminal definitions and major aspects of culture, including language and social institutions. It discusses the sources of culture and the limitations in viewing culture as nationality. This chapter highlights how culture affects the development of skills and how social representations emerge from shared meanings in the community. The objective of Chapter 1 is to enable readers to understand and overcome their own cultural conditioning. The end-of-chapter teaching materials are designed to reinforce this.

Chapter 2 introduces the cultural dynamics of time and space. These basic cultural assumptions impact many aspects of material culture, such as the sense of ownership, preference for durability, and so on. The chapter begins with a model of action based on cultural assumptions, which influences individual decision making. It then examines cross-cultural variability in perceptions of time and space. It also looks at the way we 'borrow' or integrate foreign items and customs into our societies. The last section examines intercultural hostility towards unknown people, including prejudices and negative stereotypes.

Chapter 3 explains how cultural assumptions influence human interactions. It examines how people define who they are and who others are, which is basic to any culture. A series of issues are then examined including how people differ in their attitudes towards action, how they relate thinking to action, how they deal with desires and feelings, and how they cope with rules. This chapter ends with an examination of how cultural assumptions shape actual behaviour.

The cultural process

International marketing gives a prominent place to culture, but not everything is culturally driven. Individual behaviour is influenced, but not determined by culture. Culture is one of the many layers that influence behaviour. Arguably, it is the most difficult to recognize from within and to understand from without.

Understanding what is influenced by culture is more complicated than initially expected. Culture is complex. Our understanding of other cultures is often limited, forcing us to rely on rather shallow or stereotyped ideas about other cultures. Culture is difficult to isolate. International marketers often resort to using country or nation-states as primary segmentation bases, because borders are easily definable. But few nations hold homogeneous ethnic, linguistic and religious groups.

This chapter lays the foundation for arguments that will be developed later in the book. Culture and its major elements are defined. The issue of equating culture with nationality is discussed and alternative categorizations are suggested.

1.1

Defining culture

In French the word *culture* was defined by Emile Littré in his nineteenth-century dictionary as 'cultivation, farming activity'. The abstract sense of the word probably originated in Germany where the word *Kultur* was used as early as the eighteenth century to refer to civilization. In the Anglo-Saxon world the abstract notion of culture came into widespread use at the beginning of the twentieth century. Below, we cite several definitions, each one adding to the

cultural jigsaw puzzle, to determine the main aspects of this abstract and elusive concept.

Website link 1.1

Examine other definitions of culture from the Centre for Advanced Research on Language Acquisition (CARLA): **http://www.carla.umn.edu/culture/definitions.html**.

Particular solutions to universal problems

Kluckhohn and Strodtbeck (p. 10) emphasize the following basic points:

1. '. . . there is a limited number of common human problems for which all peoples at all times must find some solution.'
2. 'While there is a variability in solutions of all the problems, it is neither limitless nor random but is definitely variable within a range of possible solutions.'
3. '. . . all alternatives of all solutions are present in all societies at all times, but are differentially preferred. Every society has, in addition to its dominant profile of value orientations, numerous variant or substitute profiles.'[1]

How does culture link the individual to society?

Ralph Linton (p. 21)[2] emphasizes the link between culture and the individual: 'A culture is the configuration of learned behaviour and results of behaviour whose component elements are shared and transmitted by the members of a particular society.' Linton also emphasizes the limits of cultural programming that society can impose on an individual (pp. 14–15):

No matter how carefully the individual has been trained or how successful his conditioning has been, he remains a distinct organism with his own needs and with capacities for independent thought, feeling and action. Moreover he retains a considerable degree of individuality. . . . Actually, the role of the individual with respect to society is a double one. Under ordinary circumstances, the more perfect his conditioning and consequent integration into the social structure, the more effective his contribution to the smooth functioning of the whole and the surer his rewards. However, societies have to exist and function in an ever-changing world. The unparalleled ability of our species to adjust to changing conditions and to develop ever more effective responses to familiar ones rests upon the residue of individuality which survives in every one of us after society and culture have done their utmost. As a simple unit in the social organism, the individual perpetuates the status quo.[2]

Culture is useful to society and to the individual. Everyday tasks are simplified by the unwritten rules we understand through participation in our society. According to Goodenough,[3] culture is a set of beliefs or standards, shared by a group of people, which help the individual decide what is, what can be, how to feel, what to do and how to go about doing it. With this definition there is no reason for culture to be equated with the whole of one particular society. It may be more appropriate to activities shared by a particular group of people. Thus, individuals may share different cultures by interacting with different groups. These people 'switch into' the culture that is operational within a given group. The term 'operational' describes a culture that is shared by those who must cooperate on a task.

Goodenough's concept of 'operational culture' assumes that the individual can choose the culture in which to interact at any given moment or in any given situation, subject to the overriding condition that the culture has been correctly internalized from past experiences. The concept of operational culture is somewhat debatable, but it has the advantage of highlighting the multicultural nature of today's societies, which include bi-nationals, multilinguals, and even people who have a particular national identity and an international professional or corporate culture. It also draws our attention to the sources of an individual's acculturation.

1.2

Elements of culture

Culture is identified by the sum of its elements, which are organically interrelated and work as a coherent set. These interrelated elements include knowledge, beliefs and values, arts, law, manners and morals and all other kinds of skills and habits acquired by members of society. These elements are acquired and also reinforced by our biology, language, social institutions and material and symbolic productions. Culture is not only a 'toolbox' but also provides some 'directions for use' in daily communal life.

As Malinowski (p. 75) states: 'We have to base our theory of culture on the fact that all human beings belong to an animal species. . . . No culture can continue if the group is not replenished continually and normally.'[4] He develops the example of eating habits, which must be regarded as both biological *and* cultural:

Cultural determination is a familiar fact as regards hunger or appetite, in short the readiness to eat. Limitations of what is regarded as palatable, admissible, ethical; the magical religious, hygienic and social taboos on quality, raw materials, and preparation of food; the habitual routine establishing the time and the type of appetite – all these could be exemplified from our civilization, from the rules and principles of Judaism, or Islam, Brahmanism or Shintoism, as well as from every primitive culture.[4]

This demonstrates how the biological need of hunger may be influenced by aspects of culture.

Website link 1.2

See more information about Malinowski, who championed the modern ethnographic method of long term fieldwork in the Trobriand Islands from 1915 to 1918: http://www.vanderbilt.edu/Ans/Anthro/Anth206/malinowski.htm.

The major elements of culture include:

a) Language.
b) Institutions.
c) Material productions.
d) Symbolic productions.

A cultural item may belong to one or more of these four elements of culture simultaneously, which then appear as different layers. For instance, music is at once a language, an institution, an artistic production and also a symbolic element.

Language as an element of culture

Language is an important aspect of culture. Linguist and anthropologist Benjamin Lee Whorf, a chemical engineer working for a fire insurance company, spent his spare time tracing the origins and grammar of American Indian languages.[5] He is the author of a seminal, and quite controversial, hypothesis, often referred to as the Whorfian hypothesis or Whorf–Sapir hypothesis. Aspects of this theory have been incorporated, either explicitly or implicitly, at many points in this book, particularly those chapters in which language and linguistic issues are prominent, including market research (Chapter 6), branding (Chapter 9), and marketing communication (Chapters 13 and 14).

Whorf maintains that the language we learn in our native community shapes and structures our world view and our social behaviour. It influences how we select issues, solve problems and act. Although the Whorfian hypothesis has been harshly criticized by many linguists, it remains a fundamental metaphor, though not a fully validated scientific theory.

Language, especially through tenses and words, shapes time-related behaviour, which in turn influences both consumer and business attitudes and behaviours, including punctuality, opening times, and bargaining. For instance, the African Bantu people, unlike most Western cultures, do not have a specific word that clearly differentiates the 'here' and the 'now'. They have a common time–space localizer (see Appendix A2.4 'Reading').

Institutions as an element of culture

Institutional elements are the 'spine' of the cultural process, linking the individual to the group. Institutions include the family, as well as political institutions, or any kind of social organization that encourages an individual to comply with rules in exchange for various rewards (e.g. being fed, loved, paid, and so on). These rules are not static and an individual may also sometimes act as a proactive agent of change within an institution.

Malinowski[4] compiled a list of seven universal principles around which institutions are formed across cultures.

1. The principle of *reproduction* integrates people around blood relationships and marriage as an established contractual framework.
2. The principle of *territoriality* integrates people around common interests dictated by neighbourhood and vicinity.
3. The principle of *physiology* integrates people around their sex, age, and physical traits or defects. This includes the sexual division of labour, sex roles, the relationship patterns between age groups, and the way minority members of the community are treated.
4. The principle of *spontaneous tendency to join together* integrates people around common goals. This includes various kinds of associations, such as primitive secret societies, clubs, artistic societies, etc.
5. The principle of *occupational and professional activities* integrates people around labour divisions and expertise. In modern societies, this includes industry organizations, trade unions, courts, the police, the army, educational institutions and religious bodies.
6. The principle of *hierarchy* integrates people around rank and status, including the nobility, the middle class and slaves, or more generally any kind of social class system or caste system.
7. The principle of *totality* integrates diverse elements into a reasonably coherent whole. The political process (e.g., feudal, democratic, theocratic, dictatorial, etc.) expresses the need for totality. Examining any one level of institution in isolation provides only a limited picture of how a culture operates. To gain a more complex picture, some researchers have begun to examine multi-level relationships between institutions and values at the individual level. One such database is the World Values Survey, which tracks basic values and beliefs of various publics within and across countries.

Website link 1.3

Visit the World Values Survey website to learn more about values and cultural changes in societies all over the world: **http://www.worldvaluesurvey.org**.

Material productions as an element of culture

The products or outputs of our society transmit, reproduce, update and improve the knowledge and skills in the community. These include physical outputs, as well as intellectual, artistic and service outputs. They include tools, machines, factories, paper, books, instruments and media of communication, food, clothing, ornaments, etc.

We often confuse an influential civilization (which corresponds to the German word *Kultur*) with a cultural community that successfully produces many goods and services. Material consumption and wealth do not necessarily equate with cultural sophistication. Any ordering of the world's cultures is purely subjective. Cultural attitudes to material goods vary enormously. For example, Kumar[6] discusses the differing world views in India and China. The Indian world view based on Brahmanism has the goal of inner spirituality. It emphasizes spirituality over achievement and does not place a high value on wealth, acquisition or production. Conversely, the Chinese world view is based on Confucian Pragmatism with the goal being harmonious social order. It emphasizes meritocracy and hard work, focusing on action in the material, rather than the spiritual world.

Symbolic productions as an element of culture

Symbolic and sacred elements determine the relationship between the physical and the metaphysical world. In some cultures, any kind of metaphysical world is denied. In other cultures, the metaphysical world is present in everyday life. Cultural communities try to define, through religious and moral beliefs, whether there is life after death, and if so of what kind. The scientific movement, especially at the end of the nineteenth century, seemed close to pushing back the boundaries of the metaphysical world. Nowadays, most scientists recognize that the metaphysical question will never be fully resolved by knowledge. What is of interest to us is not the answers to these questions, but how moral and religious assumptions in various cultures impact on individual and group behaviour.

Numerous illustrations of the strength of the symbolic dimension are given throughout the book. In the area of marketing communication, our cultural interpretation of symbols is of the utmost importance. That is, products and their advertising communicate through the symbolism of colour, shape, label, brand name, and so on, but the interpretation of symbols is strongly culture bound. Different symbolic interpretations can have dire consequences for brands. For instance, brands that incorporate lucky numbers (e.g., 8) are viewed more favourably and those that incorporate unlucky numbers (e.g., 4) are avoided by Chinese consumers.

Traditional societies have always been more consciously involved in symbolic thought and behaviour than modern societies. Since less is *explained*, more must be *related*. For example: Why does the sun shine every day? Should its disappearance be considered ominous? What should be done to satisfy it so that it goes on spreading its generous rays on the fields and rivers? The bloody ritual sacrifices in the pre-Columbian civilizations were heavily charged with symbolic content. Human sacrifices were dedicated to the sun, as were the blood and the living heart, which was pulled out of the bodies of living people.

It is a common mistake to believe that the symbolic dimension has largely disappeared in modern life. Symbols are not only related to religious and metaphysical matters; they also extend into everyday life. We use many symbols or cues that help us understand the complex world we live in.

Culture as a collective fingerprint: are some cultures superior?

Culture is a collective fingerprint of our identity. There are no objectively 'good' or 'bad' elements of a particular cultural group, it all depends on your subjective view. Cultural differences exist, but no culture is *globally* superior or inferior to another. Cultures may be evaluated and ranked, but only on the basis of evidence related to a set of 'culturally determined' criteria and for very specific segments of culture-related activities. Some people may make better warriors, others have finer aesthetic judgement, yet others are more musically gifted.

Culture is a set of *coherent* elements. Comparison might delude us into thinking we could select the best from each culture and arrive at 'ideal' combinations. However, as we will see later on, it is not quite this easy.

A joke about Europeans goes like this: 'Heaven is where the cooks are French, the mechanics are German, the policemen are English, the lovers are Italian and it is all organized by the Swiss. Hell is where the policemen are German, the mechanics are French, the cooks are British, the lovers are Swiss and it is all organized by the Italians.' Not only would it be difficult to take the best traits from a culture while rejecting the worst, but also any attempt to combine the best of several cultures could eventually turn out to be a disaster. This is because *coherence* is needed at the highest level (corresponding to *identity* at the individual level).

1.3

Culture and nationality

Nationality is one way to divide individuals into larger groups – it is operational and convenient. However, the relationship between nationality and culture is unclear. While shared culture is fundamental in building modern nation-states, it is also fundamental at the community level. As soon as nation-states began to emerge, they struggled against local particularisms, such as dialects and customs. Conflicts in large countries often had a strong cultural base, including the War of Secession in the United States, the rivalry between the English and the Scots in the United Kingdom, and the progressive elimination of local powers in the highly centralized French state. Today, we still see major struggles between different religious groups in the Middle East and other Asian countries. These conflicts relate to distinctive cultural elements, including language, values, religion, concepts of freedom, etc.

While many international marketers have equated culture directly with nation-state, there are many reasons to avoid this:

1. A country's culture can only be defined by reference to other countries' cultures. India is a country culture in comparison with Italy or Germany, but the Indian subcontinent is made up of highly diversified ethnic and religious groups including Muslims, Hindus, Sikhs, etc., and with over 20 principal languages.

2. Many nation-states are explicitly multicultural. For instance, Switzerland has four official languages, including German, French, Italian and Rumantsch, which are spoken in different regions of the country. The Swiss political system, established more than seven centuries ago, helps people to successfully manage the complex trade-off between compliance with local cultural peculiarities and a common attitude towards anything that is not Swiss.

Political decisions, especially during the last century, have imposed the formation of new nation-states, particularly through the processes of colonization and decolonization. The borders of these new states, sometimes straight lines on a map, were often set with little regard for cultural realities. Many significant national cultures, such as that of the Kurds (split between the Iraqis, the Syrians, the Turks and the Iranians) have never been accorded the right to a territory or a state.

Sources of culture

The national element is seldom the main source of culture when regarded from an 'operational culture' perspective.[3] Figure 1.1 shows the basic sources of cultural background at the level of the individual. For instance, medical researchers or computer hardware specialists, whatever their nationality, share a common specialized education, common interests, and largely the same professional culture. This is developed through common training, working for the same companies, reading the same publications worldwide and contributing to research where international cross-cultural comparability of purely scientific methods and results is fundamental.

Similarly, social class may be a distinctive source of culture, to a greater or lesser degree, depending on the country. For instance in France and England, where there are traditions of accepted birth inequalities and a strong historical orientation, social class is a very distinctive source of culture; the way one speaks immediately reveals one's social class. However, in

Figure 1.1 Sources of culture

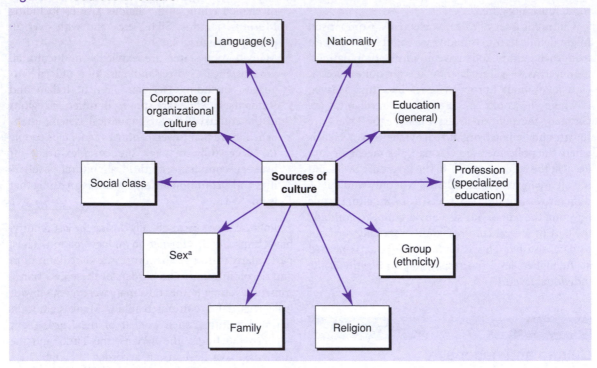

[a] In 1948 the anthropologist Margaret Mead published *Male and Female*,[7] which draws on her in-depth knowledge of several South Pacific and Balinese cultures. It not only depicts their organization of relationships between men and women, the division of labour and roles in the community, but also explains how these patterns may be compared to those of contemporary American society. *Male and Female*, which has continued to be a best-seller, is an excellent and detailed introduction to sex cultures. Although rarely mentioned in this book, which is principally concerned with territory and national culture, the difference between masculine and feminine culture is in fact the most basic cultural distinction.

the United States, Australia, Japan and the Scandinavian countries, this is not so marked. Social class, like sex, is not a territory-based source of culture.

The sense of belonging to an important ethnic group may override the feeling of belonging to a particular nation-state. The Tamil population in Sri Lanka, which makes up about 20 per cent of the total Sri Lankan population, and is mostly centred around Jaffna in the north of the island, is strongly linked with the large Tamil community in southern India (numbering 55 million), which supports them in their claim for autonomy. National cultures with specific, recognized borders are rarely fully homogeneous. The country borders are often facilitated by 'cross-border' cultures. For instance, the area around the border between France and Spain offers

continuity between the two countries: the Basque country to the west and Catalonia to the east. Other examples show that some people have been able to reach a compromise. For instance, the Alsatians in France speak mostly German-based dialects and behave in the workplace like Germans, but they lean towards a sense of French nationality and the adoption of the French lifestyle outside the workplace. People who belong to these 'cross-border' cultures generally have a privileged position as 'exporters' from one country to another.

Physical and climatic conditions are also a fairly systematic, although subtle, source of differentiation. Almost every apparently unified country is made up of a 'North' and a 'South'. Even in a country such as Sweden that is homogeneous from a linguistic, ethnic, religious and institutional point of view, has a fairly marked difference, at least for the Swedes, between the culture and lifestyle of a southern city and a northern town. This difference may not be as strongly perceived by foreigners, who are more aware of their own differences from Swedes and Sweden as a whole.

Cultural homogeneity and relevant segmentation

Most international market segments are primarily based on geographical/geopolitical divisions, which are convenient and may also be efficient segmentation criteria depending on homogeneity. However, sociodemographic variables or lifestyles may be more relevant. Often firms find it difficult to decide whether to target a transnational ethnic segment, a national segment or a cross-border regional segment. Taking the time to review the cultural literature may identify information about cultural groupings that will offer important insights into more homogeneous segments in the market.[8] Chapter 7 examines the issue of global versus regional marketing strategies.

Homogeneity clearly favours the emergence of a coherent culture in a nation-state. This may lead to the confusion of culture with country and the treatment of country as a culturally unified, coherent segment. A better understanding of the following sources of differentiation may lead to more cohesive sociodemographic microsegments:

1. Linguistic homogeneity.
2. Religious homogeneity.
3. Ethnic homogeneity.
4. Climatic homogeneity.
5. Geographical homogeneity.
6. Institutional and political homogeneity.
7. Social/income homogeneity.

The word 'homogeneity' implies one of the following:

1. The existence of a unique modality throughout the whole population (that is, only one religion, or one language) or at the very least limited diversity.
2. An accepted diversity that is officially recognized and supported by the state. For instance, an agreement for maintaining several languages (as in Canada), more or less spoken and/or understood by everybody, or several different religions (as in Germany).
3. 'Perceived homogeneity', which is the perception of acceptable differences within the national community. For instance, people may observe huge differences in wealth and income, but tolerate them for various reasons, including fatalism, indifference or on metaphysical grounds.

It is easy to see that global homogenization is unlikely. Hannerz[9] offers an alternative view of how interactions and exchanges impact cultures. He discusses the Creolization of cultures, which is a continual process where information, meanings and symbolic forms are absorbed by a culture and then transformed to make them their own. The concept and assumptions behind globalization are further discussed in Chapters 4 and 5. Logically, we might expect cultural homogeneity to directly impact national identity, but in fact the elements that tie subcultures together can strengthen nationality. For instance, Sweden is culturally more homogeneous than the United States and as such might be expected to hold a stronger national identity, but in reality it is the United States that has a stronger national identity.[10]

The concept of national culture

National culture relies on the concept of within-country homogeneity and between-country differences. Hofstede's major framework of national culture is briefly introduced here and later discussed in more detail in Chapter 2. Geert Hofstede[11] initially derived four dimensions of culture (individualism/collectivism, power distance, masculinity/femininity, and uncertainty avoidance) and later added a fifth dimension (long/short-term orientation). Hofstede's framework has been used extensively to investigate marketing issues. A more recent alternative to Hofstede's dimensions was proposed by Schwartz and colleagues[12] which incorporates three dimensions at the country level: conservatism/autonomy, hierarchy/egalitarianism, and mastery/harmony. This framework has only received limited attention in marketing.

Culture has many levels or layers, and national culture is too general to avoid the traps of cliché and stereotype. It is difficult for anyone to understand the nuances of multiple cultures. At best national culture offers a broad brushstroke. Cultures more often correspond to linguistic, ethnic, religious or even organizational entities than to nation-states. Despite its limitations, the concept of national culture can still be an interesting Pandora's box.

Website link 1.4

Visit Geert Hofstede's website to compare countries on his cultural dimensions. Try comparing your home country to a country you are studying in or would like to visit: **http://www.geert-hofstede.com/ hofstede-dimensions.php**.

Many believe that culture has a distinct imprint on personality. Personality traits exist for which the average individual in one culture scores significantly higher (or lower) than individuals belonging to another culture. This corresponds to the idea of national character or, more precisely, the concept of a modal personality. The modal personality approach largely grew out of enquiries as to why certain people are more violent, more aggressive, more domineering, and collectively more prone than others to declare war on foreign nations or to organize and implement genocide. These questions stemmed from the Second World War, especially the Nuremberg trials. Numerous empirical studies have been undertaken, particularly during the 1950s and 1960s, taking as a starting point the process of forming national character, which includes child-rearing practices, education systems, the socialization process of children, etc. The results neither prove nor disprove the existence of national character.

Others favour the idea that personality traits are largely free from the influence of culture. According to the anthropologist Ralph Linton (pp. 14–15),[2] the individual's 'integration into society and culture goes no deeper than his learned responses, and although in the adult the greater part of what we call the personality, there is still a good deal of the individual left over'. The question of whether personality is modal (culture-bound) or culture-free is not just academic. In Linton's view, individuals may have personalities quite separate from their cultural background. From a 'national character' perspective, one would expect

to meet people with an average personality that reflects their culture.

Website link 1.5

Learn more about the life of Ralph Linton: **http:// www.mnsu.edu/emuseum/information/biography/ klmno/linten_ralph.html**.

1.4

Culture and competence

Some environmental predispositions

Some cultures are considered to be more work oriented and more efficient when it comes to producing material goods. Climate has often been considered an environmental variable which has a strong influence on performance. Box 1.1 contains the beginning of Montesquieu's theory of climates.[13] While the physiological explanations are scarcely credible now, it is nevertheless a starting point for the north/south stereotype. The question is: do some countries/ climates tend to harden (or soften) people, with the result that they become more (or less) inclined towards activities of war, commerce or industry, and more (or less) efficient in pursuing these activities?

Website link 1.6

Learn about the life and works of Charles-Louis de Secondat, Baron de Montesquieu: **http://www.newadvent.org/cathen/10536a.htm**

A hot climate may directly influence culture, by physically discouraging effort and action, or indirectly influence culture through adaptation to climatic conditions. Climates may be controlled, using air conditioners and heaters. If climate has both a direct and an indirect influence, via progressive genetic adaptation and/or cultural traits acquired through education and socialization, then air conditioning is still necessary but not enough. The indirect influence is likely to combine with the direct influence to change skills and behaviours over the long term. Interestingly,

BOX 1.1

Of the difference of men in different climates

A cold air[a] constringes the extremities of the external fibres of the body; this increases their elasticity, and favors the return of the blood from the extreme parts to the heart. It contracts[b] those very fibres; consequently, it increases also their force and elasticity. People are therefore more vigorous in cold climates. Here the action of the heart and the reaction of the extremities of the fibres are better performed, the temperature of the humors is greater, the blood moves freer towards the heart, and reciprocally, the heart has more power. This superiority of strength must produce various effects; for instance, a greater boldness, that is, more courage; a greater sense of superiority, that is, more frankness, less suspicion, policy, and cunning. In short, this must be productive of very different tempers. Put a man into a close warm place, and, for the reasons above given, he will feel a great faintness. If, under this circumstance, you propose a bold enterprize to him, I believe you will find him very little disposed towards it: his present weakness will throw him into a despondency; he will be afraid of every thing, being in a state of total incapacity. The inhabitants of warm countries are, like old men, timorous; the people in cold countries are, like young men, brave. If we reflect on the late[c] wars, (which are more recent in our memory, and in which we can better distinguish some particular effects, that escape us at a greater distance of time), we shall find that the northern people, transplanted into southern regions,[d] did not perform such exploits as their countrymen who, fighting in their own climate, possessed their full vigor and courage.

[a] This appears even in the countenance: in cold weather people look thinner.
[b] We know it shortens iron.
[c] Those for the succession to the Spanish monarchy.
[d] For instance in Spain.

(Source: Montesquieu, pp. 224–5.[13])

climate has been found to have an indirect effect on a country's competitiveness. For instance, temperate countries are more likely to overpay their workers, relative to their standing on the worldwide ladder of wealth.[14]

National character and educational practices

Research into national character emphasizes the influence of education on the adult personality. Margaret Mead,[7] for instance, notes that the United States is seen as an adolescent peer culture: education favours diffuse, depersonalized authority where children face a demand for strong inner moral control. Cheerful, easy-going, informal Americans are often jokingly referred to in Europe as resembling big children. In order to study how national character is formed, education systems and child-rearing practices may be observed, especially in the early years (up to the age of 5 or 6). Key elements of personality develop during this time, due to feeding and nourishing, weaning, personal hygiene and toilet training, the degree and modes of socialization into various parts of the community (with other children, with adults, with the opposite sex), the demands and prohibitions imposed on small children, and finally the reward/sanction systems that help to orientate their behaviour.[1]

Culture and skills

Cultural background influences perceptual and cognitive skills. There are clear differences in people's perception of visual illusions. People belonging to various human groups differ in their visual inference systems, because their physical environment differs widely from group to group.[15] Some people live in a constructed environment, based on straight lines and sharp angles (especially those of modern buildings and industrial objects), whereas other people live in a more rounded and curvilinear physical setting (ibid.[15]). The daily environment shapes people's visual inference, so that the same objects are seen differently. Thus, vision is considered to be a culturally built interpretation of specific retinal signals.

Competences and skills vary across cultural groups. The first research on the intellectual abilities of non-European people was undertaken by researchers, such as Levy-Bruhl, who classified the thought patterns of primitives as 'pre-logical'. Little by little this somewhat extreme attitude, that 'primitives' could never understand things as we do ('we' being the modern, Westernized people of European culture or origin), has given way to a more reasonable position. The scores on intelligence quotient (IQ) tests remain relative to the type of questions asked and the situations evoked in the verbal part of the test (reading, memorization and understanding of texts). Even that part of the test which is quantitatively oriented (i.e., mathematics, geometry, statistics, logic), requires handling abstract and mathematical signs. No test encompasses all the possible facets of human intelligence, or offers total objectivity in the experimental and empirical methods used to evaluate them. Definitions of intelligence are culturally contingent. Intelligence levels do differ and IQ tests can have practical benefits, but IQ scores should be interpreted cautiously when tests devised by one culture are administered to people from other cultures.

1.5

Culture and social representations

The notion of social representation is used throughout this book, even where there is no explicit reference to it. For instance, the acceptance (or prohibition) of comparative advertising is related to social representations of the necessity to inform consumers, to allow price competition and even to risk the denigration of one company by another (see Chapter 14). Social representations are miniatures of behaviour, copies of reality and forms of operational knowledge used to reach and implement everyday decisions. For instance, people may use a combination of social representations in order to make their health-care decisions. In the south-west of the United States Hispanic populations concurrently use four bases of knowledge for classifying and interpreting illnesses: the traditional popular medical knowledge, which relates mainly to pain and suffering; the medical knowledge orally transmitted within Amerindian tribes; the modern (English) popular medical knowledge; and the medical scientific knowledge (established and recognized).[16] According to the seriousness of the illness and the availability of money to pay for the cure, Hispanic populations let themselves be guided either by collective representations or by scientific information, in order to choose which one of these four sources should be pursued in search of a cure.

Social representations are collective images that are progressively formulated within a particular society. Social representations of health and sickness may have a strong influence on consumption patterns. For instance, villagers in many European countries tend to moan about the invasion of urban development. This relates to the rhythm of the city versus the tranquillity of the countryside. These social representations help to explain the development of natural and organic products, direct from the farm, with no additives or industrial processing, and the diffusion of ecological ideas in modern society.

Social representations are at the intersection of the psychological/individual and social/collective levels. They serve as frameworks which help us to categorize and interpret circumstances, phenomena, individuals and theories and enable us to make decision about these issues. We interpret our daily reality through our learned social representations. While social representations may reflect our prejudices, they are dynamic, collectively verified and validated. Our social representations are constantly updated through individual behaviour and social activities or as a result of the media, public opinion polls, news summaries, court decisions and legal penalties. People derive their opinions and stimulate debate from these sources of information.

Social representations vary across societies. Therefore, they have a cultural value when we have to decide what is, what can be, how to feel, what to do, and how to go about doing it (operating culture). Social representations are less profound than basic cultural orientations, as they alter within shorter time spans (10 to 20 years versus centuries). Social representations are nonetheless important. They may oppose basic cultural orientations since their time-scale is short term and they are more suited to the urgent need for collective and individual adaptation to reality.

Questions

1. In light of the definitions of culture given in this chapter, is it possible for a culture to disappear? Why, or why not? Give an example.

2. A common problem, across cultures, is to attract/be attractive for potential partners. Discuss how, in Kluckhohn and Strodtbeck's terms, there is a range of possible solutions, and how they are differentially preferred across societies. Outline possible consequences for marketing.

3. Discuss the case of multi-language/multi-religion countries (e.g. India, Canada, Switzerland): how can people in these countries share a common culture? On which segments of culture?

4. Discuss the role of education (at home, at school and elsewhere) in the transmission of culture.

5. What is *national character*?

References

1. Kluckhohn, Florence R. and Frederick L. Strodtbeck (1961), *Variations in Value Orientations*. Westport, CT: Greenwood Press.

2. Linton, Ralph (1945), *The Cultural Background of Personality*. New York: Appleton-Century.

3. Goodenough, Ward H. (1971), *Culture, Language and Society*. Reading, MA: Modular Publications, 7, Addison-Wesley.

4. Malinowski, Bronislaw (1944), *A Scientific Theory of Culture and Other Essays*. Chapel Hill, NC: University of North Carolina Press.

5. Carroll, John B. (1956), *Language, Thought and Reality: Selected Writings of Benjamin Lee Whorf*. Cambridge, MA: MIT.

6. Kumar, Rajesh (2000), 'Confucian Pragmatism vs Brahmanical Idealism: Understanding the Divergent Roots of Indian and Chinese Economic Performance', *Journal of Asian Business*, 16 (2), 49–69.

7. Mead, Margaret (1948), *Male and Female*. New York: William Morrow.

8. Lenartowicz, Tomasz and Kendall Roth (1999), 'A Framework for Culture Assessment', *Journal of International Business Studies*, 30 (4), 781–98.

9. Hannerz, Ulf (1991), 'Scenarios for Peripheral Cultures', in *Culture, Globalization and the World System*, A.D. King, Ed. London: Macmillan.

10. Keillor, Bruce D. and G. Thomas M. Hult (1999), 'A Five-Country Study of National Identity: Implications for International Marketing Research and Practice', *International Marketing Review*, 16 (1), 65–82.

11. Hofstede, Geert (2001), *Culture's Consequences* (2nd edn). Thousand Oaks, CA: Sage.

12. Schwartz, Shalom H. (1997), 'Values and Culture', in *Motivation and Culture*, Donald Munro and John F. Schumaker and Stuart C. Carr, Eds. New York: Routledge.

13. Montesquieu, Charles de (1748), *The Spirit of Laws* (Thomas Nugent, Trans.) (6th edn). Dublin: McKenzie and Moore.

14. Van De Vliert, Evert (2003), 'Thermoclimate, Culture, and Poverty as Country-Level Roots of Workers' Wages', *Journal of International Business Studies*, 34 (1), 40–52.

15. Segall, Marshall H., Pierre R. Dasen, John W. Berry, and Ype H. Poortinga (1990), *Human Behavior in Global Perspective*. New York: Pergamon.

16. Moscovici, Serge (1988), 'Notes Towards a Description of Social Representations', *European Journal of Social Psychology*, 18 (33), 211–50.

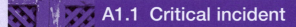

Teaching materials

A1.1 Critical incident

An old lady from Malaysia

The frail, old, almost totally blind lady appeared at every clinic session and sat on the dirt floor enjoying the activity. She was dirty and dishevelled, and obviously had very little, even by Malaysian kampong (local village) standards.

One day the visiting nurse happened upon this woman in her kampong. She lived by herself in a rundown shack about 10 by 10 feet [3 × 3 m]. When questioned how she obtained her food, she said she was often hungry, as she only received food when she worked for others – pounding rice, looking after the children, and the like.

The nurse sought to obtain help for the woman. It was finally resolved that she would receive a small pension from the Department of Welfare which would be ample for her needs.

At each weekly clinic, the woman continued to appear. She had become a centre of attention, laughed and joked freely, and obviously enjoyed her increased prestige. No change was noted in her physical status, however. She continued to wear the same dirty black dress and looked no better fed.

The nurse asked one of the rural health nurses to find out if the woman needed help in getting to a shop to buy the goods she seemed so sorely in need of.

In squatting near the woman, the rural health nurse noted a wad of bills in the woman's pocket. 'Wah,' she said, 'It is all here. You have spent nothing. Why is that?'

The woman laughed and then explained: 'I am saving it all for my funeral.'

(Source: Weeks et al., pp. 24–5.¹)

A1.2 Critical incident

The parable

The leader tells the following parable to the group, illustrating with rough chalkboard drawings if desired:

Rosemary is a girl of about 21 years of age. For several months she has been engaged to a young man – let's call him Geoffrey. The problem she faces is that between her and her betrothed there lies a river. No ordinary river mind you, but a deep, wide river infested with hungry crocodiles.

Rosemary ponders how she can cross the river. She thinks of a man she knows who has a boat. We'll call him Sinbad. So she approaches Sinbad, asking him to take her across. He replies, 'Yes, I'll take you across if you'll spend the night with me.' Shocked at this offer, she turns to another acquaintance, a certain Frederick, and tells him her story. Frederick responds by saying, 'Yes, Rosemary, I understand your problem – but – it's your problem, not mine.' Rosemary decides to return to Sinbad, spends the night with him, and in the morning he takes her across the river.

Her reunion with Geoffrey is warm. But on the evening before they are to be married. Rosemary feels compelled to tell Geoffrey how she succeeded in getting across the river. Geoffrey responds by saying, 'I wouldn't marry you if you were the last woman on earth.'

Finally, at her wit's end, Rosemary turns to our last character, Dennis. Dennis listens to her story and says, 'Well, Rosemary, I don't love you . . . but I will marry you.' And that's all we know of the story.

(Source: Weeks *et al.*, pp. 24–5.[1])

Discussion guide

1. Before any discussion, participants should be asked to write down individually on a piece of paper the characters of whose behaviour they most approve, plus a sentence or two explaining their first choice.
2. Participants may be split into small groups of four or five, to share their views and raise relevant issues.
3. The discussion should centre on the cultural relativity of values and their relation to one's own cultural background.

A1.3 Reading

Body rituals among the Naciremas

Website link A1.1

Text for this reading is located on the book website: **www.pearsoned.co.uk/usunier**.

Appendix reference

1. Weeks, William H., Paul B. Pedersen, and Richard W. Brislin (1987), *A Manual of Structured Experiences for Cross-Cultural Learning*. Yarmouth, ME: Intercultural Press.

2

Cultural dynamics 1: time and space

If we adopt Selma Lagerlöf's definition of culture as 'what remains when that which has been learned is entirely forgotten', culture may appear to be a vague and practically limited concept.[1] Its main use would be as a 'synthesis variable': an explanation that serves as a last resort. It would also serve as an explanatory variable for residuals, when other explanations are unsuccessful.

However, Lagerlöf's definition usefully identifies two basic elements of cultural dynamics at the individual level:

1. Culture is learned.
2. Culture is forgotten, in the sense that we cease to be conscious of its existence as a learned behaviour.

Yet culture remains present throughout our daily activities. Culture represents our adaptation to reality, serving as a constraint and an opportunity. Unless our natural and social environments are perfectly stable, as may be the case in primitive societies which are located in remote places and subject to no exterior interference, our culture will not stand still. As our natural and social environments change, new solutions are discovered to solve new problems.

This chapter and the next focus on a model of cultural dynamics to explain culture-related behaviour. This model is based on a set of cultural assumptions (see section 2.1), which relate to perceptions of time (section 2.2) and space (section 2.3). But these are not static, as cultures borrow from each other through time and space. Section 2.4 is dedicated to this and the corresponding changes in the importing society. The last section (2.5) is dedicated to cultural hostility. Territoriality is the organizing principle of cultures across space and hostility arises from prejudiced views

of others and the fear of having to share with members of alien cultural groups.

2.1

A model of action based on cultural assumptions

Figure 2.1 presents how basic cultural assumptions in three major areas (time, space and the concept of the self and others) influence interaction models, which shape our attitudes towards action. Fundamental assumptions about time, space, and the concept of the self and others are explained in greater detail in this chapter and the first section of the next chapter.

Cultural assumptions are statements about the basic nature of reality in response to a set of fundamental human problems. They give communities a framework for evaluating solutions to these fundamental problems, combining a cognitive dimension (*what people think*), an affective dimension (*what people like*) and a directive dimension (*what people do*).

Kluckhohn and Strodtbeck[2] categorized common human problems under six main groups:

1. What is the character of innate human nature (human-nature orientation): good or evil, neutral, or a mix of good and evil? Is this state of human nature mutable or immutable?
2. What is the relation of humans to nature and super-nature (nature orientation): subjugation to nature, harmony with nature or mastery over nature?
3. What is the temporal focus of human life (time orientation): past, present or future?

Figure 2.1 A model of cultural dynamics

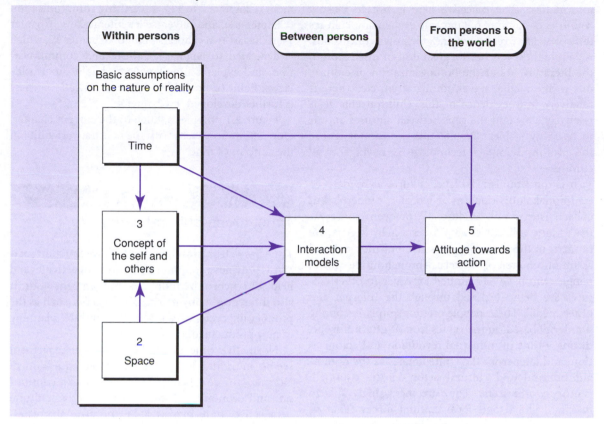

4. What is the modality of human activity (activity orientation): should people be (being), should people do (doing) or should they do in order to be (being in becoming)?
5. What is the modality of the relationship between humans (relational orientation): linearity, collaterality or pure individuality?
6. What is the conception of space? Is it considered predominantly private, public or a mix of both?

Website link 2.1

Examine a visual representation of Kluckhohn and Strodtbeck's value orientations: **http://www.toonloon.bizland.com/nutshell/values.htm#varo1**.

These common problems permeate every society. People *are* and *do*, and there are always children and parents. Some kind of family nucleus exists everywhere. But different assumptions within these categories result in different dominant responses in a particular society. We have combined Kluckhohn and Strodtbeck's approach with those adopted by other authors[2–10] to depict differences in five tables: time-related differences in Table 2.1, space-related differences in Table 2.2, the concepts of self and others in Table 3.1, interaction models in Table 3.3, and attitudes towards action in Table 3.6.

Each of the five tables highlights common problems, important solutions and dominant differences across cultures. This leads to a detailed inventory of basic differences in cultural assumptions that influence interactions. These differences are mostly the result of learned behaviour. We give some country-specific illustrations, without too often citing 'typical' cultures, to avoid stereotyping. Except for Hofstede's dimensions, which are considered mostly in the realm of 'interaction models', little empirical data is detailed, though we have at times indicated where to find such information. The objective here is not to classify countries or cultures, but rather to explain how cultures differ, and leave readers to draw their own conclusions.

While there has been a great deal of discussion in the literature about the homogenization of culture, due to the media, travel, immigration, etc., there is relatively little evidence of this. Cultural change is relatively slow and the gaps between cultures appear to be fairly stable.[7] Despite this, we cannot ignore the profound impact technology is having on all cultures.

It is too simplistic to label cultures as modern or traditional: individualism is globally 'modern', but collectivism is not 'traditional', or even 'conservative'. Many collectivist nations, especially in Asia, are modern in the technological sense, but their cultural assumptions are not Western. Throughout the world, people who have had limited exposure to other cultures are being exposed through the Internet and other media. These people are not simply becoming 'modern'; based on the values from Western Europe, during a time of industrial revolution and colonization, and later from the United States as the dominant political and cultural actor on the twentieth century world scene. They are increasingly able to integrate global and local cultural forces. That is, they may be global in one domain, but local in another.[11] The cultural assumption that 'modern' is more legitimate is highly questionable. It can lead people to imitate behaviour that is in some ways not appropriate to their own culture. As such, we try to refer to why and how a certain cultural assumption, interaction model or attitude towards action belongs to 'modern' culture.

We claim to be culturally relative. Cross-cultural learning experience involves examining a different mindset. It is possible to develop cultural awareness from reading materials written from a culturally alien perspective. Cultural assumptions are not completely in the realm of *unbewußtsein* (unconsciousness, deep-seated and inaccessible); they are rather in the realm of *unterbewußtsein*, which is located at a subconscious level, where interaction and self-questioning can reveal them.

Throughout this book, we highlight the impact of culture on specific areas of international marketing. In subsequent chapters cultural assumptions are used to explain elements of consumer behaviour (Chapter 4), market research (Chapter 6), marketing management (Chapters 7 to 11), advertising communication (Chapter 13), and buyer–seller interactions (Chapter 14). The last two chapters build on Chapter 12, which is dedicated to language, culture and communication, and explains how language shapes our worldviews. Point (e) in Table 3.3 (communication styles) is further developed in Chapter 12.

Figure 2.1 provides a guide to the current chapter. Our exploration starts with the cultural variability in the concept of time.

2.2

Time: cross-cultural variability

Time has a strong influence on how we function socially. It provides a common framework for activities and helps to synchronize individual human behaviour. It also influences many marketing concepts, such as the product life cycle, sales forecasting and the planning of new product launches.[12]

Normative time in marketing and management seems indisputable, and so is rarely questioned. Normative time is perceived as being linear, continuous and economic. However, from a cross-cultural perspective, time may well be the area of greatest difference, because (1) assumptions are very deep-seated and (2) formally, we hold a common model of clock-based time.

People's relationship with time changes across periods of history, human development, technological advances in the measurement of time, natural and social rhythms, and the prevailing metaphysical views. Each vision of time (*Zeitanschauung*) corresponds to a vision of the real world, its origins and destiny (*Weltanschauung*). Each new time pattern superimposes itself on the previous one. As a consequence, an individual's perceptions of time may result from adding or mixing different basic patterns of time. This complicates our understanding of people's relationship with time.

Website link 2.2

The Centre for Time Use Research has multinational data comparing 19 countries and how people spend their time: **http://www.timeuse.org/mtus**.

Dimensions of time orientations

Table 2.1 presents time-related cultural assumptions, which correspond to four common problems:

1. To what extent should time be regarded as a tangible commodity (economicity of time)?
2. How should tasks and time be combined (monochronic versus polychronic use of time)?
3. Should lifetime(s) be seen as a single continuous line or as combining multiple cyclical episodes (linearity versus cyclicity of time)?
4. What are the appropriate temporal orientations: towards the past, the present and the future?

Economicity of time

Time may be seen as external to us, and as such to be treated like a tangible commodity. Many European countries as well as the United States and Australia are representative of the 'time-is-money' culture, where time is an economic good. Since time is perceived as a scarce resource, people should try to allocate it in the most economically optimal way. This results in people using their time as 'wisely' as possible in scheduling or establishing timetables and deadlines. Measurement of parking meter time by units of 7.5 minutes or sport performance by the hundredths of a second is typical of precisely measured economic time with direct and explicit financial consequences. Norms tend to be very strict regarding time schedules, appointments, dates and durations.

> ### Website link 2.3
>
> Examine the gap between the way mainstream Indonesian culture and most Western cultures view the sense of time: http://www.expat.or.id/business/senseoftime.html.

Table 2.1 Time-related cultural differences

Basic problem/Cultural orientations	Contrasts across cultures
Is time money?	
(a) Economicity of time	Time is regarded as a scarce resource or, conversely, as plentiful and indefinitely available.
How to schedule tasks?	
(b) Monochronism versus	Only one task is undertaken at any (preset) time, following a preset schedule. An 'agenda society'.
Polychronism	Multiple tasks undertaken simultaneously. Appointment times, if set, are flexible. Time is less important than the context of the situation.
Is time a continuous line?	
(c) Linearity (L) versus cyclicity (C) of time	Time is seen as linear, separate blocks (L), versus an emphasis on the daily, yearly and seasonal cycles (C).
How should we emphasize past, present and future?	
(d) Temporal orientations (i) towards the past	These people consider the past as important. Resources must be spent on teaching history and building museums. Naturally, oral and written traditions are important. Their basic assumption is that their roots are implanted in the past and no plant can survive without its roots.
(ii) towards the present	These people live in the 'here and now'. Although not always enjoyable, the present must be accepted for what it is: the only *true* reality we live in.
(iii) towards the future	These people easily and precisely envisage and plan their future. They are project oriented, prepare for the long term, appreciate the achievements of science, and so on. The future is inevitably 'bigger and better'.

Attitudes towards money and the money value of time are inseparable from marketing.[13,14] A strong economic time assumption influences consumer behaviour. Products are created to 'save time' and services are based on blocks of time, including bank loans and life insurance policies. Economicity of time also has an impact on buyer–seller interactions, influencing the waiting process, the communication style and the efficiency of service.

Monochronic versus polychronic use of time

Edward Hall described two extreme task scheduling behaviours, which he calls monochronism (M-time) and polychronism (P-time).[5] Individuals working on M-time do one thing at a time and tend to adhere to preset schedules. When confronted by a dilemma (e.g. a discussion with someone that lasts longer than planned), M-time people will politely stop the conversation in order to keep to their schedule. In M-time societies, not only the start of a meeting but also its finish is often planned. Conversely, individuals working on P-time do several things at the same time, easily modify preset schedules, and seldom experience time as 'wasted'. P-time may seem quite hectic to M-time people: 'There is no recognized order as to who is to be served next, no queue or numbers indicating who has been waiting the longest' (Hall, p. 47).[5] P-time people are more committed to relationships than to schedules. When confronted with a conflict such as the one described above, they prefer to go on talking or working after preset hours rather than keep to a schedule – that is, if they have one.

The PERT (programme evaluation and review technique) method is an example from a typical M-time 'agenda culture'. PERT explicitly aims to reduce polychronic tasks (they really take place simultaneously, which is part of the problem) to provide a monochronic solution (the critical path). Management methods, originating in Western cultures, favour pure monochronic task organization. They clearly devalue polychronic tendencies, which tend to make plans and schedules rather hectic. When it comes to delays and being 'on time', precise monochronic systems give priority to meeting dates and commitments to schedules.[15,16]

M- or P-time is important for understanding buyer–seller interactions. It is also important for scheduling in almost every aspect of business, including completion times, deliveries and promotional campaigns.

David Palmer and David Schoorman[17] integrated Hall's M- and P-time with the economicity of time to distinguish three dimensions:

1. *Time use preference*: The extent to which people prefer to engage in multiple tasks simultaneously.
2. *Context*: The extent of context needed to effectively communicate. M-time is associated with low context communication, conveying only explicit meaning in messages. P-time is associated with high context communication, where the information that surrounds an event, as well as many indirectly meaningful cues, are needed to correctly interpret the message. High and low context messages are explained in detail in Chapter 13.
3. *Time tangibility*: The extent to which time is viewed as a commodity that can be bought, sold, saved, spent or wasted.

Palmer and Schoorman suggest that these three dimensions interact to produce eight types of individual temporality. In a survey of 258 middle and senior executives from 25 nations – although most were Americans – they found most executives to be Type A (44 per cent), being polyphasic, time urgent and low context, or M1 (32 per cent), being monochromic, time urgent and low context. Other patterns are likely to form with different samples from different cultures. This illustrates the importance of examining the interaction between time use, cultural factors, and individual preferences.

Linearity (L) versus cyclicity (C) of time

A strong economic view of time, when it is combined with monochronism, emphasizes the linearity of time. Time is viewed as being a line with a point – the present – at the centre. Each portion of the line can be cut into slices, which are supposed to have a certain value.

Basic religious beliefs play a key role in supporting such a linear view of time. Christianity has a one-shot interpretation of worldly existence. Only on the final judgement day will Christians know if they are to be granted eternal life. However, the Asian religions, including Hinduism and Buddhism, assume that on the death of the body, the soul is born again in another body. The belief in regular reincarnation, until a pure soul is allowed to escape the cycle and go to *nirvana*, radically changes the nature of time in a specific life. This is not 'all the time I have got', it is simply one of my 'times' across several lives. For most Asians, cyclicity is central in their pattern of time. *Nirvana* is the final release from the cycle of reincarnation. It is attained by extinction of all desires and individual existence, culminating in absolute blessedness (in Buddhism), or in absorption into Brahman (in Hinduism). Naturally, patience is on the side of the people believing in cyclical reincarnation of the soul. For Christians, it is more urgent to achieve, because their souls are given only one worldly life. But, as the New Testament puts it clearly, those who do right, even in the very last moment, will be considered favourably.

Another element that favours a cyclical view of time is the degree of emphasis put on the natural rhythms of years and seasons, the sun and the moon. This concept contrasts so-called 'modern' with 'traditional' societies, in so far as 'modern' means technology, mastering nature and, to a certain extent, the loss of nature-related reference points. Despite this, highly developed societies such as the Japanese are known for having maintained a strong orientation to nature. The floral art of *Ikebana* and the emphasis on maintaining a contact with nature, even in highly urban environments, are testimonies to their attachment to the natural rhythms of nature. Even within a country, the relationship to nature influences the model of time adopted by urban as compared with rural people.

Elements of cyclicity of time have three main origins: (1) religious assumptions about reincarnation of the soul; (2) natural rhythms of years, seasons and days; and (3) the social division of time periods, which is more arbitrary, less natural and 'given', than we assume. Time is naturally both linear and cyclical. Cultures have definite time patterns that combine both views.

Temporal orientations: past, present, future

People's perception of time tends to be related to temporal orientations toward the past, present or future. As stated by Kluckhohn and Strodtbeck (1961, pp. 13–15):

The possible cultural interpretations of temporal focus of human life break easily into the three point range of past, present and future . . . Spanish-Americans, who have been described as taking the view that man is a victim of natural forces, are also a people who place the present time alternative in first position . . . Many modern European countries . . . have strong leanings to a past orientation . . . Americans,

more strongly than most people of the world, place an emphasis upon the future – a future which is anticipated to be 'bigger and better'.

While these orientations tend to be associated with countries and cultures, they are also individual psychological traits.[18] Furthermore, societies undergoing change may temporarily underplay their basic temporal orientation, such as those experiencing rapid economic change minimizing their past orientation.

Past oriented people emphasize the past in explaining where we are now. They tend to restore old buildings, invest in museums and emphasize the importance of history at school. Many European and some Asian cultures are past oriented.

Website link 2.4

For the Aymara people living in the Andes,
the past lies ahead and the future lies behind:
http://www.guardian.co.uk/science/2005/feb/24/4.

Present oriented people focus on the 'here and now', believing that the past is over and the future is uncertain, theoretical and difficult to imagine. Religion may play an important role in pushing people towards a present orientation, especially if it emphasizes that only God decides the future. Arabic–Muslim culture has been described as fatalistic and short-term oriented.[19] As stated by Harris and Moran (p. 474):

Who controls time? A Western belief is that one controls his own time. Arabs believe that their time is controlled, to a certain extent, by an outside force – namely Allah – therefore the Arabs become very fatalistic in their view of time . . . Most Arabs are not clockwatchers, nor are they planners of time.[20]

Future oriented people focus on planning for a bigger and better tomorrow. They tend to delay immediate gratification and invest in the future. An example of this is the millions of Americans who start a specific savings account for their child's education as soon as he or she is born. Future oriented societies will tend to invest in science or technology. Americans and some Asian cultures are future oriented.

Important differences in temporal orientations were found in the Chinese Value Survey (CVS), which purposefully introduced an Eastern bias to counter the historical Western bias in value surveys.[12] The

CVS uncovered a dimension it termed Confucian Work Dynamism, which corresponds to a future orientation on one hand and a past and present orientation on the other. Later, Hofstede (p. 359)[7] in his review of the CVS referred to this as Long Term Orientation (LTO) and Short Term Orientation (STO):

Long Term Orientation stands for the fostering of virtues oriented towards future rewards, in particular, perseverance and thrift. Its opposite pole, Short Term Orientation, stands for the fostering of virtues related to the past and present, in particular, respect for tradition preservation of 'face' and fulfilling social obligations.

Countries scoring high on LTO include many Asian countries (e.g. Hong Kong, Japan and South Korea). Countries scoring low in LTO include many Western countries (e.g. Australia, Germany, USA and UK) and developing nations (e.g. Pakistan and West Africa). Although the US appears to be both future oriented and at the same time high STO, this STO could be attributed to constraints imposed by the highly organized nature of the society (e.g. quarterly reporting for companies).

The following summarizes some of the main connotations of LTO differences as cited in Hofstede (2001). In LTO cultures delayed gratification is accepted and long-term virtues such as frugality, perseverance, savings, and investing are emphasized. The most important events in life will occur in the future and persistence is an important personality trait. Conversely, in STO cultures, immediate gratification is expected, and short-term virtues such as social consumption and spending are emphasized. The most important events in life occurred in the past or present.

Several studies have found interesting correlations with these dimensions. LTO scores are strongly correlated with national economic growth and have been used to explain the dramatic growth of the East Asian economies in the latter part of the twentieth century (Hofstede, 2001).

2.3   Space *territoriality*

People are by nature territorial. They must define who has ownership and control over certain spaces. The key words for space-related cultural assumptions are 'in' and 'out', member and non-member, belonging or not. Belonging can be based on family ties or common characteristics including education, religion and professional associations. Space is the basis for the organizing principle of *territoriality*, which we mentioned in the previous chapter.

Table 2.2 contrasts space-related cultural assumptions, which correspond to four common problems and cultural orientations:

1. Whether people are insiders or outsiders (*personalization* versus *depersonalization*).
2. What the rights and obligations are for ingroup members (*ingroup orientation*).
3. Whether it is possible for outsiders to gain insider status, or a limited part of it (*concrete* versus *abstract territoriality*).
4. What the group membership conditions are for those willing to 'enter this space' (*group* versus *individualistic cultures*).

> ### Website link 2.5
>
> What level of personal space is acceptable in America? Take the elevator test to find out: http://www. everythingesl.net/inservices/proxemics_elevator.php.

Personalization versus depersonalization

The contrast between a *being* and *doing* orientation is based on the concepts of personalization and depersonalization. Personalization means that assumptions about what a person can *do* depend on who the person *is*. Since not all is prima facie visible, it will be necessary to spend time to understand who this person is. This is evident in cultures with a *being* orientation.

A 'being' orientation emphasizes belonging, based on shared characteristics, including categories:

1. those you are born into, such as gender, family, social class, ethnic background, religion, or nationality; and
2. those you currently belong to, such as age (young versus older people) and marital status.

A strong *being* orientation assumes that who the person *is*, naturally, legitimately and forcefully, influences the roles, power and capacities he or she has in society. There is a strong link between a *being* orientation and the concept of the self and others, which helps translate this concept into interaction models. A typical causal chain in a *being* orientation

Table 2.2 Space-related cultural differences

Basic problem/Cultural orientations	Contrasts across cultures
Is emphasis put on what people *do* (i.e. *doing*) or on what they *are* (i.e. *being*) based on belonging to family, age, sex, religious or social status groups?	
(a) Personalization versus depersonalization	The necessity of personally knowing a person before you can efficiently communicate and interact versus the ability to communicate easily with unknown people.
Who is a member of the group and what are the relevant ingroups?	
(b) Ingroup orientation	Belonging to the ingroup (or reference group: family, tribe, clan, club, professional society, nation, etc.) may be a *necessary condition* for being considered a reliable, *bona fide* partner.
How to gain membership?	
(c) Concrete versus abstract territoriality	What are the group membership conditions? What are the prerequisites for assimilation, if an outgroup member is to achieve group membership?
How to deal with physical space?	
(d) Group cultures with close physical contact versus individualistic cultures desiring private space	Tendency to live near to one another, and to be undisturbed by such intimacy, versus the need for private space around one's body, and to dislike intrusion into this space.

is: she is a woman, thus she belongs to the group of people in charge of reproduction and nurturing roles, thus she cannot work outside the home.

A strong *being* emphasis is evidenced by what people call themselves and others. In many traditional societies, language designates people by a term meaning 'human being'. 'Bantu' for instance, means human being. This, more or less, emphasizes that others are not *real* human beings. Without going so far, the Japanese language also divides 'we' and 'they'. Japanese people call themselves *Nihon-jin* and foreigners *Gai-jin* (those from the outside). Similarly, Pakistanis in the UK call themselves *Apney* (our own people) and white English *Gorey*.[21]

In contrast, depersonalization means that it is not necessary to know who a person *is* in order to decide what this person can *do*. Therefore it is not necessary to spend time discovering who the person is, especially if time is strongly economic. Depersonalization means that belonging to particular groups (e.g. extended family, social class, ethnic background, religion, gender, and age) is less important than their individual characteristics (e.g. abilities, talents, and education).

A strong *doing* orientation assumes that what people are *does not* naturally, or legitimately, influence the roles, power and capabilities people have in society. What is important is what people can achieve, given their individual talents and abilities. In the purest version of the doing orientation, even character and personality would be considered as unimportant in what individuals can achieve. Tasks are viewed as standard and people as interchangeable. Deeds are separated from emotions and *doing* belongs to a world of its own, radically separated from the *being*.

Ingroup orientation

Who is a member of the ingroup?

There is a natural relationship between the *being* orientation and the emphasis on group belonging, which has to do with natural law and the right of people to occupy a certain territory. The largest possible ingroups are nations. Benefits related to nationality are strongly space-related, including the right to live, work and enjoy citizenship of a definite territory. In some countries, legitimacy is primarily based on your ancestry. Nationality may be legally based on *jus sanguinis* (law of the blood) and only granted if at least one parent is a national. In other countries (e.g. Australia, France, the UK and the USA), nationality is legally based on *jus soli* (law of the soil) and granted to all those born in the country. This opposition delineates two ways of defining the content of an ingroup (in this case a national group): on the one hand, people emphasize blood and kin; on the other, they do not.

Ingroup orientation is quite complex. It involves patterns of kin-based loyalty and obligation. The family is the most basic and smallest ingroup unit. Strong ingroup orientation is most often accompanied by a rhetoric based on family relationships, with a dominant father (outside oriented), a protective mother (inside oriented) and sisters and brothers, alternately considered as rivals within the ingroup (because they are competing for parents' love, affection and preference) and allies in comparison with the outgroup (because they share the same fundamental identity; they *are* of the same kin). The family space is the house and surrounding land, which is private but not closed to outsiders, who may enter under definite conditions.

In contrast, outgroup orientation is based on the assumption of the fundamental unity of mankind, beyond the borders of ingroup spaces (e.g. families, nations and cultures). If the two orientations are roughly opposed, it is not a complete opposition. In certain cultures they coexist. For instance, Nordic European cultures combine a strong sense of national identity (ingroup) with a universal focus on mankind, manifested in their strong commitment to peace, development of the poorest nations, and international organizations (outgroup).

What does membership involve in terms of rights and obligations?

Ingroup bonds involve relationships of loyalty that do not extend beyond the borders of the ingroup space. Loyalty can be based on kinship or patronage, which is often an extended form of kinship based on symbolic adoption (taking another's child as one's own). Loyalty is based on allegiance, even in the face of conflicts with other members of the ingroup or when experiencing unfair treatment from the most powerful members. Loyalty is fundamentally non-reciprocal: people do not expect other ingroup members' loyalty because they are loyal themselves. There are no time constraints on loyalty: one may wait for 50 years to be rewarded for loyalty or one may never be rewarded.

Strong ingroup orientation increases an insider's loyalty, but simultaneously decreases the feeling of obligation towards outsiders. Morality is space related. It might, for instance, be considered as perfectly virtuous to lie to or steal from people to whom no loyalty is owed. The Mafia is a good illustration of an ingroup oriented society. Morality is based on a set of values favouring strict loyalty, treason being punished by a death sentence; the godfather who has ordered it goes to the burial ceremony because he still 'loves' the betrayer.

Ingroup orientation partly explains behavioural relativity. Some national groups have a reputation for their compliant behaviour at home (where rules are strictly enforced) and for 'looser' conduct abroad. When they are away, they no longer feel the need to observe the rules that apply at home. They do not need to respect outgroup rules, even those similar to their ingroups, since outsiders do not deserve loyalty or respect.

Ingroup or outgroup orientation has a deep influence on the system of ethics and morality in a society. Outgroup orientation values universal rules, applied to everybody. Human rights ethics are a typical feature of outgroup orientation. Objectivity and reciprocity are preferred over loyalty. Loyalty is not to the group, not to people, but to the rules and values that govern the society as a whole. This relates to personalization (people orientation) versus depersonalization (rule orientation), as discussed previously. The depersonalized approach in outgroup oriented cultures leads to a greater sensitivity to the problems of human beings far away from their own space. Their tendency to behave in a more universal way in no way means that they are less human.

These differences have a major impact on cross-cultural consumer behaviour and international business. Decision making can be quite different across ingroup and outgroup contexts in some but not other cultures. Social influence is also likely to differ across these contexts. For instance, Kelman[22] suggested three processes of social influence: compliance, identification and internalization. While most people are susceptible to informational influence through a process of internalization (depending on the relevance and congruence with persons' values), a strong ingroup orientation is likely to increase susceptibility to value expressive influence through the process of identification and reward/punishment influence through the process of compliance. These differences also have a major impact on international business, including the information needed to understand the connections between people and how contracts are made and honoured.

Pitfalls of excessive ingroup and outgroup orientations

All societies combine some elements of ingroup and outgroup orientation. For example, 'affirmative action, equal opportunity' is a strong outgroup motto typical of Western cultures. Despite this, human beings cannot freely choose their nationality. If they could, it would illustrate the purest form of outgroup orientation.

Extreme positions in either space-related assumption present drawbacks.

The pitfalls of excessive ingroup orientation include:

1. Tribalism – only kin ingroup are considered worth interacting with and caring for.
2. Localism – only people belonging to a small geographical unit are considered interesting.
3. Provincialism – only values and behaviour that are in use in the community are considered appropriate.

The pitfalls of excessive outgroup orientation include:

1. Unrealistic universalism – abandoning all borders may increase conflict.
2. Global village ethnocentrism – seeing what happens in all parts of the world does not mean that different behaviours are understood. While images are global, a common interpretation of them is not.

Concrete versus abstract territoriality

If people are very territorial, it is important to know how to gain access to them, even as an external partner, such as a business partner in a joint venture. Group membership may be gained on the basis of either concrete or abstract territoriality. The type of territoriality is largely dependent on the combination of ingroup/outgroup and the being/doing divides.

1. When ingroup and being orientation are strong, membership is generally gained on the basis of *concrete territoriality*.
2. When outgroup and doing orientation are strong, membership is based on *abstract territoriality*.

Ingroup membership based on *concrete territoriality* requires characteristics that can not be acquired by outgroup adults. Here, ingroup criteria are most likely to be related to birth, socialization and education. In cases where it is impossible to gain membership, one must behave as a friendly but realistic outsider. Outsiders often, too quickly, view cultures with an ingroup/being orientation as being narrow-minded, provincial, and hostile towards foreigners.

Membership-based *abstract territoriality* corresponds largely to Western *doing* cultures. Here, an outgroup orientation is valued. What people have *done* up to now is indicated by their curriculum vitae (CV). An interview guide in countries where affirmative action compliance is important considers it discriminatory to enquire about an applicant's age, citizenship, marital status, and birthplace. This information is not only legitimate in *being* cultures, it is essential to ascertain who the applicant *is*. Abstract territoriality is mostly based on professional achievements, evidenced by diplomas, membership of professional bodies, being an alumnus of an ivy-league university, and so on. The epitome of abstract territoriality is represented by the *golden boys*. For them *insider* trading is fraud, showing that the use of their natural ingroup advantages is viewed as evil. The space of 'golden boys' is a mix of top MBA schools, market dealing rooms and a 'club of people constantly connected worldwide'. We can only imagine the profound differences between the 'golden boy' and the Bengali farmer.

Business school graduates or those holding the title of doctor in Germany belong to these 'modern groups' that are based on doing and competence rather than being, age, sex and group membership. It is assumed that access to membership is organized on a non-discriminatory and objective basis and that it is in the interest of society as a whole because the 'best people' are doing the 'appropriate job'. However, even in a *doing* framework, relational competence never disappears in favour of pure professional competence. Managing relationships is still an important part of the *doing* competences.

Paradoxically, when abstract territoriality is very strong, it largely re-creates primitive ingroup behaviour, but based on different criteria. Even the world of academia, which is very outgroup oriented in terms of gender, nationality, religion and age, is very ingroup oriented when it comes to doctoral degrees and the journals where people publish.

Group membership assumptions are important for many aspects of international marketing, especially as a foreign firm in a national competitive environment. For instance, foreign firms entering Africa and the Middle Eastern countries may have difficulties making public relations contacts, dealing with staffing issues, and handling situations involving business ethics. Foreign firms with an outgroup orientation often have a difficult time understanding the issues surrounding the favouring of one party over another on the ground of personal relationship, which is standard practice for ingroup oriented people. In fact, these actions are often viewed as corruption by outgroup oriented people.

Group versus individualistic cultures

Territoriality also refers to possessiveness, control and authority over physical space. The 'language of space' is culturally determined. Individuals refer to culturally based rules concerning space, such as the codes concerning social distance. For example, how far should one stand from other people in order to respect their area of private space? Edward Hall[3] developed the concept of 'proxemics': the study of human use of space as a specialized elaboration of culture. In Western cultures, there are three primary zones of space: the intimate zone (0 to 18 inches; 0–45cm), the personal zone (18 inches to 3 feet; 0.45–1m), and the social zone (3 to 6 feet: 1–2m). Touch can occur for Westerners in the intimate and personal zones, but sensory involvement and communication is less intense in the social zone.

The following physical space assumptions differ across cultures:

1. What are the sizes of the three zones? To what extent do they overlap?
2. Who is allowed to enter these zones of physical space?

3. What is considered adequate sensory exchange within definite interpersonal distances?

The last question is important in marketing terms, as our sense of physical space mixes with culturally determined sensory codes, based on sight, sound, touch and smell, to give meaning to product characteristics. For instance, some Western countries (e.g. Australia, UK, USA) focus on a suppression of personal odours in public spaces, which has created a mass market for room deodorizers, antiperspirants, mouthwashes and deodorants. Although smell suppression is globally 'modern', it is not clear whether it will remain so in the future, with people striving for a more natural expression of themselves.

The list of basic space-related cultural assumptions in Table 2.2 is not exhaustive. Some other aspects need to be considered. For instance, the availability of inhabitable physical space and the density of population vary greatly across countries, with profound impact on material culture. Population density increases the importance of an assumption that 'smaller is better' or 'bigger is better'. It also influences how towns are organized and how urban and rural landscapes are integrated and interrelated and how transportation is developed.

2.4

Cultural borrowing and change in societies

It would be wrong to give the impression that cultural assumptions are purely different and exclusive. Through time and space, cultures intermingle. In fact, cultures are rarely pure, except in a few areas where people have been almost untouched by foreign influences.

An example of cultural isolation might be Japan, which during the era of the Tokugawa shoguns withdrew from all contact with outside people and cultures. The Tokugawa period lasted for more than two centuries before the Meiji era, which began in 1868 and initiated a period of increased accessibility of foreign influences to Japan. Only after the beginning of the Meiji era in 1868 did the Japanese begin to interact with Europeans. They found that the Europeans had achieved enormous advances in scientific knowledge during the previous two centuries.

The succession of these two periods, one of great isolation and one of openness towards foreign cultures, may explain the paradoxical relationship of the Japanese with international trade and marketing. In one sense they are very ethnocentric, but simultaneously they are quite capable of overcoming their ethnocentrism to become, ultimately, highly successful international marketers.

In most cases, cultures mix, even if contact is confrontational, due to territoriality and conflicting interests (e.g. religion, language, social and political systems) across borders. The perennial conflicts between the region south of the Mediterranean Sea (mostly Arab and Muslim) and the northern region (mostly Christian) are an example of this pattern of conflict and cooperation. That is, cultural encounters occur even in wartime. When besieged by the Turks in the fifteenth century, the Viennese were introduced by their opponents to a new, tasty and stimulating beverage known as coffee. It is through the Viennese as intermediaries that coffee was introduced into the West. Even during the Crusades (tenth to twelfth centuries), warriors on both sides had quiet moments during which they enjoyed each other's food.

The basic requirement for the introduction of a new cultural item (a product, a lifestyle, a word, a dance, a song) is that it looks (and in fact is) coherent with the culture that adopts it. This is why cultural borrowing is often disguised, by a change of name or by means of 'reinvention', where a local inventor/discoverer is *found*. It is fascinating to see how many countries claim credit for particular inventions (the Xerox machine, for instance) at the same time.

Website link 2.6

Find out how the Native American culture has been borrowed to the point of thievery: http://www.awakenedwoman.com/cultural_theft.htm.

There have always been different kinds of travellers (e.g. explorers, warriors, merchants, colonials) who transfer foreign innovations to their native country. Usually by accident, and sometimes by an almost systematic process, societies may find good imported solutions to their problems. For instance, jeans, as informal trousers for casual wear, have made their way to most cultures. The fabric originally came from France (*de Nîmes* – denim) and the name from Italy – short for Jean Fustian from Genes (Genoa). Afterwards this 'American' invention made its way back to Italy and most other countries of the world. In a more systematic manner, marketers have promoted many natural products as 'belonging' to their country or region. For instance, the kiwi fruit, which is largely thought to be from New Zealand, is native to southern China. Similarly, the macadamia nut, which is largely thought to be from Hawaii, is native to Australia. The macadamia nut, like many commercial food crops, is now grown throughout the world, including Australia, the USA, Israel, and many parts of South American and the African continent.

Similarly, words and concepts are often borrowed in their original form, despite being obviously related to a well-established stereotype of a particular country: *ersatz* (the high reputation of German chemistry), *leitmotiv* (German music), *showbiz* (US dominance), *élégance* (the French reputation for style), *kamikaze* or *hara-kiri* (the Japanese capacity for self-sacrifice), *mamma* (the Italian sense of the motherly role in the family). The English language has had a profound influence on Japanese marketing, especially in Japanese promotional texts and labels (Sherry and Camargo, 1987). *Mai* (English 'my'), for instance, is used extensively in compounds such as *mai homu* (my home), because the Japanese equivalent would sound too selfish and stress the private over the collective. Cultural borrowing also extends to concepts and values, including the adoption of aspects of individualism, which is discussed in more detail in the next chapter.

Although cultural opportunism is understandable, it often remains hidden by the need to maintain cultural identity. Few societies are prepared to accept that a large part of their culture is really foreign. Cultural borrowings are often disguised until they are integrated into the dominant culture. Numerous words, goods and even lifestyles (the 'weekend', for instance) have been largely borrowed. Such words as 'magazine' and 'assassin' have been directly imported from Arabic. A more systematic example is the Japanese borrowing of Chinese writing more than 15 centuries ago. This is a true example of borrowing and reinterpretation which makes this appropriation a genuine element of Japanese. At first, the Japanese did not immediately recognize ideograms (which they later called *kanji*) as representing *ideas*, but experienced them more directly as *sounds*. This led to the *kanji* pictogram system representing both ideas and sounds. They also developed two syllabaries, which represent only sounds: *hiragana* for native words and *katakana* for imported words. The *katakana* syllabary is typical of the Japanese attitude towards cultural imports: they do not object (as the French do, for instance), but at the same time they clearly signal the foreign origin of some words and concepts by writing these words in *katakana*. *Katakana* represent the same syllables as *hiragana*, which may seem an apparent waste of effort to an outsider.

Other examples of cultural borrowing are numerous: music, clothes, architecture, building techniques, food, recipes, etc. Borrowing is sometimes as pure and simple as copying. The Japanese have been remarkably skilful at borrowing European music, becoming the most important producers of musical instruments worldwide. Even castanets – an ethnically Spanish product – are made in Japan for sale in Spain. Some types of borrowing can also be viewed as product counterfeiting.

With the advent of the Internet and e-commerce, the potential for cultural borrowing has expanded exponentially.[23] For example, e-books may evolve to have built-in translators and culture-specific annotations so that they adapt to different modes of thought and reading styles.[24] In this case, the reader would have no idea of its origin. Still, there appears to be resistance to this change, even within universities, where computer competencies are much higher than in the general population.

2.5

Cultural hostility

Limits to borrowing clearly appear when it is seen as a threat to cultural coherence. This is especially true of religious practices, social morals and even daily customs. For instance, it is not easy to import polygamy or clitoral excision for babies into cultures where monogamy and child protection are strongly established practices. As previously stated, there must be a minimum level of coherence and homogeneity in cultural assumptions and behaviour if people are to integrate and live peacefully together.

In fact, cultural similarity/dissimilarity has been found to influence many aspects of international marketing, including the attractiveness of markets[25] and tourist destinations,[26] relationship development,[27] international cooperation,[28] trade relationships[29,30] and country of origin image.[31] For example, Swift examined export business managers' perceptions of cultural closeness (using 20 cultural elements, including language, religion, food, drink, politics, etc.) and found that managers tended to like those overseas markets they perceived as more similar.[25] In reality, this relationship is not as simple as it sounds. Cultural similarity is not just an objective symmetrical distance.[32] The extent of perceived similarity or distance can be influenced by many factors, including the tolerance of other cultures, the extent of interaction, cultural 'attractiveness', and geographical proximity.[32]

Racism

Racism is often confused with cultural hostility. Racism precedes cultural hostility, but cultural hostility does not necessarily imply racism. People may be hostile to those from another culture without being a racist. There is a theory behind racism: that, because of their race (i.e. physiology), some human beings are inferior in terms of intelligence, creative abilities, moral sense, or some other factor. The theories of Gobineau and Hitler's *Mein Kampf* are writings that clearly developed and propagated racist views.

> ### Website link 2.7
>
> Hitler is known as the consummate all-time terrorist – learn more through his memoir, *Mein Kampf*: http://www.roadtopeace.org/index.php?itemid=125.

Racist theory has been progressively abandoned over the last two centuries, although the differing intellectual capacity among people of different races or ethnic groups is still being discussed. Intelligence is measured by IQ tests, which are of Western/US origin. The IQ test is biased towards the countries that developed the test, as the IQ test does not take into account many skills and competences that were unknown to the authors. Moreover, studies show that the *inter-individual* variability of genetic characteristics is much larger than the *inter-racial* groups' variability (Segall *et al.*, 1990). In other words, genetic differences among Europeans, or genetic differences among South African Zulus, are significantly greater than the genetic differences between the average European and the average Zulu – a strong anti-racist argument (Ferraro, 1990).

> **Website link 2.8**
>
> Why not try a free web-based IQ test?:
> http://www.ifreeiqtest.com/.

Cultural hostility

In contrast to racism, cultural hostility does not imply prior prejudices as to who is inferior or superior according to race or culture. Culture is part of a person's heritage. There is a strong affective dimension, when a person's cultural values are threatened. This emotional response may result from:

1. Simple interactions with people whose cultural values are quite different. This may lead to feelings of unease, difficulty in communication and lack of empathy. A defensive response may develop, in terms of minor and unconscious cultural hostility.
2. Collective reactions to groups that are culturally different. Cases are so numerous worldwide that it would need many pages to list them exhaustively.

A few examples include Transylvanian Hungarians and Romanians, people in ex-Yugoslavia, Armenians of High Karabakh and Azeris of the Azerbaijan enclave in Soviet Armenia; Walloons and Flemings in Belgium; Protestant and Catholic communities in Ulster. *Identity is a matter of culture rather than race.*

It is not only territorial conflicts but also economic competition that may cause cultural hostility, especially when combined with cultural differences. For instance, some negative feelings toward the Japanese in the United States were generated by media about the large trade imbalance, combined with culturally based Japanese protectionism. Despite the large trade imbalance with China, there seems to be less economic animosity due to lower levels of protectionism. Exports from China to the United States are largely financed by the United States.

Cultural hostility directed at successful nations is often a fairly ambiguous feeling, where admiration and envy for the other's achievements go along with contempt for many traits of the envied people and an unwillingness to understand the root causes of the other's success. This may also results in naive copies of selected cultural artefacts as magical ways of becoming stronger: in *Robinson Crusoe* savages were about to eat Man Friday in order to gain his qualities.

Part 4 of this book further examines the mechanism of cultural hostility, which is sometimes increased by language and communication problems. Intercultural misunderstandings may stem from a lack of competency in the other's language, or from the natural tendency to adopt defensive stereotypes. This often results in a snowballing cultural hostility.

Questions

1. Discuss cultural variation in the solutions that have been found across societies to the four common problems listed below:
   (a) How to secure oneself (to feel secure, subjectively, and to protect oneself, objectively) against unforeseeable negative events (a grave illness, an accident, etc.).
   (b) How to treat the oldest in the community when they can no longer work.
   (c) Who should have access to education, on what criteria, and how should its cost be financed, given that the resources available for education, private and public, are not infinite? To what extent should education be given to *all* members of a particular

society, irrespective of their age, social class and personal capacities? On which bases should access to education be organized?

(d) How should couples, the basic unit for the reproduction of the species, be formed? What role should love, common ethnic or social belonging, age or (even) sex play in such a process?

2. Discuss the marketing implications of differing cultural solutions to points (a) and (b) in question 1, in terms of the existence of certain products or services, provided by the market, the state or mutual bodies, organized within the family group or by a traditional community.

3. What is the influence of space availability (mostly determined by population density in a definite country or area) on material culture? Give examples.

4. Indicate how the following products and services are 'loaded' with time, in terms of time used in consumption, time-saving device, durability, waiting time, seasonality, time projections in the past and the future, etc. (as an example, Box 7.1 describes the time load in life insurance policies):
   (a) a dishwashing machine;
   (b) a haircut;
   (c) obtaining cash from your bank;
   (d) spending two-week vacations at Club Méditerranée;
   (e) fresh orange juice versus dried orange juice (i.e. concentrated powder).

5. How would you expect consumer behaviour to vary across cultures for the five products/services above? (Cite one example per case.)

6. You try to park your car. A sign indicates that parking in this area is limited to 15 minutes. Another sign reads: 'Long term parking, 300 metres'. What do these explicit signs suggest concerning temporal culture in this country?

7. Define what would be the most important criteria for recruitment in a being oriented society as compared with a doing oriented society.

8. In most countries, police and judiciary positions are subject to a condition of nationality (being a national is a requirement for entering the service) whereas in universities and research centres positions are open to applicants regardless of their nationality. Why?

9. Find examples of cultural borrowing (in everyday life, in the press, in people's behaviour, in work as well as leisure activities, the arts, etc.).

10. The scooter was invented just after the Second World War on a Californian airport, by putting a body on a motorcycle; this allowed quick movement on the tarmac. The invention was industrially developed by the Italians in the 1950s and 1960s. In the 1970s, the Japanese began to sell scooters worldwide. What does this suggest in terms of cultural borrowing?

11. Try to elaborate on the following assertion: 'The usual traffic in marketing and business texts is that this generally starts with the American text and this is then translated into other languages or sometimes used in the original version.' What are the problems likely to be encountered by non-US educators and practitioners when using such materials? On the other hand, what are the advantages of using them?

References

1. Petit, Karl (1960), *Dictionnaire des Citations*, Paris: Marabout.
2. Kluckhohn, Florence R. and Frederick L. Strodtbeck (1961), *Variations in Value Orientations*. Westport, CT: Greenwood Press.
3. Hall, Edward T. (1959), *The Silent Language*. New York: Doubleday.
4. Hall, Edward T. (1966), *The Hidden Dimension*. New York: Doubleday.
5. Hall, Edward T. (1976), *Beyond Culture*. Garden City, NY: Anchor Press/Doubleday.
6. Hall, Edward T. (1983), *The Dance of Life*. New York: Anchor Press/Doubleday.
7. Hofstede, Geert (2001), *Culture Consequences* (2nd edn). Thousand Oaks, CA: Sage.
8. Triandis, Harry C. (1983), 'Dimensions of Cultural Variation as Parameters of Organizational Theories', *International Studies of Management and Organization*, XII (4), 139–69.
9. Triandis, Harry C. (1994), *Culture and Social Behavior*. New York: McGraw-Hill.
10. Trompenaars, Fons (1993), *Riding the Waves of Culture*. London: Nicholas Brealey.
11. Cleveland, Mark and Michel Laroche (2007), 'Acculturaton to the Global Consumer Culture: Scale Development and Research Paradigm', *Journal of Business Research*, 60, 249–59.
12. Bond, Michael Harris (1987), 'Chinese Culture Connection: Chinese Values and the Search for Culture-Free Dimensions of Culture', *Journal of Cross-Cultural Psychology*, 18, 143–74.
13. Jacoby, Jacob, George J. Szybillo, and Carol K. Berning (1976), 'Time and Consumer Behavior: An Interdisciplinary Overview', *Journal of Consumer Research*, 2, 320–39.
14. Spears, Nancy, Lin Xiaohua, and John C. Mowen (2001), 'Time Orientation in the United States, China, and Mexico: Measurement and Insights for Promotional Strategy', *Journal of International Consumer Marketing*, 13 (1), 57–75.
15. Usunier, Jean-Claude (1991), 'Business Time Perceptions and National Cultures: A Comparative Survey', *Management International Review*, 31 (3), 197–217.
16. Usunier, Jean-Claude (2003), 'The Role of Time in International Business Negotiations', in *International Business Negotiations*, Pervez N. Ghauri and Jean-Claude Usunier, Eds. (2nd edn). Oxford: Elsevier.
17. Palmer, David K. and David F. Schoorman (1999), 'Unpackaging the Multiple Aspects of Time in Polychronicity', *Journal of Managerial Psychology*, 14 (3/4), 323.
18. Usunier, Jean-Claude and Pierre Valette-Florence (1994), 'Perceptual Time Patterns ("Time Styles"): A Psychometric Scale', *Time and Society*, 3 (2), 219–41.
19. Ferraro, Gary P. (1990), *The Cultural Dimension of International Business*. Englewood Cliffs, NJ: Prentice Hall.
20. Harris, Philip R. and Robert T. Moran (1987), *Managing Cultural Differences* (2nd edn). Houston, TX: Gulf Publishing Company.
21. Chapman, Malcom and Ahmad Jamal (1997), 'Acculturation: Cross Cultural Consumer Perceptions and the Symbolism of Domestic Space', *Advances in Consumer Research*, 24, 138–43.
22. Kelman, Herbert C. (1961), 'Processes of Opinion Change', *Public Opinion Quarterly*, 25 (1), 57–78.
23. Borenstein, Severin and Garth Saloner (2001), 'Economics and Electronic Commerce', *Journal of Economic Perspectives*, 15 (1), 3–12.
24. Ohler, Jason (2001), 'Taming the Technological Beast', *The Futurist*, January–February, 16–21.
25. Swift, Jonathon B. (1999), 'Cultural Closeness as a Facet of Cultural Affinity', *International Marketing Review*, 16 (3), 183–201.
26. Ng, Siew Imm, Julie Anne Lee, and Geoffery N. Soutar (2007), 'Tourists' Intention to Visit a Country: The Impact of Cultural Distance', *Tourism Management*, 28 (5), 1497–506.
27. Anderson, Erin and Barton Weitz (1989), 'Determinants of Continuity in Conventional Industrial Channel Dyads', *Marketing Science*, 8, 310–23.
28. Van Oudenhoven, Jan Pieter and Karen I. van der Zee (2002), 'Successful International Cooperation: The Influence of Cultural Similarity, Strategic Differences, and International Experience', *Applied Psychology*, 51 (4), 633.
29. Martinez-Zarzoso, Inmaculada (2003), 'Gravity Model: An Application to Trade between Regional Blocs', *Atlantic Economic Journal*, 31 (2), 174–88.
30. Yu, Chwo-Ming Joseph and Dixie S. Zietlow (1995), 'The Determinants of Bilateral Trade among Asia-Pacific Countries', *ASEAN Economic Bulletin*, 11 (3), 298–305.
31. Wang, Chih-Kang and Charles W. Lamb Jr (1983), 'The Impact of Selected Environmental Forces Upon Consumers' Willingness to Buy Foreign Products', *Journal of the Academy of Marketing Science*, 11 (2), 71–84.
32. Shenkar, Oded (2001), 'Cultural Distance Revisited: Towards a More Rigorous Conceptualization and Measurement of Cultural Differences', *Journal of International Business Studies*, 32 (3), 519–35.

Teaching materials

A2.1 Cross-cultural scenario

Inshallah

Stefan Phillips, a manager for a large US airline, was transferred to Dhahran, Saudi Arabia, to set up a new office. Although Stefan had had several other extended overseas assignments in Paris and Brussels, he was not well prepared for working in the Arab world. At the end of his first week Stefan came home in a state of near total frustration. As he sat at the dinner table that night he told his wife how exasperating it had been to work with the local employees, who, he claimed, seemed to take no responsibility for anything. Whenever something went wrong they would simply say '*Inshallah*' ('If God wills it'). Coming from a culture which sees no problem as insoluble, Stefan could not understand how the local employees could be so passive about job-related problems. 'If I hear one more *inshallah*,' he told his wife, 'I'll go crazy.'

Question

What might you tell Stefan to help him better understand the cultural realities of Saudi Arabia?

(Source: Ferraro, p. 118.[1] Ferraro, Gary, *The Cultural Dimensions of International Business*, 5th edn, © 2006; reproduced by permission of Pearson Education, Inc., Upper Saddle River, NJ.)

A2.2 Cross-cultural interaction

Engineering a decision

Mr Legrand is a French engineer who works for a Japanese company in France. One day the general manager, Mr Tanaka, calls him into his office to discuss a new project in the Middle East. He tells Mr Legrand that the company is very pleased with his dedicated work and would like him to act as chief engineer for the project. It would mean two to three years away from home, but his family would be able to accompany him and there would be considerable personal financial benefits to the position – and, of course, he would be performing a valuable service to the company. Mr Legrand thanks Mr Tanaka for the confidence he has in him but says he will have to discuss it with his wife before deciding. Two days later he returns and tells Mr Tanaka that both he and his wife do not like the thought of leaving France and so he does not want to accept the position. Mr Tanaka says nothing but is somewhat dumbfounded by his decision.

Question

Why is Mr Tanaka so bewildered by Mr Legrand's decision?

1. He believes it is foolish for Mr Legrand to refuse all the financial benefits that go with the position.

2. He cannot accept that Mr Legrand should take any notice of his wife's opinion in the matter.

3. He believes Mr Legrand is possibly trying to bluff him into offering greater incentives to accept the offer.

4. He feels it is not appropriate for Mr Legrand to place his personal inclinations above those of his role as an employee of the company.

(Source: Brislin *et al.*, p. 158.[2] *Intercultural Interactions: A Practical Guide*, by Brislin, Richard W., Kenneth Cushner, Craig Cherrie and Mahealani Young, copyright 1986 by Sage Publication Inc. Books, reproduced with permission of Sage Publications Inc. Books in the format Textbook via Copyright Clearance Center.)

A2.3 Cross-cultural interaction

Opening a medical office in Saudi Arabia

Dr Tom McDivern, a physician from New York City, was offered a two-year assignment to practise medicine in a growing urban centre in Saudi Arabia. Many of the residents in the area he was assigned to were recent immigrants from the much smaller outlying rural areas.

Because Western medicine was relatively unknown to many of these people, one of Dr McDivern's main responsibilities was to introduce himself and his services to those in the community. A meeting at a local school was organized for that specific purpose. Many people turned out. Tom's presentation went well. Some local residents also presented their experiences with Western medicine so others could hear the value of using his service. Some of Tom's office staff were also present to make appointments for those interested in seeing him when his doors opened one week later. The meeting was an obvious success. His opening day was booked solid.

When that day finally arrived, Tom was anxious to greet his first patients. Thirty minutes had passed, however, and neither of his first two patients had arrived. He was beginning to worry about the future of his practice while wondering where his patients were.

Question

What is the major cause of Tom's worries?

1. Although in Tom's mind and by his standards his presentation was a success, people actually only made appointments so as not to hurt his feelings. They really had no intention of using his services as modern medicine is so foreign to their past experiences.

2. Given the time lag between sign-up and the actual day of the appointment, people had time to rethink their decision. They had just changed their minds.

3. Units of time differ between Arabs and Americans. Whereas to Tom his patients were very late, the Arab patient could still arrive and be on time.

4. Tom's patients were seeing their own traditional healers from their own culture; after that, they could go on to see this new doctor, Tom.

(Source: Brislin *et al.*, pp. 160–1.[2] *Intercultural Interactions: A Practical Guide*, by Brislin, Richard W., Kenneth Cushner, Craig Cherrie and Mahealani Young, copyright 1986 by Sage Publication Inc. Books, reproduced with permission of Sage Publications Inc. Books in the format Textbook via Copyright Clearance Center.)

A2.4 Reading

Language and time patterns – the Bantu case

Cultural and linguistic unity of the Bantu area

The Bantu area spreads along the southern side of a line that starts from Douala, Cameroon, by the Atlantic Ocean, and finishes at the mouth of the Tana river in the Indian Ocean. It divides northern and southern Africa. The Bantu area covers most of the southern cone of this continent.

These wide territories (several million square kilometres) are occupied by Bantu people, with the limited exception of some other small ethnic groups. The cultural unity of this people has been established on the basis of common linguistic features. As early as the middle of the nineteenth century, W. Bleek (quoted by Kadima and Lumwanu[3]) had recognized that Bantu languages shared common lexical elements and many grammatical forms. In taking Bleek's work one stage further, anthropologists, historians and linguists have tried to identify the common social and cultural traits which allow a particular area to be classified as Bantu.

Alexis Kagame[4] for instance, has studied Bantu linguistic systems, especially their underlying structures. He has collated what he terms 'compared Bantu philosophy'. The convergence of authors when describing the conception of time in Bantu cultures is quite marked.

The unification of time and space

At the heart of the Bantu's intuition of time lies the postulate of a very close relation between time and space. Within this postulate none of these basic dimensions of reality exist without the others. Alexis Kagame[4] reveals this conceptual link.

Ontologically, Bantu culture puts whatever may be conceived or said into one of four categories:

1. The being – of intelligence (man).
2. The being – without intelligence (thing).
3. The being – as localizer (be it place or date).
4. The being – modal (incidentality, or modification of the being).

The major assumption made by Kagame is that translation of Bantu words in metaphysical categories is possible. He therefore translates *ha-ntu* as the being-localizer. This common word expresses the unity of space (place) and time (date). In the Bantu language this term means both the 'there' of locus and the 'now' of time. It is an indivisible localizer, both spatial and temporal.

The localizing prefix *ha-*, which forms *ha-ntu*, and its variants *pa-ntu* and *ka-ntu* are found in the eastern zone of the Bantu territory. Its equivalent in the western zone is *va*, whereas it is *go* in the south-eastern part of the Bantu area. The idea of unification between space and time in Bantu languages is shared by Emil Pearson,[5] who has lived in the south-east of Angola since the 1920s. He writes in his book *People of the Aurora* (p. 75):

In the Ngangela language there is no word, as far as I know, for 'time' as a continuous, flowing passage of events or the lack of same. Time is experiential or objective, that is, it is that which is meaningful to the person or thing which experiences it. *Time and space are cognate incidents of eternity.* The same word is used for both 'time' and 'space' (the latter in the sense of 'distance').

'Ntunda' can either express meaningful time or meaningful space. For example: 'Ntunda kua i li' – 'There is some distance'; and 'Ntunda i na hiti' – 'Time has passed'. The related verb 'Simbula', means 'delay', the thought being of awaiting 'meaningful time'. To the European the African may seem to be idling away useful time, whereas the latter, according to his philosophy, is awaiting experiential time, the time that is right for accomplishing his objective. 'Time' is locative, something that is virtually concrete, not something abstract. The locatives 'Ha', 'Ku' and 'Mu' are used for expressing 'time' as well as 'place'. Example: 'Ha Katete' – 'In the beginning' (as to either time or place); 'Ku lutue' can mean either 'in front' or 'in the future'. 'Mu nima' can mean 'behind' as to place, or 'after' as to time.

Bantu time experience

Two significant points sharply contrast the way Bantus experience time with the Western way of experiencing it within a technological environment. First, Bantus have no theoretical substantive to designate time as an entity per se, which can be quantified and measured. Second, for Bantus, the temporal dimension is intrinsic to the event itself. It is not an abstraction as in most Occidental developed cultures. To these cultures it appears as a content which flows regularly from the past to the future, through the present; a flow in which everything moves at the same speed, being 'in time'. For Bantu people time has no real value, no meaning, without the occurrence of an event which will serve as a 'marker'. The intuition of time only becomes effective when an action or an event happens: warriors' expedition, arrival of the train, rainfall, starvation on the increase. Time then becomes individualized. It is drawn out of anonymity. It is not anybody's time which would be abstractedly defined. It is concrete time concerning people I know. Instead of considering time as a straight railway track, where events may happen successively, it will only be spoken of as 'the time of this . . .' or 'the time of that . . .', or time which is favourable for this and that. That is why, on many occasions, there is no point in giving dates, that is to refer oneself to ideal time coordinates. History is not a series of dates, but a link between various events. Everything possesses its own internal time. Each event occurs at its own time.

(Source: Usunier and Napoleon-Biguma, pp. 95–114.[6] Reproduced with the kind permission of the publisher and the co-author.)

A2.5 Exercise

World picture test

Objective

To clarify participants' understanding of countries and cultures of the world through their knowledge of geography.

- *Participants*: Three or more persons. Facilitator.
- *Materials*: Paper and pens.
- *Setting*: No special requirements.
- *Time*: At least 30 minutes to one hour.

Procedure

1. Each participant is given a sheet of paper and a pen and asked to:
   (a) draw a map of the world as best they can within a five-minute time period;
   (b) name as many of the countries as they can;
   (c) mark any country they have visited for a week or longer;
   (d) exchange papers with other members of the group and discuss what differences are evidenced in what the other person put into their drawing and/or left out of the drawing.

2. Discuss the following points:
   (a) Does a person's awareness of the shape of a country reveal that person's awareness of the shape of the culture?
   (b) When a person leaves out a country, what does this mean?
   (c) When a person leaves out a continent, what does this mean?
   (d) What country did the person place in the centre of the map and what does that mean?
   (e) When a person draws a country out of place in relation to other countries, what does this mean?
   (f) Were they better acquainted with countries they had visited?
   (g) When the person objects violently to doing the drawing, what does that mean?
   (h) How well did persons draw home countries of other group members?
   (i) What do the persons plan to do as a result of what they learned in this exercise?

(Source: Weeks et al., pp. 107–8.[7])

Appendix references

1. Ferraro, Gary P. (1990), *The Cultural Dimension of International Business*. Englewood Cliffs, NJ: Prentice Hall.
2. Brislin, Richard W., Kenneth Kushner, Craig Cherrie, and Mahealani Yong (1986), *Intercultural Interactions: A Practical Guide*. Newbury Park, CA: Sage.
3. Kadima, K. and F. Lumwanu (1989), 'Aires linguistiques à l'intérieur du monde Bantu: Aspects généraux et innovations, dialectologie et classifications', in Théophile Obenga, Ed., *Les Peuples Bantu, migrations, expansion et identité culturelle*. Paris: Editions L'Harmattan, 63–75.
4. Kagame, Alexis (1975), 'Aperception Empirique du Temps et Conception de L'histoire dans la Pensée Bantu', in *Les Cultures et le Temps*. Paris: Payot/Unesco.
5. Pearson, Emil (1977), *People of the Aurora*. San Diego, CA: Beta Books.
6. Usunier, Jean-Claude and Constantin Napoléon-Biguma (1991), 'Gestion Culturelle Du Temps: Le Cas Bantou', in *Management Interculturel: Modes et Modèles*, Gauthey Franck and Dominique Xardel, Eds. Paris: Economica.
7. Weeks, William H., Paul B. Pedersen, and Richard W. Brislin (1987), *A Manual of Structured Experiences for Crosscultural Learning*. Yarmouth, ME: Intercultural Press.

3

Cultural dynamics 2: interactions, mindsets and behaviours

Figure 2.1 in Chapter 2 illustrated that basic cultural assumptions are related to cultural models of time and space, and that both time and space influence our concept of the self and others. The first section of this chapter is dedicated to concepts of the self and others, which are central to the explanation of how people interact (section 3.2) and what leads to action, including attitudes (section 3.3), information (section 3.4), feelings (section 3.5), and rules (section 3.6). This material is organized around common problems, explained in the three tables (3.1 to 3.3) that directly relate to Figure 2.1. The final section in the chapter (3.7) discusses how basic cultural assumptions translate into everyday behaviour.

3.1

Concept of the self and others

The concept of the self and others deals with how the organization of a society is internalized by people and is reflected in the view we have of ourselves in relation to others. It is largely about people within a society responding positively and unconsciously to membership. People make assumptions about the hows and whys of their membership in society, even though they are largely unaware of it. These assumptions differ from one society to another.

The concept of the self is a modal view of what people *are* in society and therefore what they are allowed to *do*. Assumptions are often related to the main sociodemographic categories (e.g. age, sex, social class), as well as to idealized conduct in particular

roles (the perfect partner, businessman, child, etc.). These ideal patterns are depicted in books, films, TV series, and many other cultural artefacts that convey subliminal normative messages. For instance, we have an abundance of identification possibilities from films, such as *Harry Potter*, *Spiderman*, and Robert Neville in *I am Legend*. In viewing these, we constantly receive messages on how to behave. We find heroes to be desirable role models, even though we know that these characters are fictional.

The concept of the self has major implications in the area of consumer behaviour, many of which are discussed in Chapter 4. Briefly, our possessions are a major reflector of our identities. As we ascribe meaning to what we buy and consume, we strive to assert, complete, or attain our 'ideal' self through our possessions.[1]

One of the most studied aspects of self-concept across cultures is the tendency toward an independent or interdependent self-construal. Markus and Kitayama[2] identified these two relatively stable self-construals which emphasize the degree to which people see themselves as separate from or connected to others. They described the Western or individualist self as *independent*, 'containing significant dispositional attributes, and as detached from context', whereas the Eastern or collectivist self is *interdependent* 'with the surrounding context, [where] it is the "other" or the "self-in-relation-to-other" that is focal in individual experience' (p. 225)[2]. While each of us is able to draw on either aspect, the most salient aspect determines which influence is most likely in a given situation. For instance, in collectivist societies, the interdependent self is more likely to

Table 3.1 Concepts of the self and others

Basic problem/Cultural orientations	Contrasts across cultures
How should we treat unknown people?	
(a) Is human nature basically good or bad?	Unknown people are considered favourably and shown confidence or, conversely, they are treated with suspicion when met for the first time.
Appraising others	
(b) When appraising others, emphasis placed on: 　　(i)　age 　　(ii)　sex 　　(iii)　social class	Who are the persons to be considered trustworthy and reliable, with whom it is possible to do business? (i)　Older (younger) people are seen more favourably. (ii)　Trustworthiness is based on sex or not. (iii)　Social class plays a significant role (or not) in concepts of the self and others.
Appraising oneself	
(c) Emphasis placed on the self-concept perceived as culturally appropriate: 　　(i)　self-esteem: low/high 　　(ii)　perceived potency: low/high 　　(iii)　level of activity: low/high	To give the correct appearance one should behave: (i)　Shy and modest versus extrovert or even arrogant. (ii)　Power should be shown versus hidden. (iii)　Busy people or unoccupied/idle people are well regarded.
Relating the individual to the group	
(d) Individualism versus collectivism	The individual is seen as the basic resource and therefore individual-related values are strongly emphasized (personal freedom, human rights, equality between men and women); versus the group is seen as the basic resource and therefore group values are favoured (loyalty, sense of belonging, sense of personal sacrifice for the community, etc.).

be salient, leading to norms, roles and values of the ingroup becoming the 'obviously' correct way to behave.[3]

Table 3.1 presents major categories in the area of concepts of the self and others. From Table 3.1 there are four basic problems that we will discuss below: (1) How should we treat strangers; (2) How do we assess or appraise others; (3) How do we appraise ourselves; and (4) How do we relate to the group?

Is human nature good or bad?

Our attitudes to people on first contact may be positive or negative. If we assume human nature is basically good, we have a friendly and open-minded attitude toward people we do not know. When visiting the United States or Australia, Europeans are often amazed by how well they are received. It is clear that Australians have a strong positive belief about new people, who are assumed to be good. Such an attitude has a functional side in relatively new countries. Generally, twentieth-century films of the 'Western' genre portrayed 'bad' Indians and 'good' European settlers. The assumptions of this human nature orientation are fairly straightforward: 'civilized' = good; 'uncivilized' (Indians, gamblers, desperadoes) = bad.

In contrast, first contact with the Latin Europeans and South Americans can be more difficult. The novels of Colombian writer Gabriel García Márquez are typical of the view that human nature is basically bad. Trust should only be given to those who are known to be trustworthy.

Website link 3.1

Believed by many to be one of the world's greatest writers, Gabriel García Márquez is a Colombian-born author and journalist, winner of the 1982 Nobel Prize for Literature: **http://www.themodernworld.com**.

In reality, assumptions about human nature are of a dialectic nature. That is, the apparent contradiction between the two assumptions is resolved at a higher level of thinking. They would read more as:

- Human nature is basically good, but . . .
- Human nature is basically bad, but . . .
- Human nature lies somewhere between good and bad, and . . .

The two sides of each basic assumption coexist in most religions, which strive to improve individuals, especially through the social morals they develop. For ourselves, we still need culturally based reference points for evaluating others.

The dynamics of friendship involve assumptions about human nature. If human nature is assumed to be good, then friendship develops quickly but often more superficially. Since many people are supposed to be good, it is not as necessary to select a small group of 'true' friends. When it is assumed that human nature is generally bad, friendship develops more slowly owing to initial distrust. Friendships will generally be fewer, but deeper. A circle of friends may be a protective barrier against a society perceived as unfriendly, if not hostile. While human nature orientation is not directly related to action, it is related to marketing through collaboration, competition and the messages we create, which depict bad versus good characters, etc.

How do we appraise others?

We judge others in many different areas of our lives, including making friends, choosing business partners, targeting potential customers, and so on. Apart from personality traits, which we judge by intuition, we use the many available clues, such as age, sex and behaviour. How each clue is evaluated depends on our culture.

Sex is probably the most important cultural difference, because of the definite roles and self-concepts imposed on boys and girls by their culture. In *Male and Female*, Margaret Mead (pp. 7–8) says:

The differences between the two sexes is one of the important conditions upon which we have built the many varieties of human culture that give human beings dignity and stature. In every known society, mankind has elaborated the biological division of labour into forms often very remotely related to the original biological differences that provided the original clues. Upon the contrast in bodily form, men have built analogies between sun and moon, night and day, goodness and evil, strength and tenderness, steadfastness and fickleness, endurance and vulnerability. Sometimes one quality has been assigned to one sex, sometimes to the other . . . Some people think of women as too weak to work out of doors, others regard women as the appropriate bearers of heavy burdens . . . some religions, including our European traditional religions, have assigned women an inferior role in the religious hierarchy, others have built their whole symbolic relationship with the supernatural world upon male imitations of the natural function of women. In some cultures women are regarded as sieves through whom the best guarded secrets will sift; in others it is the men who are the gossips.[4]

(Copyright © 1949 by Margaret Mead. Reprinted by permission of HarperCollins Publishers. WILLIAM MORROW.)

Website link 3.2

Learn more about the life of Margaret Mead: **http://www.webster.edu/~woolflm/margaretmead.html**.

The place of women in society has changed greatly over the last century. Some basic rights, such as voting, were long denied to women. In many societies the place of a woman is still very different from that of a man. Not all that long ago, the voting rights of women were still inferior to that of men, even in advanced countries like Switzerland (in very traditional cantons). In many countries women are largely dependent on men, mostly on an economic basis. In some traditional Muslim countries women are not allowed to work outside the home, and are often not permitted to go outside alone, even to shop. Worldwide differences in the self-concept of women, and the concept of women held by men, are striking.

Youth may be associated with inexperience, doubtful character and lack of seriousness, or, by way of contrast, with open-mindedness, creativity, and the ability to change things and to undertake new ventures. Naturally, both sets of qualities are found in young people of all cultures. What is more interesting is how certain cultures, like Japan and Africa, place a higher value on older people, while others, like the United States and Australia, value younger people in society. This divergence of attitude probably occurs because the qualities typically found in the more highly valued age group are implicitly perceived as more congruent and favourable for the overall development of the society.

An emphasis on age is associated with other cultural orientations such as power distance, which is explained later in this chapter. It is also related to the dominant family models in a particular society. Where the family is nuclear and the structure is fairly weak, the parental authority will also tend to fade, as will the positive view of older age groups as being in the 'adequate' age bracket. On the contrary, where an extended family is dominated by an older patriarch or matriarch, the image of age and competence will be influenced. On average, 'modern culture' values younger people because changes are extremely rapid (e.g. TV advertising revolves around beautiful young, rough and ready young boys or yuppie-like professionals), whereas in 'traditional culture' the elders are a source of wisdom and guidance for the community and as a consequence their age is more highly valued.

All societies place people in particular strata, such as *social classes and castes*. In economically oriented societies they may divide people into the 'haves' and the 'have-nots', but other criteria may be based on birth or education, even in the absence of obvious wealth or income criteria. Like many other elements of the concept of the self and others, social class is important for consumer behaviour, as people express their real or imagined class differences by what they buy and use.

Social stratification is based on different criteria across cultures, even though social classes consistently appear across cultures. For instance, in many newer Western countries social class is based on wealth. In others, such as India, it is based on birth. In India, castes (a special order of social stratification) include four major hereditary classes into which the Hindu society is divided: the *Brahman*, *Kshatriya*, *Vaisya* and *Sudra*. In China, social class is something in between, in that it does not belong to an individual but extends to his or her family.[5]

It is not the existence of social classes that differ across societies, but the degree of emphasis placed on social stratification. In countries where the emphasis is strong, people in higher classes see themselves as *being substantially different* from those in lower classes. This can extend to speaking the language differently (or even a different language), prohibiting interclass marriages, and distinguishing oneself by specific tastes and lifestyles.

Website link 3.3

For an in-depth analysis of the Hindu caste system:
http://www.hinduwebsite.com/hinduismln_caste.asp.

How do we judge ourselves?

People hold a certain view of themselves, which is subconsciously chosen to be culturally appropriate to their ingroup. Three main areas of cultural contrasts may be identified: self-esteem, perceived potency and perceived activity.[6] The first contrast is in perceptions of self-esteem. Self-esteem can be low or high according to whether we think of ourselves as good or not good. Low self-esteem results in displaying modest and self-effacing behaviour, whereas higher self-esteem results in displaying more assertiveness and self-assurance. Asians, on average, clearly display lower self-esteem than Westerners. This does not mean that Asians deserve less esteem, but rather that they assume that they deserve less as an individual. The second contrast is in perceptions of potency. Some cultures encourage individuals to view themselves as powerful and capable of accomplishing almost any task. The third contrast is in perceptions of personal activity. When the appropriate level of personal activity is seen as high, people will boast about their being 'workaholics', will work weekends, and generally be satisfied with overworking. When, by contrast, the appropriate image of the self is based on a low level of activity, as in the Hindu case, the standard attributes of a normal self-concept will focus on few hours spent in the office, low involvement in work-related issues, and having time available for pure inactivity. These three dimensions interact, so that people who are low on self-esteem, perceived power and perceived activity feel powerless and often accept the world as it is. Conversely, people with high self-esteem, perceived power and perceived activity are more likely to be overconfident and take on difficult tasks, even to the extent of failure.

Website link 3.4

Psychotherapists try to discourage narcissism, and encourage self-esteem. Find out how the two are related: http://www.hmiworld.org/hmi/issues/Mar_April_2004/around_narcissism.htm/.

How do we relate the individual to the group?

Defining the boundaries between people and the groups they belong to, in order to ensure the smooth and efficient functioning of society, is a challenge to all societies. The concepts of individualism and collectivism are mentioned in Table 3.1, 'Concepts of the self and others', because they are deeply ingrained in the 'borders' of our self. People from individualist cultures have a more clear-cut view of where 'oneself' stops ('I, me, mine' as George Harrison's song says) and where 'others' start, whereas people from collectivist cultures have much fuzzier borders between their self and their ingroup.

The 'rice argument' is frequently used to explain the differences between individualism and collectivism. Rice growers need to coordinate the flooding of rice fields, which promotes dependence among the growers by requiring common action. Conversely, the basic staples in the West are 'individualist' cereals (wheat, barley, oats, etc.), where the farmer's achievements depend mostly on his or her own individual efforts.

Individualism is based on the principle of asserting your independence and individuality. All societies have individuals and groups, but *individualism* stresses the smallest unit as being that where the solution lies. Common individualist assumptions are as follows:

1. Initiative, effort and achievements can best be developed at the individual level, because people are *different* (divisibility).
2. Individual achievements can be added to each other without loss (the sum equals the parts: the additive model).
3. Society has to maximize individual freedom, emphasize high individual achievers, and value individuals (the freedom orientation).

These assumptions are not necessarily 'true'. One may ascribe to them because of intellectual conviction, especially assumption 1, or to get personal leeway, as

is the consequence of assumption 3. They are 'true' to the extent that they are largely a self-fulfilling prophecy. The obvious problems arise from assumption 2: collective action is simply a sum of individual effort. The process is more complex, as suggested by the collectivism assumptions:

1. Initiative, effort and achievements can best be developed at the group level, because people function in groups rather than as separate independent entities. They belong to a *common* reality (the organic view).
2. Collective achievements are fundamentally different in nature from individual achievements, and the combination of parts (if such a computation is even possible) is much greater than the parts themselves (the multiplicative model).
3. Society has to maximize group coherence and social harmony, even at the expense of individual freedom and, if need be, minimizing individual achievements (the concord orientation).

Collectivism is often associated with 'traditional culture', whereas individualism is a strong component of 'modern culture', especially in the area of consumption, which is an excellent domain for the expression of individual freedom and difference from others. Since the Middle Ages, the awareness of self has become less shared and more individualistic, which is evidenced by the growing popularity of self-oriented objects such as mirrors, self-portraits, chairs (rather than benches), etc.[7]

Modern individualism has its roots in sixteenth- and seventeenth-century England. It is based on the ideas of English and Scottish philosophers (More, Bacon, Hume and Locke) and was generated in large part by the Act of Habeas Corpus, the first legal edict forbidding the Sovereign from jailing somebody without lawful reason. The United Nations Universal Declaration of Human Rights is in the same vein: it favours an individual-based view of what is a 'good' society. The individualist view of human rights is also typical of Amnesty International, which has heated debates with some Asian governments holding a different view of what human rights are.

The individualist/collectivist divide is not always clear-cut. In individualist societies people still belong to groups, live in communities and think of themselves as integrated into a larger whole. In collectivist societies people still feel a need to express their personal identity, and strive often for individual success and self-actualization. Cooperation takes place in all societies, but people cooperate in culturally appropriate ways. Those from individualist societies are more likely to rely on individuality and rationality as motivations for cooperation, while those from collectivist societies are likely to be driven by collective rationality and social forces.[8] Similarly, conflicts need to be handled in all societies. People from collectivist societies are more likely to rely on formal rules and procedures to handle disagreements, which preserves ingroup harmony, while those from individualist societies rely more on their own experience and training to handle disagreements.[9] In an individualist society people are seen as more mature if they act in a manner that is consistent with their attitudes, whereas people in a collectivist society are seen as more mature if they can put aside their own personal feelings and act in a socially appropriate manner.[10]

Box 3.1

From Chanel chick to individualist

'Brand auntie', 'Chanel chick'

These curious turns of phrase reflect Japan's obsession with brands. From her Luis Vuitton bag to her Gucci shoes the 'Brand auntie' thinks nothing of draping herself in luxury brands from head to toe.

The 'Chanel chick' is a high-school girl with a bit of cash on her hands. She will do what it takes to get those hands on a Chanel or Hermes wristwatch (quite beyond her means at a cost of several hundreds of thousands of Yen), paying by monthly instalments if she has to. Her dinner, on the other hand, is a pre-packaged meal bought at the local convenience store.

Why do the Japanese, as represented by such chicks and aunties, cluster around these exorbitantly expensive luxury brand goods in a frenzy of consumption, where each buys exactly the same thing as everyone else?

The Japanese as a people have been dominated by conformity – the Me Too-ist obsession 'so-and-so has one, so for me not to is, well . . .'. The sharing of identical values was seen as the only way to create a comfortable society. This tradition saw the 'wa', or harmony, as most precious, and conforming with others was an unbreakable rule of communities at all levels of society. Doing something different from others, making a statement as an individual, meant 'murahachibu' – banishment from the group – not straying from the herd continues to be seen as a prime virtue in Japan. This fundamental value of 'seeking to be like others' has created a 'desire to have the same things as others', which has further evolved into a sense that one 'must have the same things as others'. The result is a society where consensus on what is good or fashionable is easily reached, and the population quickly falls into step behind recognized innovators and opinion leaders.

Chanel chicks, Gucci grandmas, and Hermes honeys

In looking at which brands became the prime targets of this brand boom, we need to understand the Japanese obsession with Europe. Impressions of 'Western Prestige Brands' tend to lean heavily towards associations with Europe, seen generally as having an image of high quality, heritage, craftsmanship, elegance, and spirituality. Europe was seen as the model of modern civilization by nineteenth-century Meiji-era literati when the country opened its doors to the outside world after 200 years of isolation and the reverberations of this interaction with the colossus of European civilization continue to echo in Japan to this day. The popularity of brands such as Luis Vuitton, Chanel, Gucci, and Hermes is without question intimately related to perceptions of the distinctive identities of each of these brands. But it is also extremely important to keep in mind that all these brands are at the same time wrapped inextricably with the generalized aspiration and obsession with European culture that has characterized Japan for the last 130 years.

(Source: Ohye, 2003.[11])

Table 3.2 Hierarchical dimensions of individualism and collectivism

	Horizontal	Vertical
Individualism	Independent self-concept See self at same level as others (e.g. Sweden, Denmark, Australia)	Independent self-concept See self within a hierarchy (e.g. USA, Great Britain, France)
Collectivism	Interdependent self-concept See self at same level as others (e.g. Isreali kibbutz)	Interdependent self-concept See self within a hierarchy (e.g. Korea, Japan, India)

The 'modern' aspect of individualist assumptions is now heavily challenged by the rise of collectivist nations in Asia and in South America, with their achievements in international trade and their high rate of economic growth. Robertson[12] links the recent economic success in many Asian nations to traits associated with Confucian Dynamism or Long Term Orientation (LTO) as discussed in Chapter 2. This is the tendency toward a future-minded mentality.[13] At the individual level, it manifests itself in scholarship, hard work and perseverance, which have been instrumental in the success of many Asian nations. Thus, it is not individualism and collectivism that predict economic prosperity alone, but the interaction between many aspects of culture. The debate between individualism and collectivism is not yet finished; like water and oil they do not readily mix: even if they seem to blend when shaken vigorously, they separate when left to settle.

Recently, variation across individualist and collectivist societies has also been recognized in terms of hierarchical relationship, leading to horizontal (emphasizing equality) and vertical (emphasizing hierarchy) dimensions of individualism and collectivism.[14] Shavitt and colleagues[15] describe the differences as follows:

1. In vertical individualist societies, people are concerned with distinguishing themselves from others to improve their standing.
2. In horizontal individualist societies, people are concerned with expressing uniqueness and self-reliance.
3. In vertical collectivist societies, people are concerned with enhancing the cohesion and status of their ingroup and complying with authorities.

4. In horizontal collectivist societies, people are concerned with sociability and interdependence.

Table 3.2 outlines the hierarchical and status motivations behind these dimensions. Shavitt and colleagues[15] detail several areas in which this combination of values is likely to have a significant influence, including how people respond to others and how they respond to the marketing mix, especially advertising message appeal and effectiveness.

3.2

Interaction models

Individualism and collectivism refer to concepts of the self and others (as assumptions located *within* persons) as well as to a model of interaction *between* people. Countries higher in individualism are more likely to be more self-sufficient and less dependent on others. They are more likely to own and use private gardens rather than using public parks for gathering, have dogs and cats that eat pet food, have insurance, and perform do-it-yourself activities, such as painting and home carpentry.[16]

Table 3.3 lists a series of other aspects of what are considered to be culturally appropriate interaction models in particular societies. Most of these factors are based on Hofstede.[16,17] Although Hofstede developed these concepts in relation to organizational issues and through collection of data at the corporate level, they are largely transferable to the society as a whole.

The impact of these dimensions of national culture on various issues has been assessed, such as

Table 3.3 Interaction models

Cultural orientations	Contrasts across cultures
Equality or inequality in interpersonal interactions	
(a) Power distance (PD)	In high PD societies, hierarchy is strong, power is centralized at the top. In low PD societies, power is more equally distributed and superior and subordinates have a sense of equality as human beings.
Interacting *with* others or *for* others	
(b) Masculinity versus femininity	In masculine societies, assertiveness and personal achievement are favoured. In feminine societies, caring for others, adopting nurturing roles and emphasizing quality of life is more important.
Dealing with uncertainty	
(c) Uncertainty avoidance (UA)	In high UA societies, there is a tendency to avoid ambiguous situations, to prefer known, stable situations, uncertainty-reducing rules and procedures, which are seen as a necessity for efficiency. In low UA societies, ambiguity does not create the same level of anxiety. Uncertainty is seen as an opportunity, where people as individuals are the engine of change, which is perceived as a requirement for efficiency.
Relying on oneself or on others	
(d) Independence versus dependence	In individualist societies, there is a tendency to be motivated by personal preferences, needs and rights and for personal goals and rational analysis to take precedence. In collectivist societies, there is a tendency to be motivated by the norms and duties imposed by the ingroup and for ingroup goals and a relational analysis to take precedence.
Developing appropriate communication with others	
(e) Communication styles	In high context societies, communication is more diffuse and the meaning of a message is derived from the context and knowledge of the speaker. In low context societies, communication concentrates on specific issues and the meaning of a message is literal and explicit. For more information see Chapter 12 on Language, culture and communication.

structure, hierarchical relationships, management of expatriate personnel and variation in motivation and consumption patterns across culture.[16,18,19] While Hofstede's four dimensions of national culture were originally derived from an empirical analysis of IBM employees, they make sense for marketing and sales and, as such, have been studied extensively in international marketing and comparative consumer behaviour. Replications show that the dimensions are fairly stable, at least in terms of the distance between cultures.[16,19,20]

National cultures and the relativity of managerial practices

The cover picture of an issue of *Fortune* magazine relating to management styles shows an American with oriental-looking eyes attempting to eat a hamburger using chopsticks. This metaphor illustrates how difficult it is to transpose elements of one culture onto another. Geert Hofstede was one of the first researchers to question the adaptability of US management theories and practices to other cultural contexts. Empirical studies for Hofstede's work were undertaken between 1967 and 1973 within IBM, a large multinational company, in 66 of its national subsidiaries.[16] Hofstede was able to derive four main conceptual dimensions on which national cultures exhibit significant differences. One of these four dimensions is *individualism/collectivism*. In collectivist countries there is a close-knit social structure, where people neatly distinguish between members of the ingroup and members of the outgroup: people expect their group to care for them in exchange for unwavering loyalty. In individualistic societies the social fabric is much looser: people are basically supposed to care for themselves and their immediate family. Exchange takes place on the base of reciprocity: if an individual gives something to another, some sort of return is expected within a reasonable time span. The three other dimensions are explained below. They correspond to the first three cells in Table 3.3.

Website link 3.5

Examine Geert Hofstede's website for his dimensions of culture: **http://www.geert_hofstede.com**.

Power distance

Power distance measures how far a society and its members tolerate an unequal distribution of power in organizations and in society as a whole. It is shown as much by the behavioural values of superiors who display their power and exercise it, as by the behavioural values of subordinates who wait for their superiors to show their status and power, and are uncomfortable if they do not.

In high power distance societies, superiors and subordinates feel separated from each other. It is not easy to meet and talk with higher ranking people, and the real power tends to be very much concentrated at the top.

In low power distance societies, members of the organization tend to feel equal, and close to each other in their daily work relationships. They cope with situations of higher hierarchical distance by delegating power. At society level, power distance translates as shown in Box 3.2.

Box 3.2

More equal than others

In a peaceful revolution – the last revolution in Swedish history – the nobles of Sweden in 1809 deposed King Gustav IV whom they considered incompetent, and surprisingly invited Jean Baptiste Bernadotte, a French general who served under their enemy Napoleon, to become King of Sweden. Bernadotte accepted and he became King Charles XIV; his descendants occupy the Swedish throne to this day. When the new King was installed he addressed the Swedish parliament in their language. His broken Swedish amused the Swedes and they roared with laughter. The Frenchman who had become King was so upset that he never tried to speak Swedish again. In this incident Bernadotte was a victim of culture shock: never in his French upbringing and military career had he experienced subordinates who laughed at the mistakes of their superior. Historians tell us he had more problems adapting to the egalitarian Swedish and Norwegian mentality (he later became King of Norway as well) and to his subordinates' constitutional rights. He was a good learner, however (except for language), and he ruled the country as a highly respected constitutional monarch until 1844.

One of the aspects in which Sweden differs from France is the way its society handles *inequality*. There is inequality in any society. Even in the most simple hunter-gatherer band some people are bigger, stronger or smarter than others. The next thing is that some people have more power than others: they are more able to determine the behaviour of others than vice versa. Some people are given more status and respect than others.

(Source: Hofstede.[21])

Masculinity/femininity

Masculinity and femininity are responses to the common problem: 'do we interact *with* others or *for* others?' The assumptions behind the masculinity/femininity divide are different: should we help people (at the risk of their being weakened by a lack of personal effort) or should we not (at the risk, for them, of being even worse off)? This dimension roughly corresponds to the dominant gender role patterns: male/assertive and the female/nurturing roles. On average, men tended to score high on one extreme and women on the other, *across* societies, but there are also significant differences *between* societies.

In masculine societies the emphasis is on assertiveness, money, showing off possessions and caring less about the welfare of others. Generally, there is a stronger role differentiation between males and females, but both boys and girls learn to be assertive and ambitious. In masculine societies people are likely to be more possession oriented. They own more expensive watches and clothing.[9] People in masculine societies (whether individualist like the US or collectivist like Japan) admire the strong, like Rambo or Vin Diesel in the US. Those who are in a weaker position find less support from society.

In feminine societies the emphasis is on nurturing roles, interdependence between people and caring *for* others (who are seen as worth caring for, because they are temporarily weak). Generally, there is less gender role differentiation and both boys and girls learn to be modest and to sympathize with the underdog. In feminine societies the welfare system is highly developed, education is largely free and easily accessible, and there is openness about admitting to problems, such as in northern European countries. People in trouble are shown patience and hope. In feminine societies people are more likely to share both large and small decisions, such as the choice of main car and everyday food shopping, and to purchase less expensive watches and jewellery.[19]

Uncertainty avoidance

A common problem for any society is how to deal with uncertainty. There are basically two ways. Societies high in uncertainty avoidance assume that uncertainty is bad and everything in society must aim to reduce uncertainty. Organizations in these societies promote stable careers and produce rules and procedures to reduce ambiguity. People in these cultures tend to be better groomed as a way of organizing their world and prefer purity in food, as evidenced by higher consumption of mineral water.[19]

Societies low in uncertainty avoidance assume that people have to deal with uncertainty, because it is inevitable. The future is by definition unknown, but it can be speculated, and people and institutions can deal with likely outcomes. People in these cultures tend to be more innovative and entrepreneurial.[21]

Uncertainty avoidance should not be confused with risk avoidance. Hofstede notes that risk is more specific than uncertainty and is often expressed as a probability that a specific outcome will occur, whereas uncertainty is a situation in which anything can happen. In fact, some people may engage in risky behaviour in order to reduce ambiguities, 'such as starting a fight with a potential opponent rather than sitting back and waiting' (p. 148).[16]

Website link 3.6

A comprehensive resource for business etiquette around the world: **http://www.cyborlink.com/besite**.

The cultural relativity of management theories

Table 3.4 shows the scores for 53 countries/regions on each of Hofstede's dimensions. Figure 3.1 presents a diagrammatic map of countries when individualism and power distance are combined. This combination of cultural dimensions illustrates patterns or clusters of countries that have a common history, such as the northern European cluster or the Anglo-Saxon cluster.

Hofstede first raised concerns about the *cultural relativity of management theories*.[17] Management theories are rooted in the cultural context where they were developed. Any simple direct transfer is problematic. For instance, Abraham Maslow's 'hierarchy of needs'[22] and McClelland's theory of the achievement motive[23] are directly related to two dimensions of US culture: its strong masculinity and individualism. People are motivated in an overtly conscious

Table 3.4 Values of Hofstede's cultural dimensions for 53 countries or regions

Country/region	Dimensions				
	Power distance	Uncertainty avoidance	Individualism	Masculinity	Long-/short-term orientation
Arabic countries[a]	80	68	38	53	–
Argentina	49	86	46	56	–
Australia	36	51	90	61	31
Austria	11	70	55	79	31
Belgium	65	94	75	54	38
Brazil	69	76	38	49	65
Canada	39	48	80	52	23
Chile	63	86	23	28	–
Colombia	67	80	13	64	–
Costa Rica	35	86	15	21	–
Denmark	18	23	74	16	46
East African region[b]	64	52	27	41	25
Ecuador	78	67	8	63	–
Finland	33	59	63	26	41
France	68	86	71	43	39
Great Britain	35	35	89	66	25
Greece	60	112	35	57	–
Guatemala	96	101	6	37	–
Hong Kong	68	29	25	57	96
India	77	40	48	56	61
Indonesia	78	48	14	46	–
Iran	58	59	41	43	–
Ireland	28	35	70	68	43
Israel	13	81	54	47	–
Italy	50	75	76	70	34
Jamaica	45	13	39	68	–
Japan	54	92	46	95	80
Malaysia	104	36	26	50	–
Mexico	81	82	30	69	–
Netherlands	38	53	80	14	44
New Zealand	22	49	79	58	30
Norway	31	50	69	8	44
Pakistan	55	70	14	50	0
Panama	95	86	11	44	–
Peru	64	87	16	42	–
Philippines	94	44	32	64	19
Portugal	63	104	27	31	30
Salvador	66	94	19	40	–
Singapore	74	8	20	48	48
South Africa	49	49	65	63	–
South Korea	60	85	18	39	75
Spain	57	86	51	42	19
Sweden	31	29	71	5	33
Switzerland	34	58	68	70	40
Taiwan	58	69	17	45	87
Thailand	64	64	20	34	56
Turkey	66	85	37	45	–
United States	40	46	91	62	29

Table 3.4 *(continued)*

Country/region	Dimensions				
	Power distance	Uncertainty avoidance	Individualism	Masculinity	Long-/short-term orientation
Uruguay	61	100	36	38	–
Venezuela	81	76	12	73	–
West African region[c]	77	54	20	46	16
West Germany	35	65	67	66	31
Yugoslavia	76	88	27	21	–
Overall mean	57	65	43	49	39
Standard deviation	22	24	25	18	22

[a] Saudi Arabia, Egypt, United Arab Emirates, Iraq, Kuwait, Lebanon and Libya.
[b] Ethiopia, Kenya, Tanzania and Zambia.
[c] Ghana, Nigeria and Sierra Leone.

(Source: Hofstede, 2001. Reproduced with permission.)

Figure 3.1 Map of 53 countries ranked on power distance and individualism indices

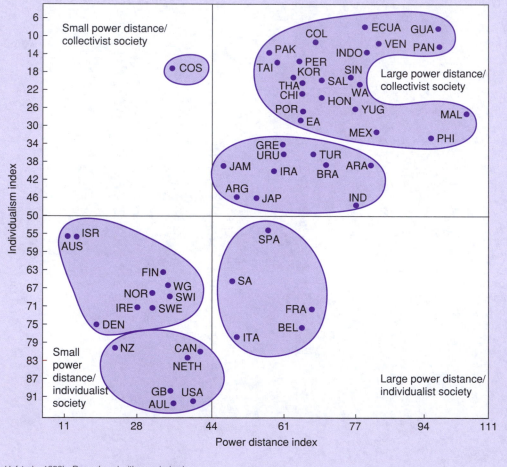

(Source: Hefstede, 1980b. Reproduced with permission.)

manner by extrinsic reasons and rewards that result from their actions. In contrast, Freudian theory, which has not been greatly applied by US management theorists, sees the individual as driven by the internal and largely unconscious interaction between the id, ego and superego. The superego (unconscious inner pilot) criticizes the thoughts and acts of the ego (conscious self-concept), which tries to control the id (unconscious forces). According to Hofstede,[17] Austria, the birthplace of Sigmund Freud and his theories, scores significantly higher than the US on uncertainty avoidance and lower on individualism. Freud's superego acts as an internalized uncertainty-absorbing device. This may explain why motivation is more related to internalized social values.

Interaction clashes

Multinational and global companies need to take cultural differences into account when they design reward systems, especially those for sales forces that cross national subsidiaries with different cultural contexts. People compare their rewards from work against others in the same market. For instance, extrinsic rewards (e.g. bonuses, gifts, holidays, monetary incentives) are more valued in masculine, individualistic countries, where there is also lower uncertainty avoidance. In contrast, intrinsic rewards are more valued in societies that are more feminine, and/or more collectivist, and/or with higher uncertainty avoidance. The choice of employee benefits available also differs depending on the level of uncertainty avoidance and power distance.[24] For instance, managers from countries with low uncertainty avoidance and power distance are more likely to offer cafeteria plans, where workers can choose how their benefit dollars are spent. This level of choice can create anxiety in people who are used to less uncertainty and are comfortable with the power being concentrated at the top. Similarly, the proportion of variable compensation for CEOs is positively related to individualism and negatively to uncertainty avoidance.[25]

Differences in dominant solutions to problems within organizations are also evident. For instance, students of various nationalities were asked to write a diagnosis and solution to a conflict between the sales and product development departments. The French saw the problem as one that the hierarchy should solve, a solution being sought from the chairperson. The Germans saw the problem as the absence of formal rules and written procedures. The English saw the problem as a lack of interpersonal communication. According to Hofstede (p. 60),[16] 'the implicit model of the organization for most French was a pyramid (both centralized and formal); for German a well-oiled machine (formalized, but not centralized); and for most British a village market (neither formalized, nor centralized)'.

Organization structures are also related to culture. In a matrix organization, for instance, there is a double hierarchical linkage (with a product division at the regional level and a subsidiary general manager at the country level). This structure is not accepted well by either the French or Germans. For the French, it violates the principle of unity of command. For the Germans, it thwarts their need for organizational clarity and is not acceptable unless individual roles inside the organization can be unambiguously defined.

Self-reliance versus dependence

Being self-reliant or dependent naturally involves assumptions about the self. For example, valuing elders in the community will tend to decrease the legitimacy of independence among younger age groups. Similarly, traditional sex roles promote the dependence of women. Even social class may encourage dependence, where people in higher social classes behave patronizingly towards those in lower classes. In industrial relations, for instance, the 'paternalist' orientation of factory owners towards their workers typifies the role of the boss as a father and the employees as 'children'.

Self-reliant people find motivation and control within themselves. Dependent people need to find outside support, motivation and control. As summarized in Table 3.5, low power distance and uncertainty avoidance combined with high individualism and masculinity will be related to more self-reliance (e.g. the US and Australia). The most extreme contrast to this is the Latin countries like Chile, Portugal or Brazil (see Table 3.4). The typical Westerner is on average more self-reliant than the average Easterner. And the typical northern European is more self-reliant than the typical Latin European.

Table 3.5 Self-reliance versus dependence

Hofstede's dimension	Influence on self-reliance/ dependence
Individualism	Increases self-reliance
Power distance	Promotes dependence
Masculinity	Increases self-reliance
Uncertainty avoidance	Promotes dependence
Long-term orientation	Promotes dependence

Two assumptions are central in developing either self-reliance or dependence among individuals. The first basic issue is whether people have an external or an internal locus of control.[26] People with internal locus-of-control have more self-reliance because they believe in their ability to manage their own world. The locus-of-control concept was developed by Rotter at an individual level, but it applies fairly well as a contrasting dimension across cultures.

Website link 3.7

Find out where you fall on the locus of control personality dimension by taking this quick and free online survey: **http://www.dushkin.com/ connectext/psy/ch11/survey11.mhtml**.

The second issue in relation to self-reliance versus dependence is the kind of family role that a particular culture favours. In Latin societies the parent–child relationship is a very strong underlying model for interaction. Even in situations which are normally assumed to be between equals, people may unconsciously and spontaneously act in parent–child roles. For instance, in conflicts a superior will easily fall into the role of a 'critical' parent – in the terms of Eric Berne's transactional analysis[27,28] – leaving their counterparts to behave in the role of a 'compliant child' by obeying, or a 'rebel child', or by leaving. Where parent–child roles underlie models of interaction, many relationships will be in the realm of dependence. Generally functional relationships will be based on filial dependence, whereas dysfunctional relationships will develop from conflicting roles.

For people who come from societies where self-reliance is standard behaviour, it is extremely irritating not to be treated as an adult, with equal rights and obligations. Many aspects of the French culture favour dependence, with the major exception of a strong individualist orientation. This results in a pattern of varying dependence, where people constantly play a game of dispute and reconciliation in teamwork and true self-reliance can only be fostered by creative activity and/or working independently.

3.3

Culture-based attitudes towards action

Action is about changing the world, even in a minuscule way. Many actions do not involve problem solving, in that they are repetitive and programmed routines. Non-routine tasks require a more complex course of action, because they:

1. Must be based on a clear sense of purpose (why act?).
2. Involve a largely unpredictable future, including elements of uncertainty and risk.
3. Need input from past experiences.
4. Imply the need to balance collective and individual interests.
5. Need to relate the hand to the brain, the heart and the mouth.

Expressed metaphorically, this last feature means that action (hand), in a cross-cultural perspective, can hardly be separated from how people think (brain), how they relate their wishes and desires to actions (located somewhere between brain, heart and mouth), and how they mix feelings (located clearly in the heart for most cultures) with deeds. Table 3.6 details the main differences across cultures in terms of attitudes towards action.

Most marketing and managerial action involves non-routine tasks that incorporate the elements listed above. This can be problematic in an international setting, as most interpretive clues are based on an individual's or organization's own cultural assumptions. Basic cultural assumptions, and combinations of these, have an influence on the way we cognitively evaluate real-world situations and issues. The following section illustrates the ways in which we all construct our reality, within our native cultural community.

Table 3.6 Attitudes towards action

Basic problem/cultural orientations	Contrasts across cultures
Why act?	
(a) The degree of fatalism: mastery versus subjugation to nature; existence and degree of legitimacy given to a Promethean (proactive) view of human life.	Some people believe that it is possible to cope with any problem or any situation. Nothing is impossible. It is evil or unconscionable when one does nothing ('master of destiny'). Conversely, others believe that fate is responsible for most actions. Destiny binds us and we should not try to thwart it. It is evil when one does not accept one's own destiny ('subjugation').
What is action?	
(b) 'Speech' versus 'deed' orientation	Some cultures value speech as action; others see speech as separate from action (do, not talk). Some cultures see a clear sequencing of the steps required for successful action; others hold a fuzzier view.
How to relate thinking to action (1)	
(c) Ideologism versus pragmatism	Ideologists take decisions from a range of solutions. Thinking patterns, communication (style of speech) and actions selected within the context of broad ideological principles (religious, political, social, legal, etc.). Pragmatists make decisions by problem solving. Precise issues must be addressed and a practical attitude is favoured. The orientation is towards getting concrete results.
How to relate thinking to action (2)	
(d) Intellectual styles	Differences in assigning a dominant role to theory (Teutonic style), empirical evidence (Saxonic style), speech (Gallic style), or modesty and virtue (Nipponic style) in assessing truthful propositions that need to be put into action.
How to relate wishes and desires to action	
(e) 'Wishful thinking' orientation (WT)	WT cultures tend to emphasize enthusiasm, imagination of the future and the capacity of desires to *shape* reality. Non-WT cultures emphasize the principle of reality. Desires and wishes have to be checked objectively against constraints of the real world.
How to relate feelings to action	
(f) Affective (A) versus neutral (N)	In neutral cultures, people separate feelings from actions. They separate friendship from business. In affective cultures, people believe that mixing feelings and actions is legitimate and useful.
How to deal with rules	
(g) Obeying practical rules versus coping with ideal rules	Rules are made and respected, discussed and implemented quite strictly. There is discrepancy between the 'ideal' rules and what people actually do. Exploring and bypassing rules is an accepted practice.

Why act?

Not everyone is preoccupied with doing, acting, being efficient and achieving tangible results that can be appraised by others. From an existential point of view this preoccupation with 'doing' is not really justified. In the long term we will all be dead.

Montesquieu's 1748 description of the Indians and Thais as *indolent nations* in *The Spirit of Laws* (pp. 228–9), illustrates a 'being' orientation:

The Indians believe that repose and non-existence are the foundations of all things, and the end in which they terminate. Hence they consider entire inaction as the most perfect of all states, and the object of their desires. To the supreme Being they give the title of immoveable. The inhabitants of Siam (Thailand) believe that their utmost happiness consists in not being obliged to animate a machine or to give motion to a body.[29]

Not only are the Indians and Siamese (the Thai people) more 'being' oriented, they also have a quite different view of their relationship with nature from Westerners (i.e. subjugation to nature rather than mastery over nature). As noted previously, their religions include belief in reincarnation. On the death of the body, the soul transmigrates or is born again in another body. Life therefore is not seen as 'one shot', but more as a cyclical phenomenon. This puts less pressure on people to be 'doing' oriented and means there is more inducement to *be* blameless and virtuous since it is these factors that will influence the status of further reincarnations. Inaction is one of the surest ways to lead a blameless life. While this orientation helps the individual to cope with reality, it may be less helpful for the complexities of living in a larger social system.[30]

Both being and doing orientations have their merits and it is obviously difficult to find supportive evidence as to whether we are reincarnated or not. Thus, it is more interesting to investigate the consequences for action. When Kumar (p. 59)[30] discusses the consequences of Brahmanism in India, he points out that the emphasis on 'thought' (being) over 'action' (doing) means that implementation receives less attention: there is 'an emphasis on developing grandiose schemes without concern for implementation at all'.

Fatalism is a belief that directly influences action, not necessarily in terms of acting less, but rather in terms of acting *differently*. It clearly posits the locus of control as being outside, in the metaphysical environment. It also provides convenient explanations for unpredictable events, which allow people to resume activity quickly after major catastrophes (earthquakes, fires, car accidents). Fatalism makes mourning easier and facilitates the acceptance of strongly negative personal events, such as a bankruptcy.

Website link 3.8

How does a determinist cross the street?: **http://www.naturalism.org/fatalism.htm#How%20Determinists.**

What is action?

Another important distinction is whether a culture tends to classify words, speeches and, more generally, acts of communication as 'deeds'. In many cultures there are popular sayings that effectively condemn speech on the basis that it is not real action ('do, not talk'). In the real world, life is more complicated. Communications are a category of act, and their potential influence on others is beyond doubt. But whether communication is considered as being significantly related to action differs across cultures.

The word 'poetry' comes from the Greek word *poio*, a verb meaning to 'make', to 'produce', to 'build'. This sheds some light on judgements of the usefulness of poetry based on different cultural assumptions. On one hand, poetry is seen as distinctly distant from action in the real world. On the other, poetry is seen as a direct source of inspiration for action. Indeed if a 'classical' model of action is assumed, i.e. one that is culturally European/Western based, the following sequence is expected to occur:

1. Analysis of the problem and the issues at stake.
2. Gathering of relevant information.
3. Listing and evaluating possible solutions.
4. Selecting the 'best' decision.
5. Implementation: While the decision tends to be more individualized, implementation is a process that involves steps that involve individual and collective action from numerous diverse agents.
6. Appraisal of the outcome, control of the difference between target and actual outcomes, and possibly feedback to a previous step in the sequence.

This sequence can be easily criticized as culturally non-universal. Even if we were to accept that this sequence is true, it would still involve a great deal of cultural relativity. For instance, the Japanese have no word for decision making, and action/decision/control processes are viewed as implementation issues.[31] This leads to the Japanese first consulting each one of a large group of people at various levels in the organization, who all comment on how to do something (not necessarily on why).

3.4

How to relate thinking to action

In relating thinking to action, the following categories are considered:

1. How should issues be addressed? Broadly, with the premise that *the parts always represent the whole*, or narrowly, considering that *focus is the key to relevance* when acting.
2. What is the basis on which a certain course of action is evidenced as the correct one: (a) data; (b) theory; (c) personal conviction; (d) virtue because it is morally correct to think and do so?

Ideologists versus pragmatists

If future partners do not share common 'mental schemes', it is difficult for them to solve problems together. For instance, buyer and seller agreements will be easier if they share a joint view of the world, especially on the following points:

1. What is the relevant information for action?
2. How should this information be sought, evaluated and fed into the decision-making process?

Ideologists will use a wide body of ideas, Marxism or liberalism, for instance, that provide them with a formal and coherent description of the world. In an ideologist framework, every event is supposed to carry meaning. Typically, ideologists will *take* decisions, that is, pick a solution from a range of possible decisions (which are located outside the person who decides).

Conversely, pragmatists first consider the diversity of real-world situations, and then derive principles inductively. Reality is seen as a series of independent and concrete problems to be solved. The issues will make complete sense when related to practical, precise

and even down-to-earth decisions. Typically, pragmatists will *make* decisions, that is, they will both decide and implement them. Decisions are enacted, not selected.

Triandis[6] suggests that complex traditional societies will tend to be ideologist, whereas pluralistic societies or cultures experiencing rapid social change will tend to be pragmatist. This distinction may also be traced back to the difference between the legal systems of *common law* (e.g. Australia, UK and USA) and of *code law* (e.g. French, German and Italian). Whereas the common law favours legal precedents set by the courts and past rulings (cases), code law favours laws and general texts that are intended to build an all-inclusive system (or code) of written rules of law. Codes aim to formulate general principles that embody the entire set of particular cases.

The ideologist orientation, which is found in southern and eastern Europe, leads negotiators to focus on a set of principles before any detailed discussion on specific clauses of the contract. They have a tendency to prefer globalized negotiations in which all the issues are gathered in a 'package deal'.

The pragmatist orientation, which is found in northern Europe and most former UK colonies, leads negotiators to define problems of limited scope, then solve them one after the other. They tend to concentrate their thinking on supportable facts (e.g. deeds, not words; evidence, not opinions; figures, not value judgements) and are willing to reach real-world decisions, even if they have to be down-to-earth ones.

Communication may be difficult when partners do not share the same mental scheme. The most unlikely situation for success is an ideologist-oriented contractor/supplier who tries to sell to a pragmatist-oriented owner/buyer. The ideologist will see the pragmatist as being overly interested in trivial details, too practical, too down-to-earth, and incapable of looking at issues from a higher standpoint. Pragmatists will resent ideologists for being too theoretical, lacking practical sense, concerned with issues that are too broad to lead to implementable decisions.

What information is relevant for action? How should it be used?

The dimensions of ideologism and pragmatism are not mutually exclusive. For instance, it would be a mistake to consider Americans as pure pragmatists with no leaning towards ideology. They are pragmatic in that they identify problems clearly and precisely as 'issues' and collect evidence systematically. Their attitude is matter of fact. To be 'down to earth' is a positive expression, whereas its French equivalent is often pejorative. But they are also somewhat ideological in their free-market/individual oriented view of the world. This view is enshrined in their Constitution, anti-trust legislation, corporate law, and so on. This ideology is generally accepted unquestioningly. It is therefore somewhat irrelevant to debate practical matters as an ideologist would. Ideology is rarely present on a daily basis, when information directly relevant to action is gathered or discussed. Thus, they are more likely to be conscious of pragmatic considerations when ideology and ideas are the object of debate.

In international business negotiations there is often a discussion of principles, but these may lead to a substantive outcome later on. The fundamental skill of diplomats (who are, in many respects, experts in matters of culture) is to obtain the acceptance and underwriting of basic principles by their counterparts, the effectiveness of which is only apparent at a later date.

3.5

Dealing with desires and feelings

In Freudian terms, management is based on the principle of reality, and not on the principle of pleasure. Therefore there is little interest in examining an individual's desires and feelings, which are considered to be purely subjective. However, in a cross-cultural perspective, desires and feelings are important. People have different ways of relating their actions to their desires and feelings. In this section we discuss (e) 'wishful thinking' (WT) orientation and (f) affective versus neutral cultures, as illustrated in Table 3.6.

How to relate wishes and desires to action

Words and deeds may be classified in two separate categories or combined. They may be in opposition to each other, in that words are empty or hollow, or complimentary, in that words influence and

sometimes cause others to act. Most acts of authority are only words.

An important issue for cultural action styles is the problematic link between what one says and what one does. WT consists in first thinking, then saying how one wants things to be, not how they are. Since nobody knows exactly how things will be in the future, a non-WT oriented person will try to say how he or she realistically thinks they will be, not how he or she wants them to be. WT is more inhibited in a culture that clearly divides words from deeds (do what you say, say what you do).

Where speech is considered an action, WT may become necessary to galvanize people towards an ideal and improbable future. WT is more prevalent in present oriented cultures, as people do not worry so much about the future. WT is a convenient way to escape from the constraints of longer-term realities by focusing on the here and now. It dodges problems to be solved, and hides divergences and possible conflicts at least in the short term.

WT is related to any action that deals with the future and with potential reality, including the listing of prices, bidding and negotiations, the management of delivery delays, attitudes towards new projects, and advertising campaigns where arguments may 'explain why' the audience should be convinced by the message.

Website link 3.9

See more examples of wishful thinking in American business: http://www.american.com/archive/2008/january-february-magazine-contents/the-dangers-of-wishful-thinking.

Affective versus neutral cultures

The contrast between affective and affectively neutral cultures is described by Trompenaars (p. 63)[32]: 'Members of cultures which are affectively neutral do not telegraph their feelings but keep them carefully controlled and subdued. Neutral cultures are not necessarily cold or unfeeling, nor are they emotionally constipated or repressed.' Trompenaars classified countries on responses to a question asking if they would express their feelings openly if they felt upset about something at work. The highest neutrality was for the Japanese (83 per cent), followed by (the former West) Germany (75 per cent) and the United Kingdom (71 per cent). The Dutch (55 per cent) and Americans (40 per cent) express their emotions more easily. Finally, Italy (29 per cent) and France (34 per cent) are clearly more affective cultures, with more people agreeing they would express their feelings openly.

The contrast between affective and neutral cultures is closely related to the being/doing divide in basic cultural assumptions and to dependence in the models of interaction. If people are strictly *doing* oriented they tend to disregard expressions of *being*. Feelings and affectivity are seen as *being* in the purely personal and private, individual domain. Thus, Anglo-Saxon cultures tend to suppress these feelings and view their direct expression as inappropriate for effective interaction.

Extremes in either affective or neutral cultural orientations are problematic. On one hand, overly suppressed emotions and feelings can lead to flawed interaction and few results. People may discover quite late that personal antipathy is a major hurdle to interaction. On the other hand, open expression of emotion may cause offence and undue delays.

The feelings/action issue is important for the choice of partners to improve communications in marketing negotiations, managing sales personnel, establishing relationships with foreign distribution channels, or preparing locally appropriate advertising materials.

Every culture has certain codes and rituals that allow for a compromise between the two extreme positions. What varies is the starting assumption:

1. Expressing emotions is legitimate and useful for action (affective cultures).
2. Expressing emotions needs to be separated from action (neutral cultures).

It needs, however, to be refined, by the addition of two further caveats. First, as emphasized by Trompenaars (1993), people have no fewer emotions in neutral cultures than in affective cultures; perhaps the contrary is true. If feelings and emotions are contained, they may build up and result in hidden negative feelings. Second, the influence of culture should not be overstated, as there is high variability in individuals' personality traits and interactions. More is universal than culture-specific in the area of feelings and emotions. Chapter 13 on language, culture and

communication explores the issue of affectivity versus neutrality in more detail.

3.6

Coping with rules

Rules and basic assumptions

A rule is an authoritative regulation or direction concerning method or procedure. Rules are formalized norms that generally comprise a scale of sanctions according to the gravity of the breach. Rules can be made which are respected, discussed and implemented quite explicitly, or there may be a discrepancy between ideal rules and what people actually do, leading them to behaviour involving the exploring and bypassing of rules.

Some typical indicators of rule-related behaviour include how people deal with speed limits, traffic lights, queuing at banks or bus stations, filling out income statements, and so on. A naive interpretation of rules would be that they are made to be respected. The real function of rules is more complex. Written rules are fairly standard across cultures; it is the way we react to them that differs. Rules need to be interpreted on the basis of our cultural assumptions and interaction models (see Table 3.7):

1. A positive human nature orientation (HNO) leads to rules where sanctions are small and often positively reinforced; with a reward for respecting the rule being preferred to a penalty. People are trusted to respect rules and they are seen to gain benefit from them. Conversely, a negative HNO leads to rules where sanctions are high and severe enforcement is carried out. People cannot be trusted to respect rules, as human nature is seen as opportunistic and basically bad.
2. The level of power distance in a particular society has an influence on both the design of rules and their implementation. Low power distance results in people having input, in some way, to the design of rules. It also leads to rules being applied with a sense of fairness and equity to everybody, including those with more power in the society. In contrast, high power distance results in people being subject to rules that are designed and imposed by others. Furthermore, these rules apply more

Table 3.7 Type of rules and behaviour according to HNO and power distance

		Power distance	
		Low	High
Human nature orientation	Good	**Pragmatic rules** (responsible compliance)	**Challengeable rules** (exploring behaviour)
	Bad	**Mechanical rules** (automatic compliance)	**Oppressive rules** (bypassing behaviour)

stringently to those with less power in society. The most powerful people are seen as being beyond the reach of rules that are designed to control 'ordinary people'.

3. Strong ingroup orientation (see Chapter 2) often leads to the syndrome that rules are 'applicable only here'. Rules do not need to be followed when outside their community.

4. The emphasis on guilt (*inner feeling* of responsibility for committing an offence) versus shame (a painful *emotion, directed to the outside*, resulting from an awareness of having done something dishonourable as a group member) influences behaviour toward rules, as well as the punishments and rewards associated with them.

Table 3.7 presents four stereotypical rule types and their relationship with HNO and power distance. In this case, the HNO assumption must be understood in a comparative way between the ruler and the ruled: 'good' means that the ruled view themselves as 'better' than or equal to the ruler; 'bad' means that the ruled view themselves as 'as bad' as or 'even worse' than their rulers.

Types of rules and rule-related behaviour

Anglo-rules, including those of northern European countries, are basically 'pragmatic' rules. People generally comply with the rule out of a sense of responsibility built on positive motivation. Rules are understood as helping society to work more smoothly and efficiently and everyone is supposed to benefit from their being respected. In this picture, people are universally at ease with their rules; even if they sometimes break them (nobody is perfect).

'Challengeable rules' are found in Italy or France where power distance is fairly high and ordinary people view themselves as having a better nature than those at the top. Since rules are mostly directed at the population from the top, without 'instructions for use', people are expected to investigate the extent to which rules can be transgressed. The only way to explore a new rule is to breach it discreetly, in order to know whether it is intended to be applied seriously, or whether it is simply one more empty threat that is neither enforced nor respected.

'Mechanical rules' are found in the German or Swiss case. They are made democratically because power distance is low, but there is distrust of people. Sanctions are explicit and implemented fairly literally. Respect for rules has a fairly mechanical and automatic side: they are applied literally.

The final stereotypical case is found in many developing and Third World countries with high power distance and negative assumptions as to the nature of human beings, powerful or not. Rules are often very strict, formal and somewhat unrealistic. Chapter 10 develops the example of foreign exchange control systems, which lead to the bypassing rules by over- or under-invoicing. Oppressive rules oblige people to bypass the law and encourage rulers towards corrupt behaviour, in that they can implement unimplementable rules with some leniency in exchange for a bribe. Oppressive rules lead to a high discrepancy between what people say they will do and what they actually do. This leads to a sort of systematic social schizophrenia, where we might see police changing money in the illegal parallel exchange market. Official rules can be complicated by opportunistic behaviour and their being difficult to respect. It is relatively easy to see local patterns of dealing with rules in any country. An examination of the basic rules relating to the functioning of society, such as traffic, queuing, and taxation, will quickly illustrate how rules are actually implemented.

People who favour universal rules are characterized by an inner compliance dynamic based on guilt, that is, self-reproach caused by an inner feeling that one is responsible for a wrong or offence. The moral punishment is to a large extent interiorized within the psyche as in the Freudian concept of *schuld* (in German: debt, fault, culpability). Conversely, people who favour relative rules are characterized by an external compliance dynamic. In this case it has to do with losing face, having one's honour threatened, and risking rejection by the ingroup members. Local rules are territory bound and concern breach of loyalty to the ingroup.

Adopting a more open view of how people attribute meaning to rules makes sense for a large array of international marketing issues. As far as consumer behaviour is concerned, rules on waiting, attitudes towards queuing, theft from stores by consumer or sales staff, the attention paid by consumers to instructions for use (e.g. pharmaceuticals and food), the attitude towards filling in market research questionnaires, giving truthful information. In fact, any ethical issue that involves social responsibility of manufacturers, service providers or consumers have to be examined with a view to their cross-cultural relativity.

3.7 Cultural assumptions and actual behaviour

As outlined in Chapter 1, all societies face common problems, and although there is a dominant solution, alternatives are always present. These alternatives can combine in a dialectic way. Japanese people are often depicted as collectivist and the Americans as individualist, but there are limits to this distinction. Who is more humane, more personal and more sensitive in interpersonal relations, more attentive and understanding than the average Japanese person? Who cares more about the community than the average American, whose objective is to 'socialize in the community'? In the United States the word 'community' is used extensively. Indeed Americans and Japanese share a common problem: that of combining individual actions and collective undertakings.[33]

This problem may be solved only by a process which is essentially dialectic. In any society there exists a dominant cultural assumption about what the *first* priority should be: either the individual (as in the United States); or the group (as in Japan) is the basic survival unit. Then come the secondary cultural assumptions, which complement the basic assumption. In the US, the community is where people integrate to build a common society, and their reciprocal links should be strictly and explicitly codified. In Japan, the utmost level of sensitivity must be developed in interpersonal relations, so that the working of the group is kept as smooth as possible.

The basic cultural assumptions described in the previous sections are in fact deep-rooted beliefs that generate basic values. Indirectly they guide our daily behaviour, but they may also clash with it. By their very nature they are subconscious, as is the process by which they shape our interaction with others and our conduct. There is some leeway for other sources of influence. For instance, we use social representations to make decisions. We are influenced by other values and other standards of demeanour, such as work rules, company codes of conduct, lifestyles or friendship patterns which work closer to the surface than basic cultural assumptions. These standards of demeanour help people to manage adjustments in the short term. They change over much shorter periods of time (10 or 20 years) than basic cultural assumptions (probably formed over centuries). This leads us to question the extent to which less profound levels of culture influence people, such as corporate culture or educational culture?

Multinational companies (MNCs) offer their employees many opportunities for intercultural exchange. As such we might expect the values shared by executives in MNCs will converge, as they spend years working with different people. In order to grasp differences in cognitive styles, Laurent asked managers of different nationalities to indicate their agreement or disagreement with the following statement (item 24 of Laurent's (p. 86)[34] questionnaire on management styles): 'It is important for a manager to have at hand precise answers to most of the questions that his subordinates may raise about their work.' Only 10 per cent of Swedes agreed. They do not feel the need for omniscient managers. In contrast, Italians (66 per cent) and French (53 per cent) believe managers should have precise answers to most of their subordinates' questions. Most Anglo-Saxon and northern European people tend to see managers as problem solvers, whereas Latin and Asian people see them more as *experts*. These differences were observed in people working in their home country. In a later study, Laurent[35] asked the same question of executives who had been working for a long time in MNCs where teams had been built up from a large number of different nationalities. We would expect a decrease in the differences between national groups of managers. Surprisingly, the situation is exactly the opposite. Laurent observed an increase of differences across national groups. This suggests that, behind superficial agreements, people's basic cultural assumptions are reinforced. When a corporate culture tries to shape a manager's (or even an employee's) daily behaviour, it may look as if it succeeds (because people are concerned about their job and career), but it only scratches the surface. It is less likely to influence values and basic cultural assumptions. Moreover, since this is forced upon them, not only do they fail to change basic cultural assumptions, but they even reinforce them.

Does this mean that international experience has no effect on managers? It is more likely that international experience will influence our 'newer view' of the way the business world works than the basic cultural assumptions that guide our behaviour. For instance, a study of Japanese and Korean manager's views on marketing tactics, including pricing, found the importance of brand names and superior product design were more similar in firms that had a high level of internationalization than those whose focus was domestic.[36] Thus, changes occur in the realm of organizational learning, rather than in our fundamental cultural assumptions.[37]

Questions

1. What do you think the cultural roots to personal modesty might be?

2. Which examples would you suggest to exemplify American individualism?

3. In many countries there is an institution called 'parliamentary democracy'. On which basic cultural values is it based, in your opinion? Is there a relationship between the development of marketing and parliamentary democracy?

4. Given country scores on Hofstede's four dimensions, what do you expect would be the problems encountered by a typical boss from country X in managing a typical employee from country Y (even at the risk of some stereotyping and sweeping generalization)?
   (a) An American boss managing Japanese subordinates.
   (b) A Japanese boss managing French subordinates.
   (c) A French boss managing Swedish subordinates.
   (d) A Swedish boss managing Japanese subordinates.

5. A conversation is in progress between a British manager and a French manager concerning a common (large) project. The project is at a very early stage (examining its feasibility, setting deadlines for construction, planning of steps in building process, etc.). The Frenchman is very enthusiastic and argues: 'Let's go, we can do it; *impossible n'est pas français!*' ['impossible is not a French word']. The Englishman feels somewhat uneasy about the turn of the conversation. Why?

6. Are there Japanese individualists? Why?

7. A sign indicates: 'Parking time limited to 10 minutes. Be fair.' Which views of time and rules does this reveal? Try to imagine signs with different information for people who have a different approach to rules.

References

1. Belk, Russel W. (1988), 'Possessions and the Extended Self', *Journal of Consumer Research*, 5, 139–68.
2. Markus, Hazel Rose and Shinobu Kitayama (1991), 'Culture and the Self: Implications for Cognition, Emotion and Motivation', *Psychological Review*, 98 (2), 224–53.
3. Triandis, Harry C. (1990), 'Cross-Cultural Studies of Individualism and Collectivism', in *Nebraska Symposium on Motivation*, J. Berman, Ed. Lincoln, Nebraska: University of Nebraska Press.
4. Mead, Margaret (1948), *Male and Female*. New York: William Morrow.
5. Wong, Nancy and Aaron Ahuvia (1995), 'From Tofu to Caviar: Conspicuous Consumption, Materialism and Self-Concepts in East-Asian and Western Cultures', in *Proceedings of the Second Conference on the Cultural Dimension of International Marketing*. Odense, 68–89.
6. Triandis, Harry C. (1983), 'Dimensions of Cultural Variation as Parameters of Organizational Theories', *International Studies of Management and Organization*, XII (4), 139–69.
7. Belk, Russel W. (1985), 'Cultural and Historical Differences in Concepts of Self and Their Effects on Attitudes toward Having and Giving', *in Proceedings of the 12th Annual Conference of the Association for Consumer Research*. Provo, UT: ACR, 754–60.
8. Chen, Chao C., Xiao-Ping Chen, and James R. Meindl (1998), 'How Can Cooperation Be Fostered? The Cultural Effects of Individualism-Collectivism', *Academy of Management Review*, 23 (2), 285–304.
9. Smith, Peter B., Shaun Dugan, Mark F. Peterson, and Kwok Leung (1998), 'Individualism: Collectivism and the Handling of Disagreement. A 23 Country Study', *International Journal of Intercultural Relations*, 22 (3), 351–67.
10. Triandis, Harry C. (1995), *Individualism and Collectivism*. Boulder, CO: Westview.
11. Ohye, Kazuko (2003), 'From Chanel Chick to Individualist', *The Issue*, Reseach International's client magazine.
12. Robertson, Christopher J. (2000), 'The Global Dispersion of Chinese Values: A Three-Country Study of Confucian Dynamism', *Management International Review*, 40 (3), 253–68.
13. Hofstede, Geert and Michael Harris Bond (1988), 'The Confucius Connection: From Cultural Roots to Economic Growth', *Organizational Dynamics*, 16 (4), 4–21.
14. Singelis, Theodore M., Harry C. Triandis, Dharm P.S. Bhawuk, and Michele J. Gelfand (1995), 'Horizontal and Vertical Dimensions of Individualism and Collectivism: A Theoretical and Measurement Refinement', *Cross-Cultural Research: The Journal of Comparative Social Science*, 29 (3), 240–75.
15. Shavitt, Sharon, Ashok K. Lalwani, Jing Zhang, and Carlos J. Torelli (2006), 'The Horizontal/Vertical Distinction in Cross-Cultural Consumer Research', *Journal of Consumer Psychology*, 16 (4), 325–56.
16. Hofstede, Geert (2001), *Culture's Consequences* (2nd edn). Thousand Oaks, CA: Sage Publications.
17. Hofstede, Geert (1980), 'Motivation, Leadership and Organization: Do American Theories Apply Abroad?', *Organizational Dynamics* (Summer), 42–63.
18. Adler, Nancy J. (2002), *International Dimensions of Organizational Behaviour* (4th edn). Cincinnati, OH: South-Western Publishing.
19. De Mooij, Marieke and Geert Hofstede (2002), 'Convergence and Divergence in Consumer Behavior: Implications for International Retailing', *Journal of Retailing*, 78 (1), 67–9.
20. Søndergaard, Michael (1994), 'Hofstede's Consequences: A Study of Reviews, Citations and Replications', *Organization Studies*, 15 (3), 447–56.
21. Steenkamp, Jan-Benedict E.M., Frenkel ter Hofstede, and Michel Wedel (1999), 'A Cross-National Investigation into the Individual and National Cultural Antecedents of Consumer Innovativeness', *Journal of Marketing*, 63 (April), 55–69.
22. Maslow, A.H. (1954), *Motivation and Personality*. New York: Harper.
23. McClelland, D., J. Atkinson, J. Clark and E. Lowell (1953), *The Achievement Motive*. New York: Appleton-Century-Crofts.
24. Oliver, Elizabeth Goad and Karen S. Cravens (1999), 'Cultural Influences on Managerial Choice: An Empirical Study of Employee Benefit Plans in the United States', *Journal of International Business Studies*, 30 (4), 745–62.
25. Tosi, Henry L. and Thomas Greckhamer (2004), 'Culture and Ceo Compensation', *Organization Science*, 15 (6), 657–70.
26. Rotter, Julian B. (1966), 'Generalized Expectancies for Internal Versus External Control of Reinforcement', *Psychological Monographs*, 80 (1), 1–28.
27. Berne, Eric (1961), *Transactional Analysis in Psychotherapy*. New York: Grove press.
28. Berne, Eric (1964), *Games People Play*. New York: Grove Press.
29. Montesquieu, Charles de (1748), *The Spirit of Laws* (Thomas Nugent, Trans.) (6th edn). Dublin: McKenzie and Moore.
30. Kumar, Rajesh (2000), 'Confucian Pragmatism Vs. Brahmanical Idealism Understanding the Divergent Roots of Indian and Chinese Economic Performance', *Journal of Asian Business*, 16 (2), 49–69.

31. Lazer, William, Shoji Murata, and Hiroshi Kosaka (1985), 'Japanese Marketing: Towards a Better Understanding', *Journal of Marketing*, 49 (Spring), 69–81.

32. Trompenaars, Fons (1993), *Riding the Waves of Culture*. London: Nicholas Brealey.

33. Kluckhohn, Florence R. and Frederick L. Strodtbeck (1961), *Variations in Value Orientations*. Westport, CT: Greenwood Press.

34. Laurent, André (1983), 'The Cultural Diversity of Western Conceptions of Management', *International Studies of Management and Organization*, XII (1–2), 75–96.

35. Laurent, André (1989), 'Cultural Shock', in *European Foundation for Management Development Annual Conference*. Marseille.

36. Lee, Jangho, Thomas W. Roehl, and Soonkyoo Choe (2000), 'What Makes Management Style Similar and Distinct across Borders? Growth, Experience and Culture in Korean and Japanese Firms', *Journal of International Business Studies*, 31 (4), 631–52.

37. Kim, Daniel H. (1993), 'The Link between Individual and Organizational Learning', *Sloan Management Review*, 36 (1), 37–50.

Teaching materials

A3.1 Critical incident

An American in Vietnam

An American in Vietnam recalls an illuminating story told him by a Vietnamese who complained about a lack of understanding between the two allies. They were discussing the fate of a province chief named Vong, once hailed by the Americans as the best province chief in Vietnam. Vong was accused of embezzling some 300,000 American dollars earmarked for an airstrip, and was tried and sentenced to be executed. It seemed a harsh sentence, considering the corruption prevalent at the time, and the American asked the Vietnamese if he agreed.

'No', the Vietnamese said, 'Vong should be executed because he's a stupid man.'

'Stupid? Because he got caught?' the American asked.

The Vietnamese impatiently shook his head. 'No, no, not because he took the money', he said. 'That is not important. But you know what this stupid man did? He pacified six more hamlets than his quota. This caused the general who gave him the quota to lose face, and that is stupid.'

The perplexed American said, 'In America, he'd get a medal for exceeding his quota.' The Vietnamese shook his head and said, 'You Americans will never understand the Vietnamese.'

Question

What aspects of the incident are significant in describing the difference in opinion between these two persons?

(Source: Weeks *et al.*, p. 22.[1])

A3.2 Rationales for section A2.1 (cross-cultural scenario) and sections A2.2 and A2.3 (cross-cultural interactions)

A2.1 Scenario: Inshallah

This scenario can best be understood by first appreciating the very different views in US culture and Saudi culture concerning 'locus of control'. In the US it is believed that ultimately people are responsible for their own destiny. If something goes wrong, it is believed, it is frequently possible for the individual to *do* something (that is, to change certain behaviour) to bring about the desired outcome. In Saudi Arabia, and indeed throughout the Arab world, people are taught from an early age that all things are subject to the direct will of Allah. All plans for the future (including, of course, business plans) are viewed with a sense of inevitability and will be realized only if God wills it. This is not to say that people in the Arab world would not work hard to help bring about the desired results. Rather, they believe that despite the effort, the desired ends will not happen unless God is willing. Perhaps Stefan would have been less frustrated if he had translated *inshallah* to mean 'if possible' or 'God willing' rather than as a knee-jerk response used to absolve oneself of all responsibility for one's actions.

(Source: Ferraro, p. 162.[2] Reproduced with permission.)

A2.2 Interaction: engineering a decision

1. There is little evidence for this in the story. While the financial benefits are relevant, to Mr Tanaka they are probably a minor consideration in the situation. Please choose another response.

2. It is quite probable that coming from a male-dominant Japanese society he does think it odd that Mr Legrand should mention his wife's opinion. However, the decision not to go to the Middle East also appears to be Mr Legrand's personal inclination so this does not fully account for Mr Tanaka's bewilderment. There is another explanation. Please choose again.

3. It is unlikely that Mr Tanaka would consider this. There are factors far removed from personal gain dominating his concern. Please choose again.

4. This is the most likely explanation. In Japanese and many other collectivist societies a person is defined much more as a collection of roles (parent, employee, servant, official) than by his or her individual identity. Therefore, fulfilling these roles to the best of one's ability is regarded as more important than one's personal inclinations. Thus Mr Tanaka would see that Mr Legrand's responsibility as a company employee would be to accept the position whether or not he is personally happy about the idea. Mr Legrand's refusal is thus bewildering and makes him think that his belief in Mr Legrand's dedication has been completely misplaced. Mr Legrand, however, comes from a culture where individual freedoms are highly valued and so exercises his right to refuse the offer with little compunction. The cultural conflict thus resides in different strengths of values applied to the roles occupied by a person in the culture.

(Source: Brislin *et al.*, pp. 177–8.[3] *Intercutural Interactions: A Practical Guide*, by Brislin, Richard W., Kenneth Cushner, Craig Cherrie and Mahealani Young, copyright 1986 by Sage Publications Inc. Books, reproduced with permission of Sage Publications Inc. Books in the format Textbook via Copyright Clearance Center.)

A2.3 Interaction: opening a medical office in Saudi Arabia

1. It is unlikely that people would sign up solely to satisfy a newcomer's feeling. There is a better explanation. Please select again.

2. If there is a considerable time lag between when a person makes a decision and the action upon it, it is possible that they may change their mind. However, there is no indication in the incident to support this. Please select another response.

3. Units of time reference differ markedly between Arab and American cultures. To an American, the major unit of time is five minutes. Fifteen minutes is a significant period of

time. To an urban Arab, the unit of time that corresponds to our 5-minute block is 15. Thus, when the Arab is 30 minutes late (by the clock), he is not even 10 minutes late by his standards. This is the best answer. Tom's patients may still arrive.

4. While the patients may be seeing their own traditional healers, they would not necessarily do so in the strict sequence suggested by this alternative. There is a more precise explanation. Please choose again.

(Source: Brislin *et al.*, p. 179.[3] *Intercutural Interactions: A Practical Guide*, by Brislin, Richard W., Kenneth Cushner, Craig Cherrie and Mahealani Young, copyright 1986 by Sage Publications Inc. Books, reproduced with permission of Sage Publications Inc. Books in the format Textbook via Copyright Clearance Center.)

Appendix references

1. Weeks, William H., Paul B. Pedersen, and Richard W. Brislin (1987), *A Manual of Structured Experiences for Cross-Cultural Learning*. Yarmouth, ME: Intercultural Press.
2. Ferraro, Gary P. (1990), *The Cultural Dimension of International Business*. Englewood Cliffs, NJ: Prentice Hall.
3. Brislin, Richard W., Kenneth Kushner, Craig Cherrie, and Mahealani Yong (1986), *Intercultural Interactions: A Practical Guide*. Newbury Park, CA: Sage.

Part 2   The integration of local consumption in a global marketing environment

© Getty Images

Introduction to Part 2

Globalization has taken place at a rapid pace over the last half-century. The continuous expansion of cross-border marketing has been backed by the progressive elimination of barriers to trade, and the emergence of a global consumer culture. Although global convergence seems undeniable, some basic traits of local consumption experience still resist change. The general objective of Part 2 is to show how global and local patterns coexist in both consumer behaviour and marketing environments. The cross-cultural approach to international marketing that is presented in Chapters 4 to 6 should enable future international marketers to understand local consumer behaviour in its full complexity. This approach allows adaptation of the design and implementation of market research across national markets when research instruments and data collection procedures are not similarly understood and do not produce equivalent findings cross-nationally.

Quite often basic concepts have been developed in a specific cultural environment. In marketing the major contributor has been the United States. As such it is necessary to investigate whether the consumer behaviour concepts and theories used cross the borders of cultures without losing part of their relevance and explanatory power. Consequently, Chapter 4 explores the cross-cultural aspects of consumer behaviour theories. It starts by assessing how culture affects consumer behaviour and highlights its influence on selected concepts such as loyalty, involvement and dissatisfaction. The chapter also examines the topic of ethnic consumption. The last section in this chapter takes as its premise that marketing is based on exchanges of meanings between marketers and consumers. This perspective makes much sense in international marketing since meaning is directly based on language, and linguistic diversity remains quite high cross-nationally.

The encounters between local consumers and increasingly globalized consumption items are complex, contradictory and sometimes problematic. Chapter 5 first explains how the trend to globalization has been ideologically supported over the last two centuries by the free trade doctrine and how this doctrine tended to view products merely as commodities and to deny cross-national variety in consumers' tastes and consumption habits. Analysis of global trends in consumption patterns shows some convergence at a broad, quantitative level: the utilitarian needs for reasonably priced, mass-produced products and services are drivers behind this fast-paced change. The emergence of a global consumer culture is based on increasing aspirations for a world-standard package of goods and services whose performance is highly predictable. However, the meaning attributed to products and consumption experiences remains to a large extent embedded in local contexts, that of shared habits within the cultural and linguistic groupings. Examples are given of how products whose consumption is becoming global, such as beer, are locally reinterpreted and vested with specific meanings, which must be taken into account when designing marketing strategy. In some cases, local consumer cultures can be strong enough to develop resistance to globalized consumption if it is perceived as detrimental to local cultural and economic interests. In most cases, however, the emergent pattern is of a mix of local and global consumer behaviour based on kaleidoscopic ways of assembling diverse consumption experiences and making sense of them in everyday life.

When market research takes place across borders, a number of survey instruments, such as questionnaires, scales, sampling techniques, interview techniques, etc., may not fit with the target contexts where data has to be collected. Chapter 6 describes the technicalities of cross-cultural market research, that is, the problems posed by the possible inequivalence of instruments and methods across research contexts. The chapter reviews equivalence issues, such as conceptual, functional, translation and measure equivalence, which are examined in successive sections and illustrated by real-life examples. The issue of samples and sampling procedures is addressed because of the need of international marketing decision makers for findings that can be consistently compared across cultures and markets. Chapter 6 also examines how local respondents may react to survey instruments and which sort of data biases result from their unfamiliarity with the chosen data collection techniques. As a consequence, international research is often less technical than domestic research in terms of scientific survey instruments and needs more inputs of action research: this is illustrated in the last section with the example of the Japanese style of researching markets.

Cross-cultural consumer behaviour

'*Sehen Sie Mercedes mit anderen Augen. Die neue E-Klasse ist da*' says a Daimler-Benz poster for their new E-Class car ('Look at Mercedes with other eyes. The new E-Class arrives'). This chapter is all about 'looking with other eyes'. It deals with the influence of culture on consumer behaviour. Looking with the 'same eyes' means that theories, underlying models, concepts and views of what consumers are, what their motives are, and how they behave are assumed to be universal. One may 'add glasses to the same eyes' so that what was previously invisible comes to light. But what Mercedes asks its potential consumers to do may be necessary: changing the eyes in order to have a different perspective. Table 4.1 sums up four perspectives, starting from the view that both consumers (the object) and underlying consumer behaviour theories (the eyes) can be either universal or specific. When reading Table 4.1, it is important to note that no cell corresponds to a better perspective than any other.

As depicted in Table 4.1, the *global perspective*, in its purest form, is now rarely found except in the text on globalization of markets by Levitt[1] and more generally when consumers are viewed as truly global. It may make sense for particular classes of consumers, such as business people travelling worldwide, and their families ('the global nomads'). The *global perspective* has been widely used and in some cases has led to the design of successful marketing strategies.

Much of the earlier and more current work in consumer behaviour takes a global perspective, where the theories and consumers are assumed to be universal. The universality of underlying theories and concepts have to be challenged, especially in international markets, but also in ethnic groups within countries (e.g. Black, Italian, Jewish, WASPs – White Anglo-Saxon Protestants, Muslim).

In the *imported perspective*, offerings are tailored to local markets and marketing environments, but basic underlying theories are not changed. The imported perspective may sometimes enable one to discover significant differences in consumer behaviour (CB) that require adaptation, but it is not always sufficient. For instance, behavioural intentions models were assumed to be universally applicable in terms of the global perspective, with attitudes and expectations

Table 4.1 Consumer behaviour in a cross-cultural perspective

		Consumer behaviour theories	
		Universal (etic)	Specific (emic)
Consumers	**Universal**	(1) Global perspective	(3) Ethnic consumption perspective
	Specific	(2) 'Imported' perspective	(4) Cultural meaning perspective

of important others influencing intentions. Then, when looked at from the imported perspective, differences in weightings were found between attitudes and expectations of important others in a predictable pattern across cultures. The attitudes of consumers in individualist cultures were more influential on intentions than expectations of important others, while the reverse was true in collectivist cultures.[2-4] Then, researchers began to look with 'new eyes' from a cultural meaning perspective, to examine whether different models better suited different cultures.[2,5]

This chapter questions the cross-cultural transportability of CB theories. This is not to say that similarities do not exist between cultures. Commonalities are demonstrated by the success of products and services designed in perspectives 1 and 2. But it is important to assess the cultural relativity of both consumers and the underlying models we apply if we really want to understand their behaviour. Since both similarities and differences exist, it is important to know what one is looking for. This decision will guide the models that apply: those that let differences emerge or those that favour the discovery of similarities. This corresponds with the etic (universal) approach and the emic (specific) approaches.[6]

Website link 4.1

Read a discussion on imagery in cross-cultural research from the emic and etic perspectives: http://www.quirks.com/articles/a1995/19950102.aspx.

Section 4.1 discusses the influence of major cultural traits on consumer behaviour. It starts with the question of whether the hierarchy of needs applies cross-culturally. Not only whether people locate their needs at different levels in the hierarchy, across cultures, but also, are the major assumptions in this model valid across cultures? The next topic is the influence of individualism and collectivism on consumers' attitudes and buying behaviour at the cultural and individual levels (i.e. independent and interdependent self-concepts that are more or less likely to be salient in individualist and collectivist cultures). Finally, the influence of institutions, social conventions, and customs on consumer behaviour is discussed.

Section 4.2 examines the impact of culture on selected aspects of consumer behaviour. Table 4.2 lists the types of cultural values and behaviours that have an impact on consumer attitudes, decision-making and buying behaviour. The table also suggests issues to be addressed in order to reach a better understanding of cultural differences in consumer behaviour. The final sections review how a selection of consumer behaviours are influenced by culture, including consumer involvement, cognitive styles, perceived risk and uncertainty and loyalty.

Section 4.3 explores post-purchase dissatisfaction further, by analysing the transferring of consumer behaviour constructs across cultures. Marketers tend to apply consumer behaviour concepts in an ethnocentric manner, whereas they would learn more by focusing on a common problem: how do cultures solve a similar problem in a different way?

Section 4.4 examines the influences of ethnicity on consumption patterns. As we argued at the end of Chapter 2, cultural borrowing is intense, and immigrants bring with them their values and behaviour. Ethnic consumption is a major dimension of cross-cultural consumer behaviour in two respects: (1) ethnic consumption has modified consumption patterns in countries opened to immigration; and (2) some ethnic products have reached world-class status by being adopted in most countries of the world, through migration and international travel.

Marketing is a process involving communication and exchange: consumers buy meanings as well as objects. Accordingly, section 4.5 focuses on the way in which cultural background influences communication and exchange. Two examples are used to illustrate this: the role of emotions in Japanese marketing and the role of symbols in linking objects and persons in the Italian style of marketing.

4.1

Culture and consumer behaviour

Although consumer behaviour has strong universal components, its cultural variations cannot be ignored. Without presenting an exhaustive list, there are some essential points of cultural influence on consumer behaviour that are worth considering in some detail:

1. Hierarchies of needs, which shape demand across product categories.
2. Culture-based values, especially individualist or collectivist orientations, which influence purchasing behaviour and buying decisions (individual versus family).
3. Institutions, which influence consumer behaviour, given that most consumption is rooted in social life, a large part of which is institutionalized.

Hierarchy of needs

Culture influences Maslow's 'hierarchy of needs' on at least two levels. First, one of the basic axioms of Maslow's theory is not true in every culture, namely, that needs at a definite level must be satisfied in order for higher-order needs to appear. Second, similar kinds of needs may be satisfied by very different products and consumption types.[7] In the hierarchy of needs, physiological needs are at the lowest level because they are the most fundamental. Then safety needs, such as being sheltered and protected from dangers in the environment, emerge when physiological needs are satisfied. Then come what Maslow calls social needs, which include friendship and love relationships. Then come esteem needs, such as the desire for respect from others, which is supported by status-improving goods. Finally, when all other levels have been satisfied, is the need for self-actualization, encompassing the development of one's full potential as a human being.

Website link 4.2

See an application of Maslow's Hierarchy of Needs to the television show 'Survivor': http://www.bpsoutdoor.com/article.php?article=psycho_effects.

First, the level of economic development influences the satisfaction of our needs. In less developed economies, people usually focus on more basic survival needs. However, some cultures (e.g. Hindu) encourage the pursuit of self-actualization, the highest level (the satisfaction of which does not neces-

sarily imply material consumption) and discourage the pursuit of lower level needs. As such, the basic need for safety, including shelter and personal protection, is not satisfied according to the same criteria in different cultures. For instance, in certain developing countries people may deprive themselves of food in order to afford a refrigerator, thereby satisfying the social status and self-esteem need before satisfying their physical need.[8] The well-documented area of conspicuous consumption also contradicts the hierarchy of needs. As noted by Solomon (p. 426),[12] the term *conspicuous consumption* was coined by Veblen, who was initially inspired by anthropological studies of the Kwakiutl Indians:

These Indians had a ceremony called a potlach where the host showed off his wealth and gave extravagant presents to their guests. The more one gave away, the better one looked to the others. Sometimes, the host would use an even more radical strategy to flaunt his wealth. He would publicly destroy some of his property to demonstrate how much he had. This ritual was also used as a social weapon: Since guests were expected to reciprocate, a poorer rival could be humiliated by inviting him to a lavish potlach. The need to give away, even though he could not afford it, would essentially force the hapless guest into bankruptcy.[9]

A similar concept also exists in modern societies, especially in the context of fundraising where appreciation banquets, kick-off luncheons and campaign parties present ritualized, symbolic gift giving which induces participants into the social dynamics of philanthropy.[10]

The potlach example suggests that consumer motivations are rooted in the dynamics of social life. Thus one of the basic axioms of Maslow's theory, that needs must be satisfied at one level in order for the needs in the next level to appear, is not true from a cross-cultural point of view.

Slightly caricatured, Maslow's picture of motivation describes an individual, starting from the belly and extending to the brain: although relevant, it cannot provide a universal view cross-culturally. There is limited support for the cross-cultural applicability of Maslow's hierarchy of needs.[11] Whereas the list of needs described by Maslow are themselves fairly consistent across cultures, their rank ordering varies, as does the way in which each need is met. Rather than needs, which have a distinct rational and utilitarian connotation, consumer *desires* may be a more useful concept for cross-cultural consumer behaviour.

Cultural dimensions

Most of the available marketing literature depicts individual consumers who make their own decisions. While this individualistic conception remains at the heart of marketing research, there is a growing understanding that our decisions are strongly influenced by social factors. For example, Bagozzi's model of goal-directed behaviour encompasses multiple sources of social influence on an individual's intentions.[12] Further, Bagozzi and Lee (pp. 229–30)[13] describe the concept of social intentions, termed 'we-intentions to perform a group act . . . In this case a person plans to participate in a joint activity, but conceives of the activity less as individuals performing personal acts that contribute to a group performance than as a group action in which one is a member of the group'. In addition to the more traditional influence of expectations of important others, group norms and social identity also influence I- and We-intentions in some cultures.[13,14]

Two areas of marketing research have a history of examining group decisions: industrial marketing and family decision making. Both literatures recognize that different people exert more or less influence depending on the importance of that decision to the group and individual. Generally, unimportant decisions are made by individuals, midrange decisions by a group, and very important decisions by a key decision maker.[15] For instance, across a range of Latin American countries, food and appliance decisions were mostly made by the wife, vacations, furniture, savings and insurance decisions were made jointly and automobiles were mostly made by the husband.[16] Both of these literatures also recognize that the final decision maker is not the only one to influence the decision.

In the CB literature, the family is often seen as an interacting group of individuals, who influence each other in their decisions. In this literature, one or two family members, almost always including the mother, are asked about family purchasing decisions. Few studies view the family as an organic entity or single decision-making unit, as opposed to a casual collection of individuals who share information and some common interests and constraints. This organic view may help to uncover the myriad of social influences within the family group, which

is more complex in studies that span cultures or countries.

The vast majority of the family decision-making literature has focused on Western families. In this literature differences in family influence have been found depending on external factors, such as the family member asked, the product type studied and the stage of the decision process, as well as internal family factors, such as the role structure within the family, spousal resources, and decision-making styles.

Social and cultural factors have also been examined. One of the most important factors is egalitarianism, which is a value system emphasizing equality. Generally, in Asia, families are more traditional in terms of the marital-role values, with the husband being expected to make the majority of decisions. Rodman (pp. 63–5)[17] identified four stereotypical types of societies where the marital power is likely to differ:

1. *Patriarchy:* A high level of paternal authority across all levels of society (e.g. India).
2. *Modified Patriarchy:* Patriarchal family norms are modified by equalitarian norms, where paternal authority is inversely related to social class (e.g. Greece and Yugoslavia).
3. *Transitional Equalitarianism:* Equalitarian norms are replacing patriarchal norms giving more normative flexibility, where personal resources are likely effect the level of influence (e.g. Germany and the USA).
4. *Equalitarianism:* Strong equalitarian values, where both husband and wife share power throughout all levels of society (e.g. Denmark and Sweden).

These types of societies reflect Hofstede's masculinity–femininity dimensions,[18] described in Chapter 3. Thus, we might expect family decision making to differ across the individualism–collectivism and masculinity–femininity divide. Highly feminine individualist cultures, such as Denmark, Norway and Sweden, share social and economic responsibilities between men and women. They have overlapping gender roles, a high level of equality and a high level of individual freedom. Highly feminine collectivist cultures, such as Chile, South Korea and Thailand, also share social and economic responsibilities and have a high level of equality, but they have less individual freedom. In Thailand, there are generally stronger family ties, there is more communication and family members have a greater influence on consumption behaviour than in Western families.[19]

In contrast, highly masculine individualist cultures, such as Australia, Germany, the UK and the USA, have large gender-role differences, lower equality and a high level of individual freedom. Highly masculine collectivist cultures, such as Hong Kong, Japan and Mexico, have large gender-role differences, lower equality and a low level of individual freedom. Japanese mothers restrict their children's consumption, allowing less autonomy, while at the same time reporting a higher level of children's influence than American mothers who encourage the development of independent consumption relatively early.[20]

Another influence from collectivism is the role of the extended family. In the East, the extended family model has survived and it has a powerful influence on many purchase decisions. Even Chinese people, who may sometimes appear quite individualistically oriented when outside their national context, remain strongly bound by their family ties. Ikels (p. 30)[21] points out two factors that have reinforced family ties:

. . . first the traditional value of interdependence both between parents and children and among the masses as a whole has never been attacked; second, the economic conditions in China, and in rural China in particular, provide the elderly with opportunities to contribute to household income while at the same time making it impossible for them to go it alone.

Independent versus interdependent self

Consumers buy objects and services for the value they provide. In valuing things, consumers may attribute private and/or public meanings. Public meanings have been defined as the subjective meanings assigned to an object by outside observers (non-owners) of that object, that is by members of the society at large.[22] Public meanings emerge through socialization and participation in shared activities and are reinforced in social interchanges. Private meanings are the sum of the subjective meanings that an object holds for a particular individual. Some of the private meanings may derive from socially shared

interpretations, but some of them are unique to the consumer because they are associated with private and even intimate experiences.

Both Asians and Westerners see the self as divided into an inner private self and an outer public self based on social roles. It is important to go beyond the individualism/collectivism divide in order to understand how the concept of self distinguishes Westerners and Orientals (and how this concept is articulated with the concept of others). The divide between individualism and collectivism may be considered as the other side of this reality, at the social rather than personal level.

Two relatively stable dimensions of the self have been proposed: *independent* and *interdependent*.[23] The *independent* self corresponds to the Western conception; it is based on the assumption of individualism discussed in section 3.1, whereby people are seen as inherently separate and distinct. The inner self is the regulator of activity and personal consumption preferences are supposed to reflect a person's tastes, values and convictions. Self-expression is encouraged, especially in the area of consumption. The slogan is 'be yourself', that is, act in accordance with your private self.[24]

On the other hand, the *interdependent* self of most Asians is based on an assumption of collectivism. People are seen as connected to each other by a multitude of overlaps and links: they share a common substance. So, as a result, identity lies in familial and social relationships. People with interdependent selves tend to value the criteria of appropriate social conduct in their consumption behaviour.

These distinctive self-concepts are not mutually exclusive. People, especially bicultural people, can easily switch between their independent and interdependent self in response to different situations.[25] All of us carry aspects of independence and interdependence; which one is used depends on the situation and reference group.[26] Consequently, people from collectivist cultures are more likely to rely on an interdependent self-concept and people from individualist cultures are more likely to rely on an independent self-concept in any given situation.

The interdependent or independent self-concept influences many aspects of consumer behaviour, including reasons for purchase,[27] impulsive buying behaviour,[28] references for consumption symbols,[29] associations embedded in persuasion appeals,[30] the persuasion of approach and avoidance appeals,[29] and emotional appeals.[31] For instance, the independent self-concept is more strongly related to purchase reasons associated with uniqueness, while the interdependent self-concept is more strongly related to reasons associated with group affiliation.[27]

Institutions, social conventions, habits and customs

Institutions such as the state, the church and trade unions also influence the marketing environment. For example, the French Catholic hierarchy has generally been opposed to Sunday trading. In Germany, trade unions strongly oppose an extension of store opening hours. In Germany, stores generally close at 7 p.m. each working day, at 2 p.m. on Saturdays, and are closed on Sundays. These hours are legally mandated and contravening shops are heavily fined. The result is that many German consumers must shop quickly on Saturday mornings. Catalogue-based mail order and online shopping are good substitutes for consumers kept at their offices during shop opening hours. As a result, mail order sales are highly developed in Germany, with giant enterprises having developed in the industry, such as Neckermann, Bertelsmann and Quelle.

Other products are institution dependent: examples include marriage-related goods such as a wedding dress or the products featured on wedding lists, or the many kinds of traditional gifts offered for specific occasions. One example is the initiative by a Parisian Catholic priest to take action against Halloween in favour of the next day, All Saints' Day, traditionally an important holiday in France. In conjunction with the French Association of Bakers, a '*Gâteau de la Toussaint*' was developed to increase respect for the day of honouring the dead, thereby creating an institution-dependent product.

Website link 4.3

Find out more on Chinese eating habits:
http://www.cuisinet.com/glossary/chinaday.html.

Of all the cultural conventions that structure daily life in the consumption domain, the most important is probably eating habits. According to Wilk (p. 372)[32]: 'Food is both substance and symbol; providing both physical nourishment and a key form of communication that carries many kinds of meanings.' Cultural variations in eating habits include:

1. The number of meals consumed each day.
2. The standard duration and the position of meals in the daily schedule.
3. The composition of each meal. Servings may differ in size, comprise various types of food (local ingredients or cooking style) and differ in the nutritional content so that people can cope with long time periods without eating.
4. Beverages that accompany meals (water, coffee, tea, wine, beer, and so on) and their functional use as a refresher, energizer, coolant, relaxer, etc.
5. The social function, whether 'fuel' or daily 'social event'. Meals may be communal events where people entertain themselves by eating and chatting together, or it may simply be a means of feeding oneself without any symbolic connotation.
6. The way it is put together. Is the food ready-made or is it prepared from basic ingredients? Do servants help prepare the meal? What is the cultural meaning of the meal being prepared by the housewife or by her husband, for whom, in which particular situations?

The list of cultural variations in eating habits is endless, because nothing is more essential, more vital and at the same time more accurately defined by culture than eating habits. Eating habits should be considered as the whole process of purchasing food and beverages, cooking, tasting, and even commenting on them.

A questionnaire was developed in western Europe to assess food-related lifestyles which includes five areas: ways of shopping (e.g. information importance, joy of shopping); quality aspects (e.g. health, price–quality relation); cooking methods (e.g. involvement, convenience); consumption situations (e.g. snacks versus meals, social event); and purchase motives (e.g. self-fulfilment in food, social relationships).[33] The questionnaire was used in Singapore, asking the member of the household who does the most cooking and shopping to fill it out: 89 per cent of respondents were female and 11 per cent of them also maids.[34] Askegaard and Brunsø (p. 80)[34] found that 'cooking patterns in Singaporean families are definitely very different from the European ones. First of all, the presence of a maid and the regular habit of dining out makes the "woman's task" more diffuse to define in terms of responsibility for the family's health and nutrition. Furthermore, the issue of carrying out tasks (maid) versus controlling these tasks (wife or husband) may cause problems in terms of who is to respond to various sections on the survey'.

In many countries, commercials advertising ready-made foods, such as canned or dried soups, faced resistance from the traditional role of the housewife, who was expected to prepare meals from natural ingredients for her family. As a result, advertisers were obliged to include a degree of preparation by the housewife in the advertising copy for such foods.

> **Website link 4.4**
>
> See an overview of cross-cultural dining etiquette:
> http://www.sideroad.com/Cross_Cultural_
> Communication/dining-etiquette.html.

4.2

The influence of culture on selected aspects of consumer behaviour

Table 4.2 presents selected aspects of consumer behaviour that are influenced by cultural differences. This table is designed to be indicative, rather than exhaustive, as there has been a dramatic increase in the cross-cultural analysis of consumer behaviour. There are more comprehensive reviews of the general literature[6,35] as well as specific literatures, such as preference for variety[36] and service experiences.[37]

We now discuss a selection of the relevant consumer behaviour constructs, including consumer involvement, decision-making styles, perceived risk and loyalty. In the next section we extend this discussion to post-purchase behaviours, focusing on consumer complaining.

Consumer involvement

Consumer involvement is generally a function of a person, a product or service and a situation.[38] Whereas personal interests differ in all cultures, situational factors are likely to be more important in determining the extent of consumer involvement in Eastern than in Western cultures. Eastern consumers value social harmony and the smoothness of relationships within the extended family. Therefore the social significance of a product is very important because it may express status, gratitude, approval or disapproval. Those products that have social symbolic value and those that are conspicuous to others are likely to have a higher level of involvement. Conversely, involvement is likely to be lower when products are used for private consumption.[39] In this case, consumers are likely to adopt a rather simple cognitive stance, favouring the physical functions of the product and being mostly concerned with price and quality.

Consumer cognitive styles

High involvement purchase decisions are generally thought to have five stages: problem recognition, information search, alternative evaluations, purchase (perhaps) and post-purchase. For habitual purchases and less involving products, these processes have either occurred in the past, or are limited in terms of effort. In addition, each of these processes is influenced by social environment and situational factors, including marketing stimuli (particularly advertising and sales promotion).

Consumer behaviour models have a rather linear, analytical and abstract style. Asian consumers tend to have a different cognitive style: the Chinese as well as the Japanese have a more synthetic, concrete and contextual orientation in their thought patterns.[39-42] For instance, information acquisition on an attribute by attribute basis is not the dominant style of information processing employed by consumers: information is processed in a more holistic way by choice alternative or some combination of attribute and choice alternative.[41]

Table 4.2 Possible impacts of cultural differences on selected aspects of consumer behaviour

Aspect of consumer behaviour	Impact of cultural differences: values involved/issues to be addressed	Section
Perception	Perception of shapes, colours and space varies across cultures.	2.3; 9.4
Motivation	Motivation to own, to buy, to spend, to consume, to show, to share, to give.	4.3
Learning and memory	Literacy levels. Memory as it is shaped by education. Familiarity with product classes shaped by education.	4.2; 4.3
Age	Do people know their exact age? Value of younger and older people in the society. Influence processes across age groups. How is purchasing power distributed across generations?	3.1
Self-concept		3.1; 4.1
Group influence	Individualism/collectivism. To what extent are individuals influenced in their attitudes and buying behaviour by their group? How does consumer behaviour reflect the need to self-actualize individual identity or to manifest group belonging?	3.1; 3.2 4.1
Social class	Are social classes locally important? Is social class belonging demonstrated through consumption? What type of products or services do social-status-minded consumers buy? Are there exclusive shops?	3.1; 4.1
Sex roles	The sexual division of labour; who makes the decisions? Shopping behaviour; who shops: he or she or both of them?	3.1; 3.2
Attitudes changes	Resistance to change in consumer behaviour (possibly related to high level of uncertainty avoidance, past orientation, fatalism), especially when change could clash with local values and behaviour (e.g. resistance to *fast-food* restaurants in France).	4.2
Decision making	Family models (nuclear versus extended family). Involvement. Compulsive buying.	4.0; 4.1 4.2
Purchase	Loyalty. Environmental factors, especially legal. Influence of salespersons on clients.	4.2 15.1 15.3
Post-purchase	Perceptions of product quality. Consumer complaining behaviour. Dissatisfaction/Consumerism.	4.3; 9.1 9.2; 9.3 10.2; 10.3; 11.3

This does not mean that Asians are less rational; on the contrary they might be more rational in their purchasing. Eastern collectivist consumers have been shown to engage in less impulsive buying than Western individualist consumers, despite having similar personal impulsive tendencie.[28] Eastern consumers (as adults) learn to suppress their internal feelings in order to act appropriately in the situation.

It seems that they are able to suppress their impulsiveness trait and act in a manner that is consistent with cultural norms.

Perceived risk

Perceived risk is an important consideration that is likely to enter into the decision-making process at the alternative evaluation stage.[43] This may be the evaluation of alternative product categories or alternative products within categories that may satisfy a need.

Perceived risk is broken into the psychological, financial, performance, physical, social and time or convenience risk.[44] In Western cultures, performance risk is highly correlated with overall perceived risk, and as such has been suggested as a good measure of perceived risk.[45] Performance risk, whether the produce performs as expected, may not be the most important type of risk in other cultures.

In Eastern cultures, consumers may be more sensitive to social risk (because a purchaser may risk the loss of face in other people's eyes), than performance or financial risks. Their tight ingroup increases the importance of social expectations, whereas it decreases the importance of personal risk. People in collectivistic cultures are more risk seeking in their financial choices than people in individualistic cultures.[46] This has been attributed to cushion theory, which suggests that social networks protects people if they take risks and 'fall'.[47]

In other cultures, physical risk has a low importance, because the mortality rate is high, and illness and death are accepted as part of this life, but perhaps not the next. This will influence the purchase of many products, including insurance, healthcare, food and transportation. In a country where road safety is not a high priority, we might see people sitting on the top of trains, or on chairs in the back of trucks, with no regard for safety issues. In this case, the more important risk associated with purchasing a car may be reliability: an engine breakdown may be seen as a disaster, because there is little or no available maintenance. These perceived risks are quite different from those experienced by the average purchaser of a car in a western European country.

It is important to note that risk is fundamentally different from uncertainty, although they have often been confused in the literature. Risk is quantifiable: it has an associated probability. Uncertainty has no associated probability; it is a situation in which anything can happen.[18] As Hofstede (p. 148)[18] points out, people may engage in risky behaviour in order to reduce ambiguity, 'such as starting a fight with a potential opponent rather than sitting back and waiting'.

Loyalty

Consumers can be loyal, repeating their purchases on a regular basis, buying the same brand or product, or buy at the same store or from the same catalogue or website. Loyal consumers prefer to be sure of what they buy. However, by doing this they reduce their opportunity to find other, and perhaps better, choices which would provide them with more value for their money. Disloyal consumers try new brands, shift from one brand to another when a new one is promoted, and take advantage of temporary price reductions. Disloyalty is the natural counterpart of loyalty (to a brand, a product, a store, etc.). What is culturally meaningful is to observe which one of these two opposite attitudes is considered as the legitimate, fundamental behaviour.

In the West, *brand loyalty* is carefully surveyed, and demographics, lifestyles or situational variables are researched. Standard behaviour is assumed to be disloyal. Consumers are likely to switch brands to test competing products, thereby fostering price competition. It is standard behaviour to respond spontaneously to advertising and sales promotion, because consumers enjoy change more than stability. They seek more variety in their purchases.[36] Variety seeking has been linked to the need for uniqueness, which is more prevalent in Western cultures.[48] It is assumed that consumers are not rewarded for buying the same brand (i.e. 'brand loyal') and/or shopping in the same store (i.e. 'store loyal').

Loyalty is a key concept in collectivist cultures, which spreads from people to product, inasmuch as products are expressions of the self. There is an unusual level of single brand dominance in many Asian markets, with one brand accounting for 40–50 per cent of market share over quite a long period of time.[49] Consumers in collectivist societies have been shown to be more loyal on average for two reasons.[50] First, they tend to rely more on information found in their reference group – often by word-of-mouth communication – rather than on media information. Second, they tend to follow the group consensus until convinced the new product is better. A rare examination of loyalty outside Western cultures reveals that consumers from China and South Korea tend to buy the same brands because these products fulfilled their experiential, social and function needs.[51]

When consumers in New Zealand (NZ) and China were asked about a recent incident when they had seriously considered switching service providers (e.g. bank, insurance company, doctor, phone company, hairdresser), the most important factor for the NZ sample was confidence, in terms of satisfaction and trust, whereas the most important consideration for the Chinese sample was time and effort, in terms of learning, switching and establishing a new relationship.[52] This illustrates the higher level of cost to switching in Eastern cultures. Not only is extra time required in developing a relationship with a new service provider, but extra time is also required in researching alternatives. The stronger reliance on word-of-mouth in Eastern cultures increases the effort required to gain the relevant information about alternatives.

It is necessary for marketing strategies to differ where consumers are fundamentally more loyal and less used to rational comparisons (such as price/quality cross-brand or cross-product comparisons), from those where consumers frequently shift brands. Uncertainty avoidance and collectivism are both positively related to loyalty, suggesting that companies entering markets with these characteristics will face more obstacles. Where consumers are more loyal, it may be necessary to build a loyal consumer base from scratch. Where consumers are less loyal, it may be more effective to persuade brand shifters to switch from other established brands, and then to try to turn the newly developed consumer base into a loyal one.[53] The extent of loyalty also has implications for brand equity. In South Korea, the most important element of brand equity in apparel was loyalty, while perceptions of quality and familiarity were more important for Americans.[54]

4.3
Investigating the cross-cultural applicability of consumer behaviour concepts

Any element of consumer behaviour is filtered through cross-cultural lenses. For example, *word-of-mouth* communication is fairly universal: in any culture, people discuss and exchange information on their consumption experiences. Where little relevant information is available, as in the case of films for instance, or new products, or when consumers have a low level of familiarity with a complex product, people tend to seek information from acquaintances. However, word-of-mouth communication is likely to be stronger in collectivist and ingroup oriented societies, where outside information provided by an impersonal marketer will be seen as less reliable than opinions from relatives and acquaintances.

The best solution for investigating cross-cultural applicability is always to start from the 'common problem' in Kluckhohn and Strodtbeck's terms.[55] For instance, why and how can consumers express dissatisfaction with products or services? The solution found in the consumer behaviour literature is based on the dominant normative solution in the West. Other alternatives must always be looked for, especially the alternative that the problem may not *have* a solution.

The example of consumer dissatisfaction

We can investigate the equivalence of consumer satisfaction and dissatisfaction by assessing the comparability of antecedent factors, formation processes and behavioural outcomes.[56]

1. What are the relevant antecedent factors that may differ? Do they include economic (buying power), temporal (time needed for purchase and consumption activities), cognitive (mental capacity available to understand and process information) and spatial (location of activities in terms of place and distance) differences, in terms of the way they are perceived and the criteria and processes used for allocation (a scarce resource in one country

may not be scarce in another)? Are the categories and substitutability of these resources comparable? Are the contextual or situational influences, such as spatial aspects, social surroundings, and tasks comparable? For instance, in Chapter 2 we looked at the variability of time and space. Where time is considered an economic resource, consumers are more likely to trade off or substitute time for money.

2. Are dissatisfaction formation processes the same, including ideal, expected, deserved and minimum tolerable product performance? Do consumers perceive discrepancies in the same way? In some cultures, such as Mexico, consumers seem to rely more on perceptions, rather than the Western model of relying on confirmation or disconfirmation of their expectations.[57]

3. Will dissatisfaction influence action in the same way, such as repeat purchasing and switching behaviour? Some cultures have a higher social desirability bias and, as such, high reported satisfaction is unlikely to lead to the same level of repeat purchase as those from cultures with a lower social desirability bias.[56]

Attitudes towards consumerism vary across national contexts and so does the importance given to the consumer movement based on the following premises:

1. Is it legitimate for consumers to make their dissatisfaction known? In societies that experienced long periods of supply shortage this is not the case; complaints are useless.

2. Is it legitimate for consumers to force a producer, whose product is of dubious quality, to close down? In other words, is it right for consumers to cause innocent workers to lose their jobs?

3. Will complaining make any difference for the individual or for society?

These questions illustrate the problems associated with issues of consumer empowerment. The defence of individual consumers has consequences for society. Thus, expressing dissatisfaction frankly and openly may be considered to be partially illegitimate.

In fact, normal practices in terms of returns and exchanges differ markedly around the world. In many countries, returns and exchanges are not possible, or only possible in very limited circumstances,

such as only those products that are unopened or have clear defects, and are accompanied by a receipt. The following are a selection of customer comments from Blodgett and colleagues (pp. 109–10):

Czech Republic: 'The policies toward returning products are similar to those applied in the USA. However, most retailers will not accept returned items . . . unless they are persuaded that you did not use the product "improperly" or in any way that is explicitly forbidden in the instructions for use.'

China: 'It is not common . . . for customers to return items that they are not satisfied with.'

Russia: 'The product can be returned if it was damaged/faulty and a customer kept purchase receipt and [had] service warranty (for example, with electronics) . . . Personal belongings such as apparel, cosmetics and beauty items, as well as leisure items (books, CDs' tapes etc.) could not be returned in any circumstances.'

Taiwan: 'It is usually not possible for customers to return an item in Taiwan.'

Kenya: 'you can not return a product once purchased and customers take their own risk. In my country customer relations is not very good . . .'

India: 'There is no customer empowerment. People realize that they are being "ripped off", but if everyone is a thief, what can the customer do.'[58]

(*Journal of Consumer Satisfaction, Dissatisfaction and Complaining Behavior*, by Jeffrey Blodgett, Donna Hill and Aysen Bakir, copyright 2006 by *Journal of Consumer Satisfaction, Dissatisfaction and Complaining Behavior*, reproduced with permission of *Journal of Consumer Satifaction, Dissatisfaction and Complaining Behavior* in the format Textbook via Copyright Clearance Center.)

While returns may be limited by lack of competition, social expectations and legislation, customer complaining should be less limited. We see dramatic differences across countries. Western consumers in general voice more dissatisfaction than Eastern consumers. For instance, South Koreans respond privately more often, including avoiding the firm's product, buying from another firm or telling others about their bad experience, as compared to Americans who tend to discuss the problem with the manager, ask for the firm to fix it and believe that telling them will help them to do better in the future.[59]

The concept of dissatisfaction seems to have different meanings, socially and individually. Richins and Verhage (p. 203)[60] found significant differences in American and Dutch consumers' beliefs about dissatisfaction with a product or a service:

Dutch consumers perceive more inconvenience and unpleasantness in making a complaint than do American consumers . . . Dutch consumers were less likely than Americans to feel a social responsibility to make complaints . . . Seemingly contradicting this finding, however, Dutch consumers are more likely than Americans to feel bothered if they don't make a complaint when they believe they should, a sort of guilt. Perhaps this seeming contradiction indicates that Dutch respondents tend to feel a personal rather than social obligation to make complaints.

The word *construct* relates to a concept that has several underlying dimensions, and may be measured quantitatively by identifying these various dimensions. The construct *consumer dissatisfaction and complaint behaviour* identifies five domains of attitude towards complaining:[61]

1. Beliefs about the effect experienced when one complains.
2. Perceptions of the objective cost or trouble involved in making a complaint.
3. Perception of retailer responsiveness to consumer complaints.
4. The extent to which consumer complaints are expected to benefit society at large.
5. The perceived social appropriateness of making consumer complaints.

It is important to think about whether each of these sub-dimensions makes sense in the cross-cultural context. In the case of developing countries micro-level (e.g. excessive prices, misleading advertising, lack of performance) and macro-level sources of consumer dissatisfaction (e.g. low income, inflation) may interact.[62] Cavusgil and Kaynak (p. 118)[62] argue that: 'In general micro-level sources appear to lead, over time, to a diffuse, latent discontent with the state of the marketplace; that is to macro-level dissatisfaction. Unsatisfactory experiences with specific products and services seem to be reflected in a disillusionment with all institutions in the society'. Further they argue (p. 122) that complaining behaviour does not have the same meaning if buyer and seller know each other personally, as either acquaintances or relatives: 'Personal relationships with vendors often prove advantageous. Usually food shoppers get to know how far they can trust a food retailer, and can negotiate prices and other terms'.

Looking with other eyes: questioning consumer behaviour

'Looking with other eyes' implies decentring yourself. For instance, European cars overwhelmingly have manual gearboxes in contrast to the dominant use of automatic gearboxes in cars in the US. As such, an automatic gearbox is not a standard feature of cars in Europe and consumers have to pay extra and wait a little longer to get an automatic car. Further, selling a car with an automatic gearbox in a European country may be difficult since Europeans consider automatic cars either as being reserved for handicapped persons or a feature of luxury cars.

If we apply the perspectives from Table 4.1, the universal or global approach provides few clues for understanding the case of manual versus automatic gearboxes. The other perspectives provide many more insights by focusing on consumer specifics. In many countries there are limitations on the licensing of drivers of automatic cars. For instance, in the United Kingdom and Australia, a person may take their driving test in an automatic car and receive a licence that is restricted to automatics. In France, people must learn and take their driving test in a manual car. The only exception is for handicapped drivers who are allowed to use automatic cars to obtain their licence. Thus, learning plays a key role in the resistance to change: having been educated on manual drive, they tend to stick to what they know. Second, many Europeans still believe that automatic gearbox cars have high petrol consumption (or poor gas mileage in US terms). Nowadays this is not true, since technology has progressed to the point where the difference is almost nil, and in fact favours automatic cars in urban traffic conditions. Third, automatic vehicles are associated with high social status. Large and expensive cars are automatic more often than medium or small cars. Fourth and probably the strongest insight is symbolic: '*c'est une voiture d'infirme*': Most people see automatic cars, in the middle range of the market, as being specifically for handicapped persons, rather than for those who are not disabled.

If we sum up on the basis of the perspectives presented in Table 4.1:

1. The *global perspective* assumes both universal theories and universal consumers. This perspective misses the specific consumer insights from the market.
2. The *imported perspective* assesses specific consumer insight assuming universal theory. This perspective allows the discovery of the social status and resistance to change arguments.
3. The *ethnic consumption perspective* applies specific theories but assumes consumers are universal. This perspective allows the researcher to identify a small 'ethnic' target, that of North American expatriates (although many of them love manual gearboxes, which to them look more sporty).
4. The *cultural meaning perspective* applies specific theories to specific consumers. It is the only perspective that reveals the symbolic argument (automatic being associated with handicap), which is the major obstacle to selling the automatic car in Europe, even though they are much more comfortable to drive, as speedy and as fuel efficient as other cars.

Radical questioning

The application of different eyes requires radical questioning. One way to question consumer behaviour cross-nationally is simply to examine motivation in each of these basic actions: to own, spend, save, buy, consume, display, share and give (see Table 4.2).

1. The *motivation to own* is based on the notion of ownership. The English verb 'to own' has no equivalent in Swahili, the dominant language in East Africa. Possession, that is, the rights of individuals over objects, is also much more limited in scope.
2. *Motivation to spend* may also be radically altered by negative views of money.
3. *Motivation to save* may be altered by a lack of future orientation, and the feeling that one should not bet on one's future (see Box 6.1).
4. *Motivation to buy* may be low when objects and material culture are discarded, independent of purchasing power, as in Hindu culture.
5. *Motivation to consume* may be largely hindered by a strong ecological stance, as in Denmark or Germany where sensitivity to environmental problems has practically eliminated plastic bottling in favour of reusable glass.

6. *Motivation to display* is naturally related to the self-concept and the prevailing pattern of property.
7. *Motivation to give* also varies across cultures: it is widely practised in Japan, where the size of the gift is codified according to the type of social exchange. Gift giving in Hong Kong, is embedded in socio-cultural influences.[63] In other cultures, however, gift-giving practices may be less frequent, based on the view that it might embarrass the recipient, be necessary to reciprocate and finally both participants may resent being obliged to participate in the ritual.

There have been many studies of gift giving. One such study found that Korean and Americans have altruistic motivation more than 50 per cent of the time, but it was higher for the American sample (86 per cent): Koreans more often gave out of obligation (17 per cent), self-interest (11 per cent), group conformity (7 per cent) and facesaving (5 per cent). Park (p. 580) cited a Korean respondent's thoughts about gift giving:

I do have a lot of occasions to give a gift for face saving. Because saving face is very important in social life, I should give a gift on those occasions in order not to lose face. But I can't afford them always. Actually, there are too many occasions to afford with my income. The most frequent gift occasions for face saving are weddings, funerals, New Year's Day and Choo Suk [Korean Thanksgiving]. When I receive a gift, I feel pressure to reciprocate sometime in the future. In fact, face saving gifts are not pleasant at all.[64]

> ### Website link 4.5
>
> See examples of business gift-giving etiquette in different cultures: http://www.businessknowhow.com/growth/cultural.htm.

4.4

Ethnic consumption

Ethnicity as a thwarted ingroup orientation

Ethnic consumption is a strong component of modern consumption culture. Ethnic products have been popularized worldwide and ethnic food and restaurants are fast growing segments in the food industry. Ethnicity reflects the internationalization of lifestyles through migration and travel.

Ethnic consumption also has a great deal to do with mixing consumption patterns of the home and host country. One of the most influential models of migrants' adaptation and adjustment processes, is Berry and colleagues' acculturation model.[65] This model is based on two dimensions: maintenance of their ethnic or home culture and their relationship with the host culture. These dimensions lead to four basic strategies:

1. *Assimilation* – acquiring the host culture while not maintaining their home culture.
2. *Integration* – acquiring the host culture while maintaining their home culture.
3. *Separation* – rejecting the host culture while maintaining their home culture.
4. *Marginalization* – rejecting both the host and home culture.

These strategies can be seen in the consumer behaviour of ethnic groups. For instance, elements of an *integration* strategy can be seen in Herbert Gans' (p. 184) description of the Italian immigrant culture's eating and consumption habits in a New York neighbourhood, which he calls 'West End':

> Their actual diet, however, bears little resemblance to that of their Italian ancestors, for they have adopted American items that can be integrated into the overall tradition. For example, although their ancestors could not afford to eat meat, West Enders can, and they spend considerable sums on it. Typically American meats such as hot dogs, hamburger and steak are very popular indeed, but they are usually prepared with Italian spices, and accompanied by Italian side-dishes. The role of American culture is perhaps best illustrated by holiday fare. Turkey is eaten on Thanksgiving, but is preceded by a host of Italian antipastos, accompanied by Italian side-dishes, and followed by Italian desserts. This amalgamation of ethnic and American food is, of course, not exclusive to the West Enders, but can be found among all groups of foreign origin.[66]

On the maintenance of culture dimension, ethnic subcultures are based on shared beliefs and habits and the sense of belonging to a specific group of people, which is different from the society at large. Ingroup orientation is central to ethnicity, but to a large extent the sense of belonging to the subcultural community is thwarted, because it is simultaneously necessary – and difficult – to identify with the values and behaviour of the dominant ingroup and the nationals of the country of residence. Hispanics in the United States have to cope with this dilemma: they have to adjust to a predominantly WASP (White Anglo-Saxon Protestant) culture, while their basic assumptions, interaction models and sense of belonging would drive them towards the Hispanic community.

Ethnicity is a matter of shared belief about a common ancestry. Bouchet's six main attributes of ethnic community are:[67]

1. a collective proper name;
2. a myth of common ancestry;
3. shared historical memories;
4. one or more differentiating elements of common culture (e.g. language);
5. an association with a specific homeland; and
6. a sense of solidarity.

Because ethnic belonging in the host country is taken from the culture's original territory and inhabitants, people often try to maintain their subculture by means of ethnic stereotyping. In marketing, this gives rise to opportunistic use where, for instance, 3M has used Scottish imagery to denote value in 'Scotch' tape, since the Scottish stereotype of supposed frugality is viewed favourably in the United States.[9]

Elements of a *separation* strategy can be seen in Ger and Østergaard's (p. 49) description of Turkish students in Denmark as more 'Turkish' than those who live in Turkey:

> Some families brought the curtains from Turkey, thinking that the curtains in Odense were too simple. Their furniture reminded the Turkish author of the 1960s urban middle class furnishings in Turkey: chandeliers, then a symbol of wealth, a prominent buffet, and 'Turkish' crochéed covers hanging from the shelves. They displayed many knick-knacks – small decorative souvenirs, currently sold for tourists in Turkey . . . Several homes had Turkish flags. One male informant, who displayed such a flag, in addition to posters of the Turkish national anthem and Istanbul, rosary beads, a Turkish soccer team key chain, and a Koran, and who was wearing a small flag pin on his sweater, explained that the Danes always have flags in their houses. Unlike 'some who try to hide the fact that they are Turks', he wants everyone to know that he is Turkish. His e-mail messages end with 'We Love Turkey'.[68]

On the more negative side, the stresses related to social adjustments to the host culture can lead to alcohol abuse.[69] This resembles a *marginalization* strategy, where a lack of clear behavioural guidelines can result in self-destructive tendencies.

The acculturation strategy

It may be wrong to equate consumers from a definite ethnic group to a specific market segment, which seeks specific products or service benefits; as noted in the section above it is more complex. The usefulness of observable ethnicity as a market segmentation basis in international consumer marketing has been questioned.

The dual cultural influences result in mixed schemas of cultural values, norms and behaviours.[70] This reflects the *integration* strategy, but we also see an *assimilation* strategy reflected in consumer behaviour. For instance, Hispanics tend to be more American than Anglo-Americans in many characteristics.[71]

Assimilation takes place when the relative influence of the culture of origin diminishes and immigrants hold faster to the values and behaviours of the country of residence. Assimilation is evidenced in the following areas: consumption patterns, employment, marriage with people originating from the host culture, participation in the political process as a candidate, and having acquaintances outside the ethnic community. The process of assimilation is a lengthy one, which may require several generations to be fully accomplished.

In the assimilation process, two mechanisms are at work.[72] The first is based on structural constraints where compliance is compulsory, not voluntary: if people drive on the other side of the road, the individual will be obliged to adapt. The second is based on the newcomer's willingness to adjust to the new culture's behaviour and rules: it depends on the enthusiasm for what the new culture brings, e.g. in terms of increased freedom and improved material status.

Ethnicity as identity

When assimilation has fully taken place, probably by the third or fourth generation, those now assimilated may share much more with the society at large than with their subcultural group. However, there is often resurgence of ethnicity; ethnicity has more to do with the evolution of identity in general rather than with the origin of one's historical identity.[67] For instance, Oswald (p. 307)[73] illustrates how Haitian consumers in the United States 'culture swap', using goods to move between one cultural identity and another as they negotiate relations between home and host cultures:

> Odette insisted she was so mainstream as to provide nothing at all about Haitian culture, having lived in the United States for 30 years and having served in the U.S. Army . . . Odette planned to hold the children's party at Chuck E. Cheese, a pizzeria chain, but invited relatives to the home for a Haitian barbecue and the ubiquitous rice and beans.

Thus ethnic consumption should be considered as a complex and unstable reality, which marketers need to look at with quite an open mind. It gives birth to strange mixtures, such as the Chino-Latino cuisine, a fusion of Asian and Cuban cuisine to be found in New York, which has its roots in the Chinese immigration to Cuba in the early 1900s.[74]

Website link 4.6

Examine a Chino-Cubano restaurant menu from New York City: **http://www.menupages.com/ restaurantdetails.asp?neighbourhoodid= O&restaurantid=1722.**

When dealing with ethnic consumption, the following points must be kept in mind:

1. Translation or spelling mistakes or inadequate wordings may be resented as offending the group's honour. For instance, a burrito has been mistakenly called in Spanish a burrada, which means 'big mistake'.[9] This results in minority groups feeling neglected because their language is misused, or at least not understood, or respected.

2. In ethnic behaviour, the status of membership, that is, the claim of being 'different' is central and may be pushed to its extreme. Smaller ingroups are stronger platforms for identification. The larger Hispanic category will be further broken into Mexicans, Puerto-Ricans, Cubans, etc.

3. The level of acculturation, or the degree to which people have learned the ways of the host culture, influences ethnic consumption. Age is also

significant: older people and less acculturated people tend to display stronger ethnic attitudes.

4. Identification needs are 'reversible', creating ambiguous and even contradictory demands. Most people belonging to ethnic communities strive for both integration into the society at large and maintenance of their specific cultural roots. In some areas of consumption, such as housing and furnishing, they may express their belonging to the larger national ingroup and in another area, such as food, they may maintain strong ethnic behaviour.

4.5

Marketing as an exchange of meanings

Consumers buy meanings and marketers communicate meanings through products and advertisements. Consumer goods are vehicles of cultural meanings and consumers choose and then make use of these cultural meanings. In order to understand this, however, we have to look with other eyes.[75] For instance, Penaloza (p. 373)[76] investigated the cultural meaning of the Old West in the United States, finding different meanings for whites and non-whites:

For whites, popular depictions of adventurous explorers, miners, and ranchers accompany those of land thieves, murderers, and forced religious converters. For Native Americans, popular depictions of hostile savages stand beside romantic naturalists and spiritualists, wealthy casino owners, and movement activists fighting ongoing battles for land, mineral, and water rights.

Marketing may be seen primarily as a process of exchange where communication, broadly defined, is central. Many of the meanings in marketing exchanges are culture based: they are intersubjectively shared by a social group.[77] Intersubjective sharing of meanings signifies that each person in the group knows that everyone else knows the cognitive schema. Therefore in the process of exchange through buyer–seller relations, marketing communications or product consumption, interpretations are made spontaneously, as if they were obvious realities, and a great deal of information in the process of marketing as exchange and communication need not be made explicit. For instance, Kragh and Djursaa

(pp. 1314–15)[78] explored the meanings carried by Danish and English dining and living rooms in which participants viewed photographs from the other country:

The English respondents complain that Danish modernist rooms look old fashioned, . . . the English respondents also think the Danish rooms are boring and bare . . . Returning the compliment, the Danes complain that the English rooms are tasteless, and pinpoint the syntactical features which convey this message: they find them overdone, with too many flowers and patterns. In addition, they find the room composition odd, missing their sofa groups with coffee tables which are integral to Danish ideas of togetherness.

Culture may be considered as a sort of *meta-language* central to the marketing process when viewed as exchange and communication. It works as a type of *game rule*, implicitly indicating how people will interact in an exchange relationship, influencing their constraints and their leeway in behaviour and decisions. The attitudinal differences toward market research between the Americans and Japanese (section 6.6) are a good example of this: what is the 'right' way (that is, legitimate or appropriate) to communicate with the market? What is the market (actual buyers versus potential consumers)? In each case the objective is seemingly the same: to collect relevant information and market data, in order to decide on marketing strategies. Two examples illustrate the differences in marketing meta-communication: the role of emotions in Japanese marketing, and the emphasis on the symbolic relationship between person and object in the Italian style of marketing.

The role of emotions in Japanese marketing

There is wide range of books on Japanese marketing, which are unfortunately written only in Japanese *Kanji* and *Hiragana*, thereby limiting access for non-Japanese (*Gai-jin*) readers. But the Japanese provide details in English in the review of the largest Japanese advertising agency, *Dentsu Japan Marketing/Advertising*. Koichi Tanouchi, a professor of marketing at Hitotsubashi University, depicts the Japanese style of marketing as being fundamentally based on emotions and sensitivity. He first insists, as many authors do, that Japan is oriented towards rice production, and is not a nation of hunters and gatherers. This means more collective organization and interpersonal sensitivity: the cultivation of rice requires the simultaneous flooding of paddy fields, which cannot be decided by an isolated landowner. This involves a strong collective solidarity, serious planning and individual tenacity. Tanouchi states that 'masculine' values are less developed in Japan than 'feminine' values, which is illustrated by the example of marital relationships in household and personal spending:

In Japan, the husband is supposed to hand all his income over to his wife. If he doesn't, he is criticized by people around him. If she complains about this to his boss in his business company, the boss is very likely to take the wife's side, and advise him to give all his salary to his wife and add that that is the best way to keep peace at home and that everyone else is doing so. The wife has the right to decide how much money her husband can have for daily lunch and coffee. Regularly, about once in a half year, Japanese newspapers carry a research report about the average amount of the money the average husbands get from their wives. Wives decide about their husbands' lunch money watching these figures (p. 78).[79]

Sensitivity and emotions seem to permeate most aspects of Japanese marketing.[76] This is evidenced by the high level of sensitivity and response to actual consumer needs and by the search for social harmony between producers and distributors. It is also prominent in Japanese sales force compensation arrangements, where collective reward systems are often used. They foster cooperation, avoid threatening individual competition and promote social harmony in the sales team (section 14.4).

The role of the symbolic link between object and person through the medium of design in Italian marketing

A specific Italian marketing style has emerged that is characterized by heavy emphasis, and corresponding financial commitment, devoted to product appearance and design. The product is intended to act as a link between producers–sellers and consumers–purchasers: both appreciate the aesthetic qualities of the object. The Italians concentrate on the style and functionality of the object, and its integration into the environment. The focal point is object symbolism and its fit with the meaning attributed to it by consumers, as such increasing importance is given to qualitative studies. The Italians are not alone in having an awareness of the symbolic meaning of possessions for consumers. But they incorporate it at

---

BOX 4.1

The functional form of the cigarette lighter

The stylized fluidity of the 'functional forms' testifies to the connotation of mental dynamics, the semblance of a lost relationship, in an attempt to reconstruct a purpose through the accumulation of signs. For example, a lighter in the shape of a pebble was successfully launched by advertising some years ago. The oblong, elliptic and asymmetrical form is 'highly functional', not because it provides a better light than another lighter, but because it fits exactly into the palm of the hand. 'The seas have polished it into the shape of the hand': it is an accomplished form. Its function is not to give a light, but to be easy to handle. Its form is, so to speak, predetermined by Nature (the sea) to be handled by man. This new purpose is the sole rhetoric of the lighter. The connotations are here twofold: as an industrial object, the cigarette lighter is supposed to recall one of the qualities of the handicraft object, the shape of which furthers the gesture and the body of man. Moreover the allusion to the sea brings us to the myth of Nature, itself cultured by man, which follows all his desires: the sea plays the cultural role of a polisher; it is the sublime handicraft of nature. As the stone rolled by the sea, furthered by the hand producing light, the cigarette lighter becomes a wonderful flint, a whole prehistoric and artisanate purpose comes into play in the very practical essence of an industrial object.

(Source: Baudrillard, pp. 82–3.[80] Author's translation.)

a high level and make it an essential element of marketing strategies. Baudrillard (1968) and his 'system of objects', which was fairly successful in France, ultimately achieved real success in Italy, where he is regarded as a guru of marketing semiology (Box 4.1).

Website link 4.7

Review a lecture given by the late Jean Baudrillard at the European Graduate School about imagery: http://uk.youtube.com/view_play_list?p=FOF40A6DB3FF31E4.

4.6
Conclusion

The other side of the poster mentioned at the start of this chapter says '*Bei Mercedes bleibt alles anders*' ('With Mercedes everything remains different'). In international marketing, where similarities abound, it is wise to examine specific differences in consumer behaviour with *different* eyes. This will provide a method of enquiry which favours the discovery of significant differences in how consumers behave across cultures and offers insights into the way consumers invest meaning into their purchases.

Questions

1. What would you expect to be the relation of *consumer loyalty* with the following cultural variables? Argue why, in your opinion, consumers having a certain cultural trait would be more, or conversely less, loyal:
   (a) strong future orientation;
   (b) strong ingroup orientation;
   (c) high individualism;
   (d) high uncertainty avoidance.

2. Discuss how a strong emphasis on group belonging in a particular culture may influence buying decisions.

3. Discuss possible cross-cultural variability in the concept of 'status-seeking consumers'.

4. Why can 'word-of-mouth communication' among people be considered as a fairly robust consumer behaviour concept cross-culturally?

5. What is ethnic consumption?

References

1. Levitt, Theodore (1983), 'The Globalization of Markets', *Harvard Business Review*, 61 (May–June), 92–102.
2. Bagozzi, Richard P., Nancy Wong, Shuzo Abe, and Massimo Bergami (2000), 'Cultural and Situational Contingencies and the Theory of Reasoned Action: Application to Fast-Food and Restaurant Consumption', *Journal of Consumer Psychology*, 9 (2), 97–106.
3. Lee, Julie Anne (2000), 'Adapting Triandis's Model of Subjective Culture and Social Behaviour Relations to Consumer Behaviour', *Journal of Consumer Psychology*, 9 (2), 117–26.
4. Lee, Chol and Robert T. Green (1991), 'Cross-Cultural Examination of the Fishbein Behavioural Intentions Model', *Journal of International Business Studies*, 289–305.
5. Malhotra, Naresh K. and J. Daniel McCort (2001), 'A Cross-Cultural Comparison of Behavioral Intention Models', *International Marketing Review*, 18 (3), 235–69.

6. Luna, David and Susan Forquer Gupta (2001), 'An Integrative Framework for Cross-Cultural Consumer Behavior', *International Marketing Review*, 18 (1), 45–69.

7. Maslow, Abraham H. (1954), *Motivation and Personality*. New York: Harper and Row.

8. Belk, Russell W. (1988), 'Third World Consumer Culture', in *Research in Marketing*, E. Kumçu and A. Fuat Firat, Eds. Vol. 4. Greenwich, CT: JAI Press.

9. Solomon, Michael R. (1999), *Consumer Behavior* (4th edn). Upper Saddle River, NJ: Prentice Hall.

10. Hanson, John H. (1997), 'Power, Philanthropy, and Potlatch: What Tribal Exchange Rituals Can Tell Us About Giving', *Fund Raising Management*, 27 (12), 16–19.

11. Mendenhall, Mark, Betty Jane Punnett, and David Ricks (1995), *Global Management*. Cambridge, MA: Blackwell.

12. Bagozzi, Richard P. (2000), 'On the Concept of Intentional Social Action in Consumer Behavior', *Journal of Consumer Research*, 27, 388–96.

13. Bagozzi, Richard P. and Kyu-Hyun Lee (2002), 'Multiple Routes for Social Influence: The Role of Compliance, Internalization and Social Identity', *Social Psychology Quarterly*, 65 (3), 226–47.

14. Lee, Julie Anne and Geoffrey Soutar (2004), 'Singaporeans I- and We-Intentions to Come to Australia', in *Australian and New Zealand Marketing Academy Conference (ANZMAC) Proceedings 2004*. Wellington, New Zealand: Victoria University.

15. Na, Woonbong, Youngseok Son, and Roger Marshall (2003), 'Purchase-Role Structure in Korean Families: Revisited', *Psychology and Marketing*, 20 (1), 47–57.

16. Harcar, Talha and John E. Spillan (2006), 'Exploring Latin American Family Decision-Making Using Correspondence Analysis', *Journal of World Business*, 41 (3), 221–32.

17. Rodman, Hyman (1972), 'Marital Power and the Theory of Resources in Cultural Context', *Journal of Comparative Family Studies*, 3 (Spring), 50–69.

18. Hofstede, Geert (2001), *Culture Consequences*. Thousand Oaks, CA: Sage Publications.

19. Viswanathan, Madhubalan, Terry L. Childers, and Elizabeth S. Moore (2000), 'The Measurement of Intergenerational Communication and Influence on Consumption: Development, Validation, and Cross-Cultural Comparison of the Igen Scale', *Journal of the Academy of Marketing Science*, 28 (3), 406–24.

20. Rose, Gregory M. (1999), 'Consumer Socialization, Parental Style, and Developement Timetables in the United States and Japan', *Journal of Marketing*, 63 (July), 105–19.

21. Ikels, C. (1983), *Aging and Adaption: Chinese in Hong Kong and the United States*. North Haven, CT: Archon Books.

22. Richins, Marsha (1994), 'Valuing Things: The Public and Private Meaning of Possessions', *Journal of Consumer Research*, 21 (3, December), 504–21.

23. Markus, Hazel Rose and Shinobu Kitayama (1991), 'Culture and the Self: Implications for Cognition, Emotion and Motivation', *Psychological Review*, 98 (2), 224–53.

24. Wong, Nancy and Aaron Ahuvia (1995), 'From Tofu to Caviar: Conspicuous Consumption, Materialism and Self-Concepts in East-Asian and Western Cultures', in *Proceedings of the Second Conference on the Cultural Dimension of International Marketing*. Odense, 68–89.

25. Fu, Jeanne Ho-Ying, Chi-Yue Chiu, Michael W. Morris, and Maia J. Young (2007), 'Spontaneous Inferences from Cultural Cues: Varying Responses of Cultural Insiders and Outsiders', *Journal of Cross-Cultural Psychology*, 38 (1), 58–75.

26. Triandis, Harry (1994), *Culture and Social Behavior*. New York: McGraw Hill.

27. Lee, Julie Anne and Jacqueline J. Kacen (1999), 'The Relationship between Independent and Interdependent Self-Concepts and Reasons for Purchase', *Journal of Euro-Marketing*, 8 (1/2), 83–99.

28. Kacen, Jacqueline J. and Julie Anne Lee (2002), 'The Influence of Culture on Consumer Impulsive Buying Behavior', *Journal of Consumer Psychology*, 12 (2), 163–76.

29. Aaker, Jennifer L. and Bernd Schmitt (2001), 'Culture-Dependent Assimilation and Differentiation of the Self: Preference for Consumption Symbols in the United States and China', *Journal of Cross-Cultural Psychology*, 32, 561–76.

30. Aaker, Jennifer L. (2000), 'Accessibility or Diagnosticity? Disentangling the Influence of Culture on Persuasion Processes and Attitudes', *Journal of Consumer Research*, 26 (4), 340–57.

31. Aaker, Jennifer L. and Patti Williams (1998), 'Empathy Versus Pride: The Influence of Emotional Appeals across Cultures', *Journal of Consumer Research*, 25 (3), 241–61.

32. Wilk, Richard (1995), 'Real Belizean Food: Building Local Identity in the Transnational Caribbean', in *Proceedings of the Second Conference on the Cultural Dimension of International Marketing*. Odense, 372–91.

33. Brunsø, K., K.G. Grunert, and K. Kristensen (1996), *The Aarhus School of Business, An Analysis of National and Cross-National Consumer Segments Using the Food-Related Lifestyle Instrument in Denmark, France, Germany, and Great Britain*, MAPP Working paper No. 35, Aarhus.

34. Askegaard, Søren and Karen Brunsø (1999), 'Food-Related Lifestyles in Singapore: Preliminary Testing of a Western Research Instrument in Southeast Asia', *Journal of Euromarketing*, 7 (4), 65–86.

35. Sin, Leo Y.M., Gordon W.H. Cheung, and Ruby Lee (1999), 'Methodology in Cross-Cultural Consumer Research: A Review and Critical Assessment', *Journal of International Consumer Marketing*, 11 (4), 75–96.

36. Herrmann, Andreas and Mark Heitmann (2006), 'Providing More or Less? Accounting for Cultural Differences in Consumers' Preference for Variety', *International Marketing Review*, 23 (1), 7–24.

37. Zhang, Jingyun, Sharon E. Beatty, and Gianfranco Walsh (2008), 'Review and Future Directions of Cross-Cultural Consumer Services Research', *Journal of Business Research*, 61 (3), 211–24.

38. Engel, James F., Roger D. Blackwell, and Paul W. Miniard (1993), *Consumer Behavior* (7th edn). Fort Worth, TX: The Dryden Press.

39. Yang, Chung-Fang (1989), 'Une Conception Du Comportement Du Consommateur Chinois', *Recherche et Applications en Marketing*, IV (1), 17–36.

40. Lazer, William, Shoji Murata, and Hiroshi Kosaka (1985), 'Japanese Marketing: Towards a Better Understanding', *Journal of Marketing*, 49 (Spring), 69–81.

41. Liefeld, John P., Marjorie Wall, and Louise A. Heslop (1999), 'Cross Cultural Comparison of Consumer Information Processing Styles', *Journal of Euro-Marketing*, 8 (1/2), 29–43.

42. Yau, Oliver H.M. (1988), 'Chinese Cultural Values: Their Dimensions and Marketing Implications', *European Journal of Marketing*, 22 (5), 44–57.

43. Quintal, Vanessa Anne (2007), 'An Investigation into the Effects of Risk and Uncertainty on Consumers' Decision-Making Processes: A Cross-National Study', University of Western Australia.

44. Stone, Robert N. and Kjell Grønhaug (1993), 'Perceived Risk: Further Considerations for the Marketing Discipline', *European Journal of Marketing*, 27 (3), 372–94.

45. Mitchell, V. (1998), 'A Role for Consumer Risk Perceptions in Grocery Retailing', *British Food Journal*, 100 (4), 171–83.

46. Weber, E., C. Hsee, and J. Sokolowska (1998), 'What Folklore Tells Us About Risk and Risk Taking: Cross Cultural Comparisons of American, German and Chinese Proverbs', *Organizational Behavior and Human Decision Processes*, 75 (2), 170–86.

47. Weber, Elke U. and Christopher K. Hsee (2000), 'Culture and Individual Judgment and Decision Making', *Applied Psychology: An International Review*, 49 (1), 32–41.

48. Drolet, A. (2002), 'Inherent Rule Variability in Consumer Choice: Changing Rules for Change's Sake', *Journal of Consumer Research*, 29 (3), 293–305.

49. Robinson, Chris (1996), 'Asian Cultures: The Marketing Consequences', *Journal of the Market Research Society*, 38 (1), 55–62.

50. Chiou, Jyh-Shen (1995) 'The Process of Social Influences on New Product Adoption and Retention in Individualistic Versus Collectivist Cultural Contexts', in *Proceedings of the Second Conference on the Cultural Dimension of International Marketing*. Odense, 107–27.

51. Kim, Jai-Ok, Sandra Forsythe, Quingliang Gu, and Sook Jae Moon (2002), 'Cross-Cultural Consumer Behavior, Needs and Purchase Behavior', *Journal of Consumer Marketing*, 19 (6), 481–502.

52. Colgate, Mark, Vicky Thuy-Uyen Tong, Christina Kwai-Choi Lee, and John U. Farley (2007), 'Back from the Brink: Why Customers Stay', *Journal of Service Research*, 9 (3), 211–28.

53. Straughan, Robert D. and Nancy D. Albers-Miller (2001), 'An International Investigation of Cultural and Demographic Effects on Domestic Retail Loyalty', *International Marketing Review*, 18 (5), 521–41.

54. Jung, Jaehee and Eun-Young Sung (2008), 'Consumer-Based Brand Equity: Comparisons among Americans and South Koreans in the USA and South Koreans in Korea', *Journal of Fashion Marketing and Management*, 12 (1), 24.

55. Kluckhohn, Florence R. and Frederick L. Strodtbeck (1961), *Variations in Value Orientations*. Westport, CT: Greenwood Press.

56. Reynolds, Nina L. and Antonis Simintiras (2000), *Establishing Cross-National Equivalence of the Customer Satisfaction Construct*, EBMS Working Paper, 2000/7.

57. Pons, Frank and Michel Laroche (2007), 'Cross-Cultural Differences in Crowd Assessment', *Journal of Business Research*, 60 (3), 269–76.

58. Blodgett, Jeffrey, Donna Hill, and Aysen Bakir (2006), 'Cross-Cultural Complaining Behavior? An Alternative Explanation', *Journal of Consumer Satisfaction, Dissatisfaction and Complaining Behavior*, 19, 103–17.

59. Liu, Raymond R. and Peter McClure (2001), 'Recognizing Cross-Cultural Differences in Consumer Complaint Behavior and Intentions: An Empirical Examination', *The Journal of Consumer Marketing*, 18 (1), 54–75.

60. Richins, Marsha and Bronislaw J. Verhage (1985), 'Cross-Cultural Differences in Consumer Attitudes and Their Implications for Complaint Management', *International Journal of Research in Marketing*, 2, 197–205.

61. Richins, Marsha (1983), 'Negative Word-of-Mouth by Dissatisfied Consumers: A Pilot Study', *Journal of Marketing*, 47 (Winter), 68–78.

62. Cavusgil, Tamer S. and Erdener Kaynak (1984), 'Critical Issues in the Cross-Cultural Measurement of Consumer Dissatisfaction: Developed Versus Ldc Practices', in *Comparative Marketing Systems*, Erdener Kaynak and Ronald Savitt, Eds. New York: Praeger.

63. Joy, Annamma (2001), 'Gift Giving in Hong Kong and the Continuum of Social Ties', *Journal of Consumer Research*, 28, 239–56.

64. Park, Seong-Yeon (1998) 'A Comparison of Korean and American Gift-Giving Behaviors', *Psychology and Marketing*, 15 (6), 577–93.

65. Berry, J.W., Uichol Kim, Thomas Minde, and Doris Mok (1987), 'Comparative Study of Acculturation Stress', *International Migration Review*, 21, 491–511.

66. Gans, Herbert (1962), *The Urban Villagers*. New York: The Free Press.

67. Bouchet, Dominique (1995), 'Marketing and the Redefinition of Ethnicity', in *Marketing in a Multicultural World*, Janeen Arnold. Costa and Gary J. Bamossy, Eds. Thousand Oaks, CA: Sage.

68. Ger, Güliz and Per Østergaard (1998), 'Constructing Immigrant Identities in Consumption: Appearance among the Turko-Danes', *Advances in Consumer Research*, 25, 48–52.

69. Caetano, Raul, Catherine L. Clark, and Tammy Tam (1998), 'Alcohol Consumption among Racial/Ethnic Minorities: Theory and Research', *Alcohol Health and Research World*, 22 (4), 233–42.

70. Lee, Eun-Ju, Ann Fairhurst, and Susan Diallard (2002), 'Usefulness of Ethnicity in International Consumer Marketing', *Journal of International Consumer Marketing*, 14 (4), 25–48.

71. Yankelovitch, Skelly and White (1982), 'Spanish USA: A Study of the Hispanic Market in the U.S.', for Spanish Television Networks.

72. Wallendorf, Melanie and Michael D. Reilly (1983), 'Ethnic Migration, Assimilation and Consumption', *Journal of Consumer Research*, 10 (December), 292–302.

73. Oswald, Laura R. (1999), 'Culture Swapping: Consumption and the Ethnogenesis of Middle-Class Haitian Immigrants', *Journal of Consumer Research*, 25 (March), 303–18.

74. Straus, Karen (1992), 'Go Hog Wild with Chino-Latino Pork Dishes', *Restaurants and Institutions*, 102 (19), 43–57.

75. McCracken, Grant (1991), 'Culture and Consumer Behaviour: An Anthropological Perspective', *Journal of the Market Research Society*, 32 (1), 3–11.

76. Penaloza, Lisa (2001), 'Consuming the American West: Animating Cultural Meaning and Memory at a Stock Show and Rodeo', *Journal of Consumer Research*, 28 (3), 369–98.

77. D'Andrade, Roy G. (1987), 'A Folk Model of the Mind', in *Cultural Models in Language and Thought*, Dorothy Quinn and Naomi Holland, Eds. Cambridge: Cambridge University Press.

78. Kragh, Simon Ulrik and Malene Djursaa (2001), 'Product Syntax and Cross-Cultural Marketing Strategies', *European Journal of Marketing*, 35 (11/12), 1301–19.

79. Tanouchi, Koichi (1983), 'Japanese-Style Marketing Based on Sensitivity', *Dentsu Japan Marketing/Advertising*, 23 (July), 77–81.

80. Baudrillard, Jean (1968) *Le Système Des Objets*. Paris: Gallimard.

Appendix 4

Teaching materials

A4.1 Exercise

'Dichter's consumption motives'

Question

Discuss the cross-cultural variability of the major motives for consumption as identified by Ernest Dichter some 30 years ago. Choose five associations between motives and associated products for your discussion.

Motive	Associated products
Power, masculinity, virility	Power: sugary products and large breakfasts, bowling, electric trains, pistols, power tools.
	Masculinity, virility: coffee, red meat, heavy shoes, toy guns; buying fur coats for women, shaving with a razor.
Security	Ice-cream, full drawer of neatly ironed shirts, real plaster walls, home baking, hospital care.
Eroticism	Sweets, gloves, a man lighting a woman's cigarette.
Moral purity, cleanliness	White bread, cotton fabric, harsh household cleaning chemicals, bathing, oatmeal.
Social acceptance	Companionship: ice-cream (fun to share), coffee.
	Love and affection: toys, sugar and honey.
	Acceptance: soap, beauty products.
Individuality	Gourmet foods, foreign cars, cigarette holders, vodka, perfume, fountain pens.
Status	Scotch [whisky], ulcers, heart attacks, indigestion, carpets.
Femininity	Cakes and cookies, dolls, silk, tea, household curios.
Reward	Cigarettes, candy, alcohol, ice-cream, cookies.
Mastery over environment	Kitchen appliances, boats, sporting goods, cigarette lighters.
Disalienation (a desire to feel connectedness to things)	Home decorating, skiing, morning radio broadcasts.
Magic, mystery	Soups (have healing powers), paints (change the mood of a room), carbonated drinks (magical effervescent property), vodka (romantic history), unwrapping of gifts.

(Source: Solomon, p. 168.[1] Solomon, Michael R., *Consumer Behavior: Buying, Having and Being*, 4th edn, © 1999, reproduced by permission of Pearson Education, Inc., Upper Saddle River, NJ.)

A4.2 Exercise

Investigating the cross-cultural applicability of a consumer complaint scale

A scale of consumer complaint behaviour (CCB) developed by Singh[2] is portrayed below. US respondents were asked to express their degree of agreement or disagreement on a six-point Likert scale on the items listed below (possible behavioural responses to dissatisfaction with a consumption experience). Factor analysis allowed three dimensions to be distinguished for CCB.

1. Voice CCB
   (a) Forget about the incident and do nothing.
   (b) Definitely complain to the store manager on your next trip.
   (c) Go back or call the repair shop immediately and ask them to take care of your problem.

2. Private CCB
   (a) Decide not to use that repair shop again.
   (b) Speak to your friends and relatives about your bad experience.
   (c) Convince your friends and relatives not to use that repair shop.

3. Third party CCB
   (a) Complain to a consumer agency and ask them to make the repair shop take care of your problem.
   (b) Write a letter to the local newspaper about your bad experience.
   (c) Report to the consumer agency so that they can warn other consumers.
   (d) Take some legal action against the repair shop/manufacturer.

Question

Investigate the cross-cultural applicability of such a scale. Since you cannot do this with a full psychometric design, conduct your investigation mostly into the meaning, situations, institutions and behaviours depicted by the items.

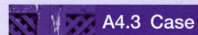

A4.3 Case

Mobile phones in the European Union

In 2002, Jean-Michel Hubert, director of the French Telecoms Regulation Authority stated that the European mobile telecommunications were considered to be in a crisis. The main reason seemed to be a relatively saturated market and low average revenue per user (ARPU), at 29 euros in Europe versus 50 euros in the USA.[3] According to the Western European Mobile Forecasts and Analysis 2003–2008 report, the number of active subscribers was forecast to grow just 5 per cent per year to 309 million.[4] However, there were 553 million mobile subscribers in the European Union (EU) in October 2007,[5] an increase far beyond EU enlargement. Providing services at lower cost has become a challenge. Cuts in tariffs have stimulated growth, but ARPU has consequently stagnated or decreased. Across Africa, the average revenue per user is $17.50 per month. In India, that figure drops to $10 a month. In western Europe and the United States, the comparable number is nowadays close to $40.[3]

Mobile sector growth in the European Union is exponential. Average penetration is 112 per cent in October 2007 (see Table 4.3 for country data), while it is 30 per cent in China and only 10 per cent in India, which are nevertheless expected to be the world's largest mobile markets by 2010.[6] In China, growth is exponential but penetration is still relatively low, partly due to the size of the population. Penetration is dependent on age, being mainly driven by youths aged 13–18, for which penetration rate often reaches 90 per cent. In terms of new sub-scribers, the European market is near saturation. For an understanding of this phenomenon, one must look first at the issue of adoption and diffusion of new technology, and second at cultural differences among European countries. There are different competitive environments in each European country, with generally three to five mobile operators and a grand total of 100 country operators for Europe as a whole (among them many national subsidiaries of Europe-wide mobile operators such as Orange or Vodafone). Price is an issue for mobile communication since it may be a relatively significant part of a person's budget, especially for young adults who do not yet earn their own living (see differences in price-mindedness across cultures in section 10.3). Depending on country, prepaid mobile communication accounts for between 40 per cent and 90 per cent (Italy and Malta) with an average 50 per cent for pre-paid and 50 per cent for monthly paid. Design and aesthetic also matter for mobile handsets (see cross-cultural differences in aesthetics and perception of design in section 8.4). Applications, mobile phones features, and content are important attributes for mobile phones users. Novelty orientation, innovative behaviour, and variety seeking also matter for mobile phones since resistance to change may vary across cultures. Users also differ in terms of their sensitivity to disturbance caused to others when using a mobile phone in social settings.

Table 4.3 Mobile phone penetration in Europe (2007)

Penetration	≥ 130%	110–130%	100–110%	80–100%
Western Europe	Italy Luxemburg	Denmark Germany Ireland Portugal Spain	Finland Greece UK Sweden	Belgium France Malta
Eastern Europe	Estonia Latvia Lithuania	Bulgaria Cyprus Czech Republic	Hungary Slovakia	Poland Romania Slovenia

(Source: CEC.[5] Adapted table, based on figures excerpted from the European Commission's 'Progress Report on the Single European Electronic Communications Market 2007' (13th Report), COMN(2008) 153 final/[SEC(2008) 356].)

Adoption of mobile phones

There is a popular theory behind the adoption of high tech consumer equipment such as mobile phones, that is, the TAM (Technology Acceptance Model), with a considerable body of scientific literature in Marketing and Information Technology as well as Management Information Systems.[7,8] The key variables behind the user adoption of new IT technology are 'perceived usefulness' and 'perceived ease-of-use'. The more usefulness consumers perceive in the technological device and the less difficulty of use they perceive, the quicker they will adopt the new technology. A number of arguments can be made on different perceptions of mobile phones according to age, in terms of both 'perceived usefulness' and 'perceived ease-of-use'. Perceptions of usefulness may increase (or not) with new features being added to sucessive generations of mobile phones. For instance, one may wonder to what extent all features of 3G handsets are (or will be) really perceived as 'useful' (especially when their price is considered).

Other key variables in the TAM model are perceived behavioural control, perceived risk, and demographics (age, gender). Perceived risk for mobile phones may relate, for instance, to electromagnetic waves near the ear potentially causing brain tumours, a sensitive topic that still has not been medically proven. Perceived behavioural control is linked to the circumstances of mobile phone use (e.g. car, restaurant, classroom, theatre, etc.) and involves safety issues and social concerns in situations where mobile phones can be perceived as making their users out of control of rather than in control of the device. Mobile operators can act in terms of increasing or emphasizing factors that are favourable to the adoption of mobile phones and decreasing those which are unfavourable. They may also segment markets according to demographics (especially age, gender) or according to business vs. non-business use, this being relevant in terms of both adoption and use. Moreover, some segments are likely to be rather transnational (e.g. young users) and relatively culture-free.

The cultural roots of the European mobile phone predicament

Zbigniew Smoreda, sociologist at *France Telecom* and researcher on the Eurescom P903 study that examined mobile habits in nine countries, explains that overall, in countries like Denmark, Germany, and the UK, the primary reason for obtaining a mobile subscription was to keep one's life organized. For the French, the primary reason was to be available at all times. However, the most striking differences were found between urban and rural settings. The city user, whether in Copenhagen or Rome, is likely to use the phone often – perhaps partly due to the complications of city life, and partly due to age (they tend to be younger).[9] From an aesthetic perspective, Samsung handset designers speak of 'global localization' and the balance of 'reason and feeling' attributes that govern the design, then subsequently the marketing process (see Table 4.4).[10]

Table 4.4 Samsung's 'reason and feeling' attributes for mobile phone design

Region	Attribute: 'reason'	Attribute: 'feeling'
Asia	High tech	Cuteness
Europe	Minimal	Emotion
North America	Durable	Dynamic

(Source: Delaney *et al.*[10])

According to the Eurescom P903 study,[11] Italians were the fastest adopters of the mobile telephone, quickly overtaking the Nordic countries where the standard was first launched. Italian youths take the credit for this; age being the 'most important factor for predicting the adoption of the mobile phone'. It is not a cliché to say that Italians are talkative, according to Alessandra Bianchini, communications head at Italian mobile operator *Wind*, it is one of the reasons that mobile phones are ubiquitous in Italy. She goes on to say that another cliché about Italians – love of family – is another reason: the mobile phone is ideal for keeping in touch with relatives and friends. In fact, mobile technology was promoted more as a tool of communication rather than business from the outset in Italy. It is not a rare sight to see young Italians chatting on their phones, perched on the back of a scooter in the midst of city traffic – phones are used everywhere. In 2002, there were 50 million mobile numbers in Italy owned by 86 per cent of the population, and one-quarter of these had multiple subscriptions. The Netherlands, where 76.6 per cent of the population are mobile users, presents a contrast to the Italian attitudes towards mobile use. In accordance with clichés about the Dutch, their use of the technology is economical: they are one of the least talkative on their mobile phones in Europe, partly due to concern over phone rates. According to Marc Gommers of mobile operator *Dutchtone*, another reason for this is the precision of the Dutch language that allows them to express themselves rapidly. There are also social norms that frown upon over-use of the phone in public; in restaurants they are banned, as they are in Denmark.[9] In France, the lack of such social norms triggered increasing frustration about the inconsiderate use of mobile phones, inciting the government to legalize mobile phone jamming in public places – a measure agreed upon by 85 per cent of the population.[12]

According to a Gartner G2 report, 41 per cent of European adults use SMS, even more than those who use e-mail (30 per cent). That figure rises in Germany, where 43 per cent of adults prefer SMS to using e-mail (29 per cent).[13] Britons send more SMS than other Europeans (31 versus 26 per month on average). Europeans overall use SMS much more than Americans. Schuyler Brown of Euro RSCG Worldwide's STAR. (Strategic Trendspotting and Research) team believes that commuting and PC use determine SMS use. European teenagers tend to use public transport, an ideal situation for chatting via SMS, whereas American teens tend to drive to school and work. Likewise, the European teen spends more time in public spaces, where time can be spent sending and receiving SMSs, compared with the American teen who is more likely to stay at home, which is likely to be equipped with a PC, wide-screen TV, and game console, competitors for time and attention deviated to SMS in Europe.[14]

However, more theory is needed for looking at in-depth cultural differences, starting at the surface before digging deeper. Meaningful cultural differences in terms of mobile phone use can be discovered by looking at consumer behaviour *in context*. Such cultural differences are related inter alia to communication patterns, individualism–collectivism, language, time orientations (monochronism/polychronism),[15] and orientation to others. Key motivations for the use of a mobile phone are its freedom dimension, its significance in making communication with others easier, the pleasure of talking (i.e. oral culture favouring speaking over writing), and the need (or conversely, the fear) of being reachable always and everywhere, that is, a permanent social connection, at least with important others who know the mobile phone number. Mobile phones also involve the possibility of disturbing others (see proxemics, section 2.3, p. 26) and the sensitivity to perceived risk for one's health (see social representations, section 1.5).

Mobile phones involve daily routines in reference to chronological time (Newtonian time). They save time (economic time) and enable immediate voice communication in order to relate to others (unorganized time). Using mobile phones enables individuals to manage activities instantaneously, much like in a polychronic use of time. Differences in time orientation between France and Germany, and their influence on use of mobile phones have been shown to be significant.[16] An initial qualitative survey was set up in order to determine the main components of mobile communication behaviour through a focus group of 20 French mobile phone users. Three main dimensions appeared to be relevant for users: freedom, contact with others, and instantaneous behaviour. Interestingly, these dimensions are located on different levels. Freedom is a means–end interpretation of a value, contact with other people a social benefit, and instantaneous behaviour a functional benefit.

In France, two time-style dimensions, economic time and tenacity, had a significant influence on the general mobile communication attitude. The link between economicity and mobile communication attitude suggested that the French associate the use of a mobile phone with the capacity to organize their own lives and to save time. The French have been described as intellectually monochronic but behaviourally polychronic. Monochronism is more associated with tenacity than polychronism, explaining why tenacity in the French time-style is negatively associated with the overall mobile communication attitude. In Germany, preference for quick return and non-organized time were found to have a significant influence on the overall mobile communication attitude. The positive link between preference for quick return and mobile communication attitude suggested that Germans associate the use of a mobile phone with instantaneous behaviour. The positive relationship between non-organized time and mobile communication indicate that mobile communication is also associated with flexible time and instantaneous behaviour. Paradoxically, the Germans, traditionally described as being monochronic and valuing organized time, positively associate mobile communication with free and spontaneous behaviour. These findings indicate that consumers are not sensitive to the same product benefits, depending on country and time-style. French consumers mostly value the economicity aspect of using a mobile phone (saving time). The Germans put more value on mobile communication to get immediate gratification and to create space in their lives for unorganized time (increasing their freedom).

Third-generation (3G) applications

Mobile phone subscribers are expected to grow from 2 billion worldwide in 2005 to approximately 3.3 billion in 2010, representing annual growth of more than 10 per cent. The forecast share of 3G subscribers should be more than 10 per cent in 2007, reaching 296 million.[17] In the European Union, the average 3G penetration was 20 per cent in 2007. Regarding mobile applications in addition to voice and text messaging, there is interest in Europe in third-generation (3G or UMTS) capability for specific applications, such as information (including maps and directions, news, and financial), m-banking, and m-trading. Most of the year-on-year growth in phone sales is attributed to these 'smart phones'.

However, overall interest is tepid. A Taylor Nelson Sofres study of 7000 subscribers in 10 European countries found that Poland and Turkey were the most likely countries to adopt 3G, while 58 per cent 'other' Europeans, and 66 per cent Britons were 'not interested' in 3G phones. Britain, one of the most mature mobile markets in world, is mainly happy with 2G phones, and is not interested in going beyond pre-pay. A 2007 survey of British mobile phone users shows that 27 per cent sent a photo in the last 12 months, but only 15 per cent listened to an mp3, 12 per cent accessed the Internet, and 10 per cent downloaded ringtones. The use of other mobile applications is quite limited with only 9 per cent sending a video clip, 6 per cent downloading music, 6 per cent paying for information, and a tiny 1 per cent watching TV.[18] The implication may be that Europeans are likely to keep their trusty old handsets, and only a minority will be interested in purchasing 3G phones.

In order to develop the 3G market, operators are seeking to increase non-voice revenue. Most of this revenue now comes from person-to-person messaging, and increasingly includes downloadable music and games.[19] Web logging (known as blogging) is now offered for mobile phone users whereby a personal webpage (known as a Foneblog by its Irish creator, www.newbay.com), complete with photos and even short videos, is created and may be viewed by other mobile phone users via WAP or a standard web browser. Many games are already available, like Sweden's Botfighters game that combines SMS and Global Positioning Systems (GPS), informing players via SMS that they are approaching another player. The first to respond to the message receives extra 'life' game points. More simple games based on sports, driving, puzzle, and arcade formats are affordable and easy to procure. A realistic example of a phone game is the Finnish football team Helsinki PK-35 pay-per-shot game whereby their approximately 3000 fans may send text suggestions from their mobile phones for game strategy, including defence and substitutions.[20] If only mobile phone users could send text suggestions regarding strategy to their mobile operators, they could help these companies at a crossroads to navigate an uncertain future.

Questions

1. How can mobile operators, software designers, and handset producers inspire Europeans to use their mobile phones for longer times and for more applications?

2. Based on the cultural differences highlighted in the case, explain how consumer behaviour for mobile phones may differ between one northern and one southern European country (your choice). Outline marketing strategies for second-generation mobile communication targeted to northern and southern European countries, that would take these differences into account.

3. What would you advise as a pan-European 3G marketing strategy for a mobile operator?

(Source: Saskia Faulk and Jean-Claude Usunier wrote this case to provide material for class discussion. The authors do not intend to illustrate either effective or ineffective handling of a business situation. The authors may have disguised certain names and other identifying information to protect confidentiality.)

© IRM/HEC, 2008   Version: (A) 2008-04-10

 A4.4 Exercise

Cross-cultural consumer behaviour and the standardization/adaptation of service offers

Based on a discussion of variations in consumer behaviour across countries, review arguments in favour of standardizing or adapting service operations in one or several of the following service industries:

- private banking;
- telecommunications;
- hairdresser;
- motor insurance;
- life insurance;
- hotels;
- haute cuisine restaurants;
- satellite launch.

You may distinguish different subsets of the service industry or different market segments within this service industry; consider two aspects in each industry:

1. whether the service and its characteristics are more or less standard worldwide;
2. whether consumer behaviour and especially the service encounter differs across domestic markets;

You may take into account the following issues in your discussion of the cross-cultural variability of service encounters and consumer behaviour:

■ Does language have an influence on the service encounter?
■ Does religion have an influence on attitudes towards the service and on the service encounter itself?
■ Do time attitudes (waiting, long-term orientation, fatalism, linear vs. cyclical views of time, etc.) have an influence on the service encounter (pre-process, in-process, post-process)?
■ Are there standards for this service industry? What is their reach?
■ How does culture influence both the service customer and the service provider?

You may Google to get some additional insights on the issues above.

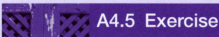

A4.5 Exercise

Multidomestic versus global

For the following industries or products discuss to what extent:

1. a world **consumer** exists (in terms of tastes and preferences, consumption habits, social taboos, local regulations influencing consumer behaviour, differences related to language, consumer learning, etc.)
2. the **products or services** offered are themselves global (similar world-wide): you may distinguish major product types within the generic product (e.g. high-fermentation versus low-fermentation beer); and
3. the **industry** itself can be considered as global (players tend to be global ones and competition takes place on a global rather than multi-local basis).
   ■ Airlines
   ■ Beer
   ■ Pharmaceuticals (ethical/prescription drugs)
   ■ Pharmaceuticals (non-prescription/over-the-counter drugs)
   ■ Tobacco (cigarettes, cigars, other tobacco-based products)
   ■ Meat-based foods
   ■ Automatic blood analysers
   ■ Mail services (delivery of letters and parcels)
   ■ Sheets and pillows
   ■ Ski lifts
   ■ Portable computers
   ■ Writing instruments (you may distinguish between pencils, ball-point pens and fountain pens)
   ■ Micro-chips
   ■ Toilet tissues
   ■ Washing machines (for cloth)
   ■ Auditing services.

This exercise can be used in relation to Chapters 5 and 7 (where the concepts of multi-domestic and global markets are explained).

Appendix references

1. Solomon, Michael R. (1999), *Consumer Behavior* (4th edn). Upper Saddle River, NJ: Prentice Hall.
2. Singh, Jagdip (1988), 'Consumer Complaint Intentions and Behavior: Definitions and Taxonomical Issues', *Journal of Marketing*, 52 (January), 93–107.
3. Anon (2002), 'La Téléphonie Européenne pour un Recentrage sur le Client', *Freesurf Actualité Hi Tech*, 21 November.
4. Anon (2003), 'News', *Analysis News*, 26 March, http://www.analysys.com/default.asp?Mode=article&iLeftArticle=1192.
5. Commission of the European Communities (CEC) (2007), *Progess Report on the Single European Electronic Communications Market 2007*. http://ec.europa.eu/information_society/policy/ecomm/doc/library/annualreports/13th/SEC(2008)356DTSVol2final.pdf.
6. Burns, Simon (2007), 'China and India Poised for Stellar Mobile Growth', *Informatics*, 6 February, http://www.infomaticsonline.co.uk/vnunet/news/2174261/china-india-half-billion-mobile.
7. Davis, Fred D., Richard P. Bagozzi, and Paul R. Warshaw (1989), 'User Acceptance of Computer Technology: A Comparison of Two Theoretical Models', *Management Science*, 35 (8), 982–1003.
8. Venkatesh, Viswanath, Michael G. Morris, Gordon B. Davis, and Fred D. Davis (2003), 'User Acceptance of Information Technology: Toward a Unified View', *MIS Quarterly*, 27 (3), 425–78.
9. Anon (2002), 'Européen et Mobile', *ORANGE Magazine* (Spring), 9–13.
10. Delaney, Mark, Jeff McFarland, Gee Hong Yoon, and Tom Hardy (2002), 'Global Design and Cultural Identity', *Innovation* (Summer), 46–9.
11. Eurescom (2001), 'ICT Uses in Everyday Life'. http://www.eurescom.de/~ftproot/web-deliverables/public/P900-series/P903/p903_newsletter_may.pdf.
12. Ó hAnluain, Daithí (2002), 'They Be Jammin' in France', *Wired News*, 23 March, http://www.wired.com/news/culture/0,1284,51273,00.html.
13. Gartner Group (2002), 'SMS Bigger than Email in Europe', 5 November. http://www.qlinks.net/quicklinks/stats12.htm.
14. Nahmany, Peggy (2003), 'Y Rn't We N2 Sms?', *PR Newswire*, 12 February.
15. Usunier, Jean-Claude and Pierre Valette-Florence (2007), 'The Time-Styles Scale: A Review of Developments and Replications over 15 Years', *Time and Society*, 16 (2/3), 349–82.
16. Valette-Florence, Pierre, Jean-Claude Usunier, and Jean-Marc Ferrandi (2001), 'Le Temps des Consommateurs: Le Cas du Téléphone Portable', *Revue Française de Gestion*, January/February (132), 112–18.
17. Dmeurope (2008), '3.3bn Global Mobile Phone Subscribers by 2010 – report', 16 April. http://www.dmeurope.com/default.asp?ArticleID=15236.
18. Anon (2007), 'Mobile Users Turned-Off by Advanced Features', *Cellular News*, 20 August, http://www.cellular-news.com/story/25516.php.
19. Phillips, Leigh (2003), 'Messaging and Entertainment Services to Boost Mobile Operator Revenue and Arpu, Report', *Europemedia.net*, 27 March, http://www.analysys.com/default_acl.asp?Mode=article&iLeftArticle=5&m=&n=.
20. Laughlin, Kirk (2002), 'Revenue at Risk: Why are ARPU's Falling in North America, but Rising in Parts of Europe?', *America's Network*, 1 March.

5

Local consumers and the globalization of consumption

Consumption habits and personal preferences across nations will always diverge. In Germany, most homes have no cupboards, because it is thought only poorer people have cupboards and not wardrobes. This way of thinking extends to Alsace, but stops in France and the Latin countries, where the convenience of both cupboards and wardrobes is recognized, and there is no implied socio-economic or class-related meaning. Nevertheless, IKEA is a highly successful global marketer despite retaining a strong Swedish brand image with its furniture names to its waitresses who serve *glögg* in traditional Swedish costume.[1]

While companies become increasingly global, consumers are still largely local. This chapter acknowledges that consumption styles converge only at a macroscopic level. Consumption patterns resemble Russian dolls, building up from home to city, from community to region, and from nation to globe.[2] It has become more important than ever to look closely at the unique elements of meaning local consumers invest in their products, services, and consumption experiences.

There are three crucial aspects promoting the globalization process. The first aspect is demand, with the convergence of consumer behaviour and marketing environments at the macro level. The second aspect is supply and competition, with the shift away from domestic industries operating in national markets, which are protected by non-tariff barriers. Many of these changes were initiated through the successive rounds of the General Agreement on Tariffs and Trade (GATT) and implemented by the World Trade Organization (WTO) and by regional trade organizations such as the European Union (EU) or the North American Free Trade Agreement (NAFTA). The third aspect is cost reduction through the globalization of products and marketing offerings. Companies react to globalization partly by shaping new strategies and partly by refining their organizational design. They do this under cost constraints, given the potential for the experience effect of available technologies and the impact of transportation costs.

The first half of this chapter explores the justifications for globalization. In section 5.1 we discuss how traditional models of international trade have been strong drivers for globalization. These models ignore local consumers' tastes for local design and manufacture, and focus on utilitarian needs for generic products. These traditional models have been used as to justify worldwide similarity. In section 5.2 the global convergence of consumption patterns is discussed. Convergence happens at the macro level for generic product categories, but it is less evident at a micro level when we examine specific products and consumer behaviours. In section 5.3 the emergence of a global consumer culture is examined, based on 'modern cultural' values that may lead to a world standard package.

The second half of this chapter explores the justifications for localization. Section 5.4 examines how products are culture bound, and how goods and services and consumption experiences are infused with uniquely local meanings. Section 5.5 examines consumer resistance to global products and consumption patterns which may threaten local interests. Finally, section 5.6 explores the kaleidoscopic patterns of local consumption in a globalizing world, that is, how consumers mix globalized products and local items in a grand *bricolage*.

5.1

Free trade doctrine and the denial of cultural variety in consumers' tastes

Ricardo's hypothesis

Traditional international trade doctrine laid the foundations for the denial of culture in international marketing. One of the seminal manuscripts on international trade is the seventh chapter of David Ricardo's *On the Principles of Political Economy and Taxation* (1817),[3] which explains why countries and traders may benefit from developing international trade.

> ### Website link 5.1
>
> See a summary of a United States Democratic Party committee hearing considering the Bush administration's claim that outsourcing is good for the US economy: **http://democrats.senate.govl**.

Ricardo considers the case of two countries, England and Portugal, and two types of goods, wine and sheets. He posits *the law of comparative or relative advantage*, arguing that a country would benefit from international trade even when it is at a competitive disadvantage for both products. By trading internationally, each country finds a better exchange ratio for the goods than provided by its domestic market. By concentrating efforts and resources on products where they have a relative advantage, both countries increase their national and global welfare.

Though visionary, many implicit assumptions in Ricardo's theory are not clearly spelled out: (1) gains from trading internationally must offset transportation, customs duties and trading costs; (2) there are constant returns to scale; (3) products should be identical, or at least perceived as such by both consumers and merchants; (4) information must be easily available and efficient enough so that merchants in the two countries may be aware of the potential gains

to be derived from international trade; and (5) there must be no other financial or government restriction or market barrier that limits international trade for these products.

The implicit assumption that products and consumers' tastes, habits and preferences are perfectly identical in the two countries or the world is a difficult one. England produced almost no wine at the time and it is doubtful that British wine had the same physical characteristics, the same alcoholic content or the same taste as the Portuguese wine. English and the Portuguese tastes in bed linen were probably distinct enough to enable them to recognize clearly which were 'their' sheets. Their fabrics and embroidery were different and natives of the two countries were likely to be aware of the origin of their sheets. Furthermore, in Britain beer tends to be the drink of choice in pubs, whereas *vinho verde* or *porto* are the favourite drinks of the Portuguese, while they listen to *fado* (guitar music). Ricardo does not think of products as cultural artefacts. Only quantity and price matter. Exchange is purely economic: goods and services are commoditized, generic, indefinitely marketable and without cultural meaning.

The cultural variable has been neglected in international trade theory and practice, which are almost purely economics based. For classical economists, national culture has an aura of inertia and resistance to change; they favour commonalities, not differences. Their theories are based on utility maximization, rather than on identity building through non-utilitarian motives.

Ricardo's theory came at the time of England's Corn Laws. He demonstrated that Britain should reduce its customs duties, thereby opening up its domestic market to foreign agricultural commodities – especially those from the colonies that were more cost competitive – and specialize in certain manufactured goods to be exported worldwide. It did not sufficiently acknowledge the human consequences, including rapid rural depopulation, social inequality, consumer frustration, stress, materialism, lack of self-sufficiency in food supplies, and threats to health and the environment.[4]

International trade theorists assume the inevitability of global change despite local consequences like job losses. But locally, people strongly defend their cultural identity and are thought of as embracing protectionism in international trade. This is illustrated in France by the *Lois Méline* introduced at the end of the nineteenth century out of a desire to protect French food supplies and French farmers, even though this meant higher costs for the consumer. This was also true in Germany where the writings of Friedrich List promoted a nationalistic approach to economic growth.

Website link 5.2

Visit the Global Trade Watch website: http://www.citizen.org/trade/.

It is difficult in practice to distinguish between protecting national/cultural interests (self-identity is enhanced by consumption) and protecting the interests of industries, which may deprive consumers of cheaper products, or even of the opportunity to buy particular products. Hence, there is a natural tendency to ignore culture or to consider it as an anecdotal variable, defending local, narrow interests rather than promoting global welfare. International business and international marketing also perceive culture as subsidiary, with weak explanatory power. Culture in the 'modern' world is considered at best an anecdote and at worst a useless constraint.[5] Ultimately, this argument relies on a macro-perspective rather than a multifaceted approach where all factors are considered.[6]

The dismal treatment of diversity in global marketing

The global product philosophy lacks the consideration of meanings invested by local consumers. This is because price is a universal concern and low-cost arguments make sense. In this utilitarian view, products are commoditized in a worldwide sphere of exchange. As explained by Kopytoff (p. 68)[7]: 'A commodity is a thing that has use value and that can be exchanged in a discrete transaction for a counterpart, the very fact of exchange indicating that the counterpart [most often, money] has, in the immediate context, an equivalent value.' As advocated by Levitt,[5] and many other authors in the area of international marketing, we might expect to see the emergence of global markets for standardized consumer products on a previously unimagined scale. In Levitt's (p. 97)[5] words it would 'not [be] a matter of opinion but of necessity'. Traditional differences in national tastes would disappear, while local consumer preferences and national product standards would become 'vestiges of the past'. Consumers worldwide would look for good-quality/low-cost products and global competitors would seek to standardize their offerings everywhere. Farewell diversity: we will not mourn your passing!

This world view contains a number of assumptions to be discussed in this and other chapters. The first concerns the strong ideology of 'standard' in the Western mind. Utilitarianism dominates consumption: people strive for a large quantity of fair-quality, low-cost products. Levitt rightly argues that low cost and high quality are not incompatible. However, this refers only to the quantitative definition of product quality, based on reliability, performance and durability. Here, quality is meant only in the sense of the word contained in the first of nine definitions given by *Collins English Dictionary* (p. 1325)[8]: 'a distinguishing characteristic, property or attribute', this does not necessarily mean superior quality to other products. Quality in the sense of 'having or showing excellence or superiority' is only the ninth and last meaning in the dictionary.

Levitt's text incorporates a section entitled 'vindication of the model T', where he clearly explains his view that 'consumption fordism' (which values assembly-line organization and continuous processes) is the only possible pattern. The second assumption deals with the continuum between traditional and modern societies. 'Traditional' is associated with the past, which is of low value in the Western view; the past is mostly seen as an impediment to effective action. This naive view of world diversity states that we are all converging towards a 'modern' lifestyle marked by standard products and consumption patterns worldwide.

The anti-diversity discourse can be found in international marketing texts where the inevitability of global preferences is presented as a simple fact. Diversity is treated as an anecdotal constraint. There are, however, non-utilitarian reasons for consumer behaviour; cultural diversity at the international level is a reality. Moreover, there are opportunities for companies that reject the 'consumption fordism' of globalization, to create differentiation and gain a competitive advantage. For instance, in 2000, the new CEO of Coca-Cola, Douglas Daft, declared a repositioning strategy based on three fundamental principles. The second of the three was to 'think locally and act locally'. Daft (p. 12), stated that:

Ours is a local business – we will think locally and act locally. We became one of the best marketers in the world because we understood that no one drinks 'globally'. Local people get thirsty, go to their local retailer, and buy locally made Coke. To think locally and act locally, we must push decision making and accountability to the local level . . . Understanding the local culture and acting on that understanding is paramount to success.[9]

5.2

The global convergence of consumption patterns

The marketing environment

The political environment worldwide has clearly converged with the steady decline of communist regimes. It is more and more difficult, given the powerful means of telecommunications, including satellite television and the Internet, to block the access of citizens to information on what is happening in their own country and in the world. Only a very few countries deny their citizens access to the Internet while some, like China and Tunisia, try to control access.

The general economic environment is to a certain extent converging, but there are major limitations in a number of areas that are important for marketing. While economic systems are converging towards a market economy, the degree of poverty of a significant group of developing countries has been increasing over the years. Legal integration has limits since legal traditions continue to differ greatly. Some legal materials are duplicated and become complex, as in the EU where laws pertaining to marketing are regulated both at EU level and at the level of member states, sometimes resulting in discrepancies, even if local regulation is supposed to comply with Europe-wide directives.

Marketing infrastructures are converging, because the standards of the marketing profession are fairly consistent worldwide. Multinational companies have heavily influenced the widespread adoption of similar practices even if to some extent tailored to local environments.

Marketing knowledge is probably the most controversial issue. It is based on Anglo-American cultural premises and seems to have been widely adopted worldwide. However, a multitude of differences, both local and cultural, reflect how marketing knowledge has been understood, sometimes misunderstood, and often transformed. Hence, management expectations about both consumers' responses and the performance of marketing tasks can be partly disproved, even in an environment to which they are apparently suited, because there has not been enough awareness and understanding of the local marketing environment.

Supply and competition are now largely globalized, with the progressive shift from domestic industries, operating in national markets protected by non-tariff barriers, to global industries. This alone is enough to explain a large part of the globalization of consumption.

General convergence at the macro-level

There is also some evidence of macro-level convergence in consumption patterns. For example, there is significant demographic convergence in the European Union: (1) the age distribution of the population comprises more older persons; (2) the size of households is constantly decreasing; and (3) the proportion of immigrants is increasing with higher concentrations in large cities (Leeflang and Van Raaij, 1995). Convergence is also seen in the sociocultural environment in terms of growing equality between men and women and increasing percentages of working women, while all over the EU health and environment concerns are on the rise. In Hofstede's terms,[10] there is a trend towards more *femininity*. Convergence in consumer behaviour can also be observed at a broad level. Services account for a larger part of the household budget and it is the fastest-growing area of international trade.[11] Demand is growing for healthcare, environmentally friendly products and services, and fun and convenience products.

Most of the empirical studies on globalization are synchronic in design; they study cross-national

Box 5.1

Savoury snacks and global law: Two different routes for globalization

Globalization can occur even when local patterns do not disappear. In the two examples below local patterns work either as an opportunity or as a constraint for the emergence of globalized product or service use.

Japan has a long tradition of savoury snacks based on local ingredients such as rice crackers (*arare* and *senbei*), dried seafood snacks (*kozakana*) and *edamame* (green soybeans lightly boiled in salt). Although these snacks still have high consumption rates among elderly people, they have lost ground to potato- and corn-based Western-style snacks: sales of traditional Japanese-style snacks decreased by 16.5 per cent between 1993 and 1997.

In a totally different field, legal practice, local legal systems have presented an opportunity for US and English law firms.[12] Due to the political nature of law, most countries restrict the practice of law to their own nationals. However, US law firms have been following the globalization of US companies, which took them along as they expanded abroad, in particular to arrange cross-border deals that maximized advantages under US tax law. By learning the intricacies of local legal systems, US law firms have adjusted to local contexts while maintaining their comparative advantage in terms of common law (the prevailing legal tradition in the United Kingdom and the United States), by assisting foreign firms willing to enter the US market or drafting international business contracts based on common law.

(Source: Adapted from Spar;[12] *Euromonitor*.[13])

similarity in consumption patterns at a precise point in time. The most logical way to study the convergence process is, however, to examine how consumption changes over several time periods. A good illustration of long-term convergence in consumption figures is that of wine, traditionally a southern European drink, and beer, traditionally a northern European drink. Wine consumption has decreased and beer consumption has increased in the south (in France, Greece, Italy, Portugal and Spain), whereas the opposite pattern has evolved in the north of Europe (in Austria, Belgium, Denmark, Germany, Luxembourg and the UK), leading to macro-level convergence.[14] Also evident is a tendency toward drinks with lower alcohol content, stricter drink-driving laws, and higher quality products. Similarly, there is evidence of increasing macro-level similarity in cross-national consumption patterns in broad commodity categories, when a utility-maximizing framework is used.[15]

Numerous detailed examples are cited in support of the globalization of consumption behaviour. Beef consumption in Japan, traditionally a fish-eating country, has developed considerably, while there has been a rise in fish consumption in traditionally meat-eating countries. There have been similar changes in relation to rice and wheat between the West and the East (see Box 5.1 for other examples).

Rather than discuss macro-level globalization, it makes more sense from an international marketing perspective to try to understand the nature of this phenomenon. With decreasing barriers to international trade over the last century, and mostly in the last 50 years, more variety has been brought to consumers in most countries of the world. In this sense, globalization increases, rather than decreases, diversity for consumers.

Evidence of consumers' globalization at a micro-level

De Mooij and Hofstede (p. 62)[16] point out that: 'International marketers would like us to believe that in the "new Europe" with a single currency, consumers will become more similar, will increasingly eat the same food, wear jeans and cross-trainers, and watch the same television programs. Reality is likely to be different.'

Buying and consumption patterns in affluent countries appear to have in fact diverged as much as converged. Across 15 European countries, preference for new cars over second-hand cars depends more on culture than on wealth.[17] Today, consumers have more opportunities for choice and are often affected by social needs. As de Mooij (pp. 58–9) states:

Clothes satisfy a functional need, whereas fashion satisfies a social need. Some personal care products serve functional needs, but others serve social needs. A house serves a functional need and a home, a social need. Culture influences the type of house in which people live, how they relate to their homes, and how they tend to their homes. A car may satisfy a functional need, but the type of car for most people satisfies a social need. Social needs are culture-bound.[18]

At the micro-level, researchers find that culture influences consumption patterns, but that this influence differs by the product type, product/service category, situational factors, and reasons for purchase.[19] First, durable household and functional products vary more by culture than non-durable sensory and personal products.[20] Similarly highly visible products, such as wristwatches, are more influenced by culture than consumer electronics.[21,22] Second, services, such as restaurants and air travel are more influenced by culture than products, such as beer, jeans, soft drinks and stereos.[23] Third, situational factors differ by product type. For instance, the frequency, the time of day, where consumers shop, the length of shopping time and the reason all vary by culture for food, but not for clothing.[24] Fourth, reasons for purchase, such as maintenance, enjoyment and defence differ by country.[25] Many other examples of micro-level differences were elaborated on in Chapter 4.

Website link 5.3

Read an article on selling Indian beer in British pubs: http://www.atimes.com/atimes/South_Asia/EC18Df02.html.

Thus, at a micro-level, evidence about the globalization of consumer behaviour relating to specific products is somewhat inconclusive. Finding convincing proof of micro-level globalization is difficult, since testing for it would include such issues as the

pace and process of globalization, the market segments involved and the geographically significant cultural areas.[26] The trend towards globalization depends partly on the specific aspect of consumer behaviour: whether buying behaviour, shopping behaviour, lifestyle, values, psychometrics and underlying attitudes, influence processes, including group influences and word-of-mouth, etc. The use of culturally unique concepts and research instruments (largely Western) compresses differences, even when cross-cultural precautions are taken. Since the concepts and theories of marketing originated from the US culture, their full ability to capture local patterns of consumer behaviour is questionable.

5.3
The emergence of a global consumer culture

There are at least four ways to interpret global consumer culture: the proliferation of transnational corporations; the proliferation of global capitalism; global consumerism; and global consumption homogenization.[4] As there is no doubt that transnational corporations and capitalism have proliferated, this section will focus on global consumerism and later on global consumption homogenization.

Ger and Belk (p. 275)[4] define global consumerism as 'a widespread and unquenchable desire for material possessions'. It is a culture in which the majority of consumers avidly desire, and therefore try to acquire and display, goods and services that are valued for non-utilitarian reasons such as status seeking, envy provocation and novelty seeking.[27] The rise in most countries of large-scale, democratized consumption as a legitimate and positively valued human activity (unlike, say, war or monastic contemplation) has led to the emergence of a global consumer culture. This is illustrated by Prahalad and Lieberthal (p. 71): 'What is big and emerging in countries like China and India is a new consumer base consisting of hundreds of millions of people. Starved of choice for over 40 years, the rising middle class is hungry for consumer goods and a better quality of life and is ready to spend.'[28] It seems in every culture there is a culturally appropriate way to justify consumption. Even in countries where purchasing power does not really allow access to goods and services, Hollywood films, with an approximate market share of 90 per cent worldwide have been a major driver of desires and aspirations, fuelling consumers' needs and envy. In many countries of the world, adding subtitles or dubbing movies is considerably less expensive than making them locally.

Website link 5.4

The computer-generated stars of the 2007 *Transformers* movie were also a product placement for General Motors vehicles: **http://www. productplacement.biz/news/product-placement/transformer-movie-incorporates-the-strongest-product-placement-in-film-history-20070717-2268-84.html**.

The world standard package and 'McDonaldized' consumption

A consumer culture guides people in defining their aspirations towards a certain set of possessions. The standard US package of goods has developed into a world standard package that includes a car and a home with refrigerators, televisions and computers. The same holds true for services, since the fast-food restaurant has become part of the world standard package. Ritzer (p. 70) describes how strongly people identify with McDonald's around the world:

In Taipei, the Golden Arches have come to have more symbolic meaning than the local temple. In Seoul, people are passionate about McDonald's as well as their opposition to it. In Tokyo, Japanese boy scouts were reported to be pleasantly surprised when during a trip they discovered that there was a McDonald's in Chicago.[29]

In the emergence of a global consumer culture, a process dubbed the *McDonaldization* of society, the word 'standard' is central.[30] 'Standard' has three meanings: (1) the same for everybody; (2) the same everywhere in the world; (3) the same for all time. The paradoxical success of the 'Classic' Coke as against the 'new' Coke is an illustration of the last point. Standard also means that product quality remains the same unless new technological developments allow improvements which complement the previous attributes.

There are four elements in the McDonaldization process[30]:

1. *Efficiency*: the McDonaldized product or service in the 'Republic of Technology'[5] offers the optimum method for getting from one point (being hungry) to another (being fed). In contrast to traditional solutions, fordist consumption values assembly-line organization and continuous processes: with the parking areas adjacent to the fast-food restaurant, a short walk to the counter, a limited menu and quick choice, finger food and speedy disposal of leftovers.

2. *Systematic quantification and calculation*: McDonald's offers more 'bang for the buck' and provides its customers with 'value' meals. Rational economic calculations based on the emphasis of price and the size/weight given for each ingredient extols the utilitarian view. In this model, quantity equals quality.

3. *Predictability*: whether in Chicago, Los Angeles, Paris, Moscow or Tokyo, we find the same Big Mac and French Fries. Consumers find great comfort in this predictability which offers neither shocks nor surprises, and reduces perceived risk. There is not much surprise in the limited range of products offered, but we know that it will be consistent over time and place. Predictable food is based on predictable, often frozen, ingredients and corporate guidelines that detail every item of the fast-food outlet.

4. *Control through the substitution of non-human for human technology*: the system is operated so that there is limited human involvement in the whole production process: rules are fairly strict and automated systems (e.g. soft drinks or ice-cream dispensers) control the exact quantity, in line with point 2. This also facilitates predictability by reassuring customers about the service McDonald's delivers.

The globalized consumption experience is only one part of the real world of consumption but it plays a dominant role because it has been consistently and heavily portrayed as 'useful' and 'good for people'. It is also publicized somewhat inaccurately since there is much more local adaptation, both in Coca-Cola and in McDonald's, than admitted by these global marketers. For instance, McDonald's has adapted elements of its menu to local tastes. In Japan there are Teriyaki burgers, in China bean sundaes, in Norway salmon burgers, and in Uruguay poached egg burgers. In addition, the same concept can mean something quite different when borrowed from another culture: 'The fast-food concept that fits the US fast lifestyle has adapted successfully to PRC's consumers' lifestyle, because less waiting and fast service do not mean to eat fast' (p. 92).[31]

Website link 5.5

The Economist has used the globalization of the Big Mac to develop a cross-national financial purchasing power indicator: http://www.economist.com/markets/bigmac.

Globalization and 'modern' culture

The most debatable aspect of globalization is the belief that we are all converging towards a 'modern lifestyle'. This view of cross-cultural buyer behaviour involves three main assumptions: (1) modernity is a given and technology is our path to a bigger and better future for all; (2) even if they differ externally, all societies, from traditional to developed, can be placed on a continuum of social change; and (3) the criterion for placing a society on the continuum is its degree of resistance to modern changes.[32]

Modern culture believes that scientific knowledge and technology are able to control nature and improve human existence. Even though it may be argued that we have already entered the postmodern era, most people still live in a modern era, marked by a strong belief in the achievements of science, its unlimited problem-solving capacity through technology and its exclusive contribution to global welfare.[33] Modernization is clear in Levitt's (p. 97)[5] view of globalization, where he criticizes multinational companies as being medieval (or pre-modern):

The multinational corporation knows a lot about a great many countries and congenially adapts to supposed differences. It willingly accepts vestigial national differences, not questioning the possibility of their transformation, not recognizing how the world is ready and eager for the benefit of modernity, especially when the price is right. The multinational corporation accommodating mode to visible national differences is medieval.

Global values in modern culture emerge because consumers throughout the world inevitably have fairly similar responses to new technologies and product innovations. 'Modern' culture is characterized by:

1. an individualist orientation, supported by the exercise of purchasing power as a demonstration of individual freedom;
2. a strong emphasis on material achievements and materialistic values, that is, a doing/having rather than a being orientation;
3. a strongly economic, 'commoditized' time;
4. a tendency to discard the past in favour of a future orientation, while expressing some frustration at not living in the present as much as one would like; and
5. a fairly high degree of utilitarianism.

For instance, household equipment tends to individualize tasks, freeing people from both the constraints and the pleasures of communal life, in a mostly urban environment where families are nuclear and the extended family separated by large distances. An increased awareness of a clock-bound and universal time, at the expense of a local and nature-bound time, accompanies the enthusiasm for innovation and change. Modern culture posits a strong future orientation: consumers quickly dispose of perfectly functional products that are quickly obsolete. Various environmental concerns typify modern cultures as countries become more polluted, the ozone layer is depleted, and global warming is an increasing cause for anxiety. Although Germany, with its *grüne punkt* (green point), still largely leads the environmental movement, the interest in 'green' products is growing worldwide. Notably, the interest is manifested in ways that are context appropriate. For instance, consumers in higher density countries such as South Korea (approximately 500 people per square kilometre) give a higher priority to product disposability and biodegradability than consumers in Germany (with 235 people per square kilometre) or the USA (with 33 people per square kilometre).[34]

The controversial claim that the 'American way of life' has universal appeal and extends 'backward' to other nations is typical of the binary way of modern thought, opposing concepts such as past/future, traditional/modern, true/false and rational/emotional.[35] In fact, true globalization has to work both ways. US consumers will have to import genuine, unpasteurized, French *foie gras* or crude milk cheese which contains relatively harmless bacteria, but also has real taste and consistency. Similarly, if globalization is to be less unidirectional, French consumers will have to develop a taste for peanut butter, American women start wearing kimonos, and Australian men swap their shorts and thongs for Bavarian *lederhosen*.

The emergence of a global 'modern' culture is often confused with the convergence of local cultures, leading to an incorrect description of globalization. A frequent mistake is to equate 'modern' with 'American': while it is true that the United States and US multinational companies have been literally the champions and heralds of modern culture in consumer goods (consumption fordism) and services, globalization is not simply the worldwide extension of the 'American way of life'. The imitation of American solutions results mostly from borrowed answers to common worldwide challenges. American society values a pioneer spirit, is less resistant, and has fewer social impediments to change than more traditional societies. When the Japanese, French or Chinese change, it is not as a result of American pressure; rather, since these societies are less socially and technologically innovative, they borrow some of their responses from the United States, while often making the United States scapegoats for the drawbacks of modernity.

Modern culture, with both high individualism and structured time patterns, implies a type of social organization centred on peer-age segments. Girls give up their Barbie dolls between the ages of 12 and 13 because it would be inappropriate to play with dolls – even sophisticated ones – when they reach adolescence. Each age class increasingly has its own identity, its own way of doing things, membership is signalled through consumption, and the shared values and behaviour transcend national borders. There is also evidence that certain age groups, such as teenagers, are allowed a 'cultural time-out', where they are expected to rebel against their cultural restraints. For instance, we see Japanese youth wearing American baseball hats backwards, watching MTV, etc. Later, when they join the workforce and start families they are expected to re-adopt culturally appropriate behaviour.

The increased adoption of modern culture cross-nationally is incorrectly interpreted as a sign of full convergence and as testimony to the progressive disappearance of local cultures. Significant elements of local cultures, such as language, writing systems, religions and relational patterns, stay visibly in the global landscape. While cultural differences rarely appear as the key explanation for behaviour, local cultures allow a deeper understanding of consumption in a specific context. Interpretation must be close to the local reality: for instance drip/filter coffee taken 'to go' or drunk with a meal (as is common in the USA), is a widely different coffee-drinking experience from espresso enjoyed with friends at a local café in Europe or Australia. Local cultures do not really disappear; rather, a new layer of common culture is superimposed on them. The very fact that the Japanese and the Chinese are not willing to change their ideographic writing system, which from a purely utilitarian perspective makes little sense, demonstrates the very deep roots of local cultures.

5.4

Local products and consumption experiences

Not surprisingly, globalized fordist consumption has a striking preference for 'culture-free' products and consumption situations. A different perspective on consumer behaviour centred on cultural meanings ascribed to things may be useful despite its limited use in international marketing texts.[36] Many more insights can be gained by actually centring on a service, product or possession and how it is used in context than through the national character approach, based on limited universal variables and the design of cultural ideals (i.e. high versus low scores on common dimensions).[37] For instance, a Japanese wedding ceremony would be practically incomprehensible to a Westerner apart from the (now shared) appearance of diamond rings and white wedding dresses. Applbaum and Jordt (p. 213)[37] describe the *pro nakôdo*, which is a commercial service for dating and arranged marriages in Japan:

Through personal contacts – that is, not through advertising – a pro nakôdo is introduced to a young man or young woman interested in being set up for arranged marriage dates . . . The pro nakôdo association meets once a month to exchange information on new registrants. At the meeting each pro nakôdo's new contribution will be photocopied and distributed among the other pro nakôdo . . . the pro nakôdos

Box 5.2

Colour television as a life statement

Television has made tremendous inroads into Chinese homes over the last ten years: penetration rates are reaching 80 per cent in rural areas and 98 per cent in cities. Television, more than any other good, represents freedom from oppression in the 'new China', and breaking with the past by access to information, in a country that has traditionally been wary of foreign influence. Ownership of a TV set plays an important role in establishing one's financial image and projects an image of personal success. Chinese people indicate that owning a colour television is a prerequisite to marriage and some couples indicate that they are willing to wait two years to be able to afford the best possible TV (a Japanese one, often several times more expensive than a Chinese colour TV). One respondent said: 'Buying a Chinese TV will give my marriage a poor start. I must wait until I can buy a Japanese TV to project the right image to my friends.'

(Source: Adapted from Doran.[38] *Advances in Consumer Research*, Kathleen Brewer Doran, copyright 1997 by Association for Consumer Research, reproduced with permission of Association for Consumer Research in the format Textbook via Copyright Clearance Center.)

bring home and place in their loose-leaf notebooks between 100 and 200 new pages each month. At the end of five years, or on marriage, whichever comes first, a person's sheet is removed from the notebook. At the time of this study, the association had slightly more than 6,500 registered clients.

If consumer culture matters, then it is likely that consumers will invest more meaning in products and services that are more bound to cultural interpretation. The question is therefore: what is more culture-free and what more culture-bound, in terms of product and service categories on the one hand, and consumer behaviour on the other?

Culture-bound products

Culture bonds arise in a number of ways, some related to the consumption situation, others to product attributes. This complexity is due to the *peculiar qualities intrinsic to the encounter between things and people*. The first aspect to examine is whether a rich (or poor) cultural context surrounds the product, including shopping for it, buying it, consuming it and disposing of it. Furniture, for instance, will be more culture-bound than consumer electronics, because there is often a local style and a local manufacturing tradition for these items. Furniture may not only be bought, but also inherited or restored, which makes less sense for an MP3 player. Consumer electronics are a typical culture-free product category because they are technology based, low in cultural context and universally used. It comes as no surprise, therefore, that consumer behaviour is very similar cross-nationally for consumer electronics.[22] An exception is in developing economies where consumer electronics do tend to become culture-bound, such as in China, where colour TV sets are invested with symbolic values that are rooted in the local context (see Box 5.2).

The more closely products relate to the *physical environment*, the more culture-bound they will be, as the physical environment influences the local material culture, which is linked to climate, density of population, housing, flora and fauna, and so on. The absence of visible cattle rearing on most Japanese islands, except Hokkaido, distances Japanese people from dairy products. Japanese people find cheese, the most sophisticated dairy product, quite a strange food; cheese conveys little meaning except that of foreignness. Similarly, local ways of building are generally based on the availability of substitute building materials (wood, cement, stones, etc.), certain craft traditions (e.g. masonry versus carpentry), and constraints (e.g. earthquakes), which explain the dominance of local technical solutions. For instance, the use of steel in bridges and urban freeways is much higher in Japan than it is in Europe where bridges are mostly built with reinforced concrete. Similarly, wood is frequently used for housing construction in the United States, whereas it is quite marginal in western Europe except in Scandinavia, and also in Australia, where most houses are built with clay bricks.

Culture bonds are strong for a product or service when there is an investment of *cultural and national background and identity* in consumption. Consuming then becomes, consciously or unconsciously, more than a simple utilitarian purchase, resulting in a preference for products made in one's own country. In terms of product attributes, the use of local materials and production processes, recipes and craft techniques reinforce the perception of compatibility, if they are known as such by consumers.

Language content is also a major constituent of the cultural content of a product, as in genuinely cultural products (e.g. songs, soap operas, films and novels), or just in written language used on or around the product, such as the packaging or brand name. For instance, the instructions for assembling IKEA furniture avoid complex multiple language explanations by using pictures alone. Pictures are visual elements which are more culture-free than written materials.

Products that involve a *relationship to others*, in terms of displaying/showing or giving/sharing, are likely to be culture-bound, precisely because this relationship is culturally coded. That is, the social situation is likely to moderate the influence of culture. The same consumer may choose different brands depending on who is involved in the decision-making process or likely to use the product.[39–41] Conspicuous-consumption items, and more generally goods having a high signal value, are culture-bound. Whereas many luxury products are globally branded, the nature of their consumption is largely local, depending at least on concepts of the self and others.[42] Products that have been consumed as a part of life since childhood are often marked by locality. Peanut butter from the USA and Vegemite from Australia are widely used local products which cannot be easily found in many countries. As such, American and Australian expatriates have difficulty obtaining them when assigned abroad.

Complex products, such as films, are logically culture-bound, because they require a high level of interpretation and knowledge of the local context in order for the film to be fully understood and enjoyed. One of the reasons for the limited global success of most countries' films is that they rely on local cues which are not easily understood by different local audiences. However, the success of American movies is based on their low contextuality, simplified char-acters, reliance on the universal appeal of violence, love, and wealth, and their simple moral dichotomy, where good struggles against evil. Even so, many Hollywood films are modified during the dubbing process to add the appropriate local context. For instance, many of the jokes were changed in the German version of the animated movie *Aladdin*. Comedy, it seems, is largely culture-bound, due to a sense of shared understanding.

The very *nature of the product* has some influence on the level of universality of needs. *Non-durables* seem to appeal more to tastes, habits and customs; therefore they are more culture-bound. Clothing, confectionery, food and household cleaners are all culture-bound. Empirical evidence seems to suggest that industrial and high-technology products, such as computer hardware, machine tools and heavy equipment, are appropriate for global strategies, as they often offer significant benefits over the previous alternatives.[43] While one could easily believe that industrial products are typically culture-free, this view is largely mistaken, because the contexts in which they are used, and the functionalities sought, depend on culture. The construction industry, for instance, is highly influenced by local cultural traditions, as well as the attitude towards time (short-term versus long-term orientation) and the perceived trade-off between the price and durability of equipment. In Europe, the difference between national markets is considerable. For instance, the market estimate for clay water pipes is 460,000 tons/year in Germany, whereas it is only 11,000 tons/year in France. In fact, clay water pipes are two or three times more expensive than cast-iron pipes; however, their durability extends way beyond the lifetime of those who decide on the investment; they may last for a century, or even several centuries. The German local authorities and/or standard-setting bodies prefer a high investment cost/extended lifetime trade-off, whereas the French seem to consider this too costly and think a century is beyond significance for public decision makers. Furthermore, the major player in France for this kind of water pipe, Pont-à-Mousson, uses ductile cast iron, a solution it has promoted widely with the water utilities. Box 5.3 provides a further illustration of how benefits of equipment goods depend on local culture.

One framework for unravelling the degree and the nature of culture bonds for products is to

Box 5.3

Time to wait

Market data were gathered for blood analysis equipment in several European countries (Germany, France, Italy, Spain, and the United Kingdom) in hospital labs. Doctors were asked to rate the importance of time to results, a reason for adopting automatic blood analysis equipment allowing speedier outcomes. Responses reflect different degrees of preoccupation with time, Germans being the most concerned with short time to results (86 per cent of German labs mentioned this as a major factor in their buying decision), followed by the British (72 per cent), the French (67 per cent), the Spaniards (55 per cent), and the Italians (37 per cent). Thus, even for organizational purchasing, underlying cultural values are different.

---

undertake a 'cultural biography' of the goods surveyed.[7] Drawing on the analogy with the life of a person, the biography of an object allows one to understand how it ultimately nests itself within a cultural milieu. Kopytoff (p. 67) describes what a 'cultural biography' of a car in Africa might entail:

The biography of a car in Africa would reveal a wealth of cultural data: the way it was acquired, how and from whom the money was assembled to pay for it, the relationship of the seller to the buyer, the uses to which the car is regularly put, the identity of its most frequent passengers and of those who borrow it, the frequency of borrowing, the garages to which it is taken and the owner's relation to the mechanics, the movement of the car from hand to hand over the years, and in the end, when the car collapses, the final disposition of its remains. All of these details would reveal an entirely different biography from that of a middle-class American, or Navajo, or French peasant car.[7]

This type of analysis may uncover new interesting product uses, especially in lesser developed nations, where necessity dictates the conversion of products to maximize their use. Some culturally bound product uses include the use of car tyres to reinforce wells during the rainy season and the use of a telephone answering machine to check for power outages which may cause heat loss at a distant residence.[44]

Unique consumption experiences

Consumption is still largely a local reality. Far from being uniquely culture related, local reality also reflects climate and customs, and the mere fact that much of our life is still shared with others who have the same kind of 'local knowledge' in the Geertzian sense.[45] There are still huge differences in the pattern of household expenditures across EU countries. The percentages spent by households in various EU countries on food in general, and specifically vegetables, chocolate and cheese, still widely differ. Consumers attribute meaning to products and services in context, especially what it means to desire, to search, to evaluate, to purchase, to consume, to share, to give, to spend, and to dispose. Consumption experiences are full of social facts in interaction with other players in the market game: manufacturers, distributors, salespeople and also other consumers. Two illustrations are given below.

Consumption as disposal

Consumption involves how we see our environment, how nature and culture affect our perceptions. Our cleaning behaviour depends on how we define clean and dirty. Many consumption acts result in product destruction, even if only because the product is obsolete or out of order.

Issues of product continuity may be observed in the example of filters for drip-coffee machines, which are white in France and yellow-brown in Germany (*naturbraun*), paper handkerchiefs, which are generally white in France and yellow-brown in Germany and toilet paper which is generally pink or white in France and greyish in Germany. The Germans express their willingness to be environmentally friendly (*umweltfreundlich*) by purchasing paper-based products whose colour exhibits their genuinely 'recycled' nature, that is, not bleached with chlorine-based chemicals that are used to whiten the paper. The same holds true for German writing and copying paper, which, because of its greyish and irregular appearance, would be generally considered by most French as 'dirty' and of poor quality. The difference in consumer experience lies in the difference of *continuity* in the ecological concern. Germans feel the necessity to be nearer to nature because they live in a country about three times more densely populated than France and they insist on strong coherence between their words and their deeds. The two peoples seem to have different ways of reconciling nature and culture: Germans are often perceived stereotypically as natural, deep and aggressive, whereas the French are thought of as sophisticated. German culture finds its expression in love for nature and a preference for isolation, whereas French culture advocates social life and shows disdain for everything that is too nature oriented.[46]

Offering wine

Offering wine is a different experience in southern Europe from what it is in the United States, Japan or northern Europe. Hosts who receive wine from their guests have to decide whether to keep it for later, or to open it immediately to share it with their guests. In France, unless the host states that the wine is not suitable to accompany the meal, the received wine will be drunk with the guests: sharing is a must and keeping the wine for oneself would imply that it may not be good enough to drink now. In many other countries it would be impolite to drink a gift with the giver, since it would mean the immediate destruction of a present that should be kept as a memory, at least for a time. The emphasis in each case is on different values: the sense of sharing on the one hand, and the sense of keeping a present as a memory of the donor on the other.

Habits, habitus and shared meaning

Culture may be viewed simply as shared habits and customs, and as shared meaning about how particular experiences are to be interpreted in context, rather than as a value system. This system of shared habits

and interpretation is often incorporated into 'common sense' (shared meaning), which translates into French as 'good sense' (*bon sens*) with a clear value judgement, or into German as 'sound understanding' (*gesunder Menschenverstand*), showing that it is the appropriate solution. Habits are central in local consumer behaviour, because they limit options, simplify interpretation and assist in attitude formation at an almost automatic level. Habits mean we do not have to scan all possible alternatives all the time and give us confidence in our decisions. But they are a largely overlooked element of consumer behaviour, probably because they are seen as passive decision making. According to Triandis,[47] habitual behaviour is almost unavoidable when we are emotionally aroused in terms of being angry or very happy. In these situations, our cognitive capacity may be depleted, making habitual behaviour very difficult to overcome, even if we want to.

A Chinese proverb says that 'habit starts with the first time'; a Western proverb that 'habit is second nature'. To become fully built into a person, habits need support in child-rearing, schooling and education systems and the whole reward–sanction system that goes with our social surroundings. Habits are ways of doing and behaving that have been reinforced by authorization and gratification, so that once the programming is forgotten they appear to be legitimate. Three examples taken from diverse contexts may be used to illustrate this.

Kaffeetrinken

The German *Kaffeetrinken* is a traditional German form of enjoyment, organized mostly at weekends or holiday afternoons with family or friends, at home or in a *Konditorei* (pastry shop serving coffee and tea) or a restaurant, at about three or four o'clock. The special relationship of Germans to coffee, sweets and cakes (*Kuchen*) has much to do with happy hours experienced since childhood, when people relax in a somewhat constrained society with a deeply internalized pressure for conforming to rules.

British fire safety systems

The United Kingdom is one of the largest markets for fire safety equipment in the world; fire alarms outside buildings are intended to attract people's attention quickly in case of fire. The excessive fire safety instructions, in both public and private buildings, are striking for many foreigners. The tradition of using wood in building and the Great Fire of London are probably historical reasons for this British phobia. The United Kingdom logically follows the European norm EN52 on fire safety equipment, which, although compulsory, is not at present respected by the Italians and the Spaniards: not only would the implementation of this regulation in all public buildings involve massive investment that Italian and Spanish state budgets cannot afford, but also in Latin countries stone is more common than wood in construction and the anguish caused by building fires has been rare.

Drinking a beer

Individuals invest meaning into their consumption experiences. Whereas aggregate data seem to demonstrate quantitative convergence, it also conceals huge qualitative divergence as far as experiences, context, perceptions and interpretations are concerned. For instance, beer is consumed in greater quantities in southern Europe than in the past, but the very experience of drinking beer still has a different meaning from that in the north of Europe: the meaning differential has not yet diminished in the same proportion as the volume differential.

Shared situations, habits and stories around beer differ across Europe. This is most obvious in the type of beer, glass preference and environment in which it is consumed. Beer differs in terms of the bitterness, froth, bubbles, sweetness and alcoholic content. For instance, most British beers are high-fermentation beers with lower alcohol content than beers on the Continent. The Bavarian *Krug* (a large jar) does not give the same 'taste' to beer as the French *demi* (a quarter-litre stemmed glass), the English pint glass or the Australian middie.

Drinking beer in Germany has a different meaning to drinking beer in the United Kingdom or in France. In Germany, beer is consumed in a *Kneipe* (tavern) or bought from a *Getränkeshop* (a nice combination of German and English to refer to a side-store to a supermarket entirely dedicated to beverages). Local beers play a dominant role in the German beer scene. In the region of Cologne, for instance, the *Kölsch* beers, comprising some 10 high-fermentation brands of beer, are seen as a reference to the place, a little like wines in France. The German returnable half-litre bottles suit a densely populated country where people

are concerned with recycling glass. German beers always refer to the purity law (*Reinheitsgebot*) of 1516.

In a British pub, drinking a pint (0.57 litres) or half-pint of beer is a different experience; the pub is a comfortable place that invites people to stay and feel at home. Since people often drink more than a single pint of beer, it must be low in alcohol. This beer can be drunk without 'getting plastered', especially if one stays for quite a long period of time. A pub is a totally different world from the French *café-bar*, with its tiled floor and its rather cold interior design. In France regular customers invest the place with their own sense of comfort and human warmth. But non-regular customers will never find in a *café-bar* the immediate comfort that they find in most British pubs.

This contrasts the Australian experience. Pettigrew (pp. 162–4) interviewed patrons at local pubs to uncover the basic symbolic values of leisure, freedom and solidarity, at least for:

Older Male: 'What you are is a person when you walk into a pub. No matter where it is in Australia, automatically you can get into such a situation where you can just be friends with a person you have never met before. It doesn't matter from one state, one pub, one environment to another.'

Older Male: 'You are in my home. This pub is my home. This place is about socialized drinking. People come down here to enjoy themselves, talk to their workmates after work, have a couple, and then go home. Kiss the dog and feed the missus. You go to work and you go to the pub, and that is home.'

Male: 'It is probably perceived that men are allowed out for beers basically and the women still stay home and look after the family, which sounds a very old attitude. Although everybody says they have changed, and things have changed, maybe they haven't.'

Another contrast is Finland where, until recently, only low-alcohol beer has been allowed to be sold in supermarkets. All other types of alcoholic drinks, including standard beer, are sold only in the state chain Alko, which has a monopoly. Alko stores have limited opening hours and are generally removed from central shopping areas. This symbolizes the effort one must make to buy beer (apart from the low-alcohol type); indicating a level of societal disapproval.[48]

Local consumer cultures and resistance to change

The Danes dominate the world market for blue cheese with their Blue Castello: a decontextualized product with an Anglo-Italian name. It is a pasteurized, inoffensive, white soft cheese, palatable for every germphobic cheese-lover. As such, it is a good candidate for promotion as a global product, and a typical progeny of fordist consumption. The British Stilton, the French Roquefort or the Italian Gorgonzola, all traditional blue cheeses, may in the long run be under threat from this global alternative.

You may wonder how much autonomy consumers have in encouraging or limiting the movement towards globalization. Naturally, we may or may not buy globalized products and services, and to this extent we 'vote with our feet'. But we also have little choice but to buy what is available, as goods are astutely brought to stores by sophisticated merchants. In this respect there could be some resistance to change, not at the level of the individual buying decision, but at more of a macro-level.

Even though we win as consumers, we may lose from globalization as citizens and workers, which leads to a preference for buying locally made products. Holt et al.[49] in a study of consumers in 12 countries (the US, UK, Brazil, China, Egypt, France, India, Indonesia, Japan, Poland, South Africa and Turkey) found that one in ten would not buy global brands if given a choice. This is despite the widespread belief that global brands are associated with high levels of quality. What this amounts to is people asking to have their 'way of life' preserved.

While some products may be global, there are strong arguments against the existence of a global consumer per se. The concept of cosmopolitanism has been oversimplified and used to depict a privileged universal, impartial and objective individual, who is above 'localism'.[50] According to Levy and colleagues (2007, p. 240)[50]: 'cosmopolitanism does not denote an intrinsic value, but represents a state of mind that is manifested as an orientation toward the outside, the Other, and which seeks to reconcile the global with the local and mediate between the familiar and the foreign'. Thus, cosmopolitans are not global, in the sense of being the same worldwide. They are still anchored in their local culture, and their behaviour depends on their purchase motivation, personality and past experiences.[51] As shown above, consumers' motivations do not easily globalize.

Consumers always 'construct' the identity of brands, even for 'global products' and they do so on the basis of their local culture and identity. One way of examining the symbolic meaning of brands is to identify the human characteristics that consumers associate with a brand. While brand personalities include some universal elements, such as competence, trendiness, excitement, sincerity and sophistication, they also include some culture-specific elements.[52,53] For instance, in more collectivist Japanese and Spanish samples the dimension of peacefulness (e.g. dependence, naiveté, mildness and shyness) emerged, while in the more individualist US sample, ruggedness (e.g. outdoorsy, masculine, Western, tough and rugged) emerged.[52] In addition, the dimension of passion (emotional intensity being fervent, passionate and intense; and spirituality being spiritual, mystical and bohemian) emerged in the Spanish sample. This it is certainly descriptive of Spanish culture. It is also interesting to note that even the apparent universal elements of brand personality show differences in their emphasis. For instance, excitement (young, contemporary, spirited and daring) also contained imaginativeness, uniqueness and independence in the US and Spain, while in Japan it included talkative, funny and optimistic. Thus, while companies might try to create a global brand personality (e.g. Coca-Cola), it may be perceived and interpreted differently in each culture.

'Global brands' in this sense are portfolios of local marketing assets, federated under a common, lexically identical name. Although Blue Castello builds on both an American referential (blue-cheese dressing) and an Italian image, it is doubtful whether people in all countries have the same kind of buying motives, product use and product image. False 'global' consumers buy false 'global' products, which they re-invest with their own culture-bound motivations and purposes. This suggests that most of the resistance will be hidden from global marketers. Box 5.4 illustrates this point.

Box 5.4

Consumer resistance to McDonald's?

France, where cultural resistance to fast food and hamburgers exists as a matter of national pride, is McDonald's fastest growing market in Europe. Having first achieved great success with a limited number of successful 'luxury' (high end of the market) fast-food stores located in the centre of major towns in France, McDonald's has now expanded to the suburbs and motorway junctions, and offers breakfast service. Anti-fast-food consumer associations have resisted the fast-food movement. Anti-globalization activists such as José Bové have caused material damage to restaurants. Nutrition specialists have shown that traditional French meals (based on diverse foods, lasting one hour) are much better for the digestion and prevent cancer of the digestive tract. Despite all this, McDonald's is popular with the young generation, especially children who will be tomorrow's adults and parents.

McDonald's has been responsive to criticisms of nutritionists in the United States. It has reduced fat, salt and sugar in its products and introduced a lean Deluxe burger with only 10 grams of fat and 310 calories against 20 grams of fat and 410 calories for the Quarter Pounder. In May 2002, the French weekly *Femme Actuelle* carried a McDonald's advertorial advising families not to eat at the restaurant more than once per week for health reasons.[54] McDonald's has also responded to attacks from environmentalists and animal rights activists by replacing the Styrofoam hamburger box in most countries with paper or a new starch-based alternative, and enforcing strict guidelines for animal husbandry. In northern Europe, McDonald's now insists on sorting its own refuse so that it can be appropriately recycled. Resisted or beloved, fast food is now an institution.

Will consumers resist the globalization process?

Globalized consumption assumes that consumers are pleased with it because it means cheap, good-quality products. The 'globalness' of a product is a cue for quality across cultures.[49] Perceived 'globalness' is positively related to perceived quality and prestige and, through them, to purchase likelihood in the United States and Korea, but only for consumers with low ethnocentrism.[55] Those with higher ethnocentrism resist globalization by paying a premium for locally made goods, voting for protectionist governments, or acting as consumer lobbyists to support public action (e.g. against fast food) in order to maintain or re-create entry barriers that protect local consumption. They may, nonetheless, be self-contradictory individuals – for instance, drinking Coke while complaining about the Americanization of society.

Globalization obviously has some drawbacks. Some have denounced the de-humanizing process in post-fordist consumption, and the possible decrease in consumption diversity which may result from the progressive replacement of local consumption by globalized offerings.[30] Others have wondered whether globalization is just going a bit too far. For instance, the continual opening up of national markets through the WTO may result in increased worldwide competition across countries that have widely different levels of social security. These countries cannot compete on a fair basis because social insurance may raise the cost of goods subject to global competition. Globalization favours the consumer, not the worker, and raises complex issues when these combine in one single citizen. As Rodrik (p. 30) argues:

'Globalization' is exposing a deep fault line between groups that have the skills and mobility to flourish in global markets and those who either don't have these advantages or perceive the expansion of unregulated markets as inimical to social stability and deeply held norms. The result is severe tension between the market and social groups such as workers, pensioners, and environmentalists, with government stuck in the middle.[56]

There are two different issues here. The first is knowing whether there are intellectual, ethical and practical reasons for protecting local cultures and consumers from the globalization of consumption patterns. As Ger (p. 122)[57] points out, opening up markets is not necessarily desirable: 'goods can delight or frustrate, cultivate or impoverish, empower or alienate, and nourish or destruct social relations for individual people and contribute to societal, cultural, health and environmental problems'.

The second issue is whether mechanisms resisting globalization actually occur at the individual and/or social level. For this issue, we can see a growing network of loosely associated individuals and groups opposed to 'globalization'. They could be seen rioting at the 1999 WTO summit in Seattle, and since then disrupting subsequent international financial and trade meetings in Washington, Davos, Nice, Bologna, Milan, Florence and Genoa. Activists fall into some-times dissonant categories, including Marxists, environmentalists, trade unionists, anarchists, cultural preservationists, advocates of fair trade, and, more recently, anti-war activists. But not all opposition to globalization is based in identifiable groups. In a recent study, we found that 15 per cent of adult consumers in the USA and 10 per cent in China had a high level of animosity towards global companies, on the basis of their economic power, cultural impact and environmental harm to the consumer's country.

Website link 5.6

Some examples of how McDonald's has reacted to anti-Americanism: http://money.cnn.com/magazines/business2/business2_archive/2002/12/01/333274/index.htm.

Global marketing is often presented as a powerful tool for promoting economic development. As Kearney (p. 64)[58] notes: 'emerging-market countries that are highly globalized (such as Poland, Israel, the Czech Republic and Hungary) exhibit a much more egalitarian distribution of income than emerging-market nations that rank near the bottom of the Globalization Index (such as Russia, China, and Argentina) . . . the general pattern of higher globalization and greater income equality holds for most

countries, both in mature economies and emerging markets'. Thus, global marketing could enhance the needs and desires of badly treated consumers who live in sellers' economies. Marketing could then favour the creation of local industries to produce consumer goods and meet their demands.

However, in a Third World consumer culture the emphasis is on hedonistic conspicuous consumption, even when basic utilitarian needs have not been met.[4] Thus, it is important to emphasize a marketing system that designs, produces and delivers products and services that increase the populations' material welfare without damaging tradition.[59] This clearly means avoiding some of the uglier consequences of globalization, such as the problems caused by Nestlé infant formula in developing countries (see section 14.5). Global consumer culture encourages individuals to interpret their needs exclusively as utilitarian needs for commodities, but people may well have non-utilitarian needs that are more tailored and localized, especially for local cultural products and products whose consumption process is part of the genuine local culture.[60]

In the case of Turkey, most modern packaged goods reach two groups of higher socioeconomic status, representing respectively 1 per cent and 4 per cent of the Turkish population, whereas international products such as Coca-Cola target a larger audience by including the lower-middle class (46 per cent).[61] This has both positive and negative influences on the socioeconomic development. On the positive side there is increased dynamism, optimism, aspirations, communications, employment and demand for education. On the negative side, marketing has accelerated the transmission of a consumption culture to the general population, increasing the desirability of Western products and leading to the purchasing of gadgets and appliances at the expense of the satisfaction of more basic needs.[61]

Preference for national products

In most developed countries, domestic products are more popular than foreign-made products. This strong preference for domestic products has been clear for many countries including Australia, western Europe, the USA and Japan. Conversely, in developing countries national products are less preferred to imported goods, especially when the products are from high-profile competent developed nations. It is important to note that this is not static. There have been changes in the preferences of Hong Kong and Chinese consumers since the handover of Hong Kong from the United Kingdom to China.[62] Consumers in both countries now have a greater preference for their own products than foreign products, including UK-made.

However, many consumers throughout the world have deep-rooted nationalistic feelings that extend to purchasing situations. There are different explanations for this preference for national products, especially in developed countries. For instance, ethnocentrism, patriotism, collectivism, and openness to foreign cultures are all significantly related to a preference for national products.[63] Consumer ethnocentrism, which is defined as beliefs about the appropriateness or morality of buying foreign-made products, has been studied extensively.[64] Ethnocentric consumers are more likely to buy domestic than foreign products.[58,65] Ethnocentrism is also negatively associated with attitudes toward global brands.[66] In addition, some consumers have deep-rooted feelings toward specific countries, because of past events, such as wars or economic histories between countries.[67] Whereas ethnocentrism is related to a tendency not to purchase any foreign products, animosity is related to the tendency not to purchase products from specific countries.

Tapping into nationalism, 'Buy National' campaigns have been used in many countries including the United States, Portugal, Japan, France, Canada, and Mexico, as well as Australia.[68] 'Buy National' campaigns should be used very cautiously as they are affected by country of origin (COO) perceptions, product categories and situations. First, we should consider the possible opposing influences of ethnocentrism and COO perceptions. Attitudes towards foreign products are negatively affected by ethnocentrism and positively affected by COO perceptions.[69] These campaigns are less likely to be effective when other countries' products are seen to have a COO appeal, such as Italian shoes or Swiss watches. The influence of nationalism is likely to differ by product category. It depends on country competencies and capabilities. Second, the influence is also likely to differ by usage situation or context. Ger and colleagues found that coffee type differs by situation in

Turkey, especially when convenience may be a factor (p. 167):

I have Nescafe all the time, all day, when I am studying. Nescafe is more practical, you can easily make it, but it takes time to prepare Turkish coffee. Turkish coffee is usually consumed after the meals. Turkish coffee reminds me of being with friends and chatting together. When you go to a neighbour or a friend, she prepares Turkish coffee and you chat while you drink. I almost always drink it with my mother or my friend. I never drink it alone (Zehra, female, 18).[70]

The effectiveness of 'Buy National' advertising was brought into question when it was found that American consumers' attitudes towards domestic products did not correspond with their purchasing behaviour.[71] Consumers are fairly rational in their product evaluations. Attempts to artificially enhance the relative quality perceptions of locally made products are likely to be ineffective. The best approach is to reinforce nationalistic feelings, and not to attempt to influence consumers in their product evaluation.

5.6   Emergent patterns of mixed local/global consumer behaviour

What emerges from the confrontation of global and local consumption is a complex pattern where the variety of consumption experiences reaches unprecedented levels. Global consumption patterns are reflected in local kaleidoscopes where myriad pieces of coloured glass are constantly rearranged into innumerable pictures.

Positioning the local vis-à-vis the global: patchworks and kaleidoscopes

As Firat (p. 111)[35] rightly observes, 'In an overwhelmingly marketized existence, individuals experience practically all aspects of their lives as consumers'. Whereas consumption was not always highly regarded by modern consumers, the postmodernist consumers pursue, with little thought, the construction of their self-image. Further, Firat (p. 115) states:

Because the postmodern consumer experience is not one of committing to a single way of being, a single form of existence, the same consumers are willing to sample the different, fragmented artifacts. The consumer is ready to have Italian for lunch and Chinese for dinner, to wear Levi's 501 blue jeans for the outdoor party in the afternoon and to try the Gucci suit at night – changing not only diets and clothes but also the personas and selves that are to be (re)represented at each function.[35]

Whether people really change their self-image so quickly may be debatable. However, most consumers assemble diverse consumption items in a very opportunistic, fragmented and idiosyncratic way, not hesitating to mix local products and ways with global products and services. There is high degree of pragmatism in postmodern consumption, in particular because budgetary constraints are still very meaningful. Fordist consumption items have their place in the patchwork: they offer good value and are often shrewdly advertised so that the potentially negative aspects of standard offerings on the consumer's self-image are largely erased. High-touch products and luxury brands play a complementary role, being the shiniest and most colourful squares of the harlequin tights of postmodern consumption. Local products are also present: they make up the bulk of the patchwork with more discreet and less shiny pieces of fabric. As shown by Box 5.5, featuring our favourite example (beer), local products are candidates for promotion at a higher level of image in other countries where they are opportunistically re-interpreted, precisely because their foreignness allows it.

A process of creolization takes place when foreign goods are assigned new meanings and uses by the buyers' culture, even if they are transferred to it without change. For instance, Kragh and Djursaa (p. 1306)[72] observe that 'traditional furniture such as English furniture of the eighteenth century Chippendale and Hepplewhite mould is found in a number of especially elderly Danish homes and kept alive as a cultural expression through the exposure to English upper-class interiors depicted in television series and films'. In this sense one can contrast the creolization paradigm, where attention focuses on the reception and domestication process of global goods in local contexts, to the Cocacolonization paradigm, where emphasis is on uniformity.[73] A good example of such localization of consumption is Disneyland Tokyo, which is a perfect replica of the American model, yet is completely 'Japanized', i.e. fully reinvested by local cultural codes.[74,75]

Central and peripheral consumption contexts

In the emergent consumption patterns, the consumption context is an important aspect of how consumers combine global 'fordist' goods and services,

---

Box 5.5

'European' beers

Typical of the diversity of the European brewing industry is how different brands in their segments are viewed from country to country. Brands which do not have their origin in a country, which are 'foreign', are invariably viewed as premium segment products. A good example of this is BSN's Kronenbourg 1664, which is sold in France as an ordinary segment beer, but is viewed in almost all other (European) markets as a premium product. As an Italian brewer puts it: 'Foreign brands command a premium price for their image of higher quality.' However, potential hazards exist for brewers in pursuing this policy: 'In Great Britain, (Belgian) Stella Artois is a premium beer, one of the most expensive beers you can get there, and people buy it because it is expensive. It is marketed and promoted that way. The British are travelling people, so now when they come to Belgium, they discover that Stella Artois is a cheap beer. So they ask themselves if it is justified to pay so much for it in Great Britain' (French brewing manager).

(Source: Steele, p. 58.[76] *Business of Europe: Managing Change*, Murray Steele, copyright 1991 by permission of Sage Publications Inc. Books in the format Textbook via Copyright Clearance Center.)

high-touch luxury brands and local items. Consumption contexts involve a certain space (i.e. certain rooms in a home), as well as particular time periods and people. A family dinner in a British dining-room or a ski vacation in the French Alps are examples of consumption contexts. Djursaa and Kragh (1998) studied the fragmented nature of globalization by distinguishing central and peripheral consumption contexts, based on in-depth, direct observation for two highly culture-bound product categories: furnishings and food. The consumption contexts of furnishings are Britain and Denmark, and the consumption contexts of food are three Arab cities: Riyadh, Jeddah and Dubai. Centrality for food is defined in terms of time of the day when a meal is consumed whereas centrality in the case of furnishings is defined in spatial terms as the room where traditional cultural values are respected because this room carries a strong culture-bound meaning. British informants clearly express the dining-room as a central consumption context and, when presented with modernist furniture for dining-rooms, indicate that:

they were pleasant enough and would be OK for kitchens or breakfast rooms, but not for 'proper' dining rooms, which for the majority of English respondents clearly had to be traditional to carry the proper cultural message of identity. In Denmark, by contrast, modernism is the cultural norm and carries our notions of identity perfectly adequately, in central rooms as well as in main homes (p. 28).[77]

In peripheral consumption contexts it is easier for a consumer to innovate by borrowing from foreign cultural contexts. Informants from the three Arab cities note that dinner, a peripheral meal, is increasingly taken in fast-food outlets, unlike their lunch, which for Arabs is the 'central' meal. A common pattern for Emiris is to go out for dinner at Pizza Hut, McDonald's or Harvey's, which have compartments for male and female members of the family to eat together, separated from other guests. In the case of dinner taken at home, 'global products also play a very significant part in the meal; as one respondent said, "Dinner is pizza and Pepsi"' (p. 30).[77]

Kaleidoscopic borrowing and the assemblage of local and global items is only possible if marketers are flexible enough to introduce some adaptations to their offerings, ignoring the Levittian criticism

of adjustment to local ways.[5] For instance, when McDonald's in Egypt suffered an anti-American boycott for its support of Israel in 2001, the company introduced the McFalafel, promoted by the singer of the hit *I Hate Israel* by Sha'ban Abdel Rahim.[78] Since then, McDonald's has been proactive about incorporating local tastes into the standard menu.

Global marketers should first target peripheral consumption contexts to successfully introduce foreign products that are not grounded in the local culture. In China, McDonald's is appropriate for a date, but not for a celebration.[79] McDonald's is not appropriate for a celebration because the prices and seating arrangements are standardized and offer no opportunity to make a special display of face to the guest of honour. Conversely, it is the standardized offering that makes it more appropriate for a date, as the man does not need to worry about the lavishness of a meal.

Borrowing can also be progressive: McDonald's has started in many countries without being open at breakfast time, as it is in most Western countries. It is now introducing breakfast offerings worldwide, which brings – from a fordist perspective – increased efficiency in terms of covering overhead costs by prolonging demand patterns over 14 or more hours. McDonald's and other fast-food outlets have succeeded in extending fordist consumption throughout the world because they have been pragmatically adaptive, partly tailoring their offering to local habits.

Complexity and ambivalence in globalized consumption patterns

Consumers search for and create meaning because they need constantly to re-build their self-image. For this reason, their search for identity through consumption must be a key concern for marketers. In a globalized world, identity-seeking consumers can pick up products from two different shelves: one that favours the locality and the ingroup orientation and another that displays desirable values, meanings and signs offered by foreign, outgroup cultures. How consumers combine local and global meanings is complex. There is much ambivalence in the search for identity in a radically modern world where local diversity based on linguistic and religious differences will not disappear for centuries.

Globalized consumption has a threefold pattern. The first component is based on modernity and on fordist consumption; it corresponds to low-cost/fair-quality, weakly differentiated, utilitarian products, embedded in fairly low-context consumption experiences. Its highest potential for success is reached when products and consumption experiences are culture-free, or consumption contexts are peripheral. Examples range from the film *Titanic* to Camay soap. Families, because they often face stricter budgetary constraints than singles, are likely to be adept in modern fordist consumption. Despite appearances and discourse, fordist marketers show major adaptations and flexibility in facing local consumption. They display much more sensitivity to local ways than is described in textbooks, and their success is more pragmatic than ideological. The second element is a postmodernist type of consumption: fragmented, continually re-assembled and re-interpreted. This can be particularly true for big brands, conspicuous consumption, younger people and yuppies. The third element corresponds to people who are aware that consumption is now a key driver for culture and that their choices as consumers will influence their culture. This radically modern type of person behaves both opportunistically and critically, with a willingness to display diversity in consumption.[30] For these consumers McDonald's is an ethnic, American restaurant.

In concluding this chapter, it may be wondered why companies should try to ignore local diversity. Rather than being a liability, it can also act as a superb opportunity for building competitive advantages based on differentiation, which are easier to defend against competitors than low-cost advantages.

Questions

1. Take mineral water as a product example and outline how 'global' mineral waters such as Perrier or Evian can coexist with quite local ones.

2. Is there a 'modern' lifestyle, common to many cultures around the world? How could it be described? What could be its principal raisons d'être?

3. 'Dating' is a very curious concept for many people. In any case it cannot be fully translated into many languages and simply means 'making an appointment'. Compare what dating means to Americans with what it means in other cultures, demonstrating how the complex process of finding a partner for life can be commercialized in different contexts.

4. List some arguments and evidence that may show that globalization of consumption and lifestyles is under way. Outline the limitations and discuss the counterarguments.

5. To what extent are 'modern culture' and individualism primary inputs in the process of globalization of consumer preferences and lifestyles?

6. Discuss to what extent 'Buy National' advertising campaigns are effective. What can they achieve? What can they not achieve?

7. The FDA (US Food and Drug Administration) prohibits the import of traditionally prepared French foie gras. FDA inspectors visit French foie gras laboratories and refuse most of them the right to export to the United States since hygiene standards are not met. For the French too much antiseptic would kill the taste and for the Americans such unpasteurized products are dangerous to one's health. Discuss the difference in understanding of what 'good food' is.

8. Compare a global film (e.g. *Spiderman* or *Lord of the Rings* or *Titanic*) and a local film on a number of aspects: story, characters, situations, atmosphere, key appeals for the viewer (action, love, violence, etc.), combination of music and sound, rhythm, type of ending, etc.

Explain why local films are most often not good candidates for reaching a global audience.

References

1. Warnaby, Gary (1999), 'Strategic Consequences of Retail Acquisition: Ikea and Habitat', *International Marketing Review*, 16 (4/5), 406–16.
2. Bell, David and Gill Valentine (1997), *Consuming Geographies*. London: Routledge.
3. Ricardo, David (1817), 'On the Principles of Political Economy and Taxation', in *Bounties on Exportation and Prohibitions on Importation*, Piero Sraffa, Ed. (1951 edn). Cambridge: Cambridge University Press.
4. Ger, Güliz and Russel W. Belk (1996), 'I'd Like to Buy the World a Coke: Consumptionscapes of the "Less Affluent World"', *Journal of Consumer Policy*, 19 (3), 271–305.
5. Levitt, Theodore (1983), 'The Globalization of Markets', *Harvard Business Review*, 61 (May–June), 92–102.
6. Aulakh, Preet S. and Michael G. Schlechter (2000), *Rethinking Globalization(s): From Corporate Transnationalism to Local Interventions*. New York: St Martin's Press.
7. Kopytoff, Igor (1986), 'The Cultural Biography of Things: Commoditization as Process', in *The Social Life of Things, Commodities in Cultural Perspective*, Arjun Appadurai, Ed. Cambridge: Cambridge University Press.
8. *Collins English Dictionary* (2003), 6th Edn. London: Collins.
9. Daft, Douglas N. (2000), 'Connecting with Global Consumers', *Executive Excellence*, 17 (10), 11–12.
10. Hofstede, Geert (1991), *Cultures and Organizations: Software of the Mind*. Maidenhead: McGraw-Hill.
11. Lovelock, Christopher and Jochen Wirtz (2007), *Services Marketing: People, Technology, Strategy* (6th edn). Upper Saddle River, NJ: Prentice Hall.
12. Spar, Deborah L. (1997), 'Lawyers Abroad: The Internationalization of Legal Practice', *California Management Review*, 39 (3), 8–28.
13. Euromonitor (1997), 'Market Report Japan: Savoury Snacks', *Market Research International*, XXXVIII (December), 111–13.
14. Smith, David E. and Hans Stubbe Solgaard (2000), 'The Dynamics of Shifts in European Alcoholic Drinks Consumption', *Journal of International Consumer Marketing*, 12 (3), 85–109.
15. Clements, Kenneth W. and Dongling Chen (1996), 'Fundamental Similarities in Consumer Behaviour', *Applied Economics*, 28 (6), 747–57.
16. De Mooij, Marieke and Geert Hofstede (2002), 'Convergence and Divergence in Consumer Behavior: Implications for International Retailing', *Journal of Retailing*, 78 (1), 61–69.
17. De Mooij, Marieke (2001), 'Convergence–Divergence', Unpublished doctoral dissertation, Universidad de Navarra.
18. De Mooij, Marieke (1998), 'Masculinity/Femininity and Consumer Behavior', in *Masculinity and Femininity: The Taboo Dimension of National Cultures*, Geert Hofstede, Ed. Thousand Oaks, CA: Sage.
19. Eshghi, Abdolezra and Jagdish N. Sheth (1985), 'The Globalization of Consumption Patterns: An Empirical Investigation', in *Global Perspectives in Marketing*, Erdener Kaynak, Ed. New York: Praeger.
20. Huszagh, Sandra M., Richard J. Fox, and Ellen Day (1986), 'Global Marketing: An Empirical Investigation', *Columbia Journal of World Business*, XX (4), 31–43.
21. Agarwal, Sanjeev and R. Kenneth Teas (2002), 'Cross-National Applicability of a Perceived Quality Model', *The Journal of Product and Brand Management*, 11 (4/5), 213–36.
22. Dawar, Niraj and Philip M. Parker (1994), 'Marketing Universals: Consumers' Use of Brand Name, Price, Physical Appearance, and Retailer Reputation as Signals of Product Quality', *Journal of Marketing*, 58 (2), 81–95.
23. Zaichkowsky, Judith L. and James H. Sood (1988), 'A Global Look at Consumer Involvement and Use of Products', *International Marketing Review*, 6 (1), 20–33.
24. Nicholls, J.A.F. and Sychey Roslow (1999), 'Oceans Apart: The Influence of Situational Factor in Grenada and Cyprus', *Journal of International Consumer Marketing*, 12 (1), 57–72.
25. Woods, Walter A., Emmanuel J. Chéron, and Dong Han Kim (1985), 'Strategic Implications of Differences in Consumer Purposes in Three Global Markets', in *Global Perspectives in Marketing*, Erdener Kaynak, Ed. New York: Praeger.
26. Jain, Subhash C. (1989), 'Standardization of International Marketing Strategy: Some Research Hypotheses', *Journal of Marketing*, 53 (January), 70–79.
27. Belk, Russel W. (1988), 'Third World Consumer Culture', in *Marketing and Development: Toward Broader Dimensions*, E. Kumçu and Fuat Firat A., Eds. Greenwich, CT: JAI Press.
28. Prahalad, C.K. and K. Lieberthal (1998), 'The End of Corporate Imperialism', *Harvard Business Review* (July–August), 70–79.
29. Ritzer, George (1999), 'Contemporary Urban Japan: A Sociology of Consumption/the Sociology of Consumption: An Introduction/Golden Arches East: Mcdonald's in East Asia', *Contemporary Sociology*, 28 (1), 68–70.
30. Ritzer, George (1993), *The Mcdonaldization of Society*. Newbury Park, CA: Pine Forge Press.
31. Anderson, Patricia M. and Xiahong He (1999), 'Culture and Fast-Food Marketing Mix in the People's Republic of China and the USA: Implications for

Research and Marketing', *Journal of International Consumer Marketing*, 11 (1), 77–95.

32. Sheth, Jagdish N. and S. Prakash Sethi (1977), *A Theory of Cross-Cultural Buyer Behavior*. New York: North Holland Publishing.

33. Bouchet, Dominique (1994), 'Rails without Ties: The Social Imaginary and Postmodern Culture: Can Post-Modern Consumption Replace Modern Questioning?', *International Journal of Research in Marketing*, 11 (4), 405–22.

34. Auger, Pat, Timothy M. Devinney, and Jordan J. Louviere (2007), 'Using Best–Worst Scaling Methodology to Investigate Consumer Ethical Beliefs across Countries', *Journal of Business Ethics*, 70 (3), 299–326.

35. Firat, A. Fuat (1995), 'Consumer Culture or Culture Consumed?', in *Marketing in a Multicultural World*, Janeen Arnold Costa and Gary J. Bamossy, Eds. Thousand Oaks, CA: Sage.

36. McCracken, Grant (1986), 'Culture and Consumption: A Theoretical Account of the Structure and Movement of the Cultural Meaning of Consumer Goods', *Journal of Consumer Research*, 13 (June), 71–84.

37. Applbaum, Kalman and Ingrid Jordt (1996), 'Notes toward an Application of Mccracken's "Cultural Categories" for Cross-Cultural Consumer Research', *Journal of Consumer Research*, 23 (December), 204–18.

38. Doran, Kathleen Brewer (1997), 'Symbolic Consumption in China: The Colour Television as a Life Statement', in *Advances in Consumer Research*, Merrie Brucks and Debbie McInnis, Eds. Vol. 24. Provo, UT: Association for Consumer Research.

39. Bagozzi, Richard P., Nancy Wong, Shuzo Abe, and Massimo Bergami (2000), 'Cultural and Situational Contingencies and the Theory of Reasoned Action: Application to Fast Food Restaurant Consumption', *Journal of Consumer Psychology*, 9 (2), 97–106.

40. Han, Sang-Pil and Sharon Shavitt (1994), 'Persuasion and Culture: Advertising Appeals in Individualistic and Collectivistic Societies', *Journal of Experimental Social Psychology*, 30, 326–50.

41. Lee, Julie Anne (2000), 'Adapting Triandis's Model of Subjective Culture and Social Behaviour Relations to Consumer Behavior', *Journal of Consumer Psychology*, 9 (2), 117–26.

42. Wong, Nancy and Aaron Ahuvia (1995), 'From Tofu to Caviar: Conspicuous Consumption, Materialism and Self-Concepts in East-Asian and Western Cultures', in *Proceedings of the Second Conference on the Cultural Dimension of International Marketing*. Odense, 68–89.

43. Peterson Blyth Cato & Associates and Cheskin & Masten (1985), *Survey on Global Brands and Global Marketing*, New York.

44. Mick, David Glen (2008), 'Degrees of Freedom of Will: An Essential Endless Question in Consumer Behavior', *Journal of Consumer Psychology*, 18 (1), 17–21.

45. Geertz, Clifford (1983), *Local Knowledge*. New York: Basic Books.

46. Gephart, Werner (1990), 'Nature–Environment', in *Au Jardin des Malentendus, le Commerce Franco-Allemand des Idées*, Jacques Leenhardt and Robert Picht, Eds. Arles: Actes Sud.

47. Triandis, Harry (1994), *Culture and Social Behavior*. New York: McGraw Hill.

48. Vrontis, Demetris and Claudio Vignali (1999), 'Bass Plc, an Assessment, Evaluation and Recommendations for Their Strategic Approach in Entering Foreign Beer Markets', *International Marketing Review*, 16 (4/5), 391–405.

49. Holt, Douglas B., John A. Quelch, and Earl L. Taylor (2004), 'How Global Brands Compete', *Harvard Business Review*, 82 (9), 68–75.

50. Levy, Orly, Schon Beechler, Sully Taylor, and Nakiye A. Boyacigiller (2007), 'What We Talk About When We Talk About "Global Mindset": Managerial Cognition in Multinational Corporations', *Journal of International Business Studies*, 38 (2), 231–58.

51. Cannon, Hugh M. and Attila Yaprak (2002), 'Will the Real-World Citizen Please Stand-Up! The Many Faces of Cosmopolitan Consumer Behavior', *Journal of International Marketing*, 10 (4), 30–52.

52. Aaker, Jennifer, Veronica Benet-Martínez, and Jordi Garolera (2001), 'Consumption Symbols as Carriers of Culture: A Study of Japanese and Spanish Brand Personality Constructs', *Journal of Personality and Social Psychology*, 81 (3), 492–508.

53. Sung, Yongjun and Spencer F. Tinkham (2005), 'Brand Personality Structures in the United States and Korea: Common and Culture-Specific Factors', *Journal of Consumer Psychology*, 15 (4), 334–50.

54. Dolbeck, Andrew (2002), 'A Quick Taste of the Fast Food Industry', *Weekly Corporate Growth Report*, November, 11.

55. Steenkamp, Jan-Benedict E.M., Rajeev Batra, and Dana L. Alden (2003), 'How Perceived Brand Globalness Creates Brand Value', *Journal of International Business Studies*, 34 (1), 53–65.

56. Rodrik, Dani (1997), 'Has Globalization Gone Too Far?', *California Management Review*, 39 (3), 29–53.

57. Ger, Güliz (1997), 'Human Development and Humane Consumption: Well-Being Beyond the "Good Life"', *Journal of Public Policy & Marketing*, 16 (1), 110–25.

58. Klein, Jill Gabrielle, Richard Ettenson, and Balaji C. Krishnan (2006), 'Extending the Construct of Consumer Ethnocentrism: When Foreign Products Are Preferred', *International Marketing Review*, 23 (3), 304–21.

59. Dholakia, Ruby Roy, Mohammed Sharif, and Labdhi Bhandari (1988), 'Consumption in the Third World: Challenges for Marketing and Economic Development', in *Marketing and Development: Toward Broader Dimensions*, E. Kumçu and A. Fuat Firat, Eds. Greenwich CT: JAI Press.

60. Sherry, John F. (1987), 'Cultural Propriety in a Global Marketplace', in *Philosophical and Radical Thought in Marketing*, A. Fuat Firat and Nikhilesh Dholakhia and Richard P. Bagozzi, Eds. Lexington, MA: Lexington Books.

61. Ger, Güliz (1992), 'The Positive and Negative Effects of Marketing on Socioeconomic Development', *Journal of Consumer Policy*, 15, 229–54.

62. Yu, Julie H. and Gerald Albaum (2002), 'Sovereignty Change Influences on Consumer Ethnocentrism and Product Preferences: Hong Kong Revisited One Year Later', *Journal of Business Research*, 55 (11), 891.

63. Sharma, Subbash, Terence A. Shimp, and Jeonghsin Shin (1995), 'Consumer Ethnocentrism: A Test of Antecedents and Moderators', *Academy of Marketing Science Journal*, 23 (1), 26–38.

64. Shimp, Terence A. and Subbash Sharma (1987), 'Consumer Ethnocentrism: Construction and Validation of the Cetscale', *Journal of Marketing Research*, 26 (August), 280–89.

65. Yang, Zhilin, Nan Zhou, and Jie Chen (2005), 'Brand Choice of Older Chinese Consumer', *Journal of International Consumer Marketing*, 17 (4), 65–81.

66. Alden, Dana L., Jan-Benedict E.M. Steenkamp, and Rajeev Batra (2006), 'Consumer Attitudes toward Marketplace Globalization: Structure, Antecedents and Consequences', *International Journal of Research in Marketing*, 23 (3), 227–39.

67. Klein, Jill Gabrielle, Richard Ettenson, and Marlene D. Morris (1998), 'The Animosity Model of Foreign Product Purchase: An Empirical Test in the People's Republic of China', *Journal of Marketing*, 62 (1), 89–100.

68. Granzin, Kent L. and John J. Painter (2001), 'Motivational Influences on "Buy Domestic" Purchasing: Marketing Management Implications from a Study of Two Nations', *Journal of International Marketing*, 9 (2), 73–96.

69. Moon, Byeong Joon and Subhash C. Jain (2001), 'Consumer Processing of International Advertising: The Roles of Country of Origin and Consumer Ethnocentrism', *Journal of International Consumer Marketing*, 14 (1), 89–109.

70. Ger, Güliz, Søren Askegaard, and Ania Christensen (1999), 'Experiential Nature of Product-Place Images: Image as a Narrative', *Advances in Consumer Research*, 26, 165–69.

71. Ettenson, Richard, Janet Wagner, and Gary Gaeth (1988), 'Evaluating the Effect of Country-of-Origin and the "Made in the USA" Campaign: A Conjoint Approach', *Journal of Retailing*, 64 (1), 85–100.

72. Kragh, Simon Ulrik and Malene Djursaa (2001), 'Product Syntax and Cross-Cultural Marketing Strategies', *European Journal of Marketing*, 35 (11/12), 1301–21.

73. Howes, David (1996), 'Commodities and Cultural Borders', in *Cross-cultural Consumption*, David Howes, Ed. Vol. 1–18. London: Routledge.

74. Brannen, Mary Yoko (1992), '"Bwana Mickey": Constructing Cultural Consumption at Tokyo Disneyland', in *Re-Made in Japan*, Joseph J. Tobin, Ed. New Haven, CT: Yale University Press.

75. Van Maanen, John and André Laurent (1992), 'The Flow of Culture: Some Notes on Globalization and the Multinational Corporation', in *Organization Theory and the Multinational Corporation*, S. Ghoshal and D.E. Westney, Eds. New York: St Martin Press.

76. Steele, Murray (1991), 'European Brewing Industry', in *The Business of Europe*, Roland Calori and Peter Lawrence, Eds. London: Sage.

77. Djursaa, Malene and Simon Ulrik Kragh (1998), 'Central and Peripheral Consumption Contexts: The Uneven Globalization of Consumer Behaviour', *International Business Review*, 7 (1), 23–38.

78. Dabbous, Dalia (2001), 'Sing a Song of Conflict', *Cairo Times*, 5 (20), 19–25.

79. Eckhardt, Giana M. and Michael J. Houston (2002), 'Cultural Paradoxes Reflected in Brand Meaning: Mcdonald's in Shanghai, China', *Journal of International Marketing*, 10 (2), 68–82.

Appendix 5

Teaching materials

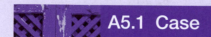

A5.1 Case

Setting the stage – Disneyland Resort Paris

Disney is the biggest entertainment company in the world with a market value of US$38 billion, and one of the oldest, continuously operating since 1923. Today it comprises filmed entertainment businesses, major media networks, publishing, theme parks, resorts, a cruise-line, real estate, and consumer products. Disney's first international park opened in Tokyo, Japan in 1983. Tokyo Disneyland opened with a flourish and continued to do well until the softening of Japan's economy in the 1990s, from which it has yet to recover. In an effort to boost attendance, the older male-oriented Tokyo DisneySea Park opened in 2001.[1] Hong Kong Disneyland opened in 2005 – about the time that Universal Studios opened China's first world-standard theme park in Shanghai.[2] There has been criticism of value-for-money at Disney parks, which total 10 worldwide, with an average admission fee of US$50. The company recently spent US$5 billion to address this concern and to build new rides and attractions to bolster falling attendance at the parks. The parks account for US$1.2 billion in operating income, which is 41 per cent of Disney's total – a significant business unit for the company.[3]

After their initial success with the Japanese park in the mid 1980s, Disney entered into negotiations with the Spanish and French governments. The French bid 'won' by enticing Disney with tax breaks, loans, and below-cost land. Disney was determined to profit more from the Paris park than it did in Tokyo, where a local operator, Oriental Land, took most of the initial risk and currently takes most of the profits. Therefore, the company staked a 39 per cent ownership in EuroDisney to operate the park, and to receive 10 per cent of admission fees, 5 per cent of food and merchandise sales, and 49 per cent of the profits.

EuroDisneyland opened in April 1992 to a host of problems, which were to continue until Disney loosened corporate constraints to fit the desires of local and European visitors. Disney's admissions and pricing policies were in the 'premium' bracket, even higher than US parks. At first, spending per visitor was half that of Japan, and hotel occupancy rates were 37 per cent.[4] French intellectuals and artists had criticized the park since its embryonic planning stages.[5] Notably, theatre director Ariane Mnouchkine coined the term 'Cultural Chernobyl' in the early 1990s, an enduring sobriquet applied to the park and other Disney ventures even today.[6] Cries of cultural imperialism were heard from the intelligentsia, the media, and farmers who protested against the expropriation of agricultural land by the government for the park. However, the French had enjoyed Disney cartoons for more than 60 years, and some supporters of the project were very enthusiastic, such as film-star/singer Yves Montand who declared: 'T-shirts, jeans, hamburgers – nobody imposes these things on us. We like them'.[7]

It's a small world – or is it?

The EuroDisney park lost US$515 million during its first year.[3] In the early days of EuroDisney, the management structure was rigid and little provision was made for local or employee participation, the prevailing Disney attitude formed by their self-ascribed infallible experience.[7] Many American managers in Paris were unaware of the many local and Asian adaptations made in Tokyo, and accepted at face value the relatively short psychic and cultural distance between the United States and France as signifying that the two cultures were similar.[8] Therefore, Disney implemented the same amusements, policies and plans in France as in the United States with some architectural changes due to the cooler weather.[9] In response to local criticism, Disney took steps to 'Europeanize' the park by adding a Discoveryland based on the writings of nineteenth-century French author Jules Verne, and by emphasizing characters of European origin such as Pinocchio (Italian), Cinderella (French) and Peter Pan (British). French managers were recruited as the issues became increasingly critical, such as the disputes with French employees, who being rather individualistic resented strict codes of conduct and dress. After a series of adaptations to the local and European markets, Disneyland Paris first became profitable in 1995, going on to become the 'number one tourist destination in Europe' in 2001, with 12.3 million visitors. Disneyland Paris follows the Tokyo parks, Anaheim, California and Orlando, Florida, to rank fifth in terms of attendance per year.[10] French visitors currently make up 40 per cent of the park's total, while 18 per cent come from the United Kingdom, 8 per cent from Germany, 8 per cent from Belgium, 8 per cent from the Netherlands and Luxembourg, 8 per cent from Spain and Italy, and 10 per cent from other countries.

There are seven on-site themed hotels with occupancy averaging 86 per cent in 2001, and about 22 others in the local area. Disneyland Paris concluded joint ventures for the construction of the three hotels that opened in Spring 2003. The hotel partners are Airtours UK Leisure Group (tour operator), Holiday Inn, and the French hospitality group Envergure. These hotels will add 1100 more rooms to the 5800-room capacity currently within the resort's seven Disney hotels. The design and décor of the new hotels draws its inspiration from the many château of the local region.

Learning from mistakes

As EuroDisney's CEO Jay Rasulo admitted, 'We had not yet had an on-the-ground experience in a multicultural environment. It was really the first park that had the majority of its guests coming from very diverse cultural backgrounds.' After near-catastrophic losses, Disney was quick to respond to customers' demands. The company reversed its ban on alcoholic beverages, adding wine to the menu. It developed more table-service restaurants, of which two employ chefs with 'Meilleur Ouvrier de France' status. Restaurants open earlier in the evening for early-bird German guests, and stay open later for Spanish night owls. Disneyland Paris is now working closely with French and European tour operators, travel agents, and transport operators who were formerly disregarded.[11] The company has forged better relations with the local and national government, to the point where it is Mickey Mouse who concludes the French national tourism advertisement with the declaration, 'J'aime la France!' The resort still needs to exercise great care in setting its prices, because continental Europeans with six weeks' paid holidays per year are necessarily more thrifty on holiday expenditures than Americans with their two-week often unpaid holidays. Europeans therefore have less to spend at the park than Disney would like. As Milhomme (p. 94)[12] emphasizes: 'In short the theme park is a short duration recreational means, with a high density spending pattern at the opposite of the recreational European pattern which aims at long duration recreational means with low density spending pattern.'

Act two: Disney Studios

Disney Studios opened in March 2001, after a three-month 'soft opening' to test the reactions of visitors. The park is divided into four areas: the Front Lot, Animation Courtyard, Production Courtyard and Back Lot, the whole comprising ten attractions. Front Lot includes a studio mock-up, complemented by film props, a restaurant and boutiques. Animation Courtyard offers visitors the chance to learn about animation, while 'Animagique' showcases clips from Disney films, and 'Aladdin' is the backdrop for a magic carpet ride. Production Courtyard is the home of the Disney Channel and allows visitors a backstage glimpse of production through the Studio Tram Tour, while Catastrophe Canyon puts visitors through an imaginary film shoot. Back Lot includes notably the Rock 'n' Roller Coaster Starring Aerosmith and the Stunt Show Spectacular featuring Rémy Julienne. Visible efforts were made to adapt the primarily American material to local and European tastes. In the Tram tour, for instance, the following actors lend their voices to the eight languages used during narration: Jeremy Irons (English), Irène Jacob (French), Isabella Rossellini (Italian), Inès Sastre (Spanish), Famke Janssen (Dutch) and Nastassja Kinski (German). An effort was made in the décor and content to include European references, for instance to the French classics *Les Enfants du Paradis* and *Les Parapluies de Cherbourg*.

Aims of the new park

Disney Studios expected to attract guests from further away, such as Scandinavia and Spain, more likely to consider the distance travelled as offset by the increased benefits. According to EuroDisney Chairperson Jay Rasulo, the Studios should increase visitor counts to 17 million yearly, up 36 per cent from 12.3 million in 2001. The park should increase the average length of stay per visitor from today's 2.4 days to 3.4, and increase return visits from 41.5 per cent.[13] The visitors attending the opening of Disney Studios could observe the improvements implemented over the past decade, including the expansion of Disney Village, and the dedicated rail station (with RER and TGV trains) bringing Paris within 20 minutes and Belgium or the United Kingdom within less than three hours. Within the immediate vicinity is an outlet mall that is open seven days per week. Disney Studios was not designed to deal with the SARS epidemic, the Iraq conflict, fears of terrorism, a disastrous summer heat wave, massive strikes and destructive forest fires, all of which increased cancellations and prompted holidaymakers to go elsewhere.[14]

Financial matters: some day my prince will come . . .

EuroDisney is still plagued with troubles. In September 2003, *The Times* reported that the park was asking one of its major investors, Saudi prince Alwaleed bin Talal, for a refinancing deal. Due to low park admissions, the company was expecting to have difficulty meeting its debt payments in 2004.[15] Walt Disney Studios reportedly cost the company US$600 million. The company reported a profit of 30.5 million for the financial year ending September 2001, 20 per cent less than the previous year.[11] Stock analysts do not appear to be interested in Disney stock. Contributing factors include a debt load that is two times equity at US$13 billion,[3] and a stock price of about €1 – one-tenth of its value a decade ago.[16] There are concerns that a debt-loaded park that is managing approximately 50 per cent more capacity in a time of slowing economies and a fast-growing theme park sector may be putting itself in danger.[16] The average visitor spends $43 per day at Disneyland Paris, which is 20 per cent lower than the figures for Orlando or Anaheim. This figure is worrying, given that theme parks make their profits from their hotels and merchandise.[16] In addition, France began in 2001 to see a slowdown in GDP growth (down to 1.9 per cent that year), caused by a climate of uncertainty and softer global economic conditions that slowed exports. At home, this has translated into higher unemployment (up to 9.8 per cent in 2002), lower inventory levels, and a lower level of business confidence.[17] Although analysts are concerned with the park's launch during an economic downturn, some point out that as an accessible, full-service, short-break destination, Disney Studios could even benefit from a softer economy.[16]

Marketing the Studios

A massive campaign for Disney Studios started in December 2001 with the slogan 'Come and live the magic of cinema'. Advertising agency Publicis focused on television, print, billboard and online advertising. The ads were rolled out in the United Kingdom, Germany, France, Belgium, the Netherlands, Spain and Italy, and were designed to differentiate the new park from the resort, which was accordingly renamed 'Disneyland Resort Paris'. According to Disneyland Paris central marketing director, Christian Darquier, Disney Studios is positioned as 'a journey behind the screen to understand how the magic of movies, television, and animation is made' whereas the resort was 'designed to make guests live out the stories behind Disney entertainment'. In an unusual move, Disney used direct marketing in the United Kingdom and the Netherlands.[18] The Disney Channel, with its headquarters within Disney Studios, is working to raise awareness of the park, just as the channel successfully did for the resort in the 1990s.

Not everybody loves Disney Studios

Disney Studios has drawn criticism from visitors who claim that the ten attractions are not enough to keep a family entertained for one half day. Other criticisms stemmed from the three rides cloned from Walt Disney World, as well as the 'tame' nature of some of the other rides.[19] Other journalists refer to the new park as 'dull', and boring for children.[16] In addition, there is continuing wider criticism of 'Hollywood' and American culture by French intellectuals and the media. A new wave of concern is sweeping France regarding American imperialism, cultural or otherwise, at a time when geopolitical considerations have focused scrutiny on the global actions of the United States. Anti-globalization activist José Bové, who went from destroying a McDonald's restaurant in the south of France to global fame as a leader of the 'altermondialiste' movement, considers himself a spokesperson for France's ambivalent attitude towards globalization. Even for those within the globalization camp, France and the United States have had several rancorous disputes over trade and foreign policy, most recently over Iraq. On a smaller scale, a journalist voiced his concern for the impacts of a tour operator's decision to change from 'Paris and the Chateaux de la Loire' to 'Paris and Disneyland'.[20] Placed within the framework of more quantitative terms, however, according to an international comparative study, the French give the United States the lowest ratings in Europe. Other nations whose citizens have flocked to the park in the past have been equally alienated by the policies of the US government.[21] This may give cause for concern that the Disney complex continues to operate in a culturally sensitive environment.

Competing with a better mousetrap

There is stiff competition among amusement/theme parks throughout Europe, of which France has its share. Parc Astérix, located 30 minutes away in Plailly, offers a unique blend of humour, thrills, history, and French and European culture. Parc Astérix has doubled its attendance, from 950,000 in 1992 to 2 million in less than a decade.[22] Two Astérix films and the release of a new Astérix album have fuelled the enduring popularity of the character in Europe, to the likely benefit of the park. The identification of Astérix as a plucky Gallic villager, standing up to the evils of empire may even inspire goodwill towards the park in times of complex international politics. Planète Futuroscope, a unique park in Poitiers, is an intense audiovisual and amusement experience themed on high technology run by a former EuroDisney executive. Three other large regional parks opened in 2003.[23] The French company Vivendi-Universal owns Universal Mediterranea, two clustered theme parks near Barcelona, Spain. The new water-themed park, Costa Caribe, boasts a new ride that attracted 1.5 million new visitors within its first four months.[13] The addition of the new park and two new hotels are part of a positioning as 'the most complete family resort in Europe'[24] thereby bringing the park into more direct competition with Disneyland Resort Paris.[16] Paramount Parks owns Terra Mitica, a history- and mythology-themed park near Benidorm, Spain. There are two Warner Bros. Movie World parks featuring Looney Tunes and superheroes like Batman – one in Madrid, Spain and the other near Bottrop-Kirchhellen, Germany. There are two European Six Flags parks, located at Flevo, Netherlands and Wavre, Belgium. Growing competition may not be a threat in itself, however, because it is likely that tougher competition in Europe may benefit Disney in the long term, by habituating Europeans to Disney-style parks.

All company-specific information and additional information can be found at the Disneyland Resort Paris corporate website: **http://www.Disneylandparis.com/uk.**

Questions

1. More than a decade later, has Disney's top management completely addressed the lack of cultural sensitivity observed at the opening of the first park in 1992?

2. Comment in more detail on the issue of holiday regulations in Europe, the United States and Japan (duration, paid versus unpaid holiday) and their impact on leisure consumption.

3. How will changing geopolitical situations affect park attendance? What can be the repercussions of a US-led conflict in the Middle or Far East?

4. Based on the case study, use cultural factors to explain why visitors from Germany make up only 8 per cent of total Disneyland Resort Paris visitors. Do you think that Disney Studios will attract more Germans than the other park? What steps could management take in order to increase the German share of the market?

5. Do you consider that the company made a wise decision in incurring debt to develop Disney Studios? Given the state of the economy, the need to continually spend on new attractions, and the rapid rate of development for other competing theme parks in Europe, do you believe this investment is justified in the long term?

Saskia Faulk and Jean-Claude Usunier prepared this case solely to provide material for class discussion. The authors do not intend to illustrate either effective or ineffective handling of a business situation. The authors may have disguised certain names and other identifying information to protect confidentiality.

(©IRM, reprinted with kind permission.)

A5.2 Case

Papa Ingvar's worries

Who can successfully market products around the world with names like 'snuttig', 'droppen', 'grimo', 'moren', 'jerker', 'mård' or 'slugis'? IKEA, the world's biggest home furnishings retail chain can use names that break some 'rules' of branding, and make a healthy profit out of it. Quirky and identifiably Swedish, the names mirror the company's image.

Small-town entrepreneur Ingvar Kamprad founded IKEA as a furniture mail-order company in Almhult, Sweden, in 1943. Since then, IKEA has expanded far from its pastoral headquarters to worldwide sales of €11.3 billion[25] from 175 outlets in 32 countries and territories.[26] IKEA is now one of the world's largest family-owned companies. Although well past retirement age, Kamprad remains active in the business, reportedly travelling to IKEA stores by economy class and public transport, in order to listen to the concerns of ordinary people – and to save a little money. His three sons have worked at the company.[27] Since 1997, revenues have grown at a rate of 20 per cent and a new IKEA store is opened, on average, each month.[28] Today, IKEA operates retail stores in countries as diverse as Austria, Australia, Canary Islands, France, Hungary, Iceland, Israel, Malaysia, Russia and Saudi Arabia, with 31 outlets in Germany, and 16 in the United States.

At the insistence of founder Kamprad, IKEA expanded rapidly without adapting its core concept to local conditions. Starting in the early 1960s, IKEA took a foothold in Sweden, then Denmark. In 1973, the company took its high-design, good quality, reasonably priced goods throughout Europe and Australasia. Today, four out of IKEA's top five markets are in Europe, the fifth is the USA. Although IKEA has concentrated on company-owned, larger scale outlets, franchising has been used in 14 countries and all stores operate on a franchising basis, regardless of ownership.

During 2003, store openings were scheduled in Germany, Australia, Hungary and Spain. Since 2000, three IKEA stores have opened in Moscow, as well as two in St Petersburg, and nine more in other Russian cities. In France, growth has been particularly impressive with a total of 23 stores since 1983 with six in the Paris region. IKEA has opened 16 stores in Germany since 2000 to total 43 German stores. In 1974, the North American expansion began; a venture that continues with plans to open 50 stores in the USA by 2013. Out of a total of 33 US stores, 23 have opened since 2000. There are now six Chinese IKEA stores and four in Japan. Recent expansion in the Asia-Pacific region is projected to continue at a significant rate. IKEA currently operates the largest warehouse in South-East Asia, which is poised to fill the expected demand.[29]

The nuts and bolts of IKEA

Founder Ingvar Kamprad formulated IKEA's vision to 'offer a wide range of home furnishings with good design and function at prices so low that as many people as possible will be able to afford them'. IKEA carries approximately 10,000 different home furnishings, garden items, plants, lighting, office furniture and supplies, household textiles, decorative items, kitchen cabinetry, toys and children's equipment, crockery and flatware, and seasonal decorations.

Product strategy

IKEA follows a standardized product strategy with an identical assortment around the world. IKEA designs all of its product lines and products, then uses a bidding process among hundreds of agreed suppliers, contracts the manufacturing job out under stiff quality-controlled conditions. Furniture and accessories are designed to fit four categories:[30]

- *Scandinavian*: simply styled, streamlined, light wood.
- *Modern*: minimalist and funky.
- *Country*: a new take on traditional European styles.
- *Young Swede*: totally simple, but functional and stylish.

IKEA's office-supply division offers office furnishings that also fit into the four categories. It operates on a business-to-business as well as a retail level, in some areas publishing its own catalogue and employing its own call-centre employees. IKEA pioneered the idea of flat-pack merchandising, which means that buyers do the final assembly for most items. It has been estimated that six times more freight space would be needed if its products were shipped already assembled, a significant cost point especially when increasing numbers of items are made in the Asia-Pacific region and control of shipping times and costs becomes critical.[30]

IKEA's shopping experience is a unique element in the marketing mix. In addition to the items they buy, shoppers have an experience at IKEA's self-contained shops. The largest stores feature a self-service restaurant with Swedish menu items, a snack bar, Swedish food boutique and a child-care centre for customers. The restaurant and café have been given central status at newer USA stores built on a clover-leaf shape, with sales floors radiating off from the food-service facilities.

Pricing strategy

The IKEA concept is based on low price, and products are designed to offer prices that are 30 to 50 per cent lower than fully assembled competing products.[30] Keeping within this constraint, IKEA responds to different customer needs using a three-level pricing strategy: low, medium and high.[30] The affordability of IKEA products is due to several business practices, including target-pricing, whereby a product is priced first then designed and sourced accordingly. Other elements of the IKEA business that keep prices low are: high-volume purchasing; low-cost logistics (hence the flat-packs), and inexpensive retail space, mainly in suburban areas. IKEA's prices do vary from market to market, largely because of fluctuations in exchange rates and differences in taxation and tariff regimes, but price positioning is kept as standardized as possible.[30]

Communications strategy

IKEA's promotions are effected mainly through its catalogues, websites, and the IKEA family loyalty programme. All stores follow a communications prototype, with catalogues, printed materials and websites designed to conform to the IKEA look. Websites (**www.IKEA.com**) are examples of tailored uniformity, featuring the same type of information on all 26 websites and seven mini-sites. However, the sites feature different photos and colours, and information based on the location and market familiarity with the concept, and many feature a choice of several languages. The seven mini-sites are standardized, simply offering contact information and map/directions (such as IKEA Saudi Arabia). The company has turned increasingly to online marketing, and has even indulged in the 'viral marketing' fad, whereby customers forwarded a promotional message to friends via e-mail and SMS.[31] Primary communications are centred on IKEA catalogues, of which 45 editions are printed in 23 languages with a worldwide circulation of over 118 million copies. The catalogues are uniform in layout except for minor regional differences. Other specialized publications include 'Smart Kitchen', 'IKEA View', 'Professional Office Furniture' and 'IKEA Summer'.[32]

IKEA advertising is designed to be unique and provocative. The company's communications goal is to generate word-of-mouth publicity through innovative and sometimes ground-breaking approaches. IKEA has featured ground-breaking advertising in several markets, earning the ire of some conservative groups. For instance, the company has used homosexual couples, just-divorced women, teenage pregnancy and marijuana as topics in its ads. Perhaps the most controversy was sparked by IKEA's Netherlands campaign featuring a male homosexual couple with their daughter. For a view of IKEA's portrayals of lesbian and gay worlds, visit: **www.commercialcloset.org** (a review of gay advertising) or **www.gfn.com** (the Gay Financial Network).

According to Irena Vanenkova, IKEA's head of public relations in Russia, a good example of innovative communications by IKEA was a competition to find a handsome cat with a Swedish heritage to enter the new Russian showroom on opening day (cats are considered to bring Russians good luck), generating publicity and goodwill through 20 publications and websites that would have otherwise cost thousands of rubles.[32] IKEA's thirtieth birthday celebrations in Switzerland were characterized by a thought-provoking use of the Swiss flag on a sombre and staid background, emblazoned with '30 years of democracy in Swiss home furnishings'. The official-looking artwork was counterbalanced by pricing offers using the number '30', such as sofas normally priced at 900 Swiss Francs selling for 30 Swiss Francs.

On a quieter front in communications, IKEA is active on environmental and social-responsibility programmes, providing the company with exposure in the press, and a themed emphasis in communications materials.

Target market

IKEA executives tend to be vague about their target markets, and the comment on the topic from the country manager for Japan, Tommy Kullberg, is typical. In an interview with *Nikkei Weekly*'s Asako Ishibashi, he stated that the company targets families with young children and young people starting a home, from virtually all social categories. These are people who tend to have a young 'mental age'.[33] Industry analysts refer consistently to first-time home buyers, young families and people renting their homes.

Distribution

IKEA has a division devoted to business travel logistics, primarily to allow company representatives to visit manufacturers in order to ensure that working conditions are optimal, and that products are made in accordance with IKEA's code of environmental and social responsibility. The primary countries of origin of IKEA products are: Sweden (14 per cent), China (14 per cent), Poland (8 per cent), Germany (8 per cent) and Italy (6 per cent). Manufacturers ship the components or finished products to large warehouses, such as the central one in Almhult, or to one of the other 25 distribution centres in 15 countries. About 30 per cent of the products are shipped directly to the stores, which are, in effect, warehouses.[30] To facilitate the shipping, IKEA developed IKEA RAIL, the only private rail freight forwarding company in Europe. The network of subcontracted manufacturers numbers nearly 1800 in 55 different countries, with 42 trading services offices in 33 countries, for which the company uses an online suppliers' portal to negotiate bids and order supplies, such as nuts and bolts from IKEA's internal supplier-to-supplier division.[34] IKEA does not offer home delivery but IKEA stores cooperate with local companies that offer small trucks for rent, or delivery and even furniture assembly services. IKEA offers a mail order service and very recently introduced an online ordering facility in some countries; however, in its first stages the cumbersome system was not well received.

IKEA's competitors?

There is no global competitor for IKEA. The company has used its relatively low prices, stylish design and offbeat image, environmental performance (no PVC products, no sweatshop workers) and immediate gratification via do-it-yourself delivery in order to attain a unique positioning. No other large company in this sector has pioneered so many supply chain innovations, including long-term and online collaboration that is spiced up with civilized competition between suppliers. No other international furniture company offers such a universal appeal. Competitors are inevitably smaller than IKEA, and may be able to compete with the Swedish monolith on one of the above points, such as low price, but not simultaneously on all of them. The experience of shopping at IKEA is likewise unique: although lacking in salespeople, store facilities present many opportunities for the shopper to maximize the benefits of shopping IKEA-style. Measuring tapes, pencils, handy order forms, desks to write on, realistic mini-showrooms, and user-friendly merchandising are examples of this. IKEA's day-trip dimension is also inimitable, with signature food service, children's entertainment and even child care.

It's a big country. Someone's got to furnish it . . . IKEA in the United States

IKEA entered the US market in 1985, quickly establishing three outlets in the north-east, and experiencing such success that a major warehouse near Philadelphia was followed by others around the country. Since 1985, 16 more stores have been opened in the United States and the company has grown to become the seventh largest furniture retailer in the country.[30] Plans call for 50 stores across the country by 2013, with nine scheduled to open or re-open within the next year or so.[30] IKEA quickly learned from its early experiences in North America. First, people considered their glasses to be too small to add ice – a singularly American habit. In addition, bed sizes needed to be changed according to standard North American measurements. Generally, furniture was made wider and larger for the USA, changing IKEA's conception of a worldwide appeal. In terms of merchandising, IKEA stores tend to display easily identifiable colour and design combinations, to guide the customer a bit more than they were accustomed to doing in Europe.[35]

To gain awareness in a relatively new market, IKEA has been inventive, including among its promotions the 'Living Works of Art' exhibit as part of downtown Chicago's 'Home Suite Home' campaign. Three couples 'lived' in the heart-shaped exhibit, made up of IKEA furniture, for several days, thereby earning US$15,000 for charitable causes.[36] Another example is the recent 'unböring' campaign in the USA that included a dedicated website, television, print, direct, outdoor and wildpostings. The 'unböring' campaign's 'manifesto' clearly places IKEA as an idiosyncratic company of Swedes, fighting 'for liberty and beauty for all'. For more on the campaign, see **www.unboring.com**.

IKEA is a complex business, comprising retail businesses, franchising, product development and design, supply-chain businesses like Schwedwood, and manufacturing management, distribution using conventional channels and IKEA RAIL, massive warehouse operations, real estate, food service operations, and even the ownership of local competitors like Habitat in the UK and France. The pan-European IKANO Bank and real estate services company is also owned by the Kamprad family. In Sweden in the 1990s, IKEA designed and sold houses. The 'Bo Klok Project' ('live smart' in Swedish) wood-frame houses were prefabricated and built with Swedish developer Skanska, in two Swedish cities. Efforts have been made to bring the project to the UK and other markets. Of course, home-buyers were given a 3000 SEK gift certificate for IKEA merchandise.[37] As a reflection of this complexity, IKEA founder Ingvar Kamprad told the Swedish newspaper *Smaalandposten* in an interview that, contrary to his earlier position as an 'engine' of growth, he now worries that the firm is expanding too quickly. In particular, he cites concern that in an economic downturn, some IKEA stores may have to close. 'Papa Ingvar', as he is known to many IKEA employees, said that he felt the responsibility for potential lost jobs was a very heavy burden.[25]

All IKEA company information and addition information can be found at the IKEA corporate website: **http://www.ikea.com**.

Questions

1. Furniture styles and home trends are usually thought to be linked to cultural attitudes and perceptions. How can a global company like IKEA successfully market its standardized products in so many countries? Based on your visit to IKEA websites for a variety of countries, give some suggestions for improvement to the communications director.

2. Why do IKEA products receive Swedish-sounding names? What is the role of IKEA's Swedish image, and its Swedish country of origin in the company's image policy?

3. How can IKEA continue long-term to market its wares to young-minded people around the world? Can the company remain true to its original mission, culture, and mass-appeal?

4. Regarding Ingvar Kamprad's worries about the firm's expansion, do you agree that the company is expanding too quickly or into too many different sectors? What marketing problems do you expect this growth will cause in the short and long term?

Saskia Faulk and Jean-Claude Usunier prepared this case solely to provide material for class discussion, originally adapted from a case prepared by Czinkota and Ronkainen, pp. 203–7.[38] The authors do not intend to illustrate either effective or ineffective handling of a business situation. The authors may have disguised certain names and other identifying information to protect confidentiality. The full version of this case is available at WS5.A.

(©IRM, reprinted with kind permission.)

A5.3 Case

McDonald's – a global cultural icon?

McDonald's is often considered to be a symbol of globalization in its American incarnation. This case study will explore people's perceptions of McDonald's in the Middle East and other regions where religion-based ideologies are rooted and anti-globalization has spread. This is a broad attempt to document the tectonic shifts that surround globalization, and how companies like McDonald's adapt, as they fight for profits and survival.

About McDonald's

McDonald's is the biggest fast food chain worldwide, operating more than 30,000 restaurants in 120 countries.[39] Current growth has been achieved primarily through franchising.[39] McDonald's topped the market share ratings of fast-food restaurants with 7.3 per cent of US market share in 2002, more than double that of the next ranked chain, Burger King.[40] The company was ranked number 17 out of the top 100 global marketers in 2007,[41] and was rated eight among 25 US 'Megabrands' in terms of domestic advertising spending.[42] In the US, the corporation developed *Chipotle* (Mexican food) and *Boston Market* ('comfort' food), while it sold *Donatos* pizzeria and closed its *Pret* chain in Japan in order to reallocate resources to McDonald's outlets. In an effort to better market its toy, books, videos, and clothing lines, the company has rebranded them in early 2004 as *McKids* in North America, Australia, China, Japan, Korea and Taiwan, with expansion planned shortly. The strategy is designed to 'connect with customers in fresh, relevant ways both inside and outside our restaurants' according to the company's marketing head, Larry Light.[43]

The company long had a higher sales growth overseas than in its home market. Europe was McDonald's second biggest market after the US. France, Germany, and the UK accounted for 75 per cent of European operating income in 2002. France and Russia accounted for most of the sales growth from 2001 to 2002 in constant currency terms.[39]

In December 2002, McDonald's posted its first ever quarterly loss. The company announced restaurant closures in several countries in the Middle East and Latin America, delaying new openings, and increasing layoffs through 2005. Poor business performance was blamed on weak economies, 'mad cow' disease, and increased competition. In 2003, Subway, a sandwich chain, overtook McDonald's as the largest fast food company in the US.[44] According to McDonald's late Chief Executive Officer Jim Cantalupo, writing in the company's 2002 annual report, 'McDonald's has lost momentum . . . and lost what it takes to make customers feel special. We have struggled to grow our business in the face of weak and uncertain economic conditions around the world. The result has been disappointing financial performance'. He stated that 'McDonald's is in transition from a company that emphasizes *adding restaurants to customers* to one that emphasizes *adding customers to restaurants*', adding 'McDonald's has a new boss . . . it's not me . . . it's the customer'.[45] During Cantalupo's tenure in 2003, the company's performance began to improve, with more of a focus on improving existing restaurants, new menu offerings, and attempts to improve service.

The operating environment for McDonald's has become increasingly threatening over recent years, with tougher competition from agile multi-brand rivals like YUM! (owners of Pizza Hut, Taco Bell, and KFC among others), Burger King, and increasing local competitors. Despite the increase in smaller, more regional chains, the top ten fast-food leaders tend to remain the same: McDonald's, Burger King, Wendy's, Pizza Hut, KFC, and others, almost exactly in that order. An example of such local competition is Marrybrown (**www.marrybrown.com.my**), a Malaysia-based fried chicken and burger chain, a shiny, clean competitor with more than 100 outlets in China, India, Malaysia, Sri Lanka, and the Middle East. Al-Tazaj ('fresh') at www.altazaj.com.sa, has grown from one Mecca-based grilled chicken restaurant, opened in 1992, to 49 units across Egypt, Malaysia, Qatar, Lebanon, and the US, where it is known as Taza. The company is owned by a Saudi Arabian poultry supplier. Philippines-based Jollibee (**www.jollibee.com.ph**) is one of the only regional fast-food chains to outstrip McDonald's in terms of market share. The chain offers a similar menu to McDonald's, with Philippine-adjusted ingredients such as sweeter, spicier, and more juicy meat-based items, locally inspired sauces, and rice. Jollibee has expanded from 467 domestic units to 25 international units, including locations in the US, Indonesia, Brunei, Hong Kong, and Vietnam. Nando's, a spicy-grilled chicken chain, has grown from a strong South African base to more than 330 stores worldwide, including 11 in Malaysia and others in the Middle East, Sub-Saharan Africa, Australasia, Canada and the UK.

US multinationals generally consider global advertising campaigns to be too challenging due to cultural differences. However, for the first time, McDonald's launched a global advertising campaign in 2003. The 100-country campaign's tagline, 'I'm lovin' it', was sung in many markets by internationally known American pop star Justin Timberlake. The German-designed ads had an edgy, urban feel to them and a hip-hop beat and style. The campaign accompanied Justin Timberlake's McDonald's-sponsored 35-country tour and recent release entitled 'I'm lovin' it'. The new ad campaign was viewed as 'hype' by many in the advertising world, who believed that the company should fix its operational and internal problems prior to embarking upon a new branding campaign.[46] Renowned ad critic Bob Garfield of *Advertising Age* called the campaign an 'embarrassing, pandering mess', calling its youth appeal 'desperate'. In his analysis of the 'I'm lovin' it' ads, the ad critic believes that it violated several principles of advertising.[47]

In 2004, McDonald's planned to modify menu items and offer new benefits to customers. In the wake of lawsuits claiming that McDonald's food made people obese and popular concerns about obesity and health, McDonald's decided to remove the 'Supersize' option from its menus, allowing extra large sized portions. The Happy Meal, which celebrated its 25th anniversary in 2004, was redesigned to offer more variety and more healthy alternatives. In Lebanon and China, greeters were hired to welcome diners at restaurants, special parking for mothers was to be introduced in New Zealand and Canada, organic milk made available in Britain, fruit cups offered in Italy, bottled water and low-fat yoghurt available in Spain, and child-care staff watched the children in Italy and the Netherlands. 'Salads Plus' was to be launched in 16 European countries in a bid to provide healthier menu offerings, although some of the salads may contain more fat than a cheeseburger. As a special offer, music downloads are planned to be offered for free upon purchase of certain McDonald's menu items in a partnership with Sony's download service, Sony Connect, in which McDonald's is said to have committed US$30 million in advertising. The company stated it is considering tie-ins with companies 'in the area of music, sports, fashion, and entertainment'.

According to a survey conducted in Gulf countries during the first quarter of 2003 by Synovate, McDonald's scored higher than other chains on last-visit satisfaction, market penetration, and market share. Market share actually increased during the period, but visits to McDonald's declined – possibly due to geopolitical tensions. The period coincided with the recent introduction of the locally inspired McArabia, grilled chicken on Arabic bread.[48] The sandwich was launched with a powerful promotional campaign that overshadowed marketing efforts for the jealously guarded Big Mac. The campaign has been viewed as an effort to 'Relaunch McDonald's in the Muslim world'.[49] The owners of McDonald's Middle East Development Company run a 'Hamburger University' training programme in Dubai for the region to reflect local training needs (Anon, 2002f). As for McDonald's in Iraq, the corporation joined the vanguard of American and multinational corporations seeking business opportunities in post-war Iraq at the Madrid fundraiser conference.[50]

Adapting to local conditions and trends

McDonald's President Jim Cantalupo said in 1991 that the company's strategy was to become 'as much part of the local culture as possible'.[51] McDonald's customizes its foods and elements of décor according to local preferences and competitive environment; however, it maintains its power as signifier of that which is American and modern. The company has made major menu modifications in line with local tastes, and has modified its marketing and public relations campaigns significantly in line with local concerns. In **China**, where McDonald's intends to open 100 new restaurants, there are plans to introduce a pork burger and shrimp McNuggets in deference to local preferences. According to McDonald's China Development Company managing director Tim Lai, 'Consumers do not go to McDonald's for Chinese-style food', in contrast with primary competitor KFC which has 1000 outlets in the country and regionally adapted Chinese-style menus.[52] McDonald's has 770 outlets in China. In **India**, where McDonald's has 56 outlets,[53] the company serves no beef, in deference to Hindu principles, and no pork in deference to Muslim principles. India is primarily Hindu, with an influential Muslim minority. Due to the strictness of vegetarianism in the country, McDonald's India practices segregation of vegetarian and non-vegetarian foods from suppliers through to service.[54] Kitchen staff who cook vegetarian food are identifiable by their green aprons. With a menu that is '75 per cent different in India' than the rest of the world, McDonald's introduced the Maharaja Mac (a version of the Big Mac made with lamb), McAlu Tikki (vegetarian) burgers, Chicken McGrill (grilled chicken with a mint sauce), Paneer Salsa Wraps, chicken tikka, and Veg McPuff (a version of Indian samosas).[55] In the context of some anti-American feeling in the country, McDonald's is not considered to be American, but Indian. In **Saudi Arabia**, with variations among Muslim other countries, the menu offers *halal* items (ingredients and meat processing in keeping with Muslim regulations). McDonald's outlets close five times per day for prayers, and close during the day through Ramadan, in keeping with the Muslim custom of fasting while there is daylight. The company introduced a version of a popular regional dish with the McArabia, grilled chicken and salad on Arab bread. In order to conform to local expectations, since its inception in Saudi Arabia in 1993, McDonald's has kept a strict 'apartheid' of the sexes in its operations. All workers are men. Women must sit separately in a glassed-off dining area from men. There are two separate lines for service, one for women and one for men, and two separate entrances.[56] McDonald's will not serve a woman, even a Western woman, who wants to eat alone if she does not have the permission of her husband or male relative. According to one report, the women's seating area is not well maintained, in contrast to the lavish appointments of the men's area.[57] Gender segregation in Saudi Arabia was confirmed by McDonald's Communications Office employee Ann Rozenich, and justified as respecting and observing local customs.[56] In Saudi Arabia, men and women are supposed to remain separate in public places, unless they are relations among whom marriage is not permitted, such as brothers or fathers.[58]

In **France** the company upgraded decors to compete with the ambience of local cafés. Themed restaurants: near sports stadiums have sports motifs, and in the mountains have chalet-like decoration. One concession to French tastes is the Croque McDo (a version of the ubiquitous Croque-Monsieur, a ham and cheese toasted sandwich). McDonald's outlets in areas with many Muslims, such as Marseille, offer fish-based promotional Ramadan menus starting in the late afternoon. McDonald's **Malaysia** made a donation composed of employees' individual donations to the Iraq Humanitarian Fund. In China, the menu has not changed much, however on offer are Spicy Chicken Filet Burger, and Spicy McWings. In **Turkey** the menu includes a Double Kofte burger (meat patties with onions and Turkish spices).[59] In **Israel**, McDonald's seven kosher restaurants are closed on the Sabbath and religious holidays. Israel also has more than 70 non-Kosher outlets.[60] Following lawsuits and concerns about health and obesity, McDonald's **UK** introduced Happy Meals offering more choices, including fruit juices and fresh fruit slices, as well as a wide variety of sandwiches. In **Mexico** the company reflected local preferences by increasing egg offerings such as McHuevo, and adding spicy peppers and refried beans. In **Japan**, McDonald's menu includes teriyaki burgers, corn soup, bacon potato pies, and a wide variety of milkshakes.

In terms of religious dietary restrictions, there are many resources that advise Muslims as to suitability of foods, including fast-food options. According to several Muslim websites, Muslims are advised to avoid 'Most items' at McDonald's and other fast-food outlets. Some McDonald's outlets in the US, Canada, UK, France, and elsewhere with many Muslim patrons purchase Halal meat, and McDonald's is experimenting with Halal chicken nuggets. In an ordinary McDonald's, however, reasons for avoiding most items include: non-Muslim staff, contamination of vegetarian burger and other vegetable/fruit offerings by unlawful ('Haram') meats or animal fat (if cooked or prepared in common area or if touched by a utensil that previously touched non-Halal meat), and dairy products contaminated by rennet (ingredient derived from the intestine). Some sweets are banned for their content of vanilla flavouring, which is commonly conditioned by alcohol.

Common factors among McDonald's community involvement programmes include World Children's Day activities, celebrations of the anniversary of the UN adoption of the Convention on the Rights of the Child, Ronald McDonald Houses located near hospitals for families of sick children, and donations to orphanages, children's hospitals, children's health organizations.

Consumer attitudes towards McDonald's

There are many more McDonald's outlets implanted in Asia than there are in the Middle East, suggesting that, among other factors, people in the Middle East may be less willing to embrace this representative of globalization. According to brand consulting firm CoreBrand head Lawrence McNaughton, 'If you hate America, it's real easy to hate Coke or McDonald's'. For him, the primary risk criteria are 'if you're in business in the Middle East and you're a cultural icon'.[61] Two surveys conducted in the months leading up to the Iraq conflict showed that although many consumers do not use consumer choices to express political views, a sizeable minority say they try to avoid buying American products. Publicis-Groupe's Leo Burnett Asia Pacific surveyed people in China, South Korea, Indonesia, India and the Philippines to uncover their beliefs about a brand's country of origin and its impact on their purchasing habits. The survey asked whether certain brands have 'my country's interests at heart'. Of all multinationals active in the region, McDonald's and Coca-Cola scored most favourably, most likely a reflection of the companies' efforts to market themselves as local companies. Two-thirds of young Asian shoppers said they bought brands they liked regardless of the brand's country of origin, but 23 per cent claimed to avoid American brands. A similar study, conducted in Europe and Canada by GMI found that in the US and Canada, at least 50 per cent of consumers said they 'distrusted' American companies – with highest proportions among French and German consumers – partially as a result of the government's foreign policy.[62]

McDonald's has made many efforts to be viewed as a local company – with local menu adaptations, sports sponsorship, and community relations seen by the company as key to success in this aspect. According to US financial analyst David Kolpak, 'The problem in Europe was the perception that any large US brand has, which is bringing the American way of eating and marketing and invading the local culture'.[63] Director of marketing and communications for McDonald's in the Middle East, Dubai-based Ricarda Ruecker, stated in a telephone interview that when threatened by boycott protests, and violence, local franchisees initiated advertising campaigns. 'We educated people; we have a 100 per cent local ownership model, 80 per cent local suppliers, we do a lot of charity. Now people understand more.' According to Brandeis University's international marketing professor Shih-Fen Chen, 'Consumer attitudes toward American brands can change quickly, if a bomb lands in the wrong place.'

Protesters targeting McDonald's seem to reject the corporation's claim that it is a 'local' company. In Indonesia, for example, where much work has been done by master franchiser Bambang Rachmadi to convince local people that McDonald's is not a foreign implant (see previous section), people protesting against the war in Iraq and other American-related issues consistently targeted McDonald's outlets, in addition to boycott campaigns and an occasional KFC or other fast-food chain attack. During one protest the 1000-strong crowd chanted 'God is great' and 'USA go to hell'. Protesters also denigrated the United Nations, Kofi Annan, and George Bush.[64] In Egypt, Essam Haraz, manager of local competitor Mo'men stated his belief that of all the fast-food chains in Egypt, McDonald's has suffered the most, due to its alleged close ties with Israel. He believed that many Egyptians felt the same way because he did not perceive that other American fast-food chains were suffering, although they had featured equally on boycott lists.[65] Ahmad Bahi Al-Din Shabaan of the Arab Popular Boycott Committee said that the committee chose as a strategy to focus a boycott on a limited number of brands, including McDonald's, Marlboro, and Coca-Cola, which 'represent the American way of life and US hegemony'.[66]

Anti-McDonald's timeline

This section will detail, in a non-exhaustive manner, violent actions and protests against McDonald's over the past five years, in selected countries. Action taken by McDonald's shortly after the attacks or protests is supplied for each time period. At the end of the section, Table 5.1 summarizes the events.

France, 1999: Anti-globalization activist José Bové set fire to a McDonald's outlet, for which he was imprisoned for 20 days. In 2003, as the prospect of hostilities in Iraq became likely, anti-war activists smashed windows and spray-painted obscenities and 'Boycott' on McDonald's outlets.[67]

McDonald's action: The corporation adopted French comic hero Astérix as corporate mascot. Astérix is a well-loved symbol of French resistance to foreign occupation, having battled Imperial Rome in a prolific comic book series.

Saudi Arabia, 2000: boycott of American products and companies inspired by perceived US support for Israeli incursions into Palestine. The call to boycott US products included the statement 'Each dollar spent buying an American product is transformed into a bullet to kill our brothers in Palestine'. McDonald's General Manager in Jeddah said that the boycott would hurt Saudi employees more than American interests, and added that some anti-Western activists were hypocrites who drive American cars while complaining about American products.[68]

McDonald's action: Saudi franchise committed during the month of Ramadan to sending 26 cents from each Big Mac sold to the Al Quds Intifada Fund,[51] helping children's hospitals in the Palestinian territories.[69] The message is 'Buy a burger and help a Palestinian child'. The BBC's Middle East correspondent termed the campaign as a 'canny marketing move, as much as a well-meaning act of charity'. Prince Mishal Bin Khalid, who heads a McDonald's licence holder, expected that the campaign should raise US$100,000.[68] The reaction to McDonald's announcement was almost immediate: several e-mails began circulating calling for Jews worldwide to boycott McDonald's for the company's perceived support for the Intifada (Emery, 2001). This was a similar situation to that of Burger King, which responded to Arab boycotters by removing its contentious outlet from a West Bank Israeli settlement. By doing so, Burger King triggered the anger of pro-Israeli groups.[70]

Egypt, 2001: US support for Israel sparks anti-American protests and boycotts. Clerics declare in fatwa that Israeli and US products should be forbidden.[69] President Hosni Mubarak was quoted by his Information Minister as saying 'People are right to boycott their [Israeli] goods, but a boycott of European or American goods must be considered in a wider and more general context'.[71] US military action sparked several boycotts and violent action. Demonstrators threw bricks and rocks at some outlets. Anxious employees at the American University outlet in Cairo hung up a poster declaring their support for Palestine.[72] The Doctor's Syndicate boycott advised people to buy nothing from any country active in Iraq. A sweeping boycott, organized by a retired professor from Washington, DC, was developed at a pan-Arab conference. According to organizer Dr Al Boyoumi, the boycott criterion is that the products 'should be symbols of US globalization', not just those one would target in an anti-war or pro-Palestinian protest. The main brands targeted were: Always, Ariel, Coca-Cola, Lay's, Marlboro, and McDonald's, and activists believed the boycott is a positive tool to encourage local businesses to take the place of foreign brands that may suffer. They also attempted to educate the public about the health and environmental impact of global brands in Egypt. The boycott marked a change in Egyptian activism – this time it was focused and understandable, as well as aligned with the common causes of foreign anti-globalization organizations. Alongside McDonald's assertion that the boycott is doing nothing to harm their business, company reports suggest that Egyptians may be wary of being seen in public at a McDonald's due to the social pressure of the boycott, but online and telephone-based orders for home delivery have soared since the beginning of the boycott.[73] Despite this, McDonald's and KFC reportedly suffered a 20–50 per cent fall in sales since the beginning of the second Intifada 19 months previously.[74] Businesspeople and government officials are concerned about the future of foreign direct investment in Egypt.[73] Egypt is the second largest recipient of US aid after Israel.[75]

McDonald's action: In 2001 the company introduced the McFalafel in its 49 outlets, with an advertising soundtrack by 'I hate Israel' hit singer Shabaan Abdel Rahim, a song considered a rallying point in an anti-American and anti-Israel boycott. In the anodyne McDonald's jingle he sang, 'If you eat a bite, you can't stop before finishing the whole roll'. Following an official complaint by the American Jewish Committee (AJC) to McDonald's, the ad was dropped after running for three weeks.[76] McDonald's US corporate office stated that the marketing decision was locally made and lacking in research. The AJC stated it was 'delighted in their responsiveness'. Egyptian fast-food chain Mo'men ('Believer'), launched in 1999, appears to do well from any disaffection from McDonald's. It has its own strong market share. The chain sells typical 'Western' fast-food items like chicken nuggets as well as traditional Egyptian offerings.[72]

Indonesia, 2002–2003: During the unrest leading to the fall of President Suharto in 1998, several McDonald's outlets were destroyed. In the wake of US forces' strikes on Afghanistan, Indonesia's highest Muslim order called on the government to sever diplomatic ties with the US. When students demonstrate against US interests, McDonald's is a common target. Protests against US military action in Afghanistan turn against McDonald's outlets. McDonald's outlet in Makassar was bombed by a militant Islamic group affiliated with Al-Qaeda in December, 2002, killing three and wounding 11 people. During the run-up to hostilities in Iraq, anti-war protesters seal doors and plaster restaurants with signs urging people not to go inside McDonald's restaurants, as well as other US food chains.[67] Since the beginning of US military operations in Iraq, McDonald's outlets were targets of demonstrations. Demonstrators stated their belief that a portion of American profits go to Israel.

Despite the highly visible local ownership campaign by owner Bambang Rachmadi, demonstrators emphasized the American-ness of the brand. They threw away McDonald's leaflets stating how McDonald's Indonesia 'Grew in the hands of Indonesian sons and daughters'.[64]

McDonald's action: Emphasis on the local ownership of franchises, proclaimed on big green banners outside the 85 restaurants (green is the colour of Islam), proclaiming: 'In the name of Allah, the merciful and the gracious, McDonald's Indonesia is owned by an indigenous Muslim'. The company hired security staff from local Islamist organizations to guard the outlets. Such organizations include Ka'bah Youth Movement, a black-uniformed group advocating the adoption of Islamic Law in Indonesia, which has been known to close night clubs perceived to transgress Islamic codes. On Fridays, staff are supplied with religious-inspired uniforms. Female employees are required to wear a headscarf. Walls are covered with photos of the Indonesian franchise owner Bambang Rachmadi on his Mecca pilgrimage. Arab music is played in outlets. In some outlets, tables are raised over straw mats so patrons can eat without shoes in the Javanese style. The menu includes the popular 'Rice Packet', rice with fried chicken, scrambled egg, and a dose of spicy Sambal sauce (Ford, 2002). American-educated Mr Bambang Rachmadi, McDonald's master franchise owner in Indonesia, described McDonald's as America's 'most significant icon'. McDonald's headquarters receives 5 per cent of revenue from the McDonald's Indonesia franchise. Food served at the outlets is mainly produced locally, and boasts a menu containing traditional ingredients like chicken and rice. 'If you destroy it [McDonald's outlet], you'll only destroy a job for a Muslim.' McDonald's Indonesia donates goats for sacrifice during Muslim Ramadan ceremonies.

Lebanon, 2002: Boycott against American goods and companies doing business with Israel. Influential Shia cleric Sheikh Mohammed Hussain Fadlallah asked Arabs to buy European or Asian products instead of American ones.

McDonald's action: Franchise owners pay for full-page newspaper advertisements declaring the franchise is fully owned and financed by Lebanese.

India, 2003: Opposition members of parliament called for a boycott of all American brands, notably Coca-Cola, McDonald's, Pepsi, and British-owned Lever. Demonstrators blocked the entrance to McDonald's outlets to protest the war and call for a boycott of American goods.

Pakistan, 2003: According to Pakistani police, an attack on McDonald's and KFC by Islamic militants was prevented by arrests. 'It's a Western cultural invasion', according to Jamaat-e-Islami representative Munawar Hasan. Jamaat-e-Islami, a powerful Islamist political party, considers the presence of the chain in Pakistan to be an 'ideological issue'. Also angering Pakistanis is the uniform requiring women to wear trousers, which is for some against Islamic principles.

McDonald's action: the company stations private security guards armed with pump-action rifles outside outlets.

Palestinian occupied territories, 2003: American-style fast-food restaurants in Ramallah were compelled to close, although the motive was not clear. Closed restaurants included US chain outlet Subway and three local copies of McDonald's and KFC.

UAE, Egypt, Jordan, 2002–2003: rumours circulated that McDonald's donates some of its profits to Israel. Boycotts against American emblems like McDonald's leave restaurants 'empty'. In Jordan, people walking into American restaurants are 'socially ostracized'.[77]

Table 5.1 Chronology of attacks on McDonald's outlets in selected countries

Location	Year	Casualties	Admitted/convicted	Weapon/means
Millau, France	August 1999	Destruction of property (McDonald's construction)	Farmers protest US agricultural tariffs in retaliation for EU refusal of US beef	Tractors, tools
Cahors, France	17 August 1999	None	Farmers against US agricultural tariffs	Blocked roads, distributed local produce
Athens, Greece	4 October 1999	Damage	Filiki Etairia group	Fire bomb
Dinan, France (Brittany)	19 April 2000	1 killed	Suspected Breton separatists	Bomb
Istanbul, Turkey	17 February 2001	None	Unknown	Bomb defused by police
Merter, Istanbul, Turkey	28 September 2001	3 wounded, property damage	Unknown	Pipe bomb
Beirut, Lebanon	Spring 2002	None	Students	Sit-ins, protests
Bahrain (2 outlets)	April 2002	'substantial' damage	Pro-Palestinian demonstrators	Stones
Oman	April 2002	Damage	Pro-Palestinian demonstrators	Smashed windows
Moscow, Russia	25 October 2002	1 killed, 8 wounded, major damage to outlet	Presumed Chechens	Bomb
Al Kharj, Saudi Arabia	20 November 2002	None	McDonald's near US military base	Fire
Dammam, Saudi Arabia	25 February 2002	None	Unknown	Fire-bomb attempt
Jounieh (Beirut) Lebanon	23 September 2002	3 cars destroyed	Unknown	Car bomb
Bombay, India	6 December 2002	23 wounded	Unknown	Bomb
Makassar, Indonesia (Sulawesi)	5 December 2002	3 dead, 11 wounded	Islamists	Bomb
Dora, Beirut, Lebanon	5 April 2003	5 wounded	Considered to be anti-American group	Bomb; 55 kg TNT found outside outlet
Istanbul, Turkey	15 April 2003	Extensive damage	Unknown	Bomb
Thessalonica, Greece	21 June 2003	Outlet destroyed	Protesters during European Union summit	Fire
Yanbu, Saudi Arabia	1 May 2004	Damage	Five Westerners, killed, shots fired at McDonald's and Holiday Inn	Gunfire
Istanbul, Turkey	19 May 2004	Car park damage	Unknown	Percussion bomb
Rome, Italy	19 May 2004	2 bombs defused; no damage	Thought to be Red Brigades	Homemade bombs

McDonald's action: Published a statement in Egyptian daily *Al-Ahram* and other publications denouncing the rumours as 'ridiculous' and stating that such rumours endanger 3000 Egyptian jobs. In other countries criss-crossed by such rumours, McDonald's franchisees issued statements that the outlets were locally owned and operated. In 2003, McDonald's introduced the McArabia sandwich, a version of a popular regional snack using Arabic bread and grilled chicken, appeasing some people by this apparent salute to local food culture. According to some reports, the introduction of the McArabia counteracted reduced sales caused by calls to boycott McDonald's. The company denied that the introduction of McArabia was related to geopolitical issues, asserting that the item had been in development for two years. McDonald's owner Rafiq Shah in Dubai pointed out that 'There is no liaison between McArabia and politics'.

Other attacks during the past several years on McDonald's have occurred in Belgium, Mexico, England, Chile, Serbia, Colombia, South Africa, and Xian, China. In the same time-frame, American-based Yum brand KFC has been attacked in Pakistan, Indonesia, Lebanon, and Greece, and Pizza Hut was bombed in Lebanon. Table 5.2 provides recent information about the number of outlets located in regions experiencing criticism against US foreign policy.

Table 5.2 McDonald's locations in sensitive spots around the globe

Country	Locations
Bahrain	8, since 1994
Egypt	More than 50 outlets and points of sale (since 1994)
Indonesia	108 since 1990
Israel	More than 80
Kuwait	34 since 1994
Pakistan	20 since 1998
Saudi Arabia	71 since 1993
UAE	28 since 1994

Local ownership is emphasized on the McDonald's Corporation website, where sentences like 'Bahraini-owned, operated, and proud to serve you' are repeated on practically every country page. In addition, each page dedicated to a gulf region country contains the statement: 'In the Arab nations, all McDonald's restaurants are locally owned and operated by Arab entrepreneurs' (for more information visit www.mcdonalds.com). Charitable actions and community campaigns are strongly emphasized on McDonald's Corporation websites, including donations to and activities with children's cancer hospitals and Red Crescent. Equally prominent on local pages of the McDonald's website are claims of the percentage of ingredients supplied locally, and the number of local workers employed.

Non-violent and violent action

Some militant Islamic websites, such as those affiliated with Al-Qaeda, have specifically designated McDonald's as a target to weaken the US economy. According to the Islamic-centred magazine *Khilafah*, McDonald's is a 'tool serving to promote the domination of the US. The chain has become an empire with fiefs around the world'.[78] 'There are people who are very, very, angry with the US and they retain their ability to strike', said Dr Achmad Abdi, Director of criminal investigations South Sulawesi, Indonesia.[79] According to an Islamic militant held in the US camp at Guantanamo, Cuba, the South East Asian Islamic group Jemaah

Islamiyah has decided to attack 'soft' targets like American-linked businesses because 'hard' targets such as military or government installations were too difficult.[78] So-called 'soft' targets thought to be desirable and easily accessible for terrorists include restaurants, hotels, shopping centres, and entertainment facilities.[80] Examples of such attacks include assaults on McDonald's, KFC and Pizza Hut outlets in several countries as well as deadly bombs at a hotel in Kenya, night clubs in Bali,[81] a J.W. Marriott Hotel in Jakarta, Indonesia, in August 2003 and simultaneous attacks on a Spanish restaurant, Jewish community centre, and a five-star international hotel in Casablanca, Morocco in May 2003.[82] In the past, 'soft' tourist targets were also deadly but were smaller in scale, such as the killing of 58 tourists at Luxor, Egypt in November 1997 and several violent incidents in Turkey in the late 1990s.[83]

A form of non-violent protest, the boycott, has been extensively used in the Middle East to protest against McDonald's itself, American presence, cultural imperialism, the US government's stance on Israel and Palestine, and the invasion of Iraq. Although companies are understandably reluctant to discuss the economic/social impacts of boycotts, the recent boycott has cost McDonald's sales in the Middle East, according to Claire Babrowski, McDonald's former Asia Pacific and Middle East/Africa president.[84] Repeated attempts by journalists at McDonald's headquarters to hear the company's view on the topic were ignored. According to Islam Online, an 'upswing' of American and Jewish boycotts has caused losses to McDonald's, and is partly to blame for the company's ill-health. A professor of economics at Al-Azhar University, Cairo, Egypt, stated that 'We should bear in mind that this is a form of waging economic war on the enemies, and war always necessitates sacrifice . . . as part of the positive results of the boycott, people will shift to purchasing local products and services . . . creating a form of [Muslim] self-sufficiency'.[85]

Beliefs about boycotts

The Arab Movement for the Boycott of American and Jewish Products spokesperson Amin Iskander stated his belief that the economic damage of the Arab boycott on American companies may be very small; however it is seen to be a 'message of protest . . . [to] mobilize popular feelings and raise awareness in the streets about the US biased attitude towards Israel'.[65] Amin Iskander is also an up-and-coming Egyptian politician. Some boycotts have the force of Fatwa – religious ruling based on the Sharia,[86] the body of Islamic law – behind them. According to Muslim scholar and president of the European Council for Fatwa and Research Sheikh Youssef Al-Qaradawi, 'Each dinar, dirham used to buy their [US] goods eventually becomes a bullet fired at the hearts of a brother or child in Palestine'.

The US Bureau of Industry maintains an anti-boycott office with examples and analysis at: **www.bxa.doc.gov/AntiboycottCompliance/Default.htm**. Calls to boycott continue today, examples of which may be consulted on the Internet at: **www.inminds.co.uk/ boycott-israel.html**.

Other boycotts of McDonald's

Global Boycott for Peace, an organization that has as a mission to 'pressure the US government, through its corporate sponsors, into becoming an international partner in maintaining peaceful and sustainable world peace and renounce militarism' lists McDonald's as among the 'Top 20 companies to boycott'. (For more information, go to **www.globalboycottforpeace.org**.) Hindus in India and abroad have called for a boycott of the company on the basis of its promotion of meat, and its use of beef flavouring in french fries in some markets. People for the Ethical Treatment of Animals have advocated a boycott of McDonald's for alleged cruel practices in the meat industry that supplies the fast food company (see **www.mccruelty.com/**).

Why McDonald's is a target

In an interview with *Foreign Policy* journal, former Chief Executive Officer of McDonald's, Jack Greenberg, was asked why McDonald's outlets were often defaced and attacked. Greenberg saw these disruptions as proof of McDonald's widespread power: 'The price of our unique success.' Greenberg added that no other service company 'touches so many people [45 million] every day in such a personal way . . . If you're going to have that kind of presence, you're going to have that kind of attention.' Greenberg stated that in his belief, many frustrations are blamed on globalization, and conveniently vented on McDonald's. 'Would I rather be the target or would I rather be number two and not be the target? . . . I'd rather be number one. . . . Because of our leadership position and our size, we are a very natural, highly visible point of discussion for good and bad.' Greenberg expressed his view that some critics of globalization should like McDonald's because it is a 'decentralized entrepreneurial network of locally owned stores that . . . adapts very well to local conditions'.[87] When *Foreign Policy* journal editor Moises Naim asked whether McDonald's could correct some misperceptions about the company, Greenberg asserted that the company is not a 'Big American company'. Rather, it is a network of local businesses owned by local entrepreneurs. 'We have become the symbol of everything people don't like or are worried about in terms of their own culture.' In 2000, more than half McDonald's sales came from outside the USA.[87] In an attempt to increase public understanding, the company has stated 'McDonald's is a global brand and is often used as a symbol in complex issues facing the world' on the McDonald's Kuwait website. Philippe Labbe, Director General of McDonald's France, stated after anti-McDonald's protests that the company was a 'Victim of its visibility'. He added that trade wars do not concern McDonald's which buys only 10 per cent of its beef outside France.[88]

Effects of the anti-US and anti-Israeli boycotts

Although companies are understandably reluctant to discuss the economic/social impacts of boycotts, the recent boycott has cost McDonald's sales in the Middle East, according to Claire Babrowski, McDonald's former Asia Pacific and Middle East/Africa president.[83] Director of marketing and communications for McDonald's in the Middle East Ricarda Ruecker said that since April, 2002, when Intifada-related tensions rose, 'We, like every global brand, suffered definitely'. Repeated attempts by journalists at McDonald's headquarters to hear the corporate view on the topic were ignored. According to Islam Online, an 'upswing' of American and Jewish boycotts has caused losses to McDonald's, and are partly to blame for the company's ill-health. In Jordan, two out of six McDonald's outlets have closed due to lack of business, and in Muscat, Oman, McDonald's sales reportedly fell by 65 per cent.[89] An industry association representing 22 mostly American fast-food chains in Egypt, Mahmoud Al-Kaissouni, claimed that sales at most member restaurants were down 20 per cent since Israel entered the Left Bank. After the eruption of the Intifada in September 2000, sales reportedly fell 5 per cent.[65] Even in cosmopolitan Dubai, it was reported that business was down at McDonald's and other American fast-food chains. In another report, sales at most American fast-food outlets were down by about 20 and 30 per cent around the Arab world in 2002.[90] The impact on local economies is often a concern when there is a boycott.

McDonald's as a subject for study

Why is there such rage and passion surrounding McDonald's? In his analysis of the company, *The Sign of the Burger: McDonald's and the Culture of Power*, academic author John Kincheloe[91] offers some explanations. He argues that dramatic differences in people's perceptions of McDonald's illustrate the company's importance as a worldwide symbol.

McDonald's has captured the imagination of people around the world, incarnating many roles: 'all-American success story':

- rampaging cultural imperialist or actor in cultural homogenization;
- symbol of America itself;
- harbinger of free market capitalism;
- symbol of aggressive American capitalism (Collins, 1998);
- exploiter of labour;
- exploiter of children;
- bellwether brand;
- sign of Western-driven economic development;
- signifier of what is 'modern';
- destroyer of the environment;
- embodiment of greedy corporatism, and so on.

José Bové, the French farmer opposed to globalization, vandalized a McDonald's under construction to protest against trade policies and bad food. Some of Bové's acclaim throughout France and in other countries came from his opposition to a widely understood symbol as powerful as a national flag, McDonald's. Kincheloe[91] analyses the company's ability to 'produce and transmit knowledge, shape values, influence identity, and construct consciousness'. Although there are limits to postmodernist analysis, the book helps in understanding how a multinational brand can inflame the passions of people everywhere.

In a similar vein, George Ritzer[92] used McDonald's as a vehicle and as a form of shorthand to describe deep sociocultural and economic changes in his book *The McDonaldization of Society*. Ritzer studied the manner in which McDonald's rationalized the processes involved in food production and service. He uses the word rationalization in the sense that processes are examined and re-designed in a more rational manner. Four factors emerge as key to the rationalization process: efficiency, predictability (standardization), calculability (quantifiable outcomes), and control (of customers, processes, and employees). According to Ritzer's thesis, McDonald's-like rationalization has taken root in other industries and institutions hoping to improve output and efficiency. As a result, consumers are trained to do some of the corporation's tasks, such as taking their food to the table and clearing the table when finished, filling the car tank with petrol rather than being served by an employee, and delivering furniture to their homes themselves instead of relying on a delivery service. Rationalization is described in the book to have irrational consequences for the company and society, such as employee turnover and phenomena that alienate people.

The ethnographic studies in James L. Watson's book *Golden Arches East: McDonald's in East Asia*[93] are illuminating in their portrayal of different meanings ascribed to the company and its products. The book shows how in Korea the chain did not expand quickly due to the perception that it affronted Korean culture. In Beijing the hamburger was considered to be a snack similar to a type of ravioli ('xianbing'), while in Japan a hamburger could not be considered a meal due to its lack of rice. The essays appear to confirm that McDonald's is considered to be a local product by many of its loyal customers, and has supplanted local institutions (such as the tea house or street vendors) with apparent ease.[94]

Thomas Friedman, foreign affairs columnist at the *New York Times*, famously contended that McDonald's fosters peace. In his book *The Lexus and the Olive Tree: Understanding Globalization*,[95] he argued that globalization is the new economic system. After checking the facts with McDonald's headquarters, he theorized that when two countries grew middle classes large enough to justify the growth of McDonald's outlets, they were not likely to go to war. That has since been proven wrong, with India and Pakistan being prime examples;

however it is notable that he chose McDonald's as a leading indicator of globalization. The 'Golden Arches theory of conflict prevention' has been amended to *Starbucks*, Friedman's new model.[96]

Leading business publication *The Economist* selected McDonald's as a relatively stable global institution to determine the value of currencies in foreign exchange markets. 'Burgernomics', as the publication calls the process, is about purchasing power parity or the ability to pay a similar amount of US dollars for goods around the world. In theory, exchange rates should converge at a point where it costs the same in US dollars and local currency to purchase a similar basket of goods in both countries. In this case the basket of goods is a Big Mac, sold in 120 countries. Former Chief Executive Officer of McDonald's Jack Greenberg said the company 'loves' the Big Mac Index, adding that 'It says something about the strength of the brand that you can do something like that and have credibility'.[87] In a similar development, the investment bank UBS created a measure of purchasing power in terms of minutes of work needed to buy a Big Mac around the world. The UBS index reflects local productivity as well as McDonald's costs in local markets where the most time is needed in Kenya, the least in the USA.[97]

Questions

1. How would you describe McDonald's global marketing strategy: is it a hard globalizer or does it adjust to local contexts? What are the reasons for its choices?

2. What is a cultural icon? To what extent is McDonald's, as a corporate name, and its product brand names (e.g. Big Mac) associated with its country of origin (the US) and to large-scale, standardized service operations?

3. Describe the ambivalent attitudes of consumers to McDonald's. Do boycotts really succeed in stopping the growth of McDonald's outside the US? Base your answer on actual data.

4. How should McDonald's react to boycotts in the short run? In the long run, how could the company avoid being considered a mere cultural icon?

Saskia Faulk and Jean-Claude Usunier prepared this case solely to provide material for class discussion. The authors do not intend to illustrate either effective or ineffective handling of a business situation. The authors may have disguised certain names and other identifying information to protect confidentiality. This case was designed to present a complex marketing situation. It presents sensitive political, cultural, economic, and religious issues, and was in no way intended to offend, nor to advocate, the cause of any party.

(©IRM, reprinted with kind permission.)

Appendix references

1. Dawson, Chester (2001), 'Will Tokyo Embrace Another Mouse?', 10 September.
2. Anon (2003), 'Working Time Needed to Buy a Big Mac', *The Economist*, 11 September, www.economist.com/markets/bigmac/displayStory.cfm?story_id=2054313.
3. Pulley, Brett (2002), 'Disney the Sequel', *Forbes*, 170 (12), 106–12.
4. Gregerson, Hal B. (1998), 'Developing Leaders for the Global Frontier', *Sloan Management Review*, 40 (1), 21–32.
5. Aupperle, Kenneth E. and Grigorios Karimalis (2001), 'Using Metaphors to Facilitate Cooperation and Resolve Conflict: Examining the Case of Disneyland Paris', *Journal of Change Management*, 2 (1), 23–32.
6. Anon (2006), 'Hey Mickey you're so fine', *The Independent on Sunday*, September 3. Retrieved 10 August 2008 from http://www.independent.co.uk/arts-entertainment/film-and-tv/features/hey-mickey-youre-so-fine--disney-and-his-draughtsmen-414503.html.
7. Kauth, Robert K. Jr (1988), 'The Myth of Cultural Imperialism', *The Freeman*, 38 (11).
8. D'Hauteserre, Anne-Marie (2001), 'Destination Branding in a Hostile Environment', *Journal of Travel Research*, 39 (3), 300–307.

9. Usunier, Jean-Claude (2000), *Marketing across Cultures* (3rd edn). London: Prentice Hall.

10. TEA/Economics Research Associates (2006), *TEA/ERA Theme Park Attendance Report*. Retrieved 10 August 2008 from http://www.themeit.com/attendance_report2006.pdf.

11. Assaoui, Mohammed (2002), 'Disneyland Paris, 2nd Edition: Case Study', *Le Figaro Entreprises*.

12. Milhomme, Albert J. (1993), 'Customized or Global, the Strategy May Not Work at Euro Disney', Tom K. Jr Massey, Ed. in *Marketing: Satisfying a Diverse Customerplace, Proceedings of the Southern Marketing Association*. New Orleans, LA, 91–94.

13. Koranteng, Julia (2001), 'European Park Owners Bullish About Future', *Amusement Business*, 113 (33).

14. Gentleman, Amelia (2003), 'Iraq Fallout, Strikes and Forest Fires Have Kept Americans and Europeans Away', *Guardian*, 9 August.

15. Hopkins, Nic (2003), 'Saudi Prince in Talks with Eurodisney over Rescue', *The Times*, 6 September.

16. Chu, Jeff (2002), 'Happily Ever After?', *TIME Europe*, 25 March.

17. Anon (2002), 'Welcome to the French Market', *US Commercial Service*.

18. Koranteng, Julia (2002), 'Disney Embarks on European Marketing Push', *Amusement Business*, 114 (11).

19. Hill, Jim (2002), 'It's Déjà Vu All over Again', *Orlando Weekly*, 3 March.

20. Guyotat, Régis (2001), 'Un Grand Salon au Rez de Chaussée', *Le Monde Diplomatique* (December).

21. Anon (2002), 'What the World Thinks in 2002: How Global Publics View Their Lives, Their Countries, the World, America', *Pew Charitable Trust*, 4 December.

22. O'Brien, Tim (2000), 'Parc Asterix', *Amusement Business*, 112 (42).

23. Chu, Jeff (2002), 'Room for the Imagination', *Time Europe*, 25 March.

24. Universal Mediterranea (2003), Press Dossier.

25. Anon (2003), 'Ikea Founder Worried over Growth', *BBC News World Edition*, 3 January.

26. Anon (2002), 'Ikea Aims to Double Revenue in Region', *Business Times*, 26 November.

27. Anon (2003), 'The World's Largest Family Businesses', *Family Business* (undated).

28. Wheatley, Malcolm (2001), 'Ikea's Financial Furnishings', *CIO Magazine* (online), 1 September.

29. IKEA (2007), *Facts and figures. IKEA Group Stores*. Retrieved 10 August 2008 from http://www.ikea.com/ms/en_US/about_ikea/facts_figures/ikea_group_stores.html.

30. Margonelli, Lisa (2002), *Business 2.0*, 3 (10), 106–13.

31. Beeler, Amanda (2000), 'Virus without a Cure', *Advertising Age*, 17 April.

32. Hatch, Denny (2003), 'Case Study, Ikea, Sweden's Jewel', 18 May.

33. Ishibashi, Asako (2002), 'Ikea Brings Back Scandinavian Design', *Nikkei Weekly Page* (online), 22 July.

34. Gilbert, Alorie (2000), 'Ikea to Build Supplier Portal', *CNET.COM*, 26 March.

35. Gilligan, Gregory J. (2002), 'Ikea on the Move', *Siam Future*, 28 July.

36. Anon (2001), 'Ikea Takes Art to a New Height with Its Suite Home Chicago Entry', *Furniture World*, June–July.

37. Slavin, Terry (2001), 'Ikea in Pre-Fabs Plan for Low-Paid', *Guardian* (online), 25 November.

38. Czinkota, Michael R. and Illka A. Ronkainen (1990), *International Marketing* (2nd edn). Hinsdale, IL: Dryden Press.

39. Datamonitor (2004), McDonald's Corporation, Datamonitor Business Information Center, Undated. www.datamonitor.com.

40. Anon (2008), 'McDonald's Bottom Line Swells, U.S. Sales Lag', *Dow Jones Newswire*, 22 April, www.smartmoney.com/bn/ON/index.cfm?story=ON-20080422-000388-0839&hpadref=1.

41. Anon (2007), '21st Annual Global Marketers, Part 1: Global Ad Spending by Marketers', *Advertising Age*, 19 November, http://adage.com/images/random/datacenter/2007/globalmarketing2007.pdf.

42. Bruene, Jim (2006), 'Top U.S Financial Brands', *Advertising Age*, 29 July, www.netbanker.com/2006/07/top-us-financial-brands.html.

43. Anon (2003), 'McDonald's Puts Mckids on Marketing Menu', *Brandweek*, 13 November, www.brandweek.com/bw/search/article_display.jsp?vnu_content_id=2028514.

44. Day, Sherri (2003), 'After Years at Top, McDonald's Strives to Regain Ground', *New York Times*, 3 March, http://query.nytimes.com/gst/abstract.html?res=F30913FB34580C708CDDAA0894DB404482.

45. McDonald's Corporation (2003), *Summary Annual Report 2002*. www.mcdonalds.com/corp/invest/pub/annual_rpt_archives/2002_annual.html.

46. Davis, Scott (2003), 'Top of Mind: McDonald's Strategy Doesn't Deliver', *Brandweek*, 10 November, www.allbusiness.com/marketing-advertising/branding-brand-development/4680724-1.html.

47. Garfield, Bob (2003), 'Why We're Not Lovin' It', *Advertising Age*, 8 September, http://adage.com/garfield/post?article_id=38296.

48. Cooper, Peter J. (2003), 'Mcdonald's', *AME Info*, 11 June, www.ameinfo.com/25009.html.

49. Anon (2003), 'U.S. Brands Stand to Suffer Should War Be Declared', *New York Times Service*, Paris, 16 March, www.taipeitimes.com/News/bizfocus/archives/2003/03/16/198307.

50. Docena, Herbert (2003), 'Dying for a McDonald's in Iraq', 22 October, www.zmag.org/content/showarticle.cfm?ItemID=4382.

51. Karon, Tony (2002), 'Adieu, Ronald McDonald', *TIME Magazine*, 22 January, www.time.com/time/columnist/karon/article/0,9565,196925,00.html.

52. Anon (2004), 'McDonald's plans to open 100 new outlets in China', *People's Daily Online* (January 15). Retrieved 11 August 2008 from http://english.peopledaily.com.cn/200401/15/eng20040115_132696.shtml.

53. Kamath, Vinay (2004), 'Big Mac to Head South, Finally!', *Hindu Business Line*, 11 February, www.thehindubusinessline.com/2004/02/12/stories/2004021202340600.htm.

54. Anon (2002), 'Animal Flavouring – McDonald's Indian Arm Says It's Clear', *Hindu Business Line*, 8 March, http://www.thehindubusinessline.com/bline/2002/03/09/stories/2002030901530600.htm.

55. Deshpade, Vidya (2000), 'McDonald's Goes More Indian', *Financial Express*, 11 September, www.financialexpress.com/fe/daily/20000911/faf10031.html.

56. King, Colbert I. (2001), 'Saudi Arabia Apartheid', *Washington Post*, 22 December, www.desert-voice.net/new_page_7.htm.

57. Manning, Nicole (2002), 'U.S. Companies Support Gender Segragation in Saudi Arabia', *National Organisation for Women Times*, Summer, www.now.org/nnt/summer-2002/gender.html.

58. Amnesty International (2000), 'Gross Human Rights Abuses Against Women in Saudi Arabia', September. www.amnestyusa.org/countries/saudi_arabia/document.do?id=D2C1FC0DC59EC51C802569610071BFEC.

59. Ford, Peter (2002), 'McDonald's in Disguise', *Christian Science Monitor*, 11 September, www.csmonitor.com/2002/0911/p02s02-wogi.html.

60. McDonald's Corporation (Undated), 'Welcome to McDonald's Israel' (webpage). www.mcdonalds.com/content/countries/israel.html.

61. Cohen, Deborah (2003), 'America's Corporate Icons Brace for War Backlash', *Reuters*, 8 March, www.commondreams.org/headlines03/0308-04.htm.

62. GMI News (2004), 'Half of European consumers distrust American companies', *GMI News* (December 27). Retrieved 11 August 2008 from http://www.gmi-mr.com/about-us/news/archive.php?p=20041227.

63. Werdigier, J. (2007), 'To woo Europeans McDonald's goes upscale', *New York Times* (25 August). Retrieved 11 August 2008 from http://www.nytimes.com/2007/08/25/business/worldbusiness/25restaurant.html.

64. Anon (2003), 'Indonesian Protesters Unswayed by Mcdonald's Defence', *ABC News*, 28 March, www.mcspotlight.org/media/press/mcds/afp280303.html.

65. Abdel-Halim, Mustafa (2003), 'Muslims Rally against U.S. Products, Big Mac Feels Backlash', *Islam Online*, 8 February, www.islamonline.net/English/News/2003-02/08/article03.shtml.

66. Athanasiadis, Iason (2002), 'U.S. Products, and Some Egyptian Ones, Still Feeling Boycott', *American Chamber of Commerce Business Monthly*, October, www.amcham.org.eg/Publications/BusinessMonthly/October%2002/reports(usproductssomeegyptianonesstillfeelingboycott).asp.

67. Kirschbaum, Erik (2003), 'Boycott of American Goods over Iraq War Gains', *Reuters*, 25 March, www.commondreams.org/headlines03/0325-10.htm.

68. Gardener, Frank (2000), 'Saudi Burgers to Help Palestinians', *BBC News*, 28 November, http://news.bbc.co.uk/1/hi/world/middle_east/1044998.stm.

69. Abu-Nasr, Donna (2000), 'Calls to Boycott U.S. Sweep the Gulf', *New York Times*, 30 November, www.hsje.org/calls_to_boycott_us_sweep_gulf.htm.

70. Karon, Tony (2000), 'Official Sandwich of the Intifada?', *TIME Magazine*, 29 November, www.time.com/time/columnist/karon/article/0,9565,89889,00.html.

71. Hassan-Gordon, Tariq (2001), 'Boycott against Israel Gathers Steam', *Middle East Times*, 18 May, www.inminds.co.uk/boycott-news-0204.html.

72. Wax, Emily (2003), 'In Egypt, Anger Replaces Admiration of U.S.', *Washington Post*, 24 March, www.commondreams.org/headlines03/0324-07.htm.

73. American Chamber of Commerce Egypt (2003), 'Boycott Campaign Thinks Bigger', April. www.amcham.org.eg/publications/BusinessMonthly/April%2003/ reports(boycottcampaignthingbigger).asp.

74. Blanford, Nicholas (2002), 'Arab Citizens Seize Boycott Banner', *Christian Science Monitor*, 7 May, www.csmonitor.com/2002/0507/p06s01-wome.html.

75. American Chamber of Commerce Egypt (2003), 'Egypt asks Washington for war damages', April. www.amcham.org.eg/publications/BusinessMonthly/April%2003/ reports(egyptaskswashingtonforwardamages).asp.

76. Anon (2001), 'McDonald's Dumps "I Hate Israel" Singer', *Jerusalem Post*, 5 July, www. inminds.co.uk/boycott-news-0076.html.

77. Cherian, John (2002), 'A Test of Resilience', *Frontline* (India), 7 June, www.frontlineonnet.com/ fl1911/19110610.htm.

78. Anon (2002), 'Antiaméricanismes', *Le Monde*, 7 December, www.concours-profils.fr/sujet-synthese-2004-1A.rtf.

79. Murphy, Dan (2003), 'U.S. Multinational Companies Wary of Backlash', *Christian Science Monitor*, 21 April, www.csmonitor.com/2003/0421/p12s01-woap.html.

80. Shannon, May (2002), 'Another Warning from Zubaydah', *TIME Magazine*, 11 May, www.time.com/time/nation/article/0,8599,236992,00.html.

81. Crock, Stan and Michael Shari (2003), 'Terrorism: A Gulf between Fear and Fact', *BusinessWeek.com*, 16 January, www.kabar-irian.com/pipermail/kabar-irian/2003-January/ 000104.html.

82. Anon (2003), 'Bomb Carnage Shocks Morocco', *BBC News*, 17 May, http://news.bbc.co.uk/2/ hi/africa/3037157.stm.

83. International Labor Organization (2001), 'The Social Impact of Events on the Hotel and Tourism Sector of Events Subsequent to September 11, 2001', Geneva. www.ilo.org/public/english/dialogue/ sector/techmeet/imhct01/imhctbp.pdf.

84. Farkas, David (2002), 'Risky Business: Claire Babrowski Runs McDonald's Most Volatile Region, Which Just Might Be Its Best Hope for Growth', *Chain Leader*, November, http:// findarticles.com/p/articles/mi_hb5682/is_200211/ai_n23722653.

85. Taja, W. (2003), 'Buying locally made US products not permissible: Scholar', *Islam Online*. No page given. Retrieved 11 August 2008 from http://www.islamonline.net/English/News/2002-07/03/ article09.shtml.

86. Streusand, Douglas (1997), 'What Does Jihad Mean?', *Middle East Quarterly*, September, www. meforum.org/article/357.

87. Naim, Moises (2001), '"Mcatlas Shrugged" (Interview with McDonald's CEO Jack Greenberg)', *Foreign Policy*, May, www.jstor.org/pss/3183188.

88. Anon (1999), 'French Farmers Bid to Banish Big Mac', *BBC News*, 20 August, http:// news.bbc.co.uk/2/hi/europe/426141.stm.

89. Pallister, David (2003), 'Arab Boycott of American Goods Spreads', *The Guardian*, 8 January, www.guardian.co.uk/international/story/0,3604,870412,00.html.

90. MacFarquhar, Niel (2002), 'An Anti-American Boycott Is Growing in the Arab World', *New York Times*, 10 May, www.commondreams.org/headlines02/0510-02.htm.

91. Kincheloe, John L. (2002), 'The Sign of the Burger, (Excerpt)', www.temple.edu/tempress/titles/ 1599_reg.html.

92. Ritzer, George (2000), *The McDonaldization of Society* (3rd edn). Pine Forge Press.

93. Watson, James L. Ed. (1997), *Golden Arches East: McDonald's in East Asia*. Stanford: Stanford University Press.

94. Collins, Samuel (1998), 'Book Review: James L. Watson, Ed. *Golden Arches East: McDonald's in East Asia*', *H-Net.org*, www.h-net.org/reviews/showpdf.cgi?path=9287903478462.

95. Freidman, Thomas (2000), *The Lexus and the Olive Tree: Understanding Globalization*. Anchor Press.

96. Thrupkaew, Noy (2003), 'Big-Mac Attack', *The American Prospect*, 31 January, www. prospect.org/cs/articles?article=mac_attack.

97. Anon (2002), 'Universal Studios, Shanghai Sign Deal', *Guardian*, 7 December.

6

Cross-cultural market research

Market research across national/cultural boundaries can be problematic. A European syrup maker ordered a survey of the Swedish syrup market from a large international market research company. Unfortunately, syrup, a solution of sugar dissolved in water and flavoured with fruit juice, was incorrectly translated as *blandsaft*, a Swedish term for concentrated fruit juice, a local substitute for syrup with much less sugar. Thus, when the results came in, they were of no use, because it was a local product rather than the product category at large that had been surveyed. This simple translation mistake may have cost the company the money allocated to the research, but had they not discovered the mistake and acted on an answer to the wrong question, it could have cost them dearly in market share as well.

Market research is about timely, relevant information. For instance, the simultaneous launch of new products into several different national markets requires research to be undertaken in multiple locations at the same time. Typical research questions may be similar to the following:

1. How should one undertake a market survey for instant coffee in a traditionally tea-drinking country like the United Kingdom or Japan? What information and data must be sought? How should the data be collected?
2. Which information-gathering technique should be used for personal care products in a country where, for instance, potential respondents resent interviews as an intrusion into their privacy, or female members of a household are not permitted to talk to strangers?

3. How should a questionnaire be translated and adapted to the cultural specificity of other countries when the starting point is a questionnaire that was originally designed for a specific country?

Even slight differences in the research question may require a different emphasis or even a different research technique to uncover the required answers. For instance, we might want to know how to increase market share, but we need to make sure that the problem (and not just the symptom) is correctly specified. Using instant coffee as an example, we might ask one of the following:

1. How can we recover the market share lost by instant coffee to ground coffee in a traditionally coffee-drinking country? This requires the investigation of consumption patterns in certain social and family situations, and the times at which people drink specific coffee-based beverages.
2. How can we increase the market share for instant coffee out of the total hot beverages market in a traditionally tea-drinking country? This requires an in-depth investigation of market segments that are likely to drink coffee in at least some consumption situations.

An understanding of the cross-cultural environment is a basic requirement in setting the research objective: therefore the objectives cannot be the same as those for domestic market research. The first section in this chapter discusses the local marketing environment and infrastructure (section 6.1) that needs to be considered in marketing research decisions.

Given the multinationalization of business, establishing the quality of research instruments, consistency of behavioural/attitudinal constructs and equivalence of samples are of paramount concern to the marketer. This chapter presents the main limits to equivalency across national/cultural contexts when undertaking cross-cultural market research. These include conceptual and functional equivalence (section 6.2), translation problems (section 6.3), measure equivalence related to different units being used cross-culturally (section 6.4), the comparability of samples and sampling procedures (section 6.5) and the equivalence problems in data collection procedures resulting from interviewers' and respondents' attitudes towards surveys (section 6.6). It also aims to provide the reader with some basic insights, drawn mostly from cross-cultural methodology in the social sciences, on how to solve these problems. The last section (section 6.7) discusses whether international market research should use a different approach from traditional, positivistic market research techniques.

6.1

Local marketing institutions and infrastructures

Observers of local marketing environments need to remember Schrödinger's cat dictum that the observation or measurement of something in itself affects an outcome (in layman's terms the dictum states that a cat in a sealed box is both alive and dead until someone observes it). We understand local environments from our own ethnocentric perspective. There is always a reference point that makes judgements implicitly comparative. For example, when local people fail to understand or appreciate the value of the interviewing process in market research, we might judge them by as uneducated. Conversely, we might try and understand their viewpoint, and gain useful information about how products and services are used by local people.

The whole marketing process is based on a series of steps or processes that need to be applied locally, in preparing for decisions (market research), developing strategy and implementing it (e.g. advertising campaigns or placing the product in distribution channels). The feasibility of marketing decisions and details of their execution are affected by local marketing institutions and infrastructures.

Market research can be undertaken in most countries of the world and international marketers will find subsidiaries of major international market research organizations or local or regional companies that offer good research services almost everywhere. While the multinational firms may not offer the full range of services in developing nations, the list of services is expanding every year. In the case of China, the lead-up to the 2008 Olympics in China has seen a dramatic increase in marketing research firms and services being offered. Research companies in China now offer a range of panel services, at least in the major cities.

Other institutional factors, such as the socioeconomic, regulatory systems and cultural systems, also need to be taken into account when conducting research across countries.[1] Burgess and Steenkamp (pp. 341–4)[1] describe these as:

1. Socioeconomic systems including macroeconomic and demographic characteristics, heterogeneity within countries, as well as social, political and economic change.
2. Regulatory systems including formal rules, levels of conformity and sanctions.
3. Cultural systems including the shared interpretive processes and understanding that influences beliefs, attitudes, habits, norms and behaviours.

Differences in these systems need to be considered when deciding the goals of the research, the information that needs to be collected and the way in which it is collected. For instance, the socioeconomic systems influence the target markets and importance of factors, such as household income and access to consumers. Regulatory systems influence the way in which we conduct marketing research and in a broader sense how we implement marketing strategies, but it also influences the rights of consumers and their expectations. As is the claim of this text, cultural systems influence most aspects of marketing and market research. The more apparent and more subtle influences of culture are elaborated throughout this chapter.

Quite apart from its technicalities, which are explained at great length in specialist textbooks, market research is a human activity that generally involves interviewers/researchers and informants/respondents as human beings. The kind of neutral, objective stance that is required from informants, who must speak their true mind without any influence from the interviewer, is difficult enough to find in countries where market research, polls and panels are well established. It is all the more difficult to find in many local environments, where willingness to answer or more generally to deliver information to strangers is low, since interviewers are seen to be hidden sellers or impolite intruders. Similarly, motivation to answer will be low when there is no local belief that answering will benefit consumers as a community, because the feedback loop that links consumer research information to product improvement and to personal interest is uncertain and complex.

6.2

Equivalence in cross-cultural research

If the type of data sought and the research procedures implemented are considered to be of general application, the main difference between domestic and cross-cultural market research lies in the difficulty in establishing equivalence at the various stages of the research process. It is not self-evident, as the Japanese style of market research shows (see section 6.6), that research procedures and the type of data sought are completely independent of the cultural context of the researcher. But this chapter first emphasizes dependence on the researched context.

The complexity of the research design is greatly increased when working in an international, multicultural and multilinguistic environment (not to mention the difficulties in establishing comparability and equivalence of data).[2-5] Even greater problems may arise when differences in sociocultural or psychographic variables imply different attitudes and behaviour when using particular types of product. For instance, research in Singapore, using a food-related lifestyle instrument that had been developed in western Europe, reveals that out of five areas (ways of shopping, quality aspects, cooking methods, consumption situations and purchasing motives), only consumption situations and purchasing motives show even a minimal level of cross-cultural validity.[6]

The many possible reasons for this include (a) different cooking patterns in Singapore, where the use of maids and eating out are more prevalent, (b) lower involvement in cooking, (c) a broader concept of convenience, (d) different beliefs in health properties of food, and (e) different use of information in the highly competitive Singaporean food sector. Thus, questionnaires need to be adapted to the context in each country (see the hair shampoo exercise in section A6.2).

Research approaches: emic versus etic

The classic distinction in cross-cultural research approaches is between *emic* and *etic*.[7,8] The emic approach holds that attitudinal or behavioural phenomena are expressed in a unique way in each culture. Taken to its extreme, this approach states that no comparisons are possible. The etic approach, on the other hand, is primarily concerned with identifying universals. The difference arises from linguistics where phon*etic* is universal and depicts universal sounds that are common to several languages, and phon*emic* stresses unique sound patterns in languages.

In general, market research measurement instruments adapted to each national culture (the emic approach) offer more reliability and provide data with greater internal validity than tests applicable to several cultures (the etic approach, or 'culture-free tests'). But use of such instruments is at the expense of cross-national comparability and external validity. The results are not generalizable to other cultural contexts. This is why we need to examine cross-national equivalence, which is inspired by the etic rather than the emic perspective. In terms of Table 4.1 the issue would be very much at the centre of the four cells; it lies somewhere between looking with the same eye at an object that is supposed to be different and changing to a slightly different eye in order to have a better look.

Levels of cross-cultural equivalence

Management must provide guidelines for the systematic collection of data, either domestic or international. It

Table 6.1 Categories of cross-cultural equivalence

A. Conceptual equivalence	B. Functional equivalence
C. Translation equivalence ■ Lexical equivalence ■ Idiomatic equivalence ■ Grammatical–syntactical equivalence ■ Experiential equivalence	**D. Measure equivalence** ■ Perceptual equivalence ■ Metric equivalence ■ Calibration equivalence ■ Temporal equivalence
E. Sample equivalence ■ Sampling unit equivalence ■ Frame equivalence ■ Sample selection equivalence	**F. Data collection equivalence** ■ Respondents' cooperation equivalence ■ Data collection context equivalence ■ Response style equivalence

(Source: Adapted from Craig and Douglas.[9] *Consumer Behavior*, 4th edn, Craig C. Samuel and Susan P. Douglas, 2001, © John Wiley & Sons Limited, reprinted with permission.)

is important to follow a precise plan that outlines the various steps of the research process, starting with a clear and concise statement of the research problem.[10] The literature now includes many papers exploring the issue of cross-cultural equivalence.[4,11–18] There are also areas where non-equivalence, causing non-comparability, may arise in comparative consumer research.[9] The various levels of cross-cultural equivalence displayed in Table 6.1 are explained in the text of the chapter, with six main categories and 16 subcategories that are further discussed in this text.

Website link 6.1

Read a discussion paper on cross-cultural equivalence in international sales negotiations: http://www.swan.ac.uk/sbe/research/working%20papers/EMBS%202000%206.pdf.

Conceptual equivalence

A basic issue in cross-cultural research is the determination of whether the concepts have similar meaning across the social units studied. The same construct may be relevant across cultures, but expressed in different ways. Problems of *conceptual equivalence* are more frequent when testing the influence of certain constructs on consumer behaviour. For instance, the hypothesis of the cognitive theory that people do not

willingly behave inconsistently may hold true in the United States while not being applicable to some other countries (conceptual equivalence). For instance, in many collectivist cultures people are seen as more mature if they can overcome their internal attitudes and emotions and act in a manner that is appropriate.[19] Conversely, in many individualist cultures people are seen as more mature if they act on their internal attitudes and emotions in a consistent manner.

Reaching true conceptual equivalence between cultures can be extremely difficult. As anthropologist Clifford Geertz (p. 59) notes:

The Western conception of a person as a bounded, unique, more or less integrated, motivational and cognitive universe, a dynamic center of awareness, emotions, judgement and action, organized in a distinctive whole . . . is, however incorrigible it may seem, a rather peculiar idea, within the context of world's cultures.[20]

Such basic concepts as beauty, youth, friendliness, wealth, well-being, sex appeal, and so on, are often used in market research questionnaires where motivation for buying many products is related to self-image, interaction with other people in a particular society, and social values. They seem universal. However, it is always advisable to question the conceptual equivalence of all these basic words when designing a cross-cultural questionnaire survey. Even the very concept of 'household', widely used in market research, is subject to possible inequivalence: in Northern Nigeria people often live in large extended family compounds or gida which are difficult to compare with the prevalent concept of household that reflects the living unit of a nuclear family.[21]

Many examples in previous chapters illustrate the practical difficulties in dealing with the conceptual equivalence of constructs used in a survey. When looking at the underlying dimensions across countries, it can often be seen that they are not equivalently weighted or articulated in the total construct. For instance, in the construct 'waiting in line' (to be served), the dimension of 'wasting one's time' may be emphasized in a time-conscious culture, whereas it may be almost non-existent in one that is not economically time-minded. In line with this, Americans are more impatient than Singaporeans, and this leads to Americans being willing to pay more for items that are available for immediate consumption.[22]

Often the conceptual equivalence of several basic interrelated constructs has to be questioned, inasmuch as they relate to consumer behaviour idiosyncrasies for the specific type of product or service surveyed. Box 6.1 shows some construct equivalence problems in the case of life insurance policies.

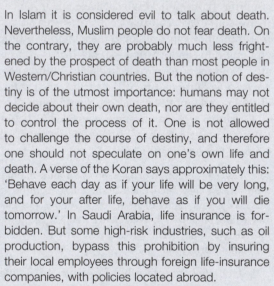

Box 6.1

A multinational survey on life insurance: conceptual equivalence problems in Islamic countries

In Islam it is considered evil to talk about death. Nevertheless, Muslim people do not fear death. On the contrary, they are probably much less frightened by the prospect of death than most people in Western/Christian countries. But the notion of destiny is of the utmost importance: humans may not decide about their own death, nor are they entitled to control the process of it. One is not allowed to challenge the course of destiny, and therefore one should not speculate on one's own life and death. A verse of the Koran says approximately this: 'Behave each day as if your life will be very long, and for your after life, behave as if you will die tomorrow.' In Saudi Arabia, life insurance is forbidden. But some high-risk industries, such as oil production, bypass this prohibition by insuring their local employees through foreign life-insurance companies, with policies located abroad.

In the Islamic world people do not like to invest and bet on the long term. Effort must be rewarded quickly if it is to be maintained. The concept of a financial product such as life insurance needs a long-term orientation and a strong individual capacity to imagine the future. Projection towards the future is a culture-related trait (see section 2.2). In Islam, you may certainly imagine how you will be tomorrow, but not at a particular place or moment. The future tense exists, but it is certainly not as accurate or meticulous as that of the English or European languages. Moreover, protection of the family and solidarity within the extended family are highly valued and work effectively. If a man dies, his brother will care for his wife and children.

The concept of life insurance is related to culture in at least the following four aspects: protection of the family and/or the individual; future orientation; betting on one's own life and death; the degree of solidarity in the family and extended family group. In Islamic countries it is important not to offend interviewees at first contact. It is better to rely on in-depth non-directive interviews and focus groups carried out principally by briefed local researchers who have a thorough personal knowledge of Islam and the local culture (the Islamic world spreads from black Africa to China). Some research questions will have to be addressed in order to prepare an adequate marketing strategy. What is the appropriate mix, for the design of the life insurance policies offered to potential consumers, in terms of death benefit (amount of money to be paid when a person under a life insurance policy dies) and annuities (a series of payments made at regular intervals on the basis of the premiums previously paid)? What term(s) should be proposed for people before they receive the benefits of their life insurance policy? How should the beneficiaries be designated? How should this offer be communicated to potential consumers through advertisement: which brand name should be adopted and which themes and advertising style should be favoured in the advertising campaign?

Many popular marketing constructs have been used in cross-cultural research settings (perceived risk, brand loyalty, Rokeach value survey, lifestyles, etc.). Some, mostly in the form of shortened scales, have been tested for equivalence across multiple cultures. Many other scales have been reduced on an ad hoc basis to be equivalent in the samples being studied, by including only the highest loading items. These scales may or may not be equivalent with other samples from the same or other countries. Thus, it is necessary to evaluate each construct and scale for the study at hand.

Generally speaking, conceptual equivalence is an obstacle to the direct use of constructs that have been specifically designed for Western cultures. The perceived risk construct, for instance, may differ in its components across cultures. As mentioned in Chapter 4, perceived risk has to be broken down into several sub-dimensions, including psychological, financial, performance, physical, social and time or convenience risk.[23] The emphasis placed on these sub-dimensions may vary across cultures. For instance, people in some cultures may give more value to the social risk of buying a car because their purchase and use of the car is mostly status oriented, whereas in other cultures people may be more concerned with physical safety because death in accidents is greatly feared. Further, it would be important to know if it was the perceptions of risk in the specific situation or the more generalized attitude toward risk that differed. Chinese students are less risk-averse than Americans, however the difference is in the perceptions of the risk, rather than the attitude towards perceived risk.[24]

Therefore it is necessary to investigate, far more frequently than is actually done, the construct validity in each culture where a cross-cultural consumer behaviour study is undertaken. The construct validity is effected by both construct bias and equivalency issues. Bias occurs when the definition of the construct differs across cultures influencing construct validity (e.g. lack of consideration of the extended family in measuring intergenerational influence across countries), whereas equivalency relates to the level of comparison or measurement of the construct.[25] The validity of the underlying constructs at the conceptual level and reliability at the empirical/ measurement instrument level should be tested by following recognized procedures outlined in the sections below.

Functional equivalence: similar products and activities performing different functions

If similar activities perform different functions in different societies, their measures cannot be used for the purpose of comparison.[26] Concepts frequently used in market surveys, such as preparing a meal, are not necessarily functionally equivalent across countries. When asked: 'What dishes do you cook, or prepare with tomato juice?' Italians and Danes give different answers. Functional equivalence problems can be illustrated taking the example of hot milk-based chocolate drinks.[27] Whereas in Australia, the USA and the UK milk-based drinks are generally considered an evening drink, best before going to sleep, in much of Latin America a 'Chocolate Caliente' is a morning drink. In this case, functional equivalence is not reached due to differences in the consumption time period and in the purpose for use: waking/energizer versus sleep/relaxer. Similarly, functional equivalence will be a problem if we compare bicycle purchases in China, where they are used mainly for transportation, with other countries, where they are mainly used for leisure.[28]

Similarly, a watch may be used as jewellery, a status symbol, or an instrument for handling time and daily schedules. The same holds true for a fountain pen. In some countries its function may be as a simple general-purpose writing instrument; in others it may be regarded mostly as an instrument for signing documents. Elsewhere it may be considered purely non-functional since it needs time and care to refill it, and often stains. Many other examples could be given, such as wine (everyday beverage accompanying meals versus beverage for special occasions), beer (summer refresher versus all-year standard 'non-water' beverage), mixed spirit drinks (a man's versus a woman's drink) and perfumes (masking bodily odours versus adding a pleasant smell after a shower).

The simple word 'coffee' covers a whole range of beverages that are enjoyed in very different social settings (at home, at the workplace, during leisure time, in the morning, or at particular times during the day), in quite different forms (in terms of quantity, concentration, with or without milk, cold or hot), prepared from different forms of coffee base (beans, ground beans, instant). The function of the Brazilian cafezinho, very small cups of coffee, rather strong and drunk every hour in informal exchanges with colleagues, cannot be compared with that of the US coffee, which is in large cups, very light, and drunk mostly at home, while in transit or in restaurants. Similarly, the meaning and even the uses of coffee in the Haya community of Tanzania are in fact significantly different to those of the global economy.[29]

One of the best ways to investigate functional equivalence is to examine the social settings in which a product is consumed. Local observational methods and focus groups are commonly employed for this purpose.

6.3

Translation equivalence

For many reasons, which are outlined principally in Chapter 12 on language, culture and communication, translation techniques, no matter how sophisticated, might prove incapable of achieving full comparability of data. Let us first make a small review of translation equivalence problems.

Website link 6.2

Find 22 humorous examples of translations gone awry: **http://www.world-time-zones.org/articles/translation.htm**.

Categories of translation equivalence

Translation equivalence may be divided into the following subcategories:

1. *Lexical equivalence*: This is what dictionaries can provide us with: for instance, one may discover that the English adjective *warm* translates into the French *chaud*.
2. *Idiomatic equivalence*: The problem of idiomatic equivalence comes when you try to translate a sentence such as 'it's warm': French has two expressions for it, either 'il fait chaud' (literally, 'it

makes warm' meaning 'it's warm [today]') or 'c'est chaud' (meaning 'it [this object] is warm'). An idiom is a linguistic usage that is natural to native speakers. Idioms are most often non-equivalent: the present continuous (i.e. I am *doing*) has no equivalent in French, except *je suis en train de . . .* , which is highly colloquial, not to be used in correct French written language. This may also be problematic for regions within a country, as Roy *et al.* (p. 207) states:

The English phrase 'high risk' can be translated as 'qiang feng xian' in the middle and northern China but as 'gao feng xian' in southern China. To Chinese from the south, the word 'qiang' has two meanings, one is related to the 'magnitude' and the other to 'strength'; as such, it can be difficult to interpret the concept 'qiang feng xian'.[28]

3. *Grammatical–syntactical equivalence*: This refers to the way words are ordered, sentences are constructed and meaning is expressed in language. English generally proceeds in an active way, starting with the subject, followed by the verb and then the complement, avoiding abstractions as well as convoluted sentences. Many languages, including German and French, start by explaining the circumstances in relative clauses, before they proceed into the action. This makes for complex sentences starting with relative clauses based on *when*, *where*, *even though*, *although*, and so on. The Japanese language has a quite different ordering of words from Western languages: verbs are always at the end of the sentence: 'Gurunoburu no daigaku no sensei desu' means: 'Grenoble of [*the*] university of professor [*I*] am', that is, 'I am a professor at the university of Grenoble'.
4. *Experiential equivalence*:[30] This is about what words and sentences mean for people in their everyday experience. Coming back to 'chaud', it translates into two English words 'warm' and 'hot': the French do not experience 'warmth' with two concepts as the English, the Germans and many others do. Similarly, the special experience of coldness in the word 'chilly' cannot be adequately rendered in French. Translated terms must refer to real items and real experiences which are familiar in the source as well as the target cultures. An expression such as 'dish-washing machine' may face experiential equivalence problems when

Box 6.2

'Reproductive health'

Cultural discrepancies are not only evidenced in factual themes, they also manifest themselves in translation difficulties: the concept of 'reproductive health' was translated into German as '*Gesundheit der Fortpflanzung*' (health of propagation). The Arabic translators invented the formula: 'spouses take a break from each other after childbirth', the Russian translators worded this in despair as 'The whole family goes on holiday' and the Chinese translators elevated themselves to the almost brilliant formula 'a holiday at the farm'. This shows that the new word-monsters, elegantly coined by the Americans, are almost non-translatable worldwide; on the other hand, they infuse international conferences with a lot of humour.

(Source: Bohnet.[31])

people, even if they know what it is, have never actually seen this type of household appliance or experienced it. Another example of experiential non-equivalence is given by the Japanese numbering system, which reflects a special experience of counting, where the numbers cannot be fully abstracted from the object being counted. Most often the Japanese add a particle indicating which objects are counted. *Nin*, for instance, is used to count human beings: *yo-nin* is four (persons). *Hiki* is used for counting animals but not birds, for which *wa*, meaning *feather*, is used, *satsu* is used for books, *hon* for round and long objects, *mai* for flat things such as a sheet of paper, textiles, coins, etc., and *hai* for cups and bowls and liquid containers in general. As a vivid illustration of translation problems, Box 6.2 shows the translation errors in the case of a major concept, 'reproductive health', for the UN World Conference on Population Development, held in Cairo in 1994.

Back-translation and related techniques

The back-translation technique is the most widely employed method for reaching translation equivalence (mainly lexical and idiomatic) in cross-cultural research.[32] This procedure helps to identify probable translation errors. One translator translates from the source language (S) into a target language (T). Then another translator, ignorant of the source-language text, translates the first translator's target language text back into the source language (S¢).

Then the two source-language versions, S and S¢, are compared.

For instance, when translating '*un repas d'affaires*' ('a business meal' in English) from French to Portuguese in the preparation of a questionnaire for Brazil, it is translated as *jantar de negocios*. When back-translated, it becomes a '*dîner d'affaires*' ('business dinner'). In Brazilian Portuguese, there is no specific expression for '*repas d'affaires*'. It is either a 'business lunch' ('*almoço de negocios*') or a 'business dinner'. One has to choose which situation to elicit in the Brazilian questionnaire: the 'business meal' has to be either at noon or in the evening in the Portuguese version. When back-translating, discrepancies may arise from translation mistakes in either of the two directions or they may derive from real translation equivalence problems that are uncovered. Then a final target-language questionnaire (T_f) is discussed and prepared by the researcher (who speaks the source language) and the two translators. In practice it is advisable to have one translator who is a native speaker of the target language and the other one a native speaker of the source language. It means that they are translating *into* their native language rather than *from* it, which is always more difficult and less reliable.

However, back-translation can also instil a false sense of security in the investigator by demonstrating a spurious lexical equivalence.[33] Simply knowing that words are equivalent is not enough. It is necessary to know to what extent those literally equivalent words and phrases convey equivalent meanings in the two languages or cultures. Another technique,

Figure 6.1 Examples of translation techniques

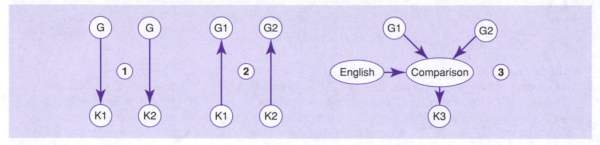

blind parallel translation, consists of having several translators translate simultaneously and independently from the source language into the target language.[34] The different versions are then compared and a final version is written. This is similar to the collaborative and iterative technique, which engages a committee or expert panel both at the initial translation stage as well as the iterative revision translation stage.[35]

Combined translation techniques, limits of translation

Parallel and back-translation can be merged, as shown in Figure 6.1. When two languages and cultures present wide variations, such as Korean and German, combining parallel and back-translation provides a higher level of equivalence.[36] For example, two Koreans translate the same German questionnaire G into two Korean versions, K1 and K2. A third Korean translator, who is unfamiliar with the original German text G, translates K1 and K2 into G1 and G2. A final Korean questionnaire, K3, is then prepared by comparing the two back-translated German versions G1 and G2. English is used to help compare them as it is widely used and more precise than either German or Korean. This example could be refined: the number of parallel translations may be increased, or back-translation processes may be independently performed.[37]

A more sophisticated solution to the problem of translation is to develop research instruments in the two cultures, and generate items, questions or other survey materials jointly in the two cultures.[32] After back-translation, or after any initial translation

process has been performed, there is an opportunity to change the source-language wording. This technique, called *decentring*, not only changes the target language, as in the previous techniques, but also allows the words in the source language to be changed, if this provides enhanced accuracy. The ultimate words and phrases employed will depend on which common/similar meaning is sought in both languages simultaneously, without regard to whether words and phrases originate in the source or the target languages. In the above example of the business meal, choosing the decentring method would imply changing the words in the source questionnaire to 'business lunch'. In any case, it remains absolutely necessary to pre-test the translated research instrument in the target culture until satisfactory levels of reliability on conceptual and measurement equivalences are attained.[38] Table 6.2 presents a synthesis of translation techniques as well as their advantages and drawbacks.

6.4

Measure equivalence

Variations in the reliability of research instruments

Variation in cross-cultural reliability of underlying instruments has already been assessed; measurement unreliability is also a threat to cross-national comparability. Investigating the problem of measurement reliability in cross-cultural marketing research for three types of consumer behaviour measures (demographics, household decision involvement and

Table 6.2 Advantages and drawbacks of translation techniques

Technique ⇒	Direct translation	Back-translation	Parallel translation	Combined techniques
Process	S ⇒ T	S ⇒ T; T⇒ S' comparison S to S' ⇒ final version T_f	S ⇒ T; S ⇒ T' Comparison T to T' ⇒ final version T_f	S ⇒ T; S ⇒ T' T ⇒ S'; T' ⇒ S" comparison S'/S", decentring of S ⇒ final version T_f
Advantages	Easy to implement	Ensures the discovery of most inadequacies	Easier to implement in S country with T translators	Ensures the best fit between source and target versions
Drawbacks/ Constraints	Leads to translation errors and discrepancies between S and T	Requires the availability of two translators, one native in S and one native in T languages	Leads to good wording in T, but does not ensure that specific meaning in S is fully rendered	Costly to implement Difficult to find the translators Implies readiness to change source-language version

Key: S = source language, T = target language (translators or versions).

psychographics) across five country-markets, utilizing three different reliability assessment methods, it is shown to be easier to obtain measurement equivalence between demographic variables than between psychographic variables such as lifestyles. For psychographic variables it may be necessary to use a more in-depth assessment method to gain a better understanding of the variable, as well as potential linkages to products. For instance, by using a 'means–ends', which begins with the core values, respondents are asked which values are important in their life.[39] Then they indicate which of a list of products make the value or feeling possible. Finally, they say how each product facilitates the value or feeling. What emerges is the value *family security* not only defined in terms of physical safety but also in terms of financial security. In this case, *family security* is linked to alarm systems through the means of safety and linked to mutual funds through financial security. The 'means–end' concept can be extended to include not only written and verbal interactions, but visual and other sensory images.[40] Mental maps can be developed and compared across cultures (Sugai, 2005).

Variations in knowledge and familiarity with products, concepts or attitudes also impact on the equivalence of measures. A warranty is perceived in a different manner in China than in the United States.[41]

In China it is viewed as an extrinsic cue of little value to the potential buyer, due to their lack of familiarity with the concept. Similarly, comparing the attitudes of respondents in two countries (the United States and Turkey) towards the people and products from three countries of origin (West Germany, Japan and Italy) using three products (cars, cameras and electronic calculators) demonstrates that the same scale may have differing reliabilities when used by the same individual in evaluating products from differing cultures.[42] As Parameswaran and Yaprak (pp. 45–6) state:

differing levels of awareness, knowledge, familiarity and affect with the peoples, products in general, and specific brands from a chosen country-of-origin may result in differentials in the reliability of similar scales when used in multiple national markets . . . Two alternative courses of action may alleviate this problem. Measures to be used in cross-national market comparisons may be pre-tested in each of the markets of interest until they elicit similar (and high) levels of reliability . . . Alternatively, one might devise a method to develop confidence interval (akin to statistical spreads based on sample sizes) around the value of the measure based on its reliability.[42]

Comparison of results across countries should be made while simultaneously analysing and checking for the reliability measures of the rating scales.

Table 6.3 Adjectives which have the same level of meaning in two languages and provide similar distances between the points of the scale

Colloquial rating scale				Formal rating scale			
US adjectives			**French adjectives**	**US adjectives**			**French adjectives**
Fantastic	20	20	Extraordinaire	Remarkably good	17	17	Très bon
Delightful	17	17	Superbe	Good	14	14	Bon
Pleasant	14	14	Très correct	Neutral	10	10	Moyen
Neutral	10	10	Moyen	Reasonably poor	6	6	Faible
Moderately poor	7	7	Assez faible	Extremely poor	3	3	Très mauvais
Bad	4	4	Remarquablement faible				
Horrible	2	2	Terriblement mauvais				

(Source: Pras and Anglemar, p. 76.[43] © March 1978 by ESOMAR® – The World Association of Research Professionals; this article first appeared in *European Research*, published by ESOMAR.)

Perceptual equivalence

As emphasized in sections 1.4 and 8.4, perception varies across cultures. Colours are perceived differently according to culture, that is, not all cultures have equivalent sensitivity to the various parts of the colour spectrum and the corresponding languages do not qualify colours in exactly the same way. In addition, the symbolic interpretation of colour varies widely (Box 8.5). The same is true for smells: the first issue in equivalence is whether people perceive them physically and mentally in the same manner; the second issue deals with the kind of interpretation they vest in these smells. When conducting research about packaging, perfumes for washing liquids, etc., where perceptive clues are important for product evaluation, it is a key research issue to formulate questions so that interviewees can express their native views on the smell or the colours. Rather than ask them whether they like a lavender smell, it is better to ask them first to recognize the smell, then to comment on what it evokes.

Metric equivalence

If the scores given by respondents do not have the same meaning, then metric equivalence is a problem. Scores may differ across cultures for a variety of reasons including the avoidance of extreme responses, humility or social desirability.[5] Unfortunately, these differences can only be checked after the data is collected, limiting the validity of cross-cultural comparisons. There are several techniques available to researchers to assess metric equivalence, including the popular multiple-group structural equation modelling,[16,44–46] and the Rasch measurement approach.[47,48]

The validity of a rating scale in a cross-cultural study is affected by the equivalence of the scales and by the homogeneity of meanings. For instance, there are problems with the use of scales in China.[28] The difficulty lies in determining lexical equivalents across languages for verbal descriptions of a scale, as the Chinese language does not readily provide good antonyms (see Table 6.3). It is also difficult to ensure that the distances between scale points, especially verbal scales, are equivalent across languages (metric equivalence). For instance, while scale anchors such as 'agree/disagree' might work well for English-speaking managers, Japanese managers might not understand them adequately.[49] Thus, it is naive to use a differential semantic scale originally written in English, Spanish or any other language and translate it lexically (simply with dictionary-equivalent words) into other languages. In this case decentred measurement is preferable, which means constructing reliable and valid scales for all the countries under survey. In this way the original wording of the scale may be changed if it provides better measurement equivalence across countries/cultures.

The metric equivalence of nine scale terms (from 'excellent' to 'very bad') across eight languages (English, Arabic, Chinese, Farsi, French, German, Korean and Spanish) reveals that: (1) some languages have fewer terms to express gradation in evaluation (e.g. Korean), whereas others have a multitude (French); and (2) there are large discrepancies in the 'value' of these adjectives, measured on a scale from 0 to 100. For instance, the Spanish 'muy malo' rates 58 per cent higher than its supposed English equivalent of 'very bad' (Sood, 1990). Therefore the best solution is not to translate scale terms but rather to start from local wordings based on scales used by local researchers. Also we need to be wary about the meaning of numbers across cultures. For instance, the numbers 2, 8 and 9 are considered lucky in China and as such may be chosen more frequently.[28] Thus, it may be advisable in some cultures to number only the end points.

One promising avenue for cross-cultural research is the use of purely visual scales that avoid the verbocentric nature of most market research instruments, which are based on words and sentences that never translate perfectly. Perhaps 'putting people back in' is best: most communication relies on images and is non-verbal, whereas thinking processes rely on metaphors to elicit hidden knowledge.[40] Instruments that allow respondents to express the mix between emotions and reason may be more useful. For instance, the use of 'smiling faces' as scales should not be limited to children, on the basis of the (unconscious) view that adults *should* use words, not pictures, and should not express their views metaphorically. Visual and verbal representations of the overlap between a person's self-identity and the identity of the group increase equivalence across cultures.[50] More sophisticated visually oriented scales, such as the self-assessment manikin (SAM), allow cross-cultural measurement with less bias than verbal scales; they further enable a better apprehension of the respondents' emotions.[51]

Another promising research method is the best–worst method proposed by Jordan Louviere and colleagues (see Marley and Louviere[52] for a more formal discussion of BWS, including formal proof of the measurement properties associated with different cognitive processes that respondents might use to make best and worst choices). This method was recently applied to measure Kahle's[53] List of Values

Table 6.4 The SVBWS task

Most Important		Least Important
○	Successful, capable, ambitious.	●
●	Protecting the environment, a world of beauty, unity with nature.	○
○	Helpful, honest, forgiving.	○
○	Devout, accepting portion in life, humble.	○
○	Clean, national security, social order.	○

and Schwartz[54] values (see Lee *et al.*[55,56]). A sample set from the Schwartz Value Best Worst Survey (SVBWS) is shown as Table 6.4.

Best Worst Scaling (BWS) requires a respondent to choose one item that the respondent thinks is the best/largest/most-x and one that is the worst/smallest/least-x from a series of sets that contain different combinations of a larger master set of items. The particular combinations that appear in each set are determined by an experimental design to ensure balanced appearance and co-appearance across the sets. BWS assumes respondents behave as if they examine every pair of items or options in each set and then choose the most distinct or maximally different pair. Respondents find it relatively easy to choose the *most* and *least* within a set.

This method has the potential to reduce response-style effects, as respondents cannot consistently use the middle points, end points, or one end of a scale. It also has the potential to reduce problems with equivalence, due to the difficulty in finding lexically equivalent verbal descriptions for a scale, metrically equivalent distances between numbers, and separating numbers from their meanings. The BWS method only has two verbal scale terms (e.g. most important and least important); it is relatively easy to find equivalent terms for 'most' and 'least' in most languages. The BWS method also has no numbers, which eliminates problems found when numbers have meanings in certain cultures, such as 2, 8 or 9 being lucky and 4 unlucky in China. Finally, the BWS method results

Box 6.3

Measuring fuel efficiency across cultures

Most Europeans use the metric system, an international standard. They measure distances in kilometres and liquid volumes in litres (one cubic decimetre). When looking at fuel consumption, they calculate how many litres are necessary for driving 100 kilometres, at a particular average speed. Fuel consumption is measured in litres/100 km. In the USA, 'gas mileage' is based on a reverse concept: given a definite fuel volume, namely a gallon, how many miles can one drive with it? For Europeans

trying to understand what miles per gallon means is somewhat nightmarish. First, they have to know which gallon it is: the British or Imperial gallon (4.55 litres) or the US gallon (3.79 litres) and whether it is a statute mile (1.609 kilometres) or a nautical mile. When they understand that it is a US gallon and a statute mile, they still have to make an inverse calculation and try to finish with 100 kilometres in the denominator in order to know whether the car has high petrol consumption or poor gas mileage.

in an interval or ratio score, depending on the scoring technique.[56]

Calibration equivalence

Calibration equivalence problems arise from different *basic* units being used as well as from *compound units* when they are based on different computation systems (see Box 6.3). For instance, a typical calibration equivalence problem relates to differences in monetary units; this is especially true in high-inflation contexts where daily prices over a year cannot be directly compared with those of a low-inflation country. Naturally, exchange rates and units of weight, distance and volume cause calibration equivalence problems. Calibration equivalence mixes with perceptual equivalence: for instance, how many colour classes are recognized by people from a particular country? This might prove useful for a packaging test or a product test. Western subjects, for example, have more colour classes than African subjects, and some primitive people have only a two-term colour language. The Bantu of South Africa, for example, do not distinguish between blue and green. Consequently they do not discriminate between objects or symbols in these colours.[57]

Temporal equivalence

Temporal equivalence is similar to calibration equivalence, in terms of calibrating dates and time periods. Information, for instance, ages at different speeds

across countries: in a country where the annual inflation rate is minimal, income and price data are comparable across years; whereas in a Latin American country such as Venezuela with a 20 per cent annual inflation rate in 2007 it is necessary to indicate on which day the data were collected and what the price indexes and exchange rates were at that time.

Website link 6.3

In 2008 the inflation rate in Zimbabwe was the highest in the world at 100,000 per cent: **http://www.guardian.co.uk/world/2008/feb/22/zimbabwe.**

Temporal equivalence also deals with differences in development levels and technological advancement: certain countries are 'equivalent' to what others were 20 years ago. Assessing time lags may be useful for making analogies: such a market may develop in South Africa now as it did in the United States 15 or 20 years ago and the product life cycle may be similar even though the two countries are at different points on the curve.

6.5

Comparability of samples

When secondary data – especially published statistical data – are sought, there may be some difficulties in comparing these data across countries:

1. Differences in categories: for instance, for age brackets, income brackets or professions.

2. Difference in base years, when some countries have no recent data.

3. Unavailable or unreliable data, the data collection procedure by the local census bureau being biased for certain reasons (non-exhaustive census, inadequate sampling procedure).

4. Sampling unit (who should the respondent be?).

Choice of respondents (sampling unit equivalence)

An important criterion for sampling is the choice of respondents. Selecting a unit of analysis is a key issue in the conceptualization of comparative research designs. The role of respondents in the buying decision process (organizational buying, family buying, information and influence patterns, etc.) may vary across countries. Several studies have found differing parental influence over children's purchases across countries. For instance, parents have a greater influence over their children's purchasing in Fiji,[58] Japan[59] and Thailand,[60] when compared to the United States. In the United States, it is not uncommon for children to have a strong influence when buying cereals, desserts, toys or other items, whereas in countries that are less child oriented, children's influence on the buying decision will be much smaller.[8] It is therefore crucially important to assess, first, the basic equivalent sampling units. This statement is as relevant for industrial markets as for consumer goods markets: when researching industrial products, it is important to compare the position, role and responsibility of industrial buyers throughout different countries.

Website link 6.4

See sampling techniques and examples of poor sampling and bias: http://www.marketresearchworld. net/index.php?option=com_content&task=view&id= 23&Itemid=1&limit=1&limitstart=1.

Representativeness and comparability of national/cultural samples

Sampling is a basic step in most market surveys. A complete census, where the whole population of interest is researched, generally proves too costly. Therefore it is advisable to infer the characteristics of the whole population from a limited sample. In this process the following tasks must be carried out:

1. Finding a sampling frame or list, where the basic population characteristics are known (a telephone directory, an electoral list, etc.).

2. Drawing a sample from this frame, by a method which may be either probabilistic or non-probabilistic.

3. Checking that the selected sample is representative of the population under study.

The main problem in the cross-cultural sampling process is the selection of comparable samples across countries. Reaching perfect comparability is very difficult, if not impossible. These limitations should be considered when interpreting research findings.

In cross-cultural research there are often two levels of sampling to consider. The first level is a sample of countries or cultures and the second level is based on samples of individuals within the chosen countries or cultures. At the first level, the research question is directly comparative. Samples of cultures should not be confused with samples of individuals.[61] There is a risk of stereotyping, whereby country characteristics are considered as individual characteristics. Mean values for each country are first compared, calculated from the scores on each question for the respondents from that country.

Samples of maximally different countries can be used to compute the average influence of cultural values on certain consumption patterns. For instance, to understand what the main cultural, sociodemographic and economic variables are that best explain the per capita consumption of a particular product or service. For instance, in a study of 26 developed countries national wealth was found to explain most of the variance in country-level adoption of technology such as mobile phones, cable television, computers and the Internet.[62] In a study of 23 countries, the evaluation of brand manufacturer websites was moderated by the countries' legal systems, individualism and their level of national identity.[63] Strategic marketing decision making often needs to assess country-level data to select target national markets and markets with low actual demand but high growth potential to deciding where to locate efforts for the future.

A cross-cultural/cross-national design may also be useful when one tries to derive an estimated market demand figure in a country where statistical sources are scarce and unreliable. For instance, it is possible to estimate a regression equation explaining per capita annual wallpaper consumption, with explanatory variables such as income per capita, percentage of home ownership, frequency of use of other wall-covering materials, etc.[64] To estimate the parameters it is possible to use a cross-section sample (data for a sample of countries, for the same year), or a pooled cross-section/time series sample, when the countries' data are available for several years. For a country where wallpaper consumption is unknown, it is then possible to compute it with the values of the explanatory variables.

A second issue is the representativeness of each sample in each unit of analysis, which may be a country, a culture, or a common language group which shares similar patterns of social interaction and communication.[65] Countries are often used as proxies for cultural units. In cross-cultural research it seems a priori relevant to follow a systematic procedure, the same in every country, to achieve reliability and comparability of data. Unfortunately, demographic definitions do not correspond exactly from one country to another. Age may, as long as people know their birth dates, but occupation, education and socioeconomic status usually do not. If data are presented in categories, say for income or age bracket, these categories will most likely not correspond exactly across countries (category equivalence). Religion and tribal membership will also have to be added to traditional demographics as they are of the utmost importance in some less developed countries.[66]

A representative sample?

A researcher may construct a sample which represents the population of interest. However, a sample split into 50 per cent men and 50 per cent women conveys a different meaning in a country where women's rights are recognized in comparison to countries where women's status is lower. The expression 'representative sample' therefore makes little sense without clarifying which traits and characteristics this sample actually represents. For instance, shopping behaviour is very different worldwide: in some places men tend to do most of the shopping, in other countries it is mostly women; this also depends on various other factors (income level, type of product, etc.). In this case, the samples must represent actual shoppers, rather than a representative number of men and women in the general population of potential shoppers.

In order to define a sampling procedure for cross-cultural research, a method must be selected so that each national sample is fully representative of the *population of interest*, and which furthermore provides comparable data across countries. There is usually limited availability of exhaustive sampling frameworks that corresponds exactly to the characteristics of the population at a global (multi-country) level.[3] This extends to the Internet. While the Internet might seem attractive to researchers, due to lower costs and faster speed in data collection, Internet sampling frames are limited by the technological capabilities of the populations of interest. These characteristics may differ dramatically from large cities to rural populations, as is the case in China.

> ### Website link 6.5
>
> See guidelines for conducting research on the Internet: http://www.ifsm.umbc.edu/npreece/Papers/Online_survey_design_ISHCI04.pdf.

In fact, sampling frames are often biased. Audience research for the BBC worldwide stresses the frequent lack of reliable or recent census data in many developing countries, including the former Soviet Union and in eastern Europe.[21] For instance, a sample drawn from the electoral list in Bolivia may overrepresent men, since women are not as likely to vote.[27] Similarly, most sampling frames in Saudi Arabia are inadequate: there is no official census of the population, no exhaustive voter registration records, and telephone directories tend to be incomplete.[67] Non-probability sampling is necessary in many countries. Often sampling frames for businesses are of better quality, since most businesses want their number on lists, such as the telephone directory, but in China these directories are often out of date and lists are likely to include only the businesses or people associated with the list supplier.[28]

Estimating sample size is also a critical step. The use of traditional statistical procedures, such as constructing confidence intervals around sample means, or hypothesis testing, is difficult to implement since such procedures require precise estimates of the variance of the population. This variance estimate is often unavailable in countries that have poor census data. The most frequently used procedure is therefore the selection of sample size, country by country, taking into account their respective peculiarities.

In establishing a framework to determine which sampling approach should be used for international studies it is stressed that the objective of the research should guide the technique.[68] For instance, if the objective is to examine similarities and differences across cultures and cross-national comparability is important, non-probability samples may be a better method to allow the researcher to create homogeneous samples. Conversely, when the objective is to describe attitudes or behaviour within specific countries, within-country representativeness is important and probability samples should be used to enable the researcher to estimate the sampling error.

Survey firms in different countries measure public opinion and survey markets with different methods: for instance, quota sampling used in most of Europe is considered less acceptable in the United States.[69] Similarly the use of RDD (random digit dialling) to construct phone samples, which is standard practice in the United States for telephone surveys, in order to include both unlisted people and recent movers, is not used in phone samples in many other countries.

Finally, one may conclude that representativeness and comparability of cross-cultural samples can be better achieved by using different samples and sampling techniques that produce equivalent levels of reliability than by using the same procedure with all samples. For example, different screening criteria are often used in North America and China to ensure that the samples were comparable.[70] In North America the objective may be to sample mainstream consumers with screening criteria including being a native English speaker, born in North America to North American parents. In China the objective may be to sample respondents who had access to consumer markets, with screening criteria including an education level that would allow a literate information search and an income level that would allow consumption.

The main problem (before any statistical procedure is implemented) is to secure equivalence in meaning: does it make sense to represent the same populations across various countries? Do the samples actually represent these populations in the same way?

6.6
Data-collection equivalence

Where primary data are concerned, discrepancies in response patterns across countries may cause data unreliability and so limit direct comparison. Let us assume that through any of the translation procedures described above we are able to develop equivalent national versions of a common questionnaire for a cross-cultural market research study, and that we have consistent and equivalent samples. We may still have to overcome response equivalence, such as the following:

1. Secrecy/unwillingness to answer (respondents' cooperation equivalence).
2. Response biases (data-collection context equivalence).
3. Differences in response style (response-style equivalence).

Sources of error measurement related to response styles are multiple and may directly create discrepancies between observed measurement and true measurement. Some basic precautions may help to avoid the generation of data with a great deal of measurement error.

Reluctance to answer: respondents' cooperation equivalence

Respondents sometimes feel that the interviewer is intruding into their privacy. They prefer not to answer or they consciously bias their answers, fearing that their opinion could later be used against them.[27] Many countries have strong privacy/intimacy patterns, where the family group is protected from external, impersonal interference. It seems the very private and reserved nature of Saudis is not conducive to personal interviews.[67] Saudis do not want to be exposed to justifying or explaining their actions when answering a barrage of questions. In the case of Afghanistan and Mozambique, Mytton (p. 26) explains that:

Protocol demands that the most senior woman of the house should be interviewed before any other female . . . In some areas of Afghanistan, women cannot be used as interviewers. In others the reverse is the case; a male stranger coming to a house would be regarded as a possible threat . . . As in Afghanistan, many respondents in Mozambique did not know their own age or that of other members of the household . . . In several areas the presence of strangers writing down information on pieces of paper while talking to people, started rumours. One rumour suggested that the survey team was registering the number of children in each household with the intention to return later and kidnap them. Research had to be delayed for meetings to be held with the local authorities in order for them to reassure people living in the area.[21]

Similarly, there are also differences in response rate from business surveys: response rates to industrial mail surveyed differed dramatically across 22 countries: ranging from over 40 per cent in Denmark and Norway to 7 per cent in Hong Kong and 11 per cent in the United States.[71] This was in spite of the efforts to motivate respondents (CEOs and Human Resource Managers),[72] including a reminder mailing, letter, photograph of the researcher and a tea bag or coffee satchel with the message 'Why don't you take a short break, have a nice cup of tea and fill out the questionnaire right now, it will only take 10–15 minutes'.

Context equivalence of data collection

Questions are never culture-free: there is inevitably a social and cultural context built into them. Contextual equivalence relates to elements in the context of the data-collection process that have an influence on responses. As Douglas and Craig explain (p. 109): 'In the Scandinavian countries, for example, respondents are considerably more willing to admit overdrinking than in Latin America. In India, sex tends to be a taboo topic.'[57] Any question that deals, directly or indirectly, with social prescription needs to be worded so that people can elaborate a response without feeling too embarrassed, and

responses have to be screened in order to know if the responses reflect actual reality or a view of what is socially desirable. Some well-disposed and open-minded interviewees may be questioned further to deliver their true view on the question.

It is possible to measure individual social desirability bias and then to use this information to adjust the results of a survey. Using items from the Marlowe–Crowne Social Desirability Scale to assess differences in convenience samples from the United States, Japan and Sweden, the US respondents show a higher level of social desirability than the Japanese or Swedish respondents.[73] Measuring social desirability, as well as the source or influencers for respondents intercepted in shopping areas in the United States, France and Malaysia, Malaysian respondents are shown to have a higher level of social desirability bias than the US or French respondents. In addition, Malaysian respondents are more strongly influenced by personal sources, such as family and friends, and US respondents are more strongly influenced by impersonal sources such as the media and government.[74] Of course, the measures of social desirability are also subject to context equivalence. For instance, the Paulhus social desirability scale includes items that are likely to be inappropriate in some cultures, such as 'I never read sexy books or magazines'. As such, they cannot be assumed to be measuring the same thing across cultures.

Biases resulting from the relationship with the interviewer

Sexual biases between interviewer and respondent are also an important source of the reluctance to grant interviews. In many traditional countries, housewives are reluctant to grant interviews to male interviewers. Ethnic bias may also exist between the interviewer and the respondent: a Chinese person may feel uncomfortable when interviewed by a Malay.[75] Much response bias may result from the interviewees not understanding that the process of interviewing them is in order to generate objective data. Informants may perceive the purpose of research as a very long-winded form of selling, especially in developing countries.[66] The objective and the process of the interview must often be explained at the beginning. When briefing native interviewers (management

Box 6.4

The weaknesses and strengths of the 'local researcher'

1. Weaknesses

(a) Often of lower intellectual ability and research experience than his or her equivalent in developed countries.

(b) Often finds it difficult to adopt neutral, objective stance with reference to informants or clients. May want to be didactic in groups and may well prefer to distort findings to reflect a more educated picture of his countrymen than exists in reality. Alternatively, may seek to distance himself from the 'average consumer' by exaggerating their foibles and lack of sophistication. He himself, especially if he is from an educated family, may be out of touch with his countrymen.

(c) He may be unwilling or unable, even for business reasons, to cross traditional barriers of class, religion or tribe.

(d) He rarely has the Puritan work ethic and does not always see the value of objective truth. Delays, shortcuts and distortion are likely.

2. Strengths

(a) He knows the country and its people. He can usually establish rapport easily and understands what is said. If he knows the Western country he can also interpret the significance of what is said, to explain differences.

(b) He knows the language. Language can be an enormous barrier, as anyone who has tried to interview through interpreters must recognize.

(c) He is immune to local ailments and is physically comfortable in the (research) environment. He can cope, through familiarity, with common problems.

(Source: Goodyear, pp. 90–91.[66])

students) in Mauritania, they asked the following question: 'What do you want us to tell the interviewee to answer?' It was necessary to explain to the interviewers that interviewing was a distanced and objective process, where interviewees had complete freedom of response. The idea of objective truth, external to personal relations, is unfamiliar to Mauritanians (Box 6.4). Furthermore, among the Mauritanian interviewers, the *Maures*, of Arabic descent, clearly explained that they would not interview black Africans. Fortunately, there were some black Africans who were potential interviewers for their own ethnic group. Strong ingroup orientation implies that group membership has to be shared between interviewer and interviewee for the process to take place.

In the same vein, Japanese managers in Indonesia tend to recruit Bataks, because their characteristics resemble those of the Japanese, although they are not necessarily liked by other Indonesians and they may perform poorly as data collectors (Maruyama, 1990). This ethnicity-of-interviewer bias has been shown to exist even within the United States where both Hispanic and Anglo-American respondents significantly bias their responses to items pertaining to the interviewer's culture; therefore it seems more appropriate to match respondent's and interviewer's ethnicity, especially for Anglo-Americans.[76]

Some respondents, especially in Latin American countries, tend to present a 'courtesy bias' by answering in order to please the interviewer.[27] Respondents tend to tell the interviewer what they think the interviewer would like to hear. This response pattern probably takes place in countries where people tend to have difficulty in answering opinion surveys and market research questionnaires. When they agree to participate, it can be from a personal feeling of goodwill towards the interviewer.

Response-style equivalence

Response-style equivalence is the final step. All the rest may be equivalent; yet our respondents may offer non-equivalent responses. The four main concerns in relation to response-style equivalence are:

1. Yea-saying pattern (and, conversely, a nay-saying pattern) or Acquiescence/disacquiescence.
2. Extreme response style/response range and middle response style.
3. Non-contingent responding (careless, random or non-purposeful).
4. Item non-response pattern.

An analysis of five-point Likert-scale questions from a 26-country study (including countries from North and South America, Asia, northern Europe, western Europe, eastern Europe and southern Europe) showed major differences in response styles that were related to cultural characteristics (Harzing, 2006; Smith, 2004). For instance, acquiescence was negatively related to individualism and positively related to power distance and extraversion. Extreme response bias was positively related to extraversion, whereas middle response bias was negatively related to power distance and individualism. Within cultural regions and countries there were also marked differences, such as Japan having much lower acquiescence bias than most other Asian countries.[77,78] Similarly, an analysis of mail survey data from 11 European countries to assess the amount of response-style bias in five-point Likert scales shows that all of the above forms of response-style responding influence some of the scales, but that in this case there was no evidence of more severe response styles in some countries than in others.[2] the scales with the most contamination measure health consciousness, consumer ethnocentrism, quality consciousness and environmental consciousness (ibid.).

First, 'yea-saying' or acquiescence is the tendency to agree with items and nay-saying or disacquiescence is the tendency to disagree with items regardless of content.[2] For acquiescence the response scores tend to be inflated with the mean score of the respondents being biased towards the positive end of the scale, and for disacquiescence the reverse occurs. When interviewing Greek and Italian housewives on their cooking behaviour this bias has an effect: there is systematic tendency in the Greek sample to give more positive answers in psychographics as well as in product-related questions than in the Italian sample.[18,79] The yea-saying bias

translates into a higher mean score on almost all questions.

Standardizing scores across cultures allows the 'yea-saying' pattern to be eliminated, although it is fairly difficult to differentiate whether people were generally striving to give answers towards the positive end of the scale or were agreeing strongly with a particular item. Thus the 'yea-saying' pattern is diagnosed only when it is consistent across almost all the questions. Balancing the items so that some are positively worded and others are negatively worded, may be helpful (Baumgartner and Steenkamp, 2001), but this approach may affect other aspects of equi-valence across countries as East Asians do not see positively and negatively worded items as opposites.[80]

Second, extreme response style is the tendency to choose the most extreme response regardless of content, while response range is the tendency to either use a narrow or wide range of categories around the mean.[2] This response pattern is systematically marked by a higher or lower standard deviation. For instance, in the United States people tend to respond with more enthusiasm, and therefore present a more extreme response style in answering, than the Japanese[81] or Koreans.[82] This could produce a bias in the standard deviation of data, increasing it artificially in cultures where people tend to overreact to questions, compared to other cultures where people may tend to suppress their opinions, either positive or negative. In responses given to scales ranging in format (3- to 10-point) by university students in Australia, France, Singapore and the United States.[83] the amount of extreme response differs by country, with France exhibiting the highest level, followed by the United States, followed by Australia and Singapore. The scales with the least extreme response style are 5- to 7-point response formats.[83,84]

Third, non-contingent responding is the tendency to respond carelessly, randomly or non-purposefully.[2] This may happen if respondents are not very motivated to answer the questionnaire.

Fourth, item non-response is an important source of bias in cross-national surveys. Respondents may be unwilling to respond to some questions, such as those relating to income or age. In a public opinion survey in eight European countries, there is evidence of non-response in relation to income being higher in the United Kingdom and Ireland, whereas the willing-ness to respond to political questions is highest in Germany and Italy.[57]

Encouraging feedback from the informant on cultural adequacy

Humans are not simple response machines. 'Criticality dissonance' is when respondents disguise and transform responses because they fear that information may be misused.[85] As shown above, international market research is full of criticality dissonance. The basic process affecting the truthfulness of responses is 'relevance dissonance', as Maruyama (p. 30)[85] states: 'the purpose of the questionnaire survey as perceived by the respondent differs from the respondent's own purpose. The questionnaire is perceived as irrelevant and useless. In such a case counter-exploitation takes place. The respondent looks for a way to manipulate the survey or interview to produce some benefit'.

For these reasons, it seems necessary to design research procedures where feedback from the informant is possible, for instance: focus groups, in-depth interviews and open-ended questions.

Unique features of cultural behaviour cause non-equivalence. It is impossible to uncover these levels of non-equivalence if the instrument and methodology prevent them from appearing. A pragmatic solution is to ask interviewees their opinion of the relevance of questions, words and concepts used in the questionnaire at the end of the normal interview process (post-test). A pre-test of questionnaires is also necessary. Multiple methods may be used to elicit feedback from respondents, including a preliminary study using in-depth interviews, focus groups to identify the appropriate product categories and help define the interview, and, after the main study, follow-up interviews to clarify unclear issues and investigate new issues.[70]

A questionnaire forced upon interviewees does not elicit information (see the hair shampoo exercise in section A6.2). If emic feedback is to be introduced, both interviewers (especially when they have not been personally involved in compiling the questionnaire) and interviewees must be put in a situation where they may comment on the questions themselves and explain what is culturally meaningful in their own context and what is not. Interviewees should be given the opportunity after the normal answering process to elaborate freely on what they think of the questions, the situations described, and so on. This orientation is slightly different from the traditional one where interviewed people are simply required to answer, not to 'criticize' the questions. Emic feedback allows an improvement in the adequacy of the source culture's constructs and instruments.

Informants should be neither overestimated nor underestimated. They cannot respond to a barrage of questions alien to their knowledge and frame of reference. Therefore the content of the research must somehow be strictly controlled and must focus on really significant issues; surveys should be parsimonious and should not ask too much from informants. On the other hand, informants need to be carefully listened to because it is they who, as insiders, have the relevant pieces of information. The same care has to be taken with interviewers: they must be properly controlled (some – not all – may cheat by guessing responses or even filling in questionnaires themselves), and adequately briefed professional interviewers may not be found everywhere.

6.7

Researching internationally

For various reasons, apart from the equivalence issues reviewed previously, international research is different from domestic research: (1) it is more difficult and more costly to implement, and the stakes are often lower than those in the domestic market; and (2) information often needs to be fed more directly into action, thus a 'hands-on' approach is to be recommended.

Website link 6.6

See ESOMAR, a worldwide organization promoting better research into markets, consumers and societies: **http://www.esomar.org**.

The Japanese style of market research

Japanese firms use market survey techniques that are quite distinct from those used by US companies.[86] While the Japanese do survey markets, they decide what to do afterwards fairly independently of the survey conclusions. For example, research was presented to Akio Morita, founder and president of the Sony Corporation, which suggested that the Walkman would not be bought by consumers: they would not buy a tape player that does not record, even a portable one. Trusting his intuition, though undoubtedly after fairly wide consultation, Akio Morita and Sony took the decision to launch the Walkman, with the success we all know about.

In fact Japanese firms take a direct interest in the realities of the marketplace and outlets. They look for information from the actual *buyers* (not the potential consumers), who are interviewed about the products they want, and how the products themselves could be better tailored to consumers' needs. The chief executive officer of Canon USA spent six weeks visiting Canon distribution networks, chatting to sales executives, customers and store managers, in order to find out why Canon cameras were not selling as well as the competition.

This attitude is quite different from the prescriptions of traditional market research, which are as follows:

1. Market research has to be representative; therefore a representative sample must be used.
2. Market research must be scientifically objective. A questionnaire (that is, a systematic but not necessarily *open-ended* information retrieval instrument) should be administered by non-participating researchers: they should not be personally involved in the consequences of the responses given by interviewees.
3. Research has to study the *potential* market, not the *actual* market (that is, real buyers and real users).
4. As far as possible, the people who undertake market research should not be the same people who ultimately decide on the marketing strategy to be adopted. There is a potential danger that the boss of Canon USA could be manipulated by customers and distributors, who might take the opportunity to demand lower prices or other benefits by over-

stating competitors' strengths. There is also the risk that by focusing on the actual market, as yet untargeted market segments could be ignored or neglected. As Johansson and Nonaka emphasize (p. 16):

Japanese-style market research relies heavily on two kinds of information: 'soft data' obtained from visits to dealers and other channel members, and 'hard data' about shipments, inventory levels, and retail sales. Japanese managers believe that these data better reflect the behaviour and intentions of flesh-and-blood consumers. Japanese companies want information that is context specific rather than context free – that is, data directly relevant to consumer attitudes about the product, or to the way buyers have used or will use specific products, rather than research results that are too remote from the actual consumer to be useful.[86]

Market research as images of reality: atomistic versus organic views

In fact, market surveys are, at best, 'photographs' of the market; they are not the market itself. At the Los Angeles County Museum of Art there is a painting by the Belgian Painter René Magritte, called 'La pipe'. It simply shows a pipe, with a thin trail of smoke coming out of it. That is (almost) all. Then: there is a short subtitle at the bottom of the painting, saying 'ceci n'est pas une pipe' ('this is not a pipe'): a very 'down to earth' way of reminding us that *images of reality* should not be confused with reality itself. We may create images of reality, especially through the media (for instance, a war reported on a TV screen) but we may also ignore large chunks of reality (especially its experiential elements).

On the other hand, we should not underestimate the power of the process of designing images of reality, especially for decision-making purposes. Scientific market research provides marketing decision makers with an image of the actual and/or potential market, consumer behaviour and the competition. Large parts of reality are beyond our limited perceptual apparatus. Let us take another example: at the Mount Wilson observatory in California, there are photographs of the stars taken using a special quality of film, with a shutter exposure of four hours. The stars in the sky are far more numerous than we will ever see with our limited vision. The same holds

Table 6.5 Atomistic versus organic approaches

Approach to reality	Atomistic	Organic
Nature of reality	Divisibility/independence	Global/indivisible/dependent
Time	Linear/divisible	Cyclical/integrative
Communication style	Explicit/low context	Implicit/high context
Interpersonal relations	Individualist/reciprocal	Collectivist/loyal
Intellectual style	Data/measurement oriented	Intellectual modesty
Proof	Validated theory (truth)	Virtue/conviction
Space	Universalist	Localist
Decision making	Formalized	Weakly structured

true for market research: from panels or, more generally, from a large and representative sample of consumers, we may derive images of the market that we will never match simply by talking with anyone who is around.

Our argument is that, across countries, marketing decision makers do not use exactly the same information for a similar decision process, and that, to a certain extent, culture influences the scope and nature of researched information, and the use of the results in the process of marketing decision making. Two basic approaches to reality may be contrasted as ideal types, the atomistic and the organic approaches (Table 6.5), which we all share, across individuals and cultures. In terms of research traditions, the atomistic view is close to distanced positivistic research, the organic view is nearer to humanistic enquiry.[87,88]

In the atomistic view we consider ourselves as being outside the real world, as observers, able to depict with a certain degree of precision workable images of the real world (atomistic), and then use them to interact with this external world. The atomistic approach leads us to consider reality as fundamentally divisible into units that display enough independence that, operationally, we can ignore the interrelations between pieces of it.

Conversely, one may emphasize that we are an integral part of this reality, to which we belong so inextricably that it is not really possible to separate oneself from the reality. We are so deeply immersed in it that it would make no sense. The organic approach assumes the indivisible nature of reality, its elements (if there are any) being fundamentally interdependent. Reality is global, rather than piecemeal.

These two approaches are complementary rather than antagonistic. However, one approach can be dominant among a group of people or a culture, or in an individual or an area of knowledge.[89] Table 6.5, which builds on Tables 2.1 to 3.5, illustrates how these approaches are linked to major categories of cultural differences, although the difference between atomism and organism is not a cultural difference.

The atomistic belief in *divisibility* favours the view that time is divisible, that the basic unit of interpersonal relations is the individual, and that communication can and must be explicit (that is, clearly separated, 'divided' from surrounding issues, topics and preoccupations). Separating emotions from actions, friendship from business, is typically an atomistic attitude towards reality, seen as divisible. Very naturally, the atomistic approach favours the perception that data orientation and measurement are the proof that a piece of reality is divisible and (therefore) exists. To illustrate the importance of measurement in the atomistic approach, let us take the case of a company that is trying to improve service *within* the company, so that it is not only front-line service providers who are concerned with service to customers. In addressing such an issue, a typical atomistic statement would be: 'To arrive at a position where excellent service is achieved will be a difficult enterprise. This primarily results from the lack of service measurement knowledge *within* the company.' In fact, scales exist only to measure service quality vis-à-vis customers, so that the atomistic solution is to try and develop a measurement instrument, because the reality of within-company service cannot be tackled in the absence of measurement instruments.

The organic approach holds the contrary assumption: it is precisely because measurement is difficult that the two issues are considered as non-separate and to be treated as a joint piece of reality. The research approach will be quite different.

On the other hand, a dominance of the organic approach favours collectivism in its strongest sense: people do not consider themselves as being separate from the group to which they belong. Their sense of belonging includes the implicit view that they are not really separable from their group. The communication style is more implicit and contextual, because the sense of the interdependence of pieces of reality is much stronger. In interpersonal relationships, loyalty is characteristic of the organic approach, whereas reciprocity, based on tabulated favours (time, amount and persons being clearly defined), is linked to the atomistic approach. To this list can be added that proof (in the sense of making it work; being accepted and being considered as a necessary piece of reality) is based on validated theory for the atomistic approach, and on arguments favouring conviction and virtue for the organic approach.

With divisible reality, linear time and individual emphasis, the atomistic approach conceives of decision making as a highly formalized process, followed by implementation, control and feedback. It is a time sequence such as we see in many managerial textbooks. Conversely, the organic approach emphasizes circularity in time and the integration of time horizons. Preparing, making decisions and implementing them are not easily seen as completely separated pieces of time reality, leading to a fairly unstructured decision-making process. Finally, the organic approach does favour 'localism', local solutions, because solutions are built within a context and there is a difficulty in conceiving universal solutions. Conversely, the data and theory orientation in the atomistic approach favours universalism, because reality, when reduced to figures, shows a fairly high degree of universality.

The case of research on international markets: doing research with limited data availability and limited resources

International business and marketing requires a greater focus on the external environmental, since this differs more across countries than within countries.

For instance, there is a need for research into government in China.[90] One specific firm divides research into vertical and horizontal studies. First, vertical market studies research the governing structures relating to the client's business including government policies, organization, and influences. For instance, an international chemical firm commissioned them to interview government officials to obtain their position on a new regulation, 'China's Environmental Regulations for Chemical Products Imports and Exports', that was threatening their business operations, so that they could develop a strategy to lobby for adoption of internationally accepted practices. Second, horizontal market surveys are more industry-specific, such as studying market opportunities, the competitive environment and consumer preferences, etc. Similarly, Tan and Lui (p. 803) discuss trends in international marketing research in Asia:

there is also a growing realization that it is not enough to monitor shifts in brand perceptions or market share. It is, in fact, far more important to possess a holistic understanding of the total operating environment (including political and economic issues) and have better appreciation of the competitors' plans and activities. This understanding results in the clients' increasing dissatisfaction with traditional marketing research as being too narrowly focused on marketing issues: research techniques and an overriding concern with data rather than analysed information . . . Market research should therefore not just be conducted in response to one apparent market threat or opportunity, but rather on an ongoing basis in order to achieve a sustainable advantage.[91]

As explained in the sections above, when research is conducted internationally, the basic conditions of market research are different from those prevailing in the domestic market. For instance, export managers in the United States most highly value information that provides market potential, followed by legal, political, infrastructure, economics and, finally, culture: they first have to establish that the country has the necessary demand, is open, will remain open, is conducive to entry, and is evolving, and then they can seek the cultural information that will improve on success.[92] Market experience, market share and availability of people and resources are generally much higher in the domestic environment than in international markets.[93]

There is a high level of uncertainty in international markets and a limited availability of objective information, both in quantity and in quality.[94] This may explain why international marketing decisions are dominated by the influence of subjective and perceptual factors. In fact, the same information can be used in different ways. Information may be used either for 'instrumental and conceptual' use or for 'symbolic' use (Diamantopoulos and Souchon, 1999). The first category is the direct application of the research to a specific problem (instrumental use) or for general enlightenment or future use (conceptual use). The second category is really a misuse of information (symbolic use), such as using it out of context, selectively disclosing information that confirms a previously held conviction or ignoring facts. In the case of some exporting companies from Austria, Germany, New Zealand, the United Kingdom and the United States, information (relating to export marketing research, export assistance and export marketing intelligence) is more likely to be used instrumentally/conceptually than symbolically, although there are differences across countries.[95] For instance, US exporters are more likely to use information symbolically than the other countries; conversely, Austrian exporters are less likely to use information symbolically than the other countries. Instrumental or conceptual use of information is more likely to increase market knowledge and performance than symbolic use.[96]

The less sophisticated nature of international marketing research has also emerged.[97] Officials of 70 companies from Wisconsin and Illinois, involved in international business, were interviewed. Mostly simple survey techniques were used: foreign market research is generally informal, with no standard procedures. Furthermore, the frequency of identifying and analysing foreign markets is much less than once a year. Sophistication increases with the higher degree of involvement in foreign markets, as measured by the percentage of export profits to total company profits. Another study confirms these findings: a large proportion of US exporters, approximately two-thirds of the companies surveyed, do not adopt a formalized marketing plan.[98] But when they do, they tend to focus on issues similar to those researched domestically and to neglect 'strategic issues relating to risks appraisal, environmental issues, cultural considerations . . . which require close contact with the foreign environment' (Koh, p. 17).[98]

The acceptance of intuition in the decision-making process is a key element of those differences. Should we continue with very in-depth research if the final decision is taken by somebody who may or may not follow the conclusions of the research? Should the researcher and the decision maker be different people or the same? These questions are raised by the cross-cultural comparison of marketing research practices.

Research on the Internet

The Internet offers many opportunities to access both secondary and primary research. First, for secondary research the Internet makes it easy to locate preliminary information about a region or country of interest, including the macro-environmental factors, such as political, legal, geographical, economical and cultural information, as well as the micro-environmental factors, such as market size, distribution systems, presence of local and global competition and consumer information. Examples of information search on competitive intelligence analysis, industry analysis, buyer behaviour and new business-to-business markets can help in the initial stages of market consideration.[99] Access to secondary information over the Internet is fast, easy and low cost, but it is also difficult to compare and validate the data and the authenticity of sources of information.

Second, for primary research the Internet offers the ability to conduct traditional surveys via e-mail, online surveys and focus groups. It also allows tracking exposure to websites, product, advertising, company information and patterns of use, such as information search patterns. The Internet's capacity for interactivity also means that it is easy to communicate directly with customers and respondents through chat rooms and bulletin boards.[91] Access to primary information over the Internet is relatively easy and cheap, but it is usually limited to Internet/e-mail users. This may be especially problematic in countries where there is low Internet access.[3]

Website link 6.7

SurveyMonkey.com is a good place to start online market research: **http://www.surveymonkey.com**.

6.8

Conclusion

International market surveys should not be constructed by simply transposing domestic research. The nature and scope of researched market information, the ways of collecting it, the accuracy of the data as well as the criteria of reliability of the data present cross-cultural variance. This holds true even when these factors are perceived as normatively quite universal. International market researchers have to reveal their own ethnocentric biases by giving feedback opportunities to their informants or to local collaborators. From this point on, a systematic search for formal equivalence may appear dangerous. Equivalence of constructs and instruments has to be established first. As Craig and Douglas (p. 85)[3] put it, international marketing researchers 'are being challenged to conduct research that is of the highest possible quality, as quickly as possible, in multiple diverse settings'.

The final recommendation is to search for the meaning, bearing in mind this advice:

1. Scientific methods provide pictures which otherwise would not be available (the 'Mount Wilson' argument).
2. But images of reality are not reality itself (the 'la pipe' argument).
3. Address the relevant questions (only those that can be articulated into decision and action).
4. Respect your informants and consider their competence as insiders as superior to yours as an outsider; but interview only those people who have something to say.
5. Keep a 'hands-on' approach to market research.
6. Culture must be examined at each step of the research process: questions, survey methods, interviews and questionnaires, informants.

Questions

1. Define the following terms:
   (a) conceptual equivalence;
   (b) temporal equivalence;
   (c) sexual bias.

2. Discuss the functional equivalence of the following products or consumption experiences. For this, choose countries/culture with which you have familiarity and experience and think in terms of benefits and those that are particularly emphasized in certain cultures:
   (a) a bicycle;
   (b) drinking a beer;
   (c) red wine;
   (d) a watch.

3. What are the obstacles for a sample of consumers to be cross-culturally representative?

4. Discuss how market size can be estimated in a country where there is little or poor statistical data available.

5. List possible benefits for a washing powder or liquid and suggest possible cross-cultural variability in the dominance of certain benefits as compared with others.

6. Suggest ways of obtaining relevant market and consumer behaviour information where potential informants are not accustomed to questionnaires and interviews.

7. How does the individualism/collectivism difference have an impact on the drafting of market research questionnaires?

8. What constraints does strong ingroup orientation put on the data-collection process?

References

1. Burgess, Steven Michael and Jan-Benedict E.M. Steenkamp (2006), 'Marketing Renaissance: How Research in Emerging Markets Advances Marketing Science and Practice', *International Journal of Research in Marketing*, 23 (4), 337–56.

2. Baumgartner, Hans and Jan-Benedict E.M. Steenkamp (2001), 'Response Styles in Marketing Research: A Cross-National Investigation', *Journal of Marketing Research*, 38 (2), 143–56.

3. Craig, C. Samuel and Susan P. Douglas (2001), 'Conducting International Marketing Research in the Twenty-First Century', *International Marketing Review*, 18 (1), 80–90.

4. Durvasula, Srinivas, J. Craig Andrews, Steven Lysonski, and Richard G. Netemeyer (1993), 'Assessing the Cross-National Applicability of Consumer Behaviour Models: A Model of Attitude Towards Advertising in General', *Journal of Consumer Research*, 19 (4), 626–36.

5. Van de Vijver, F.J.R. and Ype H. Poortinga (1982), 'Cross-Cultural Generalization and Universality', *Journal of Cross-Cultural Psychology*, 13, 387–408.

6. Askegaard, Søren and Karen Brunsø (1999), 'Food-Related Lifestyles in Singapore: Preliminary Testing of a Western Research Instrument in Southeast Asia', *Journal of Euromarketing*, 7 (4), 65–86.

7. Pike, Kenneth (1966), *Language in Relation to a Unified Theory of the Structure of Human Behavior*. The Hague: Mouton.

8. Sapir, Edward (1929), 'The Status of Linguistics as a Science', *Language*, 5, 207–14.

9. Craig, C. Samuel and Susan P. Douglas (2001), *International Marketing Research*. Chichester: Wiley.

10. Green, Paul E., Donald S. Tull, and Gerald Albaum (1988), *Research for Marketing Decisions* (5th edn). Englewood Cliffs, NJ: Prentice Hall.

11. Bensaou, M., Michael Coyne, and N. Venkatraman (1999), 'Testing Metric Equivalence in Cross-National Strategy Research: An Empirical Test across the United States and Japan', *Strategic Management Journal*, 20 (7), 671–89.

12. Cavusgil, S. Tamer and Ajay Das (1997), 'Methodological Issues in Empirical Cross-Cultural Research: A Survey of the Management Literature and a Framework', *Management International Review*, 37 (1), 71–96.

13. Green, Robert T. and Eric Langeard (1979), 'Comments and Recommendations on the Practice of Cross-Cultural Marketing Research', in paper presented at the International Marketing Workshop, EIASM Brussels, 1–16.

14. Leung, Kwok (1989), 'Cross-Cultural Differences: Individual Level vs Culture-Level Analysis', *International Journal of Psychology*, 24 (6), 703–19.

15. Poortinga, Ype H. (1989), 'Equivalence in Cross-Cultural Data: An Overview of Basic Issues', *International Journal of Psychology*, 24, 737–56.

16. Steenkamp, Jan-Benedict E.M. and Hans Baumgartner (1998), 'Assessing Measurement Invariance in Cross-National Research', *Journal of Consumer Research*, 25 (1, June), 78–90.

17. Van de Vijver, F.J.R. and Kenneth Leung (1997), *Methods and Data Analysis for Cross-Cultural Research*. Thousand Oaks, CA: Sage.

18. Van Herk, Hester and Theo M. Verhallen (1995), 'Equivalence in Empirical International Research in the Food Area', in *Proceedings of the Second Conference on the Cultural Dimension of International Marketing*. Odense, 392–402.

19. Kacen, Jacqueline J. and Julie Anne Lee (2002), 'The Influence of Culture on Consumer Impulsive Buying Behavior', *Journal of Consumer Psychology*, 12 (2), 163–76.

20. Geertz, Clifford (1983), *Local Knowledge*. New York: Basic Books.

21. Mytton, Graham (1996), 'Research in New Fields', *Journal of the Market Research Society*, 38 (1), 19–32.

22. Chen, Haipeng (Allan), Sharon Ng, and Akshay R. Rao (2005), 'Cultural Differences in Consumer Impatience', *Journal of Marketing Research*, 42 (3), 291–301.

23. Stone, R. and K. Gronhaug (1993), 'Perceived Risk: Further Considerations for the Marketing Discipline', *European Journal of Marketing*, 27 (3), 372–94.

24. Weber, Elke U. and Christopher Yr Hsee (1998), 'Cross-Cultural Differences in Risk Perception, but Cross-Cultural Similarities in Attitudes Towards Perceived Risk', *Management Science*, 44 (9), 1205–17.

25. Craig, C. Samuel and Susan P. Douglas (2006), 'On Improving the Conceptual Foundations of International Marketing Research', *Journal of International Marketing*, 14 (1), 1–22.

26. Frijda, Nico and Gustav Jahoda (1966), 'On the Scope and Methods of Cross-Cultural Research', *International Journal of Psychology*, 1 (2), 109–27.

27. Stanton, John L., Rajan Chandran, and Sigfredo A. Hernandez (1982), 'Marketing Research Problems in Latin America', *Journal of the Market Research Society*, 24 (2), 124–39.

28. Roy, Abhik, Peter G.P. Walters, and Sherriff T.K. Luk (2001), 'Chinese Puzzles and Paradoxes: Conducting Business Research in China', *Journal of Business Research*, 52 (2), 203–10.

29. Weiss, Brad (1996), 'Coffee Breaks and Connections: The Lived Experience of a Commodity in Tanzanian and European World', in *Cross-Cultural Consumption*, David Howes, Ed. London: Routledge.

30. Sechrest, Lee, Todd L. Fay, and S.M. Hafeez Zaidi (1972), 'Problems of Translation in Cross-Cultural Research', *Journal of Cross-Cultural Psychology*, 3 (1), 41–56.

31. Bohnet, Michael (1994), 'Was Wurde in Kairo Wirklich Beschlossen', *Eine Welt* (BMZ, Bonn), October.

32. Campbell, D.T. and O. Werner (1970), 'Translating, Working through Interpreters and the Problem of Decentering', in *A Handbook of Method in Cultural Anthropology*, R. Naroll and R. Cohen, Eds. New York: The Natural History Press.

33. Deutscher, I. (1973), 'Asking Questions Cross Culturally: Some Problems of Linguistic Comparability', in *Comparative Research Methods*, Donald P. Warwick and Samuel Osherson, Eds. Englewood Cliffs, NJ: Prentice Hall.

34. Mayer, Charles S. (1978), 'Multinational Marketing Research: The Magnifying Glass of Methodological Problems', *European Research* (March), 77–84.

35. Douglas, Susan P. and C. Samuel Craig (2007), 'Collaborative and Iterative Translation: An Alternative Approach to Back Translation', *Journal of International Marketing*, 15 (1), 30–43.

36. Marchetti, Renato and Jean-Claude Usunier (1990), 'Les Problèmes De L'étude De Marché Dans Un Contexte Interculturel', *Revue Française du Marketing*, 130 (5), 167–84.

37. Usunier, Jean-Claude (1991), 'Business Time Perceptions and National Cultures: A Comparative Survey', *Business Time Perceptions and National Cultures: A Comparative Survey*, 31 (3), 197–217.

38. Sood, James H. (1990), 'Equivalent Measurement in International Market Research: Is It Really a Problem?', *Journal of International Consumer Marketing*, 2 (2), 25–41.

39. Durgee, Jeffrey F., Gina Colarelli O'Connor, and Robert W. Veryzer (1996), 'Translating Values into Product Wants', *Journal of Advertising Research*, 36 (6), 90–100.

40. Zaltman, Gerald (1997), 'Rethinking Market Research: Putting People Back In', *Journal of Marketing Research*, 34 (November), 424–37.

41. Erevelles, Sunil, Abhik Roy, and Leslie S.C. Yip (1998), 'Prices and Warranties as Signals of Quality: An Investigation of Chinese Consumers', Working paper, University of California-Riverside.

42. Parameswaran, Ravi and Attila Yaprak (1987), 'A Cross-National Comparison of Consumer Research Measures', *Journal of International Business Studies* (Spring), 35–49.

43. Pras, Bernard and Reinhard Angelmar (1978), 'Verbal Rating Scales for Multinational Research', *European Research* (March), 62–7.

44. Mullen, Michael R. (1995), 'Diagnosing Measurement Equivalence in Cross-National Research', *Journal of International Business Studies*, 26 (3), 573–96.

45. Myers, Matthew B., Roger J. Calantone, Thomas J. Page Jr, and Charles R. Taylor (2000), 'An Application of Multiple-Group Causal Models in Assessing Cross-Cultural Measurement Equivalence', *Journal of International Marketing*, 8 (4), 108–21.

46. Singh, Jagdip (1995), 'Measurement Issues in Cross-National Research', *Journal of International Business Studies*, 26 (3), 597–619.

47. Ewing, Michael T., Thomas Salzberger, and Rudolf R. Sinkovics (2005), 'An Alternate Approach to Assessing Cross-Cultural Measurement Equivalence in Advertising Research', *Journal of Advertising*, 34 (1), 17–36.

48. Rasch, Georg (1960), *Probabilistic Models for Some Intelligence and Attainment Tests*. Copenhagen: Danish Institute for Educational Research.

49. Johnson, Jean L., Tomoaki Sakano, Joseph A. Cote, and Naoto Onzo (1993), 'The Exercise of Interfirm Power and Its Repercussions in US–Japanese Channel Relationships', *Journal of Marketing*, 57 (April), 1–10.

50. Bergami, Massimo and Richard P. Bagozzi (2000), 'Self-Categorization, Affective Commitment, and Group Self-Esteem as Distinct Aspects of Social Identity in the Organization', *British Journal of Social Psychology*, 39, 555–77.

51. Morris, Jon D. (1995), 'Sam: The Self-Assessment Manikin, an Efficient Cross-Cultural Measurement of Emotional Response', *Journal of Advertising Research*, 35 (6), 63–8.

52. Marley, A.A.J. and J.J. Louviere (2005), 'Some Probabilistic Models of Best, Worst, and Best–Worst Choices', *Journal of Mathematical Psychology*, 49, 464–80.

53. Kahle, L.R. (1983), *Social Values and Social Change: Adaptation to Life in America*. New York: Praeger.

54. Schwartz, S.H. (1992), 'Universals in the Content and Structure of Values: Theoretical Advances and Empirical Tests in 20 Countries', *Advances in Experimental Social Psychology*, 25, 1–65.

55. Lee, Julie Anne, Geoffrey N. Soutar, and Jordan Louviere (2007), 'Measuring Values Using Best–Worst Scaling: The LOV Example', *Psychology and Marketing*, 24 (12), 1043–58.

56. Lee, Julie Anne, Geoffrey N. Soutar, and Jordan Louviere (2008), 'An Alternative Approach to Measuring Schwartz's Values: The Best–Worst Scaling Approach', *Journal of Personality Assessment*, 90 (4), 335–47.

57. Douglas, Susan P. and C. Samuel Craig (1984), 'Establishing Equivalence in Comparative Consumer Research', in *Comparative Marketing Systems*, Erdener Kaynak and Ronald Savit, Eds. New York: Praeger.

58. Wimalasiri, Jayantha (2000), 'A Comparison of Children's Purchasing Influence and Parental Response in Fiji and the United States', *Journal of International Consumer Marketing*, 12 (4), 55–74.

59. Rose, Gregory M. (1999), 'Consumer Socialization, Parental Style, and Development Timetables in the

United States and Japan', *Journal of Marketing*, 63 (July), 105–19.

60. Viswanathan, Madhubalan, Terry L. Childers, and Elizabeth S. Moore (2000), 'The Measurement of Intergenerational Communication and Influence on Consumption: Development, Validation, and Cross-Cultural Comparison of the Igen Scale', *Journal of the Academy of Marketing Science*, 28 (3), 406–24.

61. Hofstede, Geert (2001), *Culture Consequences* (2nd edn). Thousand Oaks, CA: Sage Publications.

62. de Mooij, Marieke and Geert Hofstede (2002), 'Convergence and Divergence in Consumer Behavior: Implications for International Retailing', *Journal of Retailing*, 78 (1), 61–9.

63. Steenkamp, Jan-Benedict E.M. and Inge Geyskens (2006), 'How Country Characteristics Affect the Perceived Value of Web Sites', *Journal of Marketing*, 70 (3), 136–50.

64. Amine, Lyn S. and S. Tamer Cavusgil (1986), 'Demand Estimation in a Developing Country Environment: Difficulties, and Examples', *Journal of the Market Research Society*, 28 (5), 43–65.

65. Douglas, Susan P. and C. Samuel Craig (1997), 'The Changing Nature of Consumer Behavior: Implications for Cross-Cultural Research', *International Journal of Research in Marketing*, 14 (4), 379–95.

66. Goodyear, Mary (1982), 'Qualitative Research in Developing Countries', *Journal of the Market Research Society*, 24 (2), 86–96.

67. Tuncalp, Secil (1988), 'The Marketing Research Scene in Saudi Arabia', *European Journal of Marketing*, 22 (5), 15–22.

68. Reynolds, N.L., A.C. Simintiras, and A. Diamantopoulos (2003), 'Theoretical Justification of Sampling Choices in International Marketing Research: Key Issues and Guidelines for Researchers', *Journal of International Business Studies*, 34 (1), 80–89.

69. Taylor, Humphrey (1995), 'Horses for Courses: How Survey Firms in Different Countries Measure Public Opinion with Different Methods', *Journal of the Market Research Society*, 37 (3), 211–19.

70. Doran, Kathleen Brewer (2002), 'Lessons Learned from Cross-Cultural Research of Chinese and North American Consumers', *Journal of Business Research*, 55 (10), 823–9.

71. Harzing, Anne-Wil (2000), 'Cross-National Industrial Mail Surveys: Why Do Response Rates Differ between Countries?', *Industrial Marketing Management*, 29, 243–54.

72. Paulhus, Delroy L. (1991), 'Measurement and Control of Response Bias', in *Measures of Personality and Social Psychological Attitudes*, J.P. Robinson and P.R. Shaver, Eds. San Diego, CA: Academic Press.

73. Hult, G. Tomas M., Bruce D. Keillor, and Barbara A. Lafferty (1999), 'A Cross-National Assessment of Social Desirability Bias and Consumer Ethnocentrism', *Journal of Global Marketing*, 12 (4), 29–43.

74. Keillor, Bruce D., Deborah Owens, and Charles Pettijohn (2001), 'A Cross-Cultural/Cross-National Study of Influencing Factors and Socially Desirable Biases', *International Journal of Market Research*, 43 (1), 63–84.

75. Kushner, J.M. (1982), 'Market Research in a Non-Western Context: The Asian Example', *Journal of the Market Research Society*, 24 (2), 116–22.

76. Webster, Cynthia (1996), 'Hispanic and Anglo Interviewer and Respondent Ethnicity and Gender: The Impact on Survey Response Quality', *Journal of Marketing Research*, 33 (February), 62–72.

77. Harzing, Anne-Wil (2006), 'Response Styles in Cross-National Survey Research', *International Journal of Cross Cultural Management*, 6 (2), 243–66.

78. Smith, Peter B. (2004), 'Acquiescent Response Bias as an Aspect of Cultural Communication Style', *Journal of Cross-Cultural Psychology*, 35, 50–61.

79. Van Herk, Hester, Ype H. Poortinga, and Theo M.M. Verhallen (2004), 'Response Styles in Rating Scales: Evidence of Method Bias in Data from Six Eu Countries', *Journal of Cross-Cultural Psychology*, 35 (3), 346–60.

80. Wong, Nancy, Aric Rindfleisch, and James E. Burroughs (2003), 'Do Reverse-Worded Items Confound Measures in Cross-Cultural Consumer Research? The Case of the Material Values Scales', *Journal of Consumer Research*, 30 (1), 72–91.

81. Zax, Melvin and Shigeo Takashi (1967), 'Cultural Influences on Response Style: Comparison of Japanese and American College Students', *Journal of Social Psychology*, 71, 3–10.

82. Chun, Kl-Taek, John B. Campbell, and Jong Hae Yoo (1974), 'Extreme Response Style in Cross-Cultural Research: A Reminder', *Journal of Cross-Cultural Psychology*, 5, 464–80.

83. Clarke, Irvine III (2000), 'Global Marketing Research: Is Extreme Response Style Influencing Your Results?', *Journal of International Consumer Marketing*, 12 (4), 91–111.

84. Clarke, Irvine III (2001), 'Extreme Response Style in Cross-Cultural Research', *International Marketing Review*, 18 (3), 301–24.

85. Maruyama, Magoroh (1990), 'International Meta-marketing: Strategic Judo, Foreign User Habits and Interactive Invention', *Human Systems Management*, 9, 29–42.

86. Johansson, Johny K. and Ikujiro Nonaka (1987), 'Market Research the Japanese Way', *Harvard Business Review* (May–June), 16–22.

87. Easterby-Smith, Mark, Richard Thorpe, and Andy Lowe (1993), *Management Research: An Introduction*. London: Sage.

88. Hirschmann, Elisabeth (1986), 'Humanistic Inquiry in Marketing Research: Philosophy, Method and Criteria', *Journal of Marketing Research*, 13 (August), 237–49.

89. Usunier, Jean-Claude (1997), 'Atomistic Versus Organistic Approaches: An Illustration through Cross-National Differences in Market Research', *International Studies of Management & Organization*, 26 (4), 90–112.

90. Ya-Fei, Margaret (2000), 'Putting the Pr in Prc', *Asia Pacific Management Forum*, July/August, www.apmforum.com/columns/china5.htm.

91. Tan, Thomas Tsu Wee and Tan Jee Lui (2002), 'Globalization and Trends in International Market Research in China', *Journal of Business Research*, 55 (10), 799–804.

92. Wood, Van R. and Kim R. Robertson (2000), 'Evaluating International Markets: The Importance of Information by Industry, by Country of Destination, and by Type of Export Transaction', *International Marketing Review*, 17 (1), 34–55.

93. Grønhaug, Kjell and John L. Graham (1987), 'International Market Research Revisited', in *Advances in International Marketing*, S. Tamer Cavusgil, Ed. Greenwich, CT: JAI Press.

94. Cavusgil, S. Tamer and Yezdi M. Godiwalla (1982), 'Decision-Making for International Marketing: A Comparative Review', *Management Decision*, 20 (4), 47–54.

95. Diamantopoulos, Adamantios, Anne L. Souchon, Geoffrey R. Durden, Catherine N. Axinn, and Hartmut H. Holzmuller (2003), 'Towards an Understanding of Cross-National Similarities and Differences in Export Information Utilization: A Perceptual Mapping Approach', *International Marketing Review*, 20 (1), 17–43.

96. Toften, Kjell and Svein Ottar Olsen (2003), 'Export Market Information Use, Organizational Knowledge, and Firm Performance: A Conceptual Framework', *International Marketing Review*, 20 (1), 95–110.

97. Cavusgil, S. Tamer (1984), 'International Marketing Research: Insights into Company Practices', in *Research in Marketing*, Vol. 7. Greenwich, CT: JAI Press.

98. Koh, Anthony C. (1991), 'An Evaluation of International Marketing Research Planning in United States Export Firms', *Journal of Global Marketing*, 4 (2), 7–25.

99. Kumar, V. (2000), *International Marketing Research*. Upper Saddle River, NJ: Prentice Hall.

Teaching materials

A6.1 Case

Mobile phones in the European Union

Questions

Using the same text as in Chapter 4 (see section A4.3), answer the following questions:

1. Assuming that Orange has decided to undertake an in-depth market survey in order to decide whether to develop its market penetration in a southern European market (e.g. France or Spain), versus a northern European market (e.g. Germany or Denmark), how would you design such a survey?

2. What information is needed?

3. How would you collect it?

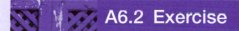

A6.2 Exercise

Hair shampoo questionnaire

You will find below a market survey questionnaire, administered by interviewers to women interviewees between the ages of 18 and 30. It was originally designed for the US market. A similar market survey, as far as the objectives are concerned, will be undertaken in other countries. Suggest cross-cultural adaptations to this instrument. In particular:

1. Review the possible problems related to the translation of the questionnaire. Suggest solutions and translate it into. . . .

2. Review the data-collection procedure, from the point of view of the interviewer as well as that of the interviewee.

3. Suggest changes in the questionnaire design and/or wording, and/or modification in survey methods, if:
   (a) the information sought is meaningless in the local context;
   (b) the required information is meaningful but the data-collection procedures are inadequate; either they will not enable you to collect the information, or else this information will be biased.
   - You must do this for at least 3 of the following countries: Algeria, Brazil, France, Germany, Thailand.

■ You should then propose a 'central' version of the questionnaire, that is, a survey instrument which enables you to collect the maximum amount of information, which could be retrieved in a reliable manner, in the largest possible number of countries. This questionnaire would then help the meaningful comparison of countries.

Questionnaire used in hair shampoo study

	Time Interview Started ....
	Ended ....
Respondent Name	Respondent No. ....
Address	
City	State ....
Telephone No	
Interviewer	
Name	
Interview Date	

Screening Questions (Part S)

'Hello, I'm .... of the Wharton School, University of Pennsylvania. We're conducting a survey on women's attitudes and opinions about hair care products.'

1. On average, how often do you shampoo your hair at home?

More than twice a week	....
Once or twice a week	....
Once or twice every two weeks	....
Once or twice every three weeks	....
Twice a month	....
Less than twice a month	....
	IF LESS THAN TWICE A MONTH, TERMINATE

2. What is your age?   ....

(IF UNDER 18 OR OVER 30 TERMINATE)

Part A

'First I'm going to show you a set of 16 cards. Each card contains the name of a benefit that a hair shampoo might provide.' (PLACE SET OF WHITE CARDS* ON TABLE IN FRONT OF RESPONDENT.)

'Please take a few moments to look over these benefits.' (ALLOW TIME FOR RESPONDENT TO STUDY THE CARDS.)

'Now, thinking about various brands of hair shampoo that you have tried or heard about, pick out those benefits that you think are most likely to be found in almost any hair shampoo that one could buy today.' (RECORD CARD NUMBERS IN FIRST COLUMN OF RESPONSE FORM A AND TURN SELECTED CARDS FACE DOWN.)

* For the wording on the cards, see CARD TEXT p. 181.

'Next, select all of those remaining benefits that you think are available in at least some hair shampoo – but not necessarily all in a single brand – that's currently on the market.' (RECORD CARD NUMBERS IN SECOND COLUMN OF RESPONSE FORM A. RECORD REMAINING CARD NUMBERS IN THIRD COLUMN. THEN RETURN ALL CARDS TO TABLE.)

'Next, imagine that you could make up an ideal type of shampoo – one that might not be available on today's market. Suppose, however, that you were restricted to only 4 of the 16 benefits shown on the cards in front of you. Which 4 of the 16 benefits would you most like to have?' (RECORD CARD NUMBERS IN FOURTH COLUMN OF RESPONSE FORM A.)

RESPONSE FORM A			
(1)	(2)	(3)	(4)
Benefits Available in Some Shampoo – Card Numbers	Benefits Most Likely to be Found in Almost Any Hair Shampoo – Card Numbers	Remaining Benefits – Card Numbers	Four Benefit Ideal Set – Card Numbers

Part B

'Now, let's again return to some of the shampoo benefits you have already dealt with.' (SELECT WHITE CARD NUMBERS 1 THROUGH 10: PULL OUT CARD 4 AND PLACE IT IN FRONT OF RESPONDENT.)

'Suppose a shampoo were on the market that primarily stressed this benefit – "produces hair that has body". If you could get a shampoo that made good on this claim, which one of the remaining nine benefits would you most like to have as well?' (RECORD NUMBER IN RESPONSE FORM B.)

'Which next most?' (RECORD.)

'Please continue until all of the nine benefits have been ranked.'

RESPONSE FORM B	
(Enter Card Numbers 1 Through 10 Excluding Card 4)	
( ) Most Like to Have	( )
( ) Next Most	( )
( )	( )
( )	( )
( )	( ) Least Most

Part C

'Now, I am going to read to you some short phrases about hair. Listen to each phrase carefully and then tell me what single words first come to your mind when you hear each phrase.'
(RECORD UP TO THE FIRST THREE 'ASSOCIATIVE-TYPE' WORDS THE RESPONDENT SAYS AFTER EACH PHRASE IN RESPONSE FORM C.)

RESPONSE FORM C

(a) Hair that has body

_____   _____   _____

(b) Hair with fullness

_____   _____   _____

(c) Hair that holds a set

_____   _____   _____

(d) Bouncy hair

_____   _____   _____

(e) Hair that's not limp

_____   _____   _____

(f) Manageable hair

_____   _____   _____

(g) Zesty hair

_____   _____   _____

(h) Natural hair

_____   _____   _____

Part D

'At this point I would like to ask you a few questions about your hair.'

1. Does your hair have enough body?
Yes _____   No _____

2. Do you have any special problems with your hair?
Yes _____   No _____
If yes, what types of problems?

_____

_____

3. How would you describe your hair?
My hair type is:
Dry _____   Normal _____   Oily _____

4. The texture of my hair is:
Fine _____   Normal _____   Coarse _____

5. My hair style (the way I wear my hair) is:
Straight _____
Slightly wavy or curly _____
Very wavy or curly _____

6. The length of my hair is:
Short (to ear lobes) _____
Medium (ear lobes to shoulder) _____
Long (below shoulder) _____

7. How would you describe the thickness of your hair?
Thick _____   Medium _____   Thin _____

Part E

'Now I would like to ask you a few background questions.'

1. Are you working (at least 20 hours per week, for remuneration)?
Yes _____   No _____

2. Are you married?
Yes _____   No _____

3. What is your level of education?
Some high school _____
Completed high school _____
Some college _____
Completed college _____

4. (HAND RESPONDENT INCOME CARD.) Which letter on this card comes closest to describing your total annual family income before taxes? (CIRCLE APPROPRIATE LETTER.)

A.	Under $9,000		E.	$30,001–45,000
B.	$9,001–15,000		F.	$45,001–60,000
C.	$15,001–20,000		G.	Over $60,000
D.	$20,001–30,000			

'Thanks very much for your help.'

Card text

Text of the 16 benefits cards (original text in English + suggested translation into French):

1. Hair stays clean a long time
2. Hair stays free of dandruff or flaking
3. Hair that looks and feels natural
4. Hair that has body
5. Manageable hair that goes where you want it
6. Hair with sheen or luster
7. Hair with no split ends
8. Hair with enough protein
9. Hair that doesn't get oily fast
10. Hair that's not too dry
11. Hair with fullness
12. Hair that's not frizzy
13. Hair that holds a set
14. Hair with texture
15. Hair that's easy to comb when it dries
16. Hair that looks free and casual

Example of a translation into French.

1. Des Cheveux qui restent propre longtemps
2. Des Cheveux sans pellicules ni noeuds
3. Des Cheveux respirant le naturel
4. Des Cheveux qui ont du volume
5. Des Cheveux souples que l'on peut coiffer à son gré
6. Des Cheveux brillants et chatoyants
7. Des Cheveux qui ne se cassent pas
8. Des Cheveux assez riches en protéines
9. Des Cheveux ne devenant pas gras trop vite
10. Des Cheveux pas trop secs
11. Des Cheveux qui ont de la plénitude
12. Des Cheveux qui ne sont pas frisottés
13. Des Cheveux tenant la mise en plis
14. Des Cheveux ayant une bonne texture
15. Des Cheveux faciles à coiffer lorsqu'ils sèchent
16. Des Cheveux naturels, en liberté

(Source: Adapted from Green *et al.*, pp. 359–62.[1])

Appendix reference

1. Green, Paul E., Donald S. Tull, and Gerald Albaum (1988), *Research for Marketing Decisions* (5th edn). Englewood Cliffs, NJ: Prentice Hall.

Part 3   Marketing decisions for the intercultural environment

© Getty Images

Introduction to Part 3

As with most international marketing textbooks, this book follows the '4Ps' model: *product*, *price*, *place*, and *promotion*. Part 3 explains how the first three Ps, product, price, and place, should be managed internationally with a view to generating the best possible compromise between large-scale operations and adapting to local markets. The last 'P', promotion, is largely treated in Part 4, since marketing communications deserve special treatment in an international context, where communication needs to be tailored because of language differences.

Multinational companies design international marketing strategies to create experience effects within the constraint of transport costs. They also use a number of production systems, such as flexible manufacturing, to gain differentiation advantages related to the customization of product offerings to local markets. Chapter 7 first deals with the supply side by examining how cost arguments explain the emergence of global strategies and the globalization of competition. On the demand side, cross-border segments are targeted in order to generate larger-scale operations. Chapter 7 explains how geographical and demographic segmentation criteria can be combined in order to segment international markets optimally.

Chapter 8 documents the strategic choice between product adaptation or standardization across national markets. It starts with a review of key arguments in favour of the standardization or adaptation of physical attributes. Physical attributes are the most sensitive to scale economies and at the same time they often require customization because of climate and other objective features of local markets. Service attributes also need to be tailored because consumer expectation regarding service quality and service performance varies across national contexts. Finally, symbolic attributes linked to product design and packaging are examined in a cross-cultural perspective that highlights the diversity of cultural interpretations of symbols by looking at attributes such as colour, figure, shape, etc.

Country of origin and brand name are two of the greatest symbolic attributes that diffuse meaning. Chapter 9 goes on to deal with the management of the images diffused by these attributes. It reviews how consumers evaluate products according to their country of origin, taking into account perceived risk related to goods produced in other countries, which may be cheaper or less prestigious in terms of design and/or manufacturing, as well as the nationalistic tendencies of consumers who prefer to buy products made in their own countries. The final section deals with the linguistic constraints of transferring national brand names onto the international scene and outlines the managerial limitations involved in the development of global brands.

In an effort to consider price other than merely *the* objective factor in the economics of international marketing, Chapter 10 examines the role of price as a central element of relational exchange; that is, a signal conveying meaning between buyers and sellers, marketers and consumers, and between companies and their middlemen. It also presents and documents the main pricing decisions that a company has to face when it sells internationally. The first perspective developed is that of bargaining, which is still widely used in many markets and remains a key ritual in buyer–seller relationships because it mixes economics and human interaction in a subtle way. Cross-cultural variation in the way consumers use price to evaluate and choose products is then discussed. The three last sections of the chapter are devoted to managerial issues in international price policy. This includes the way in which multinational companies use price policy to conquer new markets, how to enter markets where competition is avoided through cartels and price agreements, how to fight against parallel imports by unauthorized dealers, and how prices should be managed in unstable environments, which often combine high inflation, administered prices and strict foreign exchange control.

Chapter 11 focuses on the 'place' variable in the 4Ps model and consequently deals with international distribution. The Japanese *keiretsu* distribution case is used to exemplify the cultural embedding of distribution channels and the difficulty of entering foreign channels as a cultural outsider. It shows how relationships between channel members are deeply rooted in local patterns of human and economic relationships and highlights the role of distribution as a cultural filter, to be carefully considered (along with other criteria) before choosing a foreign distribution channel. Direct worldwide marketing is rapidly developing, especially through catalogue sales and through the Internet. The section dealing with direct marketing explains which products best suit direct overseas distribution and outlines some linguistic and cultural limitations to carefully consider before designing and implementing cross-border direct marketing. The final section examines cross-national variations in sales promotion methods and explains which aspects need to be customized when transferring promotional techniques across borders.

7

Intercultural marketing strategy

Globalization can occur at the market, organization and/or consumer level. It occurs mostly in markets where supply, demand and competition are increasingly global. Regional agreements worldwide and the World Trade Organization (WTO) have brought tariff and non-tariff barriers down. These are progressively being replaced by entry barriers related to scale and experience at the organizational level.

Culture imposes a natural entry barrier on consumer behaviour. It will diminish only very gradually as long as the world is composed of 'village markets' rather than one global market.

This chapter defends the idea that strategic management has to be 'global', whereas marketing management largely needs to be tailored to local contexts. Therefore, an intercultural orientation to international marketing best serves a global strategic view.

The strategic dilemma for international marketers is to achieve both low cost and differentiation in the minds of consumers vis-à-vis competitors. While differentiation may result in cost increases, there are possible compromises. Cost efficiency can be obtained in production, transport and marketing. In order to minimize costs and unnecessary differentiation, and to maximize relevant differentiation, customers should be clustered in groups sharing common characteristics. Culture is one of the main cues for clustering; however, sociodemographic criteria are also significant in an international perspective.

We need to consider the *scale* of global operations, their geographical *scope* and relevant *segments* (national versus transnational). The first section of this chapter discusses *scale*, concentrating on cost arguments as global strategies are very significant from a pure cost perspective. The second section discusses *scope*, concentrating on how global competition has progressively become the rule, due to the liberalization of world trade. The third section shows how companies have reacted to these major changes during the last 20 years and how they have been forced by the pressure from worldwide competition to standardize marketing strategies while keeping an eye on very dissimilar consumer environments. The final section deals with the *segmentation* of world markets and discusses the respective place of cross-border segments based on sociodemographics and lifestyles and geography-based cultural segments.

7.1 Cost arguments and global strategies

Trends towards global (competitive) markets

In the beginning of the 1980s, Michael Porter[1] identified a since widely accepted and applied distinction between multidomestic and global markets. According to Porter (p. 18),[1] competition becomes global when 'a firm's competitive position is significantly affected by its position in other countries and vice-versa'. When an industry is multi-domestic, separate strategies are pursued in different national markets, and the competitive scene remains essentially domestic.

Certain forces move society toward global competition, including regional integration, an ideology-free world, technological advances and borderless markets, while other forces are actively slowing the process down.[2] Rugman (p. 583)[3] even suggests that globalization 'does not, and has never, existed in terms of a single world market with free trade . . . Government regulations and cultural differences divide the world into the triad blocks of North America, the European Union and Japan'. He argues that there has been a move to regionalization rather than globalization, as most global companies earn the majority of their revenue within their home triad and adapt their products to the local market. For example: 'over 90 per cent of the cars produced in the EU are sold there; and more than 93 per cent of all cars registered in Japan are manufactured domestically' (pp. 584–5)[3].

There are some fundamental reasons for industries to remain multi-domestic, including wide differences in consumer needs and attitudes across markets, legal barriers resulting from domestic regulations (which have long been in place in the case of banking and insurance), and non-tariff barriers, which artificially maintain competition between purely national competitors (food and drug health regulations, for instance).

The trend towards global markets differs rather widely, depending on the industry. First, the influence of national regulations and non-tariff barriers varies largely across product categories. Second, the potential for experience effects also differs across product categories. For example, there is less potential for cost reduction due to volume increase in the case of perishables, such as cheeses, than for microchips. Third, there are different degrees of international 'transportability', that is, the extent to which transportation costs impinge on the degree and patterns of globalization for a particular industry. Thus, exporting may be the dominant internationalization pattern for easily transportable products such as semiconductors, and foreign direct investment may be the prevailing pattern for industries whose products are expensive to transport long distance (e.g. cement). Fourth, the trend towards globalization may be curbed in the case of culture-bound products: the globalization of foods such as cheese is slower than in the microchip industry.

In addition, globalization may not be the most profitable route for a company to take. For instance, Qian and Li (pp. 326–7)[4] caution that: 'no definitive conclusions can be drawn from past research on the relationship between foreign operations and profitability'. They suggest that increasing the scope of foreign operation should increase profits. Using data from 125 large US firms, they found that a medium global market diversification strategy performed better than a high one.[4]

As previously mentioned, pure cost efficiency can be obtained in three major areas: production, transport and marketing. Each of these is discussed below.

Production and experience effects

The potential for experience effects differs widely across product categories. The Boston Consulting Group isolated one of the main reasons for this through research into the success of various companies, including Japanese companies, in global markets. Experience effects provide companies with the ability to reduce unit costs dramatically through an increase in product quantity. The experience effects determine the relationship of unit cost to cumulated production volume according to the following formula:

$$C_n = C_1 n^{-\lambda}$$

where Cn is the cost of the nth unit; C_1 is the cost of the first unit; n is the cumulated number of units produced; and λ is the elasticity of the unit cost with respect to the cumulated production volume.

The form of the function reflects constant elasticity. Let us call k the effect of elasticity. When production is doubled, the cost (and therefore, to a certain extent, the price) will decrease by $1 - k = 1 - 2^{-\lambda}$ per cent each time the experience doubles. If, for example, k equals 70 per cent, the cost will decrease by 30 per cent when doubling the cumulated production (1 – 70 per cent = 30 per cent. Experience effects theory has been supported by empirical verification.[5] Experience effects have been estimated for diverse products and services such as long-distance telephone calls in the United States, bottle tops in West Germany, refrigerators in Great Britain, and motorcycles in Japan.

Website link 7.1

Bruce Henderson of the Boston Consulting Group brought experience curve effects into strategic management: http://www.bcg.com/publications/files/experience_curve_I_the_concept_1973.pdf.

The source of experience effects is fourfold:

1. The effects of *learning by doing*. The more a task is carried out or the more a component or a product is manufactured, the more efficiently and quickly it can be done.
2. *Scale effects*. By increasing the scale of production, the average cost can be reduced. Many industrial products, such as pocket calculators, require a large amount of research and development for product design, yet only a small quantity of raw material to be manufactured.
3. *Technological advances*. The increase in cumulated production leads technological improvement to two potential outcomes. On the one hand, production equipment may be refined. On the other hand, the product itself can be simplified and become cheaper to produce. These product simplifications are usually a result of a reduction in the number of component parts, rather than a reduction in the number of functions and the degree of sophistication, which would adversely affect the consumer.
4. *Economies of scope*. Component parts may be shared by different products. For instance, the same basic diesel engine may be used for a fork-lift truck, a small truck, a van, a car, or as an inboard motor for a boat, with a few slight adaptations. The increase in the production scale of shared components (or shared overhead costs, or any kind of shared common inputs) results in economies of scope.

Not every product has the same potential for experience effects. The potential is clearly smaller for cheese or books than for hi-fi systems or microcomputers. In the world market, the Japanese have concentrated on goods that have very high experience effects, such as motorcycles, cars, photocopiers, DVD equipment, hi-fi systems, television sets, outboard motors, musical instruments and cameras. Right from the start, Japanese companies opted for global markets, even though their domestic market for such products was itself very substantial. Competitors have

struggled to resist the competitive pressure of Japanese companies. For instance, the motorcycle industry in Europe illustrates how a lack of experience effects can inhibit innovation. In an attempt to compete with the Japanese (Honda, Yamaha, Suzuki, Kawasaki), Motobécane, a French manufacturer, launched a 125cc motorcycle some years ago. This model had a two-stroke engine that operated on a mixture of petrol and oil, since Motobécane was unable to make a four-stroke engine, like Honda, or an 'oil lube' (a device for mixing oil and petrol automatically), like Yamaha, Suzuki and Kawasaki. The motorcycle made a thick cloud of white smoke. The range of models offered remained very limited, as with other French motorcycles. The 350cc Motobécane, which could have catered to a lucrative local market consisting of the French police, was not fast or reliable enough. The company's lack of experience effects was a barrier to technological improvements. Motobécane was renamed MBK and is now a subsidiary of Yamaha.

Local players, however, can use experience effects to maintain the upper hand over transnationals by using their local identity advantage. As noted by Ger (p. 65), 'Rather than operating in the already highly competitive markets shared and dominated by the TNCs [transnational corporations], local firms can better take advantage of their potential by operating in alternative domains and "out-localizing" the TNCs, in both global and local markets'.[6]

International transportability

The unit weight, that is, dollar price per kilogram or per pound, differs widely across categories of goods, and, by extension, across the industries that manufacture them. The price of cement or basic ordinary steel products ranges from 15 cents per kilogram to several dollars per kilogram, whereas that of cars ranges from 10 dollars per kilogram (for example, a small family car at the bottom end of the market) to 60 or 70 dollars per kilogram for luxury cars at the top end of the market (large Mercedes, BMWs or Jaguars). A portable computer may reach a price of 750 dollars per kilogram (or even more), not to mention its component chips, which may climb to several thousand dollars per kilogram.

In the international transportation system, shipping charges do not follow a simple tariff, which would be directly proportional to weight. They are calculated on the basis of a mix of criteria, depending on the nature of the goods to be shipped and on the shipping line. Shipping lines are also subject to economies of scale. Transportation cost factors are influenced by the forces of competition between transportation companies, and also by the method of transportation (ship, airplane, truck or train). The mix of criteria includes weight, volume, dimensions, ease of loading and unloading, perishability, packaging and speed of delivery. Of these, weight, volume and perishability are clearly the most detrimental factors to international transportation.

Some markets remain almost exclusively multi-domestic, because goods and services cannot be transported (e.g. heavy goods and services such as hairdressing). Although transportability may have a negative influence on cross-border transactions of goods and services, it does not hamper the globalization of an industry where cross-border investments are possible. For instance, the cement industry still competes on a global basis through foreign direct investment and the sale and licensing of technology, despite the markets being regionally segmented within countries due to the high cost of transportation in proportion to basic unit price.

Transportability also relates to consumers, who may be more 'transportable' than the products or services offered to them. Ski resorts are a good example: ski slopes, buildings and equipment are not transportable, nor is snow. But potential skiers may be transported at low cost on charter flights, from countries without mountains, snow or ski resorts (provided they have some purchasing power). Consequently, in the international ski-resort industry a twofold pattern of globalization is observable. On the one hand, some world famous ski resorts, such as Val d'Isère in France, Kitzbühl in Austria, Zermatt in Switzerland and Thredbo in Australia cater to a global market. People come from many parts of the world, often on package holidays sold by tour operators or travel agencies. On the other hand, a large number of purely local ski resorts ('ski villages') in most ski oriented countries compete on a more domestic basis. This part of the industry is multi-domestic. On a scale ranging from globalized at one end and multi-domestic at the other, there are in fact many intermediate ski resorts competing on a regionally globalized basis. This is the case with

most medium-size ski resorts in the European Alps: in Austria, France, Germany, Italy, Switzerland and some eastern European countries, which compete for European skiers.

The Internet has also increased transportability in many markets. It is has been forecast that the value of e-commerce in Europe will increase from €102 billion in 2006 to €263 billion in 2011.[7] Similarly, the value of ecommerce in the United States is forecast to be more than US$250 billion in 2011.[8] According to Prasad *et al.* (p. 83): 'Benefits sought by marketers in using the Internet include improved efficiency and lower costs across supply and demand chains; improved speed, flexibility, and responsiveness in meeting customer needs; greater market access; and enhanced ability to overcome time and distance barriers of global markets'.[9] While the Internet cannot transport most physical products, it can affect communication, transactional and distribution channels.[9]

The disconnection between sourcing and marketing

When sourcing and marketing take place in geographically distant countries the most cost-efficient production sites are often export processing zones in newly industrialized countries. Consumer markets may be located in distant and remote places. The same brand may be 'made in' multiple countries, generating different country-of-origin (COO) images. This multinational production causes a 'blurring effect' for COO. Consumers, who still use country of origin as an information cue for comparing brands, are now becoming more and more aware of the actual disconnection between sourcing and marketing. Actual knowledge about a product's origin and its influence on preference for local products has recently been found to be relatively small.[10]

A world view versus a local view

There is a clear difference between customer orientation, which puts customers' needs first, and market orientation, which focuses on a larger vision of satisfying customers' current and future needs throughout the marketing value chain.[11] According to Hult and Ketchen (p. 901),[12] market orientation gives 'system-wide attention to markets (customers, competitors and other entities in the environment) throughout the organization'. Thus, a 'global strategy' implies a world view of competition and competitive advantage, not simply a belief that consumers and markets are themselves global. The issue of global strategies has been extensively documented in the strategic management literature. It is beyond the scope of this textbook (which emphasizes the cultural dimensions of international marketing) to discuss the specific issues related to global strategies in detail.

In cultural terms, the ethnocentrism of the managing team of any company is shown by the way in which it treats the domestic/national market on the one hand and 'foreign' markets on the other. This issue is not purely academic; it permeates the ways in which a company organizes its international activities and the nationalities of its top executives, as well as other more practical considerations, such as the choice of the language(s) to be spoken between its subsidiaries and the head office.

Once the company has achieved a certain level of development in foreign markets, the 'export' view and the 'international development' view can no longer coexist effectively. They are dependent on four different perspectives: ethnocentrism, polycentrism, regiocentrism and geocentrism.[13,14]

> ### Website link 7.2
>
> See the Fortune Global 500: the United States lays claim to the most global giants, followed by Japan, and France: http://money.cnn.com/magazines/fortune/global500/2007/full_list/index.html.

Two of these (ethno- and geocentrism) are somewhat irreconcilable. In terms of set theory, the domestic market is perceived as isolated from foreign markets. Ethnocentric companies view international operations as secondary to their domestic operations. A company that considers its national base as its top priority will impose its own language on its foreign subsidiaries. It will supply the domestic market first when production capacity is overstretched. It will never invite a non-national on to the board of directors unless this person shares the company's native language and culture. Conversely, a geocentric company, which considers its domestic market as belonging to the world market in the same way as any other domestic market, will make the opposite choices. It has been argued that the nine determinants of international marketing cycles are gradually declining: political stability, government policy, ideology-driven economy, fear of colonialism, marketing transfer issues, lack of infrastructure, North–South dichotomy, East–West dichotomy and product life.[15] A geocentric perspective is dependent on a truly borderless world.

Regiocentrism and polycentrism are more moderate perspectives. A regiocentric company is more open to global marketing than an ethnocentric one. However, this perspective also recognizes that regional marketing strategies may be necessary to better meet customer needs. Cultural factors still strongly inhibit the development of a homogeneous market.[16] Regional trading blocs can be used as building blocks to world trade. It is important to acknowledge differences within the bloc. Finally, a polycentric company recognizes that differences occur in overseas markets. Each country is accepted as one of many ethnocentric places which may have their own marketing policies and programmes.

When companies distance themselves from an ethnocentric attitude and adopt one of the other perspectives, by virtue of their management style and corporate culture, they develop genuinely offensive and defensive marketing strategies in foreign markets. Such a strategy manifests itself in flexible reallocation of resources from one market to another. For instance, a company will relocate to market Y, where it holds a solid position, as a reaction to a large competitor launching a price offensive in country X. This type of situation is conceivable in strongly oligopolistic markets where several (five to ten) large multinationals control the world market, as is true in the food industry or the liquefied gases industry.

Nevertheless, stiff competition may give way to forms of cooperation between large companies from developed countries. The theory developed by Kenichi Ohmae, head of the Tokyo office of McKinsey Consultants, in his book *Triad Power: The Coming Shape of Global Competition*,[17] emphasizes the need for companies that want to survive international competition to have a solid base in the market area of each of the three major industrialized regions collectively known as the 'triad': North America, Japan and Europe. Ohmae further suggests that in each of these regions companies should establish links of international division of labour with neighbouring developing countries. Companies in Latin America are natural subcontractors for North American companies. South-East Asian countries subcontract for Japanese firms. The same cooperation pattern should occur between African countries and European companies. To ensure this necessary tripolar presence, Ohmae advocates that alliances should be built between companies belonging to one of the developed market areas. Most of these companies, even if they are large, cannot individually afford to make the necessary investment that would ensure full presence in each of the three regions.

Prioritized markets often remain undisguised. To avoid the trap of 'collective unconsciousness', companies must reflect on how prioritized markets relate to corporate culture, as well as to the search for market and business opportunities, and to the decision-making process. Some European companies still supply their domestic market as a priority on the basis that this market is the 'home base'. There are consequences to this, as follows:

1. It leads to a bias in *product design.* The modest sales records of certain European cars, mainly French and Italian, in the North American) market can, at least partially, be attributed to local French and Italian motor regulations which bias the design of cars, and make them inappropriate for use in America. In France, the speed limits on highways and stiff road taxes that vary according to engine size have caused manufacturers to shy away from producing large cars and sports cars. The same holds true in Italy, where the high cost of petrol has led manufacturers to produce cars which are too small according to American public opinion. This has dissuaded car manufacturers in those countries from building high-speed luxury sedans, a gap in the market that was mostly filled by the Germans and the Swedes, before the Japanese came out with their Lexus and Acuras.

2. Home-base oriented companies often suffer from an international reputation of being unreliable with respect to *delivery dates.* This is due to the marginalization of foreign markets, which are considered as a provisional outlet to be approached when the home market is depressed. It leads to a consistent preference for supplying domestic rather than foreign customers. Even though a foreign customer may have ordered before a domestic customer, they will systematically be forced to wait and will only receive delivery after the domestic customer has been satisfied. A genuine respect for delivery dates would have led to a more equitable outcome.

As soon as domestic demand increases, the prioritization of national markets implies that production capacity will cease to be used for supplying foreign customers. As a consequence, there is a general risk that attempts to set up stable business relationships with customers and intermediaries in foreign markets will be hampered. Typically, foreign agents will only be visited when business at home is slack, and will be let down (as will foreign customers) as soon as the home market situation improves. This attitude fails to satisfy the essential precondition for effective international development.

The world market share concept: global size and diagnosis of economic market share

Calculating its world market share helps a company to prevent itself from becoming ethnocentric when defining its position vis-à-vis the competition. Competition is seen from the outset as global. Box 7.1 illustrates the dangers of overemphasizing domestic market share.

Diagnosing a particular company's situation within world markets requires evaluating the following criteria (even though estimates may be only approximate):

1. Size of world market (volume, units, sales figures).
2. Company's production size.
3. Company's share of world market.
4. Minimum world market share necessary to remain competitive, considering potential experience effects.

The world market for fork-lift trucks was roughly 200,000 units per year. Fenwick held only 2 per cent of this market. 'Competitive' market share could be estimated to have been 10 per cent, or 20,000 trucks

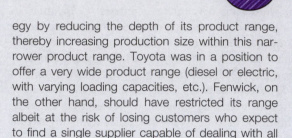

Box 7.1

Fenwick, a synonym for fork-lift

Fenwick is the leading French company for fork-lift trucks, At one point in time, the company controlled 40–50 per cent of the French market, but nearly went bankrupt because it lacked international clout. This company only produced 4000 fork-lift trucks per year, whereas its global competitor, Toyota, produced 35,000 and its main east European competitor, Balkankar (a Bulgarian company), 70,000. This had a negative effect on Fenwick's unit costs. Fenwick should have adapted its marketing strat-

egy by reducing the depth of its product range, thereby increasing production size within this narrower product range. Toyota was in a position to offer a very wide product range (diesel or electric, with varying loading capacities, etc.). Fenwick, on the other hand, should have restricted its range albeit at the risk of losing customers who expect to find a single supplier capable of dealing with all their requirements.

---

a year. Fenwick was therefore well below the required global size. In view of this, it should have reduced its range to either diesel or electric fork-lifts and to a limited range of sizes so that production could have been much greater in a more specialized world market.

There is no precise rule for estimating the 'competitive' world market share. This figure depends on the optimum size of production, which in turn depends on the potential for experience effects for a specific product or service. Experience effects are enhanced by the following factors:

1. Product/service is mass produced.
2. Product/service involves a production process with large initial fixed costs (in R & D, and/or in production facility investment, and/or in initial marketing costs).
3. Added value of product/service is high, in relation to entire production cycle.
4. Product/service is in a fairly open international market; any producer may sell throughout the world without facing prohibitive transport costs, customs barriers, statutory restrictions or market barriers (e.g. differences in taste).

The easiest empirical solution for evaluating 'competitive' market share is to examine the competitors and determine the size of those who operate most effectively. Limits on international size arise in various areas; for example cement (very high transport costs compared to its price), pharmaceuticals (statutory restrictions), foodstuffs (taste differences), etc.

As far as services are concerned, the potential for experience effects is much smaller, since in many cases services must be performed in a direct relationship with the consumer and are often intangible, which means they cannot be held in stock. In addition, their geographical market area is often fairly local and they are subject to local customs and ways of life, such as the type of food and service found in a restaurant or the kind of service offered by hotels.

Global markets as learning opportunities

Global markets work as a set of coherent opportunities through markets that are at different product life-cycle (PLC) stages and through experience cumulated across national markets. According to PLC theory, national markets at various development stages offer different kinds of opportunities.[18] If, for instance, the market for wallpaper is saturated in developed economies, it may just be opening up in newly industrialized countries. PLC theory clearly indicates the way in which sourcing and marketing activities should be disconnected. PLC theory, in conjunction with the world market share concept, assists in identifying what to supply, from where, and in which countries to market.

Global markets are also full of learning opportunities. The internationalization process has been presented mostly as a learning and experiencing process.[19] Since the cultural variable is fundamental to this learning process, some markets may be used

Box 7.2

Stimorol and Hollywood

A Danish chewing-gum company, Dandy A/S, which produces Stimorol, encountered difficulties in selling its products in France. Dandy was particularly successful at producing chewing gum. Hollywood France (owned by the US company General Foods/Kraft) was less successful in the production of this type of product, but had better access to the major distribution outlets (hypermarkets). In fact, only large companies are able to have their products referenced, that is, registered as products accepted for sale by the channel.

Referencing requires the payment of large 'entry fees' to the hypermarkets, which are only semi-legitimate. Dandy of Denmark and Hollywood ended up forging a cross-competence alliance whereby Dandy produces Hollywood products and markets Hollywood products through Dandy's international sales organization, and Hollywood markets Dandy's Stimorol brand in France and produces the Dandy stick products.

(Source: Hollensen, 1991, p. 736.)

almost purely as learning opportunities. When Procter & Gamble invaded the Japanese market for baby nappies (diapers), initially it was a great success. Its market share subsequently dropped sharply against the main Japanese competitor Kao. P & G did its best to survive against the harsh competition from Kao and other Japanese producers, to satisfy the demanding Japanese consumers and to make its way through the Japanese *keiretsu* distribution system (see Chapter 11). P & G's experience in Japan has made it only too aware of the competitive threat of Japanese producers. The company realized that it would face harsh competition if Japanese producers were to decide to expand to world markets. This has already helped it resist the internationalization of Kao, which, to date, has not succeeded in becoming a global competitor to P & G.

Global markets may also be seen as opportunities for partnership: with local consumers, with distributors and perhaps even with competitors (Box 7.2).

Opportunities exist for local firms to create niche markets, where their local identity and culture is an advantage. Ger[6] outlines three localization strategies by concentrating on: (1) local contexts as an alternative to modern global contexts; (2) information goods; (3) goods for the less affluent world. For the first strategy Ger (p. 76) suggests that:

Local firms can reinvent, reconstruct, and repackage local products, services, and places . . . They can produce a variety of 'toys' for the global consumer seeking diversity

(the affluent cosmopolitans in modernizing domestic markets as well as in foreign markets). LCs [local companies] can offer alternative products for the non-conformist or ethically concerned consumers. LCs can offer prestige by providing the unique, the exotic, the unusual.[6]

A local company can become a global player, but Ger suggests that it should aim to start in a foreign market or simultaneously in local and foreign markets. It needs to think and act both locally and globally, by either creating a niche at home or an alliance as a global player. Several winners at the annual Australian Multicultural Marketing Awards have managed to excel using these tactics.[20] Wilkinson and Cheng (p. 118) describe the success of one of these winners:

Techmeat Australia, an award winner in 1994, was started by a Korean immigrant who realized that Australian butchers and abattoirs were discarding cuts of meat considered delicacies in his home country. He now exports A$2 million worth of meat to Korea every year.[20]

Similarly, computer maker Lenovo (incorporated in Hong Kong) chose a map of the world with symbolic landmarks, such as the Sydney Opera House, Statue of Liberty and Eiffel Tower, to represent its vision on its Chinese-language homepage, along with the slogan 'in step with global technology'.[21]

The Internet is radically changing existing business models and established ways of doing business in international markets.[22] According to Susan Douglas

(p. 106),[22] 'firms can instantly "go global", targeting a specific market segment worldwide, or reach customers by building a network of Internet sites in different languages throughout the world'.

7.2

The globalization of competition

Evidence from macroeconomic data over long periods of time

There is little doubt about the globalization of competition. Market areas do not depend mainly on consumer preferences. Their reach is more strongly influenced by potential supply and by trade barriers, whether tariff or non-tariff, and also by opportunities of economies of scale and experience effects. Clear evidence from macroeconomic figures shows that competition is globalizing both worldwide and regionally.

International trade continues to expand despite the effects being felt worldwide from the American sub-prime mortgage crisis, tension in the Middle East and terrorism. From 2000 to 2006 the annual rate of increase for world trade was 5.5 per cent, compared with 2.5 per cent for world production and 3.0 per cent for world GDP.[23] Since 1995 there has only been one year, 2001, when merchandise exports increased less than the world gross national product (GNP) for the nations involved in international trade.[23] This points to a long-term trend: an increase in the scale of production.

Industrial productivity accompanies the efforts to make international markets freer and the growth of international trade. The value of world merchandise trade rose by 60 per cent from US$7.3 trillion in 2003 to US$11.8 trillion in 2006.[23] The economic linkage between countries and therefore competition between companies has continued to grow. A comparable evolution may be observed, at an even greater pace, regionally. Distances are becoming less significant and the move to worldwide globalization has its roots in regional operations.

During the 1960s and 1970s, the growth of intra-regional international trade within Europe was much faster than the overall world trade growth. In more recent years, Asia and the transitional economies have been doing much better than Europe with significantly higher import and export expansion in merchandise trade, in real terms.[23] In 2006, the European Union's merchandise imports and exports both increased by 7 per cent. This shows a reversal of the recent trend towards economic slowdown. The entry of the transitional economies into the EU has most likely changed this trend.

Evidence from business and industries

Many companies have been compelled to globalize their business. One example of this is Black & Decker, which was compelled to go global due to fierce competition from the Japanese power-tool maker Makita. The reasons for this are stated by Saporito (p. 24) in *Fortune* magazine, reporting the strategic move of Black & Decker towards globalization: 'Makita is Black & Decker's first competitor with a global strategy. It doesn't care that Germans prefer high powered, heavy-duty drills, and that Yanks want everything lighter. Make a good drill at a low price, the company reasons, and it will sell from Baden-Baden to Brooklyn.'[24]

Website link 7.3

Find a brief analysis of the six main globalization debates: **http://www.sociology.emory.edu/ globalization/debates.html**.

Michael Porter[1] analysed the change in patterns of international competition. He found that there is a shift from multi-domestic industries to global ones. Porter is not referring to consumer-led globalization but to a strategic move by companies trying to integrate activities on a worldwide basis, to gain competitive advantage over their competitors at various levels of the value chain.

Nevertheless, globalization depends on continual efforts to dismantle, or at least reduce, trade barriers. The establishment of the WTO in 1995 was a major move towards freeing trade in products and services and improving the institutional mechanisms for solving trade disputes between countries.

The globalization of the Japanese economy and other Asian countries is a real threat to both the US and Europe. Therefore, free trade can be maintained and expanded only if a certain equilibrium in the balance of trade between nation-states makes it possible to maintain low trade-barrier environments in favour of globalization within industries. In this respect the WTO seems to have been established as an organizational framework governing international competition, building on the rules of the GATT treaty, rather than a major breakthrough towards free trade worldwide. It provides increased competition in the area of services, by relaxing national barriers in a number of service industries (telecommunications, insurance, banking, etc.). It also provides more homogeneous rules concerning industrial property (patents and trade marks), thereby making it easier for brands to achieve global coverage.

> ## Website link 7.4
>
> See the World Trade Organization (WTO): the only global international organization dealing with the rules of trade between nations: **http://www.wto.org**.

It is important to globalize in an efficient and controllable manner.[25] Cultural similarity is significantly related to many aspects of business, including the level of affinity,[26] communication, trust and relationship development,[27] successful cooperation,[28] a tendency to consume similar goods,[29] a more positive country of origin image[30] and a lower cost of doing business.[29] The distance to regulative, normative and cognitive levels can also be broken down.[31]

7.3
Globalization of international marketing strategies

While artificial entry barriers are disappearing, global markets remain more ideal than real, especially when one looks at consumption patterns. Subhash Jain (p. 8)[23] examined the academic papers on standardization over the last 40 years, concluding that:

- across-the board standardization is inconceivable;
- the decision on standardization is not a dichotomous one between complete standardization and customization; rather there can be degrees of standardization;
- although a variety of internal and external factors impinge on the standardization decision, the product/industry characteristics are paramount;
- standardization is most feasible in settings where the marketing infrastructure is well developed.

So how can products and marketing strategies faced with fierce world competition, as well as consumer resistance to the globalization movement become globalized? There are three major characterizations of international business strategy:

1. *Standardization-adaptation* of market offerings (marketing mix elements).
2. *Geographical concentration-dispersion* of the structural or organizational aspects of the value chain.
3. *Financial integration-independence* of the competitive processes (planning, implementation and control).[32]

Standardization-adaptation of international market offerings

Prior to Buzzell's classic article, 'Can you standardize multinational marketing?',[33] natural entry barriers related to culture were seen as very high, requiring adaptation to national markets and offsetting the potential advantages of scale economies. Buzzell clearly showed that, with the decrease of purely artificial trade barriers, large international companies could create natural entry barriers unrelated to culture through economies of scale. Since then, there have been numerous texts that have sought to advise business people how to make the best choices between standardization and adaptation of marketing policies to foreign markets. This literature advocates either 'hard' or 'soft' globalization:

1. 'Hard globalizers' see globalization as a new 'paradigm' for international marketing.[34] According to Hampton and Buske (p. 263)[34] 'consumers in increasing numbers demonstrate that they are willing to sacrifice specific preferences in product

features, function and design for a globally standardized product that carries a lower price'. They
also report that there is a shift to the global marketing paradigm since the process of adapting
products to national wants and needs contradicts
their global convergence.

2. 'Soft' partisans of globalization see it as a necessary, but environment-constrained trend. The
physical conditions of a country, as well as the laws
relating to product standards, sales promotion,
taxes, or other aspects of production, may affect
the standardization of marketing programmes,
especially in developing countries.[35]

Consumer wants in various national markets
are not really considered by either soft or hard
globalization: differences are either denied (hard) or
treated as an external constraint (soft). Behind the
globalization debate there is a quite practical issue
in terms of the everyday life of companies: the traditional dilemma between production flexibility and
the (marketing) tendency to customize products to
diversified needs. Factory managers prefer to be
inflexible, for low-cost purposes, whereas marketing
managers favour as much tailoring to customers'
needs as possible. Current developments in factory
automation allow for products to be customized
without major cost implications.[36] New strategies
have been found to serve diversified needs, to customize products and at the same time to maintain
low costs owing to economies of scale and experience effects. A modular conception of products
permits shared economies of scale as far as components are concerned, whereas lagged differentiation
maintains a high scale of production for as long as
possible in the production process and organizes
cheap final customization either in the factory or
in the distribution network (see Box 7.3).[37–39] Why
is it necessary to maintain such a strong 'paradigm
for action' emphasis on globalization if consumption
patterns are not clearly globalizing and if adjusting
to global competition is reconcilable with tailoring
products and marketing strategies to national
markets?

First, many companies believe that standardization will result in higher performance. Zou and
Cavusgil[40] surveyed companies in the United States
to assess the influence of self-reported standardization on perceived performance (both strategic and
financial). The standardization of promotions and
products are perceived to affect both aspects
of performance. However, other studies have found
that a firm's performance is indifferent to standardization versus adaptation.[41] This relationship
is more complicated, being dependent on the fit
between strategy and context.

Second, these beliefs are often acted upon. For
example, case studies of western European and US
companies operating in central-eastern European
countries show that Western companies rely heavily
on standardization even when market conditions
seem to favour localization.[42] Managers typically
under-adapt their market offerings to foreign
markets.[43]

Third, many companies place more importance
on their home markets: Wright's interviews with
managers from US and Japanese companies found
the 'existence of ethnocentric orientations in both US
and Japanese firms because of the prevailing assumptions by headquarter firms about the importance of
their home markets' (p. 352).[44]

Organizational aspects of globalization

The reasons for globalizing marketing activities are
largely organizational. Although there is evidence of
some savings in manufacturing costs, the financial
pay-offs for hard globalization are, at best, dubious
when one considers the financial performance of
companies as a whole.[45,46] MNCs that grew fast
worldwide in the 1960s and 1970s did so by granting
a large degree of decision-making autonomy to their
subsidiaries in their home markets. Subsidiaries were
asked to replicate the corporate values and organizational practices of the parent company and also
encouraged to completely adjust to the local market.
Later on, subsidiary managers used the message that
'our market is unique' to defend specific, nationally
designed marketing policies. Hence they defended
their autonomy even at the expense of sometimes
rather fallacious arguments. In the 1980s and 1990s
MNCs probably needed to shift their organizational
design towards more centralization.

Parent companies wanted to have a more unified
implementation scheme of new, more centrally

Box 7.3

Standardized components and mass customization

The use of standardized components in the production process, much like the modular design of products, enables manufacturers to postpone final product differentiation. Identical components may be shared by diverse end-consumer products: for example, the same plug will fit various appliances. 'Modules' are standardized components designed to be suitable for a wide variety of possible uses, allowing for a significant reduction in the quantity of components.

Lagged differentiation is illustrated by the crystal glassworks at Saint Louis which have only a limited number of basic moulds for producing all their glassware while finishes (size, engraving, decoration, etc.) are applied at the end of the line to plain glass products. Unfinished glasses of different sizes and shapes are mass produced.

Similarly, the same cream cheese Tartare is packaged in different ways at the end of the production line: in aluminium foil for individual servings, in a plastic tub, canned or wrapped. In other cases, a cheese will be flavoured differently (cherry, walnut, port wine, rose or other flower perfumes, etc.). Some packagings are standardized, such as plastic containers which can be used for melted cheese as well as various types of fresh cheese.

Canson & Montgolfier manufactures papers of different weight on 2.20 metre wide and several hundred metre long rolls. This 'upstream' operation requires large-scale investment and a high level of technology, and has limited flexibility. As far as possible, each type of roll is manufactured in batches (several times a year) and stored before its final processing. Cutting, shaping and finishing is carried out on standard rolls, which are then customized to the required formats and styles of each country. At Petit-Bateau, which manufactures traditional knitwear, the knitting is done on unbleached yarn. Dying is applied to the yarn subsequently. Likewise, standardized patterns permit the creation of a large number of different clothes. At Dim, a lingerie manufacturer, hosiery is produced undyed. The dye, which is subcontracted, is applied at the last possible opportunity on untreated standard products. This allows flexible tailoring to the different shades sought by consumers. Irons by SEB-Calor are all manufactured with the same moulds, which gives rise to 100 different models, according to function, colour, casing, voltage and brand name. Christofle's Arab cafetières, designed exclusively for the Middle East, are manufactured with the same stamping moulds as other cafetières (Deher, 1986).

The Planter's Company, a unit of Nabisco, chose cosmetic customization when it retooled its old plant in Suffolk, Virginia, to satisfy the increasingly diverse demand of its retail customers. Wal-Mart wanted to sell peanuts and mixed nuts in larger quantities than Safeway or 7-Eleven did, and Jewel wanted different promotional packages than Dominick's did. In the past, Planter's could produce only long batches of small, medium, and large cans; as a result, customers had to choose from a few standard packages to find the one that most closely met their requirements. Today the company can switch quickly between different sizes (Gilmore and Pine, 1997).

(Sources: Deher, p. 66;[36] Gilmore and Pine, p. 94.[38])

designed international marketing strategies, responding to the globalization of competition. Procter & Gamble did this in Europe by introducing the Eurobrand concept, consisting of a common brand name and a basic marketing strategy for most western European countries (see Box 7.4). After a long period of centralization, P & G is now giving slightly more weight to localization, especially with regard to advertising and branding.

Global companies willing to recentralize their operations since the 1980s tend towards some authoritarianism from headquarters, especially when they adopt the 'hard' version of the globalization creed. Often the globalization of consumption is

Box 7.4

Procter & Gamble's European managers react to Eurobrands

Comments of some managers in national subsidiaries:

'We have to listen to the consumer. In blind tests in my market that perfume cannot even achieve breakeven.'

'The whole detergent market is in 2-kilo packs in Holland. To go to a European standard of 3 kg and 5 kg sizes would be a disaster for us.'

'We have low phosphate in Italy that constrains our product formula. And we just don't have hyper-markets like France and Germany where you can drop off pallet loads.'

A P & G General Manager's comments to European headquarters:

'There is no such thing as a Eurocustomer so it makes no sense to talk about Eurobrands. We have an English housewife whose needs are different from a German Hausfrau. If we move to a system that allows us to blur our thinking, we will have big problems.

Product standardisation sets up pressures to try to meet everybody's needs (in which case you build a Rolls-Royce that nobody can afford) and countervailing pressures to find the lowest common denominator product (in which case you make a product that satisfies nobody and which cannot compete in any market). These decisions probably result in the foul middle compromise that is so often the outcome of committee decision.'

(Source: Bartlett.[47])

---

presented as indisputable because it is much easier to 'sell' the recentralization policy within the organization. Kashani[48] gives the example of the Danish toy company Lego, which was facing a leading competitor in the United States. The competitor, Tyco, sold its toys in plastic buckets instead of Lego's elegant see-through cartons, which were standard worldwide. When asked by the management of the US subsidiary to package in buckets like Tyco, which was gaining market share, the head office rejected the request. After two years and a massive loss of share in the US market, Lego's headquarters in Billund (Denmark) decided to create a newly designed bucket. Not only was the share erosion in the US stopped, but the bucket was introduced worldwide and proved to be a great success.

The two main elements to globalization at an organizational level include the centralization of elements of the value chain (e.g. functions such as research and development, logistics and distribution and after-sales service) and the centralization of financial responsibility. Each of these is discussed below.

Geographical concentration-dispersion

The concentration-dispersion characterisation of international marketing can be traced to Porter's 'design' framework,[1] which argued that multi-national firms should configure the optimal value-chain, such that scale and national comparative advantages are exploited, while still being responsive to local needs.[40] The focus is on the geographic 'concentration' vs 'dispersion' of the value-chain activities, such as research and development, logistics, distribution and after-sales service. For instance, Craig and Douglas (p. 7) describe the configural advantage of News Corporation's Fox network as follows:

In the United States, News Corporation's Fox network typically ends up fourth in the rating wars with the three established networks, ABC, NBC, and CBS. However, outside the United States, the picture is quite different. In addition to establishing a fourth television network, Rupert Murdoch is building a strong configuration of satellite and cable companies around the world. The extensive geographic network of operations allows content developed for the Fox television network in the United States to be aired on News Corporation's vast satellite network, which consists of BSkyB in the United Kingdom, Star TV in Asia, and ISkyB in India, as well as through satellite- and terrestrial-based networks in other countries where News Corporation has strategic alliances. This vast network gives News Corporation a strong configural advantage over the three U.S. television networks – one that is very costly and difficult to replicate.[49]

Concentration of value-creating activities can increase economics of scale and accumulations of specialized knowledge. In contrast, geographically dispersed value-creating activities provides greater contact with both customers and competitors, which allows more rapid response to competitive innovations, and tailoring of offerings to meet local customer needs.[49] Geographical dispersion also allows more flexibility to respond to macroeconomic and market conditions, such as swings in foreign exchange, economic or political conditions, labour unrest and so on.[49]

Financial integration-independence

The *integration-independence* characterization of international marketing is concerned with the extent to which competitive moves are planned, implemented and controlled in a global manner.[50] At one end, a firm treats its subsidiaries as an *integrated network*, and, as such, may decide to cross-subsidize its competitive position across countries. On the other end, a firm treats its subsidiaries as independent profit centres, responsible for their own markets.

The relationship between headquarters and subsidiaries in the defining of any marketing strategy is complex. Too much autonomy results in purely local solutions with few economies of scale and an absence of worldwide coordination; at that point, strong action is needed. This was the case in Black & Decker's gamble on globalization, as noted by Saporito (p. 26):

Globalization did not go down well in Europe for one good reason: Black & Decker owned half the market on the continent, and an astounding 80 per cent in the U.K. European managers asked: 'Why tamper with success?' But Farley (B & D new chairman) believed that the company was treading water in Europe – sales failed to grow last year – and that Makita's strategy made globalization inevitable . . . Those who don't share Farley's vision usually don't stay around long. Last year he fired all of his European managers.[24]

This was combined with a complete turnaround: Black & Decker acquired the GE small appliance division and a Swedish company producing woodworking tools, and changed the company name to B & D, as well as the logo. B & D recentred a large part of its business on self-powered tools with built-in batteries. It ended up making a strong comeback.[51]

It is the patterns in the globalization of competition which impose changes in organizational design (recentralization), rather than the globalization of consumption patterns. In this process, negotiations and compromises between headquarters and subsidiaries are constant. As Kashani (p. 92)[48] emphasized: 'the way global decisions are conceptualized, refined, internally communicated, and, finally implemented in the company's international network have a great deal to do with their performance'. Local managers naturally tend to emphasize the uniqueness of local consumption patterns and marketing environment (legal, distribution networks, sales promotion methods and so on). The headquarters of successful global companies are flexible rather than authoritarian in dealing with their subsidiaries' assumed or real uniqueness. For instance, they commission research rather than flatly ignore a subsidiary's arguments and they take new ideas and suggestions from the most talented and dynamic subsidiaries, rather than rejecting their advice outright.

In fact, international marketing programmes have experienced a trend towards greater standardization, but this needs to be differentiated, according to: (1) the elements of the marketing mix considered; (2) the type of market, such as whether it is a developed or undeveloped country; (3) the type of product, such as consumer or industrial goods; and (4) the control exerted over the subsidiary, whether it is wholly owned or a joint venture.

A review of the literature shows that brand and product characteristics are generally more standardized than pricing, sales, distribution and promotions.

For instance, in Turkey, product characteristics, brand name, positioning and packaging are the least adapted elements; price, promotion and distribution are more tailored to the local environment (Ozsomer *et al.*, 1991). Adaptations mainly occur in non-core elements, including labelling, instructions, and selection of the appropriate product-mix and creative execution.[42]

The type of market and market similarities will also influence the standardization of offerings. Similarities in consumer preferences, as well as environmental factors, such as the cultural, economic, legal and infrastructure environment, will all assist in the level of feasible standardization.

The level of standardization in US multinational companies operating in Europe varies by product category.[52] There has been a decrease in the degree of standardization for consumer durables and industrial goods, and an increase for consumer non-durables. Most studies report industrial products as more standardized than consumer products and that high technology and branded premium luxury goods are more likely to be standardized. The caveat here is that there is no conclusive evidence, and common practice is not equivalent to best practice.

The degree of standardization is larger in wholly-owned subsidiaries than in joint ventures.[53] In many cases, standardization is implemented incrementally by transferring existing products at headquarters or in important subsidiaries. Subsidiaries continue to have a considerable degree of power in relation to product and promotion transfer in consumer goods multinationals.[54] In most cases, market needs are assessed by the subsidiary itself, which then uses the worldwide product portfolio as a resource base. In developing countries, subsidiaries initiate product transfer in 85 per cent of the cases, whereas in developed markets this drops to only 63 per cent. This suggests that worldwide or regional headquarters exert more authoritative pressure for standardization across developed markets, especially in Europe. In the transfer process some adaptation is made to local requirements. In addition, cultural differences between headquarters and subsidiaries can affect performance. For instance, Hewett and Bearden (p. 60)[55] show that 'in more collectivistic cultures, trust takes on greater importance in motivating cooperative behaviours' as compared to more economic type rewards.

Website link 7.5

See how the Japanese animation industry is attempting to break down cultural barriers: **http://www.atimes.com/atimes/Asian_Economy/ DL12DK01.html.**

Globalization belongs to the realm of organizational discourse rather than to actual international marketing. Rather than a 'hard' global marketing strategy, it is possible to adopt an intercultural marketing strategy which has basically the same goals but is more respectful of local culture and attempts to serve purely national as well as transnational market segments.

Culture-related experience is all the more important since natural entry barriers relating to consumer behaviour and marketing environments diminish very gradually and only in the long term. Language-related differences, for instance, remain. Therefore, global marketing strategies must be implemented cautiously, especially in culture-bound industries: local knowledge has to be generated, by research, by organizational learning, by hiring 'cultural' insiders or by acquiring local companies with culture-specific business experience.

7.4

Market segments

Intercultural marketing is about localizing as much as globalizing: it aims to customize product and marketing strategies to customer needs within the framework of a global strategy. Intercultural marketing tries to balance cross-national differences requiring mandatory local adaptation and cross-national commonalities which are conducive to the development of size and experience effects. To do this, the international marketer needs to define country clusters where similar marketing policies can be followed (for a review of country clustering, see Holzmüller and Stöllnberger[56]).

Website link 7.6

See Tourism Australia's website. It identifies a market segment that it believes can be targeted across cultures: **http://www.tourism.australia.com/ content/Research/Market%20Segmentations/ Japan_Segmentation_Study.pdf.**

Taking advantage of the desire for assimilation and cultural identification: the case of cultural products

Cultural products such as music, literature and films are strongly suffused with local particularities. Books, music and films are, however, three products where global marketing has been successfully employed. The success of Harlequin romantic novels, Harry Potter and *The Lord of the Rings* films has been remarkable: profound attraction has bypassed the filter of national cultures. The romantic and melodramatic adventures of Harlequin heroes target a lonely female public eager for tenderness in the majority of urban centres. Similarly, the meanings conveyed by the adventures of Harry Potter extend far beyond British culture.

Cultural products that build on fairly universal feelings and lifestyles are the ones to which standardized marketing policy can be applied. In the recording industry, marketing techniques, particularly with regard to collections of popular music, have generally evolved in a similar fashion across industrialized nations, with increased large-scale distribution or specialized chains, similar promotion channels and advertising, and a global standardization of product presentation. The recipe for global success is, however, less easily applicable than it seems: American country music has failed in its attempt to achieve major success in continental Europe. Its only real international development has taken place in Australia, despite some success in the United Kingdom. One reason for this is that no significant segment of the European population can identify with the images portrayed by the music from the American West and the symbols of a pioneer tradition. On the other hand, the Australian outback, with its jackaroos and jillaroos, is similar in many respects to the American West with its cowboys and cowgirls, and has given birth to an Australian musical tradition whose roots are in country music.

Intercultural marketing is facilitated when the conditions for product identification are present in the target market. Consumers buy the meaning that they find in products for the purpose of cultural identification, based on the desire to assimilate to a certain civilization, as in the case of ethnic consumption (see section 4.4). Such identification was the reason that record companies began to market classical music on a large scale in the form of collections. In the 1980s, market surveys showed that owning a collection of classical music recordings, combined with a superficial knowledge of the most famous pieces, promoted a personal image of stability and respectability for people aged between 25 and 40, projecting an image of successful integration in professional and social lives. As a result, certain record companies launched mass-market compilations of classical music. Their marketing strategy was to implement the strict rules of global marketing: same product, same packaging, same price and same type of communication. These compilations, however, became less successful in the 1990s when classical music ceased to be a major element in the acquisition of respectability.

Apart from their utilitarian aspects, McDonald's Big Mac and Coca-Cola are sources of meanings that provide their buyers with fantasized cultural adaptation to a desired way of life. Rock music represents a tolerant and leisurely way of life for many young Europeans and Asians. Identification with these symbols is one of the necessary conditions for being *trendy*, or 'cool'. The international marketing of rock music achieves even greater success where certain values (e.g. individualism, strong desire for equality) are already present in the potential market segment; in this case young people between the ages of 10 and 25.

Cultural identity involves two mutually contradictory desires: one is to identify oneself with the national or home culture, and the other is to identify with an exotic or foreign culture. This creates ambivalence and makes it necessary to cluster countries or consumers who share certain meaningful cultural characteristics. Such clusters form cultural affinity zones and cultural affinity classes.

Cultural affinity classes and zones

The intercultural marketing approach not only concentrates on geography- and nationality-based criteria but also takes into account consumer attitudes, preferences and lifestyles that are linked to age, class and ethnicity, occupation, and so on. Many studies have used these bases to identify international market segments, including demographics,[57] psychographics and values,[58–65] quality of life,[66] attitudes,[67] behaviour,[68] brand loyalty[69] and situation.[70]

Geographical cultural affinity zones correspond to a large extent to national cultural groups, while cultural affinity classes exist in terms of other segmentation bases. For instance, people between the ages of 15 and 20, in Japan, Europe and the US, form a cultural affinity class. They have a tendency to share common values, behaviour and interests, and tend to present common traits as a consumer segment; their lifestyles converge worldwide irrespective of national borders. As such, we see lifestyle convergence in teenagers in Europe who spend time watching MTV. Carey et al.[71] surveyed 7- to 12-year-olds around the world in the ABC Global Kids Study, tracking their lifestyle and consumption patterns. A pictorial response scale was used when interviewing children on emotions and preferences while product usage was reported more frequently by mothers, rather than children. Worldwide, children basically seem to share many common dreams and aspirations; they tend to have significant purchasing power and participate actively in family decision making for a number of product categories.

De Mooij and Keegan (pp. 118–19) reviewed comparative lifestyle research in Europe and Asia, finding multinational target groups across the United Kingdom, France, Italy and Germany:

Each of these target groups represents a distinctive segment across the different nations. Members of the social milieus within a multinational target group sometimes have more in common than with many of their fellow countrymen. In spite of these similarities, there are of course, differences. Similar values may translate differently at the local level.[72]

The Survey Research Group (SRG) attempts to monitor cross-border changes in lifestyle in Asia by conducting lifestyle surveys in Hong Kong, Malaysia, the Philippines, Singapore, Thailand and Taiwan. Similarly, changes in lifestyles across social milieus in European countries are monitored through extensive surveys, such as the ACE (Anticipating Change in Europe) study, CCA (Centre de Communication Avancée), Eurostyles and Sinus Gmbh 'Social Milieus'.

Lifestyle convergence can also be observed for gender-based segments on a worldwide basis; Tai and Tam[73] review the change in lifestyles of female consumers in Hong Kong, Taiwan and China on a number of issues such as the perception of women and their roles, family and home orientation, health and environment. They find that women in the People's Republic of China tend to be quickly influenced by Western values and are increasingly becoming similar to both Hong Kong and Taiwanese female consumers. Similarly, gender was found to be a useful segmentation criterion for travel agencies in Turkey.[74]

The practical difficulty is in combining geography-based cultural affinity zones and demographics and lifestyle segmentation criteria (cultural affinity classes). You may wonder, for instance, if consumption behaviour, values and lifestyles among 15- to 20-year-olds are more homogeneous across Europe or Asia than in relation to other age groups in the same zone. A review of the international marketing segmentation literature revealed that only 8 of the 25 studies used responses from individual consumers.[75] In addition, a number of conceptual and methodological issues need to be addressed in future studies including construct equivalence, level of aggregation, and choice of segmentation basis.

Cultural affinity classes are probably an ideal means of defining an international target for standardized products, in so far as they create a sense of belonging to a common age, gender or income group across different countries. Many different methods have been suggested for international market segmentation based on some form of cultural affinity.[76–79] Furthermore, the development of new media such as the Internet and satellite television channels will help the international launch of products targeted at the same cultural affinity classes across different countries.

Accordingly, market research should survey consumer segments as cells in a matrix, with countries in columns and cultural affinity classes in rows. If similar behaviour is observed by market researchers for a particular row across the different cells of the matrix with regard to key consumer behaviour figures (e.g. consumption of soft drinks, organization of personal time, time spent listening to the radio or watching television, etc.), the emergence of a common consumption culture and a cross-national segment may be detected. If, on the other hand, different cultural affinity classes in different countries adopt similar behaviour across international

Figure 7.1 A hypothetical map of the zones of cultural affinities in Europe

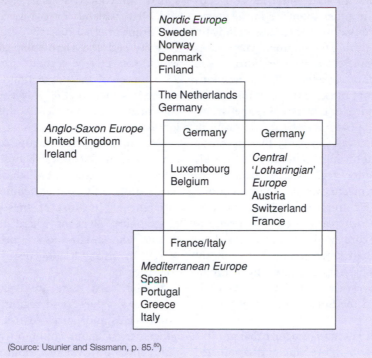

(Source: Usunier and Sissmann, p. 85.[80])

contexts, marketing communication will have to be modified to facilitate the process of diffusion from one country to another. If a drink, for example, is popular among 25- to 30-year-olds in one country and among 50- to 60-year-olds in another country, this indicates a weak affinity of national cultures.

Attempts to market products globally also highlight cultural affinity zones in which the same marketing strategy with the same type of products can be successfully implemented. In Europe, for example, two of these zones are quite separate (see Figure 7.1) – Scandinavia and the Mediterranean countries. A third zone encompasses the central European countries and Great Britain, which serve as a bridge between northern and southern Europe, while retaining their own distinct personality. Despite the traditional isolation of the United Kingdom, there are fewer differences between the United Kingdom and Denmark or Sweden than between the UK and Italy or Spain. Accordingly, an item successfully marketed in the United Kingdom is more likely to repeat this success in the Netherlands or Denmark

than in southern Europe. The long-established differences between Anglo-Saxon and Latin culture are reinforced by the religious divide between Protestants and Catholics. Cultural affinity zones display similar characteristics for easily identifiable criteria such as language, religion, family life patterns, work relations and consumption patterns. Intercultural marketing begins by choosing one of the main countries from a cultural affinity zone as a 'lead country' that will be used as a base for market entry and diffusion of strategy, with only minor adaptation for other countries throughout the zone. Marketing teams can interact with each other across zones within a regional area, especially when countries lie at the border of two zones. As an example, Figure 7.1 offers a *hypothetical map* of the zones of cultural affinities for western Europe.

The operational mapping of cultural affinity zones can be based on cultural as well as marketing criteria related to the product category, such as consumer behaviour, price levels, attitude towards innovation, opening hours in distribution outlets, etc. When a product is launched internationally, the new product will be launched first in lead countries and subsequently marketed in other countries in the zones. For instance, a record that may be successful in Latin European countries during the summer, when waves of holidaymakers come from all over Europe, will have a greater chance of spreading into Nordic countries once visitors from those countries return home and go into music stores to buy the songs they heard on holiday. Equally, a band may be so successful in a single country, such as Germany, that its music spreads into neighbouring countries. It spreads rapidly in the border regions, for example in Belgium, because of media overlap. The launch of a new product through cultural affinity zones can take from 18 months to two years, which is a relatively long period of time compared with the standard life cycle of a song, generally a few months.[80] The concept of 'lead country' has been used successfully by multinational companies such as Procter & Gamble when they developed the Eurobrand concept in the mid-1980s.

In addition, we also need to recognize that product information can now be more rapidly disseminated than ever via the Internet, which may influence the stability of segment membership.[81] Austin and Reed (p. 590)[82] state that: 'Almost 10 million (14 per cent) of America's 69 million children are now online with over 4 million children accessing the Internet from school and 5.7 million children going online from home.' This may dramatically affect the potential for segmentation in the future.

National versus regional differences

Sovereign states have very dissimilar sizes: China (9,600,000 km^2) is more than 232 times the size of Switzerland (49,293 km^2), even though both countries are significant international players on the world scene. Geographical location is related to culture: for instance, on average, islands tend to develop more homogeneity than continental countries. A special case is that of mega-countries such as the United States, Canada, Brazil, China and India because their internal diversity is fairly large. Even smaller countries, such as the United Kingdom, Spain, Italy, Sweden and France, exhibit a strong North/South

paradigm which is reversed in the southern hemisphere for countries such as Argentina, Australia and New Zealand. Even tiny Switzerland displays significant internal diversity, especially between the French- and the German-speaking communities, which respectively account for 20 per cent and 75 per cent of the population. Therefore, national differences are not the only source of variance in consumer behaviour across different geographical locations.

Regional differences in large countries with multi-ethnic and multicultural backgrounds can explain differences in consumer behaviour.[83] Researchers have consistently found significant within-country differences.[84–87] Most of these have to do with geographical divisions where geography, a shared history and a common ethnic background has served to create homogeneous groupings within countries.[87]

In the USA, there are regional differences in consumers' values[85] and regional differences in innovativeness and perceived risk, as well as cultural adherence, religious commitment, and fateorientation.[88] In South America, both regional differences within countries and value similarity across countries were found. Lenartowicz and colleagues[87] used the Rokeach Value Survey (RVS) to examine the importance of regional subcultures in Brazil and Colombia and their value similarity with consumers in Uruguay and Venezuela. They found significant differences between regions in the relative importance of values, concluding that 'geography, a shared history and a common ethnic background might be as important in defining cultural subgroups as religion and language' (p. 1006).[87] In Canada, differences have been found between English and French speakers in the same location. For instance, Laroche and colleagues[89] investigated consumers in Montreal, Canada, finding differences in pro-environmental knowledge, attitudes and behaviours between primarily French and primarily English speakers. They found that French-Canadians know more and are more concerned about environmental issues, whereas English-Canadians are more likely to recycle and are willing to pay more for environmentally friendly products.

However, regional differences within countries, even if perceived more clearly by nationals than by foreigners, are most often much smaller than international differences. For instance, among Belgian and Polish consumers of chocolates, at least two of the five segments surveyed were driven by nationality: the first segment was made up of 87 per cent Belgian consumers and the second made up of 91 per cent Polish consumers.[84] It was also found that a subcultural design was not appropriate for Poland. Similarly, English female Quebecers were found to be more similar to French female Quebecers than to English female Ontarians (all of these being Canadian females) in the benefits they seek from a brassiere.[90] These findings support the idea of the assimilation model, where the cultural values of the immigrants tend to merge with those of the locally dominant cultural group. This supports geography as an operational basis for international marketing segmentation.

7.5
Conclusion

When building clusters of countries ('cultural affinity zones') that can be approached with a regionally standardized marketing strategy, marketing professionals should take into account basic cultural variables such as language, institutions, membership in a regional grouping, and basic cultural traits as described in Chapters 2 and 3. However, some sociodemographic characteristics such as sex, age and income also provide a sound basis for transnational marketing strategies in terms of 'cultural affinity classes'. Thus international marketing segments must be defined in order to allow for the best possible compromise between national/cultural and sociodemographic characteristics.

Questions

1. Describe how experience effects induce firms to standardize products. Provide examples.

2. Select a multinational company annual report and find evidence of globalization (global decisions, global products, globalization of competition, consumption patterns, management procedures, etc.).

3. Why does globalization take place more clearly on the supply side than on the demand side?

4. For the following industries/products, discuss to what extent: (a) a world consumer exists; (b) the product or services offered are themselves global (similar worldwide); and (c) the industry itself can be considered as global:
   - airlines;
   - tobacco;
   - meat-based foods;
   - sheets and pillows;
   - pharmaceuticals.

5. What are zones of cultural affinity?

6. Discuss the relative importance, for segmentation purposes, of sociodemographic variables, such as age, sex, income, habitat, etc., in comparison with cultural variables based either on nationality or values.

References

1. Porter, Michael E. (1986), 'Changing Patterns of International Competition', *California Management Review*, XXVIII (2), 9–39.
2. Sheth, Jagdish N. (2001), 'From International to Integrated Marketing', *Journal of Business Research*, 51, 5–9.
3. Rugman, Alan (2001), 'The Myth of Global Strategy', *International Marketing Review*, 18 (6), 583–88.
4. Qian, Gongming and Ji Li (2002), 'Multinationality, Global Market Diversification and Profitability among the Largest Us Firms', *Journal of Business Research*, 55 (4), 325–35.
5. Day, George S. and David B. Montgomery (1983), 'Diagnosing the Experience Curve', *Journal of Marketing* (Spring), 44–58.
6. Ger, Güliz (1999), 'Localizing in the Global Village: Local Firms Competing in Global Markets', *California Management Review*, 41 (4), 64–83.
7. Favier, Jaap (2007), 'Europe's Ecommerce Forecast: 2006 to 2011', *Forrester Market Research*, 1, 1–7.
8. Mulpuru, Sucharita (2006), 'U.S. Ecommerce: Five-Year Forecast and Data Overview', *Forrester Market Research* (1), 1–15.
9. Prasad, V. Kanti, K. Ramamurthy, and G.M. Naidu (2001), 'The Influence of Internet-Marketing Integration on Marketing Competencies and Export Performance', *Journal of International Marketing*, 9 (4), 82–110.
10. Usunier, Jean-Claude (2002), 'Le Pays D'origine du Bien Influence-t-il Encore les Évaluations des Consommateurs?', *Revue Française du Marketing*, 189/190 (2002/4–5), 49–65.
11. Hult, G. Thomas M. and David J. Ketchen Jr (2001), 'Does Market Orientation Matter? A Test of the Relationship between Positional Advantage and Performance', *Strategic Management Journal*, 22 (9), 899–906.
12. Hult, G. Thomas M., David W. Cravens, and Jagdish Sheth (2001), 'Competitive Advantage in the Global Marketplace: A Focus on Marketing Strategy', *Journal of Business Research*, 51, 1–3.
13. Perlmutter, Howard V. (1969), 'The Tortuous Evolution of the Multinational Corporation', *Columbia Journal of World Business*, 4 (1), 9–18.
14. Wind, Yoram, Susan P. Douglas, and Howard V. Perlmutter (1973), 'Guidelines for Developing International Marketing Strategies', *Journal of Marketing*, 37 (April), 14–23.
15. Sheth, Jagdish N. and Atul Parvatiyar (2001), 'The Antecedents and Consequences of Integrated Global Marketing', *International Marketing Review*, 18 (1), 16–29.
16. Malhotra, Naresh K., James Agarwal, and Imad Baalbaki (1998), 'Heterogeneity of Regional Trading Blocks and Global Marketing Strategies: A Multicultural Perspective', *International Marketing Review*, 15 (6), 476–506.
17. Ohmae, Kenichi (1985), *Triad Power: The Coming Shape of Global Competition*. New York: Free Press.
18. Vernon, Raymond P. (1966), 'International Investment and International Trade in the Product Life Cycle', *Quarterly Journal of Economics*, 80 (2), 191–207.
19. Johanson, Jan and Jan-Erik Vahlne (1977), 'The Internationalisation Process of the Firm: A Model of Knowledge Development and Increased Market Commitments', *Journal of International Business Studies*, 8 (1), 23–32.
20. Wilkinson, Ian F. and Constant Cheng (1999), 'Multicultural Marketing in Australia: Synergy in Diversity', *Journal of International Marketing*, 7 (3), 106–25.
21. Lane, K.P., I. St-Maurice, and C.S. Dyckerhoff (2006), 'Building Brands in China', *McKinsey Quarterly*, 35–41.
22. Douglas, Susan P. (2001), 'Exploring New Worlds: The Challenge of Global Marketing', *Journal of Marketing*, 65 (1), 103–07.
23. Jain, Subhash C. (2007), 'State of the Art of International Marketing Research: Directions for the Future', *Journal for Global Business Advancement*, 1 (1), 4–19.
24. Saporito, William (1984), 'Black & Decker's Gamble on Globalization', *Fortune*, 14 (May), 24–32.
25. Matthyssens, Paul and Pieter Pauwels (2000), 'Uncovering International Market-Exit Processes: A Comparative Case Study', *Psychology and Marketing*, 17 (8), 697–719.
26. Swift, Jonathan B. (1999), 'Cultural Closeness as a Facet of Cultural Affinity', *International Marketing Review*, 16 (3), 182–201.
27. Anderson, Erin and Barton Weitz (1989), 'Determinants of Continuity in Conventional Industrial Channel Dyads', *Marketing Science*, 8, 310–23.
28. van Oudenhoven, Jan Pieter and Karen I. van de Zee (2002), 'Successful International Cooperation: The Influence of Cultural Similarity, Strategic Differences, and International Experience', *Applied Psychology*, 51 (4), 633.
29. Yu, Chwo-Ming Joseph and Dixie S. Zietlow (1995), 'The Determinants of Bilateral Trade among Asia-Pacific Countries', *A.S.E.A.N. Economic Bulletin*, 11 (3), 298–305.
30. Wang, Chih-Kang and Charles W. Lamb Jr (1983), 'The Impact of Selected Environmental Forces Upon Consumers' Willingness to Buy Foreign Products', *Journal of the Academy of Marketing Science*, 11 (2), 71–84.
31. Xu, Dean and Oded Shenkar (2002), 'Institutional Distance and the Multinational Enterprise', *Academy of Management Review*, 27 (4), 608–18.

32. Lim, Lewis K.S., Frank Acito, and Alexander Rusetski (2006), 'Development of Archetypes of International Marketing Strategy', *Journal of International Business Studies*, 37 (4), 499–524.

33. Buzzell, Robert D. (1968), 'Can You Standardize Multinational Marketing?', *Harvard Business Review* (November–December), 102–13.

34. Hampton, Gerlad M. and Erwin Buske (1987), 'The Global Marketing Perspective', in *Advances in International Marketing*, S. Tamer Cavusgil, Ed. Vol. 2. Greenwich, CT: JAI Press.

35. Hill, John S. and Richard R. Still (1984), 'Adapting Products to L.D.C. Tastes', *Harvard Business Review* (March–April), 92–101.

36. Wind, Yoram (1986), 'The Myth of Globalization', *Journal of Consumer Marketing*, 3 (Spring), 23–6.

37. Deher, Odile (1986), 'Quelques Facteurs de Succès Pour la Politique de Produits de l'entreprise Exportatrice: Les Liens entre Marketing et Production', *Recherche et Applications en Marketing*, 1 (3), 55–74.

38. Gilmore, James H. and B. Joesph Pine II (1997), 'The Four Faces of Mass Customization', *Harvard Business Review*, 75 (1, January–February), 91–101.

39. Stobaugh, Robert and Piero Telesio (1983), 'Assortir la Politique de Fabrication à la Stratégie des Produits', *Harvard-L'Expansion* (Summer), 77–85.

40. Zou, Shaoming and Tamir Cavusgil (2002), 'The G.M.S.: A Broad Conceptualization of Global Marketing Strategy and Its Effect on Firm Performance', *Journal of Marketing*, 66 (4), 40–56.

41. Theodosiou, Marios and Leonidas C. Leonidou (2003), 'Standardization Versus Adaptation of International Marketing Strategy: An Integrative Assessment of the Empirical Research', *International Business Review*, 12 (2), 141–71.

42. Schuh, Arnold (2000), 'Global Standardization as a Success Formula for Marketing in Central Eastern Europe', *Journal of World Business*, 35 (2), 133–48.

43. Dow, Douglas (2006), 'Adaptation and Performance in Foreign Markets: Evidence of Systematic under-Adaptation', *Journal of International Business Studies*, 37 (2), 212–26.

44. Wright, Len Tiu (2001), 'Intercontinental Comparisons in Marketing Strategy', *International Marketing Review*, 18 (3), 344–54.

45. Samiee, Saeed and Kendall Roth (1994), 'The Influence of Global Marketing Standardization on Performance', *Journal of Marketing*, 56 (April), 1–17.

46. Whitelock, Jeryl and Carole Pimblett (1997), 'The Standardization Debate in International Marketing', *Journal of Global Marketing*, 10 (3), 45–65.

47. Bartlett, Christopher (1983), *Procter & Gamble Europe: Vizir Launch*. Boston, MA: Harvard Business School.

48. Kashani, Kamran (1989), 'Beware the Pitfalls of Global Marketing', *Harvard Business Review*, 67 (October), 91–98.

49. Craig, C. Samuel and Susan P. Douglas (2000), 'Configural Advantage in Global Markets', *Journal of International Marketing*, 8 (1), 6–26.

50. Hofstede, Geert (1976), 'Nationality and Espoused Values of Managers', *Journal of Applied Psychology*, 61 (2), 148–55.

51. Li, Tiger (1990), 'Black and Decker's Turnaround Strategy', in *International Marketing Strategy*, Hans B. Thorelli and S. Tamer Cavusgil, Eds. Oxford: Pergamon Press.

52. Picard, Jacques, Jean-Jacques Boddewyn, and Robin Soehl (1989), 'U.S. Marketing Policies in the European Economic Community: A Longitudinal Study, 1973–1983', in *Dynamics of International Business*, Reijo Luostarinen, Ed. Vol. 1. Helsinki: Proceedings of the 15th Annual Conference of the European International Business Association.

53. Ozsomer, Aysegul, Muzzafer Bodur, and S. Tamer Cavusgil (1991), 'Marketing Standardisation by Multinationals in an Emerging Market', *European Journal of Marketing*, 25 (12), 50–64.

54. Hill, John S. and William L. James (1991), 'Product and Promotion Transfers in Consumer Goods Multinationals', *International Marketing Review*, 8 (4), 6–17.

55. Hewett, Kelly and William O. Bearden (2001), 'Dependence, Trust, and Relational Behavior on the Part of Foreign Subsidiary Marketing Operations: Implications for Managing Global Marketing Operations', *Journal of Marketing*, 65 (4), 51–66.

56. Holzmüller, Hartmut H. and Barbara Stöllnberger (1994), 'A Conceptual Framework for Country Selection in Cross-National Export Studies', *Advances in International Marketing*, 6, 3–24.

57. Anderson, Patricia M. and Xiahong He (1999), 'Culture and Fast-Food Marketing Mix in the People's Republic of China and the USA: Implications for Research and Marketing', *Journal of International Consumer Marketing*, 11 (1), 77–95.

58. Boote, Alfred S. (1983), 'Psychographic Segmentation in Europe', *Journal of Advertising Research*, 22 (December–January), 19–25.

59. Hamel, Gary and C.K. Prahalad (1985), 'Do You Really Have a Global Strategy?', *Harvard Business Review*, 63 (4), 139–48.

60. Kahle, Lynn R., Gregory Rose, and Aviv Shoham (1999), 'Findings of L.O.V. Throughout the World, and Other Evidence of Cross-National Consumer Psychographics: Introduction', *Journal of Euro-marketing*, 8 (1/2), 1–13.

61. Kale, Sudhir H. (1995), 'Grouping Euroconsumers: A Culture-Based Clustering Approach', *Journal of International Marketing*, 3 (3), 35–48.

62. Kamakura, Wagner A., Thomas P. Novak, Jan-Benedict E.M. Steenkamp, and Theo M.M. Verhallen (1993), 'Identification de Segments de Valeurs

Pan-Europe èns par un Mode Le Logit sur les Rangs avec Regroupements Successifs (Identifying Pan-European Value Segments with a Clusterwise Rank-Logit Model)', *Recherche et Applications en Marketing*, 8 (4), 30–55.

63. Kropp, Fredric, Marylin Jones, Gregory Rose, Aviv Shoham, Bella Florenthal, and Bongjin Cho (1999), 'Group Identities: A Cross-Cultural Comparison of Values and Group Influences', *Journal of Euromarketing*, 8 (1/2), 117–31.

64. Steenkamp, Jan-Benedict E.M. (2001), 'The Role of National Culture in International Marketing Research', *International Marketing Review*, 18 (1), 30–44.

65. Wedel, Michael, Frenkel Ter Hofstede, and Jan-Benedict E.M. Steenkamp (1998), 'Mixture Model Analysis of Complex Samples', *Journal of Classification*, 15 (2), 225–44.

66. Peterson, Mark and Naresh K. Malhotra (2000), 'Country Segmentation Based on Objective Quality-of-Life Measures', *International Marketing Review*, 17 (1), 56–73.

67. Verhage, Bronislaw J., Lee D. Dahringer, and Edward W. Cundiff (1989), 'Will a Global Strategy Work? An Energy Conservation Perspective', *Journal of the Academy of Marketing Science*, 17 (2), 129–36.

68. Askegaard, Søren and Tage Koed Madsen (1998), 'The Local and the Global: Exploring Traits of Homogeneity and Heterogeneity in European Food Cultures', *International Business Review*, 7 (6), 549–68.

69. Yavas, Ugur, Bronislaw J. Verhage, and Robert T. Green (1992), 'Global Consumer Segmentation Versus Local Market Orientation: Empirical Findings', *Management International Review*, 32 (3), 265–73.

70. Gehrt, Kenneth C. and Soyeon Shim (2003), 'Situational Segmentation in the International Marketplace: The Japanese Snack Market', *International Marketing Review*, 20 (2), 180–94.

71. Carey, George, Xiaoyan Zhao, Joan Chiaramonte, and David Eden (1997), 'Is There One Global Village for Our Future Generation? Talking to 7–12 Year Olds around the World', *Marketing and Research Today*, 25 (1), 12–16.

72. De Mooij, Marieke K. and Warren Keegan (1991), *Advertising Worldwide*. Hemel Hempstead: Prentice Hall.

73. Tai, Susan H.C. and Jackie L.M. Tam (1997), 'A Lifestyle Analysis of Female Consumers in Greater China', *Psychology and Marketing*, 14 (3), 287–307.

74. Koc, Erdogan (2002), 'The Impact of Gender in Marketing Communications: The Role of Cognitive and Affective Cues', *Journal of Marketing Communications*, 8 (4), 257–75.

75. Steenkamp, Jan-Benedict E.M. and Frenkel Ter Hofstede (2002), 'International Market Segmentation: Issues and Perspectives', *International Journal of Research in Marketing*, 19 (3), 185–213.

76. Kale, Sudhir H. and D. Sudharshan (1987), 'A Strategic Approach to International Segmentation', *International Marketing Review*, 4 (2), 60–70.

77. Kreutzer, Ralf Thomas (1988), 'Marketing Mix Standardization: An Integrated Approach in Global Marketing', *European Journal of Marketing*, 22 (10), 19–30.

78. Souiden, Nizar (2002), 'Segmenting the Arab Markets on the Basis of Marketing Stimuli', *International Marketing Review*, 19 (6), 611–36.

79. Ter Hofstede, Frenkel, Jan-Benedict E.M. Steenkamp, and Michel Wedel (1999), 'International Market Segmentation Based on Consumer-Product Relations', *Journal of Marketing Research*, XXXVI (February), 1–17.

80. Usunier, Jean-Claude and Pierre Sissmann (1986), 'L'interculturel au Service du Marketing', *Harvard-L'Expansion*, 40 (Spring), 80–92.

81. Kumar, V. and Anish Nagpal (2001), 'Segmenting Global Markets: Look before You Leap', *Marketing Research*, 13 (1), 8–13.

82. Austin, M. Jill and Mary Lynn Reed (1999), 'Targeting Children Online: Internet Advertising Issues', *Journal of Consumer Marketing*, 16 (6), 590–602.

83. Garreau, Joel (1981), *The Nine Nations of North America*. Boston, MA: Houghton Mifflin.

84. Januszewska, Renata, Jacques Viaene, and Wim Verbeke (2000), 'Market Segmentation for Chocolate in Belgium and Poland', *Journal of Euromarketing*, 9 (3), 1–25.

85. Kahle, Lynn R. (1986), 'The Nine Nations of North America and the Value Basis of Geographic Segmentation', *Journal of Marketing*, 50 (April), 37–47.81.

86. Lenartowicz, Thomasz and Kendall Roth (2001), 'Does Subculture within a Country Matter? A Cross-National Study of Motivational Domains and Business Performance in Brazil', *Journal of International Business Studies*, 32 (2), 305–25.

87. Lenartowicz, Thomasz, James P. Johnson, and Carolyn T. White (2003), 'The Neglect of Intracultural Variation in International Management Research', *Journal of Business Research*, 56 (12), 999–1008.

88. Gentry, James W., Patriya Tansujah, L. Lee Manzer, and Joby John (1987), 'Do Geographic Subcultures Vary Culturally?', in *Advances in Consumer Research*, Michael J. Houston, Ed. Vol. 15. Provo, UT: Association for Consumer Research.

89. Laroche, Michel, Marc-Alexandre Tomiuk, Jasmin Bergeron, and Guido Barbaro-Forleo (2002), 'Cultural Differences in Environmental Knowledge, Attitudes, and Behaviours of Canadian Consumers', *Canadian Journal of Administrative Sciences*, 19 (3), 267–83.

90. Calantone, Roger, Michael Morris, and Jotindar Johar (1985), 'A Crosscultural Benefit Segmentation Analysis to Evaluate the Traditional Assimilation Model', *International Journal of Research in Marketing*, 2 (3), 207–17.

Appendix 7

Teaching materials

A7.1 Case

Bollywood

'Why me?' grumbled Nico Rogosky, account executive for Pentagram Asian films North America. When Bollywood producer Anjali Kumar called to ask him to take over the marketing and distribution of two new 'Bollywood' films, he suggested she contact a South Asian film marketing expert like *Eros*. 'No, no', she had breezily said, 'we don't want to plug the films to your Indian minority market as usual. We want to make crossover films to appeal to other ethnic groups and the general public. I called you for a different approach.'

Nico had spent the entire afternoon viewing two Bollywood hits with his Indian equivalent, just to get an idea of the genre. So, he mused, sipping a searing-hot green tea, they want us to market their movies, then DVDs and videos, and maybe cable. The company also asked for advice on producing films directly for the North American market. Nico had enjoyed talking over dinner with his Indian counterpart from Kumar Film, a sophisticated chain-smoker named Rishi, who had studied business in Florida. Now sitting comfortably at his home office, Nico listened to the conversation he had recorded.

Nico's conversation with Rishi

Nico: I could see the actors were lip-synching, it was embarrassingly obvious!

Rishi: We'll cut the singing out of the films for you. Everyone knows that actors can't sing, and a handful of back-up singers sing for all the Bollywood stars. Actually, no one cares: back-up singer Lata Mangeshkar has more worldwide sales than the Beatles. Actors Shah Rukh Khan and Aamir Khan sold out London's Wembley Arena with backup singers singing 100 per cent of the concert!

Nico: It was incongruous, though, all those songs interfering with the story line.

Rishi: Actor and film producer Shahrukh Khan famously said that if he had produced *Gladiator*, he would have Russell Crowe singing songs in it.[1] Film star Aamir Khan said that in a movie, the songs hold an emotion, and squeeze the juice from it . . . It's just pure Bollywood.

Nico: The sexual tension between the lovers was unbearable, but the most we saw was some kissing. I would have expected them to, like, hop in bed at that point.

Rishi: Yeah, some say we're prudes, that we're censored. We're conservative, but not prudish. So metaphor, imagery and song/dance routines express sexual undercurrents. That film was quite explicit, actually. You have a lot of people here in the US who would appreciate our level of modesty in films.

Nico: The movies were fabulous, but the story and character development were weak.

Rishi: When I've spoken with film critics from your country, from England, and from France, they all say we're 'exuberant', 'melodramatic', 'earthy'. But film snobs prefer 'over the top', 'predictable', 'unrealistic', and 'superficial'. Our films are life, only more pretty. We don't pretend we're intellectuals or artists. A lot of our audiences are in far-flung villages, workers who spend a day's wage at the ticket office. We give them beauty, glamour, romance, music . . . escape. That is what your troubled people are now seeking too.

Nico had seen *Bend it like Beckham*, *Monsoon Wedding*, and other 'Asian' films that were hits in the USA and the UK, like *Crouching Tiger, Hidden Dragon*, but nothing like this. They want to appeal to Americans? For the art-house crowd there shouldn't be an issue, thought Nico. Indian style is 'in', henna, piercing, yoga, ayurveda, tattoos, and so on have become mainstream, and South-Asian inspired music like Bhangra and Asian Underground are played regularly in dance clubs.[2] But what will the archetypal housewife in Idaho think of Bollywood movies? On the other hand, the conservative right should love the movies. Nico smiled, remembering their recent boycotts of Hollywood stars for their political stances and the boycotts for alleged sexual and homosexual allusions in Disney children's films.

What about the growing communities of immigrants who tend to be more conservative (at least where their families are concerned) than mainstream Americans. A lot of them have felt marginalized over the past few years, and may be seeking self-affirmation elsewhere than Hollywood. *You know, Rishi and his colleagues might just stand a chance with a little help from us*, was Nico's surprising thought before sitting down to read more about Bollywood.

Bollywood: A preview

In the world of film, there are two giants: the United States and India. In terms of films produced per year, India's Mumbai (formerly Bombay, hence 'Bollywood') is the leading lady. In 2001, India produced 1013 films, while Hollywood films numbered 739 (Anon, 2002a). Any similarities between the two end there. It is estimated that Mumbai alone produces about 800 Hindi films per year, with other Indian cities producing the rest. Worldwide revenues for Bollywood in 2002 were estimated at US$1.3 billion, while Hollywood totalled US$51 billion.[3]

According to legend, Bollywood films resemble the fragrant, heady *masala* mixture of black pepper, cumin, cloves, cardamom, and other spices used in cooking. *Masala* films are a mixture of elements to keep audiences interested: song, dance, action, romance and comedy. It is a film genre of its own: the product of Indian village theatre, Victorian drama, and opera. Films commonly comprise three hours of romance, travel, courtship, marriage, tragedy and redemption, played to the backdrop of sumptuously appointed and colourful sets. (For more information, go to **www.bollywhat.com**.)

The stars, like Madhuri Dixit, Rani Mukherjee and Hrithik Roshan are gorgeous, and they express their emotions with a frantic sincerity in words and in lip-synched songs that appear to put the plot on hold. The music uses primal rhythms, and the tunes are catchy, accompanied by sinuous dances featuring dozens of costumed dancers. The plot may shift from place to place, with surprising interludes shot in beautiful locations like Scotland, Australia, Switzerland or New Zealand.

The storyline usually begins with a boy meets girl premise, however one of the two is from the 'wrong' social background. There is a coincidence that brings star-crossed lovers together, then fate thwarts them with death. Weeping mothers, archetypal families, giggling sisters, stereotypical characters and slapstick roles complete the *masala* film recipe. That is the legend. The reality of Bollywood films has changed in recent years, for artistic and more prosaic business and marketing reasons.

Bollywood is often accused of taking 'inspiration' from Hollywood productions partly because Hollywood is India's primary recognizable reference for wealth, style, and fashion This perception is only one-way. However, Bollywood films have yet to cross over from 'ethnic' South Asian cinema to main street cinema. Leading producer Ashok Amritraj does not believe that a Hindi film can have mass appeal in the USA.[4]

Others point to *Lagaan* and *Monsoon Wedding*, two Indian films with critical and box-office success. *Lagaan* featured a cricket game that put oppression into play between poor Indian villagers and their sneering colonial overlords (go to **www.lagaan.com** for more information). It was shortlisted for the Best Foreign Film Award at the Oscars, nominated Best Foreign Language Film at the Academy Awards, and won seven India International Film Awards.[5] It also made money: US$2 million at US and UK box offices.[6] *Monsoon Wedding* (2001), which featured an arranged marriage in New Delhi, won a Golden Lion at the Venice Film Festival. The film earned over US$30 million worldwide, and was the highest grossing Indian film to date in the United States at US$13,882,786. In an attemtpt to increase acceptance of Bollywood films, Sir Andrew Lloyd Webber's musical *Bombay Dreams* will probably be as much of a hit on Broadway as it has been in London.

Bollywood holds obvious potential, with an annual growth rate of 12.6 per cent (compared to Hollywood's 5.6 per cent). Some Bollywood hits boast a return on investment of 25 per cent or more. Possibly the most persuasive argument in favour of Bollywood is the general claim that 'half of humanity' views Bollywood films – in 2001, 3.6 billion tickets were sold worldwide. By way of comparison, Hollywood sold 2.6 billion tickets. New forms of distribution are contributing to Bollywood's profitability: in 2001, DVD, video and satellite television sales totalled US$108 million, an increase of 25 per cent from the previous year.[3]

Bootlegged DVDs and videos inundate India's domestic and expatriate markets worldwide within days of a Bollywood film release, costing the Indian film industry US$75 million in 2002, or 60 per cent of the market value.[7] Bollywood lost over US$140 million.[8] from pirated soundtracks. However, management consultants KPMG International predict that gross revenue should rise to US$1.97 billion by 2007 due to consolidation and quality over quantity in films.[9]

Up until 2001, film making was not recognized as an 'industry' in India. Therefore, about 40 per cent of Bollywood's finances originated in organized crime, according to the police.[10] A string of film-worthy murders and scandals made clear that Bollywood glamour, power and money laundering were attractive to the mob. Producers now seek funding from banks and international corporations, forcing a new professionalism that includes proper marketing plans and newer marketing tools like in-film product placements and 'marketing the film like a brand' activities and public relations, and merchandising.[11] (For more information on Bollywood marketing tactics, visit **www.indiafm.com**.)

Hollywood itself believes in the potential of Bollywood: Columbia TriStar Motion Picture Group distributed *Lagaan* and *Mission Kashmir* in the United States, and is slated to distribute many more. Twentieth Century Fox has committed to marketing and distributing Hindi films by Bollywood producer Ram Gopal Verma. Hyperion Pictures is collaborating in a US–Bollywood feature called *Marigold*.[10] Bollywood film, video and DVD distributors in the United States target the 'Desi' communities (Indian, Pakistani, Sri Lankan and Bangladeshi), and increasingly the Middle Eastern and Russian communities where the genre is very popular.[12]

Indian films have slowly but surely become an international commodity. An estimated 10–15 million Indian expatriates known as Non Resident Indians (NRIs) live in the United Kingdom, the United States, Asia and Africa. Their annual income totals approximately

US$375 billion, and they are said to account for 40 per cent of all Bollywood production profit. The large South Asian communities in the USA and UK account for 55 per cent of international ticket sales and, understandably, Bollywood films incorporate NRIs into their stories in an effort to keep the interest of expatriates.[13,14] This apparently alienates the average viewer in India, however.

Hindi cinema has for years enjoyed a strong following independent of the South Asian expatriate communities in the Gulf region, Egypt, Russia and certain eastern European countries, and some African nations. Afghanistan was once one of the biggest markets for Hindi films, and the first films to play after the fall of the Taliban were Hindi.[15] Because of their relatively modest and subtle portrayal of the female body and sexual acts, Hindi films have long been favoured by distributors in Arab countries.[13] The fact that many Bollywood stars are Muslim is also helpful. Indian films have long had a 'cult' or 'art house' following in wealthy countries as well.[16] Since 2001, the Indian government has demonstrated greater commitment to export efforts, and has participated in more film festivals and exhibitions.[17] Technological change has played a role in the 'internationalization' of Bollywood films, with satellite television beaming around the globe.

However, things started to go wrong when Bollywood was on the brink of attaining respectable status. Some reports estimate that only 7 per cent of films in 2001 made a profit.[18] In 2002, 98 per cent of films were box office failures, with the notable exception of the horror film *Raaz*, incurring a loss of US$58 million.[19,20] (For a survey of Bollywood's lucrative 'horror' phase, go to **http://sify.com/entertainment/movies/horror/index.php**.) The Indian government announced that it was to loosen its protectionist laws on cinema imports, opening the floodgates to Hollywood films. Across India, 500 cinemas closed in 2002 and in the first half of 2003 the industry was thought to have lost US$2 million to US$8 million.[20] Bollywood appeared to be at a crucial turning point.

As actor Akshay Kumar observed, Indian audiences no longer imperatively seek *roha-dhona* (tears and family oriented emotion) at the cinema because they receive high doses of it from television soap operas.[21] Analysts have reported audience fatigue with re-hashed formulas and high ticket prices.[20] Producers have responded to a perception that audiences want a change by making thrillers and horror films (all containing song and dance routines). Suspense films have all but taken over from the well-worn Bollywood romantic formula. However, they are conducive to good music, and romance may be integrated into the plot to keep the audience happy, according to trade analyst Vindo Mirani.[20]

In a nod to 'Western' films, recent films have included fewer songs or no songs at all, in addition to far away locations – such as Los Angeles where Sanjay Gupta directed *Kaante*, a US$2.2 million thriller featuring four Bollywood idols and an all-American cast and crew. The film, recorded in English and Hindi, received mixed reviews in India. It was closely modelled on Hollywood hits *Usual Suspects* and *Reservoir Dogs*. According to reports, the producers of *Kaante* plan two US releases of the film: a full-length version intended for South Asian expatriates, and a shorter one (minus songs) for the general public.[4] Other films have met the same cut before release abroad – *Asoka*, the story of the emperor-turned-Buddhist monk, is an example where songs and dances have been cut for European release.[22]

Questions

1. What is culture-specific and what is universal in Indian films? Which features of Indian films would a Western audience not be capable of understanding?

2. Is there a market for Indian movies in the United States? In Europe? What are the target audiences (ethnic groups versus general audience)?

3. Should Nico Rogosky and Pentagram accept Anjali Kumar's offer to take over the marketing and distribution of two new 'Bollywood' films? If yes, what should Nico ask Anjali and Rishi to do if he wants to minimize the risk of failure?

For images and profiles on some major Bollywood stars, go to the following sites:

Aishwarya Rai: **www.imdb.com/name/nm0706787/**
Arjun Rampal: **www.imdb.com/name/nm0992000/**
Shahrukh Khan: **www.imdb.com/name/nm0451321/**
Rani Mukherjee: **www.imdb.com/name/nm0611552/**

Saskia Faulk and Jean-Claude Usunier prepared this case solely to provide material for class discussion. The authors do not intend to illustrate either effective or ineffective handling of a business situation. The authors may have disguised certain names and other identifying information to protect confidentiality.

(©IRM, reprinted with kind permission.)

A7.2 Case

Muslim Cola – cola wars or cola crusades?

During the prelude to the recent American-led invasion of Iraq, some consumers boycotted American products and brands. In the Philippines, ten leading products were targeted, including Coke, McDonald's, Citibank and Starbucks. Among the reasons given by boycott leaders was 'disgust and revulsion' at the invasion (Anon, 2003a). In some Russian and German cities, restaurant patrons were told that Coke was unavailable because of the current political situation.[23] Other countries with active boycotts discussed in the press included Argentina, Egypt, France, Greece, India, Indonesia, Italy, Malaysia, Pakistan, Saudi Arabia, Tunisia and Yemen. Almost without exception, Coca-Cola figures prominently in the boycotted product lists. Coca-Cola has itself been targeted in a long-standing boycott over its bottling plant in occupied Palestine.[24] For years boycotts in support of the Palestinian Intifada have been in effect, as well as boycott threats in opposition to the Bush Administration's international trade stance on biotech foods and other issues.[25]

Coke's prominence on boycott lists points to its paradigmatic status as an American brand. Variations on the Coca-Cola logo have been used as an image on anti-war posters, and in puns, as in 'COLA-teral Damage' by the Belgian group STOPUSA.

Muslim colas

Mecca Cola (**www.meccacola.com**) was launched by Tunisian-born entrepreneur Tawfik Mathlouthi in November, 2002. Although its packaging is similar in colour and style to that of Coca-Cola, its philosophy is diametrically opposed to the drinks monolith: its logo is 'No more drinking stupid – drink with commitment!', and 'Don't shake me, shake your conscience!' The French company claims that 10 per cent of its net profits will be sent to Palestinian children's charities, plus another 10 per cent to European charities favouring international peace and Palestinian causes. Mecca drinks (including Tonic,

Classic, Mentha and Vanilly) are distributed in Australia, Belgium, Canada, France, Germany and the United Kingdom, according to the company.[26] In Great Britain, orders are brisk at over 2 million bottles per month.[27] Mecca Cola 'sponsored' the million-strong peace march in London in February 2003, handing out 'Not in my name' t-shirts and Mecca Cola.

Across the Channel, Qibla Cola made its appearance in February 2003. According to the Qibla Cola website (**www.Qibla-cola.com**), British entrepreneur Zahida Parveen founded the company to offer 'real alternatives to global consumer brands that support unjust policies'.[28] Like Mecca Cola, Qibla's offerings resemble those of Coca-Cola, and Qibla is the Arabic word for the direction to pray to Mecca, but the company is more than a nod at Mecca Cola. The company promotes Qibla Cola, Qibla Fantasy (orange and mango), Qibla 5 (lemon and lime, named for the five pillars of Islam), and spring water to 2.5 million Muslims in Britain, with an eye on Indonesia, Pakistan and Bangladesh.[26] The company works with Islamic Aid, a registered charity that is to receive 10 per cent of net profits. Qibla notes that it broke even after only two months, an exceptional performance for a start-up.[29] In an interview, Qibla CEO Zafer Iqbal proffered that the products' packaging and taste parallels with Coca-Cola were intended to 'leverage' Coke's global image and make consumers aware of Islamic alternatives like Qibla.[29] Company spokesperson Abdul Hamid Ebrahim stated that the company's inspiration came from Iran's ZamZam Cola, a company that profited from a leading Iranian cleric's ruling that Coke and Pepsi were 'un-Islamic'.[26]

ZamZam cola has a leading market share of 47 per cent in its home country Iran, a net income of US$176 million last year and more than 7000 employees in 17 factories.[30] It is distributed throughout the Middle East, and in some African and European countries, notably Denmark. The company was Coke's long-term partner in Iran, prior to the Islamic Revolution. In the autumn of 2002, ZamZam produced more than 10 million bottles to meet rising demand in Saudi Arabia, spurred on by anger over American support for Israel.[31] As a consequence of boycotts and the advent of competitors like ZamZam, sales of Coca-Cola and Pepsi-Cola fell from 20 to 40 per cent in some Middle Eastern countries in 2002.[32]

There are other Muslim Colas dedicated to taking market share from Coke, including Pakistan's Salsabeen (promoted through pamphlets distributed after Friday prayers), Morocco's Star Cola, and French MuslimUp (**www.muslim-up.com**). All these cola companies face similar problems. They are up against the world's most valuable brand, Coca-Cola, valued at more than US$70 billion.[33] For all but ZamZam, securing capacity contracts with bottling plants has proven difficult. Distribution is a problem, with supermarkets often reluctant to take on a new 'niche' product with an unsure future. Distributors are also concerned about the capacity of cola suppliers to meet demand at a consistent quality level. As a result, these alternative colas are often sold in small family-owned shops in areas populated by immigrants.[34] It is unlikely that any of the Muslim colas poses a real threat to the entrenched hegemony of Coke, however. As one consultant has put it, if the market for Muslim colas gets too big, Coke will simply buy them up, just as it did with start-up cola company Thumbs Up in India.[34]

Questions

1. Some analysts believe that companies like Qibla and Mecca are not capable of long-term market share, and that their initial success is due to publicity that will quickly fizzle out. Is this a likely scenario, given the competitive environment in which they operate?

2. Some Muslims object to the 'commercialization' of Islam, as represented by these cola companies' marketing strategies. Should these Muslim cola companies target a wider audience? If so, how? Give them some marketing ideas.

3. If you were the CEO of the leading company (Coca-Cola) how would you react to the emergence of Muslim colas? In non-Muslim countries? In Muslim countries? Same question if you were the CEO of the longstanding challenger (Pepsi-Cola)?

Saskia Faulk and Jean-Claude Usunier prepared this case solely to provide material for class discussion. The authors do not intend to illustrate either effective or ineffective handling of a business situation. The authors may have disguised certain names and other identifying information to protect confidentiality.

(©IRM, reprinted with kind permission.)

 **A7.3 Case**

Odol

When Manfred Hansen took over as marketing director of Lingner and Fischer in 1985, the company held a meagre 15 per cent of the oral care market in Germany – half of what the leader, Procter & Gamble, could claim. Known since 1997 as SmithKline Beecham, the company now commands a 30.4 per cent share of oral care while P & G's slice has shrunk to 13.8 per cent according to AC Nielsen. And Mr Hansen has kept his promise to be the leading oral care company in Germany, while becoming No. 1 in Switzerland and Austria as well.

SmithKline managed this turnaround through savvy marketing, including extending the familiar Odol and Dr Best brand names, bringing a fresh positioning to whitening products and paying close attention to consumer needs in areas such as packaging, where it eliminated wasteful wrapping entirely. The company also achieved its success in Germany by keeping an eye on global strategies while giving local managers some autonomy. 'SmithKline Beecham is acting much faster and takes greater risks than P & G', said a marketing manager at the now pacesetting company. 'We are in constant touch with headquarters in order to understand market situations in other countries, [but] fortunately headquarters leaves us freedom to act in our market, taking into consideration the local situation.'

Becoming the market leader in toothpaste, a $545 million category in Germany and hotly contested by rivals P & G, Colgate-Palmolive Co. and Elidda-Gibbs hasn't been easy. Newcomers barely get a chance to survive; Henkel's thera-med, launched in 1979 is a rare exception. So SmithKline and Mr Hansen proceeded cautiously, testing its toothpaste in a year-long trial in two German cities, Bad Kreuznach and Buxtehude, of the names Odol med 3, Aquafresh med 3 and – extending the name of its existing toothbrush line – Dr Best med 3. It soon became evident that consumers favoured Odol med 3, a brand name under which the company had marketed a mouthwash concentrate since 1893. Not coincidentally, Odol is category leader in mouthwash with a 70 per cent share in Germany, 80 per cent in Austria, and 60 per cent in Switzerland. 'Odol's brand name is extremely strong; consumers have had confidence in the product for 100 years', Mr Hansen said. 'We used this name because of the brand capital it has. Our headquarters ensures that each subsidiary uses international experience, but if we can be more successful with a local brand name, we use it.' For example, in Spain, the Aquafresh brand is marketed under the name Binaca Med 3.

SmithKline's eventual success in toothpaste was an even harder-won fight considering Odol med 3's premium price. The toothpaste was marketed for 25 per cent more than the average in Germany, but the price was justified by its attributes, such as three-prong protection against cavities, plaque and periodontal disease. After notching a 4 per cent market share in 1989, its first year, Odol med 3 climbed to 6 per cent in 1990 with the introduction of a mint line extension. By 1993, share was still climbing despite the fact that SmithKline was spending only $8–$10 million on advertising – half of what P & G was laying out for its Blend-a-Med brand. Odol also got a boost from SmithKline's move in 1991 to strip away cumbersome packaging and sell the tubes without an outer box. 'We take our consumers very seriously', Mr Hansen said. 'When we noticed that consumers were reacting to unnecessary packaging, we acted immediately.'

The stripped-down package was touted in an amusing campaign from Grey Advertising, Düsseldorf, SmithKline's agency of record in oral care for 15 years. The spot mimicked a striptease act with the toothpaste unburdening itself of its outer wrapper as an audience of animated teeth yelled out cheers and catcalls. Mr Hansen, in fact, said its close relationship with Grey was a major reason for its conquest of German-speaking countries. 'We are one team', he said. 'We have integrated the agency – the account people as well as the creative team – totally in our marketing, and we discuss with them everything from product policy to marketing strategy, prices and distribution.' Grey, then, was part of SmithKline's decision to create a special package shaped like a tooth for Odol med 3 in Germany. This development also helped the base brand reach its current 9 per cent market share in Germany neck-to-neck with Blend-a-Med. The package is being used as a template in other markets, Mr Hansen said.

What put SmithKline finally over the top was its whitening line extension, Odol med 3 samtweiss. At the time of its introduction, in 1996, whitening toothpastes were considered an also-ran in the category, used mainly by smokers and coffee and tea drinkers, and they claimed only a 5 per cent segment of the total toothpaste market in Germany. Mr Hansen and his team aimed to change that with advertising that argued against consumers' notions that whiteners damage teeth and are abrasive. Further, the message was that everyone with yellowing teeth should try Odol med 3 samtweiss. In a single year the strategy propelled the toothpaste's German share to 6.8 per cent and rocketed SmithKline's overall toothpaste share to 15.8 per cent. That sent competitors, including Henkel and Colgate, scrambling to introduce whiteners, which are just now about to hit store shelves.

But SmithKline wasn't finished yet. There were still toothbrushes to consider. Although the company had sold a toothbrush under the Dr Best name since 1953, the brand's share languished at 5 per cent of the German market in the mid-1980s, and Mr Hansen said the company was considering spinning it off. 'We even discussed selling the brand', he revealed, 'but I fought for its survival because market research showed us the Dr Best name had a recognition level of over 70 per cent. What we needed was a product advantage.' The break came in 1988, in the form of a new brush with a floating neck and a flexible handle that massaged the gums without injuring them. Grey then set to work: the agency sought, and found, a real Dr Best, a dental professional from the US who appeared in TV ads that showed the toothbrush working on a tomato without damaging its delicate skin.

Not surprisingly, P & G and Colgate followed with products of their own – but not until SmithKline had leapt into the leadership position in toothbrushes with a 39.8 per cent share, up from a mere 5 per cent in 1985 when Mr Hansen began his initial assault.

(Source: Reprinted with permission from the November 1997 issue of *Advertising Age*.[35] International copyright © Crain Communication Inc. 1997.)

Questions

1. Which aspects of the German marketing environment explain the success of Odol med 3 in terms of consumer response to the brand's innovations?

2. Why can a market like Germany be a lead market for packaging innovation in general?

3. Discuss the issues involved in transferring part of Odol's recipe for success to near national markets (France, the United Kingdom), especially the tooth-like packaging.

A7.4 Exercise

Dangerous Enchantment

First read the short extract from *Dangerous Enchantment*, the evocative title of the novel by Anne Mather (1966). Harlequin books are worldwide bestsellers. They have been translated into 15 languages and read by countless people in many countries. Therefore, they can be considered a truly 'global' cultural product. This short extract has been chosen for its capacity to illustrate the Harlequin style.

The next day Julie had collected herself. She was glad in a way that she had seen the woman with Manuel. At least it brought home to her more strongly than any words could have done the completely amoral attitude he possessed.

Marilyn had seen the television as well, however, and said: 'I say, Julie, did you see that Manuel Cortez is back in England?'

Julie managed a casual shrug. 'So what?'

'Darling, really!' Marilyn gave her an old-fashioned look. 'Surely you aren't as indifferent as all that! I know you refused a date with him, but I'm sure that was more because of Paul Bannister than anything else.'

Julie tossed her head. 'I really can't see what all the fuss is about. Paul would make four of him!'

'You must be joking!' Marilyn giggled. 'Get you! I didn't know Paul was becoming such a dish all of a sudden. Why? What's changed him?'

Julie refrained from replying. She had no desire to get involved in an argument about Paul when it meant her stating things that in actual fact were not true. It was no use pretending about Paul's attractions; he was handsome, yes, and tall, yes, and young; but there was nothing particularly exciting about him and Julie could never understand girls who thought men's looks were enough. She had known many men, and in her small experience personality mattered far more than mere good looks.

However, during her lunch break she did borrow a newspaper from Miss Fatherstone in the hope that there might be more particulars about the woman with Manuel, but there was not. There was a picture of him at the airport, and a small article, and that was all.

When they left the building that evening it was snowing, and an icy wind was blowing, chilling them to the bone. Julie, wrapped in a loose dark blue mohair coat, hugged her handbag to her as she started along towards the main thoroughfare accompanied by Donna and Marilyn. She wore knee-length white boots, but between the place where her boots ended and the place where her skirt began she felt frozen, and she wondered whether for the winter at least she should go back to normal-length skirts.

Her hair was blowing about her face, for she was wearing no hat, and she walked straight into the man who stood purposely in her way.

'I'm sorry . . .' she began hastily, a smile lightening her face, and then: 'You!'

Manuel smiled, and her heart leapt treacherously into her throat. She had let go of Donna's arm in her confusion, but both Marilyn and Donna were staring open-mouthed. Manuel took Julie's arm, and said smoothly: 'You will excuse me, ladies,' in a mocking tone, and drew Julie across the pavement to the familiar green Ferrari.

'No, wait!' began Julie, but it was no use. Manuel had the car door open and was propelling her inside, his hard fingers biting cruelly into her arm.

'Don't argue,' he said, for all the world as though it was a natural occurrence that he should meet her from work.

Julie did not want to create a scene in the street, so she climbed into the luxurious warmth of the car and sliding across out of the driver's seat, she allowed him to slide in beside her. He slammed the door, flicked the ignition, and the car moved silently forward, purring like a sated panther.

She stole a glance at him as they turned into the main thoroughfare, and saw, with a sense of inevitability, that far from changing he was much more attractive than she remembered. He turned for a moment to look at her as they stopped at some traffic lights, and said: 'How have you been?'

Julie contemplated her fingernails. 'Fine. And you?'

He shrugged, and did not reply, and she felt like hitting him. How dared he sit there knowing that she must have seen him with that girl yesterday! She looked out of the car window, suddenly realizing that she was allowing him to drive her heaven knows where, and she was making no comment.

'Where are you taking me?' she asked in a tight little voice.

'Home,' he said lazily. 'Where do you think? I thought I would save you the journey on such a ghastly night. Tell me, how do you stand this climate? It's terrible. Me, I like the sun, and the sea, and warm water to swim in.'

'Don't we all?' remarked Julie dryly. 'This will do.' They had reached the end of Faulkner Road.

Manuel shook his head. 'What number?'

'Forty-seven. But please, I'd rather you didn't drive along there. It would only cause speculation, and if you should be recognized . . .' Her voice trailed away.

'That's hardly likely tonight,' remarked Manuel coolly, and drove smoothly to her gate where he halted the car.

'Thank you, señor.' Julie gave a slight bow of her head, and made to get out, but Manuel stopped her, his fingers biting into her arm.

'Aren't you pleased to see me?' he asked mockingly. Julie looked at him fully. 'No, not really.'

'Why?'

'Surely that's obvious. We have nothing to say to one another.'

'No?'

'No.' Julie brushed back her hair as it fell in waves over her eyes. It glistened with tiny drops of melted snow and she was unaware of how lovely she was looking.

Manuel shrugged, and lay back in his seat. 'Go, then.'

Julie felt furious. It always ended this way, with herself feeling the guilty one. Well, he wasn't going to get away with it! She swung round on him.

'Don't imagine for one moment that I've been brought home believing your little tales', she cried angrily. 'I know perfectly well that the reason you have brought me home is because you could hardly take me to the apartment when you already have one female in residence!'

Manuel stared at her, a dull flush just visible in the muted light of the car rising up his cheeks.

(Source: Mather, pp. 89–92.[36] Text copyright © 1966 by Anne Mather; permission to reproduce text granted by Harlequin Books S.A.)

Questions

1. Identify the main sociodemographic characteristics of the target audience for such books.

2. Identify from the text (situation, characters and the relations between them) how, and to what extent, this text effects people in such a way as to manipulate feelings and emotions that are widely shared by the world population.

3. Define the target audience for Harlequin books, in terms of cultural affinity class(es).

Appendix references

1. Rose, Steve (2001), 'Sheer Khan', *Guardian*, 20 October.
2. Kaushal, Raj (2003), 'The Rise and Rise Of "Desi" Beats', *Telegraph*, 13 September.
3. Anon (2002), 'Bollywood vs Hollywood', *Businessweek*, 2 December.
4. Chabra, Aseem (2002), 'How Original Is Bollywood?', *Rediff on the Net*, 31 October, www.rediff.com/entertai/2002/oct/31bolly.htm.
5. Anon (2002), 'Lagaan Scoops Bollywood Awards', *BBC News*, 6 April, http://news.bbc.co.uk/1/hi/entertainment/film/1915331.stm.
6. Anon (2002), 'Bollywood Hopes for Oscar Dollars', *BBC News*, 13 February, http://news.bbc.co.uk/2/hi/business/1818660.stm.
7. Sternstein, Aliya (2003), 'Bully for Bollywood!', *Forbes Global*, 28 April.
8. Mather, Anne (1966), *Dangerous Enchantment*. London: Harlequin.
9. Pearson, Bryan (2003), 'Analyst Sez Bollywood's on Track to Bounce Back', *Variety*, 23 March.
10. Kripalani, Manjeet and Ron Grover (2002), 'Bollywood: Can New Money Create a World-Class Film Industry in India?', *Businessweek*, 2 December.
11. Anon (2002), 'Movie Marketing Comes of Age', *Business Standard*, 21 March.
12. Amdur, Meredith (2003), 'Koch Lorber Lines up Bollywood DVD Series,' *Variety*, 10 July.
13. Anon (2000), 'New York Marketing Information. The Indian Influence', Dentsu Young and Rubicam, Inc., 10 July.
14. Shah, Deepa (2002), 'Hooray for Bollywood', *Observer*, 24 March.
15. Anon (2001), 'Bollywood Eyes Afghan Market', *BBC News*, 27 November, http://news.bbc.co.uk/2/hi/entertainment/1679115.stm.
16. Gahlot, Deepa (1999), 'Why the World Loves Hindi Movies', *Himal: The South Asian Magazine*, September.
17. Episcopo, Jo (2001), 'Bollywood Comes to Cannes', *BBC News*, 15 May, http://news.bbc.co.uk/1/hi/entertainment/film/1331700.stm.
18. Jatania, Lynn (2002), 'Hollywood/Bollywood', *Sidekick Magazine*.
19. Cooper, Louise (2003), 'Bollywood Struck by Horror', *BBC News*, 23 April, http://news.bbc.co.uk/1/hi/business/2969101.stm.
20. Pearson, Bryan (2003), 'Love, Song, Dance . . . And Suspense', *Variety*, 16 February.
21. Jha, Subhash K. (2002), 'Hollywood, Bollywood-Style!', *Rediff on the Net*, 28 March, www.rediff.com/entertai/2002/mar/28bolly.htm.
22. Malcolm, Derek (2001), 'A Song and a Dance', *Guardian*, 25 October.
23. O'Flynn, Kevin (2003), 'Americans and Dollars Not Welcome', *Moscow Times*, 26 March.
24. Anon (2003), 'Qibla Shows Its Bottle', *The Publican*, 7 May, www.thepublican.com/story.asp?sectioncode=6&storycode=30238.
25. Cowen, Richard (2003), 'EU Official Sees Boycotts If US Files Biotech Suit', *Forbes*, 6 May.
26. Hundley, Tom (2003), 'New Colas Hope to Make Money Off Muslim Rancor', *Chicago Tribune*, 5 February.
27. Jeffery, Simon (2003), 'Is It the Real Thing?', *The Guardian*, 5 February.
28. Qibla Cola (2003), Qibla Cola Company Ltd. www.qibla-cola.com/index2.asp.
29. Datson, Trevor (2003), 'Muslim Cola – Idealism or Marketing Froth?', *Reuters* (online), 30 April.
30. Fernandez-Fanjul, Eufrasio (2002), 'Zamzam Cola Crece Con La Ola Antiyanqui', *El Mundo*, 8 September, www.elmundo.es/nuevaeconomia/2002/139/1031386792.html.
31. Anon (2002), 'Iran Takes on Cola Giants', *Asia Times*, 17 October, http://www.atimes.com/atimes/Middle_East/DJ17Ak06.html.
32. Theodoulou, Michael, Charles Bremner, and Daniel McGrory (2002), 'Cola Wars as Islam Shuns the Real Thing', *The Times*, 11 October, www.timesonline.co.uk/tol/news/world/article1172816.ece.
33. Ries, Al (2003), 'Coca Cola Gets It Right with "Real"', *Advertising Age*, 20 January.
34. Majidi, Nassim and Christina Passariello (2003), 'After Iraq, Cola Wars Heat Up', *BusinessWeek*, 17 April, www.businessweek.com/bwdaily/dnflash/apr2003/nf20030417_5930_db039.htm.
35. *Advertising Age* (1997), November.
36. Mathur, Arti (2003), 'India Looks to Uk to Stem Piracy', *Variety*, 29 May.

8

Product policy 1: physical, service and symbolic attributes

Should products be adapted for foreign markets or standardized? In the 1960s, the Japanese carefully researched the demographic, economic, sociocultural, politico-legal and physical environments in the Arabian Gulf countries and adapted their products to suit the needs of local markets. By doing so, they were able to take over the dominant position formerly held there by Britain.[1]

As Katsikeas and colleagues argue (p. 881): 'superior performance for the MNC subsidiary depends on the presence of fit between a standardization strategy deployed and environmental conditions. . . . Similarities (differences) in the regulatory environment, technological intensity and velocity, customs and traditions, customer characteristics, PLC stage, and competitive intensity in the MNC's home and host markets drive the deployment of standardized (customized) marketing strategies.'[2]

As discussed in Chapter 7, standardization and adaptation are not alternate strategies. Most companies in fact include some standardization and some adaptation of their products.[3] For instance, Coca-Cola and McDonald's customize the non-core elements of their products when required. The effectiveness of the strategy depends on many factors related to the four elements of the marketing mix.[4] Those relating to the product policy will be discussed in this chapter and the next.

Product customization may also result in market differentiation, thus creating a competitive advantage vis-à-vis actual competitors, raising entry barriers for potential competitors. So the message is: standardize as much as feasible and customize as much as needed.

This chapter and the next (which is devoted to the product's brand name and national image) propose a decision-making framework for the adaptation-standardization of various product attributes, including the *physical characteristics*, design, form, colour, function, packaging, brand name and 'made-in' label. An assessment is made of the potential for adaptation and standardization at different levels of *product attributes*, including physical attributes, service attributes and symbolic attributes (through colour, shape, country of origin, brand name and so on).

The first section of this chapter sets out a systematic model to clarify the choice between adaptation and standardization of product policy. It can be applied successively to each existing national market, as well as to markets where a company intends to set up new business. The second section is devoted to the physical attributes of the product. The third section deals with the standardization/adaptation of service attributes. The fourth section relates to symbolic attributes.

The ancient Greek word 'symbol' refers to an object cut into two halves. Both the host and the guest kept their halves and later passed them on to their children. When the two halves were reunited, the owners could be recognized by their halves, as these were proof of the previously established hospitality bond. The symbol therefore replaces, represents and denotes another entity by means of a conventional relationship or a suggestion, the evidence of which has usually been lost. The connotative meanings of symbols are culture based and, as such are interpreted differently across countries.

Other important symbolic attributes include the brand name and the national images linked to the product and its country of manufacture. Chapter 9 elaborates on the linguistic issues in converting a national brand into an international brand. It also discusses issues with global brands, either worldwide or regionally based.

8.1

Adaptation or standardization of product attributes

The product element of the marketing mix is often cited as the most standardized element, but within the product element there are various attributes that are more or less likely to be standardized. For instance, a survey of 500 large multinational UK companies in five sectors (including manufacturing, services, transportation and communication, construction, and retail and wholesale), revealed the elements of the marketing mix that were most standardized. For the product element, most companies reported standardizing product quality (78 per cent), brand name (72 per cent), image (71 per cent), performance (67 per cent), size and colour (54 per cent) and packaging and styling (52 per cent), while fewer standardize variety, design and features (48 per cent), pre-sales service (45 per cent), after-sales service and warrantees (43 per cent), and delivery and installation (42 per cent) (Vrontis, 2003). The same companies reported that the most important reasons for adapting the marketing mix included culture (92 per cent), market development (87 per cent), competition (84 per cent), laws (82 per cent), economic differences (78 per cent), sociological consideration (74 per cent), customer perceptions (71 per cent), technological consideration (60 per cent), political environment (53 per cent), level of customer similarity (49 per cent), marketing infrastructure (44 per cent) and differences in physical conditions (39 per cent) (ibid.).

From a consumer point of view, Hult and colleagues[5] compared the importance consumers place on 16 product attributes in France (a developed market) and Malaysia (an emerging market), finding that only two attributes (product quality and appearance) received high emphasis for both samples. In Malaysia, consumers relied more on the core product attributes and in France on the image and service attributes when evaluating grocery products and clothing.[5] In reality, consumers do not buy the product itself; they buy the benefits they hope to derive from the product. A product can be defined as a set of attributes that provide the purchaser or user with actual benefits. Con-sumers from different countries may assign different weights to similar product attributes. For instance, German consumers value ecological attributes more than British consumers.[6]

There are three layers of product attributes that are more or less applicable to standardization:

1. *The physical attributes* (size, weight, colour, etc.). Standardization of these attributes provides the greatest potential for cost benefits since economies of scale are made principally at the manufacturing stage.
2. *Service attributes* (maintenance, after-sales service, spare parts availability, etc.). These attributes are fairly difficult to standardize, as expectations and circumstances for service delivery differ widely from one country to another. Furthermore, most services are performed in direct relation to *local* customers, so service attributes are more dependent on culture.
3. *Symbolic attributes.* These often comprise the interpretive element of the physical attributes. A colour is simultaneously a chemical formula for a painting or a coat, and also the symbolic meaning conveyed by the material. Symbolic attributes affect the choice to adapt and/or standardize in a fairly ambiguous manner. It is confusing when consumers show a strong liking for domestic goods based on nationalism and also show a fascination for foreign cultures and their goods. Therefore, when adapting or standardizing symbolic attributes, the requirements for national identity symbols will sometimes intermingle with those for symbols of exoticism.

Table 8.1 proposes a systematic description of the arguments in favour of adaptation on the one hand and standardization on the other. Distinctions can be made according to the different levels of physical, service and symbolic attributes. Some arguments originate from within the company, which can benefit from changes in its way of operating. Other arguments are related to external constraints

Table 8.1 Factors influencing adaptation or standardization of product attributes

Product attributes	Arguments in favour of adaptation	Arguments in favour of standardization
Physical attributes	**1** Cost-reducing adaptations Local standards, hygiene and safety regulations, local marketing knowledge, consumer behaviour, marketing and physical environments	**2** Experience effects Economies of scale International standards International product use
Services attributes	**3** Limited savings related to scale Local peculiarities in service, maintenance and distribution	**4** Significant learning effects 'Mobile' clientele
Symbolic attributes	**5** Unfavourable image of imported products, company, nationality or brand name Inadequate meaning conveyed by colour, shape, etc.	**6** Favourable image of imported products, company, nationality or brand Exotic or ethnic appeal Demands for 'universals'

imposed by the environment, market characteristics and consumer behaviour. The influence of these factors may require a company to either adapt or standardize its offerings. In Table 8.1, each internal cell is numbered. Each concept is elaborated on using this cell number reference system throughout the chapter.

Website link 8.1

McDonald's serves the Maharaja Mac in India, the McLobster in Canada and the McShawarma in Israel: **http://www.trifter.com/practical-travel/budget-travel/mcdonalds-strange-menu-around-the-world.35517.**

8.2

Physical attributes

Chapter 7 mentions that experience effects, and accordingly the cost reductions related to cumulated production, clearly weigh in favour of standardization (cell 2). Despite this, current empirical evidence finds that neither standardization nor adaptation is inherently superior. There are, of course, many factors that influence the decision.

A comprehensive review of the literature found that quality, design and features were the most standardized product-related elements, while product lines, branding and packaging were at least partially adapted to foreign markets.[7] Despite this, even for the more highly standardized elements (e.g. product quality), no consistent positive relationship between standardization and performance has been found.[8] This is notable, since quality is one of the two product attributes that have been found to be equally important to consumers in a developed and emerging market.[5]

Cost-reduction adaptations may compensate for the loss of cumulated volume through adaptation (cell 1). For instance, the success of Japanese pick-up trucks in developing countries is due to product simplifications in suspension, engine and gearbox, which the Japanese achieved at a lower cost. However, this situation is rare. It is common that product simplifications fail to achieve their goals. Historically, Ford and General Motors developed a 'bare bones' model T type of vehicle to sell in developing countries. They both failed. In the 1980s, Jean-Jacques Servan-Schreiber designed a special computer for developing countries, financed by the French government. It also was a total failure. In these cases, the advantages resulting from 'simplifications' did not sufficiently reduce costs to offset a reduction in economies of scale, and the loss of product functionality was not appreciated by consumers. As simplified products may not be advantageous in terms of cost, the learning process for local consumers and the effect of the local context on this learning process may become the central concerns for the international marketer.[9,10]

Compulsory adaptation

Compulsory adaptation of physical attributes is often related to national regulations and standards (cell 1). Certain countries use standards which seem to operate as non-tariff trade barriers. For instance, Germany is known for its use of an exhaustive system of over 30,000 industrial standards (DIN), which are determined by standard-setting committees. German manufacturers are strongly represented on the boards of these committees. Nevertheless, DIN standards are by no means intended as non-tariff barriers.

Some examples include:

1. *Industrial standards for supply of electricity*: voltage, frequency of alternating current (50 versus 60 Hz), shape of plugs, etc. differ by region if not by country.
2. *Safety standards*: in the motor industry lighting, brake systems and vehicle safety often differ by country. For instance, the Corsa is one of the most widely sold cars of all time. It is sold in approximately 80 countries and manufactured on five continents. Its name, body style, suspension and/or engine are modified to meet local standards. The Corsa is called Vauxhall/Opel Corsa in Germany, Chevrolet Chevy (Corsa) in Mexico, Buick Sail in China and Holden Barina in Australia. However, these variations on a theme lead to increased production costs, documentation and country-specific spare parts. Consequently, it is difficult to control marketing management.
3. *Hygiene regulations*: the food processing, chemicals and pharmaceutical industries adapt to comply with hygiene legislation. Producers of *foie gras* exporting their produce to the United States have to obtain FDA (Food and Drug Administration) hygiene certification. For this they have to allow the FDA to inspect their laboratories for bacteria as well as method of production. FDA inspectors

often require *foie gras* to be pasteurized and the laboratories disinfected with an antiseptic detergent. This inevitably affects the taste and conflicts with the traditional image of a home-made quality product. French *foie gras* producers have set up laboratories in the USA where the product is prepared according to US hygiene standards. Even a product as common as Coca-Cola faces different regulations, including very different requirements for the use of artificial sweeteners across countries and the necessity to include an expiry date in some countries (e.g. France), but not others (e.g. Holland).[11]

Countless regulations influence the need for adaptation (packaging, labelling, sizes, advertising, sales promotion, etc.). In many countries, public or mutual bodies offer to assist companies by examining the issues of conforming to the technical aspects of foreign standards. Despite this, a good number of companies fail to consider the issue of adapting products to foreign markets for ethnocentric reasons. Newcomers to the export business often do not start by considering the loss of standardization; their first concern is being forced to adapt to technical standards.

In fact, obligatory adaptations are often minor in comparison to the required adaptations to differences in consumer behaviour and in the national marketing environment. Three main issues should be considered:

1. *Consumption patterns*: consumer tastes, frequency of consumption, the amount consumed per helping, etc. differ. The size of a cereal box and the style of packaging that preserves the product depend in part on whether consumers eat 50 grams of cereal a day, or if they consume larger amounts but less frequently. Even products which are supposed to be the epitome of international standardization are subject to customization for local tastes (see Box 8.1). Not only does Coca-Cola add different levels and types of sugar in different countries to account for differences in taste, but consumers also treat the product differently. For instance, Coke is served in the USA with lots of ice, whereas in Tromso, Norway it is kept in warmers.[11] While there are definite national trends, it is also important to remember that market segments exist within and across countries. Allio and Allio[12]

Box 8.1

'Pizza relativity'

'Pizza relativity' is a reality in today's world. During in-depth interviews at Hewlett Packard in Grenoble, France, several American expatriates mentioned they occasionally travel to Geneva, Switzerland (100 miles/160 km away) just to eat at Pizza Hut (although, unfortunately for them Pizza Hut has since ceased operating in Switzerland). There are many traditional pizzerias in Grenoble (the town has a very large Italian population), and yet these American expatriates prefer the taste, crust, toppings and style of American pizza. When attending a congress in Milan, I discovered that Italian pizza (at least at the restaurant where I ate it) is very different from what I am used to eating in Grenoble even though they are made by Italian cooks in both contexts: the crust is much thicker and there is less topping. My most recent pizza experience is that of the oily Brazilian pizza (which I have only tried twice).

Conclusion: Pizza, like 'Chinese' food, is largely local. This is often because of the lack of genuine ingredients, but also because taste is local. Local views of what is genuine and traditional are mostly based on fantasies about the 'true' pizza or the 'genuine' Peking duck.

---

described the successful introduction of Coors beer in Puerto Rico, after using local market research knowledge to identify the segment with the most potential (young, upper income, urban). Their major competitor, Budweiser, lost market share because it continued to target the entire market, and ignored unique aspects of local Hispanic culture. In fact, van Mesdag[13] argues that food is part of a group of products (visual art, music, architecture, social behaviour, clothing, etc.) that are not easily globalized. He proposes the 'duration-of-usage' hypothesis, where products that evolved in times when countries did not readily communicate are more difficult to standardize.

2. *Climate and the physical environment* are often important, and sometimes neglected factors that cause necessary adaptation (cell 1). Motor vehicles must be specifically designed to withstand the harsh Scandinavian winters or the warmth and humidity of the Ivory Coast. The possible range of physical environments where the product will be used must be taken into account. For example, the quality of road surfaces and the existence of tracks suitable for vehicles. The diversity of physical environments is often the cause of unexpected failure (Box 8.2). The range of elements that constitute potential demands for adaptation need to be taken into consideration at the strategic design stage. This is not always an obvious step to

take. Ethnocentrism is often the rule in product design.

3. *Adapting products to local product usage.* A number of variables have to be considered in order to ensure buyers use the product properly, such as level of literacy, technical knowledge and ability to use written information (such as ingredients or instructions). Lack of attention to these variables caused problems for Nestlé in the Third World with its infant formula: adding impure water and failing to boil water made the product dangerous for consumption, even though the powder leaving Nestlé's factories was sterilized. Consumers, on average, tend not to read instructions thoroughly enough and try to use items, especially consumer durables, before actually taking the time to learn how to operate them. German manufacturers tend to create specially adapted features designed to prevent consumer misuse; for instance, when a dish-washer knob is turned anti-clockwise instead of being turned clockwise, or when the machine is switched on when the water tap is off. In Germany, where the sense of uncertainty avoidance is quite strong (section 3.2), a product is called *idiotensicher* ('idiot proof') when all possible product design adaptations have been made to avoid the negative consequences of any imaginable misuse. Adaptation to possible misuses is related to the issue of product liability, where quite different

Box 8.2

Adaptations to the physical environment

A European drinks manufacturer decided to widen the range of one of its product lines with a giant-size version, to actively promote it in several markets, the United States in particular. After completion of production facilities, the new model was launched. The company then realized to its horror that it had forgotten one small detail: the giant-size bottle was a couple of inches too tall for the shelves in the vast majority of American stores. You can imagine the result: the sales promotion activities that were planned had to be cancelled, there was discontent among the distributors and the sales force lost a great deal of motivation while a new mould was hastily manufactured.[14]

Quaker Oats has an established share of the Cameroon market: it has been carefully adapted in line with consumption habits. It is easily made into the gruel that the Cameroons call *paf* or *pap*. It is usually eaten with maize or tapioca. In addition, Quaker uses metal packaging which is perfectly suited to the preservation of the product in the Cameroon climate. The shelf life of the can is about 10 years, even in a tropical country. Cameroon itself is not a wholly typical tropical country since in Douala, for instance, there is an annual rainfall of 7 metres. The can ensures that the product is preserved despite the humidity. It does, however, rust, and even though the product itself is not affected, certain retailers refuse to repurchase Quaker Oats because their previous stock may have partially or completely rusted.

(Sources: Adapted from Giordan, p. 110;[14] Camphuis, 1984.[15])

legal solutions are found from one country to another. For instance, Windshield sun visors made in Spain and sold in that country do not need to bear a special warning sticker, reminding users not to drive with the visor down. Spanish drivers are not considered to be more foolish than any other nationality. Conversely, for export, especially to the United States, they must display such an explicit warning: in case of an accident, the manufacturer could potentially be held liable. In his book, *Remove Child before Folding*, Jones[16] lists 101 'wacky warning labels' on products designed by litigiously paranoid American businesses, including 'Do not use while sleeping' on a hair dryer; 'May cause drowsiness' on sleeping tablets, 'Harmful if swallowed' on a fishing lure, and 'If you do not understand, or cannot read, all directions, cautions and warnings, do not use this product' on a bottle of drain cleaner.

Website link 8.2

See examples of remarkable warning labels such as 'Danger: Avoid Death', 'Do not iron while wearing shirt' etc: http://www.mlaw.org/wwl/index.html.

Requirements for international standardization

Sometimes national requirements lean toward international standardization (cell 2). This may occur in four situations:

1. There are industries where *international standards* tend to develop from technical standards originating in individual countries. For instance, in the field of oil drilling, the API (American Petroleum Institute) standards are enforced worldwide. Every oil company, whether American or not, must follow the API standards. Oil-drilling equipment manufacturers are also obliged to design their products in accordance with these standards. However, the number of industries with worldwide standards remains limited. The adoption of foreign/international standards can even prove to be problematic for selling in the country of origin. For instance, a European iron and steel company obtained certification from ASME (the American Society of Mechanical Engineers) for the very thick steel plate used in nuclear and petrochemical plants. In this small industry the company had a quite substantial world market share. ASME

certification was recognized worldwide since most nuclear plants use licensed American technology. When the company subsequently sold its heavy steel plates for use in German and French electricity utility plants, the American standards were not considered acceptable and it was forced to adapt to German and French standards.

2. Some products achieve 'international usage' such as aircraft suitcases (Samsonite of Belgium and Delsey of France), portable computers, duty-free articles, etc.

3. *Innovative products* often experience an international diffusion process.[17] High R & D costs are initially incurred for many innovative products, and the benefits from many technical products are not greatly affected by culture (e.g. DVDs). The pace of innovation diffusion is largely enhanced by the strength of 'early adopter' groups. These groups may also have a high level of exposure to international travel and to new products in the countries where they are first launched. By word-of-mouth communication, they transfer knowledge of the product to their non-travelling compatriots. They facilitate positive reactions from other consumers, who are not exposed to these new products, in the first phases of the adoption process: awareness, interest, evaluation, testing. More generally, international travel accelerates the process of diffusing standardized innovation. There is also some evidence that consumer innovativeness is higher for people from countries with lower uncertainty avoidance, higher individualism and more masculinity.[18]

4. The final point in cell 2 encompasses the basis of Levitt's[19] assertions about the globalization of markets. According to Levitt, certain aspects of ways of life would tend towards uniformity with differences in cultural preferences, national taste, standards and the institutional business environment being remnants of the past. Levitt argues that the so-called ethnic markets are a good example: Chinese food, country music, pizza and jazz now tend to be found worldwide. Although Levitt claims that he does not advocate systematic disregard for local or national differences, he overestimates the worldwide convergence of taste for global products, as emphasized in Chapters 5 and

6. Whatever value judgements are made about the all-inclusive tendency towards homogenization of world cultures, consumer segments and product categories, this issue must be raised for each company, on the basis of careful research in relation to its product, consumers and markets. For instance, Schuh[20] points out that while market conditions favour customization in Central Eastern Europe, the extra cost may not pay off as many of these countries have small markets which are rapidly changing due to massive investment from Western retailers, media, banks, etc.

Trend towards international standards

The costs required for adapting to national standards are very high since adaptation also implies the replication of test and certification procedures in many countries. In the pharmaceuticals industry, the cost of bringing a new drug onto the market is estimated at US$230 million in the United States, $150 million in Europe and $125 million in Japan. Countries still follow somewhat different routes for granting market entry to new pharmaceuticals. For instance Japan, requiring only 18 months, appears liberal in contrast with the US Food and Drug Administration, but given the relative brevity of initial trials in Japan, approval covers only the first six years, after which the manufacturer must reapply.[21]

Fortunately, there is a definite trend towards common standardization worldwide, especially with ISO (International Organization for Standardization) standards; some of these are now widely applied, such as the standards on quality, the ISO 9000 series. European technical standardization is participating in this movement, which stems from the EC Treaty, especially Article 30, which prohibits quantitative restrictions on imports from other member states and measures having an equivalent effect (that is, this is mainly a form of protectionist standardization). For instance, the *Cassis de Dijon* ruling firmly established the 'home country rule', whereby a product should not be barred from being imported into an EU country when it conforms to the standards of the EU country in which it is produced. The EU countries are engaged in a European standardization process through three Brussels-based organizations: CEN

(Comité Européen de Normalisation), CENELEC (Comité Européen de Normalisation pour les produits Electriques et Electroniques) and ETSI (European Telecommunications Standards Institute). This largely stems from the 1985 EC White Paper, which identified technical barriers as one of the main obstacles to the achievement of a single market in Europe.

Product standards are in fact a very complex strategic issue (much more so than depicted here), since they have a definite influence on the competitive strategy of the firm.[22] Issuing compatibility of standards over time (multi-vintage compatibility) and across competitors is very important in high-technology industries (e.g. computers, consumer electronics and telecommunications). There are examples where promoting a standard and licensing it to competitors (Matsushita's VHS) proved a better strategy than keeping a monopoly on one's own standard (e.g. Sony's now defunct Betamax VCR). Interestingly, it appears that Sony has learned from its costly Betamax VCR defeat. In early 2008, Toshiba was forced to abandon its HDDVD rival to Sony's Blu-ray high definition DVD standard. This time around Sony licensed its Blu-ray technology to competitors, while Toshiba largely kept the HD-DVD technology in-house. Other examples show that it was more efficient to keep the technology under total control, as Xerox did for its proprietary photocopying technology before the patent expired. But technology products are not the only items for which product standards need to be considered as part of their marketing strategy. For instance, Vertinsky and Zhou (p. 250)[23] examined forest product firms, finding that their choice to obtain Forest Stewardship Council (FSC) certification 'was to defend or create market access to markets with influential buyers' groups (e.g. the UK) or markets where environmental groups have strong influence on public opinion and the government (e.g. The Netherlands and Germany)'.

Website link 8.3

See how Sony won the High Definition DVD format war: http://knowledge.emory.edu/article.cfm?articleid=1128.

Service attributes

World export in commercial services increased by 12 per cent from 2005 to US$2.76 trillion dollars in 2006.[24] There are many factors driving this expansion including the WTO, protective measures (intellectual property rights, copyrights, trademarks, etc.), changing government attitudes, trading blocks, technology and changing demographics (e.g. more women in the workforce).[25]

Despite this, there are still many barriers for companies that wish to export services. In fact, the export of services is more highly regulated than the export of products. Managers regard regulatory barriers as more important than barriers internal to the firm (e.g. limited resources) or unfavourable markets (e.g. competitive environment or weak demand).[26] Many of these barriers are not transparent to outsiders and are difficult to negotiate. Informal barriers, such as official harassment to support local policy objectives (e.g. delays in delivery of work permits or excessive administrative fees to ease local unemployment), private harassment for personal gain (e.g. customs delays alleviated by 'fees' and 'donations' to family members of high ranking civil servants) and red tape for no apparent reason (e.g. inefficient public administration) are more problematic to managers than formal barriers.[26] In light of this, service exporters should adopt 'world class' practices from corporate structure and process to information networks and public relations strategies in order to comply with the regulatory environment.

Services may stand alone, or be part of a product offering. Service attributes include the following:

1. Repair and maintenance, after-sales service.
2. Installation.
3. Instruction manuals, information and guidance on how to use item.
4. Other related services (demonstrations, technical assistance).
5. Waiting time, delivery dates (and respect for them).
6. Guarantees (repair or replacement of goods).
7. Spare parts availability.
8. Return of goods, whether defective or not.

Box 8.3

Who's afraid of injections?

What is more standard in appearance than a syringe and an injection? There are, however, significant differences in the methods used to avoid causing pain to the patient. For intra-muscular syringes, there are two different ways of administering an injection. They correspond to two basic service attributes (correct injection of the substance, avoidance of pain):

1. Only the needle itself is stuck in, then the body of the syringe (the cylinder containing the substance and the plunger driving it) is fixed into the base of the needle, in accordance with a technique known as *luerslip* (this method is used in America). The first question asked by an American nurse is: how does it come apart? (Service attribute.)
2. French, Italian and Spanish doctors and nurses prefer (and are used to) using the fully assembled syringe. The American method would probably involve the risk of causing the patient more pain when connecting the two parts of the syringe after the needle has been implanted (an operation they are not used to doing). The service attribute required of the syringe is therefore based on its lightness and being in one piece, which is provided by a bolt system (*luerlock*). The first question asked by a French, Italian or Spanish nurse is: does it hold tight?

Further service attributes relate to who is legally permitted and professionally qualified to administer an injection and where it is possible to buy syringes. In Italy – in contrast to other European countries – syringes are on general sale, even in corner shops. They are available in blister packaging at the supermarket. Traditionally, many housewives actually give injections to members of their family.

(Source: Excerpt from a discussion with Beckton Dickinson, a world leader in single-use medical items – consumables.)

Adaptation of service in light of local conditions

The extent of service attributes differs according to the type of good being serviced. Service attributes are essential for industrial equipment and many consumer durables. Although it might not seem so, they also have a significant role to play in the field of consumer non-durables. Service requirements differ widely from country to country (cell 3) because they are related to environmental factors such as:

1. Level of technical expertise.
2. Level of labour costs, which is decisive in the balance between durability and reparability. For instance, Africans are experts at repairing and even revamping totally worn-out cars.
3. Level of literacy (this may render instruction manuals useless).
4. Climatic differences: certain climates increase difficulty of performing maintenance operations because of temperature, humidity, etc.

5. Remoteness of locations, which can render services difficult and costly to perform (e.g. servicing a gas turbine in the middle of the Amazonian forest).
6. Different ways of performing a seemingly identical service (see Box 8.3).

Actual services in developing countries are more traditional and of a limited technical level, at least when viewed by technologically developed countries. In societies where shortages are common, recycling is essential: African shoemakers, for instance, are experts at making shoe soles from used tyres. There is no lack of technical expertise and craftsmanship in developing countries; it is expressed differently, and relates to the prevailing economic conditions. In many African countries for instance, a lot of maintenance is done by small mechanical workshops, which succeed in repairing cars but take a long time to do so; although their repair methods may not be orthodox, they do work. Service instructions issued by car manufacturers naturally need some adaptation. It is better to show mechanics how to do a job than to send them a free 800-page book on maintenance operations. Services are generally delegated to distribution channels. The shortage of available and/or adequate channels and the small size of distribution outlets are obstacles to services, particularly in developing countries.

Even across developed countries, differences in the service offered by distribution channels are much greater than may be expected. The daily and weekly shop-opening hours vary widely. They may range from less than 60 hours per week total opening time in northern Europe and Australia to more than 100 hours per week in southern Europe and the United States. This affects attitudes towards distribution services; for example, where weekly store-opening hours are limited, people tend to turn to the Internet or mail order. Where a husband and wife are at work during shop-opening hours, an elderly parent with different service requirements may have to do the shopping for them.

From a customer perspective, differences have been found in service expectations, service evaluations and service reactions.[27]

Service expectations are the reference points from which consumers judge performance. The SERVQUAL is the most commonly used framework to assess service quality, as it measures the gap between expectations and evaluations of performance, which influences satisfaction.[28] It includes five dimensions: tangibility, reliability, assurance, responsiveness and empathy. From an etic perspective, these dimensions have been found to be important across cultures. From an emic perspective, additional dimensions have been found. For instance, Raajpoot[17] found that personalization, formality and sincerity were also important in some cultures. Generally, it has been found that US consumers have higher overall service quality expectations than consumers from other countries, commonly explained by the service environment and level of individualism.[27]

Service perceptions and evaluations also appear to differ across countries. For instance, Japanese consumers (high context/collectivist) rated service perceptions, in the same superior service condition, lower than US consumers (low context/individualist).[29] Some differences have also been found in the factors that influence service evaluations. For instance,

consumers from low-context Western cultures placed more emphasis on the tangible cues, whereas those from high-context Eastern cultures placed more emphasis on the intangible cues.[30]

People also react differently to service failures across cultures. For instance, consumers from Western cultures are more likely to complain than those from Eastern cultures.[31] Whereas compensation from a service failure positively influenced Western and Eastern consumers, it only influenced repurchase intentions and word of mouth for the US sample.[32] Customers from more collectivist or uncertainty-avoidant countries have a greater intention to give positive word-of-mouth after a positive service encounter, but if they receive a negative service encounter they tend not to give negative word-of-mouth, complain, or even switch.[30] The reverse is true for consumers from more individualist and lower uncertainty-avoidant countries. According to Zhang and colleagues (p. 219): 'Northern Americans may be more result-focused and pragmatic in their reactions to service experiences.'[27]

In a business setting, word-of-mouth may be more important in Japan than in the United States: when searching for a service in Japan and in the United States, buyers from Japanese and US firms use a number of personal information sources. Japanese companies have been found to use 340 per cent more referral sources than US firms when purchasing services in the United States. While US firms use more referral sources when purchasing in Japan, the Japanese firms still use 78 per cent more referral sources overall.[33]

Culture and the waiting experience

An important aspect of service is waiting to be served: to obtain maintenance or spare parts, to receive cash in a bank or to be served in a restaurant. In waiting, people have to deal with time, rules and power. The cultural assumptions concerning time are central to the waiting experience: people with a strong economic time pattern (see section 2.2) may experience waiting as a waste of time, a painful moment with negative emotions. For instance, Chen and colleagues (p. 291)[34] found that 'people from Western cultures are relatively less patient and therefore discount the future to a greater degree than do people from Eastern cultures, and thus Westerners value immediate consumption relatively more'.

Waiting is organized in queues to varying degrees and the rules concerning the waiting process are more or less respected according to culture (see section 3.6). Another important aspect of waiting is power: where power distance is strong, it seems almost legitimate to let the least powerful wait, with jumping the queue as standard behaviour for the most powerful. In fact, rather than jumped, the waiting line is bypassed: important consumers have direct access to the service. On the contrary, in the US, where low power distance and strong economic time prevail, waiting lines are well organized and everybody is treated fairly, following the principle of 'first come, first served'. Box 8.4 presents the Japanese attitude towards waiting in various service situations.

Waiting time can be reduced or increased according to the level of service personnel available; it can therefore be adapted according to the locally prevailing assumptions about time. In Europe, where time is, on average, slightly less economic than in the US, fast-food outlets are not as quick. People are not as preoccupied with waiting time. In the US, many pizza restaurants give a free pizza to customers who have waited more than a set amount of time (e.g. 10–30 minutes) for their order; in most European countries this practice is not necessary, because people do not resent waiting and may even value waiting time in a restaurant as a sign of careful preparation. Similarly, Rowley and Slack (p. 375) discuss differences in airport departure lounge environments across countries:

US airports have much more of a sense of urgency and activity (or a 'buzz') than airports in other parts of the world. Elsewhere the sense is more one of leisure and luxury, calm and relaxation. These messages are subtly conveyed through the way in which retail outlets are arranged, the attitudes of service agents and the nature of promotional messages.[35]

Another service attribute is the type of rules that apply to waiting and the degree to which the waiting lines are organized. In many countries, waiting is not organized at all and the principle 'first come, first served' finds no translation. Since people are used to unorganized waiting, they know that they will have to fight those who jump the queue,

by shouting, threatening them or jumping the queue themselves. For instance, the contrast between French and Swiss ski resorts, especially at peak time, is striking: whereas in France the absence of waiting corridors results in untidy crowds, in Switzerland the waiting process remains fairly peaceful and organized even if the waiting time is slightly longer. It comes as no surprise that American tourists travelling to Europe see the service quality image of French ski resorts as significantly lower than that of the Swiss and Austrian ski resorts, particularly as concerns honesty and friendliness.[36]

Cultural assumptions and service encounters

The service encounter implies a person-to-person relationship, in maintenance as well as in restaurant or other services. To this extent, the prevailing cultural norms apply in service encounters as they apply in any social interaction. Even though much is shared, especially from a normative point of view (availability, courtesy, willingness to give information), social codes concerning adequate service vary according to culture. Edward Hall (pp. 58–9), for instance, explains how, when staying in a hotel in downtown Tokyo, he was completely mystified by a problem with his room:

I had been a guest for about ten days and was returning to my room in the middle of an afternoon. Entering the room I immediately sensed that something was wrong. Out of place. Different. I was in the wrong room. Someone else's things were distributed around the head of the bed and the table . . . I checked my key again. Yes, it really was mine . . . At the desk, I was told by the clerk, as he sucked in his breath in deference (and embarrassment?) that indeed they had moved me. My particular room had been reserved in advance by somebody else. I was given the key to my new room and discovered that all my personal effects were distributed around the new room almost as though I had done it myself.[37]

Later Hall was to discover that, in contrast to the United States where being moved in such a way is almost an insult, in Japan it was tangible evidence that, after some days, he was treated as a family member, somebody belonging to the group of familiar clients, who can be treated in a relaxed and unceremonious way.

There are many situations where 'good' service is not self-evident. A case in point is when people are asleep on a plane when a meal is served. As far as the Japanese are concerned, the steward must wake those who are asleep so that they do not miss the meal, whereas Westerners prefer not to be disturbed in their sleep.[38] Naturally, the best solution, whatever the culture, would be for the steward to wait and serve the person sleeping as soon as he or she awakes; but such treatment is rarely possible because of schedule constraints.

An important cultural aspect of the service encounter is the *doing/being* divide. Hall (p. 109),[37] contrasts the French and the Americans: 'The French as a rule are much more involved [than the Americans] with their employees and with their customers and clients as well. They do not feel they can serve them adequately unless they know them well.' The first sentence is questionable: to many foreigners, service quality in France (as in other Latin countries) appears poor in comparison with the United States. Many American visitors perceive the commitment of

---

Box 8.4

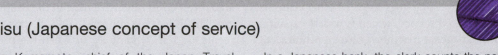

Sabisu (Japanese concept of service)

Misako Kamamoto, chief of the Japan Travel bureau recounts her experience guiding Japanese tourists overseas:

'When I take a group of Japanese tourists to a restaurant in Europe for the first time, I make a point to advise them in advance as follows: "Quite apart from the problem of whether the food suits the Japanese palate, you must be resigned to the fact that it takes a good deal of time to have a meal in a European restaurant." . . . some members of the party are bound to start complaining despite the warning that I have given them. "Why are European restaurants so slow in serving us? Please ask them to speed up the service." Some get so impatient that they stand up and leave, saying, "I don't want to wait for dessert or coffee. I can't stand a restaurant which gives such bad service." In a European restaurant, the essence of good service is to give the guests plenty of time to enjoy conversation together with the meal. So it makes sense that dishes are served with long intervals in between.

Japanese tourists who go shopping in Paris invariably return full of complaints because they were not treated like "gods" as in Japan. "The sales clerks take the attitude that they are doing you a favor by 'allowing you to buy'. They are so curt. What do they think customers are, anyway? The sales clerks have absolutely no interest in doing business. When I asked a clerk to show me something of a different color or different size, she acted annoyed and said brusquely, 'We have none.' She didn't even try to search."

In a Japanese bank, the clerk counts the notes by himself and puts them all together in a tray for the client, . . . few Japanese take the trouble of counting the notes on the spot . . . The Japanese usually consider that it is impolite to distrust anyone and believe that the other party will most naturally live up to the trust placed in him. In restaurants and hotels, Westerners do not make payment until they have thoroughly examined the bill, item by item and make sure that the sum is correctly totalled. In contrast the Japanese have always believed that restaurant and hotel bills are correct. Therefore, even when they are overseas, they assume the same and make payment without examining the bill. This habit sometimes becomes a trouble.

When they travel by train in Europe, the Japanese are struck by the quietness of the stations which are so unlike the noisy Japanese stations. There is no bell or loudspeaker signaling the departure of a train. Their first reaction is, "It's so nice and quiet." But this soon gives way to anxiety. "Why is it that there is no bell notifying us of the departure? It would be a lot of trouble if we missed the train," some say. . . . Whereas European railways give priority to silence and their rule is to have travelers enjoy a quiet journey, Japanese railways seem to think that their mission is to provide passengers with all kinds of information via blaring loudspeakers.'

(Source: Kamamoto, pp. 26–7.[38])

French service providers towards their clients as quite low. The real key is in Hall's second sentence: '*unless they know them well*'. In societies where *doing* is strongly emphasized, as in the United States, waiters and other service providers are task-centred rather than person or relationship-centred. It is no real problem for them to serve *unknown* people. To many French or Latin eyes, North American service appears the exact opposite of Hall's judgement, friendlier, more attentive and more dedicated than in European countries, especially in southern Europe. So, in a *being*-oriented society, known customers are shown attentive and friendly service, whereas unknown customers may well be neglected.

Another interesting question is whether customers prefer automated service, which is widely expanding (e.g. automatic teller machines, ticket machines, etc.), or to be served by real, flesh-and-blood people. A *being* orientation implies a preference for personnel in contact whereas the *doing* orientation favours automated service, which is purely task oriented. The dimension of affectivity versus neutrality (see section 3.5), an important aspect of Trompenaars' (1993) relational orientation, can be combined with the *doing–being* divide for describing possible preferences, as in Table 8.2: affectivity creates a preference for personnel in contact, because human relationships in the service encounter are preferred to service automation. Naturally, all this is based on cultural ideal types; other factors, such as age and level of education, have a strong influence on individual acceptance of automated service; older people and less educated persons have more difficulties in dealing with automated service devices, which they do not consider user friendly.[39]

Factors in favour of service standardization

The decision to adapt services to diversified international requirements implies little cost (cell 3), since it is far easier to reach increasing returns from economies of scale for a product's physical attributes than for its service attributes. On the other hand, there can be substantial learning effects with service attributes. For example, various management procedures such as stocking spare parts or hotel laundering may be standardized.

In certain cases (cell 3) adapting service attributes leads to cost savings because locally supplied services are far less comprehensive than in the country of origin. This is feasible either when local service requirements are less demanding or when the product has been intended to be almost maintenance free. In this case it will also be designed to stand up to 'untrained' users. Physical attributes will then interact with service attributes within the product as a whole.

However, service standardization (cell 4) is required when the clientele are internationally 'mobile'. Customers move with their service requirements. The global success of truck manufacturers from northern Europe (DAF, Volvo, Scania, Mercedes) is due in part to their ability to offer a standardized service in a range of countries and on sites along the routes that are most commonly taken by international truck drivers. For instance, an engine or a gearbox can be completely overhauled within a specified period of time at any location on the route. The same holds true for McDonald's restaurants where service is to a large extent standardized worldwide: customers know what they will find in terms of service, whether

Table 8.2 Cultural dimensions and automated service

		High			
		Being		**Doing**	
Dimensions	**Affectivity**	1.	Strong preference for personnel in contact	3.	Like(s) the machine but would like personnel also
	Neutrality	2.	Do(es) not like the machine but do(es) not like people either	4.	Strongest preference for purely automated service

they enter a McDonald's in Tampere, Finland, Osaka, Japan or Montauban, France.

8.4

Symbolic attributes

The symbol can be defined linguistically as the sign that designates a relationship which is non-causal (as opposed to the *indicator*) and non-analogous (as opposed to the *icon*). The *Oxford English Dictionary Online* defines 'symbol' as 'Something that stands for, represents, or denotes something else (not by exact resemblance, but by vague suggestion, or by some accidental or conventional relation)'. Any animate or inanimate object may be a basis for making a symbolic association. A fox may be a symbol of cunning, whereas an oak may be a symbol of strength. The use of the words 'may be' recognizes the fact that not every culture makes identical associations. Either there are no foxes or oaks, or other interpretative meanings are applied. Symbols work as a powerful means of suggestion and evocation. The symbolic aspects of consumption are important to consumers: the social meaning of many products is more important than their functional utility or at least as important, e.g. clothes or perfumes. As Solomon emphasized (p. 320): 'Symbolic interactionism focuses on the process by which individuals understand their world. It assumes that people interpret the actions of others rather than simply react to them.'[40]

Most symbols are not universal; they may be understood and used by a large part, but not all, of the world population. One of the rare symbols to transcend cross-cultural boundaries is that of left and right, with a positive value put on the 'right' side, which is seen as the adequate way, as correct and true, or as being in accordance with moral or legal behaviour.[41] In French (*droit*) or German (*Recht*) the same word is used for designating both the right side and law.

In terms of adaptation/standardization, two different issues should be addressed:

1. The relationship between symbolic attitudes and national product images, with respect to product category, company and brand names and country of manufacture (see Chapter 9).

2. Divergent symbolic interpretations. Meanings are principally conveyed by the packaging and outward appearance of a product. If a symbolic attribute which was ethnocentrically conceived has a very different and highly negative interpretation in the target culture, adaptation is required (cell 5). For instance, symbolic associations linked to objects or colours may vary considerably across countries and cultures. Carlsberg had to add a third elephant to its label in Africa, since two elephants seen together are considered an ominous sign.[42]

Link between symbols and culture

The link between symbols and culture comprises seven successive steps. The starting point is conceptual: colours, for example, are wavelengths of light reflected by objects; a set of waves of different frequencies produces a colour spectrum. If it is stated that an object is red, this means the following:

1. It soaks up all received light except red.
2. The language has the term called 'red', which designates a certain part of the spectrum that reflects the object (which has no colour as such).
3. Our perceptual apparatus – eyes, retinas, optical nerves, brains – are capable of identifying the wavelengths.
4. Through a learning mechanism, both linguistic and visual, we have learnt to recognize this colour as 'red' since early childhood; that is, to qualify it by imitation of all the other people who also designate this colour as 'red'.

Perception results from a culture-based adaptive process (points 2 and 4 above). Numerous experimental studies have shown that certain peoples have a less discriminating perception of colour (their vocabulary and identification is more restricted). They 'mix up' certain 'colours' that other peoples can distinguish. It has also been shown that sensitivity to visual illusions (shapes and length) varies according to culture, particularly as a result of the effects of syncretism. Suggestive visual associations result from our daily environment. Our native physical environment shapes our perceptual universe (see section 1.4). In the case of pictorial perception, Cohen[43] distinguishes two questions: (1) 'What do people see when they look at this picture?' and (2) 'What does the picture mean?' The second question refers to meaning, interpretation and symbolism, but the first question, which has to be answered first, refers to what people *actually see*. Western pictorial conventions representing three-dimensionality on a plane, for instance, are based on arbitrary codes: smaller objects, and higher objects in the picture plane, are meant to be farther away; an overlapped object is supposed to be farther away, and the rules of 'perspective' are applied in the form of convergence of lines. As explained by Cohen (p. 219):

A picture of an empty bowl in front of a child was supposed to show that the child was hungry and malnourished. The two cues which should have indicated three-dimensionality were overlap and size. But when individuals in the target market were shown the picture, they thought the bowl was an empty washbowl. This was because the bowl was in the foreground and was large in size compared with the child.[43]

In order to move on from the *percept* (i.e. the subjects are able to formulate verbally what has been shown to them) to the *symbolic image*, three steps must be added to the four previously set out. The cultural process intervenes at each of these three final steps:

5. An association has been established between a certain colour, form, smell, shape, etc. and a suggested meaning, as in the two parts of the Greek symbol (see the introduction). Initially there can be a highly tangible link: for example, the colour brown may be tainted by a negative sense in the connotation of waste, since it may be concretely associated with excrement.
6. This link is ignored; there are two complementary parts but the way they are related has been forgotten: why in most Western countries is blue the colour for little boys and pink for little girls? The association is important for choices in baby-related markets.
7. Then there is social overspill through education, advertising, the mass media, literature, magazines – in short, throughout society and indeed even to packaging and marketing communication in general. The symbol shares the characteristics of a language. It conveys rich and diversified meanings, full of nuances, and its messages are often implicit.

It conjures up a set of evocations, suggestions and interpretations that are almost subconscious yet still very real in the minds of consumers. This set of interpretations is to a large extent specific to each national culture. For example, does orange juice have to be yellow, orange or slightly red, full of pulp or clear, thick or very fluid, in order to evoke different product attributes: the sense of its being a nature-based/non-artificial drink, its dietary qualities, an image of refreshment, healthy for children as opposed to being intended for adults?

Images diffused by symbolic attributes

Symbols, in their capacity as signs with suggestive power that is non-causal and non-analogous, rely on natural elements: colours, shapes, locations, materials, everyday objects, animals, countryside and elements of nature, famous characters, etc. In certain cultures a lake is a symbol of love, blue is a symbol of virginity. Most commonly the 'natural' backgrounds of symbols appear fairly arbitrary, in so far as the original link has often been lost or transformed, as and when the symbol became widely used. The interpretation of symbolic messages conveyed by attributes, such as colour, shape and consistency, may differ significantly between the marketer's culture and the consumer's culture. Williams and Longworth[44] cite the case of the Coral Sea tuna fishery in Australia, where the government spent money to develop exports to Japan. The fishing operation was unable to obtain a high price for its fresh tuna air-freighted to Japan, because the Japanese had a problem with the colour of the fish. After investigations were conducted in the Tsukiji central wholesale market, it appeared that the negative interpretation was related to the meat colour, which evidenced a non-Japanese origin; this resulted in the Australian tuna consistently being sold at a discount. Today, Australia selects and sends only the more compatibly coloured Southern Bluefin tuna into the highly priced sashimi (raw fish) market in Japan. Australia is the second largest exporter of Bluefin Tuna to Japan with 21 per cent of the market in 2006.[45]

Ethnocentrism is instinctive in all symbolic thought. It is therefore quite inevitable, especially when it is present in the consumer's culture. In the case of ethnic products, it may even be of some use to marketers in order to maintain genuineness. However, inappropriate (or even poor) use of backgrounds that diffuse symbolic images that are not adapted to the local consumer presents a danger for international marketers. Inappropriate use of symbolic meanings may be based on the best possible intentions on the part of the marketer but may result in the worst consequences for users: for example, the skull and crossbones symbol, used in most Western countries to represent lethal dangers posed by electricity, poison, steam, etc., is a symbol of potency in many African countries.

Symbolism of colours, shapes, numbers, etc.

White is the colour of birth and in the West usually refers to a happy life event, whereas in China it symbolizes mourning. Conversely, the colour black symbolizes death in the West, perhaps because its darkness suggests fears that the sun will not return, whereas it is an everyday colour in China.

Hidden behind each symbol is one or more material support. Red, for example, is the colour of blood: it can evoke and suggest meanings that differ widely depending on the culture (see Figure 8.1). Every culture has an image of blood, which feeds part of the symbolic content of the colour red (see Box 8.5). Naturally, the colour red can be linked to substances other than blood – certain flowers, for instance. Use of red as the dominant colour on a product or its packaging must therefore be very carefully considered beforehand (cell 5 in Table 8.1).

Associating symbols

The following examples illustrate symbolic associations. Symbols which are diffused by the design of a product or its packaging may be associated with the intrinsic qualities of the product itself.

The Italian company Olivetti produced a typewriter that was such a beautiful object that a New York museum displayed it in its modern art collection. This typewriter proved to be a commercial failure in the United States even though the Americans liked its appearance. Potential purchasers found that its design did not inspire an image of robustness (cell 5). Furthermore, in Anglo-Saxon societies there is often a puritanical attitude that work is an activity required by duty, which is sometimes arduous and should be more painful than enjoyable. This beautiful and enjoyable object was incompatible with such an attitude.

Coca-Cola decided to adapt the name 'Diet Coke' to 'Coke Light' or 'Coca-Cola Light' when it found that in some countries the word *diet* connoted the need for weight-reduction rather than minimizing weight gain.[11] In other countries, legal issues with the word *diet* have diminished its use as a label.[46] Now Coca-Cola uses the word 'Light' in almost one-third of countries, including Germany, Spain, Argentina, Mexico and Brazil.

In many cases, symbolic associations may work even though, from a rational point of view, individual symbols are somewhat contradictory: consumer interpretation of symbolic associations take the form of an impressionistic halo rather than a detailed content analysis. An example is a German *Weissbier* (a beer brewed with wheat instead of barley), called

Figure 8.1 An example of diverging symbolic interpretations

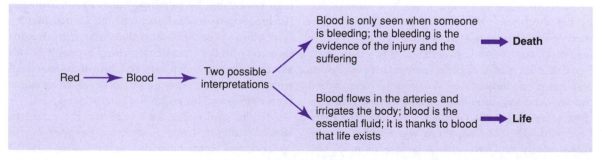

Box 8.5

Colours, things, numbers and even smells have symbolic meanings . . . often not the ones you think!

Green, America's favorite colour for suggesting freshness and good health, is often associated with disease in countries with dense green jungles; it is a favorite colour among Arabs but forbidden in portions of Indonesia. In Japan, green is a good high-tech colour, but Americans would shy away from green electronic equipment. Black is not universal for mourning: in many Asian countries it is white; in Brazil it is purple, yellow in Mexico, and dark red in the Ivory Coast. Americans think of blue as the most masculine colour, but red is more manly in the United Kingdom or France. While pink is the most feminine colour in America, yellow is more feminine in most of the world. Red suggests good fortune in China but death in Turkey. In America, a candy wrapped in blue or green is probably a mint; in Africa, the same candy would be wrapped in red, our colour for cinnamon . . . in every culture, things, numbers and even smells have meanings. Lemon scent in the United States suggests freshness; in the Philippines lemon scent is associated with illness. In Japan the number 4 is like our 13; and 7 is unlucky in Ghana, Kenya and Singapore. The owl in India is bad luck, like our black cat. In Japan, a fox is associated with witches. In China, a green hat is like a dunce cap; specifically it marks a man with an unfaithful wife. The stork symbolizes maternal death in Singapore, not the kind of message you want to send to a new mother.

(Source: Copeland and Griggs, p. 63.[47])

Oberdorfer. It claims on one side of its label to be brewed according to the Bavarian purity law dating back to 1516, whereas the other side of the label boasts 'ice-rifing' (*sic*), 'our new *coole* art to brew beer' (*coole* is a germanification of 'cool', which evokes positive values of quietness and relaxation in many non-English speaking cultures, and 'ice-rifing' probably evokes a late crop of hops which provides a more bitter taste). Associating (local) tradition and (foreign) modernity is in general no major problem: in daily life, consumers themselves experience the complex mix of modern and traditional, local and foreign values and behaviours.

A French company exported a cheese from the Pyrenees to West Germany. A shepherd surrounded by his sheep was depicted on the packaging. This picture was directly related to what was shown in the television commercial. In France, this image conveyed the idea of a natural manufacturing process and home-made qualities. A consumer test carried out in Germany, after the initial failure of the product, showed that the Germans associated the shepherd with dirt. The shepherd was withdrawn and subsequently replaced with a picture of mountain scenery. The product was then able to undergo a successful relaunch. In this example the problem stems from the association of symbolic opposites: country/mountain, dirty/clean, natural/artificial. Clearly, in this case, the symbolic associations of the French and the Germans are very different.

Colours may also be associated with particular product categories or product attributes. Purple, for instance, is perceived as expensive in Asian cultures, but inexpensive in the United States. Black is perceived as demonstrating trustworthiness and high quality in China.[48] Colours may also be associated with countries, the products of which are supposed to be the most likely to have this colour dominant on their packaging. By gathering data in four countries (China, South Korea, Japan and the United States), Jacobs and colleagues[48] show that Asian nations associate red with the United States, but US people do not associate their country with red; purple is associated with France, and the four cultures reviewed associate both France and Italy with the colour green.

Madden and colleagues[49] explored the extent to which students from East Asia, Europe, North America and South America like various colours, the meanings they associate with colours and how they would match colours for a logo by testing. They found that blue, green and white share similar meanings and are well liked across countries, while black and red, although also liked, hold different meanings across countries. For instance, red was perceived as active, hot and vibrant across all countries, but in the PRC and Taiwan it was also perceived as pleasant. In addition, when students were asked to match colours for a product logo, the colours paired with red differed considerably. It was paired with black (for the United States and Brazil), with white (Colombia, Hong Kong, China and Taiwan) and with yellow (Austria, Canada and China).

Exotic, ethnic and universal appeals

Certain factors weigh in favour of the standardization of symbolic attributes (cell 6 in Table 8.1): favourable perception of imported products, positive association with the country of origin (perfume with France, fast food with the United States, etc.) and other factors are examined in detail in the next chapter. Many people buy a small slice of American life when they enter a McDonald's restaurant, a touch of French romance when they buy Cacharel perfume, or an instant of German *gemütlichkeit* when they drink a Löwenbräu beer. In these consumption experiences, ethnic product symbolism is associated with exotic appeal for the consumer; thus, symbolic attributes must be kept standardized even though the product or its surrounding services are to a certain extent adapted to local markets.

Website link 8.4

View symbols from all over the world:
http://www.whats-your-sign.com/index.html.

A good example of a purely standardized product is the 'Classic Christmas Cake' sold worldwide through mail order by Collin Street Bakery from Corsicana, Texas. The advertisement, sent by mail worldwide, emphasizes that they still bake the 'Deluxe cake true to the Old-World recipe brought to Corsicana, Texas from Wiesbaden, Germany in 1896, by master baker Gus Weidmann'; it boasts the richness of the ingredients ('a full 27 per cent rich pecans') and claims to deliver in 196 countries. Associating symbols of tradition (Old World), genuineness and American richness, they have a full register of images that work worldwide (and claim to do so!). Some brands also try to build on universal symbols: Coca-Cola has always successfully avoided being associated too strongly with an American image by creating a strong brand association with youth, sports and leisure situations, all universal themes. Packaging consistency is a solution for products that want to diffuse a universal image and build on a highly standardized offering: Coke uses the same red and white logo in each country, and its bottle design is consistent across markets. Similarly, McDonald's never strays from its yellow arches. The symbolic interpretation then shifts from the parts to the whole: rather than relating to interpretations of yellow and arches in particular cultures, it diffuses a message about McDonald's worldwide.

For the designer of product attributes that convey appropriate symbolic meanings, the following recommendations can be made:

1. When conducting research on possible standardization before a product launch, it is preferable to choose symbols that have a universal or near-universal value (as far as they exist).
2. Since there is very great diversity in the interpretations and associations of symbols, product and packaging standardization must be systematically preceded by product and packaging tests carried out in each national market, using local informants.

Questions

1. List basic attributes of a perfume at the three levels (physical, service and symbolic). Indicate how the interpretation of symbolic attributes of perfumes may differ cross-culturally.

2. What are basic attributes of Coca-Cola (physical, service and symbolic) in its original US context? Coca-Cola is adapted to suit local tastes and its advertising, although based on core advertising themes and guidelines, is customized for local audiences. Why?

3. How can a company make compromises between worldwide product standardization and customization to local markets?

4. Why is service adaptation across markets necessary? Outline basic reasons.

5. People in a queue may be told how long they still have to wait before being served. What are the possible interpretations by consumers of such information?

6. You have been asked to choose a colour and a design for a fire extinguisher. What are the standard colour and signs used in your native culture. Assess whether they are cross-culturally transferable. Answer the same question for a coffee package.

7. Are there universal, or near-universal, symbols? To what extent can they be used in a marketing strategy? Provide examples.

References

1. Tuncalp, Secil (1990), 'Export Marketing Strategy to Saudi Arabia: The Case of British Exporters', *Quarterly Review of Marketing*, 15 (2), 13–18.

2. Katsikeas, Constantine S., Saeed Samiee, and Marios Theodosiou (2006), 'Strategy Fit and Performance Consequences of International Marketing Standardization', *Strategic Management Journal*, 27 (9), 867–90.

3. Vrontis, Demetris (2003), 'Integrating Adaptation and Standardisation in International Marketing: The Adaptstand Modelling Process', *Journal of Marketing Management*, 19, 283–305.

4. Baalbaki, Imad B. and Naresh K. Malhotra (1995), 'Standardization Versus Customization in International Marketing: An Investigation Using Bridging Conjoint Analysis', *Journal of the Academy of Marketing Science*, 23 (3), 182–94.

5. Hult, G., Tomas M., Bruce D. Keillor, and Roscoe Hightower (2000), 'Valued Product Attributes in an Emerging Market: A Comparison between French and Malaysian Consumers', *Journal of World Business*, 35 (2), 206–20.

6. Diamantopoulos, A., B.B. Schlegelmilch, and J.P. Du Preez (1995), 'Lessons for Pan-European Marketing? The Role of Consumer Preferences in Fine-Tuning the Product-Market Fit', *International Marketing Review*, 12 (2), 38–52.

7. Theodosiou, Marios and Leonidas C. Leonidou (2003), 'Standardization Versus Adaptation of International Marketing Strategy: An Integrative Assessment of the Empirical Research', *International Business Review*, 12 (2), 141–71.

8. Shoham, Aviv (1996), 'Marketing-Mix Standardization: Determinants of Export Performance', *Journal of Global Marketing*, 10 (2), 53–73.

9. Amine, Lyn S. (1993), 'Linking Consumer Behavior Constructs to International Marketing Strategy: A Comment on Wills, Samli, and Jacobs and an Extension', *Journal of the Academy of Marketing Science*, 21 (1), 71–7.

10. Wills, James A., Coskun Samli, and Laurence Jacobs (1991), 'Developing Global Products and Marketing Strategies: A Construct and a Research Agenda', *Journal of the Academy of Marketing Science*, 19 (1), 1–10.

11. Dana, Leo-Paul and Brenda M. Oldfield (1999), 'Lublin Coco-Cola Bottlers Ltd', *International Marketing Review*, 16 (4/5), 291–8.

12. Allio, David J. and Robert J. Allio (2002), 'Coors Light in Puerto Rico: Battling for Local Dominance in a Global Market', *Strategy and Leadership*, 30 (6), 13–17.

13. van Mesdag, Martin (2000), 'Culture-Sensitive Adaptation or Global Standardization – the Duration-of-Usage Hypothesis', *International Marketing Review*, 17 (1), 74–84.

14. Giordan, Alain-Eric (1988), *Exporter Plus 2*. Paris: Economica.

15. Camphuis, Pierre-Arnold (1984), 'Launching a Product on the Cameroon Market', Internship report, Ecole Supérieure De Commerce De Paris.

16. Jones, Bob Dorigo (2007), *Remove Child before Folding: The 101 Stupidest, Silliest, and Wackiest Warning Labels Ever*. New York, NY: Grand Central Publishing.

17. Raajpoot, Nusser (2004), 'Reconceptualizing Service Encounter Quality in Non-Western Context', *Journal of Service Research*, 7 (2), 181–201.

18. Baumgartner, Hans and Jan-Benedict E.M. Steenkamp (1996), 'Exploratory Consumer Buying Behavior: Conceptualization and Measurement', *International Journal of Research in Marketing*, 13 (2), 121–37.

19. Levitt, Theodore (1983), 'The Globalization of Markets', *Harvard Business Review*, 61 (3), 92–102.

20. Schuh, Arnold (2000), 'Global Standardization as a Success Formula for Marketing in Central Eastern Europe', *Journal of World Business*, 35 (2), 133–48.

21. Pahud de Mortanges, Charles, Jan-Willem Rietbroek, and Cort MacLean Johns (1997), 'Marketing Pharmaceuticals in Japan: Background and the Experience of US Firms', *European Journal of Marketing*, 31 (8), 561–82.

22. Shapiro, Carl and Hal R. Varian (1999), 'The Art of Standard Wars', *California Management Review*, 41 (2), 8–32.

23. Vertinsky, Ilan and Dongsheng Zhou (2000), 'Product and Process Certification: Systems, Regulations and International Marketing Strategies', *International Marketing Review*, 17 (3), 231–52.

24. World Trade Organization (WTO) (2007), *International Trade Statistics 2007*. www.wto.org/english/res_e/its2007_e/its07_trade_category_e.htm.

25. Javalgi, Rajshekhar G. and D. Steven White (2002), 'Strategic Challenges for the Marketing of Services Internationally', *International Marketing Review*, 19 (6), 563–81.

26. Kostecki, Michel Maciej and Marcin Nowakowski (2002), 'Regulatory Barriers to Export of Services: A Managerial View from Poland-Based Export Firms', *Argumenta Oeconomica*, 12 (1), 17–51.

27. Zhang, Jingyun, Sharon E. Beatty, and Gianfranco Walsh (2008), 'Review and Future Directions of Cross-Cultural Consumer Services Research', *Journal of Business Research*, 61 (3), 211–24.

28. Parasuraman, A., Valarie A. Zeithaml, and Leonard L. Berry (1988), 'Servqual: A Multiple-Item Scale for Measuring Consumer Perceptions of Service Quality', *Journal of Retailing*, 64 (1), 12–40.

29. Laroche, Michel, Linda C. Ueltschy, Shuzo Abe, Mark Cleveland, and Peter P. Yannopoulos (2004), 'Service Quality Perceptions and Customer Satisfaction: Evaluating the Role of Culture', *Journal of International Marketing*, 12 (3), 58–85.

30. Mattila, Anna S. (1999), 'The Role of Culture in the Service Evaluation Process', *Journal of Service Research*, 1 (3), 250–61.

31. Liu, Ben Shaw-Ching, Olivier Furrer, and D. Sudharshan (2001), 'The Relationships between Culture and Behavioral Intentions toward Services', *Journal of Service Research*, 4 (2), 118–29.

32. Wong, Nancy Y. (2004), 'The Role of Culture in the Perception of Service Recovery', *Journal of Business Research*, 57 (9), 957–63.

33. Money, R. Bruce, Mary C. Gilly, and John L. Graham (1998), 'Explorations of National Culture and Word-of-Mouth Referral Behavior in the Purchase of Industrial Services in the US and Japan', *Journal of Marketing*, 62 (October), 76–87.

34. Chen, Haipeng (Allan), Sharon Ng, and Akshay R. Rao (2005), 'Cultural Differences in Consumer Impatience', *Journal of Marketing Research*, 42 (3), 291–301.

35. Rowley, Jennifer and Frances Slack (1999), 'The Retail Experience in Airport Departure Lounges: Reaching for Timeless and Placelessness', *International Marketing Review*, 16 (4/5), 363–75.

36. Ofir, Chezy and Donald R. Lehmann (1986), 'Measuring Images of Foreign Products', *Columbia Journal of World Business* (Summer), 105–8.

37. Hall, Edward T. (1976), *Beyond Culture*. New York: Doubleday.

38. Kamamoto, Mitsuko (1984), 'Japanese Concept of Service', *Dentsu Japan Marketing/Advertising* (January), 26–9.

39. Simon, Françoise and Jean-Claude Usunier (2007), 'Cognitive, Demographic, and Situational Determinants of Service Customer Preference for Personnel-in-Contact over Self-Service Technology', *International Journal of Research in Marketing*, 24 (2), 163–73.

40. Solomon, Michael R. (1983), 'The Role of Products as Social Stimuli: A Symbolic Interactionism Perspective', *Journal of Consumer Research*, 10 (December), 319–29.

41. Cohen, Judy (1996), 'The Search for Universal Symbols: The Case of Right and Left', *Journal of International Consumer Marketing*, 8 (3/4), 187–210.

42. McCornell, J.D. (1971), 'The Economics of Behavioral Factors in the Multinational Corporation', in *Combined Proceedings of the American Marketing Association*, Fred E. Allvine, Ed., p. 260.

43. Cohen, Judy (1995), 'Toward a Theoretical Understanding of the Impact of Culture on Pictorial Perception', in *Proceedings of the Second Conference on the Cultural Dimension of International Marketing*. Odense, 213–45.

44. Williams, Stephen C. and John W. Longworth (1989), 'Factors Influencing Tuna Prices in Japan and Implications for the Development of the Coral Sea Tuna Fishery', *European Journal of Marketing*, 23 (4), 5–24.

45. Infofish (2007), Tuna Market Report – Bluefin – January 2007. www.infofish.org/marketreports/tuna-bluefin0107us.html.

46. Coleman, Zach (1999), 'Foreign Markets Develop Taste for Coke Light', *Atlanta Business Chronicle*, 10 May.

47. Copeland, Lennie and Lewis Griggs (1986), *Going International*. New York: Plume Books/New American Library.

48. Jacobs, Laurence, Charles Keown, Reginald Worthley, and Ghymn Kyung-Il (1991), 'Cross-Cultural Colour Comparisons: Global Marketers Beware!', *International Marketing Review*, 8 (3), 21–30.

49. Madden, Thomas J., Kelly Hewett, and Martin S. Roth (2000), 'Managing Images in Different Cultures: A Cross-National Study of Color Meanings and Preferences', *Journal of International Marketing*, 8 (4), 90–107.

Teaching materials

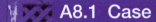

A8.1 Case

Movies worldwide

The world market for feature films has been dominated by the United States for more than 50 years. Hollywood, *MGM*, *Warner Bros*, and the roaring *20th Century Fox* lion are names, images, and sounds with worldwide recognition. Examples of 60 years of creative work by US studios may be seen on *TCM/TNT Turner Classic Movies* (**www.turnerclassicmovies.com**). Despite the criticism that films are too commercialized, with scenarios overly influenced by focus groups, the average Hollywood release remains a worldwide success. *Ben Hur*, *Star Wars*, and *Titanic* are examples of global hits that have done more than sell tickets around the world. They also reached the status of artistic myths in their categories (epic, science fiction, and disaster, respectively). The *Harry Potter* films (released by Warner Bros.) are a more recent example of Hollywood's massive impact around the world. *Harry Potter and the Chamber of Secrets* is the third highest international grosser in history.[1] In Norway, one in five people saw the second film, having booked weeks in advance of the opening night. Twelve million Germans have seen the film. In Japan, adults, to whom the film is primarily marketed, are as fanatical about it as children.[2] *Harry Potter*, as a franchise, is more profitable than blockbusters *Star Wars*, *Titanic*, and *Matrix*[3] (see **www.harrypotter.warnerbros.co.uk/**).

What many non-American US movie viewers ignore is that some films succeed at home but not abroad, and vice versa. Robin Williams did very well globally in *Good Morning Vietnam*, *Mrs. Doubtfire*, and *The Dead Poets Society*. However, his US health system drama *Patch Adams* failed overseas. According to Duncan Clark, international theatrical department head at Sony, certain formats are thought to fail abroad, such as black, urban, and historical themes, as well as baseball and football films.[4] At home, filmmakers try to target different ethnic markets in addition to the mainstream. Since marketers are targeting youth, English now is the language of ethnic-oriented films (Spanish or Chinese subtitles may be available, so as not to alienate older viewers), however the theme of the screenplay may differ. Action and adventure movies are more successful among Asian-American audiences, for example.[5] Film makers tend to select their cast, and particularly their stars, with a view to attracting international interest in their films. A respected source for directors is the Hollywood Reporter's 'Star Power' classification for the international box office. In 2002, the top five actors were Tom Cruise, Julia Roberts, Tom Hanks, Mel Gibson, and Jim Carrey. Non-white actors are thought to hold little attraction for overseas markets, apart from Will Smith, Denzel Washington, and Jackie Chan.[4]

Movie imports

In most cinema markets around the world, the majority of films are imported, reaching 78 per cent in Italy and 93 per cent in Egypt (Anon, 2003). The market share of American movie films is very high (most often above 50 per cent). They reach summits of 90 per cent in Scandinavia, and for the European Union as a whole 78 per cent in 2002,[6] up from 66 per cent in 2001.[7,8] Even in supposedly 'resistant' countries like France, the share of American films is above 50 per cent, or approximately eight times more in value than the combined imports of films made in other European countries.[9] In Spain, domestic film production is stagnant, accounting for 12.5 per cent of admissions, while American films accounted for 70 per cent.[10] Films from central and eastern Europe, the Mediterranean Basin, and Latin America generally account for a market share of about 1 per cent in the European Union, making the EU more impenetrable to filmmakers other than those from the US, Canada, Australia, and Japan. It is likely that a combination of cultural protectionism and poor distribution systems create conditions for market dominance of US films in Europe.[7,8] Interestingly, there are historical differences. In the 1950s, German, French, and Italian audiences had a marked preference for their own national productions. Up until the 1980s, it was rare that the same film would share top ten status in Germany, France, and Italy. However, since that time, 40 per cent of the top ten films in these three continental European countries are the same Hollywood films.[11] Between 1996 and 2002, the top five films in terms of box office receipts were either British or British-American co-productions like *Bridget Jones's Diary* (2001), *Notting Hill* (1999), *James Bond: The World is Not Enough* (1999), and *Bean – the Ultimate Disaster Movie* (1997).[12]

Hollywood's hegemony

Hollywood's hegemony was won primarily thanks to its massive home market, which allowed studios to recover their costs domestically, freeing up resources for expensive stars, special effects, and marketing – which averages US$25 million per film.[13] Having recovered production costs in their home markets, Hollywood studios can sell their films relatively cheaply to foreign distributors. In fact, three-quarters of film distributors around the world are American-owned.[14] making the top ten film studios also the top ten global distributors. Around the world, US distributors have the leverage to do what is illegal at home: 'Blockbooking', forcing theatres or distributors they do not own to buy packages of lower quality films in order to obtain a desirable hit film.[13] The appeal of Hollywood films around the world is not so surprising considering that Hollywood producers have always had to appeal to different ethnic, religious, and social groups in their heterogeneous home market. In addition, many 'Hollywood' directors of the present and past are not American at all. Examples are many, including Taiwanese Ang Lee (*Hulk*, *The Wedding Banquet*), British Sam Mendes (*American Beauty*), German Roland Emmerich (*Independence Day*, *The Patriot*), and British Ridley Scott (*Gladiator*, *Alien*). Another element that increased acceptance of US films among non-native speakers of English was the adoption of an introspective, non-verbal style in interpreting roles. This style (known as the 'Method') originated in nineteenth-century Russian theatre and is diametrically opposed to the Shakespearean tradition that emphasizes eloquence. As a by-product of the 'Method' style of Marlon Brando, James Dean, Robert DeNiro, and others, Hollywood films are easily understood even when one's knowledge of English – or the quality of subtitles – is poor. It is helpful that Hollywood's American-ness can tap into the most prominent country-brand equity in the world to increase its potency.[15]

Table 8.3 Top two films by gross box office receipts per country/region 1996–2002

Country	Top grossing film	Second grossing film
Australia (2002 only)	*Star Wars: Episode 2* (USA)	*Lord of the Rings: Fellowship* (USA/New Zealand)
European Union (1996–2002)	*Titanic*, 1997 (USA)	*Harry Potter and the Sorcerer's Stone*, 2001 (USA)
France (2002 only)	*Astérix et Obelix: Mission Cléopatre* (France/Germany)	*Harry Potter and the Chamber of Secrets* (USA)
Italy (2002 only)	*Pinocchio* (Italy/France/Germany)	*Lord of the Rings: Fellowship of the Ring* (USA/New Zealand)
Japan (2002 only)	*Harry Potter and the Sorcerer's Stone* (USA)	*Monsters, Inc.* (USA)
Korea (2002 only)	*Marrying the Mafia* (Korean)	*The Way Home* (Korean)
Latin America (1996–2002)	*Central do Brasil*, 1998 (Brazil/France)	*El Hijo de la Novia*, 2001 (Argentina/Spain)
Spain (2002 only)	*Spider-Man* (USA)	*Harry Potter and the Chamber of Secrets* (USA)
USA (2002 only)	*Spider-Man* (USA)	*Star Wars: Episode 2* (USA)

(Source: Based on Lange and Newmann-Baudais, World film market trends[16]; Focus,[12] Marché du Film, Observatoire Européen de l'Audiovisuel (**www.obs.coe.int**).

US concerns about declining share of global movie market

Although American film productions account for about 85 per cent of world film audiences,[10] some in Hollywood are increasingly concerned about dependence on world markets. In 2001, market share of American films fell by 16 per cent against local films around the world, and local films were bigger hits than US films in Korea, France, India, and other countries. Hollywood has its sights trained on the Asian markets (Japan, India, and China) and related markets (Arab countries, North Africa, East Africa, Indonesia, Iran, and South Asia) comprising over 75 per cent of the world's population.[17] Hollywood is actively seeking to acquire films from around the world with a more global appeal and to this end Sony and Miramax have acquisition executives seeking Chinese-language films in Hong Kong.[18] More and more Hollywood studios are giving a more international flavour (and appeal) to their films by co-producing abroad or by filming extensively on location in target markets. Africa, for example, is considered to be a safe bet by some Hollywood studios due to an almost total lack of cultural protectionist measures, and little resentment of America and the concept of an 'American Hero'. *Tears of the Sun* and *Emma's War* were filmed on location, and Disney's *Lafiya* is intended to interest Africans and Black Americans.[19]

Cultural protectionism

American film marketers need to take into account the cultural protectionism in some European countries and others, including Indonesia, Brazil, and Korea. Protective duties, import quotas, and screening time quotas are common tools used to protect local film production.[11] The French film industry receives approximately US$400 million per year in subsidies, an amount that has been growing each year. Other European countries with a cultural subsidy structure, such as Spain and Italy, are with France the most prolific of Europe's film producers.[20] In an effort to preserve the smaller, fragmented film industries around the world, Canada and 35 other countries have joined trailblazing France to negotiate a 'cultural exception' within the World Trade Organization, and the adoption of UNESCO's global convention on cultural diversity.[10] Hollywood has paid for protectionism of its own, too. The massive motion picture industry lobbying of Washington pushed hard for a decision favouring copyright extensions for creations like Disney's Mickey Mouse in *Steamboat Willie* (soon to expire). The US Supreme Court recently upheld a law extending to a total of 70 years after the creator's death, or 95 years in the case of creations owned by corporations.

Non-American films are beginning to attain better acceptance in the United States. *Crouching Tiger, Hidden Dragon* won the second highest number of Oscar awards, grossed US$100 million in North America despite American's traditional dislike for subtitled films. *Crouching Tiger, Hidden Dragon* is one of the 'breakthrough' films signalling the increasing acceptance of foreign films in the USA. Another such film is *Life is Beautiful*, the surprising humorous drama directed by Italian Roberto Benigni, where again a subtitled, foreign-language film succeeded in mainstream cinemas across North America to become the top grossing foreign language film in history, with more than US$43 million in receipts.

The film's key cultural components

Traditionally the movie industry is local. It is a multi-domestic industry, dealing with local actors, local scripts, and the indigenous language. Most films produced worldwide are targeted for local or regional audiences. Egypt and India are major movie film producers. Indian films are viewed from the Middle East to East Asia. Apart from the work of well-known filmmakers like Satyajit Ray, the bulk of Indian films is unknown to a non-Asian audience. Films essentially reflect the local cultural scene of the country where they were made. The local scene means familiar landscapes, clothing, institutions, scenes, urban sites, and ways of interacting between people. A film also features products because product placement has become a way of increasing film budgets everywhere, resulting in the presentation of local products or global ones distinguished by a local touch. In Hong Kong, films feature the names of companies that purchased product placement more prominently than they do the names of the film stars.[21] Local cues portrayed in films, such as the US legal system inherent to courtroom dramas, are most often unfamiliar to foreign viewers and generate an impression of the unknown, which may be positive (exoticism) but is usually viewed negatively. Films that are popular usually reflect the values held by the audience. In Germany, for instance, a rather collectivist and duty-oriented society gradually evolved post-war into one that valued self-determination and pleasure-seeking. This change in value orientation was reflected in an increasing popularity of the *James Bond* series, John Wayne films, *Jaws*, and *Superman* where the protagonist drives the narrative to fulfil his own goals and the main values of the work are 'fun'.[11]

Films are about storytelling (e.g. drama, comedy), through a visual and spoken narrative based primarily on language. This causes one of the key problems when selling films worldwide: how will speakers from other linguistic contexts understand a Mexican or a Japanese film if it is still in its original language. Generally, when Hollywood studios produce films intended for international markets, they intentionally minimize the dialogue and simplify it, so translations are easier to make, and narrative cues are embedded in the context.[22] Partly for this reason, filmmakers emphasize the visuals of a film when the overseas market is targeted. Most countries either use dubbing or subtitles. Dubbing is more costly to implement because it requires specialized professionals to draft a text that fits, as well as actors to dub the voiceover that replaces the original voice soundtrack. In the case of Disney's animated films like *Tarzan*, musical soundtrack dubbing may bankroll international stars like Phil Collins singing in five major languages, including two types of Spanish (Castilian and American), with local stars doing the dubbing in smaller markets.[23] Dubbing is very popular in most European countries, where industries have grown up around the activity in large countries like Italy, Germany, France, Spain. Dubbing is also popular in Asia. Viewers of dubbed films are accustomed to the inevitable mismatch between actors' lips and their dubbed pronouncements. Smaller countries tend to use subtitles because the dubbing process is too costly. In Finland for instance, most films are subtitled in Finnish and Swedish, the two official languages. US viewers have never accepted dubbed films, with *Crouching Tiger, Hidden Dragon* and *Amélie* being notable exceptions. They also dislike watching subtitled foreign language films. Perhaps more importantly, US distributors consider foreign-language films as more suited to the niche 'art-house' cinema circuit than the mainstream. This, among other factors, explains the very low market share of foreign films in the US, where more than 97 per cent of the films viewed are locally produced.[9]

Story-telling is also culturally meaningful, whether scripts put emphasis on fine-grained psychological relationships between characters (e.g. Swedish films by Ingmar Bergman), historical topics, action films, mob and gangster films, kung fu, or any kind of drama that is meaningful to the audience. The film script may finish with a happy ending or not. According to Czech-born Hollywood director Milos Forman (*One Flew over the Cuckoo's Nest, Ragtime*), the main difference between US and European films is that Hollywood likes happy endings and 'macho fairy tales', while Europeans prefer more ambiguity and realism.[24]

There are also a number of other components for a film, including music, soundtrack, and images. The most significant cultural component in a film is in the interaction between the key characters: their communication style typically reflects a context-bound interaction style. When people interact with Al Pacino in *The Godfather*, it cannot at all be compared with people interacting with Toshiro Mifune in the *Seven Samurai*. (For more information, go to **www.sprout.org**.)

The global film: the exception rather than the rule

The market for films is not per se a global market. There still will remain some important market barriers related to language and culture. However, the market is far from being a purely multi-domestic one. As noted above, imports are considerable and viewers are eager to watch foreign films. Many spectators like both national films (identity enhancing) and foreign (mostly American) films. There is a greater chance that a film will reach a worldwide audience if a story is rather simple and universal, relatively context-free and easy to capture. An example of this is Japanese filmmaker Akiro Kurosawa's *Seven Samurai*, a global success later adapted by Hollywood as *The Magnificent Seven*, a Western deprived of its Japanese context, with a larger global reach than the original film. Filmmaker Jean-Jacques Annaud (www.jjannaud.com/) has produced films that reached a worldwide audience because apart from their artistic quality, they eluded certain cultural obstacles (such as *La Guerre du Feu*, devoid of language, as was an interpretation of Jack London's *The Bear*). The popularity of animated films, such as *Finding Nemo* and *The Lion King*, may in part be due to their lack of particularistic cultural cues. *The Lord of the Rings* series (www.lordoftherings.net/), although filmed on location in the Southern Island of New Zealand, has no context-bound cues for the spectator apart from those from J.R.R. Tolkien's fantasy works. Appeals are also important to establish when targeting wider audiences: violence, action, science fiction, sex and eroticism, and suspense are likely to appeal broadly and in different cultures. In an international business analysis of film, six characteristics of American films were identified as: a fast pace, sexual tension, graphic violence, repetition of a fable or storyline, and a happy or spectacular ending.[13] Less likely to appeal worldwide are family intrigues, psychological dramas, social criticism, and moral narratives – more likely to characterize European films.

Questions

1. Why have American films been so successful over the last half century? Outline what you consider to be the key success factors for a film (type of story and genre; actors; directors, pace, music, and so on). Was the fascination for the American culture and way of life the prominent reason for that success? What was the contribution of the American melting pot with its huge diversity of migrants' origins to the creativity and global outlook of the American film industry?

2. What is the future of local films? Should they still target a local language and culture audience? Is there any future for local movie industries? Why? Take country examples if you wish.

3. If you were a ROW (rest-of-the-world, that is, non-US) film director willing to reach a wider audience how would you go about increasing your chances of being accepted by the audience in more countries?

4. Are films primarily artistic pieces or are they mere commodities? Should filmmaking be seen as an industry or as an art? If compromises are possible how would you devise them?

In order to answer the questions, you may use the web-based information in addresses mentioned below. If you want more information you may conduct a key word search on www.google.com, and generally you will find it.

General: **www.screendigest.com/**: the pre-eminent source of business intelligence, research and analysis on global audiovisual media;
Box office data for films: **www.boxoff.com/** and
www.boxoff.com/scripts/newsviewstory.asp?ID=4397
Research guide in film studies (from Yale University, with links to industry data for many countries): **www.library.yale.edu/humanities/film/industry.html**

On the US film industry: **www.zeal.com/category/preview.jhtml?cid=317854**
On US/EU market shares: **www.culture.fr/culture/actualites/politique/diversite/wto-en3.htm; www.suite101.com/subjectheadings/contents.cfm/307**

On French films: **http://perso.club-internet.fr/hwelty/France/FrenchMovies.html; http://www.unf.edu/groups/spinnaker/archives/2002/feb27/french.html; http://www.indiewire.com/biz/biz_020306_WorldCine2.html**

About Jean-Jacques Annaud: **www.rottentomatoes.com/p/JeanJacquesAnnaud-1040523/**

On Fnnish films: **http://www.film.prodigybiz.com/; http://www.preview-online.com/jan_feb/feature_articles/focus_on_finland/**

About Chinese, Asian and Australian films: **www.heroic-cinema.com/www.htm; www.expatsinchina.com/culture/movies/; www.the-trades.com/column.php?columnid=622; http://fpeng.peopledaily.com.cn/200005/22/eng20000522_41353.html** (WTO entry and the Chinese film industry)

About films in Egypt and Italy: **http://kvc.minbuza.nl/uk/theme/film/**

About Japanese films: **www.lisashea.com/japan/movies/mov_main.html; www.cdjapan.co.jp/movie/jmovie/;**

www.japanreference.com/Art_&_Culture/Cinematography/index.shtml;
www.jinjapan.org/today/culture/culture15.html;
www.giapponegiappone.it/japan/culture/cinema.htm

About the pros and cons of dubbing: **www.cnn.com/SHOWBIZ/Movies/9908/26/
life.is.beautiful/**

About Iranian films: **www.netiran.com/Htdocs/Clippings/Art/951215XXAR05.html**
(a debate with Abbas Kiarostami)

Saskia Faulk and Jean-Claude Usunier prepared this case solely to provide material for class discussion. The authors do not intend to illustrate either effective or ineffective handling of a business situation. The authors may have disguised certain names and other identifying information to protect confidentiality.

© IRM/HEC, 2003   Version: (A) 2003-09-04

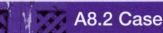

A8.2 Case

Fast food – Halal or Haram?

It was a crowded table at this noisy North African KFC outlet. Kader and four of his friends lounged comfortably in their chairs, eating and talking at a leisurely pace. After a range of references to France, movies, friends, and cars, the lunch companions launched into a discussion of the calls for an American boycott.

'I've been boycotting Israeli products for ages, that's why I don't drink Coke', stated Ahmed. 'Oh, come on: that's just one of a million rumours going around by email, you can look at any "rumours" website to find out the truth', retorted Fadi, 'As for me I drink Pepsi because they refused to go into Israel while others did.'

Kader sensed an opportunity: 'Look at you both, if you really are so politically aware, why are you wearing Nike shoes and smoking Marlboros? You should be embarrassed!' Ahmed laughed as he answered 'Mr. Kader, my friend, what are you doing enjoying your KFC food, then? It's an American company isn't it?' 'We all know that, what a lot of people don't realize is that everyone in that kitchen is an Arab, all the food comes from Arab suppliers, all . . .' Fadi interrupted, 'How do you know? How do any of us know? You believe what they say in their ads? Did you check with their suppliers? My friend, you, and all of us, are in the dark.' Taking a deep puff on his cigarette, Ahmed stated emphatically: 'I agree with all the calls to boycott, I don't want to support the Americans. As they say "by buying American products you cause Palestinian blood to flow" but what would I smoke, what would I wear, where would I eat? You tell me where there are some good local "light" cigarettes.' He squashed the cigarette in the ashtray. 'And where are the great Arab clothes designers and shoe manufacturers? When I'm at home I like Starbucks even though the head of the company's a Zionist, and THAT's not a rumour, bro'. Let's face it, we don't have a choice. Look, my shoes are counterfeit Nike's, and at least I don't go to McDonald's.'

Fadi snorted, and pointed his finger at Kader. 'Look, Ahmed, you are my friend, I wouldn't say anything bad about you, but you think that not going to McDonald's is going to help the Palestinians? The Iraqis? You know I don't normally eat here, you invited me. I don't believe that by wearing a Tommy Hilfiger shirt I'm oppressing Palestinians. Why don't you start your own clothes and shoes company, then I would know it's really "Arab" ', he added quietly. Kader shook his head, and said 'Come on guys, let's not wear each other out. It's true, though, that instead of Hilfiger you could choose a European company, at least they're not as bad. Diesel is cool. Puma is cool. I read that the guy who runs Hilfiger is a racist, did you know that? Marlboro addicts should switch to smokes like Gauloises Blondes.' Then he lightly touched each friend on the arm, adding 'Guys, guys, we can do better, the point is we don't have to be slaves to American marketing. What's the big deal? We can make a little sacrifice on favorite brands compared with the price that Palestinians pay in blood.' Fadi had been quiet for a while. Suddenly, he spoke out 'You know, I heard this Lebanese girl speaking, she started a pro-boycott organization. She said that boycotting American products isn't just about hurting the American economy, she said it's more about getting the Americans to understand that their interests lie with us, 200 million Arabs, instead of the 4 million Israelis!'.[25-27]

Fast food restaurants in the Middle East and other sensitive parts of the world have been hit by boycotts, criticism, and direct violence. Starbucks, McDonald's, Pizza Hut, KFC, and others are pawns in the global game of traditionalists versus progressives, of conservatives versus liberals, of protectionism versus globalization. Fast food companies have been the target of religious edicts, protests, vandalism, and aggressive competitive tactics, some of which have been openly supported by governments.

Globalization in the Middle East

The Middle East is a particular case of development. Most economies in the Middle East are state controlled. Many are young states with a colonial legacy, and some were Cold War battlefields. The concept of Arab nationalism restricts some countries in an inflexible frame of reference. In some cases, the legitimacy of Middle East governments is challenged by their peoples' perception that they are passive in the face of the regularly televised humiliations of Palestinians, and foreign influence in countries like Afghanistan and Iraq. Various conflicts have justified large expenditures on arms, reducing resources for education and social benefits. These factors combine to create a polarized ideological environment where pro-globalization pragmatists may be in opposition to Islamists. Such conditions are not conducive to good business.

As Arab nationalism has worn thin over the last two decades, the opposing forces in Arab societies have become more visible. Those likely to welcome globalization and its manifestations like McDonald's into their countries tend to be more affluent. Those on the lower end of the social scale are more likely to embrace ancient identities based on cultural, religious, ethnic, or linguistic differences. In his book *Jihad vs. McWorld*, Benjamin Barber[28] attempts to understand these opposing forces. 'McWorld', or globalism, offers integration into a larger economic system, and access to credit, markets and technology. 'Jihad', a term Barber uses loosely to describe tribalism, represents the fragmentation of societal identities, with 'Jihad' offering its proponents a local identity, sense of community, and solidarity against perceived outsiders. Jihad being the compelling ideology of the 'losers' of a capitalist economic system, it is also the ideology of the majority, of the masses. With the cosmopolitan exception of Dubai, these two axes describe the tensions within which foreign-owned or -influenced businesses must operate in the Middle East, representing a complex marketing environment.

Fast food has quickly established itself as a growing trend in the Middle East. In Saudi Arabia, for example, fast food outlets account for 15 per cent of all food-service sales, compared with 32 per cent in the US. However, sales by fast food outlets have grown by 10 per cent per year over five years. Table 8.4 gives an idea of the fast growth rate of the fast food market in Saudi Arabia.

Table 8.4 Number of fast food outlets in Saudi Arabia (1990–2002)

Food type	1990	1997	2002
Burger	95	181	268
Chicken	17	70	151
Coffee/baked goods	16	61	244
Ice cream	24	174	309
Pizza	49	136	209
Sandwich/Arabic	11	50	112

(Source: McNulty.[29])

In Egypt, fast food has become a part of daily life. According to a recent study done in Cairo, 23 per cent of the city's population buy foreign branded fast food at least twice per week. The main consumers were teenagers and adult males, and consumption mainly took place via home or office delivery (Zayed, 2004). Fast food outlets have become ubiquitous in the Middle East with the exception of Syria. Table 8.5 gives an idea of the degree to which fast food outlets have become part of the landscape.

Table 8.5 Non-exhaustive list of fast food outlets in predominantly Muslim countries

	Domino's Pizza	Hardee's Restaurants	Subway	Burger King	McDonald's
Bahrain	4	6	–	3	8[h]
Egypt	8	14	–	–	>50[d]
Indonesia	–	–	–	–	108
Jordan	1	–	–	5	–
Kuwait	5	–	16	47	34[e]
Lebanon	4	10	3	8	–
Malaysia	19	–	2	21	–
Oman	–	–	1	–	–
Pakistan	1	–	9	–	21[g]
Qatar		4	6	6	–
Saudi Arabia	36	24	13	35	71[c]
Turkey	32	–	3	98	111[a]
United Arab Emirates	6	21	32	21	25[f]

(Sources: **www.dominospizza.com**; **www.hardeesrestaurants.com**; **www.subway.com**; **www.bk.com**; **www.mcdonalds.com**.)

Other food service chains with significant presence included at the time of writing KFC with 207 units in Indonesia,[i] 128 in Malaysia,[j] and 36 in Egypt;[k] *Pizza Hut* with 66 units in Saudi Arabia[l] and a strong presence elsewhere; and *Burger King* with 47 units in Kuwait, 35 in Saudi Arabia,[m] and 21 in the United Arab, Emirates (UAE), Allied-Domecq-owned *Baskin Robbins* developed 133 units in Saudi Arabia.[n] According to the website, *Subway* has 9 units in Iraq, although most were temporarily closed.[o]

Notes:
a. **http://www.mcdonalds.com.tr/restoranlar/restoranlar.asp**.
b. Murphy, 2003.
c. **http://www.mcdonalds.com/countries/**.
d. **http://www.mcdonalds-egypt.com/**.
e. **http://www.mcdonalds.com/content/countries/kuwait.html**.
f. **http://www.mcdonalds.com/content/countries/United Arab Emirates.html**.
g. **http://www.mcdonalds.com.pk**.
h. **http://www.mcdonalds.com/content/countries/bahrain.html**.
i. **http://www.kfcindonesia.com**.
j. **http://www.kfc.com.my/outlets/index.html**.
k. **http://www.egyptyellowpages.com.eg/index.asp**.
l. **http://www.pizzahutsaudia.com**.
m. **http://www.bk.com**.
n. **http://www.baskinrobbins.com**.
o. **http://www.subway.com**.

Religious edicts (fatwa)

Prominent Muslim scholars have issued religious edicts (fatwa) against the consumption of American products in Egypt, Qatar, Syria, Kuwait, and other countries. Sheikh Youssef Al-Qaradawi, Muslim scholar and president of the European Council for Fatwa and Research, has issued several fatwa calling for a Muslim boycott of Israeli and American products, stating that 'To buy their goods is to support tyranny and oppression. It's a duty not to do that'.[30] The Grand Imam of Islam's highest authority, Al-Azhar, stated that it is 'forbidden' not to follow the boycott of Israel and the supporters of Israel ('America is a second Israel'[31]), issuing a fatwa on the subject.[30] In a more precisely worded fatwa regarding franchises, Dr Mohammad Saeed Al-Bouti of Damascus University's Sharia school said that 'American products which must be boycotted are those whose revenues go to the US such as American cigarettes and restaurants. There are too many of these companies in our countries'. He specified that products produced in Islamic countries according to franchise agreements were forbidden because a portion of revenues from these products was given to the American company.[31] Other fatwas issued regarding the anti-Israel/anti-US boycotts have been issued by Dr Fu'ad Mukhaymar, head of the Egyptian Sunni Egyptian Institutions, and Dr As-Sayed Nuh, Kuwait University professor.[31]

Vandalism, protests and violence

The destruction of a fast food outlet, defacing of its facade, breaking windows, and graffiti are common ways of expressing one's disagreement with all that is represented by US fast food operations. McDonald's windows were broken by angry pro-Palestinian demonstrators in Oman, and an outlet in Bahrain was defaced by stone-throwing youth.[32] KFC was attacked in Pakistan, Indonesia, Lebanon, and Greece.[33]

Burger King, McDonald's, and Starbucks were the sites for sit-ins and protests in Beirut, where they blocked access to the counters and held pro-Palestinian messages in their hands.[32] Pizza Hut was bombed in Lebanon.[33] KFC was bombed in 2001 in Makassar, Indonesia.[10] In 2003, protesters closed the KFC outlet in Palu, Indonesia to express their resistance to a war in Iraq.[10] Students in Beirut protested in front of Starbucks outlets and handed out leaflets to inform people of Starbucks' chief executive's pro-Israel stance. A bomb exploded outside KFC in Pakistan in December 2001, causing no injuries. A KFC outlet was destroyed in Cairo by anti-American protesters.[30] Mobs attacked several KFC outlets in Karachi, Pakistan in 2003. The company decided against further expansion in Pakistan in the short term, preferring to invest in less risky locations. At McDonald's in New Delhi, protesters closed the outlet, screaming 'America off our soil!'.[34]

Muslim food prescriptions

'Halal' is the Arabic word for 'Lawful', being food that is produced in the manner stipulated in Muslim Holy texts. In the case of restaurants, 'Halal' mainly applies to meats, dairy products, and other items contaminated by meat (**www.eat-Halal.com**; **www.zabihah.com**). Halal directives pertain mainly to slaughter, when the animal should be killed by a Muslim who invokes the name of Allah as the animal dies. Death should be caused by a slit throat causing the animal to bleed to death. The slaughterhouse should be supervised by a pious Muslim man.[35] In Europe, the largest Halal meat processing plants are in Belgium. Some Muslims insist that meats be Zabihah in addition to Halal: that the owner of the meat-processing business is a Muslim, that the animal was fed exclusively on a vegetable diet and not treated with growth hormones, that the animal be hand-slaughtered and not stunned.[36] Devout Muslims are generally advised by Muslim organizations to avoid 'Most items' at fast food outlets, although some fast food chains attempt to purchase some Halal ingredients (**www.eal-Halal.com/eatingout.shtml**). Muslims are advised to avoid particularly non-Halal pizza restaurants where there is a 'high risk' of contamination from pork products and meat by-products in cheese toppings. In France the many Muslim patrons often justify KFC purchasing Halal meat, although the company does not publicize the fact nor do they display their Halal certificate (which is on hand in the kitchen if a Muslim wanted to inspect it), for fear of alienating other customer segments. The Halal market was estimated at US$150 billion in 2002. Food industry experts have predicted that the Halal food trend will grow, with demand rising and increasing numbers of food suppliers and restaurant operators seeking Halal certification.[37] Table 8.6 puts Muslim food restrictions in the context of the world's other major religions.

New Muslim-based competition

In some countries, local Muslim and Halal operators have stepped in to attract Muslim customers, due to the expressed reluctance of some Muslims to frequent fast food outlets. Reasons cited by Muslims for avoiding fast food and prepared foods generally include preparation and service by non-Muslim staff, contamination of vegetarian and vegetable/fruit offerings by unlawful ('Haram') meat products, animal fat, gelatin, wine vinegar, enzymes, emulsifiers, non-Halal rennet (as used in cheese and other dairy products), and vanilla-laced sweets because vanilla essence may contain alcohol.[35] In France, there is a definite trend towards offering Halal fast food on the American fried chicken and hamburger model. The kitchen equipment and menu at outlets named among others 'ChickenSpot' and 'Paris Fried Chicken' resembles that of KFC and McDonald's, and the equipment is identical to that used by KFC. A similar phenomenon is visible in Canada, Singapore, Australasia, and the UK. In the UK, for example, Chicken Cottage, a Halal fast food chain, currently has 62 outlets and has doubled in size within the past two years (**www.chickencottage.co.uk/2003/contact.htm**). In Egypt, a local entrepreneur started Mo'men ('believer' in Arabic) in 1998 as a substitute for McDonald's. The chain, reported to be 'doing well', with outlets that are 'always packed', serves burgers and chicken nuggets, along with some traditional Egyptian items.[38] All machines and equipment used by Mo'men restaurants are American-made.[30] Mo'men offers vegetarian items that cater to Christians fasting for Lent, and a variety of festive menu items following the Muslim Eid festival.[39] In other countries, such as Malaysia and Singapore, restaurants apply for Halal certification from an official Muslim organization. In Malaysia, for example, KFC and Pizza Hut are advised by a 'Syariah Council' that oversees the supply chain and food production and service to ensure that all are Halal.[40] In Singapore, the Majlis Ugama Islam Singapura inspects and provides certificates for Halal products and services (**www.muis.gov.sg**).

Boycotts targeting fast food chains

As stated in several reports, fast food is often a target of boycotts because it is far from being a necessity, particularly when there are local brands as alternatives. Recent Arab boycotts are considered to be an extension of the original anti-Israel boycott, which is still technically in force in some countries (**www.proislam.com/muslim_boycott.htm**; **www.petitiononline.com/sb2002/petition.html**). Boycotts intensified and took on different forms in the run-up to the hostilities in Iraq, with Malaysians focusing on Coca-Cola and Pepsi, Thai Muslims setting up 'US product free zones', Moroccans calling for a US dollar boycott, and Egyptians boycotting McDonald's specifically for its alleged Jewish ties.[31] In Bahrain, a major supermarket chain removed American products from the shelves, replacing

Table 8.6 Food restrictions of Muslims compared with other major religions

Islam	Ingredients	Preparation	Consumption
Food guidelines stem from the Koran, the Hadith, and cultural traditions	No pork or pork by-products, such as gelatin; No carnivorous animals with fangs or claws; No donkeys, elephants, or monkeys; No alcohol.	Meats should be from animals slaughtered by a Muslim who invokes Allah; Slit throat/bleeding is the preferred slaughter method; Stunning animal prior to slaughter is not proper; Halal foods should be prepared separately from *Haram* foods, with different utensils.	The daylight fasting period must be respected during Ramadan (one of the 'Pillars of Islam'); According to tradition, women should eat separately from men, particularly when guests are present (some regions); According to some traditions men should eat first, a sacrifice should be made at the time of Ramadan.
Judaism Food guidelines established in the Old Testament (Leviticus)	Ruminants with cloven hoofs are fit for consumption ('Kosher'); No pork or pork by-products; No animal hindquarters to be eaten; No horsemeat, no seafood lacking fins and scales.	Separate preparation of meat and dairy products; No food preparation work or washing up to be done on the Sabbath; Animal should be slaughtered rapidly by a God-fearing man.	Meat and dairy products should not be consumed at the same meal; There are clear traditions about foods to be consumed at certain feast days.
Christianity Bible and the Pope (Catholics), the Patriarch (Orthodox) or denominational authority	Catholics should avoid meat on Fridays; Orthodox fasting may prescribe avoidance of olive oil or other ingredients.	Fasting or deprivation should be practised during Lent; The Orthodox Church has prescriptive rules for extended and frequent fasting, more than other Christians.	
Hinduism Regulations stated in the Code of Manu	Meat is not encouraged but allowed according to cultural traditions; No beef; In the case of Jainism, no living creatures should be consumed.		
Buddhism	It is accepted that people can and often must take lives of other living creatures in order to continue living. It is desirable to reduce the extent of the slaughter as much as possible, however. Serious Buddhists avoid meat.		

them with alternatives produced by companies not affiliated with the US.[41] In Pakistan, KFC chief executive Rafiq Rangoonwala said that during the beginning of hostilities in Afghanistan and Iraq, sales at KFC outlets dropped by 5–10 per cent, but soon regained earlier levels.[42] In Egypt, Jordan, and some Gulf countries, in-store sales were down but home delivery stayed the same or even rose, suggesting that some customers were simply avoiding the social pressure of being seen at the restaurant.

Some people supported boycotts for their perceived cultural benefits, such as protecting local culture from 'American culture'. Regarding fast food franchises, Muslim economist Dr Monzer Kahf bemoaned American fast food replacing 'Our traditional hommos, fool, sharwerma, falafel/ta'miyyah, kebab, booza, and other traditional fast food you see all over the Muslim land from Morocco to Malaysia and Indonesia'.[31]

The context of fast food chain boycotts

In its original form the anti-Israel boycott was initiated on 2 December 1945 as a means of refusing any kind of Arab support to Israel. The original goal of the boycott was to isolate Israel from other countries, particularly its geographic neighbours. The boycott originally operated on three levels: companies trading directly with Israel, companies that do business with Israel, and companies that do business with companies trading with Israel (Bard, 2004). Companies allegedly operating on all or some of these three levels were listed by Arab governments to facilitate their identification by local traders. 'The boycott of Israel was designed to destroy the state,' according to Yoram Sheni, Israeli Foreign Ministry division head. Companies were forced to choose between trading with Israel or the more populous Arab countries. In one example, Coca-Cola traded with Israel starting in the mid-1960s (earning blacklist status in the Arab world until 1992) while Pepsi-Cola traded with the Arab world and was barred from trading with Israel until 1992.[43] In 1977, during the Carter Administration, the Congress made it illegal for US companies to participate in the boycott.[44] Since then, contrary to expectations, trade between Arab countries and the US has continued to improve.

In 1994, six Gulf Cooperation Council states announced that they would no longer follow the secondary boycott. The beginnings of the peace process reduced the power of the boycott, and indeed dismantling the boycott was one of the conditions set out in peace treaties between Israel, Egypt, Jordan, and the Palestinian Authority. The boycott was estimated to have cost Israel some US$40 billion in lost trade as well as a 'psychological impact'.[43] As a result of Israel's violent response to the Intifada in 2001, the Arab League's Boycott Office revived its activities at the behest of Arab leaders in Damascus, with the notable absence of influential Arab countries like Egypt and Jordan.[44] The statement they issued said that the boycott was a 'peaceful, legal and noble' action to support Palestinians.

Why do they care? The transnational aspect of Muslim cultures

When the French government declared in January 2004 that Muslim headscarves were to be banned from schools, there were vocal demonstrations all over the world. Muslim women and men in Egypt, Indonesia, Lebanon, the Palestinian territories, Syria, the UK, and the USA joined French demonstrators to protest against the ban. This event illustrated the solidarity felt by Muslims around the world on certain issues, particularly where Islam meets the 'West'. In what some thinkers have referred to as the transnational nature of Islam, or 'active pan-Islamic consciousness', Muslims tend to be concerned for the welfare of Muslims in other countries. Founder of Pakistan and poet Sir Muhammad Iqbal wrote on the topic: 'Our essence is not bound to any place; . . . . Nor any fatherland do we profess except Islam'.[45]

Partly for this reason, there is widespread concern among Muslims everywhere about the Palestinian issue, and the US-led conflict in Iraq.

The Muslim world, which will comprise one-third of humanity by 2025, is far from monolithic. Ethnic, racial, and nationalist differences often bedevil efforts at unity. Within Islam the religious distinctions, such as those between Sunni and Shi'a, are divisive. Differences aside, Muslims generally hold themselves to be members of a global community, or Ummah. Despite the manifold historical, regional, and national differences in Islamic institutions and interpretations of the Koran, Shari'a (Islamic Law) and Hadith (Traditions of the Prophet), there are commonalities in the stated beliefs of politicized Islam centred on the rejection of material capitalism. The rise of Islamist beliefs and the search for an Islamic foundation for political and economic life is most likely a reaction to the perceived secularization brought on by 'Modernity'.[46]

Political Islamic movements appear to agree on protesting against the invasion of foreign capital, culture, and goods. The founder of the internationally active Muslim Brotherhood and father of political Islam, Egyptian Hasan Al-Bana, declared in 1928 that Europeans were using materialism and other devices to foster atheism among Muslims. Today, the Muslim Brotherhood is considered to represent mainstream Islam in Egypt and Jordan, providing a credible opposition. In a similar vein, the Iranian Ayatollah Khomeini said that the pro-capitalist policies of the Shah allowed American capitalists to enslave Iranians and aimed to destroy Islam and its sacred laws. In his book *America and the Third World War*, Osama Bin Laden challenged Muslims to rise up against the intentional spread of Westernization, which he said destroys Muslim rights.[45] Organizers of anti-American boycotts, such as activists, religious leaders, and students, argue that Israel is the beneficiary of taxes paid by US corporations via US foreign aid.

An issue that appears to unite Muslims the world over is support for the Palestinians, hence their vocal political and economic support for Palestinian and anti-Israeli causes. Both rejection of Western material culture and support for Palestine have been important in understanding a backlash against McDonald's and other overtly 'Western' and American brands which intensified during Israeli campaigns in the West Bank and Gaza following the beginning of the so-called 'Second' or 'Al-Aqsa' Intifada, initiated on 29 September 2000.[47] Support for the Palestinian struggle is often cited by Muslims around the world as reason to reject Israel and perceived supporters of the state of Israel. The Palestinian issue has united the 21 members of the Cairo-based League of Arab States (known as the Arab League) for years, notably through its support of the Israel boycott. Apart from media reports of Muslim statements to this effect, official sources confirm this view, such as the pronouncements of clerics and political leaders in Iran. The Egyptian State Information Service published a report in English, for example, making economic arguments that the best way to condemn Israel is via a boycott.[48] In the United Arab Emirates and elsewhere in the Arab world, phrases like this are common on websites, leaflets, and email messages: 'The penny you spend to buy these products amounts to another [Israeli] bullet for the body of our brave Palestinian brothers'.[32]

As a result of Israel's response to the Intifada and the Arab League's call for it, a boycott was announced in Saudi Arabia and lists were circulated of American products and their non-US substitutes. As in many recent boycotts, news of it spread via the Internet, e-mail messages, SMS, voicemail messages, newspaper editorials (even in state-run newspapers) mosque sermons, and fliers.[41] In a related development, Burger King opened an outlet in the Ma'aleh Adumim Mall in 1999. The mall was located in a settlement in the occupied territories. After an Arab boycott and letter-writing campaign to Burger King, the company closed its controversial outlet. McDonald's has so far refused to open branches in the West Bank.[49]

Questions

1. Why have fast food restaurants been so successful outside their country of origin, the United States? Consider basic, universal aspects of consumer behaviour in your arguments.

2. How does religion affect consumer behaviour, especially concerning eating habits, food products and beverages? Take examples from different great religions. What kinds of problems are involved for fast food restaurants to take into account religious prescriptions concerning food? What kinds of responses are given by fast food companies in terms of product and service adaptation?

3. To what extent are fast food in general and fast food restaurants in particular associated with (a) globalization; (b) Westernization; (c) modernization; (d) threats to local cultural identities? How could fast food restaurant chains handle their marketing communications in order to avoid boycotts and reduce violence against their outlets?

4. Comment about the ambivalence of Muslim-based fast food competition.

Saskia Faulk and Jean-Claude Usunier prepared this case solely to provide material for class discussion. The authors do not intend to illustrate either effective or ineffective handling of a business situation. The authors may have disguised certain names and other identifying information to protect confidentiality.

This case was designed to present a complex marketing situation. It presents sensitive political, cultural, economic, and religious issues, and was in no way intended to offend, nor to advocate, the cause of any party.

© IRM/HEC, 2008   Version: (A) 2008-04-16

Appendix references

1. Guider, Elisabeth (2003), 'Warner Bros. Hits $1 Billion B.O. Overseas', *Variety*, July 22nd, www.variety.com/article/VR1117889759.html?categoryid=1278&cs=1.

2. Hooper, John, Jonathan Watts, Jon Henley, John Aglionby, John Gittings, Giles Tremlett, David Fickling, Luke Harding, Jo Tuckman, and Andrew Osborn (2002), 'World Wide Wizard (Harry Potter)', *The Guardian*, 8 November, http://film.guardian.co.uk/features/featurepages/0,,835664,00.html.

3. Arlidge, John (2003), 'Harry Potter and the Crock of Gold', *The Observer*, 14 June, www.theage.com.au/articles/2003/06/13/1055220769388.html.

4. Waxman, Sharon (1990), 'Hollywood Attuned to World Markets', *Washington Post*, 26 October, www.washingtonpost.com/wp-srv/inatl/longterm/mia/part2.htm.

5. Fitzgerald, Kate (2003), 'Hollywood and the Demographic Revolution', *AdAge*, 15 July.

6. Lumiere (2003), 'In 2002 European Films were Unable to Repeat the Exceptional Performance Achieved in 2001', 21 March. www.obs.coe.int/about/oea/pr/lumiere_mar03.html.

7. Focus 2002: World Film Market Trends (2002), *Cannes Market*, Undated. www.obs.coe.int/online_publication/reports/focus2002.pdf.

8. Lange, André (2003), 'Harry, Billy, Amélie . . . And the Others?', *Cannes Market*, Undated, www.obs.coe.int/online_publication/reports/focus2002.pdf.

9. Center for Strategic and International Studies (CSIS) (2001), *Culture and Globalisation*, Undated.

10. Riding, Alan (2003), 'Filmmakers Seek Protection from U.S. Dominance', *The New York Times*, 5 February, http://query.nytimes.com/gst/fullpage.html?res=9E07E0DE1E38F936A35751C0A9659C8B63.

11. Garncarz, Joseph (2002), 'Germany Goes Global: Challenging the Theory of Hollywood's Dominance on International Markets', in *Media in Transition, Globalisation and Convergence: An International Conference*, MIT, Cambridge, Massachusetts.

12. Focus 2003: World Film Market Trends (2003), *Marché du Film*, Undated. www.obs.coe.int/online_publication/reports/focus2003.pdf.

13. Fuma Shapiro, Simona (2000), 'The Culture Thief', *The New Rules*, Fall, www.newrules.org/journal/nrfall00culture.html.

14. ABN Amro (2000), *Filmspace: Behind the Scenes*, 12 September.

15. Anholt, Simon (1999), 'Getting on the Brandwagon', The IFC review of private investment in developing countries (Presentation), Fall, www.ifc.org/ifcext/publications.nsf/attachmentsByTitle/IMPACT_Fall1999/$FILE/Impact+Fall+1999.pdf.

16. Lange, André and Susan Newmann-Baudais (2003), 'World Film Market Trends', *Focus*, Marché du Film, Observatoire Européen de l'Audiovisuel, www.obs.coe.int.

17. Kapur, Shekhar (2002), 'Dying Cowboy, Pouncing Tiger', *Mail & Guardian* (South Africa), 30 August.

18. Anon (2001), 'Hey, World! Hollywood's Coming!', *Telegraph* (London), 31 March, www.telegraph.co.uk/arts/main.jhtml?xml=/arts/2001/03/31/bfgrit31.xml.

19. Kariuki, John (2003), 'Africa at Large: Hollywood Goes to War in Africa', *The East African* (Kenya), 23 June, www.afrika.no/Detailed/3748.html.

20. Dollt, Andreas (2003), 'Cinema Statistics: The Upward Trend in Cinema-Going Came to a Halt in 2002', *Statistics in Focus: Industry, Trade and Services*, 3 April, www.eds-destatis.de/en/downloads/sif/np_03_08.pdf.

21. Chew, Eugene (1999), 'Life Goes On: The 1999 Hong Kong Film Festival', *Toto Cinema Matters*, Undated, http://peteg.org/toto/hkff2.htm.

22. Anon (2001), 'Interview with Howard Stringer, Chairman and Ceo of Sony America', *Frontline*, Public Broadcasting Service (USA), June, www.pbs.org/wgbh/pages/frontline/shows/hollywood/interviews/stringer.html.

23. Groves, Don (1999), 'Disney Goes Ape with Tarzan Dubs', *Variety*, 14 June, http://genesisfan.net/tarzan/disney-goes-ape-with-tarzan-dubs.html.

24. Gaydos, Steven (2000), 'Forman Brings Euro Touch to U.S. Movies', *Variety*, 10 January, www.variety.com/article/VR1117760682.html?categoryid=13&cs=1.

25. Blanford, Nicholas (2002), 'Arab Citizens Seize Boycott Banner', *Christian Science Monitor*, 7 May, www.csmonitor.com/2002/0507/p06s01-wome.html.

26. Kilani, Hala (2002), 'Grassroots Campaign Takes Aim at U.S. Economy', *The Daily Star* (Beirut), 13 April, www.lebanonwire.com/0204/02041306DS.htm.

27. Smucker, Philip and Nicholas Blandford (2002), 'Arab States Vent Rising Wrath', *Christian Science Monitor*, 22 April, www.csmonitor.com/2002/0422/p01s04-wome.html.

28. Barber, Benjamin R. (1992), 'Jihad vs. Mcworld', *The Atlantic Online*, March, www.theatlantic.com/politics/foreign/barberf.htm.

29. McNulty, Brian (2002), 'The Food Service Market in Saudi Arabia', *IMES Ireland*, 16 February.

30. Abdel-Halim, Mustafa (2003), 'Muslims Rally against U.S. Products, Big Mac Feels Backlash', *Islam Online*, 8 February, www.islamonline.net/English/News/2003-02/08/article03.shtml.

31. Taja, Waheed (2002), 'Buying Locally Made U.S. Products Not Permissible: Scholar', *Islam Online*, 3 July, www.islamonline.net/English/News/2002-07/03/article09.shtml.

32. Cox, James (2002), 'Arab Nations See Boycotts of U.S. Products', 26 June, www.usatoday.com/money/world/2002-06-26-arab-boycott.htm.

33. Murphy, Dan (2003), 'U.S. Multinational Companies Wary of Backlash', *Christian Science Monitor*, 21 April, www.csmonitor.com/2003/0421/p12s01-woap.html.

34. Kennedy, Miranda (2003), 'America Off Our Soil', The Nation, 19 May, www.thenation.com/docprint.mhtml?i=20030602&s=kennedy.

35. Eliasi, Jennifer R. and Johanna T. Dwyer (2002), 'Kosher and Halal: Religious Observances Affecting Dietary Intake', *Journal of the American Dietetic Association*, 102 (7), 911–13.

36. Muslim Consumer Group (MCG) (2003), 'MCG Criteria for Zabiha Meat', 10 August. www.muslimconsumergroup.com/news.htm.

37. Pells, Richard (2002), 'American Culture Goes Global, or Does It?', *The Chronicle Review*, 12 April, http://chronicle.com/free/v48/i31/31b00701.htm.

38. Wax, Emily (2003), 'In Egypt, Anger at U.S. Displaces Admiration', *Washington Post*, 24 March, www.commondreams.org/headlines03/0324-07.htm.

39. Classic Cairo (2002), 'Ceramics and Sandwiches', 16 April. www.cairolive.com/newcairolive/classic/26-2-2002.html.

40. KFC Holdings Malaysia (2004), Syariah Advisory Council of KFCH. www.kfcholdings.com.my.

41. MacFarquhar, Niel (2002), 'An Anti-American Boycott Is Growing in the Arab World', *New York Times*, 10 May, http://query.nytimes.com/gst/fullpage.html?res=9C02EFD81130F933A25756C0A9649C8B63&scp=1&sq=anti+american+boycott&st=nyt.

42. Zia, Amir (2003), 'U.S. Food Sells Fast in Pakistan Despite Boycott', *Reuters U.K. Top 100*, 31 July.

43. Arnold, Michael S. (1999), 'Boycott Wars with Burgers', *Jerusalem Post*, 13 September.

44. Bard, Mitchell (2004), 'The Arab Boycott', *American–Israeli Cooperative Enterprise*, www.us-israel.org/jsource/History/Arab_boycott.html.

45. Robinson, Francis (2002), 'Islam and the West', *Royal Society for Asian Affairs*, www.rsaa.org.uk/Robinson.pdf.

46. Zubaida, Sami (1998), 'Muslim Societies: Unity or Diversity?', *International Institute for the Study of Islam in the Modern World Newsletter*, www.isim.nl/files/newsl_1.pdf.

47. Aide Sanitaire Suisse aux Palestiniens (ASPP) (2001), *Chronologie 2000–2001*. www.assp.ch/page/history/hist11.html.

48. Egyptian State Information Service (ESIS) (2002), 'Economists Say Boycott Best Weapon against U.S., Israel', 13 April.

49. Maranz, Felice and Evan Greenstein (1999), 'Maleh Adumim Outlet Elicits U.S.–Arab Boycott Threat', *Jerusalem Post*, 6 August.

9

Product policy 2: managing meaning

Brand equity is a measure of the overall value of a brand.[1] The set of associations that surround a brand is referred to as customer-based brand equity. Thus, a name can convey a great deal of information and make a substantial contribution to brand equity, as Leclerc and colleagues (p. 263) point out:

What do Klarbrunn waters, Giorgio di St Angelo design wear and Häagen-Dazs ice cream have in common? All three are successful brands, and all are not what they seem. Klarbrunn is not the clear mountain-spring mineral water from the German Alps that its brand name suggests; it is American water bottled in Wisconsin. Giorgio di St. Angelo design wear is not the latest fashion from Milan but the product of U.S. designer Martin Price. And Häagen-Dazs is not Danish or Hungarian ice cream; it is American ice cream made by Pillsbury with headquarters in Minneapolis.[2]

This chapter directly complements the preceding one as it deals with the symbolic attributes that are linked to brands and national images. These issues are more significant for a company that is planning to establish a brand on the international market, as it is easier to avoid basic errors in relation to the choice of a brand name when starting from scratch. Correcting mistakes once brand goodwill has been created can prove a costly and tricky operation. A brand, even one that has a poor impact, may be an asset due to marketing that resulted in brand awareness and associations. Further, consumers are often confused by changes in a brand name. Changes to brand names, if they are possible, risk wasting time and incurring expenditure.

This chapter begins by discussing the interplay of images, including the product's country of origin, the company name and/or the brand name of its products. This complex interplay of images warrants closer analysis. When beginning with an unestablished brand, it is possible to choose favourable images that transfer across cultures, and are suitable for the product category and the national segments being targeted.

Consumer evaluation of product quality has been documented by a great number of empirical studies, as has been the perception of certain product attributes, according to their country of origin (COO). While the impact of COO has often been overestimated, it is still an important variable that can be used to convey information about a brand. The second section of this chapter reviews studies dealing with the country-of-origin paradigm. These studies suggest consistent answers to such questions: Are 'Buy British' or 'Buy American' advertising campaigns successful? Do consumers have strong preferences for their national products? Which countries are best perceived and on which attributes? Do countries' images change over time?

Section 9.3 addresses the issue of the conversion of national brands into international brands. The linguistic obstacles that are met in this conversion are examined. The question of 'global' brands is also documented since this is becoming a significant issue in international marketing.

9.1

National images diffused by product origin and brand name

Complexity of national images diffused by product

There is an important relationship between images of products and the symbols diffused by their nationality. For instance, for the purchasers of Swedish cars, who pay twice as much as for comparable cars from other countries, the symbolic label 'Made in Sweden' suggests reliability and long life, removing fear of mechanical failure. The influence of a product's nationality on consumer evaluations were first studied with respect to the 'made in' label, that is, the origin label put on products. But the 'made in' label is not the only element that contributes to consumer perception of product nationality. The following elements all contribute to such perceptions (Figure 9.1):

1. Image of national products versus imported or international products.
2. National images of generic products (e.g., yoghurt calls to mind the Balkans, perfume evokes France, a pair of jeans the United States).

Figure 9.1 Several layers of country-, company- and brand-related product image

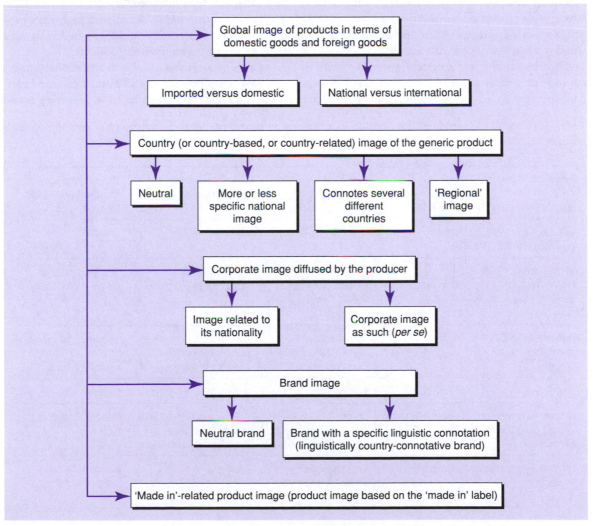

3. Image diffused by brand name.
4. Image of 'made in' label depicting manufacturing origin; origin labelling is mandatory in international trade.
5. National image of manufacturing company.

In most cases a product category is not clearly associated with only one country. For example, wine is not only associated with France. Many other countries have strong associations with one or more varieties, including other European countries (e.g. Germany, Italy, Spain and Portugal), as well as newer winemaking countries (e.g. Australia, Argentina and Chile). There are also regional associations with wine, such as Burgundy, Bordeaux, Rhone, Sonoma Valley, Hunter Valley, and Margaret River. In fact, many products, especially those based on local natural resources, have strong associations with countries and regions. For instance, in Europe, furniture made of natural pine wood is often associated with Scandinavia.

The desirability of products associated with a country or region differs by product category and consumer group, so companies must be careful about the image they wish to convey. For example, Loeffler[3] found that, for France, Germany, Italy and Spain, the quality of foreign cars are judged to be significantly lower than for corresponding domestic cars. However, foreign cars are evaluated in a different way to domestic cars in Germany: they are seen as lower quality, but superior in emotional aspects (more interesting and fascinating). This may help explain why Americans prefer German-named burger restaurants to American ones.[4]

The stereotypes associated with national images are not confined to Western cultures. For instance, Japanese consumers associate Germany and France with long history and tradition, Switzerland and Australia with rich nature, California and Brazil with abundant agricultural products, the United States and Germany with advanced industrial technology, and France with sense of design and high-class products.[5] These associations can lead to higher perceptions of quality for compatible products.

As can be seen from Table 9.1, national images operate on multiple levels and as such can send confusing messages to consumers. The following broad

Table 9.1 Some examples of the combined influence of brand name and country of origin on product image

Product	National image of generic product	National image of manufacturer	Country evoked by brand name label	Country image diffused by 'Made in' label
Shalimar (perfume by Guerlain)	French	French	India/Orient	French
Kinder (milk chocolate bars made by Ferrero)	Swiss and other countries	Italian (but manufacturer's name, Ferrero, rarely appears)	German (means 'children' in German)	'Made in' hardly visible – often Italy
National (vacuum cleaner made by Matsushita)	Neutral	Manufacturer's name (Matsushita) does not appear	National brand makes people believe that product is local	'Made in' label hardly visible – different national origins
Coca-Cola	International	American	America	Neutral
Kremly (yoghurt by Chambourcy, part of Nestlé)	Balkan/Bulgarian Slav	Looks French, but is a worldwide brand of Nestlé Switzerland	Kremly (name and graphics) evokes Kremlin, a Slavic image	'Made in' label is local
Brother (typewriters by Brother)	Neutral	English/American (in fact a Japanese company)	International	'Made in' label is indicates of origin

normative guidelines for management of a product's national image are developed for the four levels illustrated in Table 9.1:

1. *National image of generic product*: images that correspond to what is locally valued in each country should be diffused (imported or national) for the product category concerned. This can lead to the adoption of a name from the target country, due to strong nationalistic feelings.

2. *National image of manufacturer*: if the product category is generally associated with a specific country of origin, the brand name should be designed accordingly. For example, a manufacturer of machine tools should not be reluctant to adopt a German name, because of the favourable association of German-sounding names with technical reliability.

3. *Country evoked by brand name label*: the visibility of the company name, the brand name and the 'made in' label should be adjusted depending on their respective ability to convey the desired symbolic meanings.

4. *Country image diffused by 'made in' label*: it is often advisable to reduce the physical size of the 'made in' label, if the perception of the country of origin proves negative for local consumers (provided such reduction is permitted, or ignored, by local regulations). On the other hand, it should be enlarged in cases where the opposite perception prevails.

9.2

Consumer product evaluation according to country of origin

The use of 'country of origin' attribute

Consumers use the manufacturer's country of origin (COO) symbolically. In other words, they use it as an associative link: Germany = robustness, France = luxury, Italy = beauty, etc. The French pronunciation of a brand name positively affects the perceived hedonism of the product and negatively affects its perceived utility.[2] In an actual product taste test, where consumers have direct sensory experience of the product, foreign branding changes

consumers' perceptions of the product (in this case yoghurt).[2]

To date, more than 300 articles have been published on COO over the last 35 years, with a great deal of diversity in countries (as origins), product categories and consumers surveyed (in terms of demographics and nationality).[6] In the early years COO effects were often assessed in isolation: it was the only factor that differed between product choices in early experiments. The basic objective of many of the early studies was to demonstrate that the COO cue actually influenced consumer evaluations. Attempting to determine in which direction and why was only a secondary objective in the first studies.[7] This made the effects seem stronger than they would be under more realistic circumstances.[7] During the early 1980s to early 1990s researchers began to review the effects of COO in relation to other extrinsic and intrinsic product attributes, such as price, perceived risk, etc.[7-9] By the early 2000s several integrative reviews provided some important insights regarding the transfer of influence to the real world.[10-13] In the real world consumers are likely to be influenced by multiple intrinsic and extrinsic cues, only one of which is COO. As expected, the influence of COO is lower when other cues, such as product, price, and warranty information are included in the information presented to consumers.[13] In fact, the average effect of COO on perceptions of quality and reliability halves when multiple attributes or cues are added to the COO information.[12]

Some key COO influences have been established:

1. COO has a stronger influence at the earlier stages of the decision-making process. The effect is stronger on perceptions of brand quality than on attitude toward the product or purchase intention.[12,13] For instance, based on a meta-analysis of 52 COO studies, Peterson and Jolibert[12] reported that the average effect of COO on quality/reliability was 0.30, whereas its average effect on purchase intentions was 0.19 for single-cue studies and only 0.03 for multi-cue studies. Thus, as the consumer moves closer to a choice COO has less impact.

2. COO is more often used as a reliable cue of brand quality than to infer quality.[14] For instance, Agrawal and Kamakura[14] examined the objective quality of 13 products (chosen from the 1980–94

US Consumer Reports) to assess whether perceived differences were due to actual differences in objective quality across firms representing different countries or to a halo effect in favour of products made in some countries. First, they found that countries differed in the objective quality of their durable consumer electronic goods: products originating in Japan had significantly higher objective quality than those originating in the US, Europe and Korea, and that the Korean products had significantly lower objective quality than those from the US, Japan and Europe. They then used this information to re-examine 12 previous COO studies that reported the perceived quality of similar products, adding the objective quality scores. They found that COO had no significant impact on the prices companies charged, after controlling for the objective quality of the goods. This gives support to COO being used as a reliable cue or summary for brand quality, rather than as a halo effect.

3. COO also functions as a symbolic cue, with emotional value: It is seen as the right or normative way to do things.[13,15–18]

Stereotypical country images

Throughout COO studies one finds a relatively small number of stereotypical images that are fairly consistent across consumer nationalities. For instance, the image of the robustness of German products, the image of France as associated with luxury goods, the image of Korean products as being cheap. However, even these shared perceptions are restricted and unstable. Italians do not have the same image of their products as do consumers from other countries.

There are many perceptions of COO that are not shared by consumers of different national cultures. Often, differences in relationships between countries (similarity of culture and language, past colonial links, etc.) lead to differences in the perceptions of the others products.[19] For instance, the image of a country, in political, economic, cultural and social terms, may influence the willingness of foreign consumers to purchase that country's products independently of their perceived quality.

Animosity toward another culture, which has been defined by Klein and colleagues (p. 90)[17] as 'the remnants of antipathy related to previous or ongoing military, political, or economic events', has been found to influence the purchase of products from that country. For instance, Chinese consumer animosity toward Japan negatively influenced consumers' purchase of Japanese products (ibid.). In a series of studies, animosity has been found to influence purchase intentions but not product quality judgements.[17,20] Those high in consumer animosity chose not to purchase goods from a specific country because of past events, such as wars or economic histories between countries.

Consumers may also be unwilling to purchase products originating from a country under a dictatorship or one that acts in contravention of certain internationally recognized rules (as with countries that use child workers), even if these products fit their needs. Wang and Lamb[21] asked 94 US nationals about their readiness to purchase products from different countries (36 in all). They also asked them to identify the political, cultural and economic environment of each country. In this way they were able to demonstrate that variables related to the sociopolitical image of a country partially explained consumer readiness to purchase products from that country. American consumers were more prepared to buy products from politically democratic countries, such as those in Europe, Australia and New Zealand. However, country images may become partly divorced from the image of their products. Imagine, for instance, the case of a country under a non-democratic governing regime that nevertheless produces some excellent goods which are exported to democratic countries, as is the case with China.

Further, the overall level of industrial development of a country also influences the evaluations of its products by foreign consumers. For instance, consumers from industrialized countries (e.g. Canada) evaluated products from highly industrialized countries more positively than from newly industrialized countries.[22] Similarly, consumers from a range of industrialized–industrializing countries (e.g. Japan, Taiwan, South Korea, and India) evaluated products from the same four countries, finding that India (the least industrialized country) had the poorest image in terms of quality, creativity, design and technological level.[23]

Industrial buyers are also influenced by the level of development of the country from which they buy products. For instance, US industrial buyers were found to be more willing to source from industrialized (e.g. Japan, Sweden, Taiwan, West Germany) than industrializing countries (e.g. Brazil, China, Poland), except in the case of Mexico where buyers experienced with this trade partner rated it much better than for other industrializing countries.[24] US purchasers were also more ready to buy from foreign suppliers who had established warehouses or sales offices in the US, irrespective of the COO. The very fact of having already done business with industrial suppliers from less favourably perceived COOs, such as Latin American countries, causes experienced purchasers to hold a higher image of their products and quality than that held by inexperienced industrial importers.[25]

Nevertheless it remains clear that vendors located in less favourable foreign environments may be cheap and reliable suppliers, as long as they are carefully evaluated and given a fair opportunity to perform. In sum, the cost of their *learning* should be shared with their customer, and subsequently both will benefit.

Website link 9.1

See what constitutes an image of a country?:
http://www.brandingstrategyinsider.com/2008/03/branding-the-co.html.

How does product image change over time?

Another important issue in relation to COO image is whether there are changes in these images over time and, if there are, at what rate they occur. The response to this question seems to be yes, and the rate seems to be fairly rapid. This was particularly true of products originating from Japan and new industrial Asian countries, such as Korea and Taiwan.[26] Many studies confirm the dramatic improvement of the image of Japan as a COO. At the beginning of the 1970s, Japanese products were seen

as being of dubious quality; they were backed by rather restricted guarantees and poor after-sales service. By the end of the 1970s, however, they were seen as having improved significantly as far as quality was concerned.[27–29] Today, there are many prestigious products from Japan, including the Lexus automobile. In general, Saudi consumers rate Japanese products very highly with respect to central product attributes, followed by American and German products, and then by products from the UK, France and Italy, which tend to be perceived as lower quality.[30] More recently, a similar improvement is seen with the acceptance of South Korean and Taiwanese products. The length of time required for image revision depends on the efforts made by a country and its manufacturers to improve image.

Consumer characteristics and perceptions of COO

Many factors may moderate the influence of COO on consumer evaluation, including customer awareness of COO, their knowledge of and familiarity with the product, their consumer ethnocentric tendencies and the product category and risk perceptions.

As a result of the expansion of multinational firms, some companies sell the same products under identical brand names in different countries throughout the world. These products actually have widely differing national origins, not necessarily that of the COO of the parent company. Sony products, for example, can just as easily be 'Made in France', 'Made in Germany' or 'Made in Thailand' as 'Made in Japan'. Consequently 'COO' information is increasingly ambiguous to consumers. In many countries, it is now sufficient to have the origin mentioned in customs documents, rather than on the merchandise itself. Consequently, consumers are less informed about the origin of products, especially when it is unfavourable. New, uninformative labels have emerged such as 'made in Europe', or 'made in Asia' as well as humorous origin labels such as 'made in nowhere', or complex indications such as 'assembled in . . .' from 'US made (parts)'. As a result, consumers are largely unaware of the COO of many products and find it increasingly less important to assess where their purchases came from.[31] For instance, only 49 per cent of 40 American brands and 22 per cent of 44 non-American brands were correctly classified as to their origin by a national sample of adult Americans.[32] However, the influence of the COO evaluation cue is stronger where the consumer is unfamiliar, lacks knowledge or is not motivated to process the information about a product category. In this case, they use the available COO information as a quality cue.

Consumer ethnocentrism represents 'the beliefs held by consumers about the appropriateness of purchasing products originating in a foreign country' (Shimp and Sharma, p. 280[33]). It represents the beliefs held by consumers about the appropriateness, indeed morality, of purchasing foreign products.[33,34] Thus, highly ethnocentric consumers are likely to believe that purchasing imported products harms the domestic economy and causes unemployment. In addition, consumer age has been identified as a variable that significantly correlates with ethnocentrism. In particular, older consumers were found to be much more ethno-centric than their younger counterparts.[35] Similarly, older consumers are also likely to have more animosity toward specific countries.[20,36,37]

Consumer ethnocentrism has been shown to influence consumers' attitudes and perceptions about foreign products.[34,35,38,39] Generally, there is a positive relationship between ethnocentrism and domestic products, and a negative relationship between ethnocentrism and foreign products.[38,40–45] However, the relationship between ethnocentrism and foreign products has been less consistent; preference depends on the product category.[38] Even different products coming from the same country produced varying patterns of acceptability.[34,46] For example, people from Australia might like French perfume, but dislike French cameras, or even French wine, as Australia generally produces a heavier wine. Certain products are considered more 'ethnic', more typical of certain countries;[47] consumers tend to associate countries and products: Italy and pizza, Germany and machine tools, Britain and puddings. Thus, domestic companies may benefit from ethnocentrism, but foreign companies may not necessarily find resistance to their offerings.

A sound hypothesis which has been forwarded by several studies is the mediation of perceived risk to explain the influence of the COO on consumer evaluations. Either consumers perceive a lesser risk for national products, which would explain the preference for national products, or they perceive a lesser risk for the products of certain countries with a favourable image.

Consumers that come from high versus low uncertainty avoidance countries may also use COO information differently. Consumers from high uncertainty avoidance countries evaluated 'uncertain' COO quality images (Russian cameras and Japanese Vodka) less positively and had weaker behavioural intentions than those from low UA countries, but for 'certain' COO quality images (high quality = Russian vodka and Japanese cameras) there was no difference.[48]

9.3

National, international and global brands

Branding is an important tool used to differentiate products. The recognized benefits include expanding sales, increased profits, greater longevity, greater power with distributors and the ability to survive adverse economic conditions.[49] However, there are also possible negative consequences that need to be acknowledged. For instance, Naomi Klein in her book *No Logo: No Space, No Choice, No Jobs*[50] argues that the focus on branding has led to significant downsizing and outsourcing that is displacing manufacturing with the service sector and reshaping the world of work. She cites this as one of the reasons behind the backlash against the 'brand bullies' such as McDonald's and Nike. Interestingly, she also comments on the branding of activism and the need to point out that: 'there are more than two worlds available, to expose all the invisible worlds between the economic fundamentalist of 'McWorld' and the religious fundamentalism of 'Jihad' (p. 10).[50]

The majority of brands throughout the world were originally conceived on a national level and not as international brands. Even among US brands, only a small number have achieved international recognition. For instance, Rosen and colleagues studied 650 US brands and their international scope (available internationally, the age of the brand, etc.) and their general conclusion is that 'despite all the talk about the internationalisation of marketing efforts, the international diffusion of US brands is actually rather limited and . . . that most US brands are not marketed abroad' (Rosen *et al.*, p. 17[51]).

Most brands are related to a specific linguistic context. Their evocative power is dependent on the language of the country and markets where they were originally launched. In Europe, the vast majority of all brands are still national, if not purely local, in their appeal.[52] However, certain brands are launched as international brands, right from the start. In the 1960s a Japanese car manufacturer with increasing export sales decided it was necessary to have a name suitable for international markets: Toyota, with its three syllables which can be pronounced in any language, was the name finally selected.

International companies face three situations in terms of international brand names:

1. *Ex nihilo* creation of a brand name, especially for new products with high global potential. It must be pronounced and understood in a similar way across diverse linguistic and cultural contexts.
2. Management of a large brand portfolio resulting from both external growth by acquisitions of local players and multiple layers of branding (e.g. corporate names, category brands, product names). Such brand portfolios are increasingly being simplified, in order to avoid spreading brand advertising budgets too thinly over a large number of names. Only a few of these names will become transnational brands. The appropriate course of action is to nominate the best applicants in translinguistic terms, taking into account local brand equity and the attachment of both local consumers and local marketing teams to brands that often have a rich history.
3. Assessment of the potential for an international extension of regional brands developed by a subsidiary based in the lead country for a region.

Transposition of national brand name for international purposes

The brand name of a given product is often the name of the company that manufactures it. Since the brand name is historically related to the founders of the company, symbolically it would be difficult to change. Companies such as Procter & Gamble (with names that are difficult to pronounce in many languages) have followed a twofold brand strategy. Product brand names, such as Ivory, Camay, Pampers, Vizir and Tide, have been promoted almost independently from the Procter & Gamble company name (look at the respective sizes of the names on the packaging) and the Procter & Gamble name has been colloquially simplified so that it can be more easily memorized and verbalized, either to simply Procter or to P & G.

Website link 9.2

See which P&G brands are sold in different countries: http://www.pg.com/company/who_we_are/global_products.shtml.

An example of lack of adaptation is the leading French company for iron and steel and heavy mechanical equipment during the 1970s and 1980s, Creusot-Loire. It branded and sold its products under the company's name in many countries in the world, including the United States. Unfortunately, American customers found this name difficult to pronounce, for the following reasons:

1. Throaty French 'CR' sound hardly exists in English.
2. 'EU' is a typically French diphthong, unpronounceable for Americans.
3. 'S' must be pronounced 'Z' because it is located between two vowels (French rule!).
4. 'O' is a very open sound.
5. 'T' is, in this case, a mute consonant and must therefore be ignored in pronunciation.
6. 'OI': once again a typically French diphthong (unknown in English).
7. 'R' is a hard 'r', almost unused in English.
8. 'E' is a mute vowel at the end of the word, and therefore must be ignored in pronunciation.

Naturally, such a brand name is difficult to memorize for most customers in many countries. Moreover, such difficult brand names can be a serious obstacle to clear communication between buyer and seller, creating confusion when discussing business on the phone. It is therefore essential to be prepared to carry out the necessary brand name modification.

While there may be limited benefits from global standardization for many aspects of communication, there seem to be strong arguments for corporate branding, including increased market efficiency, reduced advertising and inventory costs, and convenient identification for people travelling internationally.[53] For instance, Melewar and Saunders[54] examined the benefits sought from a global corporate visual identity system (CVIS), which consists of company name, symbol/logo, typography, colour and slogan. They surveyed British MNCs with subsidiaries in Malaysia, finding that the perceived benefits of CVIS standardization include increased sales, consumer goodwill, consumer familiarity, consumer awareness and market share. However, the diversity of national regulations and the rarity of brands with similar spellings in most national markets make it difficult to register a standardized brand across a large number of countries.

The options for the transposition of an existing name range from translation, to transliteration, to creating a new transparent brand are as follows:

1. *Simple translation* is rarely used as it may result in a disaster in relation to meaning,[55] scattered brand image, and inability to create international brand recognition.
2. *Transliteration* is better as it attempts to reconstitute the connotative meaning in the target language that exists in the source language (i.e. language of brand's country of origin). For example, the American hair care product Silkience (Gillette) is sold under the same brand name in Germany, under the brand name Soyance in France and under the brand name Sientel in Italy.[56]
3. The best type of brand is the *transparent* brand, such as Sony, which is suitable everywhere. The name Sony arose from a real 'shooting down' of the company name by the brand name of its products.[57] The original name of the firm (Tokyo Tsuhin Kogyo – Tokyo Industrial Telecommunication Company) was changed to Sony as soon as the brand name of its products proved to be successful.

Linguistic aspects of brand

Brands are signs based on sounds, written signs (letters or pictographs) and visual elements (logotype, brand design). The linguistic content of a brand name has an influence on its verbal, auditory and intellectual meaning, and its interpretation by consumers.[58] The brand name is often associated with a copyrighted design. Visual elements also comprise how a brand is written (alphabet, characters, ideographs). Table 9.2 shows which branch of linguistics should be used to appreciate how the sound, spelling and design of a brand name travel from a source to a target linguistic context. A brand name should generally be relatively easy to pronounce. A simple rule is that the brand name should not exceed three syllables, each composed of one consonant and one vowel. Chinese mostly has such simple successions of one consonant and one or two vowels,[59] whereas German and Dutch often have many successive consonants (up to seven in a row in German) and French sometimes has long strings of vowels.

When considering the sound or phonological aspects of an international brand, one should check that the sound pattern corresponds to phonemes that are pronounced in all major languages (phonetics) and that it does not use unique sound patterns of the source language (phonemics). The name Hewlett-Packard, for instance, is far from perfect and is better when shortened to HP. The English 'th' or the French nasalized triphthong 'oin' (don't try it!) are among such difficult combinations. Japanese, on the other hand, is a formidable language for international brands because it is composed exclusively of phonemes that are recognized by virtually all languages in the world, and it eschews successive consonants. Denotative meaning, such as that of Milka chocolate, which directly relates to milk, is lost in most other languages; understanding of this meaning is limited to Anglo-Saxon and Germanic languages which use this root (etymology) and to speakers of English as a second language. Similarly, connotative meaning is generally lost when a product crosses borders: the detergent Tide was once sold in France (the name being pronounced *teed*) but nobody had the slightest knowledge of the idea of powerful tidal waves washing clothes that was evoked by the brand in English-speaking markets. Evidence suggests that

Table 9.2 Brand cues and meaning transfer

Brand cue	Element of meaning		Branch of linguistics concerned
Sound		L	
– Assemblage (vowels	⇨ Pure sound	I	Phonology (phonemics/phonetics)
and consonants)	⇨ Denotative meaning	N	
	⇨ Connotative meaning	G	
– Tonality		U	Etymology
		I	Semantics / Rhetoric
Written name		S	
– Alphabetic letters ⇨ sounds	Sounds ⇨ words ⇨ ideas	T	Semantics
– Pictographic writing	Pictograph design ⇨ ideas	I	Semiology
	Pictograph design ⇨ symbols	C	
Design			
– Assemblage of words (brands	– Descriptive	F	Grammar
and slogans)	– Suggestive	I	Rhetoric
– Icons (causal and analogous sign)	– Humorous	L	Semantics
– Symbols (untraceable linkage)	– Claim supportive	T	Semiology
	– Oneiric	E	
	– Ethnic	R	

meaningful names are easier to recall than meaningless ones.[60]

Written brand names are generally based on the alphabet: people first read sounds, then decode words and finish with ideas. A third of the world's consumers use ideographic writing systems; they go directly from pictographs to ideas. Sounds for a definite written item vary: people in various parts of China and Japan use similar ideographs which they recognize as having the same meaning but which are pronounced quite differently. However, even with the Roman alphabet, the use of identical letters may result in a brand sounding different, according to the linguistic context: the Danone brand of yoghurt is spelled Dannon in the US because consistency of pronunciation is preferred to consistency of spelling.[61] Given the wide differences in tonicity across languages, a brand such as Coca-Cola cannot be considered global as far as sound patterns are concerned: many languages, such as French have little tonicity, whereas others like Mandarin need tonicity to be understood.

Brand design also has an influence on its verbal, auditory and intellectual meaning. For instance, Whiskas (a Mars brand) has a translinguistic iconic value because it uses a cat's head to suggest its favourite user; but the colours are likely to be interpreted differently across cultures. Brand names are

usually associated with a copyright design and the graphic composition of a logo conveys as much meaning as the letters of the brand name. Similarly, as Cabat (p. 344) notes, the IBM trademark is inseparable from its graphics in its evocative ability to communicate with the consumer:

The letters of the IBM logo are actually obtained by the superimposition of characters known as 'Mecanes' and of a 'blind' (alternate slats of coloured bands). The blind is in this case the informative image of the letters IBM, their morphological determinant . . . It thereby becomes the sign of computer language, binary-based. The 'Mecanes' are typesetting characters whose square serif evokes industrial production and rooting in the mechanical world.[55]

The imagery of the IBM brand logo is translinguistic, and therefore offers a truly international ability to convey meaning. The link between brand and drawing is an intimate one. How, for instance, is the Coca-Cola brand name stored in consumers' minds? As eight letters, as the traditional design of the Coca-Cola words or the Coke bottle, or as a combination of them? Trademark legislation around the world varies in this respect. In some countries trademarks can only be composed of alphabetic letters and their design must be separately registered under the design and patent laws if they are to be effectively protected; in the US a trademark may be bereft of any linguistic content and can be registered solely under trademark laws. There is no systematic need, in the US and many other countries, for additional registration of a trademark's design.

Website link 9.3

Find the links to the trademark authorities of various countries: **http://www.worldwide-trademark.com**.

Linguistic devices for brand names

Table 9.3 shows various linguistic devices that can be used in creating brand names. Whether by accident or design, advertisers and marketers strive to give some punch and evocative capacity to their brand names. Of course this is done, as much as possible, in line with the symbolic connotations that they intend to communicate in relation to product attributes and, inevitably, it is done in a particular source language.

Table 9.3 Linguistic characteristics of brands

Characteristics	Definitions and/or examples
I Phonetic devices	
1. Alliteration	Consonant repetition (**C**oca **C**ola, **Coc**oon)
2. Assonance	Vowel repetition (K**a**l K**a**n, V**i**z**i**r, **O**m**o**)
3. Consonance	Consonant repetition with intervening vowel changes (**W**eight **W**a**t**chers, Tic Tac)
4. Masculine rhyme	Rhyme with end of syllable stress (Max Pax)
5. Feminine rhyme	Unaccented syllable followed by accented syllable (Am**eri**can **Air**lines)
6. Weak/imperfect/slant rhyme	Vowels differ or consonants similar, not identical (Bl**ack** & D**eck**er)
7. Onomatopoeia	Use of syllable phonetics to resemble the object itself (Wisk, Cif, Wizzard)
8. Clipping	Product names shortened (Chevy for a Chevrolet, Deuche for a Citroen Deux Chevaux, Rabbit for a Volkswagen)
9. Blending	Morphemic combination, usually with elision (Aspergum, Duracell)
10. Initial plosives*	/b/, /c-hard/, /d/, /g-hard/, /k/, /q/, /t/, (Bic, Dash, Pliz, Pim's)
II Orthographic devices	
1. Unusual or incorrect spellings	Kool-Aid, Decap'Four
2. Abbreviations	7-Up for Seven-Up
3. Acronyms	Amoco, Amro, DB, Cofinoga, Lu, BSN
III Morphological devices	
1. Affixation	Jell-O, Tipp-Ex
2. Compounding	Janitor-in-a-Drum, Vache-qui-rit
IV Semantic devices	
1. Metaphor	Representing something as if it were something else (Arrid); simile was included with metaphor when a name described a likeness and not an equality (Aqua Fresh, Longeurs et Pointes, Head and Shoulders, Tendres Promesses)
2. Metonymy	Application of one object or quality for another (Midas, Ajax, Uncle Ben's, Bounty)
3. Synecdoche	Substitution of a part for the whole (Red Lobster)
4. Personification/ pathetic fallacy	Humanizing the non-human or ascription of human emotions to the inanimate (Betty Crocker, Clio, Kinder)
5. Oxymoron	Conjunction of opposites (Easy-Off, Crème de peinture)
6. Paranomasia	Pun and word plays (Hawaiian Punch, Raid – insecticide, Fédor – orange juice)
7. Semantic appositeness	Fit of name with object (Bufferin, Nutella)

* An initial is said to be plosive if, to produce this sound, one needs first to stop the flow of air completely, then audibly release the air previously compressed.

(Source: Adapted from Vanden Bergh *et al.*[62])

There are four main categories of linguistic device: phonetic devices (sound, perceived orally), orthographic devices (relating to writing, perceived visually), morphological devices (adding morphemes to the brand-name root) and semantic devices (the figure produces meaning, perceived through culture-based interpretations).

The linguistic devices set out in Table 9.3 make it possible to understand what constitutes the pure linguistic capacity of a brand; independently of the established goodwill (brand recognition may be high for linguistically unadapted but long-standing brand names). The issue for brand marketers is whether these advantages are transposable into other linguistic contexts. The alliteration of Coca-Cola transposes well, but the composition of the words Janitor-in-a-Drum, or even the juxtaposition of opposites (Easy-Off), do not. This is because Coca-Cola does not require a basic comprehension of the words that make up the brand name. Where understanding of complex linguistic figures is required, brand names are difficult to translate and, more generally, to transpose. As a rule, the linguistic devices in categories I and II are the more 'translinguistic'. A good number of the devices in category IV are not at all translinguistic, especially # 1, 4, 5, 6 and 7.

Semantic issues: intended versus unintended meaning

As shown above, meaning can be lost when a brand crosses borders. Nestlé (*Nestele*: 'little nest' in the Alemanic dialects of the southern German-speaking area) is lost in most of the world's languages and people probably cannot understand why the logo presents a bird in a nest. Beiersdorf's 'Uhu' brand for glue sticks is based on the German name for eagle owl. Most intended meaning does not extend much beyond the source language area. It is, however, not a major problem if consumers in other linguistic areas memorize the sound of brand names easily and invest them with new, positive meanings.

Unintended negative meaning is the most dangerous. The brand name should not have an unfortunate meaning in a different linguistic/cultural context. However, checking the translinguistic capacity of a brand name is by no means universal practice. There is no shortage of examples: the German hair spray Caby-Net launched on the French market (*cabinet* is a toilet in French); the Japanese gun, Miroku, the name of which has several meanings including 'look at your bottom' in French. The examples of certain American cars in South American markets are also famous. The Chevrolet (Chevy) Nova (the intended meaning was 'new') translates into Spanish as 'does not work'. The Ford Pinto meant 'tiny male genitals' in Brazil. Kellogg's renamed its Frosted Flakes as Sucrilhos for Brazil, and its Cocoa Krispies as Crokinhos; similarly it had to change its Bran Buds brand name in Sweden, so that Swedish people did not read that they were to be served 'grilled farmer' in their breakfast bowls.[63] The type of research that must be carried out is straightforward: it is necessary to interview a group of consumers from the target country about the perceptual effects of the intended names and sometimes it is necessary to interview several depending on the number of dialects with potential for unintended meanings.

The case of Asian ideographic writing systems

The scope of the discussion has thus far been limited to the framework of languages based on the Roman alphabet where letters correspond to sounds and sounds to ideas, but almost one-quarter of the world's population reads logographic characters, including Chinese, Japanese and Korean.[64] Reading logographs relies more on visual processes, which affects consumer memory,[64–66] as well as brand attitudes.[67–69] Recall is better when Westerners speak the words and Chinese write the words down, suggesting that verbal information is encoded in a visual manner in Chinese and a phonological manner in English.[68] Similarly, visual branding is more easily integrated in memory for Chinese speakers, while auditory branding is more easily integrated for English speakers.[64] Thus, certain types of translations are likely to work better in different cultural contexts.

Zhang and Schmitt[69] put forward a framework to examine issues for creating or translating English to Chinese brand names. They explored the boundaries by examining the effects of the degree of emphasis on the English name compared with that placed on the Chinese name in a dual writing situation and the presence of prior types of brand translations in the same product category. Similarly, Hong and colleagues[70] explored the effect of phonetic translations into Mandarin for familiar and unfamiliar brands on perceptions of quality in Singapore. They found that the phonetic translation performed better for an unfamiliar brand, but for a familiar brand it was better to keep the original name.

Global brands wanting to reach these markets face a difficult task. Even Coca-Cola is not known exactly by this name in China since the simple translated name would have a negative connotation; Coca-Cola is transliterated as 'ke kou ke le' in Mandarin and 'ho hau ho lohk' in Cantonese (in terms of approximate sound equivalence), which conveys the meaning of 'tasty and enjoyable/happy'.[71] In fact, Chinese characters are pronounced differently according to the dialect spoken (Mandarin, Cantonese, Hokkien, etc.), and there is a large number of homonyms (same pronunciation, but written differently to indicate the distinct meaning). For instance 'gong' corresponds to many different meanings ranging from work to attack to palace, depending on the characters.[65] Thus, there are many possibilities to select from when transposing Roman-letter brand names into Chinese characters.

In East Asia, and especially in China, calligraphy and meaning become much more important than in standard Western branding. Schmitt and Pan,[65] list the factors needed for a brand to have a positive connotation in China:

1. characters with favourable sounds, which can be pronounced in about the same way in as many regions as possible, while avoiding the pitfalls due to tonality;
2. characters that convey favourable meaning, if possible related to the brand's advertised qualities;
3. a balance between *yin* (even number of strokes) and *yang* characters (odd number of strokes);
4. a favourable content in terms of lucky numbers such as 8;
5. suitable calligraphy for the brand; the calligraphy must convey certain visual signs that fit with the brand imagery, such as in the case of the Volkswagen 'Cheep': a character was used that evoked an imaginary slope that the jeep had to climb.

Consequently, Pepsi-Cola is transposed into Chinese characters meaning 'hundred happy things' and Mercedes-Benz becomes 'Benchi', with two characters meaning 'striving forward fast'. However, such transposition is not possible for all brands. In some cases, when the transposition of sounds is deemed more important than the transposition of meaning (it may be difficult to find a chain of characters that do both), the brand name may sound very similar to the sound of the Western version, such as 'nifeya' for Nivea, but the meaning level may be very poor. For Nivea the assemblage of characters means 'girl-not/Africa-second rank/Asia'.[71]

Francis and colleagues[72] examined brand names used by 49 Fortune 500 companies that manufactured consumer products available in China or Hong Kong. They found that most brands were leveraged in some way. That is, 44 per cent sounded similar, 22 per cent had similar meanings, and 10 per cent used their English brand names. In addition, while most brand names attempted to convey benefits (74 per cent) only 11 per cent shared the same benefits across languages. Thus, firms appear to localize their brand names in China. Localization may be necessary when there are large linguistic and cultural differences. Data from an AC Nielsen Retail Audit in China suggests that domestic brands are increasing in sales and, while the average price is lower than for multinational brands, the gap is narrowing.[73]

In Japan, the issue is both less and more complicated since the Japanese are familiar with the Western alphabet (*romaji*) but they also use the Chinese characters (*Kanji*), and two syllabaries, the *hiragana* for Japanese words and the *katakana* for foreign loanwords (which use the same syllables as the *hiragana*, but with a slightly different calligraphic style that signals the foreign origin). These alternative writing systems carry different associative meanings which must be carefully monitored in order to convey appropriate subliminal messages: (1) as to the origin of the product: *kanji* and *hiragana* will look more Japanese while *romaji* and *katakana* signal foreignness; (2) as to the product category: high-tech products will best be written in *katakana* which connotes modernity, whereas traditional products are best served by *Kanji*; (3) as to the consumer universe implied by the writing style:

hiragana have a feminine image and are used frequently for beauty products and cosmetics.[65]

Functions of brands according to national contexts

The trade name has a number of functions for the consumer such as *identity* (it guides consumers when making their choice), *practicality* (it works as a summary of information about product characteristics), *guarantee* ('signature of the manufacturer'), *personalization* (brand name allows consumers to express their individuality through their purchases) and an *entertainment* function because the brand allows the exercise of free choice and enables consumers to satisfy their needs for freshness, arousal, and surprise.[74] For the producer, the brand fulfils two essential functions: *positioning* within the competitive scene and *capitalization* of image and advertising expenditure over the long term.

These functions are very differently valued across countries, to the extent that some functions of the brand can be almost non-existent in certain national contexts. Accordingly, in France there is a certain social mistrust of brands, especially by public authorities: they supposedly increase prices, constituting entry barriers to possible competitors and thereby limiting competition.[75] Furthermore, being set up on the basis of large cumulative advertising expenditure, they are said to increase the price of the product to the detriment of the consumer. Contensou (p. 249)[75] shows that in fact these fears are groundless and further points out that 'inflationary tendencies have no connection to brand development and the multiplication of products sold under brand names'. Kapferer (1989), taking the same defensive attitude towards brand names, has shown that they support the actual intentions of the manufacturers, their achievements to the benefit of consumers and that without effective attempts to foster product quality, brand images cannot be sustained.

In contrast to France, Japan seems to be a country where brands are very highly valued. Yoshimori (pp. 277–8) explains this:

In feudal Japan, the brand was not distinct from the name of the ancestral house itself. This name had great importance, to the extent that everything was done to protect its good image, and above all to perpetuate it. Anyone who tarnished that reputation even through mere carelessness was obliged to rectify the damage through dying . . . [Yoshimori then gives examples of Japanese executives who have recently committed suicide because they believed that through their actions or negligence they had tarnished the reputation of their company] . . . a trading company, or any such firm, was not merely an economic entity; it also constituted a religious community which transcended the physical life of the family that controlled it. Ancestors occupied an almost divine place: it was therefore believed that the preservation and advancement of kamei, the name of the ancestral house, was an almost religious obligation since it (kamei) was the concrete translation of the presence of ancestors.[57]

The brand in Japan is a real figurehead of competitive struggle. Abbeglen and Stalk[76] show how, during the 1950s, the Honda brand name destroyed the Tohatsu brand (which today is completely unknown). They also describe in great detail the episodes in the Homeric quarrel between Honda and Yamaha at the start of the 1980s, which ended with a victory for Honda. In the United States, as in Japan, brands are central to competition. Brand marketing occupies a stable position in the strategies of US companies, but also one which is constantly changing, as are market shares. The vigour of the brand can only be built on 'tidal waves' of sales promotion and advertising as well as on consistent efforts towards improvement of product quality. Dupuy and Thoenig[77] compared brand status in the United States, France and Japan. They noted that brands in France have a much weaker status than in Japan and the United States.

Differences in national distribution systems explain to a large extent the degree of brand-related competition. In Japan, the *keiretsu* distribution system (see section 11.1) enables producers to control distribution channels and therefore to direct the brand name principally towards the relationship with the consumer. Alpert and colleagues[41] surveyed buyers in relation to their behaviour towards pioneer and me-too follower brands. While they found that both Japanese and US buyers accepted about the same proportion of pioneer brands (~63 per cent), they reported being offered dramatically different numbers by the manufacturers: in Japan, about half of all new brands offered were pioneer brands, while in the United States only 14 per cent were pioneers. A possible explanation is that the Japanese suppliers better understand the retailers' preferences and try to meet them.

In France, where large-scale distribution is involved in conflicts with producers, the channels develop their own brands. For instance, large-scale retailers in France (hypermarkets) have created their own private labels over the last 20 years. Distributors' brands do not need any product-related advertising expenditure and tend to compete with manufacturers' brands. This leads to an inflation of distributors' brands and private labels, which compete against established manufacturers' brands.

International and global brands

International brands share a common trait of long-term orientation. The main objective of the brand is to establish brand goodwill or equity over time through consumer brand awareness and recognition. When products share very similar attributes and performance, a well-known brand may have the edge by virtue of its reputation and the consumer loyalty it has created. Accordingly, Procter & Gamble has retained some brands such as Ivory soap for more than a century. Camay soap is also nearing this age: the brand's name, that is, not the formula of the product, which has been regularly updated. Thus, public recognition of international brands is usually based on *considerable cumulative advertising expenditure*. They are often supported by the history of a prestigious company (for cars, Mercedes, Jaguar, Ferrari, Cadillac, etc.).[78]

Website link 9.4

Find an interactive table of the Top 100 global brands: **http:bwnt.businessweek.com/ interactive_reports/top_brands**.

Brands can be aligned with the local consumer culture, a foreign consumer culture or a global consumer culture.[79] Alden and colleagues[79] examined ads from India, Thailand, Korea, Germany, the Netherlands, France and the United States, finding

that most associate the brand with the local consumer culture (59 per cent), or global consumer culture (22 per cent), while only 4 per cent aligned the brand with a foreign consumer culture. Their definition of foreign consumer culture is fairly strict, in the sense that an association was only classified in this category if it was clearly from an identifiable country. If it was seen as 'Western' for instance, it would be classified as a global association, as it was 'not associated with a single country (local or foreign), but rather a larger group generally recognized as international and transcending individual national cultures' (p. 80[79]). Which associations are more effective is a more difficult question. Consumers may value localized international brand names, as well as international brands that convey foreign benefits.[80] For instance, Reebok customizes its image to national differences with a meaningful name (translated as *dashing step*) which has no foreign image; while Nike maintains a standardized image of 'fitness and performance' in all markets.[80] The brand name Nike has no special meaning in Chinese, but it does have a distinctly Western image which sounds appealing.

In order to be successfully aligned with a foreign consumer culture, brands need to have a *basic credibility which is based on a national image*.[81] Marlboro (cigarette) is associated with an American image, the Marlboro cowboy. Similarly, Chanel No. 5 is based on the image of French *luxe* and *haute couture*, conveyed by the character of Gabrielle Chanel (Coco). Buitoni is understood as Italian pasta and Johnny Walker as whisky from Scotland. Despite this, in each country, consumers 'repaint' the international brand image with their own local images.[82]

As noted in the introduction to this chapter, the interplay between brands and national images is a game of complex meanings (Table 9.1): there must be some degree of caution prior to making the affirmation that a brand is universal. Coca-Cola's name is adapted in Chinese to avoid negative connotations. Low-calorie sugar-free Coke is called Diet Coke in the US, but Coca Light is becoming more prevalent around the world. The word *diète* conjures up the image of a strict diet or the need to lose weight. Brand images combine with the product's origin and the manufacturer's name, which is also a brand. A name like Brother offers a fairly good combination of interpretive meanings because the Brother name diffuses an English/international image that hides the Japanese origin of the manufacturer. Brother manufactured electronic typewriters and items with no 'ethnic' relation to a specific country. Finally, the concept of brotherhood supports the image of reliability, faithfulness and loyalty of an object with which people may work closely.

A basic condition for belonging to the very narrow club of global brands is to have built brand equity over a number of years by considerable advertising spending based on consistent core themes (consistent both over time and across countries). Building a global brand is expensive, but valuable. The value of the Coca-Cola brand is estimated at US$70.5 billion, Microsoft at $65 billion, and the Marlboro brand name at $22 billion.[83] Advertising remains the key investment for developing brand awareness, although advertising spending has been claimed not to be an absolute necessity for creating brand equity, with such examples as the Body Shop or Häagen-Dazs having developed their brands through events, sponsoring and retail shops.[84]

The second condition is that the brand's image must have been carefully monitored over time. This requires considerable sophistication in the management of meaning. For instance, PepsiCo assesses its brand by examining recognition (awareness) and regard, which is made up of four components (brand reputation, affiliation, momentum and differentiation).[85] In Spain the company found that awareness is increasing and among those who are aware regard is growing (i.e. a healthy brand), but in Australia, there is little increase in awareness, even though regard is growing among those who are aware.[85] Thus, using this model, Pepsi can identify the aspects of the brand they need to address, such as increasing brand awareness in Australia.

Although some people try to defend the idea of global brands,[86] it is a somewhat blurred and probably even deceptive concept. There can only be a limited number of brands known by consumers in several countries throughout the world simultaneously (a few dozen, perhaps one or two hundred at most). As Kapferer (p. 169)[87] notes, there is still hope for local brands: 'The essence of local brands' strength is their being local, which means a considerably-felt proximity that goes far beyond the local brands' advantage to an extensive and well-known distribution network developed through time, by canvassing the country and delivering a faster service to customers'.

Many companies promote both global and local elements. Contrary to the global-brand building of McDonald's, Ronald McDonald is used as a point of differentiation in each market: he celebrates Christmas in Europe, Chinese New Year in Hong Kong, promotes wine in France and fish filets in Australia.[88]

However, it is the perceptions of globalness that often drive consumer behaviour. For instance, Steenkamp and colleagues.[89] surveyed consumers in the United States and Korea to assess perceived brand globalness (PBG). They found that PBG influences the likelihood of brand purchase through three sets of beliefs, that 'globalness' (a) signifies better quality, (b) provides status and prestige, or (c) provides a way to become part of a global consumer culture.

As was pointed out in Chapter 5, global brands are more likely to be portfolios of basically localized marketing assets (consumer franchise and goodwill based on images which are in fact heterogeneous), a mere collection of local brands, federated under a *lexically equivalent single name*. The brand name may not even be pronounced similarly in different linguistic areas, a factor which can be critical for radio advertising, for example.

The management of global brands is complex. As such, Douglas and colleagues[90] propose a brand architecture framework, based on the geographic scope, product scope and the level in the organization at which the brand is used. This framework is designed to search for ways to reduce the number of brands and improved efficiency and harmonize brand strategy across product lines and country markets.

The global brand, like the global campaign, requires a large amount of creative time and investment. A brand is a *sensitive asset of symbols*, suggested and maintained by diversified marketing communications: sponsoring, advertising, communication, public relations, communication through the product itself or even the style of outlets. This mix of marketing communications must be carefully managed, so that the public never feels betrayed in those beliefs that have been invested in the brand. Alain Etchegoyen (p. 55) describes the Louis Vuitton brand image in the following way:

There is no mythology without gods or demi-gods. That is why one must not expect gods to collapse into the melting pot of the market. Some products have to keep at a distance so that other products appear to come from somewhere else. The brand can only remain influential at the expense of maintaining a sacred fire. The imaginary Eden of carefully tended [brand] images will not withstand the boorish hell of bar codes [products].[91]

Furthermore, the complexity of trademark law must be considered on an international level. Despite the move towards a standard of foreign trademark protection which binds WTO member countries, there are still many differences across countries. Gillespie and colleagues[92] examined the patterns of protection internationally. They found that groups of countries differed in their treaty participation and varied in their local trademark legislation. For participation in foreign treaties, developed countries (83 per cent) and transitional economies (79 per cent) had a higher rate (83 per cent) than NICs (newly industrialized countries) (53 per cent) or LDCs (less developed countries) (45 per cent). There were also differences in trademark legislation, such as procedures to contest the application before it is approved, the legitimacy of prior use to stop a potential pre-empter, and the necessity to use the product to maintain the trademark after approval. Developed countries and newly industrialized countries (NICs) rated higher than less developed countries (LDCs) and transitional economies.

Website link 9.5

Read about emerging issues in intellectual property from the World Intellectual Property Organization: **http://www.wipo.int/about-ip/en/studies/**.

In short, the costs and the legal complexity of managing a global brand remain extremely high. Creating an international brand is an undertaking that should be considered as a long-term target, especially when starting from scratch. Yoshimori (p. 279) quotes Akio Morita's (Sony Chairman) 1955 reply to an American client who requested that Sony manufacture transistor radios for him as a subcontractor. Morita refused to manufacture 100,000 of them and, allegedly, said:

> Fifty years ago your brand name was probably as unknown as ours is today . . . Today I decide the first stage for the next fifty years of my company. In fifty years I can promise that our name [Sony] will be just as famous as your company's is today.[57]

Questions

1. Discuss the international transferability of the following assemblages (product, company, country of manufacture, brand name).

Generic product	Company name	Brand name	Made in
Pizza	Dr Oetker	Pizza Rustica	Germany
Computer chip	Intel	Pentium	United States
Drilling tool	Bosch	Fuchsschwanz	Spain
Car	Daewoo	Daewoo/Nexia	South Korea
Tomato sauce	Mars	Dolmio	The Netherlands
Insecticide	Bayer	Baygon	Germany

2. A very large German food company, Dr Oetker, still sells its products in France under the name Ancel (the brand name of a French company taken over many years ago). Why?

3. Discuss the relationship between a country's image (through its people, its history, its political and social situation, etc.) and the image of products known to be made in this country.

4. Discuss the possible international extension of the following companies and/or brand names:

■ Müller (German yoghurts)
■ Barilla (Italian pastas and cookies)
■ Procter & Gamble
■ Teysseire (French syrups)
■ Kuoni (a Swiss tour operator)
■ Schimmelpenninck (Dutch cigars and cigarillos)
■ Ishikawajima Harima Heavy Industries (a Japanese industrial equipment company)
■ Roi des Montagnes (French dried mushrooms)
■ Hewlett-Packard
■ Douwe-Egberts (a large Dutch food and tobacco company)
■ Club Méditerrannée (a French tour operator)

5. Given the increasing importance of China as a consumer market, Nestlé has decided to stop using the Chambourcy category brand name for milk-based products used worldwide, which is a brand with great recognition in Europe and Latin America. The name was deemed too difficult to transfer into the Chinese linguistic context. Furthermore, Nestlé maintained advertising spending at three levels (corporate name, category name and product name) and decided to use the Nestlé name directly for all its milk-based products in addition to a brand name for the particular product in some cases. Discuss the marketing and management implications of such a decision.

References

1. Keller, Kevin Lane (1998), *Strategic Brand Management: Building, Measuring and Managing Brand Equity.* Upper Saddle River, NJ: Prentice Hall.
2. Leclerc, France, Bernd H. Schmitt, and Laurette Dubé (1994), 'Foreign Branding and Its Effects on Product Perceptions and Attitudes', *Journal of Marketing Research*, 31 (2), 263–70.
3. Loeffler, Michael (2002), 'A Multinational Examination of the "(Non-)Domestic Product" Effect', *International Marketing Review*, 19 (5), 482–98.
4. Harris, Richard Jackson, Bettina Garner-Earl, Sara J. Sprick, and Collette Carroll (1994), 'Effects of Foreign Product Names and Country-of-Origin Attributions on Advertisement Evaluations', *Psychology and Marketing*, 11 (2, March/April), 129–44.
5. Nishina, Sadafumi (1990), 'Japanese Consumers: Introducing Foreign Products/Brands into the Japanese Market', *Journal of Advertising Research*, 30 (2), 35–45.
6. Nebenzahl, Israel D., Eugene D. Jaffé, and Jean-Claude Usunier (2003), 'Personifying Country-of-Origin Research', *Management International Review*, 43 (4), 383–406.
7. Bilkey, Warren J. and Erik Nes (1982), 'Country-of-Origin Effects on Product Evaluations', *Journal of*

International Business Studies (Spring–Summer), 89–99.
8. Papadopoulos, Nicholas and Louise A. Heslop (1993), *Product and Country Images: Research and Strategy.* New York: The Haworth Press.
9. Samiee, Saeed (1994), 'Customer Evaluation of Products in a Global Market', *Journal of International Business Studies*, 25 (3), 579–604.
10. Jaffé, Eugene D. and Israel D. Nebenzahl (2001), *National Image and Competitive Advantage: The Theory and Practice of Country-of-Origin Effects.* Copenhagen: Copenhagen Business School Press.
11. Nebenzahl, Israel D., Eugene D. Jaffé, and Shlomo I. Lampert (1997), 'Towards a Theory of Country Image Effect on Product Evaluation', *Management International Review*, 37 (1), 27–49.
12. Peterson, Robert A. and Alain Jolibert (1995), 'A Meta-Analysis of Country-of-Origin Effects', *Journal of International Business Studies*, 26 (4), 883–900.
13. Verlegh, Peeter W.J. and Jan-Benedict E.M. Steenkamp (1999), 'A Review and Meta-Analysis of Country of Origin Research', *Journal of Economic Psychology*, 20, 521–46.
14. Agrawal, Jagdish and Wagner A. Kamakura (1999), 'Country of Origin: A Competitive Advantage?',

International Journal of Research in Marketing, 16 (4), 255–67.

15. Askegaard, S. and Guliz Ger (1998), 'Product-Country Images: Toward a Contextualized Approach', *European Advances in Consumer Research*, 3, 50–8.

16. Batra, Rajeev, Venkatram Ramaswamy, Dana L. Alden, Jan-Benedict E.M. Steenkamp, and S. Ramachander (2000), 'Effects of Brand Local and Nonlocal Origin on Consumer Attitudes in Developing Countries', *Journal of Consumer Psychology*, 9 (2), 83–96.

17. Klein, Jill Gabrielle, Richard Ettenson, and Marlene D. Morris (1998), 'The Animosity Model of Foreign Product Purchase: An Empirical Test in the People's Republic of China', *Journal of Marketing*, 62 (1), 89–100.

18. Smith, N. (1990), *Morality and the Market*. London: Routledge.

19. Yaprak, Attila (1987), 'The Country of Origin Paradigm in Cross-National Consumer Behavior: The State of the Art', in *World Marketing Congress*, Kenneth D. Bahn and M. Joeseph Sirgy, Eds. Blacksburg, VA: Academy of Marketing Science.

20. Klein, Jill Gabrielle (2002), 'Us Versus Them, or Us Versus Everyone? Delineating Consumer Aversion to Foreign Goods', *Journal of International Business Studies*, 33 (2), 345–63.

21. Wang, Chih-Kang and Charles W. Lamb Jr (1983), 'The Impact of Selected Environmental Forces Upon Consumers' Willingness to Buy Foreign Products', *Journal of the Academy of Marketing Science*, 11 (Winter), 71–84.

22. Ahmed, Sadrudin A., Alain d'Astous, and Jelloul Eljabri (2002a), 'The Impact of Technological Complexity on Consumers' Perceptions of Products Made in Highly and Newly Industrialised Countries', *International Marketing Review*, 19 (4), 387–407.

23. Khanna, Sri Ram (1986), 'Asian Companies and the Country Stereotype Paradox: An Empirical Study', *Columbia Journal of World Business* (Summer), 29–38.

24. Thorelli, Hans B. and Aleksandra E. Glowacka (1995), 'Willingness of American Industrial Buyers to Source Internationally', *Journal of Business Research*, 32, 21–30.

25. Saghafi, Massoud M., Fanis Varvoglis, and Tomas Vega (1991), 'Why US Firms Don't Buy from Latin American Companies', *Industrial Marketing Management*, 20, 207–13.

26. Jaffé, Eugene D. and Israel D. Nebenzahl (1989), 'Global Promotion of Country Image: The Case of the 1988 Korean Olympic Games', Reijo Luostarinen, Ed. in *Dynamics of International Business*, vol. 1, Proceedings of the 15th Annual Conference of the European International Business Association. Helsinki, Finland, 358–85.

27. Darling, John B. and F. Kraft (1977), 'A Competitive Profile of Products and Associated Marketing Practices of Selected European and Non-European Countries', *European Journal of Marketing*, 11 (7), 519–37.

28. Kamins, Michael A. and Akira Nagashima (1995), 'Perceptions of Products Made in Japan Versus Those Made in the United States among Japanese and American Executives: A Longitudinal Perspective', *Asia Pacific Journal of Management*, 12 (1), 49–68.

29. Kraft, Frederick B. and Kae H. Chung (1992), 'Korean Importer Perceptions of Us and Japanese Industrial Goods', *International Marketing Review*, 9 (2), 59–73.

30. Bhuian, Shahid N. (1997), 'Saudi Consumers' Attitudes Towards European, US and Japanese Products and Marketing Practices', *European Journal of Marketing*, 31 (7), 467–86.

31. Usunier, Jean-Claude (2006), 'Relevance in Business Research: The Case of Country-of-Origin Research in Marketing', *European Management Review*, 3 (1), 60–73.

32. Samiee, Saeed, Terence A. Shimp, and Subhash Sharma (2005), 'Brand Origin Recognition Accuarcy: Its Antecedents and Consumers' Cognitive Limitations', *Journal of International Business Studies*, 36 (4), 379–97.

33. Shimp, Terence A. and Subash Sharma (1987), 'Consumer Ethnocentrism: Construction and Validation of the Cetscale', *Journal of Marketing Research*, 24 (August), 280–89.

34. Sharma, Subash, Terence A. Shimp, and J. Shin (1995), 'Consumer Ethnocentrism: A Test of Antecedents and Moderators', *Journal of the Academy of Marketing Science*, 23 (1), 26–37.

35. Witkowski, Terrence H. (1998), 'Consumer Ethnocentrism in Two Emerging Markets: Determinants and Predictive Validity', *Advances in Consumer Research*, 25, 258–63.

36. Klein, Jill Gabrielle and Richard Ettenson (1999), 'Consumer Animosity and Consumer Ethnocentrism: An Analysis of Unique Antecedents', *Journal of International Consumer Marketing*, 11 (4), 5–24.

37. Nakos, George and Yannis Hajidimitriou (2007), 'The Impact of National Animosity on Consumer Purchase: The Modifying Factor of Personal Characteristics', *Journal of International Consumer Marketing*, 19 (3), 53–72.

38. Balabanis, George and A. Diamantopoulos (2004), 'Domestic Country Bias, Country-of-Origin Effects, and Consumer Ethnocentrism: A Multidimensional Unfolding Approach', *Journal of the Academy of Marketing Science*, 32 (1), 80–95.

39. Mascarenhas, Oswald A.J. and Duane Kujawa (1998), 'American Consumer Attitude toward Foreign Direct Investments and Their Products', *Multinational Business Review*, 6 (Autumn), 1–9.

40. Alden, Dana L., Jan-Benedict E.M. Steenkamp, and Rajeev Batra (2006), 'Consumer Attitudes toward Marketplace Globalization: Structure, Antecedents and

Consequences', *International Journal of Research in Marketing*, 23 (3), 227–39.

41. Alpert, Frank, Michael Kamins, Tomoaki Sakano, Naoto Onzo, and John Graham (2001), 'Retail Buyer Beliefs, Attitude and Behaviour toward Pioneer and Me-Too Follower Brands: A Comparative Study of Japan and the USA', *International Marketing Review*, 18 (2), 160–87.

42. Javalgi, Rajshekhar, Khare Virginie, Andrew Gross, and Robert Schere (2005), 'An Application of the Consumer Ethnocentrism Model to French Consumers', *International Business Review*, 14 (3), 325–44.

43. Klein, Jill Gabrielle, Richard Ettenson, and Balaji C. Krishnan (2006), 'Extending the Construct of Consumer Ethnocentrism: When Foreign Products Are Preferred', *International Marketing Review*, 23 (3), 304.

44. Reardon, James, Chip Miller, Irena Vida, and Irina Kim (2005), 'The Effects of Ethnocentrism and Economic Development on the Formation of Brand and Ad Attitudes in Transitional Economies', *European Journal of Marketing*, 39 (7/8), 737–54.

45. Yang, Zhilin, Nan Zhou, and Jie Chen (2005), 'Brand Choice of Older Chinese Consumer', *Journal of International Consumer Marketing*, 17 (4), 65–81.

46. Herche, Joel (1992), 'A Note on the Predictive Validity of Cetscale', *Journal of the Academy of Marketing Science*, 20 (3), 261–4.

47. Usunier, Jean-Claude and Ghislaine Cestre (2007), 'Product Ethnicity: Revisiting the Match between Products and Countries', *Journal of International Marketing*, 15 (3), 32–72.

48. Lee, Julie Anne, Ellen Garbarino, and Dawn Lerman (2007), 'How Cultural Differences in Uncertainty Avoidance Affect Product Perceptions', *International Marketing Review*, 24 (3), 330–49.

49. Kotler, Philip, Ang Swee Hoon, Leong Siew Meng, and Tan Chin Tiong (2003), *Marketing Management: An Asian Perspective* (3rd edn). Singapore: Pearson.

50. Klein, Naomi (2002), *No Logo: No Space, No Choice, No Jobs*. London: Macmillan.

51. Rosen, Barry Nathan, Jean J. Boddewyn, and Ernst A. Louis (1989), 'US Brands Abroad: An Empirical Study of Global Branding', *International Marketing Review*, 6 (1), 7–19.

52. Wilsher, Peter (1992), 'Diverse and Perverse', *Management Today* (July), 32–5.

53. Onkvisit, Sak and John J. Shaw (1989), 'The International Dimension of Branding: Strategic Considerations and Decisions', *International Marketing Review*, 6 (2), 22–34.

54. Melewar, T.C. and John Saunders (1998), 'Global Corporate Visual Identity Systems: Standardization, Control, and Benefits', *International Marketing Review*, 15 (4), 291–308.

55. Cabat, Odilon (1989), 'Archéologie De La Marque Moderne', in *La Marque*, Jean-Noel Kapferer and Jean-Claude Thoenig, Eds. Paris: MacGraw-Hill.

56. Czinkota, Michael R. and Illka A. Ronkainen (1990), *International Marketing* (2nd ed.). Hinsdale, IL: Dryden Press.

57. Yoshimori, Masaru (1989), 'Concepts et Stratégies de Marques au Japon', in *La Marque*, Jean-Noel Kapferer and Jean-Claude Thoenig, Eds. Paris: McGraw-Hill.

58. Usunier, Jean-Claude and Janet Shaner (2002), 'Using Linguistics for Creating Better International Brand Names', *Journal of Marketing Communications*, 8 (4), 211–28.

59. Huang, Yue Yuan and Allan K.K. Chan (1997), 'Chinese Branding Name: From General Principles to Specific Rules', *International Journal of Advertising*, 16 (4), 320–35.

60. Robertson, Kim (1989), 'Strategically Desirable Brand Name Characteristics', *Journal of Consumer Marketing*, 6 (Fall), 61–71.

61. Colombat, Catherine (1997), 'Danone Imprime sa Marque sur la Planète', *L'Essentiel du Management*, April, 74–80.

62. Vanden Bergh, Bruce, Keith Adler, and Lauren Oliver (1987), 'Linguistic Distinction among Top Brand Names', *Journal of Advertising Research*, 27 (4), 39–44.

63. Giordan, Alain-Eric (1988), *Exporter Plus 2*. Paris: Economica.

64. Tavassoli, Nader T. and Jin K. Han (2002), 'Auditory and Visual Brand Identifiers in Chinese and English', *Journal of International Marketing*, 10 (2), 13–28.

65. Schmitt, Bernd H. and Yigang Pan (1994), 'Managing Corporate and Brand Identities in the Asia-Pacific Region', *California Management Review*, 36 (4, Summer), 32–47.

66. Tavassoli, Nader T. (1999), 'Temporal and Associative Memory in Chinese and English', *Journal of Consumer Research*, 26 (2), 170–81.

67. Pan, Yigang and Bernd H. Schmitt (1995), 'What's in a Name? An Empirical Comparison of Chinese and Western Brand Names', *Asian Journal of Marketing*, 4 (1), 7–16.

68. Schmitt, Bernd H. and Shi Zhang (1998), 'Language Structure and Categorization: A Study of Classifiers in Consumer Cognition, Judgement and Choice', *Journal of Consumer Research*, 25 (2), 108–22.

69. Zhang, Shi and Bernd H. Schmitt (2001), 'Creating Local Brands in Multilingual International Markets', *Journal of Marketing Research*, XXXVIII (August), 313–25.

70. Hong, F.C., Anthony Pecotich, and Clifford J. Schultz (2002), 'Brand Name Translation: Language Constraints, Product Attributes, and Consumer Perceptions in East and Southeast Asia', *Journal of International Marketing*, 10 (2), 29–45.

71. Wilke, Margaritha (1994), 'Der Werte Name – Die Marke auf Chinesisch', *Der Neue China*, 21 (3, September), 15–16.

72. Francis, June N.P., Janet P.Y. Lam, and Jan Walls (2002), 'Executive Insights: The Impact of Linguistic Differences on International Brand Name Standardization: A Comparison of English and Chinese Brand Names of Fortune-500 Companies', *Journal of International Marketing*, 10 (1), 98–116.

73. Ewing, Michael T., Julie Napoli, Leyland F. Pitt, and Alistair Watts (2002), 'On the Renaissance of Chinese Brands', *International Journal of Advertising*, 21 (2), 197–216.

74. Lambin, Jean-Jacques (1989), 'La Marque et le Comportement de Choix de L'Acheteur', in *La Marque*, Jean-Noel Kapferer and Jean-Claude Thoenig, Eds. Paris: McGraw-Hill.

75. Contensou, François (1989), 'La Marque, L'efficience Économique et la Formation des Prix', in *La Marque*, Jean-Noel Kapferer and Jean-Claude Thoenig, Eds. Paris: McGraw-Hill.

76. Abegglen, James and George Stalk Jr (1986), 'The Japanese Corporation as Competitor', *California Management Review*, XXVIII (3, Spring), 9–37.

77. Dupuy, François and Jean-Claude Thoenig (1989), 'La Marque et l'Échange', in *La Marque*, Jean-Noel Kapferer and Jean-Claude Thoenig, Eds. Paris: McGraw-Hill.

78. Hsieh, Ming H. (2002), 'Identifying Brand Image Dimensionality and Measuring the Degree of Brand Globalization: A Cross-National Study', *Journal of International Marketing*, 10 (2), 46–67.

79. Alden, Dana L., Jan-Benedict E.M. Steenkamp, and Rajeev Batra (1999), 'Brand Positioning through Advertising in Asia, North America and Europe: The Role of Global Consumer Culture', *Journal of Marketing*, 63 (January), 75–87.

80. Fan, Ying (2002), 'The National Image of Global Brands', *Journal of Brand Management*, 9 (3), 180–92.

81. Shalofsky, Ivor (1987), 'Research for Global Brands', *European Research* (May), 88–93.

82. Clark, Harold F. Jr (1987), 'Consumer and Corporate Values: Yet Another View on Global Marketing', *International Journal of Advertising*, 6, 29–42.

83. Interbrand (2003), 'Best Global Brands', *Business Week*, 2 August.

84. Joachimsthaler, Erich and David A. Aaker (1997), 'Building Brands without Mass Media', *Harvard Business Review*, 75 (1, January–February), 39–50.

85. Kish, Paulette, Dwight R. Riskey, and Roger A. Kerin (2001), 'Measurement and Tracking of Brand Equity in the Global Marketplace', *International Marketing Review*, 18 (1), 91–6.

86. Peebles, Dean M. (1989), 'Don't Write Off Global Advertising: A Commentary', *International Marketing Review*, 6 (1), 73–8.

87. Kapferer, Jean-Noel (2002), 'Is There Really No Hope for Local Brands?', *Journal of Brand Management*, 9 (3), 163–70.

88. Lindstrom, Martin (2000), 'Global Branding Versus Local Marketing', *Clickz Network Solutions for Marketers*, 23 November, www.clickz.com/showPage.html?page=832711.

89. Steenkamp, Jan-Benedict E.M., Rajeev Batra, and Dana L. Alden (2003), 'How Perceived Brand Globalness Creates Brand Value', *Journal of International Business Studies*, 34 (1), 53–65.

90. Douglas, Susan P., C. Samuel Craig, and Edwin J. Nijssen (2001), 'Executive Insights: Integrating Branding Strategy across Markets: Building International Brand Architecture', *Journal of International Marketing*, 9 (2), 97–114.

91. Etchegoyen, Alain (1990), *Les Entreprises Ont-Elles Une Âme?* Paris: Editions François Bourin.

92. Gillespie, Kate, Kishore Krishna, and Susan Jarvis (2002), 'Protecting Global Brands: Toward a Global Norm', *Journal of International Marketing*, 10 (2), 99–112.

Appendix 9

Teaching materials

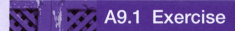

A9.1 Exercise

Interpreting symbolic attributes

Below are physical attributes for different products; try to imagine how they could be diversely interpreted symbolically in different cultures (you do not need to indicate which interpretation corresponds to a particular culture, but simply to emphasize probable divergence of interpretation across cultures in general).

- A car/colour black
- Orange juice/thick (pulpy)
- Blue Cheese (*Penicillium glaucum*)
- Beer/frothy
- Orange juice/colour deep orange
- Car/automatic
- Apple juice/vitamins added
- Refrigerator/ice dispenser
- Cheese/packed in a wooden box
- Car/diesel engine

For further guidance, see Zeithaml[1] and also Solomon (pp. 67–73).[2]

A9.2 Case

Soshi Sumsin Ltd

Sammy Soshi's first assignment for his new job with Soshi Sumshin Ltd was to recommend a new name for the firm's line of electronic products. Sammy had completed his MBA at Emory University in May 2002 and had returned to Seoul, Korea, to work in his father's firm. Soshi Sumsin manufactured a line of electronic products which included VCRs, stereos and televisions. Mr Soshi (Senior) got involved in electronics manufacturing when he agreed to manufacture television components for an American manufacturer in 1980. Eventually, he was producing a full line of television sets, as well as VCRs and stereo equipment for three American firms. In addition, he had been marketing his own line of products in the Korean market starting in 1992 under the Sumsin brand name.

Mr Soshi felt that his firm was now ready, both in terms of manufacturing know-how and capital, to enter international markets under his own brand name. The American market was chosen as the first target because of its size and buying power, and an introduction date of April 2003 was tentatively set. Being unfamiliar with the American market, Mr Soshi relied heavily on his son, Sammy, to help with marketing decisions.

The first problem Sammy tackled was the selection of a brand name for the line. His father had planned to use the Sumsin name in the American market. Sammy pointed out that failing to carefully consider the effect of a brand name in a different culture could cause major marketing difficulties at a later stage. He cited the Tatung experience as a case in point. Tatung was a Taiwanese maker of televisions, fans and computer terminals. When the company entered the American market it did not even consider changing its brand name. The Tatung company had a favourable connotation in Chinese and was known in the company's oriental markets. However, in the United States, not only was the name meaningless, but it was difficult to know how to pronounce it.

Because of these difficulties, Tatung's American advertising agency finally decided to emphasize the strangeness of the name, and it launched a campaign based on a play on words to help customers pronounce Tatung. Each ad carried the query, 'Cat Got Your Tatung?' Sammy believed that a lot of effort that should have been placed on the product itself had been spent on overcoming a bad trade name.

Sammy cited a second example of problems resulting from a poorly chosen brand name. Another Taiwanese company, Kunnan Lo, introduced its own brand of tennis rackets in the American market in 1987. Recognizing that their own name would present problems in the American market, they decided to select an American name. Ultimately, they decided on the name Kennedy; it was quite similar to their company name, and it was certainly familiar in the United States. However, after initial promotional efforts, it quickly became apparent that Kennedy was not a neutral name. Many tennis players were Republicans, and for them the Kennedy name had negative connotations. As a result, the name was changed to Kennex, a neutral, artificial word that was still similar to the company name. However, Kennex also quickly proved to be unsatisfactory, because of some confusion with the name Kleenex. To eliminate this confusion, the name was finally changed to Pro-Kennex, which provided both a tennis tie-in and retention of a root similar to Kunnan Lo. The waste of resources in the series of name changes would have been better avoided.

Determined to avoid the mistakes of these other companies entering the American market, Sammy Soshi carefully evaluated the alternatives available to his company. The first was his father's preference – to use a company family name. However, Sumsin was somewhat difficult for English-speaking people to pronounce and seemed meaningless and foreign. Soshi was equally unfamiliar and meaningless, but he was also afraid that Americans would confuse it with the Japanese raw fish, *sushi*.

A second alternative was to acquire ownership of an existing American brand name, preferably one with market recognition. After considerable research, he chose the name Monarch. The Monarch company had started manufacturing radios in Chicago in 1932 and Monarch radios had been nationally known in the 1940s. The company was badly hurt by television in the 1950s, which reduced the size of the radio market appreciably. The company was finally wiped out by the invasion of inexpensive transistor radios from Asia in the 1960s. The company filed for bankruptcy in 1972. Sammy found that he could buy the rights to the Monarch name for $50,000. The name was tied in with electronic products in the public's mind, but he wondered how many people still remembered or recognized the Monarch name. He also wondered whether this recognition might be more negative than positive because of the company's failure in the market.

A third alternative would be to select a new name and build market recognition through promotion. Such a name would need to be politically and socially neutral in the American market and ultimately in other foreign markets. It had to be easy to pronounce and to remember with a neutral or favourable meaning to the public. The possibilities might be considered.

The first was Proteus, the name of an ancient Greek sea god. This name would be easy to pronounce in most European languages, but was almost too neutral to help sell the product. The other alternative was Blue Streak, again, an easy name in English, but not necessarily in other European languages. Sammy felt that the favourable connotation of speed and progress might provide a boost for the products to which it was applied.

(Source: Adapted from Cundiff and Hilger, pp. 440–42.[3] Cundiff, E.W. and Hilger, M.T., *Marketing in the International Environment*, 2nd edn, © 1988, reproduced by permission of Pearson Education, Inc., Upper Saddle River, NJ.)

Questions

1. Evaluate the alternative names being considered by Sammy Soshi. Which name would you recommend?

2. Whatever new name is chosen, should Soshi Sumsin adopt the same name in the Korean market?

3. What are the advantages of selecting different brand names, as appropriate, in each foreign market?

4. Enumerate the characteristics that should be possessed by a good international brand name.

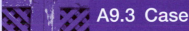

A9.3 Case

Derivados de Leche SA

Derivados de Leche SA, founded in 1968, was the first firm to market yoghurt in Mexico. It distributed yoghurt under the brand name Delsa only in Mexico City, primarily in a limited number of upper-income areas. The company was family owned, and the capital was all local. For the first five years, Delsa was sold in food stores, particularly in the newly developing supermarkets, without any advertising or other promotion. Yoghurt was a new, unfamiliar food product in the Mexican market, but Delsa depended primarily on word of mouth to provide product recognition.

In 1983, a number of laws regulating foreign investment in Mexico were modified under a single new 'regulation of foreign investment' law. According to this law foreign investors were welcome in Mexico on a joint labour basis so long as the foreign ownership share did not exceed 49 per cent. Labour-intensive industries that helped to decentralize population were particularly welcome. It was many years before this affected the yoghurt market, but eventually three multinationals entered on this joint venture basis, changing the structure of the market dramatically.

The first new brand, Chambourcy, was introduced by a joint venture subsidiary of Nestlé which had operated in Mexico since 1935. This company, Industrias Alimentacias Club SA, was a major Mexican food producer with 7000 employees. Chambourcy was launched with a strong promotional campaign and wide distribution. The following year, in 1989, a subsidiary of the French food firm, BSN-Gervais, launched its Danone yoghurt in the Mexican market.

Danone was also heavily supported with promotion. Finally, in 1995, a third multinational entered the market. Productos de Leche SA was 51 per cent owned by Mexican capital and 49 per cent by the Borden Company of the United States; it entered the Mexican market with two brands of yoghurt, Darel and Bonafina.

By 2001, the management of Derivados de Leche SA was becoming concerned about its future position in the yoghurt market. All three multinational competitors were aggressive marketers and promoters and were strong financially. Although the foreign ownership was a minority (49 per cent), management was dominated in each case by the minority ownership, so that management was competent and professional. In the short term, Delsa benefited from the primary demand creation activities of the multinationals. In 1998, Delsa sales reached almost 1600 tons, and by 2001, grew to 3800 tons. But Delsa's market share had dropped from over 95 per cent in 1985 (there were some other, very small, Mexican-owned competitors) to only 21 per cent in 2001.

The three multinationals shared 77.5 per cent of the market. If the trend continued, it was feared that Delsa's share of the market might drop so low that it would provide very little product recognition. And it was possible that ultimately sales volume would stabilize and per-haps even decline.

By 2002, Delsa management was faced with the grim reality of competition from financially strong and aggressive, professionally managed multinationals. Delsa managers felt that pricing could not be blamed for this loss in market share; the sales price of Delsa was slightly below that of its competitors. A major handicap for Delsa was its failure to promote recognition of its brand name. Although Delsa had been pulled along in the market by the initial marketing efforts which were designed to create a primary demand for yoghurt, the marketing efforts of the competitors were now focused almost entirely on selective brand name promotion. Delsa management had concentrated its efforts on getting the product into retail outlets and main-taining good relationships with dealers; no effort had been made to create consumer recogni-tion and franchises through advertising and other promotion. Management was made up of the family members who owned the company; they brought little professional training to the job.

Owner-managers of small and medium-sized firms in Mexico tended to run their busi-nesses for quick, short-term profit rather than long-term development. New capital invest-ment was needed to enlarge the production capacity, and serious consideration needed to be given to investing in a promotional campaign to build and maintain Delsa brand recognition.

Delsa was considering applying for a government-subsidized loan to double its production capacity from 4000 tons per year to 8000 tons. These loans were available only to 100 per cent Mexican-owned manufacturers, but were limited to the financing of manufacturing facilities. Delsa's marketing manager wanted to emphasize the local Mexican ownership of Delsa and to increase the firm's advertising budget from $40,000 to about $200,000. He also wanted to redesign the package so as to include some statement that indicated the brand was of pure Mexican origin. Delsa's owners wanted to put pressure on the Mexican government to limit the food processing industry to 100 per cent Mexican-owned firms. It was not known what the possibilities were of getting such legislation passed.

(Source: Adapted from Cundiff and Hilger, pp. 335–6.[3] Cundiff, E.W. and Hilger, M.T., *Marketing with International Environment*, 2nd edn, © 1988, reproduced by permission of Pearson Education, Inc., Upper Saddle River, NJ.)

Questions

1. What are Delsa's strengths and weaknesses in competing with multinationals?

2. What is the impact of 'country of origin' on demand for yoghurt?

3. What recommendations can you make to strengthen Delsa's market position?

Appendix references

1. Zeithaml, Valarie A. (1988), 'Consumer Perceptions of Price, Quality and Value: A Means–End Model and Synthesis of Evidence', *Journal of Marketing*, 52 (July), 2–22.
2. Solomon, Michael R. (1994), *Consumer Behavior* (2nd edn). Needham Heights: Allyn and Bacon.
3. Cundiff, Edward W. and Marye Tharp Hilger (1988), *Marketing in the International Environment*. Englewood Cliffs, NJ: Prentice Hall.

The critical role of price in relational exchange

At first sight, price appears to be anything but 'cultural'. In appearance, it is usually a figure, a number or a unit. And so price is often assumed to be an intrinsically objective element of exchange and an issue reserved for rational economic factors. But price has a more subjective element. It is a signal that conveys meaning and as such is perceived in quite different ways across cultures and across individuals. The subjective and perceptual aspects of price are examined in section 10.1.

Price is an important component of communication between buyers and sellers. It is also an element in short-term or long-term bonding. Price is a decisive element of social interaction between buyer and seller; it is a way of evaluating offerings, it endorses their agreement and shapes their relationship, whether short or long term. In section 10.2 bargaining is examined as a classical, primitive and widespread relationship between buyer and seller, particularly prevalent where there is no compulsory price labelling. In modern mass markets, the primary influence wielded by customers on price usually takes the form of a 'take it or leave it' bargain with quasi-anonymous sellers. This all or nothing attitude contrasts with the more 'friendly' concept of price in bargaining and relational exchange, where each party wants both parties to make a good deal, ending with a 'win–win' outcome: economic transactions inevitably have a human relations component. Section 10.3 deals with situations where the price is clearly marked and hence known by customers, who are then in a position to appraise the price–quality ratio.

The last three sections of the chapter present company attitudes in international market pricing decisions. An anthropomorphic approach is used whereby companies and markets are considered as interacting parties to an exchange. Companies are led to distort and manipulate prices between domestic markets, either to increase consumer brand loyalty in certain markets through offensive strategic pricing, or to avoid parallel imports which undermine their local distribution system (see section 10.4). Price can also be used as a tactical weapon vis-à-vis competitors in particular national markets (see section 10.5). Finally, price can be manipulated because of an inflationary environment or by over- or under-invoicing in order to close price-sensitive deals (see section 10.6).

This chapter does not consider the strictly economic aspects of price, such as the relationship between price and costs in international marketing or the law of one price, which states that, in the absence of transport, transaction-related costs and price discrimination, trade takes place in only one market and only one price prevails. Nor does it discuss the influence of exchange rate variance on price strategies in international marketing. However, you will find some information on these issues on the website, including an interesting paper by Froot and colleagues analysing price differences across countries over the last 700 years.

Website link 10.1

The iPod Index shows in which countries it is best to buy an identical iPod: http://www.comsec.com.au/public/news.aspx?id=809.

Table 10.1 Price-based signals

Meaning conveyed by price in	by . . .	Section
Buyer–seller interactions	Bargaining rituals, price offers and relationship development	10.2
Consumer behaviour	Differences in consumer price-mindedness across cultures	10.3
Product evaluation	To what extent is quality inferred from price?	10.3
(Tough) competition	Signalling willingness to compete by dumping prices	10.4
Target market(s)	Showing commitment to customers in a target market through attractive pricing	10.4
Distributors (grey markets)	Signalling desire to avoid parallel imports from opportunistic distributors who disturb international price policy and may damage brand image	10.4
(Peaceful) competition	Signalling willingness to enter a market with cartels 'peacefully'	10.5
Price increase policy	Meaning conveyed by price in high-inflation contexts	10.6
Relationship to suppliers	Overcoming barriers for supplier to receive real price by over- or under-invoicing	10.6

10.1

Price as a signal conveying meaning

Prices may be considered to be fairly objective in most consumer goods and consumer durables markets where goods are sold in mass distribution outlets that allow price comparison between stores. In such cases, the meaning conveyed by the price evolves mostly around the value of the good and the money transfer.

Prices become more central to the relationship between buyers and sellers, and to companies and their customers, distributors or competitors in the following conditions:

1. Price is not displayed.
2. It is not necessarily the seller who announces the first price.
3. There is no clear market reference for what would be a 'fair price'.
4. A particular price is understood by both the seller and the buyer as taking place within a series of transactions (i.e. past, present and future).
5. Prices for particular transactions are not necessarily meant to cover even marginal cost.
6. Prices may be distorted by inflation and government price regulation.
7. Total price is a combination of direct and indirect prices (e.g. product price plus price of maintenance, spare parts, updates, etc.).

These seven points are examples of situations where price is more 'relational' than 'economic'. As shown in Table 10.1, price can convey meaning and be an object of interaction between the various participants of the market situation, that is, manufacturers, distributors, consumers and competitors.

10.2

Bargaining

Limits of price as an element of social relations: bargaining versus no bargaining

The importance of bargaining is often underestimated because, in many countries, consumers are used to prices that are clearly displayed. If the price is not right, the product will not be bought. In most cases, people no longer bargain – or at least they appear not to. Bargaining is either legally prohibited or strictly controlled in most developed countries. Most sales of consumer products take place within oligopolistic distribution channels offering merchandise from producers also organized in oligopolies. In direct relations with customers, prices are unilaterally set by vendors and are therefore non-negotiable. Bargaining at the supermarket checkout is rare and liable to result in confusion or embarrassment.

However, once the price reaches a substantial level, people in developed countries return to bargaining as a way to maximize the value to both consumer and retailer. In many retail contexts, exchange still takes place through bargaining, e.g. new and second-hand cars, furniture, property, construction activities and industrial machinery.[1] Bargaining is also common in informal retail contexts, such as garage sales or flea markets, where the value of the transaction is often insignificant to both vendor and consumer.[2,3] Bargaining in these contexts is not just motivated by rational economics, as Hermann (p. 56) writes, 'the practice of small-scale bargaining is significant for a number of reasons . . . it provides a degree of empowerment, both pecuniary and psychological, in that individual actors can influence the price of goods through their knowledge of consumer goods and skill in negotiation'.[2]

In most developing countries, for example Thailand, India, the Philippines and the Middle East, bargaining is still the rule, even for items of low value or little vital interest. Weak purchasing power considerably increases the importance of bargaining. In certain African markets (e.g. Mauritania), where sugar is sold by the 'lump' and carrots by the 'slice', and island economies (e.g. Marshal Islands), where cigarettes are sold by the 'stick', bargaining is essential for survival. Moreover, people may not be pressed for time; the rewards of bargaining in relation to its cost are fundamentally different in developing and industrialized nations. Finally, bargaining has a fun dimension as well as a human one, possibly because of its similarity to role-playing. The human dimension exists because bargaining and commerce generally are contemplated with more seriousness in developing countries than in industrialized ones where commercial interaction has been largely 'depersonalized', particularly in the case of consumer goods. This is in fact one of the major reasons that bargaining is either legally prohibited or socially restricted in developed countries. As stated by Allen (p. 49):

It has conventionally been supposed that bargaining is socially disadvantageous, on the grounds that it breeds hostility, rivalry and distrust . . . While it is true that there is always an element of suspicion as to the real value of the commodity (and subsequently of the price), this suspicion never turns into an open conflict if the bargainers intend to conclude the sale. Any bargainer, whether seller or buyer, is careful not to offend his partner, for fear of putting an end to the transaction. Thus, though initiated by suspicion, bargaining tends rather to eliminate it, instituting instead an atmosphere of common interest and trust, which often leads to a lasting client relationship. In this way it cements community relations, rather than subverts them.[4]

Website link 10.2

See Haggling 101; tips for getting better prices: **http://abcnews.go.com/business/story?id=4610552**.

Ritual aspects of bargaining

Brand marketing is, by definition, not conducive to bargaining. Self-service and other non-personalized services do not allow people living in modern societies with advanced distribution systems to experience the rituals involved in bargaining. These rituals pose challenges to the uninitiated. They are independent of, yet complementary to, price negotiation. People who bargain more are no less rational – they are rational in a different way.

A Lebanese anthropologist, Khuri (p. 701), described the rituals involved in bargaining in the Middle East by emphasizing that such interaction always begins with standard signs of respect, affection, common interest and trust. As soon as a potential buyer shows interest in an item and requests information, the seller replies vaguely:

Between us there is no difference; we share the same interest, price is not what pleases me, what pleases me is to find out what pleases you; pay as much as you want; brothers do not disagree on price; for you it is free; it is a gift.[5]

Nothing in the above quote should be taken literally. No potential customer from the same culture would do so. This introductory incantation signals a social bond of mutual interest and trust through metaphorical kinship, likely to create an impression of friendliness and fraternity. The potential customer then insists that a price be indicated. The vendor hesitates and, perhaps, proposes a price after having presented and lauded the merits of his product at great length. Contrary to Western bargaining, potential customers should not pretend to doubt the qualities of the item because that could make them seem ignorant and therefore more vulnerable. The discussion continues with each party holding a price (i.e. maximum for sellers and minimum for customers) below or above which no transaction can take place. The potential buyer suggests a price, but is not necessarily willing to pay it. After an agreement has been reached, the transaction then takes place and the buyer purchases the item for cash. However, the bargaining operation could have been conducted just to seek information on the price. This is one instance where the bargaining activity is partly disconnected from the sales activity.

Bargaining may be disconcerting for people who are used to displayed prices and who, as a result, do not envisage entering into any sort of pleasant economic interaction merely to obtain information. When prices are not displayed it may be embarrassing for potential buyers to ask for them, because doing so may latently signal their difficulties in affording the purchase, thus exposing their low purchasing power. Roeber (p. 49) explains how asking the price is associated with class perception in the context of Zambia:

Working people, I was told, were 'sufferers'. The meaning of that word was best explained by the man who stated vehemently, 'If you have to ask the price of something, you are automatically a sufferer' . . . there was another category of people, the *apamwamba* or 'big shots', who did not have to ask for the price of commodities. They always had money to buy what they needed.[6]

The relationship between bargaining and price display is obvious. Wherever the law forces the vendor to display prices clearly, the practice of bargaining will diminish. It is understandable that people who have lost the habit of personalized commercial relations – if indeed they ever had it – may be embarrassed in these situations where affection and economics, and friendship and self-interest, are implicitly communicated, almost simultaneously. The novice bargainer also risks provoking the seller's hostility if the seller gets the impression or wishes to give the impression of being 'taken for a ride' by the buyer. It is for these reasons that bargaining can cause anxiety and tension for novice bargainers, often to the point where they will completely avoid bargaining.[7] In fact, what remains of bargaining in Western societies is disguised behind 'rational' arguments such as quantity and cash discounts, stock liquidation operations and auctions of discontinued items. Moreover, bargaining could smear the image of the distribution channel as well as that of the goods it sells. Prus (p. 146) quotes certain remarks made by Canadian vendors:

'We're flexible, where if they're getting a larger order and they suggest it, we'll give a little . . . Some customers feel that they have to have a discount to buy it.' (*Sales manageress, luggage.*)

'You can dicker in furniture, appliances, carpeting, something like that, here. But not on the smaller things, like clothing, giftware, shoes.' (*Department store salesman.*)

'Normally I try not to dicker. I am quite firm on the prices. I've found that dickering can be rather awkward. It is awkward for the merchant and the customer. And it is especially awkward if other people are around. If you can stay away from dickering, you can also avoid an image as someone who will go down. I have been known to dicker, but it is something I try to avoid.' (*Women's clothing.*)[8]

Declaring prices

Cavusgil[9] noted that international pricing is not a topic that lends itself to easy generalization. Export pricing must first address the unique nature of the individual firm or buyer with whom one is dealing. He takes the example of the Middle East where 'Regal Ware, a producer of kitchen appliances and cookware, uses a higher list price in such markets to leave a margin of discretion' (p. 505).[9]

In a culture where bargaining is expected, proposing a price is a tug-of-war exercise. Who will give way, the seller or the customer? Who should be the first to make concessions by virtue of the position of strength that is internalized within the society? At least four items play a major role in answering these questions:

1. Initial power position of each party.
2. Degree of urgency for either buyer or seller to close deal.
3. Importance of negotiation margin from start. The initial suggested price must leave room for further discussion. It could be in the vendor's interest to

Box 10.1

Price levels and buyer–seller relationship

Scenario 1

The seller wishes to offer a fair price from the start, close to the final price, expecting it will win the customer's loyalty. This should convince the buyer of the vendor's honesty, openness and genuine desire to do business. If the customer shares these European, American or Australasian values and decides to cooperate, an agreement is quickly reached and each party is satisfied.

Scenario 2

The same vendor suggests the same price, close to the final price, as a sign of goodwill towards the buyer. The buyer who comes from a different culture (such as India or Pakistan) is embarrassed: his boss expects him to obtain the greatest possible

discount from the seller. His role centres on the price rebate rather than on the price level. The announced price, close to the final price, leaves buyer and seller with little satisfactory negotiating room, therefore no deal is made.

Scenario 3

The vendor announces a much higher initial price, leaving room for negotiation from the start. This allows the buyer to demonstrate skill in a mutually beneficial bargaining exercise and enables both parties to increase the long-term value of their social relationship. The final agreed price is very close to that in Scenario 1. With the buyer interested mostly in the rebate and the seller in the price level, both can achieve greater satisfaction than in Scenario 1.

exaggerate the first price in order to leave the customer some room to manoeuvre. For instance when dealing with a buyer whose performance is subject to confirmation by superiors, that buyer is supposed to obtain a discount. The buyer's job is to reduce the price so, ironically, the vendor would be wise to open negotiations with an exaggerated price (see Box 10.1).

4. Type of social process by which buyer and seller progressively adjust their price. In the case of competitive bidding situations based on a tender offer, an excessively high price would eliminate that vendor from the short list of pre-selected candidates.

10.3

Price and consumer evaluations

Culture-based appraisal of quality and price

Consumers tend to use price as a proxy or cue for quality, especially when other criteria are absent. Price plays a major subjective role in the assessment of quality when:

1. It is very difficult to measure quality objectively. There is no generally accepted method of measuring the objective quality of a product, and much less so for a service.
2. Perceived quality of a product is even more difficult to measure than quality itself. The concept of quality is subjective but not irrational. It is based on an evaluation of both intrinsic product attributes, such as taste or physical characteristics, and extrinsic product attributes, such as advertising, brand, and price.
3. Perceived quality combines with other evaluation criteria (e.g. perceived monetary and non-monetary prices) to form a perceived value that shapes and determines the consumer's decision to buy or not.[10]

Price perceptions include both monetary and non-monetary aspects. Perceived monetary price means that consumers may not recall the exact price, but may have framed in their minds a simplified, general impression (i.e. 'it is expensive' or 'it is not that expensive after all') in comparison to a reference price range. This price impression needs to be sufficiently close to consumer expectations if they are to buy.[11] Maxwell[12] found support for this in India and the United States. In both countries, the perceived acceptability of price influenced the probability of purchase by increasing the perceived value of the product (i.e. jeans).

Consumers' perception of a non-monetary price may be better understood in terms of Becker's[13] conclusion that the objective price is not the only *sacrifice* accepted by consumers when purchasing a product. Other *sacrifices*, such as time spent shopping or cooking, are often included in the perceived price. Maxwell[12] also measured the acceptability of other costs, including discussing the purchase with friends and travelling on buses for long periods of time. Interestingly, these other costs were less acceptable to Indians than Americans.

Consumers do not build these subjective evaluations of quality and monetary and non-monetary price through irrational individual idiosyncrasies but through unconscious submission, in their everyday lives, to social representations dictated by their cultural upbringing. For instance, Erevelles and colleagues[14] examined the influence of price on perceived risk as part of a larger study with students from Hong Kong and the United States. They found that price perceptions had more influence on risk perceptions in the United States in relation to a car purchase. Becker's[13] model is firmly rooted in American society and culture. Therefore, some elements are not cross-culturally equivalent; a costly 'sacrifice' in one country may be true enjoyment in another. To cite a few examples of common aphorisms (note: the reverse of each is also defensible):

1. 'It is important to measure time, time is money' (see section 2.2): therefore, perceived non-monetary price will be higher in general for economic-time minded consumers.
2. 'Home-made food is the best': this saying could, for instance, influence the perceived quality of frozen foods even though there is no reason why their objective qualities (e.g. taste and nutritional value) should not be better.
3. 'Where there is pleasure, time doesn't count' (French proverb).

Certain representations directly influence the perceived non-monetary price of a product, particularly the desirability/non-desirability or the convenience/inconvenience of an element of the perceived non-monetary price. Put simply, the price of a nail is not easily separable from the non-monetary price

involved in driving it in, including the risk of hitting one's finger in the process. Non-monetary price reflects costs related to time spent, the search itself, psychological risk, etc. These costs shape the consumer's perception of the sacrifice involved in the consumption experience in exchange for the satisfaction to be derived from it.

Non-monetary price varies a great deal across cultures. A trip to buy a product or the preparation of meals may be perceived as enjoyable in certain cultures and reflects no perception of sacrifice or non-monetary price awareness. However, the same task may be perceived as being tedious in other cultures. Ackerman and Tellis[15] argue that Chinese consumers place more importance on the monetary sacrifice and less on the time sacrifice than US consumers, due to the Chinese social norm of frugality and sophistication in money. It is also likely that time is more important than money to many US consumers, especially for small purchases like grocery items. Similarly, the rapid expansion of the 'do-it-yourself' market is related to a marked preference for doing small jobs oneself instead of requesting the services of a professional. In France, this preference can be traced to a social representation in a high power distance society, where being served is negatively valued. The French concept of *égalité* tends to associate service with servitude and humiliation. The French fiscal system has long corroborated this by offering tax rebates to people engaging in 'do-it-yourself', while restricting the opportunity of hiring domestics to the very upper classes.

Relationships between objective quality and price, and choice strategies

It is to be expected that price and quality strongly correlate in a competitive market. However, many empirical studies show that the actual relationship between price and objective quality is fairly low, probably because consumers are imperfectly informed about the price and quality of competing products (for a review, see Fauld *et al.*[16]). Quality is often revealed through product use, that is, through post-purchase rather than pre-purchase information cues. Objective quality is based on characteristics that can be measured by consumer tests like those carried out by *Consumer Reports* magazine such as durability, performance and safety features. Measures of the objective price–quality relation are based on correlations between quality evaluations, carried out by consumer magazines, and the price of the product.

Website link 10.3

See Consumer Reports website:
http://www.consumerreports.org/cro/index.htm.

In the United States, Oxenfeldt,[17] in the earliest study on the topic, ranked 35 products from best to worst based on two dimensions (price and quality) in comparative product tests in *Consumer Reports* between 1939 and 1949. Price and objective quality were rather weakly related with a rank correlation of 0.25. Sproles[18] found a positive correlation for 51 per cent of the 135 products retained in the study. In other words, high price was not necessarily related to high quality. For 35 per cent of the products he found no correlation and for 14 per cent a higher price was related to low objective quality. Similarly, Riesz[19] found a positive rank correlation of 0.26 between price and objective quality among 685 categories of products. Curry and Riesz[20] studied price quality over product life cycle for 62 durable products. Their findings indicate that when both low-quality/high-price and high-quality/low-price brands were introduced early in the product life cycle, the inconsistent relationship between price and quality tended to stabilize over time.

The same conclusion has been found in a wide variety of countries. For instance, in Japan the mean price–quality relationship reached -0.06[21] and -0.18 in the automobile industry.[22] In the case of consumer durables, a slightly positive price–quality correlation was found across five countries (Australia, Canada, New Zealand, the United Kingdom and the United States), ranging from 0.18 to 0.35.[14] This illustrates that there generally exists a positive but weak correlation between objective price and objective quality. Price is a variable, but generally positive indicator for quality.

Obviously, there are differences in the price–quality relationship across product categories, as some products are more difficult to assess prior to purchase

than others. For instance, it is not possible for consumers to assess whether a German Miele washing machine, which is three times more expensive than a machine branded by Zanussi – Italian arm of the Swedish Electrolux group – lasts three times longer before they purchase one. Similarly, for personal computers, performance only explained 30–40 per cent of the deviation in price.[23] To take account of this, Nelson (1970) categorizes products as having search attributes that are relatively easy to evaluate prior to purchase, and experience attributes that are only evaluated after purchase. Darby and Karni[24] extended this to include credence attributes that cannot be confidently evaluated even after purchase.

The ability – due to the availability of information, experience and access to expertise – to judge objective product quality is likely to differ across cultures and individuals. For instance, for urban Chinese, the price–quality relationship is stronger for durables than for non-durables (which are easier to judge prior to purchase), and inexperienced consumers tend to infer more quality from price than experienced ones.[25] Similarly, in Turkey, where objective quality information is less commonly available to the general population, price is considered a good or fair indicator of quality for 75 per cent of the consumers Yucelt and Firoz[26] surveyed; a high price is relied upon as an indication of higher quality.

A recent meta-analysis on the price-*perceived* quality relationship conducted by Völckner and Hofmann[27] showed some interesting differences between countries. European countries showed a stronger positive relationship between price and perceived quality compared to North American countries. Similarly, less developed countries such as India and China also showed a stronger relationship compared to the North American countries. However across all countries the relationship was relatively weak. Similarly, Jo and Sarigollu[28] found that Japanese consumers had a much stronger positive relationship between price and perceived quality compared to Australian consumers.

Consumers generally have difficulty establishing a clear price–quality relationship, especially when quality is only revealed after the purchase, as in the case of products with experience and credence attributes. Furthermore, in order to form their perceptual evaluation of total price – monetary as well as non-monetary – consumers need a better understanding of the costs involved in using the product.[10] Often, in the absence of information based on actual product use, they are forced to resort to simplified formulae to guide their choice. The results of an experiment by Schindler and Kibarian[29] illustrate a simplified influence of price by varying the price endings (using 99 or 00) in a controlled advertising experiment. They found that consumers were more likely to perceive the price as relatively low if it had a 99 ending versus 00 ending. In addition, the 99 ending also had a negative effect on perceptions of quality. More recently, Suri and colleagues[30] examined price endings in the US and Poland, finding that US consumers perceived 99-ending prices as more 'fair' than the Polish did. They also noted that 99-ending prices were more frequently used in the US.

Tellis and Gaeth[31] depict three basic choice strategies when the consumer has a better knowledge of price than of quality. In the first strategy, *best value*, people use a rational standpoint to choose the brand with the least overall cost in terms of price and expected quality to maximize the utility that will be derived. In the second strategy, *price seeking*, price is used as a proxy for the unknown quality, leading the consumer to choose the highest-price brand (i.e. the consumer makes an attribution of quality from the price). In the third strategy, *price aversion*, people choose the lowest-price brand in order to minimize immediate costs (i.e. they are risk averse). The salience of these three models depends on the consumer's situation, that is, the amount of information they have, their capacity to establish price–quality relations, and their experiences. These relations and strategies were observed in the US, but different attitudes in making strategic choices are to be expected according to the consumer's national culture.

Cultural dimensions of price–quality evaluation and consumer choice strategies

Some dimensions of price appear to be fairly universal, including price–quality relationships, prestige sensitivity, and value-consciousness.[32] It is generally accepted that consumers are reasonably rational and if sufficiently motivated they attempt to evaluate, as objectively as they can, the price–quality relationship. Yet this idea of the best price–quality relationship is depicted in various ways, for example, by minimum levels of quality and maximum levels of price, below or above which consumers will eliminate a product from the set of products they will consider.

1. *Northern European consumers*: The price levels in Northern European shops and also the robustness and durability of products may be surprising. A possible explanation is that these countries are primarily Lutheran, a form of Protestantism that favours a lifestyle imbued with a certain austerity in terms of material well-being. Goods should be expensive in order to limit their consumption (see Box 10.2) and people prefer them to last, in line with an austere, thrifty and utilitarian outlook on life. For instance, furniture for homes should be sturdy and long-lasting. This means that people rarely buy furniture and when they do they are looking for the best price–quality relation, where the minimal level of quality is relatively high, thus eliminating a range of possibilities even where the price is low enough to enhance the price–quality relationship. IKEA's strategy corresponds to this type of choice (see the case study A5.2 at the end of Chapter 5).

2. *Southern European consumers*: Purchasing power in southern Europe is somewhat lower than the north European average. People stay outdoors more because the climate is warmer. Social life often takes place outdoors and is materially much less austere, hence the more pronounced taste for seasonal fashions and for appearance and show. In addition, the Catholic doctrine is rather ambiguous about money, and has little to say about the price–quality ratio. Moreover, the Catholic Church has never been preoccupied, either explicitly or implicitly, with the price and quality of material possessions. The Catholic religion is not a 'lover of money' and could therefore be said to implicitly support spending. Like all idealistic systems with a worldly dimension, the Catholic doctrine manages to sustain the paradox of being anti-money but not anti-expenditure. This is the complete opposite of the Protestant paradox of thrift that considers expenditure as a catalyst for

Box 10.2

The Puritan paradox

I fear, wherever riches have increased, the essence of religion has decreased in the same proportion. Therefore I do not see how it is possible, in the nature of things, for any revival of true religion to continue long. For religion must necessarily produce both industry and frugality, and these cannot but produce riches. But as riches increase, so will pride, anger, and love of the world in all its branches. How then is it possible that Methodism, that is, a religion of the heart, though it flourishes now as a green bay tree, should continue in this state? For the Methodists in every place grow diligent and frugal; consequently they increase in goods. Hence they proportionately increase in pride, in anger, in the desire of the flesh, the desire of the eyes, and the pride of life. So, although the form of religion remains, the spirit is swiftly vanishing away. Is there no way to prevent this – this continual decay of pure religion? We ought not to prevent people from being diligent and frugal; we must exhort all Christians to gain all they can, and to save all they can; that is, in effect, to grow rich.

(Source: Speech by Methodist minister John Wesley at the end of the eighteenth century, a few years before the Industrial Revolution in Britain. Quoted by Weber[33]; last sentence italicized by Weber.)

poor morality but still favours the accumulation of wealth. The difference exists in where the shame lies: for the Catholic, spending is not really shameful, but money is, and the religion rejects money while accepting its pleasures. For the Protestant, excessive or conspicuous spending is shameful.

Max Weber (p. 31)[33] emphasized the relative benevolence of the Catholic Church, 'punishing the heretic, but being lenient with the sinner', in contrast to the Reformed Church, which imposes stricter rules and regulations. The Catholic influence lacks the austerity and rigour of Protestantism. In a way, it accords free will to material choice, as in the famous quotation from the Bible, 'Render unto Caesar the things that are Caesar's' (Mathew 22:15). Consequently, the Latin (Catholic) consumer is more diverse, particularly in relation to displaying social class. In Latin society, social classes are more distinct and buying has the function of reinforcing one's social image. Given that there are marked differences in buying power, one would expect diversified choice strategies among consumers. For example:

1. Snobbish consumers who, by definition, buy the most expensive foods (i.e. the Veblen effect of preferring high prices).
2. Consumers who are more concerned about price and who would automatically buy the least expensive items (i.e. price-averse consumers).

3. Consumers who use price–quality relations, in line with the Latin temperament that includes a propensity for intellectual logic and rationality.

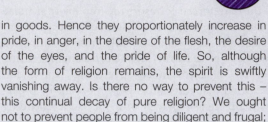

10.4

International price tactics

Price manipulation

Vendors may use pricing to serve three interrelated objectives: (1) profits, (2) sales, and (3) market interactions. While profits and sales objectives are clear, marketing interactions are also profit objectives as their focus is on relations with other market actors (i.e. customers, distributors, competitors, regulatory authorities) in order, ultimately, to make a profit. Table 10.2 identifies 11 pricing objectives under these three categories.

Price is a tactical tool in local markets and a strategic tool in face of global competition. Price tactics in domestic markets must take their place within a global strategy of cost domination based on the search for economies of scale and experience effects (see Chapter 7) or differentiation, which is obtained by designing a product offering that has been differentiated from competitors or tailored to local markets (see Chapter 8).

Table 10.2 Pricing objectives

	Objectives
Profit	(1) Maximize company profits
	(2) Reach target profits
Sales	(3) Increasing unit volume
	(4) Attain sales figures
	(5) Increase cash flows
Interaction	(6) Develop new markets
	(7) Maintain customer loyalty
	(8) Achieve greater market stability
	(9) Attain price parity with competitors
	(10) Eliminate competitors
	(11) Promote the image of the company and/or its products and/or brands

Keegan[34] described three possible positions for international strategic pricing:

1. *The extension/ethnocentric position*: a single global price based on the factory price of the goods, with the customer being charged for insurance, freight and customs costs.
2. *The polycentric adaptation position*: local subsidiaries fix their own prices according to local market conditions.
3. *The intermediate geocentric inventive position*: the subsidiary takes into account local competition and seeks to maximize the firm's total income through international coordination of tactical pricing.

These positions can be related somewhat simplistically to Stöttinger's[35] results. Stöttinger interviewed 45 seasoned European international business managers to assess 'best practices', finding that all but three firms set international prices centrally, in line with an extension/ethnocentric position. The others decentralized pricing decisions for different reasons. Stöttinger (p. 49)[35] explained that one company holds different strategic positions in their domestic and international markets: 'domestically the firm is known as a low-price, mass market manufacturer, internationally it is positioned in the premium segment', in line with the intermediate geocentric inventive position. The other two companies are mainly active in Eastern Europe, 'as respondents put it – in-depth knowledge of the market situation and the customer's financial conditions govern the pricing policy' (p. 50),[35] in line with a polycentric adaptation position.

Price can also be used against competitors. Prices can be manipulated and distorted between markets as long as customer or distributor disputes can be avoided. In fact, consumers cannot always arbitrate, because of transaction costs, complexities of international trade operations for private people, customs regulations and technical standards. However, agents are often tempted to arbitrate for consumers. Agents can reduce the transaction costs and rapidly gain experience in such practice. For example, certain agents may specialize in re-importing products sold at lower prices in a neighbouring market.

Suppliers face many difficulties in pricing goods and services. For instance, large international customers place increasing pressure on suppliers to offer them global-pricing contracts to reduce inefficiencies in obtaining prices in multiple locations.[36] This poses many problems for suppliers, who may have difficulty in passing on their full costs, especially when parts or services are also transferred among divisions that may be located in different countries. Stevenson and Cabell (p. 81)[37] suggest a two-stage approach that first identifies the cost drivers which cause costs to increase or decrease and then allocates costs to products, or regions, by the drivers: 'For example, in marketing a cost driver would be the number of shipments made to a particular region, number of orders entered, or sales calls made in a region; these drivers are used to allocate costs'. After all of the costs are accumulated, they can then be allocated to products and regions.

Signalling willingness to compete: domestic markets, export markets and dumping

Who gets the lowest prices? This question requires consideration when a company operates in different national markets, where the opportunity exists to increase profits through price discrimination. It naturally presupposes that buyers or distributors have no possibility of arbitrage. That is, buying where cheapest, either for consumption or for resale at a higher price in another national market. Other reasons for price discrimination across national markets may be found among the 11 pricing objectives in Table 10.2.

A basic international pricing issue is price discrimination between domestic and foreign markets, which depends on the positions of the respective markets on the company's cost curve. For a firm to maximize its profit, it must sell its products at a price greater than or equal to the marginal cost (i.e. in addition to the total cost of producing one extra unit). In practice, people refer to the cost price based on total costs. However, in industries where overheads are high – such as aerospace, chemicals and steel – direct costing (i.e. variable costs directly related to production) may be used.

When a completely new aircraft is launched with initial fixed expenses of US$5 billion, or a new car with overhead costs of US$1 billion, is the domestic market or the export market supposed to 'pay' for the depreciation of these sunk costs? This is a very important question and calls for a number of subjective considerations. Should the domestic market or other exclusive markets pay for its loyalty or, on the contrary, should it benefit from price cuts as compensation and encouragement for loyalty? If potential car purchasers in Britain were aware of the surcharge they pay, about 20 per cent higher than the European average, perhaps they would show less loyalty to their national carmakers.

Figure 10.1 addresses the problem of where to situate the domestic and export markets respectively on the horizontal axis of the cost curve. Because sales,

Figure 10.1 Dumping and the relationship between unit costs and cumulated production

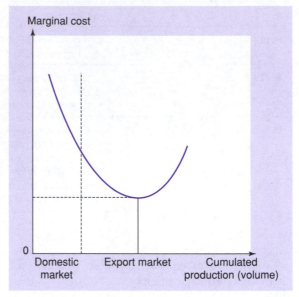

whether domestic or export, usually take place simultaneously, the problem is one of subjective (but stable) conceptualization of the bases of the cost curve, as it corresponds to exported quantities. It is this concept that leads directly to the practice of dumping. Article VI of the General Agreement on Tariffs and Trade (GATT) prohibits dumping where it prejudices the production of one of the contracting parties.

Website link 10.4

Find the WTO anti-dumping gateway: **http://www.wto.org/english/tratop_e/adp_e/adp_e.htm**.

It allows certain countries to impose anti-dumping taxes on dumping prices. The United States has regularly exercised this clause, especially on European and Japanese steel exports. Dumping is based on the following assumptions:

1. One role of the domestic market or other exclusive markets is to recover sunk costs. These markets should therefore be situated on the ascending part of the cost curve in relation to the *x*-axis signifying quantity.

2. In placing the home market in this zone, the remaining zone where marginal costs decrease

would be reserved for foreign markets where competition is supposed to be more open or where
prices that are more attractive are offered. It is,
however, worth remembering that the company's
home market is its competitors' foreign market.

3. Dumping assumes that foreign markets are like
rubbish bins. This is true except in the situation
where the aim is to assume the role of a predator,
momentarily flooding the market with the intention of raising prices after a sizeable market share
has been secured.

Showing commitment in a target market: gaining market share through pricing

Slashing prices in the short term may appear to be an
attractive strategy for obtaining new clients, building
customer loyalty, and increasing market share. This
could even result in the consumer being trapped
if prices are subsequently raised and if competitors,
who have lost market share, are not prepared to
engage in a price war to regain their previous share.
Competitors will therefore often accept the new
status quo and products will be priced high.

Slashing prices is a price tactic when viewed from
the perspective of a single market. Across markets,
however, it is the implementation of a global strategy.
The Japanese are unsurpassed in the art of initially
penetrating a market through price rebates in order
to obtain a sizeable share in it. Johansson and
Nonaka (p. 592) described the pricing strategies of
Japanese firms as follows:

The general theme was one of seeing the entry into a market as a long-term 'investment' and market penetration
was accordingly a much more important pricing objective
than quick profit taking with a skimming approach. Several
of the firms employed a version of the 'experience curve
pricing strategy' where a relatively low price was expected
to lead to large volume and future cost savings. It became
rather clear that individual markets were not seen as 'profit
centres' but rather as pieces in one large global puzzle.
By generating sufficient funds at home and in selected
country markets where the share positions were strong,
the lower returns emanating from a low price penetration
strategy in newer markets could be sustained over a
relatively long period.[38]

As an example, Japanese car manufacturers
entered the European-dominated African markets
about 30 years ago offering relatively cheap, reliable,
air-conditioned cars. Because their objective was not
to eliminate competitors, the Japanese left room for
European cars after having acquired the lion's share
of the market, which they did by raising prices. The
benefits of this strategy were threefold: they calmed
hard-pressed rivals, raised their profit margins, and
finally avoided the risk that their relatively low pricing would lead to a lasting unfavourable image of
their products.

Avoiding parallel imports: combating grey markets and opportunistic distributors

According to Palia and Keown (p. 37)[39] a grey market
occurs when an 'exporter knowingly or unknowingly
sells to an unauthorized agent who competes directly
with the sole agent appointed by the exporter within
the same territory'. Grey markets are based on parallel
imports that hamper the effectiveness of marketing
strategies in certain national markets. For instance, if
a company sells at a discount to a Central American
distributor, because local consumers cannot afford
European or US price levels, goods risk being shipped
back from Central America to the United States and
sold there through unofficial channels.[40]

Website link 10.5

See regional restrictions on DVDs and the formation
of grey markets: http://www.mbs.edu/home/jgans/
papers/dvd.pdf.

Fragmented national markets are geographically
proximate in regions, including Europe, West Africa,
Latin America, and South-East Asia. Once different
price levels are set in neighbouring countries, consumers and some distributors seek cheaper supplies
across the border, making the manufacturer compete
with its own products. If the price differential is
large enough to offset transaction costs, unauthorized intermediaries may compete with sole agents or
exclusive dealers in national markets where a specific
marketing strategy has been defined (see case A10.2).
They therefore benefit from brand advertising and
marketing strategies carried out by the company and
its regular dealers, without having to contribute to
cover these costs and are thus able to cut their own
prices and margins.[41]

Interestingly, Myers[42] found that the number of markets served and monetary issues, such as the form of currency and inflation rate fluctuations, did not impact grey market activity. However, internal and external control issues, such as distribution control and integration of channels, centralization of decision making and product standardization (i.e. a lack of interesting adaptations) were all related to lower grey market activity. After reviewing the legal controls for grey marketing, Clarke and Owens suggest that (p. 285): 'Marketers may be best served by minimizing the conditions which create gray markets or looking for nonlegal response alternatives.'[43]

Many companies that manufacture home appliances and consumer durables struggle to control the ultimate destinations of their products. For instance, Belgian, Dutch and French agents in cities close to the German border sometimes buy from German wholesalers instead of their domestic distributor, who may sell at a higher price. When price policies implement country-specific prices they should consider all the opportunities that may exist for consumer and/or distributor arbitrage. As Weigand (p. 53)[40] emphasized, consumer arbitrage is often affected through holiday travel: 'An English tourist taking a holiday in Miami bought a place setting of bone china made in Britain. She didn't pay Britain's substantial value added tax. Further the dollar was cheaper that day.' Weigand also noted that British manufacturers recognize that these personal imports affect their domestic sales. However, they have not found a way to stop them.

The same problem applies to products whose novelty is their major selling point. For example, a new DVD movie may be released in the US prior to its European release, therefore creating a potential grey market in Europe. In such cases, this will be difficult to avoid because a segment of European movie buffs will know when the DVD becomes available and will happily pay a premium to be among the first to own it. Opportunists who organize the parallel market pocket the inflated profit margin. To combat this, distributors place region-specific code restrictions on DVDs, although this has been only marginally successful due to the introduction of multi-region DVD players.

In China censors' restriction of the import of foreign music increased the opportunity for grey markets. In 2001, censors only approved about 700 titles.[44] It has been reported that more than 90 per cent of CDs sold on mainland China may be illegal copies.[44] In this case the music industry is partly responsible, as most of the CDs are not pirated but resold old stock that did not sell in the US.[44] While several companies, including Warner and Atlantic, now destroy all unsold albums in-house, piracy continues to be an issue.

Piracy is extremely difficult to combat worldwide.[45] Brand counterfeiting of consumer goods not only costs the brand owners monetary sales, but also has the effect of eroding the brand's value as the counterfeit products are of inferior quality.[45] The entertainment industry has been one of the most affected by piracy in the past few years, predominantly due to the ease of obtaining pirated media via the Internet. The Motion Picture Association of America estimates that the US motion picture industry collectively lost US$6.1 billion to piracy in 2005, and 38 per cent of that was to Internet piracy.[46] A recent analysis of cross-national piracy rates indicated that piracy of American movies was higher in collectivist countries, but is not affected by income.[47]

While the costs of lost sales are obviously massive, the industry has yet to find a cost-effective way of restricting digital duplication of their intellectual property. For instance, most attempts at copy-protecting music CDs have been either circumvented by consumers or caused consumer backlash due to incompatibility with audio systems.[48] Perhaps the most innovative attempt at combating piracy has been pioneered by rock groups such as 'Nine Inch Nails' and 'Radiohead'.[49] In 2007, Radiohead offered their album *In Rainbows* as a download from their website, giving fans the option to pay whatever they wanted for the music, or even pay nothing at all.[50] Similarly, Nine Inch Nails offered nine tracks of the album *Ghosts I-IV* as free downloads from their website. The effectiveness of this new business model at combating piracy remains to be seen.

The objective of monitoring product price positioning across markets is a difficult issue. In some countries, agents may be forced to sell at prices lawfully dictated by producers. In others, legislators may consider such practices contrary to effective competition. Resale price maintenance laws prohibit the producers from imposing prices on agents, even though this may be required by marketing strategy. Firms then manoeuvre around these laws through recommended retail price labelling, thus controlling an agent's discretionary margin. Even so, the agent could still sell the product at an offer price (e.g. to promote the agent's store) and conflict with the producer's pricing strategy.

Exclusive distribution agreements in home markets would appear to be a plausible solution to the grey market issue. But the implementation of such exclusivity clauses is somewhat difficult. In the US, there is some reluctance to limit competition by granting enforceable exclusivity rights to dealers, as this limits their control. Parallel importers, competing with authorized dealers in leading brands, like Cartier and Seiko, were accorded an almost complete victory by the K-Mart ruling handed down by the US Supreme Court (*Kmart Corp. v. Cartier, Inc.*, 486 U.S. 281 [1988]). However, in 1998 the Supreme Court clarified its opinion in the *L'Anza* case, where it ruled that after the first legal sale, the copyright owner no longer has the right to control distribution, which means they cannot prevent unauthorized importation of products bearing their brand name.[43]

European Union legislation also restricts exclusive distribution agreements. EU competition rules (e.g. Article 85 of the Treaty of Rome) prohibit any kind of market-sharing agreement by which a company could limit the sales of its distributors exclusively to a domestic market. In order to increase competition across EU countries, Article 85 and several jurisdictional decisions of the European Court of Justice have legitimized parallel imports. A company cannot prevent its 'exclusive' German distributor from selling to Italian customers, even if the company has also appointed an 'exclusive' distributor in Italy. Because it is difficult to prevent distributors from seeking arbitrage opportunities, grey markets have developed in Europe and other areas, seeking to overcome the many non-tariff barriers whenever price differentials offset the costs of parallel importing. Chaudhry and Walsh (p. 18)[51] reviewed the price and legal environments of the pharmaceutical industry in the EU, concluding that the European Court of Justice 'will continue to use Article 30 and the Exhaustion of Rights Doctrine to support the gray market'. In general, we expect that grey marketers will be able to continue to obtain their licences.

Possible solutions to the grey market issue, that is, solutions that may counter parallel imports, are as follows:

1. *Reduce the price differentials between markets*: lower the price in a national market where it is too high and/or inflate it where it is too low, in order to offset enough of the price differential, so that there is little profit in parallel importing. This, however, may be at the expense of the global coherence of the marketing strategy in either one or both countries. Authorized dealers, provided that they have a cost advantage, could be encouraged to engage in a price war with parallel importers in order to drive them out of the market.[41] Similarly, authorized dealers could scale down their promotional expenses in order to regain advantage over the grey dealers.

2. *Materially alter the product*: the official product should be favourably differentiated against the parallel imported product. If changes are only superficial, importers and consumers will not be fooled. If changes are more significant, economies of scale are lost. Other possibilities entail changing minor product attributes: extended warranties can be granted only to authorized dealers, so that parallel importers will offer products with little or no after-sales service and guarantee.[41] A label 'not for export' or 'for domestic sale only' may be attached to the packaging (which also clearly identifies the national origin). This may prevent some dealers from re-exporting, but the effectiveness of these labels is very limited, since in most countries it is not legal for a manufacturer to prohibit the export sales of its own products.

3. *Educate the dealer*: weaker dealers may be prime targets for grey market attacks and may, at first, react with an outburst of anger, because it may seem to them that the manufacturer is making excess profit at their expense. Explaining why such price differences exist is part of the manufacturer's role although the dealer may not consider such explanations to be credible.[52]

4. *Terminate the dealer agreements* (or threaten to do so) when the dealer buys from unauthorized parallel sources. Weigand (1991, p. 59) cites the case of Apple, which prints the following statement: 'Any Apple dealer or VAR (Value Added Retailer)

found to be in violation of the mail-order or transhipping prohibitions will be stripped of its authorized status.'

5. *Buy back the grey market goods*: this is positively perceived by authorized dealers, who feel actively protected by the brand owner. Generally, this solution is possible only when a permanent solution to parallel imports has been found and is quickly implemented after a short – and costly – buy-back period.

6. *Sell products under a different name*, leaving the foreign distributors to promote the products, or develop a unique trademark in each country.[43] The danger here is loss of benefits from a global trademark.

7. *Target different consumer segments*, determined on the basis of degree of risk aversion.[41]

Finally, it is important to emphasize the risk that consumer perceptions of product positioning may be adversely affected by discrepancies in price for the same good across markets. Ibison (p. 13) described the problem for Daimler Chrysler in Japan:

There was surprise at Daimler Chrysler Japan when executives saw a television advertisement promoting a model they were not due to launch in Japan for another four months. The advertisement – for the C-class Mercedes – was not part of the German/US auto group's planned marketing strategy. Nor were the prices, which were 30 per cent cheaper than they were planning to charge. In fact, the commercials, the press conference and the news stories were all generated by a savvy Japanese car dealer who had latched on to one of last year's most tempting arbitrage opportunities: the weak euro. The dealer had travelled to Europe, where C-classes had already been launched, bought 20 from a dealer in Germany, shipped them back to Japan and put them on his forecourt.[53]

Not only has the perception of the reference price and positioning for Mercedes changed, but there will be real difficulties if there is a product recall, as there will be no way to trace the purchasers. In addition, it is estimated that it reduced the potential sales by up to 12 per cent, decreasing profitability and potentially the services that can be offered.

For informed consumers – currently a rather rare species – buying in the home market is no longer attractive when they become aware that home market prices are artificially inflated. Despite the ubiquitous Internet, average consumers tend to be ignorant of international price differentials, and even when informed, they resign themselves to the tariff and non-tariff barriers that 'imprison' customers in their home market. This situation is changing rapidly, however, as regional integration speeds up in South America, Europe and South-East Asia. Consumers are slowly becoming aware of the price levels for similar goods and services in neighbouring countries. They are also being offered increased opportunities for buying abroad, with no customs duties or clearance formalities.

Pricing and the Internet

It has been forecast that the value of e-commerce in Europe will increase from €102 billion in 2006 to €263 billion in 2011.[54] Similarly, the value of e-commerce in the US is forecast to be greater than US$250 billion in 2011.[55] The industries that have taken the most advantage of this new economy include financial services, retailing and the news industry; in addition, health care and pharmaceuticals, automobile manufacturers, energy suppliers and distributors, and agriculture and food are all emerging industries that are at early stages of e-commerce development.[56]

Undoubtedly the Internet offers consumers easier access to comparative information than do retail stores; however tales of the demise of the retail store appear to be exaggerated.[57] Indeed, a recent study demonstrates that more money is spent in retail stores than Internet stores.[57] Furthermore, despite the ease of comparing information online, the vast majority of online consumers purchase from the first site they visit, including 89 per cent for books, 84 per cent for toys, 81 per cent for music and 76 per cent for electronics.[58] In addition, the price is not the main consideration for business buyers, as only 30 per cent of business buyers reported lower prices as the key benefit of online purchasing; other key factors include lower transaction search costs and automating information to track inventory and make better decisions.[58]

The Internet has become almost a necessity, rather than an advantage for firms. According to Porter (p. 78): 'The more robust competitive advantages will arise instead from traditional strengths such as unique products, proprietary content, distinctive physical activities, superior product knowledge, and strong personal service and relationships.'[59] Similarly, Ancarani[60] cautions firms to avoid the 'commodity trap' by taking advantage of the increased information and advances in technology rather than being pressed by the potential power of consumers. These factors will allow firms to better differentiate their products. For instance, the increased ability to track and profile online customers presents the opportunity for firms to refine market segmentation, and use 'price discrimination, dynamic and smart pricing, product and price versioning, price bundling and unbundling' (p. 680).[60]

10.5
Market situations, competition and price agreements

Ideal versus actual competition

The status of price in the exchange process may be viewed in different ways: (1) as an objective equilibrium point of a contract between two parties, or (2) as the instrument of a social relationship, a subjective equilibrium resulting from the interaction between buyer and seller. In classical economic terms, the social exchange relationship disappears behind Adam Smith's 'invisible hand' of the market. However, it is debatable whether human nature tends more to alliance or competition; both are aspects of human nature. The invisible hand assumes that the nature of competitors is to battle each other fiercely; however, human nature may well tend, at least sometimes, more towards agreement to divide territory between companies and sign pacts, albeit of limited duration.

On the worldwide market for household care products five main firms compete strongly against each other: Procter & Gamble, Colgate-Palmolive, Unilever, Henkel and the Kao Corporation of Japan. They compete head-to-head for market shares on some segments, brands and national markets, whereas in other areas and for other brands armistices have been implicitly signed. Competition patterns should therefore be analysed on a per case basis. A complex reality hides behind the normative

position 'it is essential to be competitive'. To varying degrees, competition and alliances between companies will always occur.

The code that constrains newcomers to the competitive scene (e.g. a national market) is even more complex, as it determines how they should behave towards already established players. Large newcomers frequently face a combined attack from all the firms, whether domestic or foreign, already present in a national market. The current incumbents may, for instance, lower their prices or spread rumours about the newcomer's product/service policies and long-term commitment to local customers. This results in poor competition, which may be detrimental to customers. An example of such hidden agreements existed in the French fire safety market, where a norm stricter than the European standard (EN 54) barred outsiders from entering the market. As a result, prices for fire detectors in France are double those in Britain. For all these reasons, the customization of marketing strategies must be carried out according to *actual* rather than *ideal* competition patterns.

Market situations and competition-avoidance patterns

Competition is not necessarily self-perpetuating. The dynamics of competition may lead to the concentration of supply amongst a limited number of companies and therefore to an actual decrease in the sum total of competing forces. For instance the trend toward concentration has been seen throughout western Europe, with the combined market share exceeding 50 per cent for the top three in grocery retailing.[61] In Finland, a high market share locally and an increasing number of industry-wide stores were associated with higher mark-ups.[61]

Conversely, in the US, effective institutions were introduced at an early stage (e.g. the US antitrust legislation and the Sherman Act) to oversee the proper functioning of competition, to discourage dominant positions and the establishment of monopolies through mergers and acquisitions. However, as Cateora (p. 128)[62] emphasized, perhaps with some exaggeration: 'Except in the United States, 20th century orientation toward competition has been to avoid it whenever possible.'

Website link 10.6

Read an antitrust case: USA versus Microsoft:
http://www.usdojogov/atr/cases/ms_index.htm.

Conversely, DeMarco[63] argues that while monopolies should be monitored for exclusivities and discrimination including prices and supplies, we have insufficient evidence to condemn them. Prior to the Second World War, one of the large German cartels, Interessen Gemeinschaft Farben, brought together three major chemical and pharmaceutical companies, Bayer, BASF and Hoechst, which now operates under the Sanofi-Aventis logo. All three are now at the forefront of the world chemical and pharmaceutical industry. Japanese *zaibatsus*, such as Mitsui and Company, Mitsubishi Group and Sumitomo Group have existed for centuries. Typically, one extended family controls groups of companies that may encompass businesses as diverse as banking, car production, trading and shipbuilding. The Americans prohibited *zaibatsus* after their victory over the Japanese in 1945, which simply caused them to evolve into today's *keiretsus*.

Competition between companies in Japan is often savage. Abegglen and Stalk[64] demonstrated this using the motorcycle industry as a case in point. Honda was far behind Tohatsu in the 1950s but completely overtook them; in 1964 Tohatsu went bankrupt. After entering the motor vehicle sector during the 1960s, Honda's motorcycle business suffered a relative loss of competitiveness because of Yamaha, which achieved almost the same market share in 1981. At the beginning of the 1980s, Honda decided to attack Yamaha. Whereas Honda introduced 81 new models

and ceased production of 32, reflecting 113 changes in product range in all, Yamaha 'only' introduced 34 new models and withdrew three, reflecting 37 changes. This strategy, in combination with a fierce attack on prices and distribution led to the collapse of Yamaha at the start of 1983. In addition to substantial losses, Yamaha announced redundancies and a restructuring programme, as well as a reduction in stocks. Yamaha's chairperson was forced to publicly acknowledge his failure.

Foreign companies seeking to establish themselves in Japan often underestimate this fierce domestic competition (for illustration see Tsurumi and Tsurumi,[65] for the case of Fujifilm and Kodak). This competitive strategy is one of the principal sources of Japanese strength when they enter foreign markets.

An industrialist's vocation is not to enjoy competition as an end in itself. Competition is imposed by the public sector opening up frontiers and ultimately by competitors themselves. If companies possess the legal and informal means to reduce competition, they will do so. This perspective remains true as long as the type of agreement is stable and the conditions remain mutually beneficial.

A German economist, Von Stackelberg[66] had the idea of combining supply and demand situations to construct a typology of markets. He distinguished buyer and seller according to whether they number one, several or many (see Table 10.3).

Every country has a few monopolies and some markets where pure and perfect competition reigns. In addition, each country has a large number of oligopolies that are usually producers of large-scale consumption and durable consumer goods, and oligopolies, and bilateral oligopolies that are usually producers of industrial input goods, such as steel,

Table 10.3 Basic forms of markets according to Von Stackelberg (1940)

		Sellers		
		One	**Some**	**Many**
Buyers	**One**	Bilateral monopoly	Contradicted monopsony	Monopsony
	Some	Contradicted monopoly	Bilateral oligopoly	Oligopsony
	Many	Monopoly	Oligopoly	Pure competition

chemicals, rubber, and capital goods. What varies, as a function of culture, is the social approval or disapproval of these market forms. Local decision makers need to determine whether monopolies may be desirable or dangerous for the community. Foreign intruders will be seen positively, from the consumer's point of view, or negatively, from the local competitor's point of view, because ultimately consumers are often also employees whose employment may be put at risk by the competition.

Americans are often shocked by the amount of protection European governments provide to their flagship companies. The Airbus–Boeing saga is typical of conceptual differences that partly derive their roots from culture. The Europeans consider that government loans – often viewed as sunk costs – were used wisely in view of the success of the Airbus aircraft, the number of jobs created, the positive effects on the trade balance and the preservation of a previously threatened European civil aeronautic industry. However, for the Americans it was a costly mess that helped no one: Boeing's success was challenged by disloyal competition, European taxpayers were burdened and international trade rules were distorted. Without Airbus, Boeing would be in quasi-monopoly situation, exacerbated by the McDonnell Douglas merger in 1997; a potential problem caused by lack of competition.

10.6

Managing prices in highly regulated environments

Over the last 20 years or so, the annual inflation rate has attained double digits in some countries, sometimes exceeding 100 per cent per year, causing monthly or daily changes in prices. In 2007, the country with the highest inflation rate was Zimbabwe; in July of 2007 it hit 7634.8 per cent. High inflation may constrain pricing policies, because prices cannot be increased daily or weekly to adjust for inflation.

The case of high-inflation countries

At the national level, price stability is based on macroeconomic policies as well as cultural values. The requisite discipline is based on: (1) future time orientation, which provides the monetary authorities with a perspective of continuity in fighting inflation; (2) control of the creation of money and credit; and (3) a belief in free market forces that may keep price increases under control because of active competition. Such a belief is, in general, related to individualism and low power distance.

One of the main reasons for persistently high inflation is that it benefits some actors in the economic system. Inflation transfers wealth fairly smoothly from some social strata to others. It appears that high inflation countries are also high in power distance (see Table 3.3). With some notable exceptions (such as Japan), the higher a country's power distance, the higher its inflation rate. The typical case for high inflation is a developing country with a semi-authoritarian government and heavy financial regulation (e.g. price controls on most goods, foreign exchange control, strict import controls and high duties). High power distance at the societal level is expressed in bureaucratic controls and restricted freedom for businesses, unless they have the appropriate connections at the top.

High inflation rates cause the local non-convertible currencies to weaken systematically against stable and convertible foreign currencies, because of constantly decreasing nominal purchasing power. Furthermore, the exchange rate is maintained at unrealistic levels. This results in a parallel foreign exchange market; illegal but generally tolerated by the authorities. In comparison with official exchange rates, parallel rates are favourable to foreign currency sellers and unfavourable to buyers. In Iran in 1993, following a period of very high inflation, the official exchange rate was about 1500 rials more than the grey market exchange rate, before it was decided to align the official rate. In such situations, foreign exchange controls serve the purpose of enriching the most powerful who can buy foreign currencies at the favourable official rate, while restricting the capacity of local exporters to receive a real price, because exporters are obliged to sell export receipts in hard currencies at the usually overvalued official rate.

Inflation is supposed to be combated by price control, an expression of the power of regulatory authorities over companies. Where there is high power distance, there tend to be oppressive rules (see section 3.6). Price increases, so vital for a company's survival, may be delayed by public authorities even though last month's or last week's inflation rate may have caused the entire industry to go into the red – costs soared while sales stagnated because of controlled prices. For instance, the Brazilian automobile industry was subject to 'staircase' price increases by which Volkswagen, Fiat or Ford are suddenly allowed to increase their price by 50 per cent or more. The strong present orientation of the Brazilian public authorities' action favours high inflation, as is the case in many Latin American countries.

Such countries possess a high-inflation culture, where consumers and companies adapt to the changing situation. Consumers delay buying after price increases occur and buy very large quantities just before they are thought to occur, because price increases are not officially announced. If possible, they stock up with items bought during favourable periods. The threat of an imminent price increase is used to motivate customers to buy 'now'. Customers must also have a present orientation and a readiness to buy at the best possible moment, for instance purchasing 'inflation bargains' because they are currently cheap, rather than because they are actually needed. Such customer opportunism may be problematic for the consumers themselves, because they tend to be too price-minded, neglecting other important criteria in their decision-making process. Companies, by contrast, do not depend on consumers for defining prices. The key for price policy, which is mostly short term, is to negotiate price increases with public authorities. Pricing depends more on government authorization than on customers and competition.

The terms of discussion with price regulatory authorities is highly relational and manipulative, rather than strictly economic. In order to obtain optimal price increases, companies argue about losses incurred because of price limitation for which they have to be compensated. Cost prices declared to regulatory authorities tend to be systematically overestimated and losses exaggerated in order to obtain as favourable a new price as possible. A company will argue for a substantial price increase so as to have a 'reserve' before the next increase. Naturally, this whole process fosters inflation rather than slows it down. Another way of obtaining the necessary price allowances – although illegal and unethical – is to propose a 'baksheesh' (i.e. kickback) or some favours to the civil servants in charge of price control within the public administration.

Over- and under-invoicing

As explained above, many high-inflation countries have legislation aimed at controlling prices. The control may take effect at retail, wholesale or production levels, or at several levels simultaneously. Price increases may be curbed, limited or even frozen. Trade profit margins may be monitored. The rationale for price control is usually a basic mistrust of free market mechanisms, often augmented by a long-established tradition of state intervention in the economy.

Foreign exchange regulations also influence the practice of over- and under-invoicing. When countries experience balance of trade and balance of payments problems, they often use administrative decrees aimed at stopping the outflow of foreign currency. Local exporters are often forced to repatriate their earnings in foreign currencies as soon as possible and to exchange them for local currency at sometimes derisory exchange rates. Local importers are also under close scrutiny. The necessity of purchasing abroad is assessed before they may receive foreign currency to pay suppliers. Furthermore, they are often obliged to deposit a guarantee that may be more than the equivalent of their foreign purchase. This sum is deposited at the central bank for a specified period prior to payment, with little or no interest. Where strict foreign exchange controls are enforced, local currency may not be converted into foreign 'hard' currencies.

Two reasons induce firms to practise under- or over-invoicing. First, where there is a high level of political risk, as is the case with many developing countries, local businesspeople seek to transfer funds to foreign banks as fears of political upheaval increase. Second, local businesspeople may wish to expatriate money through under-invoicing, simply because they need cash to buy a prohibited or scarce product or equipment for their production facilities and particularly for the manufacture of products for export.

Verna[67] described various cases of over- and under-invoicing in international trade, relating to differences in currency convertibility. A totally convertible currency may be used in all international commercial and financial operations, irrespective of the object, place, or sum. Only a limited number of countries enjoy total convertibility of their currencies. Where the local currency is non-convertible, over- and under-invoicing is likely to occur,[67] whereas when quantitative restrictions are enforced, smuggling is more likely. Local businesspeople ask foreign customers to under-invoice, foreign suppliers to over-invoice, and then wait for the extra money to be paid into their bank account abroad.

Currency black markets thrive in countries where the national currency is totally non-convertible. For this reason, there may be huge discrepancies between the black-market exchange rate and the official central bank rate. Exporters who are obliged to go through official channels lose major benefits from their transactions. Either they must sell foreign currency at the abnormally low official rate, or they must buy foreign currency for their purchases at the abnormally high parallel rate. Hence the temptation for local exporters to under-invoice and have the fully convertible balance transferred to a foreign bank account. To ensure these machinations work smoothly, the local exporter should have complete confidence in the foreign customers or an effective means of pressurizing them.

Over-invoicing works in a symmetrical way for imports. When local importers ask for an import licence from their national authorities, the face value should be as high as possible to increase the allowance for buying foreign currency. Importers ask their suppliers to over-invoice and to transfer the extra money into a convertible foreign account to maximize their overall profits. For example, Verna (p. 115) noted:

An import licence will authorize the importer to order goods from a foreign supplier; a specified amount in foreign currency is paid by the local authorities in the name of the importer. In return, the importer should refund the authorities in local currency, at the official rate, and also pay customs duties on arrival of the goods. To obtain such an import licence may be a sort of 'windfall' because it allows the importer to buy foreign goods at a better price than is offered on the free market, mainly through the (favourable) exchange rate differential between the official and black markets ... import licences can sometimes be transferable. They then become objects of exchange and even the subject of an auction ... to the extent that some governments, which have become aware of this trade, sell import licences to the highest bidder.[67]

Website link 10.7

Learn about the black market of Zimbabwe:
http://www.news.com.au/heraldsun/story/.

Questions

1. To what extent does price bargaining involve friendship?

2. What is the relationship between bargaining and 'modern culture'?

3. Discuss 'economic rationality' from a cultural point of view.

4. How may price levels reflect Protestant as opposed to Catholic values?

5. What are the limitations on a consumer in displaying obvious price-mindedness when shopping? How do these limitations relate to culture?

6. In certain countries, smuggling is fairly legitimate: customs officers are not very concerned with arresting smugglers, consumers buy smuggled products knowingly, and smugglers are known by everyone for what they do. Why and under which circumstances is this so? What are the consequences of smuggling being accepted as a legitimate activity?

7. With the abolition of duty-free shopping in 1999, increasingly rapid travel to France by car (including train–car travel by Eurostar), and the loosening of import 'allowances' for wine and spirits, UK citizens continue to buy massive quantities of drinks in Calais, France. In Calais, just 33 km (20 miles) from Dover, French stores have special areas for these British day-trippers. Excise duties on alcohol are higher in the United Kingdom than in France. What are the consequences for the UK brewing industry and its distribution channels? How could the brewing industry respond?

8. Is over- or under-invoicing legal? Why is it sometimes unavoidable?

References

1. Sharma, Varinder M. and Krish S. Krishnan (2001), 'Recognizing the Importance of Consumer Bargaining: Strategic Marketing Implications', *Journal of Marketing Theory and Practice*, 9 (1), 24–37.

2. Herrmann, Gretchen M. (2004), 'Haggling Spoken Here: Gender, Class, and Style in Us Garage Sale Bargaining', *Journal of Popular Culture*, 38 (1), 55–81.

3. Sherry, John F., Jr (1990), 'A Sociocultural Analysis of a Midwestern American Flea Market', *Journal of Consumer Research*, 17 (1), 13–30.

4. Allen, David Elliston (1971), 'Anthropological Insights into Customer Behavior', *European Journal of Marketing*, 5 (3), 45–57.

5. Khuri, Fuad I. (1968), 'The Etiquette of Bargaining in the Middle-East', *American Anthropologist*, 70 (4), 693–706.

6. Roeber, Carter A. (1994), 'Moneylending, Trust, and the Culture of Commerce in Kabwe, Zambia', *Research in Economic Anthropology*, 15, 39–61.

7. Trocchia, Philip J. (2004), 'Caving, Role Playing, and Staying Home: Shopper Coping Strategies in a Negotiated Pricing Environment', *Psychology and Marketing*, 21 (10), 823–53.

8. Prus, Robert C. (1989), *Making Sales: Influence as Interpersonal Accomplishment*. Newbury Park, CA: Sage Publications.

9. Cavusgil, S. Tamer (1990), 'Unravelling the Mystique of Export Pricing', in *International Marketing Strategy*, Hans B. Thorelli and S. Tamer Cavusgil, Eds. (3rd edn) Oxford: Pergamon.

10. Zeithaml, Valarie A. (1988), 'Consumer Perceptions of Price, Quality and Value: A Means–End Model and Synthesis of Evidence', *Journal of Marketing*, 52 (3), 2–22.

11. Jacoby, Jacob R. and Jerry C. Olson (1977), 'Consumer Response to Price: An Attitudinal, Information Processing Perspective', in *Moving Ahead with Attitude Research*, Y. Wind and P. Greenberg, Eds. Chicago: American Marketing Association.

12. Maxwell, Sarah (2001), 'An Expanded Price/Brand Effect Model: A Demonstration of Heterogeneity in Global Consumption', *International Marketing Review*, 18 (3), 325–43.

13. Becker, Gary S. (1965), 'A Theory of the Allocation of Time', *Economic Journal*, 75 (299), 493–517.

14. Erevelles, Sunil, Abhik Roy, and Stephen L. Vargo (1999), 'The Use of Price and Warranty Cues in Product Evaluation: A Comparison of U.S. and Hong Kong Consumers', *Journal of International Consumer Marketing*, 11 (3), 67–91.

15. Ackerman, David and Gerard Tellis (2001), 'Can Culture Affect Prices? A Cross-Cultural Study of Shopping and Retail Prices', *Journal of Retailing*, 77 (1), 57–82.

16. Fauld, David J., Orlen Grunewald, and Denise Johnson (1994), 'A Cross-National Investigation of the Relationship between the Price and Quality of Consumer Products: 1970–1990', *Journal of Global Marketing*, 8 (1), 7–25.

17. Oxenfeldt, Alfred R. (1950), 'Consumer Knowledge: Its Measurement and Extent', *Review of Economics and Statistics*, 32 (4), 300–316.

18. Sproles, George B. (1977), 'New Evidence on Price and Quality', *Journal of Consumer Affairs*, 11 (Summer), 63–77.

19. Riesz, P. (1978), 'Price Versus Quality in the Marketplace', *Journal of Retailing*, 54 (4), 15–28.

20. Curry, David J. and Peter C. Riesz (1988), 'Price and Price–Quality Relationships: A Longitudinal Analysis', *Journal of Marketing*, 52 (1), 36–51.

21. Yamada, Yoshiko and Norleen Ackerman (1984), 'Price–Quality Correlations in the Japanese Market', *Journal of Consumer Affairs*, 18 (2), 51–65.

22. Johansson, Johny K. and Gary Erickson (1985), 'Price–Quality Relationships and Trade Barriers', *International Marketing Review*, 2 (3), 52–63.

23. Lilien, Gary and Eunsang Yoon (1989), 'Success and Failure in Innovation – a Review of the Literature', *IEEE Transactions on Engineering Management*, 36 (1), 3–10.

24. Darby, Michael R. and Edi Karni (1973), 'Free Competition and the Optimal Amount of Fraud', *Journal of Law and Economics*, 16 (1), 67–86.

25. Veeck, Ann and Alvin C. Burns (1995), 'The Formation of Beliefs in a Price–Quality Relationship: A Study of Urban Chinese Consumers', *Asian Journal of Marketing*, 4 (1), 47–61.

26. Yucelt, Ugur and Nadeem M. Firoz (1993), 'Buyers' Perception of the Price–Quality Relationship: The Turkish Case', in *Proceedings of the 6th World Marketing Congress*. Istanbul: Academy of Marketing Science, 564–68.

27. Völckner, Franziska and Julian Hofmann (2007), 'The Price-Perceived Quality Relationship: A Meta-Analytic Review and Assessment of Its Determinants', *Marketing Letters*, 18, 181–96.

28. Jo, Myung-Soo and Emine Sarigollu (2007), 'Cross-Cultural Differences of Price-Perceived Quality Relationships', *Journal of International Consumer Marketing*, 19 (4), 59–74.

29. Schindler, Robert M. and Thomas M. Kibarian (2001), 'Image Communicated by the Use of 99 Endings in Advertised Prices', *Journal of Advertising*, 30 (4), 95–99.

30. Suri, Rajneesh, Rolph E. Anderson, and Vassili Kotlov (2004), 'The Use of 9-Ending Prices: Contrasting the USA with Poland', *European Journal of Marketing*, 38 (1/2), 56–72.

31. Tellis, Gerard J. and Gary J. Gaeth (1990), 'Best Value, Price-Seeking, and Price Aversion: The Impact of Information and Learning on Consumer Choices', *Journal of Marketing*, 54 (2), 34–45.

32. McGowan, Karen M. and Brenda J. Sternquist (1998), 'Dimensions of Price as a Marketing Universal: A Comparison of Japanese and U.S. Consumers', *Journal of International Marketing*, 6 (4), 49–65.

33. Weber, Max (1958), *The Protestant Ethic and the Spirit of Capitalism*. New York: Charles Scribner's Sons.

34. Keegan, Warren J. (1984), *Multinational Marketing Management*. Englewood Cliffs, NJ: Prentice-Hall.

35. Stöttinger, Barbara (2001), 'Strategic Export Pricing: A Long and Winding Road', *Journal of International Marketing*, 9 (1), 40–63.

36. Narayandas, Das, John Quelch, and Gordon Swartz (2000), 'Prepare Your Company for Global Pricing', *MIT Sloan Management Review*, 42 (1), 61–70.

37. Stevenson, Thomas H. and David W.E. Cabell (2002), 'Integrating Transfer Pricing Policy and Activity-Based Costing', *Journal of International Marketing*, 10 (4), 77–88.

38. Johansson, Johny K. and Ikujiro Nonaka (1990), 'Japanese Export Marketing: Structures, Strategies, Counterstrategies', in *International Marketing Strategy*, Hans B. Thorelli and S. Tamer Cavusgil, Eds. (3rd edn). Oxford: Pergamon.

39. Palia, Aspy P. and Charles F. Keown (1991), 'Combating Parallel Importing: Views of Us Exporters to the Asia-Pacific Region', *International Marketing Review*, 8 (1), 47–56.

40. Weigand, Robert E. (1991), 'Parallel Import Channels: Options for Preserving Territorial Integrity', *Columbia Journal of World Business*, 26 (1), 53–60.

41. Tan, Soo J., Guan H. Lim, and Khai S. Lee (1997), 'Strategic Responses to Parallel Importing', *Journal of Global Marketing*, 10 (4), 45–66.

42. Myers, Matthew B. (1999), 'Incidents of Grey Market Activity among U.S. Exporters: Occurrences, Characteristics and Consequences', *Journal of International Business Studies*, 30 (1), 105–26.

43. Clarke, Irvine III and Margaret Owens (2000), 'Trademark Rights in Gray Markets', *International Marketing Review*, 17 (3), 272–86.

44. Gough, Neil (2003), 'Zombie Discs: Retail Companies and Retailers Dump Them on Scrap Dealers, but Unwanted "Saw-Gash" Music Cds Find a Ready Market in China', *Time Asia*, 161 (4), www.time.com/time/magazine/article/0,9171,409647,00.html.

45. Green, Robert T. and Tasman Smith (2002), 'Executive Insights: Countering Brand Counterfeiters', *Journal of International Marketing*, 10 (4), 89–106.

46. Motion Picture Association of America (MPAA) (2005), '2005 U.S. Piracy Fact Sheet', www.mpaa.org/USPiracyFactSheet.pdf.

47. Walls, W.D. (2008), 'Cross-Country Analysis of Movie Piracy', *Applied Economics*, 40 (5), 625–32.

48. Van Wijk, Jeroen (2002), 'Dealing with Piracy: Intellectual Asset Management in Music and Software', *European Management Journal*, 20 (6), 689–98.

49. Leeds, Jeff (2008), 'Nine Inch Nails Fashions Innovative Web Pricing Plan', *The New York Times*.

50. Tyrangiel, Josh (2007), 'Radiohead Says: Pay What You Want', *Time*, 1 October.

51. Chaudry, Peggy E. and Michael J. Walsh (1995), 'Managing the Gray Market in the European Union: The Case of the Pharmaceutical Industry', *Journal of International Marketing*, 3 (3), 11–33.

52. Cavusgil, S. Tamer and Ed Sikora (1988), 'How Multinationals Can Counter Grey Market Imports', *Columbia Journal of World Business*, 23 (4), 75–85.

53. Ibison, David (2001), 'Weak Euro Lets Top Car Dealers Go Far in Japan: Parallel Imports Luxury Prices Cut', *Financial Times*, 10 (January), 13.

54. Favier, Jaap (2007), 'Europe's Ecommerce Forecast: 2006 to 2011', *Forrester Market Research*, 1, 1–7.

55. Mulpuru, Sucharita (2006), 'U.S. Ecommerce: Five-Year Forecast and Data Overview', *Forrester Market Research* (1), 1–15.

56. Penbera, Joseph J. (1999), 'E-Commerce: Economics and Regulation', *S.A.M. Advanced Management Journal*, 64 (4), 39–47.

57. Keen, Cherie, Martin Wetzels, Ko de Ruyter, and Richard Feinberg (2004), 'E-Tailers Versus Retailers: Which Factors Determine Consumer Preferences', *Journal of Business Research*, 57 (7), 685–95.

58. Baker, Walter, Mike Marn, and Craig Zawada (2001), 'Price Smarter on the Net', *Harvard Business Review*, 79 (2), 122–27.

59. Porter, Michael E. (2001), 'Strategy and the Internet', *Harvard Business Review*, 79 (3), 63–78.

60. Ancarani, Fabio (2002), 'Pricing and the Internet: Frictionless Commerce or Pricer's Paradise', *European Management Journal*, 20 (6), 680–87.

61. Aalto-Setälä, Ville (2002), 'The Effect of Concentration and Market Power on Food Prices: Evidence from Finland', *Journal of Retailing*, 78 (3), 207–16.

62. Cateora, Philip R. (1983), *International Marketing* (5th edn). Homewood, IL: Richard D. Irwin.

63. DeMarco, C.W. (2001), 'Knee Deep in Technique: The Ethics of Monopoly Capital', *Journal of Business Ethics*, 31 (2), 151–64.

64. Abegglen, James and George Stalk Jr (1986), 'The Japanese Corporation as Competitor', *California Management Review*, 28 (3), 9–27.

65. Tsurumi, Yoshi and Hiroki Tsurumi (1999), 'Fujifilm–Kodak Duopolistic Competition in Japan and the United States', *Journal of International Business Studies*, 30 (4), 813–30.

66. Von Stackelberg, H. (1940), *Die Grundlagen Der Nationalökonomie*. Berlin: Springer Verlag.

67. Verna, Gérard (1989), 'Fausses Facturations et Commerce International', *Harvard-l'Expansion*, 52 (Spring), 110–20.

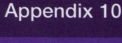

Appendix 10

Teaching materials

A10.1 Case

Saito Importing Company

Some years ago, Saito Importing Company, located in California, USA, brought in a shipment of wood carvings from Bali, Indonesia. At the time, the official exchange rate was 78 Indonesian rupias per US dollar. The 'black market' rate (as viewed by the Indonesian government), or 'free market' rate (as viewed by most of the rest of the world), was approximately 1300 Indonesian rupias per US dollar.

The seller requested a letter of credit for one-half the value of the shipment, to be provided by a US bank and confirmed by an Indonesian bank, and stipulated that the balance be wired to a New York bank account.

Obviously, the 'half' that was received in New York had many times the value of that received in Indonesia. The money in the bank account in New York was available for the seller to invest, to purchase goods for shipment to Indonesia or elsewhere, or to use if leaving Indonesia. Money held in Indonesia at that time could be used for such purposes only with the approval of the government. What the Indonesian exporter did was, of course, illegal under Indonesian law.

Saito Importing Company did not receive the goods until over a year later. Since Bali does not have a port which will accommodate ocean-going vessels, the letter of credit specified that transhipment was allowed. In the process of transhipment, the goods travelled around much of the world and were delayed while waiting for on-going vessels at points of transhipment.

When the wood carvings finally arrived in the US, Saito Importing Company declared the actual price paid for the goods, and indicated to customs why there was a discrepancy between purchase price and the value shown on the documents. The American company did not do anything illegal under US law.

(Source: Duerr, p. 310.[1] Reproduced with kind permission.)

Questions

1. Should the US company have refused to agree to make the payments as requested by the Indonesian exporter? What would have been the expected effect on the Indonesian exporter's price?

2. What effects would you expect the unrealistic official exchange rates had on Indonesian exports?

A10.2 Case

Riva International

Françoise Gain, the *directrice du marketing* at Riva in Brussels, Belgium, received astonishing results from the consumer panels and distributor panels for September and October 2008. It appeared that sales in Belgium and France of one of its main products, the Nutrifying Complex Crème Riva, were 20 per cent lower than the production level in the Belgian factory, which supplied both markets. No signs of excess inventories in the distribution in France or Belgium were noticed by the sales force during visits to the distributors.

Riva Belgium was the subsidiary of Riva Products Corporation, a large US-based multinational, whose main business lines were related to the cosmetics and beauty care industry. The Belgian subsidiary was in charge of both the French and the Belgian markets. In 2003 a scientific breakthrough by the corporate R&D laboratories had led to the development of a new skin care cream. Several patents had been filed and registered to protect the property. In Europe, the industrial use of these patents had been licensed to Riva Belgium, which began producing and selling the new skin care cream in February 2005. Sales increased quickly, and Belgian and French consumers received the new product, liking both its efficiency and good price–quality ratio. Following instructions from international headquarters, the output of Riva Belgium was intended exclusively for supplying the Belgian and French markets as well as the markets of French-speaking Africa.

In January 2008 the English subsidiary of Riva, UK Riva Ltd, started producing the same Nutrifying Complex Crème product. Hefty investments had been made in the English factory to ensure the best quality and a large production capacity. This product had been launched at the top end of the market for skin care cream. It was priced high and supported by heavy advertising and promotional expenses. After a promising start, deliveries had been falling off since August 2008. Actual deliveries to English distributors steadily diverged from target sales.

Françoise Gain knew about this situation as she had been engaged as an internal consultant in the launch of Nutrifying Complex Crème Riva in the United Kingdom. However, what worried her most in November 2008 was the gap between sales to consumers in France and Belgium and ex-works shipments. She informed Jacques Graff, chief executive of Riva Belgium and a member of the international board.

At first he did not seem to be bothered by such a gap, and showed little interest in the issue: 'Françoise, you know: panel data, what does it mean really? Our product sells well and that is all that matters! Tell your panel company to reconsider their samples and their data collection procedures, and you will see that everything is in fact normal.'

Françoise Gain nevertheless took the decision to undertake an audit by an external consultant. His findings exactly confirmed those of the panels and brought evidence of no sizeable excess inventory at the distribution level. It followed from the auditor's investigations that deviations were ascribed mostly to deliveries to two large wholesalers, which ranked among the five largest customers of Riva Belgium.

One month after his talks with Françoise Gain, Graff received a confidential note, issued by the chief executive of UK Riva Ltd. It stated that a member of his sales force had accidentally seen, at an English wholesaler, a carton containing Nutrifying Complex Crème Riva with country-of-origin label 'Made in Belgium'. The wholesaler had been evasive if not reluctant to tell the sales representative where it came from. Jacques Graff asked Françoise Gain to come to his office, and handed her the note without comment.

'I am not surprised by this note', answered Françoise. 'On the contrary, it is evidence for my suspicions about parallel imports of our Belgian products to England. I have noticed that the sales figures that vanished from Belgium and France precisely equalled the drop in deliveries of UK Riva Ltd. It is now quite clear that some of our wholesalers export to English distributors and that, before doing this, they do not warn our sales and marketing group. I examined the cost structure of UK Riva production and found that our product made in Belgium could be sold by Belgian wholesalers to English distributors at a profit. Belgian distributors may price it at 15 per cent below the English list price, even though there are transport costs.'

'How is that possible?' asked Graff, amazed.

'The English Nutrifying Complex Crème Riva was launched with heavy production and promotion costs', explained Françoise Gain. 'It is positioned at the high end of the market. It is priced higher than any of the competing products. I told them, before the launch, that this retail price level was too high. They disapproved. The finance department at UK Riva Ltd wanted a quick return on investment, taking into account the large cash outflows at the start. The marketing people, backed by the advertising agency, claimed the opportunity to seize a segment which was at the very top end of the market and which had been, up to then, neglected by competitors. Consequently my opinion was put aside.'

Jacques Graff started to pace back and forth. 'As a chief executive of the Belgian subsidiary, I am delighted. Our plant works at full capacity. But, as a member of the international board, I cannot let the English subsidiary plunge. What can we do?'

'One thing is certain', answered Françoise Gain. 'We cannot prevent our customers, namely independent wholesalers, from exporting to England if they wish to do so. As for the English distributors, one cannot blame them for seizing a better-priced offer and simultaneously taking advantage of the promotional effort of UK Riva! I know it is more easily said than done, but you should have defined, a long time ago, an international pricing strategy at the international board level.'

'It is never too late to do the right thing! Françoise, please prepare a report on your suggestions to cope with this parallel import problem of Nutrifying Complex Crème Riva', said Graff in conclusion.

Questions

1. What are the reasons for these parallel import problems?

2. What can be done to stop wholesalers exporting to the UK?

3. Is it necessary to change the marketing strategy of Nutrifying Complex Crème Riva, particularly its price? If so, where and how should it be implemented?

4. How should one organize a coordinated international marketing strategy across national markets? Prepare the report requested by Graff.

(Source: Adapted from a case written by Alain Ollivier, Ecole Supérieure de Commerce de Paris.)

A10.3 Case

Taman SA

At Taman SA, a Spanish company, orders systematically exceed production. Is this a result of the marketing and sales department's expertise, the lack of production capacity, or the inability of the production department to plan demand peaks effectively? Nobody knows the exact answer.

To tell the truth, one should excuse both the production department and the sales department. The market for high-technology products, in which Taman has built a strong European share, is growing rapidly, at about 50 per cent per year. Taman's competitors face similar problems.

In spite of a rather elaborate cost accounting system, accountants may endlessly argue about the real direct and total cost price of a given order. Diverse and changing factors tend to blur the calculation of costs, such as the allocation of R&D expenses, the cost of components, shared expenses between different orders, the price–volume relation, etc.

The director of marketing and sales and the director of production and operations are constantly in conflict. Conflicts focus on such cases as that of Magnusson AB. Magnusson AB is a new customer from whom Taman has never, up to now, received an order. Following technical tests of Taman products by Magnusson people at their factory, and after a successful certification procedure, Magnusson is ready to place a fairly large order.

The marketing and sales director argues that getting a new client is something you have to pay for. The director of production and operations considers that the largely positive margin that this order brings is smaller than that of other orders. Besides, he fears that it could disturb the production schedule for the coming weeks and consequently that it could result in numerous delivery delays.

Question

Describe this problem in about 30 lines. What ways and means would you suggest to these two directors for solving their conflict and/or serving their customer base better?

A10.4 Case

AIDS – Global ethics and the pricing of AIDS drugs

The text for this case is located on the book website (**www.pearsoned.co.uk/usunier**) at Chapter 10.

Appendix reference

1. Duerr, Mitsuko Saito (1989), *International Marketing and Export Management*, Gerald Albaum, Jesper Strandskov, Edwin Duerr and Lawrence Dowd, Eds. Reading, MA: Addison-Wesley.

International distribution and sales promotion

This chapter considers the elements of the marketing mix which are crucial in 'pushing' the product towards the customer. The elements that help to 'push' the product to the customer are as follows: (1) the distribution channels; (2) sales promotion; and (3) the sales force (examined in Chapter 14). The focus of this chapter is on the cross-cultural perspective, while acknowledging that some elements of channel and sales promotion apply universally across countries and cultures.

We examine the reputedly complex and difficult Japanese distribution system. Western distribution channels tend to be depersonalized, simplified, and efficient. Section 11.1 describes how the Japanese *keiretsu* distribution system is physically rooted in the Japanese landscape and explains how it also depends on the Japanese national character. Although the distribution channels provoke negative reactions from the non-Japanese, or *Gai-jin*, they are deeply embedded in Japanese business customs. Non-Japanese companies have condemned the channels on the grounds that they favour Japanese goods and producers and act as a barrier to the entry of imported goods. Some of these disparaging comments have been frequently voiced at the WTO international negotiations; however, these comments reveal ignorance of the deep roots of *keiretsu* in the Japanese culture. Since channels involve a direct relationship with final customers, servicing and informing them, they reflect deep cultural idiosyncrasies.

The next two sections present the criteria for selecting foreign distribution channels (section 11.2) and examine the role of distribution as a 'cultural filter' (section 11.3). Section 11.4 relates to the considerable expansion of direct marketing worldwide; it explains how catalogues and direct marketing tools must be adapted for cross-border use and discusses how the Internet can be used for direct marketing.

The last topic in this chapter, sales promotion (section 11.5), has some universal objectives: to let potential consumers try the product, to facilitate repurchasing, to increase the frequency of purchases, to reach a new segment of consumers, to reinforce brand loyalty, and so on. Sales promotion has developed a number of techniques, which have been well documented. Although this whole range of techniques is known in most countries, there is wide variation in their degree of local legitimacy and legal acceptance.

11.1

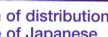

Cultural dimension of distribution channels: the case of Japanese *keiretsus*

Distribution and Japan

Japan is an insular and heavily populated country, with only a small proportion of inhabitable land. A population of over 127 million people is effectively concentrated into an area of roughly 60,000 square kilometres. Despite this, there are more retail outlets in Japan (1.30 million) than in the United States (1.14 million), while the average number of employees per retail outlet is 13 in the United States versus only six in Japan.[1-3] The distribution system is highly fragmented, with numerous retail firms with many levels of wholesale and semi-wholesale operations which form a complex, and sometimes confusing network.

Wholesalers and semi-wholesalers play a central role in Japan, where the distribution system is very fragmented. Historically, the manufacturing sector was made up of small businesses which lacked sufficient marketing and management capabilities. This sector was supported by distributors who provided outlets, funding, raw materials and working capital. Similarly, at the other end of the chain, the wholesalers and semi-wholesalers added their expertise to the retail sector which was very fragmented. In the 1970s Japan instituted the large-scale retail store law, which was revised and in fact strengthened in 1979: the law limits the size of stores and requires the approval of smaller-scale retail stores before a new large store (500 square metres or more) may open. Recent deregulation has seen a decline in the number of retail stores. While foreign retailers, such as Wal-Mart, Carrefour, Metro and Costco have been able to enter the Japanese distribution system, small stores continue to be important for to the Japanese, especially for reasons of convenience.

The retail trader has a close relationship with the customer. Many consumers go shopping on foot or by bicycle; a very viable option considering the level of traffic congestion, town centre speed limits of 20 kilometres per hour, and an absence of car parks due to shortage of space.[4] As a result, they get to know each other well.

The high level of purchasing power in Japan contrasts with the quantitative limitations on consumption due to the lack of space. The area available actually restricts many forms of consumption. For instance, it is not possible to drive long distances, as in Australia, Europe or the US simply because roads and motorways would become completely jammed. Purchasing furniture or household goods is also limited by the availability of habitable space. However, as a means of reinforcing this restriction in a positive way, the Japanese are extremely keen on detail, aesthetics, quality and service.[5] They demand extensive services from their retailers, even if they have to pay for them. Accordingly, they benefit from a wide range of services that make life easier for the Japanese consumer:

1. Daily opening times of up to 12 or 13 hours.
2. Very restricted periods of closure during the year.
3. Free home delivery.
4. Easy, unquestioned acceptance of returned goods.
5. Credit accounts with monthly payments for regular customers.

The compensation for the retailer is in higher gross profit margins; about 30 per cent higher than the European average.[4]

The Japanese system

This strong relationship – service and loyalty, willingness to pay for the retailers, commitment to their customers – is passed along the entire distribution structure. Shimaguchi describes the principal characteristics of the relationships within the Japanese system of distribution by distinguishing both the practice of and the philosophy behind the system of vertical control in the distribution system known as *keiretsuka ryutsu*, or *keiretsus*.[6] This may be approximately translated into English as 'distribution channel arrangements' or 'integrated marketing networks'.[7]

The practical aspects revolve around a widespread and extremely complicated system of discounts. Rebates operate on three levels:

1. to encourage sales promotion (to increase new consumers, support for products that sell badly, clearing expensive stocks);
2. as rewards (for favourable product placement in the shop window or on the counter); and
3. as a means of control (limiting sales of competing products, reducing rate of return, paying cash or within a short period of time, respecting 'recommended' prices, etc.).

These rebates are calculated either on a percentage basis or on a flat rate. Rebates are often confidential and encourage retailers to believe that they are receiving more than others. However, to avoid frustration and jealousy, many producers have encouraged more explicit rebate systems.

The *tegata* system is the second aspect of these sales practices. *Tegatas* are deferred payment systems, based on promissory notes which allow the offer of extended credit periods to the operator at the next stage of the channel. The relationship between two successive layers in this vertical distribution network can be described as (financially) 'protected/obliged'. Trade credit is largely and liberally extended throughout the whole distribution system, similar to Italy and France, but unlike the US and Germany, where payment times are much shorter. Payment periods range from 60 to 120 days and sometimes to 180 days. Glazer (p. 20)[8] remarks that 'everybody uses them [promissory notes] and some are referred to as "pregnancy" notes, in that they may not become due for nine months and more'. The practice of deferred payments has a snowball effect, whereby everybody in the network, financially strong or not, is threatened by notes that become uncollectable. Accounts receivable are made more onerous by the *tegata* practices. Financial reliance becomes not only an individual, but also a collective issue: if one member fails, this may lead to a chain reaction of bankruptcies.

The Japanese distribution system is heavily influenced by the nation's cultural traditions and legal systems. As Pirog and colleagues (p. 3)[9] point out, 'a culture that extols individualism will place fewer social obligations on the dyad than one emphasizing social reciprocity'. They also cite difficulties in using the courts to uphold the law, which is 'typified by the absence of discovery, prohibiting class action suits, contingency fees, and limited damage awards tend to make "arms length" deals risky' (p. 5).[9] This facilitates long-term relationships bound by trust.

Japanese distribution's commitment vis-à-vis service to consumers

The right to return unsold products is extremely liberal because consumer complaints are seen as opportunities for learning rather than as a problem. Learning begins with the consumers at the end of the chain because retailers cannot afford to hold in stock products that have been returned by customers. As Johansson and Nonaka (p. 33) point out, the dedication vis-à-vis consumer complaints is real:

In Japan, when a customer complains, the sales clerk realizes that the customer has a problem, and then tries to understand exactly what it is. She first empathizes with the customer and adopts the customer's viewpoint to gain a clear understanding of what the customer's problem is.

This means listening more than talking, and avoiding judgmental or critical remarks.[10]

Since distributors receive products to sell rather than order them, they are given the capacity to provide full feedback from the consumer to the manufacturer. If the producer does not receive an explicit order from the distributor, the producer will send a *mihakarai-okuri*, which is a delivery based on the producer's estimate of the level of stock held by the intermediary. The wholesalers accept these deliveries, although sometimes grudgingly. They then have to try to sell these extra consignments within their network. This presupposes the fairly liberal right the intermediary and consumers have to return goods, even when they are not defective.

A further aspect of the Japanese method of distribution is the high frequency of deliveries. Shimaguchi[11] explains this high frequency (retailers and wholesalers are in contact daily) in terms of limited financial resources, powerful competition and a tradition of frequent personal contact between those who trade with each other. As a result, the wholesalers are obliged to sell to retailers in small quantities and at short and regular intervals. Although wholesalers have a tendency to regard the system as inefficient, they accept it because on a global level it achieves an economic compromise between increased delivery costs and decreased inventory costs. It is worth noticing the similarities with the *kanban* system of just-in-time deliveries in the field of industrial procurement and subcontracting. One might expect these quasi-affective relationships between channel members to translate into non-aggressive price negotiations and ultimately into non-competitive pricing. Nothing of the kind occurs: the whole distribution system is very much concerned with price levels. Distributors enforce competition without the need to shift frequently from one supplier to another in order to compel them to keep product prices as low as possible. Thus, Weigand (p. 24) notes:

As a consequence of the Japanese commitment toward their employees, Japanese sellers must view prices as a highly flexible marketing instrument. The notion of marginal pricing and the importance of selling at prices that contribute to costs is well understood both by businessmen and by academicians . . . Prices may be cut at any level in the marketing channel by firms that must have sufficient immediate income to meet their unavoidable costs, but the move ultimately will affect the retailers' cost of goods.[12]

Furthermore, the setting of an initial price in Japan is a key decision. Raising the price afterwards may be as difficult as reducing it. The Japanese place a high symbolic meaning on price; a price reduction may spoil the image of the product, especially when it is intended as a gift.[13] In fact, Japanese traders in the distribution system fight over price a great deal, in spite of their loyalty to each other; this, in turn, stimulates demand.

'Traders ... try to resolve their disputes flexibly, not necessarily based on formal contacts but on their mutual trust and confidence which has been built up by human relationships and a long, stable continuity of transaction' (see Kuribayashi p. 55).[14] The personal relationship and human association between the members of the system clearly introduce an emotive element. It is further supported by the practice of gifts. Twice a year, in July at *ochugen* and in December at *oseibo*, the companies send out an enormous number of presents whose cost, importance and nature conform to a complex code.[11] This practice is further reinforced by business lunches and trips with clients, occasions that aim to win their friendship rather than to discuss business, which would be considered the height of bad manners.

In addition to the practices cited above, producers often give support to the distribution channels in the area of sales promotion, for example by sending out extra demonstrators and salespeople to supermarkets, or 'kits' for product presentation within the department. There are incentive schemes for retailers, who are offered bonuses such as a *kabuki* show, a weekend in Hong Kong or even a week in Hawaii. Although such practices do exist in other countries to varying degrees (see Box 11.1), sources agree that in Japan they exist in the strongest and most systematic form.[11,12,14]

Traditional Gai-jin criticisms of the Japanese system of distribution

Numerous converging criticisms of the Japanese distribution networks are made by foreign firms. There are, first, complaints that the distribution system amounts to collusion with Japanese public authorities trying to protect local business. Cateora (p. 622),[15] for instance, explains the case of the Coca-Cola company when it introduced Fresca in Japan: 'The Japan Soft Drink Bottlers Association staged an anti Coca-Cola campaign in which they charged unfair marketing practices. Then, when the Coca-Cola company applied to introduce Fresca, the association put so much pressure on various Japanese ministries that the company withdrew the application.'

A second argument against *keiretsu* distribution is that it creates such a chain of affective relationships operating vertically between producers, wholesalers and retailers that foreign producers find the systems impenetrable. One of the most heavily criticized aspects is the *itten itchoai* system ('single outlet, single account'), which requires retailers to order only from specified wholesalers and prohibits these same wholesalers from selling to other retailers, thus restricting competition to the wholesale stage. In the same way, numerous territorial restrictions (exclusive distribution arrangements) are reinforced by the setting up of dealerships for specified areas, which cooperate amongst themselves and increase the producer's ability to impose marketing strategies.[16] As a consequence, Japanese distribution systems are resented as one of the main obstacles encountered by foreign firms seeking to penetrate the Japanese market and even a cause of failure.

Third, Japanese channels are supposed to be inefficient: long, costly, complex and imposing an ultimate surcharge on the consumer. The main reason for their continued existence, despite their inefficiency, must be the Japanese wish to exclude foreign competition, to protect 'Japan Inc.'. For this reason, the Japanese system of distribution has become a major target of criticism from abroad.

Is the Japanese system of distribution impenetrable?

Czinkota and Woronoff[7] emphasize that the *keiretsus*, which also exist in the production system, aim to 'keep it all in the family': subcontracting networks are institutionalized, whereas elsewhere they would be fluid and informal. Shimaguchi (p. 58) described the main factors, deeply ingrained in the Japanese

Box 11.1

'Master's' retailers at Dunlop France (a subsidiary of Sumitomo Rubber): *keiretsu* distribution in France

The sports division of Dunlop France (a subsidiary of the Japanese Sumitomo Rubber) manufactures and markets tennis balls. It has developed a system of privileged relationships with its dealers, which is very much like the *keiretsu* system.

The object is to select a limited number of retail shops that procure their articles from Dunlop France. In exchange for certain commitments, retailers receive advantages from Dunlop France. Dunlop aims to improve its brand image and to increase consumer brand awareness. Which retailers may apply for the 'Master's' label? They must be independent retail stores; this excludes large specialized sports shops and hypermarkets. They should have a good reputation with potential buyers and be recognized as experts in tennis equipment; they must also offer product lines for golf and squash. Moreover, they must enjoy total freedom of procurement.

'Master's' retailers enjoy beneficial trading conditions, as in *keiretsu* distribution. Dunlop France is committed to informing them of new products before other retail stores, and supplying them with the new products first. Finally, Dunlop France

publishes a complete list of the 'Master's' points of sale in the specialized tennis press (*Tennis de France* and *Tennis Magazine*). These benefits naturally imply some obligations for retail stores. Retail stores commit themselves to maintaining a defined level of inventory and products on display, both tennis rackets and tennis balls as well as lines for golf and squash. They also commit themselves to sell at least 70 per cent of their tennis balls annually under the Dunlop brand name.

Moreover, the retailer must report any remarks made by consumers that may lead to improvements in the quality of new products to Dunlop France. Ultimately, the retail store manager provides a sponsor (usually a well-known tennis professional) with Dunlop France rackets and balls. Presently, about 150 stores bear the 'Master's' label. Dunlop France ensures that the selected stores fulfil their obligations. The outcome, as far as brand awareness and brand image are concerned, proves quite satisfactory, especially for tennis rackets.

(Source: Adapted from Zeller, pp. 33–4.[17])

mentality, which underlie the *keiretsu* distribution system:

A well-known Japanese psychoanalyst, Doi, wrote a famous book in 1973, entitled *Amae-no-kozo*, that is 'the anatomy of dependence'. Apparently *amae* is a unique feature of Japanese society, which is diffused throughout society, including the distribution channels. *Amae* is 'the indulgent, passive love which surrounds and supports the individual in a group, whether family, neighbourhood, or the world at large. Close dependency and high expectancy of others in a group seems to be the way of life in Japan'.[11]

Building and maintaining group bonds, which is called *amae*, is crucial in Japanese society.[18] It means that relationships between channel members are not depersonalized, even when members belong to different companies. Frequent visits from suppliers

(producers and/or wholesalers) to retailers are required for maintaining close human relationships in the channels and fostering the quality of the services rendered to the ultimate consumers.

A vertical structure is virtually inevitable in view of the Japanese mentality. The notion of social status is central to Japanese culture. In the field of interpersonal relationships there are three distinct levels: the *sempai* are elderly, highly respected, addressed by their name and the suffix *san*; younger, less experienced people (*kohai*) are addressed by their name with the suffix *kun*; colleagues on the same level in the hierarchy (same age, experience and seniority) are the *doryo* and should be addressed without a suffix. The determination of social status is extremely important and is one of the major reasons behind the widespread practice of exchanging business cards.

Vertical relationships exist between organizations in much the same way as between individuals.

The Japanese are fairly long-term oriented and their sense of time (*Makimono* time, see section 2.2) emphasizes continuity, stability and perseverance. According to Inagaki (quoted in Turpin[19]), persistence is instilled into Japanese people by their mothers from early childhood. A survey based on a representative sample of 3600 Japanese (over 16 years old) shows that, among the 10 preferred words of the Japanese, *doryoku* (effort) ranks first, *nintai* (persistence) second and *kanjo* (tenacity) ranks fifth. As a consequence of its long-term orientation, Japanese business is much more turnover oriented than profit oriented. Japanese companies tend, as far as possible, to accept business as soon as the sales price covers direct costs and begins to cover fixed costs. This fact is illustrated by Hanawa (quoted by Shimaguchi):

'Kami yori usui Kosen' (margins thinner than paper) is a common saying in Japanese business circles. In certain cases, with a complete disregard for producers' price lists, Japanese distributors end up bargaining machines after harsh negotiations at a price lower than listed. Why such low margins? There is a Japanese business philosophy which believes that 'A deal done is better than none'.[11]

The Japanese themselves admit that the *keiretsu* system is infused with a sense of conservatism, and that it does not lead to innovation.[11,14,16,20] Yet they appreciate the distribution system (a very relational and human sector, everywhere in the world) in the warm, sensitive and emotional tradition which permeates marketing and business in Japan.

The question of whether *keiretsu* distribution is intentionally a barrier to the entry of foreign goods on the Japanese market is a difficult one. It seems to be an accusation against the Japanese for what is essentially their way of being. As stated above, they are themselves quite critical of their distribution system. According to Ishida (p. 322):

the formation of distribution keiretsu in oligopolistic markets for highly differentiated products has the following consequences: (1) elimination or reduction of interbrand and intra brand price competition, (2) strengthening of barriers against new entrants to the market, (3) restriction of dealer independence with a consequent loss of business enthusiasm, innovation, and rationalisation, and (4) preservation and strengthening of oligopolies.[16]

In fact, Japan is slowly becoming less *keiretsu*-bound. Dedoussis (p. 7)[21] notes: '*the continuing enthusiasm* for certain Japanese practices such as loose functional, and even hierarchical, demarcations, and development of Keiretsu-like inter-firm alliances in other countries attests to the need for scrutinizing the "end of Japanese management" argument'. The global economy has made cheaper, quality products widely available to Japanese consumers. The long economic slump provided opportunities for foreign retailers to acquire the operations of failed Japanese retailers, giving them access to the market. Today, discount retailers, such as Wal-Mart and Costco (USA) and Carrefour (France) are established in the Japanese retail system. Younger consumers are more likely to shop at large discount stores, because they are more price-conscious, less tied to traditional bonds and better able to access cars.[9] These new discount stores cut out the middle of the distribution channels, determine their own merchandise assortments and pay in cash rather than depending on credit.

There are also cases where change in the *keiretsu* structure was forced by external factors. For instance, the 1995 earthquake in Kobe devastated a major sector of Kobe's distribution infrastructure. After reopening, wholesalers described some advantages of ending longstanding *keiretsu* relationships and having the right and autonomy to shift to new marketing channels.[22] Rawas and colleagues' (p. 111)[22] survey of wholesalers in the region identified five features that appear to be crucial to improved wholesaler performance: 'promoting strong collaboration, offering trustworthy information, accommodating a variety of needs, supporting the mission and determining the [uniform] price'. While these features illustrate added efficiency, they also illustrate the necessity for strong bonds and trust within the distribution system.

Overcoming the barrier of Japanese distribution

Many real-life examples show that the barriers imposed by Japanese distribution channels may be overcome by foreign companies. The US pharmaceutical company Shaklee directly transferred its door-to-door sales system from the US to Japan.[23] Shaklee

Box 11.2

Rosenthal in Japan

Rosenthal, a German company, exports porcelain, fine glassware and trinkets, which sell quite well on the Japanese market, more as gifts than for the buyer's use. The range of products offered in Japan is somewhat different to that in other countries: more emphasis is put on tea-related objects, which can be offered as presents, than on dishes. Rosenthal constantly surveys the Japanese market, in order to adapt its product range to Japanese tastes and to find those items which could best be sold in Japan. Over the last 20 years, Rosenthal has established close relations with its Japanese distributors. They are frequently invited to visit Rosenthal's production facilities in Germany.

Rosenthal assists them a great deal in displaying its products on store shelves and maintains a full-time team of window dressers in Japan. The main dealers, large department stores, are visited at least once a week. Moreover, Rosenthal has initiated a special training session for Japanese retailers: each year a group of Japanese retailers is invited to a 10-day session in Germany, all expenses paid, to learn how to advise customers. Retailers greatly appreciate this support, and willingly push Rosenthal's products, especially since margins are significant.

(Source: Dupuis and de Maricourt, p. 152.[4])

noticed that there was no legal rule requiring vitamins and nutritive pills to be sold only through medical doctors or pharmacists. It was only a custom: no regulation had formally imposed it. Japanese pharmaceutical companies observed the phenomenal growth of Shaklee's sales but were unable to react. They were afraid of damaging relations with their traditional intermediaries, especially wholesalers and retail pharmacists, who they relied on for the sale of their drugs. Another US-based pharmaceutical company, Bristol-Myers, also implemented a similar door-to-door sales programme, with its Japanese joint-venture partner.[15] The product was sold in a box that contained toothpaste, analgesics and other home remedies, and was offered to households on the basis of consignment sale. That is, every six months a salesperson visited the household, replenished the collection and collected payment for the products that had been used. Many other large pharmaceutical companies from Western countries have been able to enter the Japanese market by adapting to local conditions, such as increasing the number of salespeople per physician fourfold.[24]

US companies, such as Williams Sonoma, successfully circumvented the *keiretsu* distribution system via catalogue sales and limited retail stores of their own.[13] Cases like Rosenthal (see Box 11.2) or ComputerLand (case A11.1) clearly prove that Japanese distribution channels are penetrable for foreign companies. Moreover, the Japanese distribution system is changing, especially under the harsh competitive forces within the Japanese and global market. As Ohmae[23] stated, it is not a 'stone statue', nor are there written rules that prohibit change.

Dealing with the Japanese distribution system

Successful entry into Japanese channels without disrespecting the uniqueness of Japanese culture is a slow process consisting of five stages[6,9,13]:

1. *Find a Japanese partner.* This is the key to the unique cultural environment. The *sogoshosha* (trading companies) are potential partners, provided that they do not represent competing Japanese producers or export the products of a Japanese competitor, and they are not related to a larger group (*zaibatsu*) which has competing lines of products. An important choice is to decide whether to become allied with a company in the same industry or in a non-related industry. A choice of the same industry may provide a smooth beginning (in that the two partners share the same

business culture), but it may prove much more dangerous in the long run. The Japanese local partner may become a competitor on world markets through new products originally designed by the joint venture and then transferred to the Japanese partner's main operations.[7] Finally, the partner must be competitive and effective and be prepared to assist in dealing with the complexities of the local market and distribution system.[22]

2. Find an *original position* in the market, either by offering a significantly higher level of quality or a significant price advantage, or by emphasizing the exoticism of the product as being foreign and imported. It should be noted that Japanese firms produce goods with few if any defects. Channel members and customers expect quality in all goods and services.

3. Identify alternative opportunities for distribution channels. Philips, for instance, has succeeded in splitting its sales of electric shavers and small household appliances between two different types of channels: large department stores and chains on the one hand, small retailers on the other.

4. Be patient, aim for the long term and be prepared to wait for a long pay-back period.

5. Be aware that it is necessary to adopt the mentality of Japanese distribution channels. Build a network of personal relationships, develop loyalty, and spend time and resources building relationships of trust. As Rawwas and colleagues (p. 112)[22] note: 'entrants must adapt to the practices of the prevailing local environmental conditions by accommodating the various needs and developing personal, agreeable, and long-lasting relationships with other channel members, customers, and employees. To maintain strong relationships, entrants may also consider involvement, commitment and patience as benchmarks for success in working with the Japanese'.

11.2

Criteria for choosing foreign distribution channels

Goldman[25] studied the transfer of retail formats in China, finding that six transfer strategies were appropriate under different conditions:

1. *Global niche protection* (as-is transfer, to protect a global niche);
2. *Format-pioneering opportunity* (many changes, to fit a 'leading edge' country for transfer to similar countries);
3. *Opportunism* (many changes, to exploit host opportunities fully);
4. *Format extension* (few changes, transfer from home to compatible countries);
5. *Portfolio based extension* (few changes, transferred from most similar country); and
6. *Competitive positioning* (few changes, to gain superior entry over strong local competition).

Deciding which of these strategies is more appropriate should be based on many factors both inside (e.g. ethnocentric versus geocentric perspectives) and outside a firm, in terms of other companies and relationships.[26,27]

A survey of Canadian firms with export sales, found that 63 per cent used the same channel as in their home market.[28] Firms need to fully evaluate alternatives before extending their existing change. The method for selecting channels abroad is based on a checklist of issues that have to be dealt with in the choice of foreign distribution channels.[29,30] The '9-Cs' criteria that seem most significant are as follows:

1. *Consumers and their characteristics.* Some geographical segments in a foreign market may be more import oriented. Channels serving these segments should be preferred. For example, the French beer Kronenbourg entered the US and was initially available only in the centre of New York, then went on to reach the whole metropolis including the suburbs. People within the centre of New York consume large quantities of imported as well as US beer, so they were seen as an easier entry target. Five years later Kronenbourg became available throughout the US. Similar regional roll-outs can be done on the basis of cultural similarity or focusing on countries with low uncertainty avoidance.[31] Groups of countries may also differ in their preference for certain retail functions.[32] For instance, one of the consequences of long-term orientation is being sparing with resources. This leads to a preference for self-serve merchandise and may lead to lower acceptability of e-commerce.

2. *Culture*. This point has already been considered in relation to Japanese distribution networks. Distribution is the element of the marketing mix most deeply rooted in culture, because it is closely related to everyday life and human relationships (even in large-scale, self-service, apparently depersonalized stores). For instance, Griffith[33] studied the meanings of the market bazaar in Amman, Jordan. He found that the ties to culture and self-identification were so strong that this created a barrier to newer distribution techniques. The next section describes in more detail the impact of culture on selected aspects of distribution.

3. *Character*. It is important that the image projected by the channel, its sales methods, shop locations and clientele, should correspond to the image and character that the product is intended to convey. The success of Louis Vuitton Malletier is based on the large-scale investment in a global network of exclusive retail outlets, located in high-profile areas in major cities throughout the world. Conversely, Blockbuster failed in Germany when it tried to fight the pre-established image of video rental stores and to create a family oriented image. In Germany, video stores are not places children enter, as up to one-third of the titles are pornographic.[34] Transferring an image from one country to another can be difficult. While the image of Marks & Spencer, as a conservative, middle-class store, may be projected similarly across countries, other interpretations of their position may differ, including store reputation, quality and range, which were more positive in Britain than in Spain.[35]

Local consumers may also remain faithful to their traditional distribution outlets for specific segments of consumption. In Spain, despite the continuous development of hypermarkets, consumers make a clear distinction and prefer to purchase perishable goods such as fish, fresh fruit and vegetables, meat and bread in traditional stores.[36]

4. Necessary *capital* relates to the issue of the financial resources that are necessary to start and maintain a channel (e.g. fixed capital, working capital, possible initial losses that will need to be financed).

5. *Cost*. This criterion is strongly linked to capital, but relates more to trade margins than to overhead costs. It depends largely on the respective positions in relation to the strength of producers and distributors. In the UK, for instance, food distribution is in the hands of a very limited number of large store chains, such as Tesco, Sainsbury and Asda.[37] These giants exert pressure on major manufacturers to bear part of the costs, particularly those relating to storage. They also request smaller, more frequent deliveries with mixed items. A similar situation exists in France where the powerful hypermarkets impose constraints on producers which increase their overheads. For instance, they impose payments of fixed commissions in return for the right to carry the reference number, layout of the displays by the producer's own staff, direct help in sales promotion, etc.

6. *Competition* arises in channels either through competing products being placed side by side on shelves, or through competitors refusing other producers access to the distribution channels. For instance, American manufacturers of caustic soda (used in the manufacture of glass, steel and chemical products), were incapable of successfully entering into the Japanese market despite their price advantage.[7] The Japanese union of caustic soda manufacturers formed a cartel that apparently set the level of imports, specified which trading company was to work with which American supplier and bought up the cheap American imports in order to sell them with the assistance of its members. The success of the operation was twofold, they received the profit in place of the American exporter and still managed to keep control of their market. The American exporters were equally unsuccessful in their attempts to deal directly through small distributors, since the industrial users of the product were concerned about the risk of isolating themselves from their main source of supply (the Japanese) if they ordered directly from American exporters.

The power of competition somewhat depends on the concentration of retailers, which is likely to differ across cultures. For instance, in Australia two department stores account for 82 per cent of the market and in the US the top five account for 65 per cent, whereas in Japan the top three only account for 32 per cent.[38,39] Larger retail groups hold more power in the channel. This level of power led to higher price mark-ups in Finland.[40]

7. *Coverage* is another significant element. It is important to cover markets that are widely scattered. Markets that are very concentrated tend also to concentrate competition, since demand attracts supply. The coverage in terms of product range, size and options must also be considered, especially when channel members look for complementary products, spare parts and so on. Product coverage varies across countries according to channel type. For instance, a French *droguerie* does not sell the same products as a US *drugstore* or a German *Drogerie*, or an Australian *pharmacy*, although there is overlap between product ranges.

8. *Continuity*. It is vital that channels that require investment do not turn out to be unusable for some reason (e.g. bankruptcy or financial difficulties, recapture of market share by more aggressive competition, introduction of legal prohibitions on sale of products through the channel, etc.). Continuity may be hampered by slick competitors. For instance, one American firm lost roughly half its local sales in South America.[29] Two of its European competitors had unofficially agreed to force the American company out of the market. One of the two, which was selling a wide range of products, forced the distributors to stop representing the even wider range marketed by the American company. The other competitor purchased shares in the company that distributed the American products.

   Continuity makes initial channel choice that much more important. Research shows that consumers choose where to shop based on similar criteria across cultures. For instance, in Canada, the US and Norway good service, wide selection, low prices and good quality all have a significant influence on the choice of shopping centre.[41] Of course, there are segments of consumers to be considered in and across countries.

9. *Control*. The ideal situation is where the company creates its own distribution network. This ensures maximum control. Large companies should consider integrating their own distribution abroad, particularly when the product differentiation is large (i.e. where there are few substitutes) or where the network assets are transaction specific, such as a product which requires lengthy training for the consumer as well as the seller.[42] Another alternative is to control by equity, via a carefully drafted contract (the written base), or preferably through long-established trusting relationships with the local distributor (personal verbal base). For example, Caterpillar sells worldwide without sales subsidiary companies, by using a dealership system. Some Caterpillar dealers have been in business for more than half a century. If ownership is not practical, control of marketing may be maintained through a hybrid channel strategy, where sales and distribution are managed by foreign channels but sales promotion is managed by the producer.[43] This is the most favoured option in the personal computer industry in Europe.[43]

11.3
Role of distribution as a 'cultural filter'

Culture at the interface between shoppers and stores

Distribution forms subtle relationships with consumers by means of direct contact. People get into the habit of buying certain products which are backed by fixed services, at clearly defined times, in particular shops. Table 11.1 presents guidelines for exploring how distribution is affected by the prevailing cultural patterns in a definite country/culture context. The table refers to specific sections in other chapters where some of the underlying rationales have already been exposed. Naturally, culture explains only part of the variance in distribution systems; another part is related to shoppers and their sociodemographic characteristics, or to economic conditions.

Shopping behaviour differs in many ways according to culture. The first point to consider is whether the shopping experience is a cost or benefit. Is it viewed as a cost in terms of using precious time (strong economic view), or as a benefit in terms of the whole shopping experience. The differences in

Table 11.1 Influence of culture on some aspects of distribution vis-à-vis shoppers

Selected aspects of distribution	Traits that *may* differ according to country/culture
(1) Shopping behaviour	Is time spent shopping experienced as wasted? (economic time; section 2.2) Is return of goods standard behaviour? (complaining behaviour; section 4.3) Who is the shopper? (sex roles, age, etc.) Degree of loyalty to the shop and the shopkeeper (section 4.2)
(2) Opening hours	Religion-based arguments in favour of restricted store opening hours Femininity-based arguments (store personnel should not be exploited)
(3) Product range	Products may be banned because of religious or legal prescriptions
(4) Willingness to service consumers	Human nature is good (friendliness towards shoppers) versus bad (indifference)/negative view of service to others (section 8.3)
(5) Waiting lines	Compliance with rules (see Tables 3.3 and 3.6 and section 8.3)
(6) Thefts by consumers or personnel	Ethical behaviour – ingroup orientation (see sections 2.3, 3.6 and 14.6)
(7) Self-service versus personnel in contact	See section 8.3

opening hours in northern and southern Europe clearly illustrate the influence of culture on the distribution system. In northern Europe, Sunday is sacred and a prevailing feminine orientation strives towards protecting store employee quality of life (which would be spoilt by long opening hours). Product scarcity can also influence the utility of the shopping experience. For instance, in eastern Europe, people seem less concerned about the shopping environment, than in western countries.[44] Similarly, Chilean consumers mostly focus on the utilitarian aspect of making purchases, whereas US consumers are more likely to visit malls for the hedonistic purpose of social interaction.[45] Aspects of culture also influence store loyalty. For instance, consumers are more loyal if they come from a strong uncertainty avoidance or collectivist culture, or if they are male.[46]

Religious or social beliefs may lead to some products being legally banned from particular outlets. For instance, in France basic drugs, and more generally used drugs such as aspirin, can be sold only through pharmacies; in the US, as in many countries, drugstores sell basic medicines. These practices correspond to differing views on whether people can be trusted to self-medicate. French legislators do not trust patients and require them to proceed through doctors and pharmacists, whereas the US system assumes people can distinguish between common ailments and serious afflictions. Another example concerns the distribution of beer in Turkey, a Muslim country. Prior to June 1984, beer was considered a non-alcoholic beverage and sold in coffee-houses. When beer consumption increased sixfold between 1969 and 1983, religious authorities placed pressure on the government to reclassify beer as an alcoholic beverage (which it undeniably is). Beer was banned from being advertised on radio and television and its sale was prohibited in outlets that did not have the required permit to sell alcohol. Prohibiting the sale of this beverage in coffee-houses resulted in a dramatic drop in beer sales in Turkey.[47] Similarly, in the US the sale of liquor is restricted to state-owned stores in some states; the most restrictive being Utah with its large Mormon population.

Wide differences also exist in perceptions of waiting and service. In the US and Japan it is standard practice in supermarkets for staff at cash registers to help customers pack their purchases. In many cases, an employee is specifically assigned to packing. In most of Europe, where mass distribution is oriented towards low price rather than service, customers pack their things as they pay.

Theft by customers or store employees is an important phenomenon in distribution that has to be understood on a country by country basis in light of cultural differences. Naturally, economic constraints (purchasing power per capita) play a certain role, but they do not explain everything. For instance, in France and Italy theft is more common than in Greece, which has lower per capita income. In some countries, theft is not a problem because it is clearly understood as evil by everybody. The kind of consensus which brings about this result is hard to explain, and probably even harder to replicate. Where the rate of theft to sales amounts to several per cent, it cannot be explained simply by poverty. Theft is regarded by some as a sport and is implicitly understood as a legitimate way of social redistribution. Another explanation is strong ingroup orientation whereby ethical behaviour is limited to the ingroup. For instance, in countries where retailers are immigrants belonging to a particular foreign group, shoplifting in these stores may not be considered to be evil, but rather as recovering one's own goods from the outsider. Theft may also be situation specific, as in the case of digital music and video downloading via the Internet. Generally, taking a music CD from a store would be considered stealing, while, in contrast, downloading the same CD off the Internet is considered acceptable by many. The only difference is in the method of obtaining the product rather than the principle.

Website link 11.1

Find out just how long it took Oscar-nominated movies to be pirated to the Internet:
http://torrentfreak.com/detailed-piracy-stats-for-oscars-nominated-movies-080205.

Influence of culture on relationship between channel members

The relationships between domestic producers and distributors may be stronger, more loyal and collaborative, or weaker, more unstable and conflictual, depending on the country. Strongly established links between members of domestic channels generally make entry more difficult for foreign firms. The French invented the concept of the hypermarket and benefit from a distribution set-up that is effective, powerful and strongly independent of producers. It is so strong that products bearing the store name compete head to head with producer brands, creating an atmosphere of conflict between producers and distributors where loyalty is difficult to maintain. The system is inherently susceptible to penetration by imports, as foreign suppliers are perceived as more flexible and a good alternative to domestic producers. At the other extreme, Japan is the place where links between producers and distributors are traditionally very strong and positive. Central to this are the *keiretsus* of distribution, true vertical relationships, mixing business and emotion in typically Japanese fashion, as described in section 11.1. These networks are based on a powerful sense of loyalty, with many services being rendered by one party for the other, and therefore more difficult for foreign companies to penetrate. This is influenced by a long-term orientation, which positively affects distributor commitment.[48] It is also influenced by the focus on interdependence rather than dependence, discussed in Chapter 3. In fact, stronger performance of Western importers has also been linked to higher levels of interdependence, investment, relational norms and trust.[49]

Kale and McIntyre (1991) posit a series of hypotheses on channel relationships based on Hofstede's[50] four cultural dimensions. First, during the initiation phase, companies from high uncertainty avoidance (UA) societies will be biased in favour of finding partners with solid reputations and who can offer written performance guarantees. Conversely, in the case of weak UA, partners will be sought more informally and more flexibility will be shown in negotiations. In addition, firms in highly individualist and masculine cultures (e.g. the US) will tend to choose partners on objective criteria, negotiate the terms of the agreement from an adversarial standpoint, and engage in new relationships as well as relinquish old ones on the basis of economic criteria. Conversely, partners from collectivist and relatively feminine societies (e.g. South Korea, Taiwan, Thailand) will be more relationship centred and will expect more harmony in the partnership, and dissolution will be less aggressive and less frequent. Next, during the implementation phase, high power distance (PD) will lead firms to use coercion in their influence attempts, whereas low PD firms will avoid coercion, prefer face-to-face communication to memos and engage in consultative rather than unilateral decision making.[51] High individualism and masculinity will result in more frequent and manifest conflicts between channel members, as well as lower levels of cooperation. In contrast to these prepositions, they cite a senior Coca-Cola executive in Japan explaining that: 'Once the partnership was in place, it wasn't just the Coca-Cola company selling in Japan; it became a family, a spirit of togetherness, of common purpose.'

Relationship elements also affect direct selling effectiveness (e.g. Amway), but they are more important and coherent in collectivist countries, such as China, than in Western countries, such as Australia.[52] Even firms who establish distribution relationships in similar countries will experience different value systems. For instance, Canadian retailers have to face different values when they enter the US market. Americans are significantly more competition oriented (more achievement oriented, more risk taking) and more oriented towards a Protestant work ethic than Canadians. Canadian retailers are less individualistic and masculine and higher in power distance and risk avoidance than American distributors.[53] These findings are largely consistent with the Kale and McIntyre[51] hypotheses in distinguishing competitive/confrontational distribution scenes from collaborative scenes: 'The executives frequently commented that Americans were found to be much more competitive than Canadians. Frequently the executives voiced comments typically used to describe battles such as "It was all out war" or "Their arsenal was impressive"' (O'Grady and Lane, p. 8).[53]

Conflict is more likely when channel members belong to different cultures and are separated by cultural distance. However, high quality support systems, including frequent visits, tend to reduce decrease this conflict.[54] In addition, a large expatriate population may help to smooth the process. In the case of Greek exporters (collectivist/high UA and PD) and their British importers (individualistic/low UA and PD), relationships are fairly stable with a low degree of conflict and few communication issues, except on pricing issues.[55] This is reinforced by the fact that, among the British importers, there are a good number of Greeks or Cypriots.

There is also evidence that leadership styles are not transferable across cultures. For instance, in the US a supportive leadership style leads to higher cooperation, followed by a participative and directive style. In Finland, the participative style leads to the most cooperation, followed by supportive and directive leadership styles. Finally, in Poland a supportive leadership style is positively related to cooperation, while a directive style is negatively related to cooperation. In Poland, the directive style may be too closely related to the previous communist system.[56]

11.4

Direct marketing worldwide

Jean-Claude is one in several million direct marketing purchasers throughout the world who annually buys a Christmas cake (a Deluxe medium, 2 3/4 pounds) from Collin Street Bakery in Corsicana, Texas. The product is baked following the traditional recipe of Gus Weidman, a Bavarian who emigrated to the United States at the end of the nineteenth century. Jean-Claude buys it by credit card and it is delivered to his home in Switzerland within a month. This is just one simple example of worldwide direct marketing. Lands' End, one of the leading US direct marketers worldwide, sends its products to more than 170 countries, while large European mail-order companies such as Otto Versand, Quelle, Bertelsmann and La Redoute have developed important crossborder operations, especially in Europe.[57] The development of international credit cards and the consequent facilitation of international payment have greatly decreased the transaction costs for both consumers and cataloguers. Restricted opening hours for stores may be an incentive for consumers to buy direct: Germany and Austria, two countries where store opening hours have been historically strictly limited in comparison to other developed countries, rank first and fourth worldwide as regards catalogue sales per capita;[58] the German catalogue industry is the strongest in the world, relative to country size.

There are several issues involved in direct crossborder selling. First, logistics issues: direct mail can be sent from the domestic country, from within the target country, or from a third country to reduce mailing costs while keeping speed and security of delivery at a fair level. Although it may seem the easiest solution to mail from within the target country because the local language and culture will be understood better, there may be constraints in the local postal service that make it more advantageous to mail from a third country. This can prove cheaper in terms of mailing costs.[59]

The second major issue in cross-border direct marketing involves regulation, mainly postal regulations, customs and privacy issues, all of which are largely country specific.[60] However, regulations are becoming more and more standardized at the regional level, as in the EU where a European Union Postal Service was implemented in 1998 after six years of preparation. Customs may be a problem, since goods intended to reach the foreign customer by a specific date (e.g. Christmas) can be delayed by customs authorities; this is less likely when goods are shipped to industrialized nations.

The third issue is the availability of mailing lists, and their degree of reliability in terms of names and addresses, especially when they are not regularly updated. Rosenfield[61] makes an international comparison of direct marketing in the USA and in other countries, and states that the marketing is different rather than better. Mailing costs in the USA are comparatively low, but mailing lists are sometimes of marginal quality, causing a low net response rate. Among the European countries, France appears to be the most high-tech country for direct mail but with expensive lists; Germany also has very high standards and world-class technology but German lists are subject to stringent privacy rules (*Datenschutz*); Italy, on the other hand, with its inefficient postal service, is a relatively difficult context for direct marketing. In Latin America, Argentina and Chile are favourable countries with fairly good infrastructures, but Brazil lags behind because of postal and telecommunication problems.

Direct marketing has to be adapted for language and cultural reasons. The text, for catalogues, letters and so on, is generally prepared with the help of locals or even directly in the target country to ensure appropriateness of language. Some catalogues advertise in English worldwide. Examples are the World's Best, from Baltimore, or Shepplers, which sells Western wear; they target an affluent English-speaking

audience and use international mailing lists or selective national mailing lists. The Lands' End catalogue contains a four-page leaflet called 'Lands' End Glossary' which explains the basics in Arabic, German, Japanese and Spanish. Language adaptation must also target the addressee's name: 'Jean', a boy's first name in French, is a girl's first name in English, so that sometimes Jean-Claude receives international direct mail addressed to 'Mrs' or 'Ms'.

The source culture is often indicated by the origin of the mail, the letter or the stamp, and it may be desirable to emphasize the culture if it is positively valued in the target country (there is a strong association of the source country with the products sold and a positive evaluation of it as a country of origin). Conversely, it may be better to fully localize operations when the name must be local: Germany's Bertelsmann sells books and records in France under the name 'France Loisirs', because the original company name is not positively associated with cultural products in France. The Bertelsmann's book club operates in various European countries (Germany, France, the UK) and adapts its operations to suit each country, within the same basic formula (a two-year subscription with a minimum purchase of one book every three months). The catalogues are adapted for each market; in France its sales force consists of 500 representatives, a method that is totally ineffective in the UK. They have no shops in the UK but France and Germany maintain a network of 200 and 300 shops respectively.[59]

Ethics are a problem in international direct mail. Concerns with privacy, and the possible fraudulent uses of mailing lists, are major concerns in a number of countries. Germany and New Zealand have very strict privacy regulations but other countries are more lenient. Even in neighbouring countries, such as the United States and Canada, ethical views on direct marketing differ. Canadians tend to have more power distance than Americans and resent letters written in too direct a style; therefore, letters have to be written differently for Canadian audiences.[62]

Direct marketing and the Internet

Today, most countries have access to the Internet. It is estimated that as of December 2007 there are over 1.3 billion Internet users, around 20 per cent of the world's population.[63] Saskin[64] estimates that there is a new Internet user every two seconds.

Direct marketing increasingly uses the Internet as a global medium. Many companies (e.g. Urban Outfitters) use their website to provide detailed product information, along with the ability to make online purchases. Some companies are entirely Internet based, with no bricks-and-mortar shopfronts at all. Amazon.com is perhaps the most widely recognized of these companies. Amazon started as an online bookstore and is now more like an online department store which will deliver around the world. Lands' End, like many other direct mail companies, has a website from which anything in the catalogue can be ordered fast and efficiently with the click of a keyboard. 3M's website sells products, and provides access to detailed information on its products and worldwide operations.

Website link 11.2

Make your own Marketing Across Cultures t-shirt on Zazzle: **http://www.zazzle.com.**

The concept of mass-customization and user-designed content has flourished on the Internet. One example of this is Zazzle.com, a website that allows its users to create their own merchandise (e.g. posters, clothing, mugs, etc.) or buy merchandise created by others. Content creators receive a commission for every one of their items sold, which naturally encourages them to get more people to buy, effectively making them a salesperson for the company. Recent research indicates that individualist cultures are more likely to purchase customized products online, compared to collectivist cultures.[65] Interestingly, those collectivist consumers who do purchase customized products online are less price sensitive than individualistic consumers.[65]

Despite the growing number of firms and buyers that transact over the Internet, there are still a number of limitations. The first key issue surrounds the network infrastructure, which was initially built for US national defence purposes and was then developed by academic users. The commercial development of the web is a formidable challenge,

because the numbers of servers have to be regularly increased and jams on the web can cause lengthy delays. The second issue concerns safe Internet credit card payment. Internet theft is increasing, despite the rapid development of anti-theft devises, including encryption, the use of credit cards and the presence of specialized intermediaries between supplier and customers. Many potential customers see this as a problem. There is still relatively limited use of anonymous electronic cards for online purchases,[66] making identity theft a continuing issue.

The Internet is not limited to its purchasing potential. It offers great benefits in terms of instantaneous information exchange, sending company information to internal customers (employees and intermediaries), sending product information to customers, allowing instantaneous transactions with customers, and providing marketing and sales support and information to internal users.[67]

Only a limited number of products can be sold on the Internet because virtual shopping lacks the full-scale experience of real shopping, especially the human encounter and the opportunity to see and buy the product directly. Speciality consumer goods are the most likely to be successfully marketed over the Internet, as consumers are generally well informed about the product prior to purchase.[68] For example, the website americanaexchange.com specializes in finding and selling antique and rare books. In addition, Kwak and colleagues (p. 35)[69] discuss the benefits of trial over the Internet: 'over the past few years, new internet music startups like CDNow, N2K, MP3.com, and Liquid Audio have revolutionized the way the industry and consumers transact . . . via numerous product trials and free information for the product on the web that are not typically available offline'.

The lack of ability to really experience some types of products over the Internet may explain the failure of some virtual shopping galleries, which ceased operating within a few months of being launched onto the market. The word 'virtual', often advertised as if it were an 'open sesame', is far from innocent:

The technology of virtual simulation cannot but reinforce this risk of de-realization by giving a pseudo-concrete and pseudo-palpable character to imaginary entities . . . On one hand, thus, they constitute tools to command complexity, propitiating a better intelligibility, on the other they have a certain propensity to encourage latent forms of illusion and even schizophrenia. The more we recur to simulation as a scriptural means and as a way of inventing the world, the greater the risk to confound the world with the representations we make of it. (Queau, pp. 98–9[70]; cited by Ribeiro, p. 499[71])

Many major international organizations and companies are producing websites in multiple languages. The proportion of people accessing the Internet in English has dropped from 49 per cent in September 2000 to 30 per cent in November 2007.[72,73] There are still many problems with translations and speed in countries with low levels of infrastructure.

Even when the website is largely global, there are issues with different rules and regulations for conducting business over the Internet. Cox (p. 64) highlights logistic hurdles within the EU:

The challenge for the EU is to come up with meaningful rules for financial services and e-commerce without strangling the nascent Internet economy in the cradle. A case in point: if a company wants to set up accounts with the same bank in different EU countries, as many as 900 signatures are required.[74]

Website link 11.3

World Internet Stats is a good resource for examining global online trends: http://www.internetworldstats.com/stats.htm.

Both domestic and international legal issues are difficult to manage on the Internet, including the content of cyberspace contracts, collecting taxes for online transactions on a national basis, protecting intellectual property, stopping certain types of information from appearing, protecting consumers, location of legal jurisdiction, location of buyer, seller, or both.[75] Recently, Internet taxation issues have been attracting more attention.[76] Malaysia has shown concern about losing tax revenues from e-commerce transactions.[77] In 2001, the United Kingdom vetoed plans to introduce legislation on e-commerce in the

EU as it will be impossible to enforce VAT on non-EU companies (Anon, 2001).

As an article in the *Economist* (p. 18) put it:

Here is this amazingly useful, if disruptive, thing, built from the bottom up by idealists, largely self-regulated and beyond the reach of governments or big companies. It is a nice idea. Sadly, the Internet is neither as different nor as 'naturally' free as wired Utopians claim. The sheer pervasiveness of the Internet makes it impossible for even the best-intentioned of regulators to keep out. Such issues as privacy, consumer protection, intellectual property rights, contracts and taxation cannot be left entirely to self-regulation if e-commerce is to flourish. And, as the judge's ruling in favour of a break-up of Microsoft has just confirmed . . . antitrust action may be even more important online than off.[78]

11.5

Sales promotion: other customs, other manners

Sales promotion techniques are fairly universal, but their use and the conditions of implementing them vary cross-nationally and depend on cultural variables (see Box 11.3). Sales promotion targets some basic marketing objectives that are cross-culturally valid. It aims to engage the consumer in any of the following: (1) initial trial; (2) initial purchase; (3) an immediate purchase; (4) re-purchase; (5) an increase in frequency of purchase; and (6) entering point of sale. Promotional techniques combine the sales proposal with the following:

1. Discounts or rebates of various kinds: time-limited price discounts, coupons, 'in-pack' money-off, reimbursement offers, etc., mostly directed at immediate purchase.
2. Competitions: games, contests, lotteries, sweepstakes, etc.
3. Collection devices of various kinds (membership reward and stamps), oriented towards increasing the frequency of purchase and building consumer loyalty.
4. Free samples or some kind of cross-product offer, for the purpose of consumer trial especially.
5. Gifts: 'in-pack' gifts, purchase with purchase, reusable packaging, product bonus, etc.

Box 11.3

Global transferability of sales promotions: Lego examples

A case in point is Lego A/S, the Danish toy marketer which undertook American-style consumer promotion in Japan some years ago. Earlier, the company had measurably improved its penetration of US households by employing 'bonus' packs and gift promotions. Encouraged by that success, it decided to transfer these tactics unaltered to other markets, including Japan, where penetration had stalled. But these lures left Japanese consumers unmoved. Subsequent investigation showed that consumers considered the promotions to be wasteful, expensive, and not very appealing. Similar reactions were recorded in other countries. Lego's marketers thus got their first lesson on the limitations of the global transferability of sales promotions.

Lego was involved in a global promotion with Shell Oil, since promotional Lego toys were designed exclusively to be distributed at Shell's 44,000 service stations worldwide. The material for this global promotion was the same worldwide but the tactics used, including giveaways, cash-back coupons and discount coupons, were decided locally.

(Source: Kashani, pp. 92–3[79]; Koranteng[80].)

Cross-national differences in use of sales promotion techniques

The first question to be addressed is: who is the target? Often the target is not only the end consumer. Sales promotions may also be targeted at store personnel, to encourage them to stock a product, display it in a favourable position, or promote the product to the end consumer. This may be especially relevant to low-cost, commodity-type products that consumers need reminding to buy, such as batteries. Gifts (e.g. camera or vacation) may be offered from the battery producer, which encourage personnel to place them in a favourable position within the store. Directing promotions at the store may be more effective in less developed countries, where the final buyers are limited to the choices offered within a store. Similarly, it might be advisable to target the purchaser, rather than the end user, where people have servants who shop for food and household supplies.[81]

A second question is whether a technique is considered ethical. Sales promotion regulations differ cross-nationally according to various assumptions about what is moral or immoral and what is fair or unfair in the relationship between a merchandiser/sales promoter and a customer/shopper. Most developed countries strictly regulate sales promotion in order to prevent abuse.[82] There is also some fear that

sales promotion costs could result in overpricing of products. AC Nielsen tried to introduce money-off coupons in Chile that had to be sent to the manufacturer for reimbursement.[7] The supermarket union opposed the promotion on the grounds that it would raise costs unnecessarily and recommended its members not accept the coupons.

The areas in which ethical issues are mostly raised are competitions, gifts and cross-product offers. The United Kingdom and the United States are the most favourable countries for sales promotions.[82] Anglo-Saxon countries are generally more liberal than other countries, especially for competitions: most kinds of lotteries, free draws and sweepstakes are legally permitted. In most Anglo-Saxon countries, private betting (bookmakers) organizations are permitted, whereas in most other countries, betting (horse races, lotteries) is state controlled, since it is seen as immoral for private individuals to benefit from organizing lotteries and betting games. Italy authorizes lotteries and sweepstakes where prizes are not in cash but in kind. Prizes in competitions are often limited to small amounts, as in The Netherlands, which severely restricts the attractiveness of sales promotion competitions. France allows competitions, but they are carefully controlled so that no purchase is needed to enter the competition. The European Union has tried to harmonize these

Table 11.2 Cross-cultural adequacy problems for selected sales promotion techniques

Technique	Culture-related features that may affect implementation
Coupons	Level of literacy, consumer and retailer sophistication/low social status implied
Contests and sweepstakes	Legal requirements/prizes must suit target market tastes
Price offers	Absence of price labelling and display/bargaining/trade misuse
Stamps and collections	Future orientation needed/high inflation/level of channel sophistication
Free samples	Interpretation of gratuity/trade misuse/theft of sampled products
Gifts (in, on or near packs)	Legal requirements/theft by channel employees or customers

regulations several times, but so far there has been no uniform agreement. The intention is to abolish a number of 'outdated' restrictions, including a ban on free samples and limits to discounts (was 33 per cent in Belgium). Member states would still be allowed to decide on many other factors, including bans on discounts prior to seasonal sales, selling below the retailer's actual costs, etc.

Many national regulations prohibit gifts or limit their value. In France, the value of a promotional gift cannot be higher than 7 per cent of the retail price. The idea behind this prohibition is that consumers should buy products, not gifts. Collectors' items, such as gifts, are subject to the same kind of regulatory ceiling: the value of the collector's item associated with the purchase is often legally limited, especially those targeted at children.

Sales promotions that encourage an initial trial, such as cross-product offers and purchase-with-purchase offers, are often controlled by national legislation. It is more difficult for consumers to judge value when they pay for two products at the same time.

Some sales promotion techniques are fairly consistant cross-culturally, since they appear less questionable. For instance, (a) free samples as a way to induce people to try the product, (b) discount on the next purchase as a way to induce consumers to repeat their purchase, (c) point-of-purchase materials and product demonstrations as a way to increase consumer knowledge of the product, (d) free food tasting to induce trial, etc. However, some countries object to sales promotion techniques in general because of the risk of consumers being misled. Whereas some countries believe in personal responsibility and

trust consumers to seek and evaluate information (e.g. Australia, the UK, the US), others have less confidence in the capacities of individuals to make free and responsible choices (Latin-European and northern European countries). In Scandinavian countries sales promotions face the greatest obstacles, since every promotion has to be approved by an official body.

Sociocultural factors influencing implementation of sales promotion techniques

Table 11.2 presents a series of sociocultural factors that influence the implementation of sales promotion techniques. The level of literacy is obviously an important variable since promotion often includes important text. For instance, if the target market is largely illiterate, people are unlikely to respond to coupons. The level of literacy becomes crucial when the purpose of the campaign is consumer education. In this case, visual and oral promotion should be given preference. Promotional campaigns in some African countries travel from village to village showing promotional films, while the operator distributes free samples of the product. Conversely, where there is increasing education and political awareness, promotional campaigns should emphasize this. For instance, Thailand's state-owned oil company Bang Chak Petroleum, which offered two oranges or a copy of the Thai constitution as promotional gifts, was more successful with the constitution booklet.[83]

Retailer sophistication is required when the promotional techniques need some follow-up, such as redeeming coupons or dealing with stamps or collectors' devices. In this case, the retailer is the intermediary between manufacturer and the final consumer. They need to be organized in terms of stocking coupons, reckoning, ordering premiums, etc.

If prizes are given, they must suit the target market's tastes (e.g. cars or bicycles, small or large household items, sporting equipment or more practical appliances). This is especially important in competitions where the prizes are advertised. Whenever legally possible, cash is the most universally acceptable prize, since it allows further free spending. However, in many countries cash prizes are not allowed, or are limited to small amounts.

Unethical trade behaviour vis-à-vis the manufacturer is possible in a number of ways. For instance, retailers can decide to sell what were supposed to be free samples, or they can pocket money-off offers by increasing prices. Retailers' employees can remove samples, gifts or premiums for themselves or others. Strict control of the retailers involved in a promotion is required wherever such opportunistic attitudes are foreseeable.

Promotional techniques can be associated with images of social status. In Hong Kong the response to coupons is very positive, whereas the use of stamps is popular in Thailand; both of these locally popular techniques being associated with middle-class status.[81] In other countries, coupons or discounts can be associated with low-class status (e.g. in Australia), because the implied price consciousness suggests an image of low purchasing power. On the other hand, promotional techniques based on a price reduction cannot be implemented in countries where consumer bargaining is common, as basic prices are not displayed. A rebate only has meaning in relation to a clear market price. In such cases, it is better to target channel members rather than the end user. For instance, retailers can be offered a rebate for quantity sold over a certain period of time.

Some promotional techniques require extended involvement, such as collectors' devices, stamps or self-liquidating premiums, refunds after a series of purchases, etc. Cultures with a present time orientation respond poorly to these techniques, which require delayed gratification.[81] Similarly, high inflation is very detrimental to any sales promotion whose rewards are not immediate. For instance, the face value of coupons, discounts and other rebates may have little meaning after a few weeks have gone by (necessary for printing, distribution and claiming the rebates). To put this in perspective, Zimbabwe's inflation rate reached 165,000 per cent in early 2008.

Finally, it is necessary to check that the purpose of the promotional technique is understood locally (the problem of conceptual equivalence). For instance, in countries where much of the population grew up under communism, it may be difficult to understand the motives behind free samples. The basic rationale, that a producer wants consumers to try a product in order to have them buy it, is not self-evident. A free sample is understood either as a sign of poor quality ('they give it because they cannot sell it') or as a sign of the naivety of the manufacturer ('let's take as much as possible'). P & G experienced major problems with free samples in Poland, where some people ignored them, and others broke into mailboxes to take them. It is noteworthy that price reductions are by far the most popular sales promotion technique.[82]

Questions

1. A distribution formula is successful in the United States; you are asked to extend it through a franchise system to several countries around the world. How would you devise a policy for those franchisees who want the standard recipe to be adapted for their home market in the following areas: size of the store, personnel recruitment, servicing, stocking, brands represented, display, store name, etc.?

2. What are the ways in which retailing know-how is transferred internationally?

3. Discuss the distinguishing features of the Japanese distribution system.

4. Why do exporting firms tend to have somewhat different distribution channels abroad compared to their domestic markets, apart from the peculiarities of the local distribution systems?

5. Until recently, the typical store in Germany was open every day, from Monday to Friday, 9 a.m. to 6.30 p.m. They closed at 2 p.m. on Saturday and all day Sunday. Once a month there was a special shopping Thursday when stores were open until 8.30 p.m. Conversely, opening hours in the United States are much longer and some supermarkets are open 24 hours a day, seven days a week. Store employees in Germany are highly unionized and unions are traditionally opposed to any increase in opening hours. To what extent do time-related cultural differences explain the huge difference in store opening hours between Germany and the United States?

6. Using a local catalogue (from your own country), explain how (in terms of language, size, photographs, prices, product information, delivery and payment conditions, etc.) it should be adapted to a culturally remote market with a similar level of economic development (choose the target market) if it were to be sent to potential customers in that context.

7. Discuss how store size can be related to culture.

8. Explain how cultural values can have a negative impact on self-service and automated service in general (that is, without personnel in contact with the shopper/consumer).

9. Based on available statistics, review key differences in the retailing systems in EU countries.

References

1. Euromonitor (2004), 'Department Stores in the USA', *Euromonitor International*, www.marketresearch.com.
2. US Census Bureau (2002), *2002 Economic Census Geographic Area Series Retail Trade*. www.census.gov/econ/census02/guide/EC02_44.HTM.
3. METI (2002), *Results of the Census of Commerce*. www.meti.go.jp/english/statistics/tyo/syougyo/index.html.
4. Dupuis, Marc and Renaud de Maricourt (1989), *France/Etats-Unis/Japon, Trois Mondes, Trois Distributions*. Paris: Ecole Supérieure de Commerce de Paris.
5. Turcq, Dominique and Jean-Claude Usunier (1985), 'Les Services Au Japon: L'efficacité . . . Par La Nonproductivité', *Revue Française de Gestion* (May–June), 12–15.
6. Shimaguchi, Mitsuaki and Larry J. Rosenberg (1979), 'Demystifying Japanese Distribution', *Columbia Journal of World Business*, 14 (1), 38–41.
7. Czinkota, Michael R. and Jon Woronoff (1991), *Unlocking Japan's Markets*. Chicago, IL: Probus Publishing.
8. Glazer, Herbert (1968), *The International Business in Japan: The Japanese Image*. Tokyo: Sophia University.
9. Pirog, Stephen F., Peter A. Schneider, and Danny K.K. Lam (1997), 'Cohesiveness in Japanese Distribution: A Socio-Cultural Framework', *International Marketing Review*, 14 (2), 124–34.
10. Johansson, Johny K. and Ikujiro Nonaka (1996), *Relentless: The Japanese Way of Marketing*. New York: HarperCollins.
11. Shimaguchi, Mitsuaki (1978), *Marketing Channels in Japan*. Ann Arbor, MI: UMI Research Press.
12. Weigand, Robert E. (1970), 'Aspects of Retail Pricing in Japan', *MSU Business Topics*, 18 (Winter), 23–30.
13. Montgomery, David B. (1991), 'Understanding the Japanese as Customers, Competitors and Collaborators', *Japan and the World Economy*, 3 (1), 61–91.
14. Kuribayashi, Sei (1991), 'Present Situation and Future Prospects of Japan's Distribution System', *Japan and the World Economy*, 3 (1), 39–60.
15. Cateora, Philip R. (1983), *International Marketing* (5th edn). Homewood, IL: Richard D. Irwin.
16. Ishida, Hideto (1983), 'Anticompetitive Practices in the Distribution of Goods and Services in Japan: The Problem of Distribution Keiretsu', *Journal of Japanese Studies*, 9 (2), 319–34.
17. Zeller, Eric (1989), 'Masters Thesis', 'Stratégies d'Internationalisation des Enterprises de l'Industrie du Sport' ('Internationalisation Strategies in the Sports Industry), Ecole Supérieure de Commerce de Paris, 33–34.
18. Nakane, Chie (1973), *Japanese Society*. Berkeley: University of California Press.

19. Turpin, Dominique (1990), *World Competitiveness Report*. Lausanne: IMD/World Economic Forum.

20. Yoshino, Michael Y. (1971), *Marketing in Japan: A Management Guide*. New York: Praeger.

21. Dedoussis, Vagelis (2001), 'Keiretsu and Management Practices in Japan – Resilience Amid Change', *Journal of Managerial Psychology*, 16 (2), 173–88.

22. Rawwas, Mohammed Y., Kazuhiko Konishi, Shoji Kamise, and Jamal Al-Khatib (2008), 'Japanese Distribution System: The Impact of Newly Designed Collaborations on Wholesalers' Performance', *Industrial Marketing Management*, 37 (1), 104–15.

23. Ohmae, Kenichi (1985), *La Triade, Emergence D'une Stratégie Mondiale De L'entreprise*. Paris: Flammarion.

24. Pahud de Mortanges, Charles, Jan-Willem Rietbroek, and Cort Johns, MacLean (1997), 'Marketing Pharmaceuticals in Japan: Background and the Experience of US Firms', *European Journal of Marketing*, 31 (8), 561–82.

25. Goldman, Arich (2001), 'The Transfer of Retail Formats into Developing Economies: The Example of China', *Journal of Retailing*, 77 (2), 221–42.

26. Alexander, Nicholas and Hayley Myers (2000), 'The Retail Internationalisation Process', *International Marketing Review*, 17 (4/5), 334–53.

27. Ford, David (2002), 'Solving Old Problems, Learning New Things and Forgetting Most of Them: Distribution, Internationalisation and Networks', *International Marketing Review*, 19 (3), 225–35.

28. McNaughton, Rod B. and Jim Bell (2001), 'Channel Switching between Domestic and Foreign Markets', *Journal of International Marketing*, 9 (1), 24–39.

29. Cateora, Philip R. (1993), *International Marketing* (8th edn). Homewood, IL: Richard D. Irwin.

30. Czinkota, Michael R. and Illka A. Ronkainen (1990), *International Marketing* (2nd edn). Hinsdale, IL: Dryden Press.

31. Lee, Julie Anne, Ellen Garbarino, and Dawn Lerman (2007), 'How Cultural Differences in Uncertainty Avoidance Affect Product Perceptions', *International Marketing Review*, 24 (3), 330–49.

32. De Mooij, Marieke and Geert Hofstede (2002), 'Convergence and Divergence in Consumer Behavior: Implications for International Retailing', *Journal of Retailing*, 78 (1), 61–9.

33. Griffith, David A. (1998), 'Cultural Meaning of Retail Institutions: A Tradition-Based Culture Examination', *Journal of Global Marketing*, 12 (1), 47–59.

34. Simmonds, Kenneth (1999), 'International Marketing: Avoiding the Seven Deadly Traps', *Journal of International Marketing*, 7 (2), 51–62.

35. Burt, Steve and Jose Carralero-Encinas (2000), 'The Role of Store Image in Retail Internationalisation', *International Marketing Review*, 17 (4/5), 433–53.

36. Nueno, José Luis and Harvey Bennett (1997), 'The Changing Spanish Consumer', *International Journal of Research in Marketing*, 14 (1), 19–33.

37. Child, Peter N. (2002), 'Taking Tesco Global', *The McKinsey Quarterly*, www.mckinseyquarterly.com.

38. Euromonitor (2003), 'Department Stores in Japan', *Euromonitor International*, www.marketresearch.com.

39. Euromonitor (2003), 'Department Stores in Australia', *Euromonitor International*, www.marketresearch.com.

40. Aalto-Setälä, Ville (2002), 'The Effect of Concentration and Market Power on Food Prices: Evidence from Finland', *Journal of Retailing*, 78 (3), 207–16.

41. Severin, Valerie, Jordan J. Louviere, and Adam Finn (2001), 'The Stability of Retail Shopping Choices over Time and across Countries', *Journal of Retailing*, 77 (2), 185–202.

42. Anderson, Erin T. and Anne T. Coughlan (1987), 'International Market Entry and Expansion Via Independent or Integrated Channels of Distribution', *Journal of Marketing*, 51 (1), 71–82.

43. Gabrielsson, Mika, V.H. Manek Kirpalani, and Reijo Luostarinen (2002), 'Multiple Channel Strategies in the European Personal Computer Industry', *Journal of International Marketing*, 10 (3), 73–95.

44. Griffen, Mitch, Barry J. Babin, and Doan Modianos (2000), 'Shopping Values of Russian Consumers: The Impact of Habituation in a Developing Economy', *Journal of Retailing*, 76 (1), 33–52.

45. Nicholls, J. A. F., Fuan Li, Carl J. Kranendonk, and Tomislav Mandakovic (2003), 'Structural or Cultural: An Exploration into Influences on Consumers' Shopping Behavior of Country Specific Factors Versus Retailing Formats', *Journal of Global Marketing*, 16 (4), 97–115.

46. Straughan, Robert B. and Nancy D. Albers-Miller (2001), 'An International Investigation of Cultural and Demographic Effects on Domestic Retail', *International Marketing Review*, 18 (5), 521–41.

47. Miller, Fred and A. Hamdi Demirel (1988), 'Efes Pilsen in the Turkish Beer Market: Marketing Consumer Goods in Developing Countries', *International Marketing Review*, 5 (1), 7–19.

48. Kim, Keysuk and Changho Oh (2002), 'On Distributor Commitment in Marketing Channels for Industrial Products: Contrast between the United States and Japan', *Journal of International Marketing*, 10 (1), 72–97.

49. Skarmeas, Dionisis A. and Constantine S. Katsikeas (2001), 'Drivers of Superior Importer Performance in Cross-Cultural Supplier–Reseller Relationships', *Industrial Marketing Management*, 30 (2), 227–41.

50. Hofstede, Geert (1980), *Culture's Consequences: International Differences in Work Related Values*. Beverly Hills, CA: Sage.

51. Kale, Sudhir H. and Roger P. McIntyre (1991), 'Distribution Channel Relationships in Diverse Cultures', *International Marketing Review*, 8 (3), 31–45.

52. Luk, S., L. Fullgrabe, and S. Li (1996), 'Managing Direct Selling Activities in China: A Cultural Explanation', paper presented to *EIRASS, Third*

Recent Advances in Retailing and Consumer Sciences Conference. Telfs, Austria, 1–18.

53. O'Grady, Shawna and Henry W. Lane (1992), 'Culture: An Unnoticed Barrier to Canadian Retail Performance in the United States', paper presented at Academy of International Business Annual Conference. Brussels.

54. Shoham, Aviv, Gregory M. Rose, and Fredric Kropp (1997), 'Conflicts in International Channels of Distribution', *Journal of Global Marketing*, 11 (2), 5–27.

55. Katsikeas, Constantine S. and Nigel F. Piercy (1991), 'The Relationship between Exporters from a Developing Country and Importers Based in a Developed Country: Conflict Considerations', *European Journal of Marketing*, 25 (1), 6–25.

56. Mehta, Rajiv, Trina Larsen, Bert Rosenbloom, Jolanta Mazur, and Pia Polsa (2001), 'Leadership and Cooperation in Marketing Channels: A Comparative Empirical Analysis of the USA, Finland and Poland', *International Marketing Review*, 18 (6), 633–66.

57. Akhter, Syed H. (1996), 'International Direct Marketing: Export Value Chain, Transaction Cost, and the Triad', *Journal of Direct Marketing*, 10 (2), 13–23.

58. Mühlbacher, Hans, Martina Botschen, and Werner Beutelmeyer (1997), 'The Changing Consumer in Austria', *International Journal of Research in Marketing*, 14 (4), 309–19.

59. Desmet, Pierre and Dominique Xardel (1996), 'Challenges and Pitfalls for Direct Mail across Borders: The European Example', *Journal of Direct Marketing*, 10 (3), 48–60.

60. Rawwas, Mohammed Y., David Strutton, and Lester W. Johnson (1996), 'An Exploratory Investigation of the Ethical Values of American and Australian Consumers: Direct Marketing Implications', *Journal of Direct Marketing*, 10 (4), 52–63.

61. Rosenfield, James R. (1994), 'Direct Marketing Worldwide: One Man's Perspective', *Journal of Direct Marketing*, 8 (1), 79–82.

62. Graves, Roger (1997), '"Dear Friend" (?): Culture and Genre in American and Canadian Direct Marketing Letters', *Journal of Business Communication*, 34 (3), 235–52.

63. Anon (2008), 'World Internet Users', World Internet Usage Statistics, 27 March, www.internetworldstats.com/stats.htm.

64. Saskin, Rose (2001), 'Beyond Multilingualism', *World Trade*, 14 (6), 52.

65. Moon, Junyean, Doren Chadee, and Surinder Tikoo (2008), 'Culture, Product Type, and Price Influences on Consumer Purchase Intention to Buy Personalized Products Online', *Journal of Business Research*, 61 (1), 31–9.

66. Hodges, Mark (1997), 'Is Web Business Good Business?', *Technology Review*, 100 (6), 23–32.

67. Quelch, John A. and Lisa R. Klein (1996), 'The Internet and International Marketing', *Sloan Management Review*, 37 (3), 60–77.

68. Tian, Robert G. and Charles Emery (2002), 'Cross-Cultural Issues in Internet Marketing', *Journal of American Academy of Business*, 1 (2), 217–24.

69. Kwak, Hyokjin, Richard J. Fox, and George M. Zinkhan (2002), 'What Products Can Be Successfully Promoted and Sold Via the Internet?', *Journal of Advertising Research*, 42 (1), 23–38.

70. Queau, Philippe (1993), 'O Tempo Do Virtual', in *Imagem-Maquina*, André Parente, Ed. (34th edn). Rio de Janeiro: Editora 34.

71. Ribeiro, Gustavo Lins (1997), 'Transnational Virtual Community? Exploring Implications for Culture, Power and Language', *Organization*, 4 (4), 486–505.

72. Cutitta, Frank (2002), 'Language Matters', *Target Marketing*, 25 (2), 40–44.

73. Anon (2008), 'Top Internet Languages', *World Internet Usage Statistics*, 27 March, www.internetworldstats.com/stats7.htm.

74. Cox, Anthony (2000), 'Europe EU Faces Tall Task in Regulating E-Commerce', *Bank Technology News*, 13 (6), 63–64.

75. Zugelder, Michael T., Theresa B. Flaherty, and James P. Johnson (2000), 'Legal Issues Associated with International Internet Marketing', *International Marketing Review*, 17 (3), 253–71.

76. Waltner, Charles (1999), 'Web's Days as Tax-Free Zone Are Numbered – as E-Commerce Booms, the Battle over Internet Taxation Standards Starts Heating Up', *InternetWeek*, 6 (December), 26–30.

77. Kasim, Sharifah and Anuja Ravendran (2001), 'Tackling Tax Issues in E-Commerce Activities (Hl)', *Computimes Malaysia*, July, 1.

78. *Economist* (2000), 'Leaders: Regulating the Internet', 10 June, 18–20.

79. Kashani, Kamran (1989), 'Beware the Pitfalls of Global Marketing', *Harvard Business Review*, 67 (5), 91–8.

80. Koranteng, Juliana (1997), 'If the Web Is So Worldwide Why Is It Mainly in English?', *Advertising Age International* (May), 16.

81. Foxman, Ellen R., Patriya S. Tansuhaj, and John K. Wong (1988), 'Evaluating Cross-National Sales Promotion Approach Strategy: An Audit Approach', *International Marketing Review*, 5 (4), 7–15.

82. Boddewyn, J.J. and M. Leardi (1989), 'Sales Promotion: Practices, Regulation and Self-Regulation around the World', *International Journal of Advertising*, 8 (4), 363–74.

83. Wentz, Laurel (1997), 'Global Village', *Advertising Age International* (October), 1–3.

A11.1 Case

ComputerLand in Japan

ComputerLand recognized that it would need a Japanese partner in order to enter the Japanese market. Because of government regulations and attitude, it probably would not have been possible to obtain permission to establish a wholly owned subsidiary. Additionally, the complexities of the Japanese market would have made development of franchises there very difficult. (Both McDonald's and Kentucky Fried Chicken entered the market with Japanese partners.)

ComputerLand wanted a partner who had experience in both procurement and distribution of computer products. Following talks with a number of companies, Kanematsu-Gosho Ltd emerged as the top candidate. Kanematsu-Gosho was a major trading company, had experience in the desired areas, and already had business dealings with IBM. ComputerLand entered into negotiations with the Japanese company in order to try to develop a joint venture. The discussions, which lasted for nine months, were detailed and difficult. The Chairman of ComputerLand was concerned that if his Vice-President went to Japan to negotiate, he would be at a disadvantage trying to operate in a different culture. He therefore insisted that the negotiations be held in the United States by telephone from Japan.

This made it difficult for the Japanese to negotiate. The Japanese decision-making process requires much more consultation and agreement with the company than would normally be necessary in European and American firms. There were long delays and a lot had to be done through e-mail and fax. Among other things, the Japanese government had to be persuaded to allow the American partner to have a 50 per cent ownership rather than the customary (at the time) minority position. The agreement was finally concluded, with ComputerLand contributing knowledge, trade mark and technology and Kanematsu-Gosho contributing cash to start the joint venture, ComputerLand Japan Ltd. The Vice-President of ComputerLand then went to Japan to head the operation as Vice-President and Resident Director. A number of policy and operational problems had to be solved.

In the United States, franchisees were required to pay cash before merchandise would be shipped to them. An attempt was made to follow this policy in Japan. Retailers in Japan, however, are used to receiving credit from wholesalers – often for 90 days or even longer. A cash-in-advance policy proved to be impossible in Japan, so the company eventually went to a 10-day-open-credit policy.

In the United States, franchises were given only to individuals, not to corporations or other businesses. This was done so that the stores would be personally managed by the owners. ComputerLand Japan was not able to find sufficient individuals who had or could obtain the necessary cash. Eventually the policy was changed to allow a company to own a minority interest. As in Europe, store locations and format were also a problem. Within the United States, ComputerLand insisted that the minimum size for a store was 2000 square feet (185 m²), a busy location accessible and visible to a large amount of traffic, and with a parking lot in the rear. This was simply not possible in most locations in Japan.

It was also difficult to attract top-quality employees to work for a foreign company in Japan. Finally, there were simple coordination issues between proprietor-owned ComputerLand and large, publicly owned Kanematsu-Gosho. In spite of these difficulties, ComputerLand Japan was very successful, growing to 50 franchises with annual sales of US$50 million. It was assisted greatly by the fact that, for the first two years of operations, ComputerLand had exclusive distribution rights for the IBM PC in Japan.

Over the years, Kanematsu-Gosho found it increasingly difficult to continue to accept elements of ComputerLand's policy. Additionally, it felt that the American partner was simply exercising too much control. When ComputerLand offered to buy the company out, Kanematsu-Gosho agreed. The operation then became a wholly owned subsidiary of the United States corporation. Eventually, this subsidiary was sold to one of the franchisees, who continues to operate it under a licence agreement with ComputerLand.

(Source: Written by John T. Sakai, former Vice-President of ComputerLand. Reproduced with the kind permission of the author.)

Questions

1. Was it wise for ComputerLand to insist on holding the negotiations in the United States? What were the advantages and disadvantages for each of the parties? Why did Kanematsu-Gosho agree to the location?

2. Analyse the differences between the Japanese and American distribution systems as they appear in this case. Which elements of the 'ComputerLand model' are transferable to Japan?

3. When exporting to another country or setting up a joint venture there, how can you decide which of the local customs and business practices should be accepted, and which of your home country practices should you introduce?

 **A11.2 Case**

Virtual beehive – online marketing of US honey

The first official record of beekeeping stretches back 5000 years, to Ancient Egypt, where beekeepers navigated their bees up or down the Nile, depending on the season. Today, itinerant Chinese families and their bees track blooming flora for thousands of kilometres across the country in rented vans. Rural poor women in Malaysia cultivate the bees that pollinate coffee plantations and provide pungent honey. American beekeepers winter with their bees in Texas, and summer with them in the North Dakota plains. Argentinean landowners use low-cost labour to keep bees on their extensive lands.

Beekeeping has always been a specialized business. The demand for bee products, including honey, bee pollen, royal jelly, propolis (adhesive used for comb placement and repair), and beeswax has been quite steady throughout history. In the past beekeeping was prized because of the sweetening and medicinal properties of honey, medicinal uses for other hive products, as well as the wax used in a myriad of ways, including candles, adhesive, and hairdressing. The beekeeper's life today is in some ways more difficult than it was in the past, without the steady patronage of the religious and medical orders. Today, there are more competing products, such as corn syrup and aspartame. There are more low-cost producers, many in developing countries. The rationalized business practices of international retail conglomerates demand massive quantities, making packers and intermediaries necessary for small producers. However, now in their fifth millennium, beekeepers may finally have found through the Internet a way to keep more of their scanty margins for themselves, instead of profiting packers, agents, and exporters.

Beekeeping, a fragmented sector

Supply is subject to weather, the length of the flower blooming season, and bee disease control. Smaller beekeepers tend to leave the field because costly technology is increasingly needed for pest control, management of newly immigrated bees, and pesticide use in the environment.[1] For these reasons, among others, beekeepers tend to consolidate, however they remain a small agricultural grouping with little political muscle and low bargaining power. Under these conditions, prices tend not to be stable and currently follow a downward trend: US prices in 2000 were half those in 1997.[2,3] Yet in the USA 40 per cent of honey produced comes from smaller beekeepers, hobbyists and part-timers.[4] Smaller producers may improve their chances for survival by joining a cooperative, like the almost 90-year-old Sioux Honey Association, from Sioux City, Iowa.

Risk management in a risky business: the cooperative

The oldest beekeepers' cooperative is best known under its 'Sue Bee' brand (from 'Sioux'), and is the largest honey marketer in the world (second to Sue Bee in terms of market share is a German company).[3] In addition to continuing sales to retail outlets and online, the cooperative is focusing on manufactured food plus the food service segment (ibid.). By featuring the Sue Bee logo on its label, a food processing company is likely to boost the image of its sauces, prepared foods, condiments, or beverages. Use of honey in these products is at an all-time high.[3] (Visit Sue Bee Honey at **www.suebee.com**.)

Biggest importers of US honey 2001

The US National Honey Board (NBH) is concerned with promoting sales of US honey abroad. It has collected the following data concerning the ranking of US honey export sales:

1. Germany
2. Korea
3. Canada
4. Yemen
5. Saudi Arabia
6. United Arab Emirates

(Source: NHB.[5])

The marketing environment for honey

Before the rise of the Internet, buyers and honey processors/packers spent a great deal of time negotiating their bulk honey contracts. What may have then taken up to 30 days may now be concluded during a 30-minute online bidding process. Increased consolidation of retail businesses and food suppliers has placed bulk honey sellers at a disadvantage. For instance, retail buyers often demand slotting fees (to get the product on the shelf and, often, to keep competitors off) and pay-to-stay fees (to keep the product on the shelf). It is estimated that some Canadian packers pay 10 per cent of their total costs on these fees.[1] Retail buyers expect to pay a low price for high volume, with accompanying food safety assurances in writing (ibid.).

The honey market is diverging between a high-end, speciality product and a low-end, low-cost, relatively undifferentiated, 'generic'-type product.[1] Honey is assailed by direct and indirect competitors for sweeteners (such as sugars, fruit concentrates, rice sweetener, and molasses) and spreads (such as fruit-based, nut-based, or chocolate-based spreads) which often make their own health- and nutrient-related claims. The entry of low-cost producers like China, Argentina, and Mexico onto the honey stage has made retail buyers even more cost-conscious, as has the increased market share of countries like India, Vietnam, Turkey, and Hungary. The participation of China and Argentina in the US market has lessened due to fees that raise prices. Both countries allegedly were dumping honey on the US market within the past decade and now pay anti-dumping fees, and, in the case of Argentina, countervailing duties. (For a complete presentation of the commercial honey industry, see **www.agric.gov.ab.ca/livestock/apiculture/honey_book.pdf**.)

Table 11.3 USA honey imports from China, Argentina, Canada, Mexico, and Other: pounds imported through December, 2004

Country	2000	2001	2002	2003	2004
Argentina	98,918,160	53,950,832	13,174,534	15,961,790	4,378,161
China	53,546,855	48,603,333	17,097,663	42,793,773	61,800,126
Canada	29,289,354	21,083,039	44,430,094	27,804,493	21,881,442
Mexico	4,550,132	8,735,508	23,283,075	17,737,202	7,079,206
Other	7,883,157	24,627,842	93,840,265	100,761,135	83,609,884

(Source: NHB.[4,6])

The positioning of honey in the USA

The US National Honey Board (NBH at **www.nhb.org**) used in-depth face-to-face interviews to determine the positioning of honey in the USA. Respondents were asked questions regarding factors such as interest/intent, believability, and uniqueness relating to three positioning statements, 'Livens up the Flavor of Any Meal', 'Nature's Healer', and 'Nature's Original Sweetener'. The top performer in the tests was 'Nature's Healer',[7] a positioning that successfully differentiates honey from other options due to respondents' beliefs in its 'healthiness' (35 per cent), 'providing more benefits than artificial sweeteners' (27 per cent) and 'promoting healing' (25 per cent).[7] Despite performing well otherwise, the 'Nature's Healer' positioning elicited the lowest 'believability' score of the three positioning statements tested, however media reports of scientific findings relating to honey should increase believability over time. The findings show that, on average, honey is used in US households 1.5 times per week and that most honey consumers buy honey 2–3 times per year. It appears that many consumers would like to use honey more often, but do not know of ways to do so. Based on the research findings, the positioning strategy was refined. The new statement was 'Honey: the natural daily choice to enhance health and well being',[8] a positioning concept designed to address food and 'pharmacological' uses. To support this, the NHB committed its resources to encourage research on honey-related issues (including honey's antimicrobial, antioxidant, and healing properties, and its nutrient content) to communicate the findings to targeted consumer segments as well as the food processing industry.

Whatever the positioning of the product, online marketing may help smaller and bigger producers alike, particularly in challenging marketing conditions. In the USA, the National Honey Board's **www.honeylocator.com** offers the potential honey purchaser 300 types of US honey on its menu, while the producers' sub-sites offer even more.[9] The types of honey depend on the flora where bees collected nectar. This determines the colour (white to dark brown), taste, and aroma. Thus nectar collected from mesquite results in a different honey from that collected from lavender. A search for 'orange blossom', for instance, returned 55 companies.

Buyers may search the site using honey variety, market segment, or postal code. The pages located display contact information, product lists (usually pollen, royal jelly, kosher honey, organic honey), markets (bakery, retail, foodservice, wholesale, for export, brewery, food manufacturing), and export markets. As is vital with a searchable database, the suppliers are encouraged to stay current through various means, such as the bi-weekly 'Beemail' newsletter, contests for suppliers like 'Show me the honey', and supplier links. Canadian cooperative Beemaid Honey is Canada's biggest and one of the oldest honey marketers. The company maintains a large site in its worldwide marketing efforts at www.beemaid.com.

Honey exporters may list themselves on online commercial directories, such as usaexporters.net, where company profiles and links may be provided. On a simpler level, such as the Panhellenic Confederation of Agricultural Cooperatives at **www.paseges.gr**, interested importers may find a list with links to email addresses for more information. Honey producers or marketers may opt for banner advertising on other related sites, such as the US-based **www.localhoneyforsale.com**, or even a cooking or tourism site. In addition to export oriented sites, the web boasts many informative beekeeping sites, some of which offer advice on apiculture problems, such as **www.gardenweb.com** where beekeepers may solicit comments about how to clean a hive or which queen bees to purchase. A vast resource for beekeepers and honey purchasers is **www.beehoo.com**, a site in English and French with linked directories to exporters and hive suppliers. Another resource in English, French, Spanish and German is Apiservices at **www.beekeeping.com**, where one may access academic journals, exporter directories, classified ads, and a honey web ring. With all the possibilities offered online, rural Spanish beekeepers, beekeeping apprentices in Nepal, and isolated Australian apiaries have the potential to sell directly to buyers, anywhere in the world . . . or do they?

Questions

1a. Visit sites in at least four different languages from the list below, or from your own searches. Comment on the obstacles of selling honey internationally online, in terms of language, shipping, trust, hygiene and import regulations, etc.

Argentina	Austria	Canada	France
www.cipsa.com.ar www.apicultura.com.ar www.parodiapicultura.com.ar	www.gourmetpantry.com/honey	www.intermiel.com	www.lunedemiel.fr www.abeillestore.com www.biomiel.com www.ruchersdelorraine.com

Germany	Greece	Italy	Mexico
www.honig.de www.schwarzwaldhonig.de	www.melinas.gr www.add.gr	www.montioni.com	http://www.natura.com.mx/ subsex/mielyderiv.html

Netherlands	New Zealand	Spain	USA
www.export.nl	www.honeynz.co.nz	www.hispamiel.com	www.honeylocator.com www.suebee.com www.burlesons-honey.com

1b. Of the sites you visited, which did you consider to be most effective at selling honey long term? Discuss the reasons for your choice, keeping in mind that in the long run the site is only as good as its suppliers.

2. Discuss whether the National Honey Board's (NHB) positioning concept, 'Honey: the natural daily choice to enhance health and well being' would be effective outside the USA. Use one country as an example, as well as the NHB's criteria (believability, interest/intent, and differentiation) in your answer.

3. Which honey markets are targeted by honeylocator.com? How could the site be modified to effectively target other potential markets? Consider the role of marketing the site on the Internet as part of your answer.

Saskia Faulk and Jean-Claude Usunier prepared this case solely to provide material for class discussion. The authors do not intend to illustrate either effective or ineffective handling of a business situation. The authors may have disguised certain names and other identifying information to protect confidentiality.

© IRM/HEC, 2006   Version: (A) 2006-04-08

Appendix references

1. Alberta Agriculture, Food and Rural Development (2001), *Competition for World Honey Markets: An Alberta Perspective*, Report Two, April. www.agric.gov.ab.ca/livestock/apiculture/honey_book.pdf.
2. Foreign Agricultural Service (FAS) (1998), *Honey Situation and Outlook in Selected Countries*.
3. Karg, Pamela J. (1999), 'Taking Flight', *Rural Business and Cooperative Development Service*, 66 (5), 8–12.
4. National Honey Board (NHB) (2002), *Honey Industry Facts*. www.honey.com/honeyindustry/statistics.asp.
5. National Honey Board (NHB) (2002), *Exports from the United States*. www.honey.com/honeyindustry/statistics.asp.
6. National Honey Board (NHB) (2006), www.nhb.org/intl/4country.
7. National Honey Board (NHB) (2001), 'National Honey Board Positioning Report Phase II', September. www.nhb.org/download/industry/positioning_report_2.pdf.
8. National Honey Board (NHB) (2001), *2000 Strategic Plan* (online). www.nhb.org/info-pub/board/SP/SP2000.pdf.
9. Sanford, M.T. (2002), 'Selling Honey on the World Wide Web', *Bee Culture*, March.

Part 4   Intercultural marketing communications

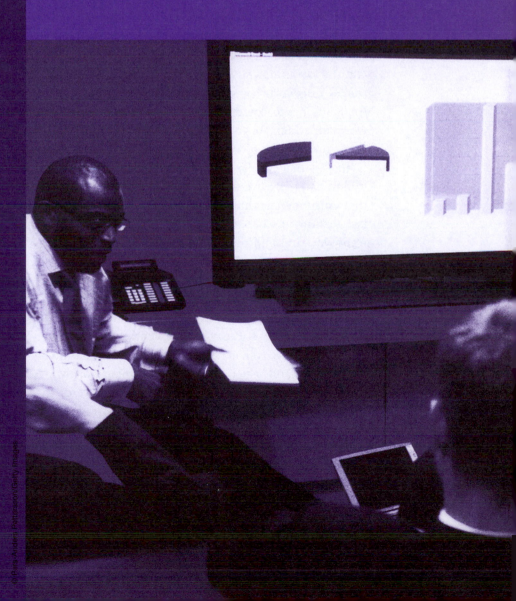

© Brian Andrew Pieters/Getty Images

Introduction to Part 4

Language plays a central role in marketing communications when they take place in an international and multilingual context since communication styles as well as world views are deeply influenced by the structure of languages. This section reviews and examines some of the major types of marketing communication tools, including advertising, personal selling, and public relations. These tools not only aim to communicate with customers, but also with all stakeholders in the market, including middlemen, business partners, public authorities, and even competitors.

Communication is never language-free. That is why Chapter 12 presents intercultural communication, both verbal and non-verbal, and explains how language shapes our world views, inasmuch as the words we use and the way we assemble them in speech correspond to particular assumptions and experiences about the world in which we live. This can lead to ethnocentrism, which is a spontaneous tendency to refer to our own beliefs and values when interpreting situations and trying to make sense out of experience. Stereotyping is another way to reduce unfamiliarity by oversimplifying foreign traits. Therefore, it comes as no surprise that misunderstandings in intercultural communication are quite frequent. The last section in Chapter 12 explains how to avoid cultural misunderstandings and improve communication effectiveness in international business, especially when using interpreters.

The main tool for communicating marketing messages to customer audiences is advertising. For reasons of image consistency, many companies want to promote their products globally through standardized advertising campaigns that use the same advertising strategy and execution worldwide. Thus, the question to be answered before transferring campaigns cross-nationally is: which elements should be localized and which ones can be similar worldwide? Chapter 13 first examines the general influence of culture on attitudes towards the social utility of advertising, especially when advertising adopts a comparative stance. International companies have to make decisions in two main areas, advertising strategy (information content, advertising appeals, etc.) and advertising execution (characters and roles represented, visual and textual elements, etc.). Based on a review of cross-cultural studies of advertisements, the chapter explains the extent to which both strategy and execution can be standardized or should be localized. The focus is then on the development of global media resources and the globalization of advertising agencies.

A lot of marketing information is also communicated directly to market stakeholders, that is, presented and explained directly by the sales force or indirectly through intermediaries or business partners in foreign markets. Chapter 14 starts by explaining what 'commerce' means from an intercultural perspective, that is, the ways and means to effectively communicate with the market in both directions, rather than in a one-sided exchange as is largely the case with advertising. This chapter develops a number of issues that are central to personal selling in an international perspective, including how to network in business markets, buyer–seller interactions, how cultural differences affect the management of the sales force, public relations across cultures and, last but not least, the issue of bribery and business ethics in an international context.

12

Language, culture and communication

Glen Fisher, a distinguished scholar in the field of intercultural relations, has described a conversation with a Latin American friend about the words used in English and Spanish for business relations. His friend first remarks that in English the word 'business' is positive. It connotes the fact of being 'busy' and emphasizes doing things. Expressions such as 'getting down to business' highlight people who have a responsible concern for their work. Fisher (p. 148) further explains that:

In Spanish the word is 'negocio' . . . The key is the 'ocio' part of the word, which connotes leisure, serenity, time to enjoy and contemplate as the preferred human condition and circumstance. But when harsh reality forces one from one's 'ocio,' when it is negated, then one has to attend to 'negocio'. The subjective meaning is obviously much less positive than in English.[1]

In this chapter, several such examples show how a linguistic/cultural group, through words or language structure, express a definite world view; *eine Weltanschauung* as the Germans express it. The anthropologist and linguist Benjamin Lee Whorf went even further, arguing that language shapes our world views, our behaviour towards others and our manner of acting. Language is obviously a major component of culture. However, it is for many reasons underemphasized in international business literature. First, language seems to be translatable through dictionaries and professional translators. Unfortunately, part of the message which is culturally unique is lost in the translation process (as the Italian proverb says *traduttore traditore*, translator betrayer). Second, international business literature is in general centred on decision

making and strategy formulation rather than the implementation of decisions. Language is important mostly in the implementation phase because implementation is largely based on communicating with others, including buyers, employees, colleagues, superiors. The logic of the planning stage can overlook the significance of language and communication, because these items are related to implementation. The third argument is that language differences have been systematically underestimated in international business literature because of an understandable bias on Western culture. Since English has traditionally been the *lingua franca* of international business there were no major reasons for native speakers of English to learn foreign languages. There is much more motivation for people from China, France, Germany, Italy and Japan to take the question of language seriously.

In this chapter we review the main aspects of language and communication that have both a direct and an indirect impact on international business operations:

1. Verbal communication styles and their relationship to contextual factors.
2. Non-verbal communication, especially through gestures and eye and body language.
3. The way language shapes and reflects particular world views.
4. Ways of dealing with language differences in international business.

Awareness is even more necessary than knowledge in relation to the impact of language and communication differences on international business. Given the variety of national and regional languages, one cannot expect to be able to speak and write them all. Even multilingual businesspeople will frequently be faced with language contexts in which they have little or no proficiency. What is needed then is awareness that large chunks of reality will always be partly hidden from non-native speakers.

12.1

Verbal communication: the role of context

'Verbal' implies words and sentences and, in most of what follows, spoken discourse, rather than written communication. Written communication is a special case and it is treated in more detail in Chapter 13, which focuses on advertising.

In this chapter, verbal is opposed to non-verbal communication. Verbal language has a prominent place in communication, perhaps because it is largely explicit and therefore more easily amenable to consciousness. Thus, linguistic differences are perceived as one of the main causes of intercultural communication misunderstandings, though certainly not the only one. Where differences in the coding/decoding process are ignored by the communicators, they may persist throughout the whole interaction process. Instead of disappearing, they may become more marked, even when people seem to be better acquainted with each other. Non-verbal communication, which is often said to occupy a dominant place in our understanding of the communication, is likely to exacerbate any misunderstandings.

A first distinction in language-based communication is whether the messages sent by the speaker are explicit. That is, can they be taken literally rather than interpreted 'in context'. Setting messages 'in context' would imply that what is literally said has to be in some way reinterpreted using various cues taken from the context, particularly the cultural context, of the speaker.

The context of language-based communication

The communication mode that first springs to mind is the verbal mode. Phrases and words in a single language have (more or less) a precise meaning; or at least this is the assumption necessary to believe that a listener can receive a clear message from a speaker. This assumption allows us to avoid the time-consuming task of constantly verifying that the message received is the same message that was sent. However, the communication mechanism incorporates several elements:

1. Even in an exchange that is primarily verbal, part of the message is non-verbal, including gestures, gesticulations, attitudes, etc. The issue then is to know to what extent non-verbal/implicit messages (which will be discussed in the next section) *mix* with verbal/explicit messages.
2. Communication integrates feedback mechanisms to verify or improve the clarity of messages. In many cultures, the accuracy of the communication process needs to be checked by various means, including repetition, paraphrases, interruption, etc.
3. In most cases, communication is dependent on its context, including who says it and where and when it is said. Contextual factors may distort what actually seems to be said literally.

The use of the word 'context' and the emphasis that is put on the role of context in communication derive from Edward T. Hall, an American anthropologist (see Bluedorn,[2] for an interesting interview with Hall). During the 1940s Hall studied the culture and social integration of Hopi and Navajo Indians. He first advised diplomats in the 1960s, and then, later on, businesspeople in their dealings with other cultures. This naturally led him to an interest in intercultural communication, a field where he has been a major contributor during the last 50 years. Hall is the kind of individual who is fascinated by foreign cultures, sometimes showing a certain prejudice in their favour and against his own native culture.

Although Edward Hall does not precisely define context, the following components can reasonably be presumed: location, people involved (age, sex, dress, social standing, etc.), and the context of the conversation itself (at the workplace, in a showroom, during a round of labour negotiations, during a sales visit). He (Hall, p. 79)[3] contrasts high context (HC) and low context (LC) in the following way: 'a high-context (HC) communication or message is one in which most of the information is either in the physical context or internalized in the person, while very little is in the coded, explicit, transmitted part of the message. A low-context (LC) communication is just the opposite; i.e. the mass of the information is vested in the explicit code.

Context will often influence communication without the participants being aware of it. For example, cultural prejudices may intervene, with such unspoken questions as: *does this young speaker deserve trust?* The relationship assumed by a particular culture between age and credibility may be positive, negative or neutral, and therefore have an impact on the flow of communication. Another important issue is whether it is necessary to know one's conversation partner relatively well to be able to talk seriously to him or her about business. This relates to the intensity of the personalization, or conversely the depersonalization of the communication process.

Context brings together the sum of interpretation mechanisms that originate within a culture and allow the message to be explained. In his collection *The Snows of Kilimanjaro*, Ernest Hemingway[4] tells a story, entitled 'A Day's Wait', in which a young boy is told that he has a fever of 102 – in degrees Fahrenheit – though he does not know that the temperature was measured on this scale. Since he had previously been in France, he thinks of the temperature as being on the Celsius temperature scale, and asks: 'About how long will it be before I die?' His mother does not understand his interpretation and explains that people do not die of a fever of 102. The young boy goes on arguing: 'I know they do. At school in France, the boys told me you can't live with 44 degrees. I've got 102.' Finally his mother understands that he has been waiting all day to die and she explains that, like kilometres and miles, temperature can be measured on different scales, and what is 37 degrees on one thermometer is 98 on another.[4]

Low-context cultures and explicit communication

As explained above, in certain cultures communication is based on low context and explicit messages. These messages are almost 'digital' and could be translated into simple computer units (bytes). The Swiss, for instance, have a reputation for talking quite literally, with explicit messages and low context. This implies a great deal of precision in the verbal aspect of

communication, implying precision with respect to time commitments and so on. Thus, in Switzerland a speed limit is interpreted literally as just that. The speed limit on motorways is 120 kilometres an hour, and when a driver is caught speeding by the police, a speedometer error of 6 per cent is allowed and then the fine is given in proportion to the speed violation. When a patient arrives late for a doctor's appointment in certain Swiss cantons, he or she has to pay a small cash penalty and reschedule the appointment if the doctor is unavailable.

These two examples should be taken for what they are: not as illustrations of an unhealthy preoccupation with punctuality, exactness and respect for rules, but as evidence of a tight social order, a highly organized social system that is costly to run but is also greatly beneficial for all. In the case of the health service, a Swiss doctor who has made a preliminary assessment over the phone with a patient will schedule their time together very precisely. If each party makes an effort to keep the appointment, the result is a genuine saving. The patient will also avoid a long period in the waiting room, exposed to the germs of the other patients.

Appointments are one example of explicit messages that in low-context cultures must be taken literally. Another example is the following seller's message to a potential buyer: 'I can offer you a price of $140 per package of 12, to be delivered in cases of 144 within five weeks.' Among the cultures with explicit communication and low context are the Germanic cultures (Germany, Switzerland and Austria), North American cultures (Canada and the US) and the Scandinavians.

Contextuality of communication is partly related to whether the language itself expresses ideas and facts more or less explicitly. English is a precise and fairly context-free language. This holds especially true for 'international English'. The *lingua franca* of international business is context-free, rendering it impoverished, but at the same time precise.

Japanese is less precise than English or French. Personal pronouns are often not explicitly expressed in Japanese, and the number of tenses is much smaller, especially in comparison to French. In Japanese, both spoken words (that is sounds) and written words (based on *kanji*, or pictographs) often have multiple meanings, so that the listener needs some kind of contextual clarification. Sometimes,

Japanese people write the *kanji* (ideographs) briefly on their hand to make clear what they are saying.

Naturally it would be a mistake to say that certain languages are vague and others precise. The real world is more complex. One must look carefully at the *structure* of the language. German has many verbs that have quite different meanings according to context. It is easy to discover many examples in German–English dictionaries. For instance, the verb *absetzen,* according to context, means to deposit or deduct a sum, take off a hat, dismiss an official, depose a king, drop a passenger, sell goods, stop or pause, or take off (a play).[5] The same holds true for the Finnish language. Even though the Finns, like many northern Europeans, have a reputation for their explicitness in communication, Finnish has a very special language structure which renders context useful in communication. They use 16 cases which virtually replace all the prepositions used in other languages. Even proper nouns can be declined (i.e. to be inflected for number, case or gender) using these cases.

All languages share a common objective: they have a common problem to solve, which is conveying meaning in an appropriate way from person to person. However, they achieve it differently, relying to varying degrees on precise words, structured grammar or, in contrast, on contextual indications of how ambiguous meanings should be made precise.

High-context cultures favour a more diffuse communication style

A notion that helps an understanding of the differences in context-related communication styles is the distinction between specific and diffuse. In low-context cultures, people tend to focus on specific issues and address their counterpart in a specific role (as a buyer for instance); not necessarily impersonally but with a specific view of what the person before them has to do. In high-context cultures, people generally address broader issues and move easily between different conceptions of their counterpart (as a private person, as a buyer, as a potential friend). Diffuse in style should not be equated with 'confused' in communication, even though people from high-context cultures may at times appear complicated to those from low-context cultures.

Among the high-context cultures, according to Hall,[3] are the Latin American, Middle Eastern and Japanese cultures. In Japan, context plays a significant role. One example is the rules of politeness. Their manner of speaking shifts in register, between more than 20 subtly different forms, according to the age, sex and social position of the conversation partner, as well as the relative positions of the speakers in the social hierarchy (pupil/teacher, buyer/seller, employee/employer). The exact word 'no' does not exist in the Japanese vocabulary; a '*yes*' in certain circumstances can actually mean 'no'. Keiko Ueda[6] distinguishes 16 ways to avoid saying 'no' in Japanese. The range of possible solutions varies from a vague 'no', to a vague and ambiguous 'yes', a mere silence, a counter-question, a tangential response, exiting (leaving), making an excuse such as sickness or a previous obligation, criticizing or refusing the question itself, saying 'No, but . . .' or 'Yes, but . . .', delaying answers ('We will write you a letter') and making apologies. Woodward[7] illustrates how this virtual absence of 'no' in Japan manifests itself in e-mail contacts. She quotes Hans Boehm, managing director of the German Association for Personnel Management in Dusseldorf (p. 15): ' "I know that Japanese people are very, very polite and never say 'No' . . . So, I encourage them to say 'No' when they mean no. And I double-check with them to make sure when they say 'Yes' they mean yes." The nuances in the tone of voice are lost in e-mail messages, so when dealing on important issues with Japanese associates, Boehm always follows up with a phone call.'[7]

People from high-context cultures which use implicit messages cannot communicate effectively unless they have a fairly good understanding of their conversation partner. Impersonal dealings (e.g. a person who comes for a day to discuss a contract, rapidly gets to the heart of the matter, and uses the limited time available for discussion to focus on crucial matters) will make people from high-context cultures feel ill at ease and impede their conversation. People from high-context cultures are more socially oriented, less confrontational, and more complacent about life than people from low-context cultures.[8]

A misunderstanding between the two communicators may come up over their differences of opinion as to what is truly important. On one hand, a person from a high-context/diffuse communication culture will prefer spending some time chatting about life in general with the very purpose of getting to know their negotiating partner. On the other hand, a person from a low-context/specific communication culture will prefer to get straight down to business with the aim of avoiding wasting time on chatting and proceeding directly to a rational discussion of the project.

Occasionally, some cultures, which fall in the middle range, may shift from an explicit/specific to an implicit/diffuse communication style, and vice versa. The UK and France are examples of such a tendency. The British practice of 'understatement' values complicity between people at the expense of clarity. French has often been considered as a good language for diplomacy, because it can be alternately vague and precise, according to the kinds of words and style chosen. Sometimes French can be written with very precise words, with simple sentences (subject verb complement), but it can also be styled in a very vague manner, starting with long dependent clauses describing circumstances and possibilities.

Communication on the Internet

The Internet is far from being immune to the language-based difficulties wrought by high- versus low-context cultures. For instance, MacLeod (p. 37)[9] notes: 'Sentences written in Japanese need to be formal, whereas an informal tone is suitable for the U.S. Translation also throws up questions of length. Each page of English may need up to two pages in German. In some Asian languages, not only are the characters larger than in English, they also read from right to left.' A common practice in the US is to automatically address others by their first name. The same is true in Iceland and Canada, as well as Australia. In more formal countries, such as Germany, Austria, Switzerland and Sweden as well as many Asian countries, you would never address a new contact by their first name unless invited to do so.[10]

Moreover, high-context languages are the ones that are growing most rapidly on the Internet, including Japanese, Chinese and Arabic. The percentage of English language online has dropped from 49 per cent in September 2000 to 30 per cent in November 2007.[11,12] The next most common languages used on the Internet are Chinese (15 per cent), Spanish (9 per cent), Japanese (7 per cent) and French (5 per cent).

The environment of the Internet allows marketers to customize information targeted at different cultures. This should include both verbal and non-verbal content that is congruent with specific cultures.[13] The use of a visitor's language symbolizes respect for the culture.[14] increasing the potential bond. In addition, non-verbal content should also be adapted. For instance, local values, symbols and even local heroes could be incorporated into the site, based on the visitor location.[13]

While the Internet is a largely low-context medium, it allows for a great deal of flexibility in the type of information it contains. For instance, McDonald's websites differ dramatically across countries, with high-context country sites (China, Korea, Japan) being quite different from low-context country sites (Germany, Denmark, Sweden, Norway, Finland and the US), including:

1. More animation, especially people vs. simple highlighting effects.
2. Promoting collectivist vs. individualist values.
3. Showing food products with people vs. lifestyles of individuals.
4. Featuring links that encourage exploratory process oriented vs. clear goal oriented navigation.
5. Offering many menus, opening in new browsers (parallel) vs. only a few menus opening in the same browser (linear navigation).

Finally, we cannot ignore the importance of e-mail communication, which lends itself to low-context communication. As such, we need to be very conscious of the receiver's cultural background. As an example, Woodward (p. 15) quoted Jeanne Poole, manager of international HRM benefits and systems for PQ Corp:

You should be very careful [in e-mails] not just start out in a cold business-like manner with some cultures . . . If I am dealing with the Dutch, I don't have to be so careful; I can just get right to the point in my e-mail. If, on the other hand, I am dealing with our Chinese or Latin American friends, I am always more careful about how I begin my message to them. I build up to the topic by saying things such as, 'I hope you are doing well. We haven't talked in a while. I just wanted to take a minute to chat with you about something that came up.'[7]

The cultural context of communication styles

So far, the discussion has been mostly about low- and high-context communication and their relationship to precision in languages, as well as to the specificity or the diffuseness of the communication focus. However, verbal communication styles include a series of other elements: tone of voice, frequency and nature of conversational overlap, speed of speech, degree of apparent involvement in what one says, emphasis on talking versus emphasis on listening, digressive and indirect speech styles, etc. These are marked by cultural norms which implicitly define what is 'good' communication ('good' meaning appropriate between members of the cultural community in so far as they share the same code).

There are at least three areas where communication style is strongly culture-bound:

1. The style may reflect a self-concept. In cultures where the self-concept is strong, one may expect a communication style based on talking and self-assertion; where, on the contrary, suppression of the self is valued, a modest, listening communication style is likely in a participant, all other things being equal (especially purely individual personality characteristics).

2. Communication styles reflect a view of what is appropriate interaction. The Latin style of interruption is a lot about showing interest. Latins often find themselves speaking when others have not finished their sentence. Those who have some familiarity with the Anglo-Saxon and the Nordic communication styles may feel uncomfortable about what could seem an overlap or even an interruption, even though it is really well intentioned. In Latin cultures, interruption and overlap show empathy with the other speaker and shared interest in the topic. Furthermore, Latins are (or they believe they are) able to speak and listen at the same time.

3. Communication styles also reflect the appropriate emphasis put on talking and listening respectively, according to cultural norms. Japanese top executives often behave like a 'sphinx': they are almost pure listeners. Their role is to hear people. With some exceptions, Japanese bosses often display a mediocre talent for making public speeches and appear to be poor spokesmen. Whereas the Japanese tend toward a 'two listeners' communication style, the Latin cultures tend toward a 'two speakers' communication style. In Japan, silence is in fact valued as a full element of communication. It conveys messages, which, although implicit, may be interpreted through contextual factors. In a novel entitled *Shiosai*, the Japanese writer Yukio Mishima features a young fisherman, Shinji, who takes his salary back to his mother, a widow with another younger son. Shinji's salary is the family's only resource. Mishima (p. 52)[15] recounts: 'Shinji liked to give his pay envelope to his mother without uttering a word. As a mother, she understood and always behaved as if she did not remember it was pay day. She knew that her son liked to see her looking surprised.'

Many messages are included in silent communication, and, in general, Europeans and Americans tend to fear them much more than Asians do. The issue of shared meaning attributed to communication behaviour inside the cultural group is important, whether the values are positive or negative. Silence may be experienced positively, as a moment for listening (especially to what is 'not said'), or negatively as a sign of possible loss of interaction, as a time-waster, or even as a sign of possible animosity on the part of the conversation partner. Similarly, conversational overlap may be seen as diluting the clarity of exchange, mere impoliteness, a lack of interest in what one says, or as fatuous on the part of the overlapper. Conversely, it may be interpreted as a sign of empathy, a quick time-saving feedback, or even a necessary sign for pursuing the exchange.

As we hope to have shown, the rules for achieving 'good' communication are largely cultural. The feeling that the flow of messages is going smoothly between two conversation partners is based on their ability to avoid a 'bad' conversation, where messages would be altered or interrupted. The value judgement

BOX 12.1

The language of friendship

The American finds his friends next door and among those with whom he works. It has been noted that we take people up quickly and drop them just as quickly. Occasionally a friendship formed during school days will persist, but this is rare. For us (Americans) there are few well-defined rules governing the obligations of friendship. It is difficult to say at which point our friendship gives way to business opportunism or pressure from above. In this we differ from many other people in the world. As a general rule, in foreign countries friendships are not formed as quickly as in the United States, but go much deeper, last longer and involve real obligations. For example, it is important to stress that in the Middle East and Latin America your 'friends' will not let you down. The fact that they personally are feeling the pinch is never an excuse for failing their friends. They are supposed to look out for your interests. Friends and family around the world represent a sort of social insurance that would be difficult to find in the United States. We do not use friends to help us out of disaster as much as we do as a means of getting ahead – or, at least, of getting the job done. The United States systems work by means of a series of closely tabulated favors and obligations carefully doled out where they will do the most good. And the least that we expect in exchange for a favour is gratitude.

The opposite is the case in India, where the friend's role is to 'sense' a person's need and to do something about it. The idea of reciprocity as we know it is unheard of. An American in India will have difficulty if he attempts to follow American friendship patterns. He gains nothing by extending himself in behalf of others, least of all gratitude, because the Indian assumes that what he does he does for the good of his own psyche. He will find it impossible to make friends quickly and is unlikely to allow sufficient time for friendships to ripen. He will also note that as he gets to know people better, they may become more critical of him, a fact that he finds hard to take. What he does not know is that one sign of friendship in India is speaking one's mind.

(Source: Hall.[16] Reproduced with permission.)

on the means that are 'good' or 'bad,' appropriate or inappropriate, is largely based on unconscious cultural standards. In a domestic setting, people agree implicitly on the appropriate rules of communication. In an intercultural situation, people have to allow themselves the informal opportunity to discuss and establish the rules of their communication (what is called meta-communication). It is quite clearly a difficult task. Box 12.1 illustrates the substantial difficulties involved in clarifying the rules of communication about what friendship means and involves.

Communication rules can be especially sensitive when problems occur. For instance, Sugimoto[17] studied cross-cultural norms of apologies. He describes the two forms of apology in Japan, the *sunao* apology, which is a sort of gently submissive apology given with good grace, and a sincere form of apology, which is more from the heart. These apologies are codified in Japanese conduct manuals, which provide many readily usable apologetic expressions. Conversely, most Westerners tend to favour direct, spontaneous and unformulaic apologies, and sincerity is conveyed through original expressions.

Simintiras[18] stresses that the inequivalence of argument patterns are barriers to cross-cultural sales encounters. He puts forward that arguments need to be equivalent in both the statements and the inferences if they are to be comparable (p. 41): 'Establishing statement equivalence requires examination of, among other things, conceptual, functional, category, language, temporal, contextual and response style equivalence.'[18] While this is difficult, there are some possible solutions for people who need to communicate with those from high-context language cultures, including repeating the message, clarifying and asking for clarification, trying to understand, or, as Simintiras suggests, using culture-free, logical arguments (i.e. logically valid sentential statement patterns).

12.2

Non-verbal communication

Since much of what is exchanged in communication is only implicitly meant, rather than talked about, non-verbal communication is largely used as an interpretative framework, which allows people to overcome the shortcomings of verbal communication. The rules, rites and usage of non-verbal communication are culture-bound. When businesspeople from different cultures communicate, they also exchange elements of non-verbal communication. This constitutes a large part of what Edward Hall[3] calls 'context', which is used in the decoding of implicit messages. The elements of context can be separated into four levels:

1. Non-verbal communication such as gestures, gesticulations, eye contact, etc.
2. The analogical components of verbal messages, such as a way of saying 'yes' that makes it mean 'no', profuse thank-yous that contain a meaning other than their 'digital' content precisely because of their excess, etc.
3. Messages are often emitted unknowingly by the speakers according to their personal characteristics of age, size, weight, sex, dress, and so on. All of these characteristics are encoded in the culture of the speaker, and decoded by the listener using his or her own cultural programme.
4. Elements of interpretation dictated by the circumstances of the conversation, including type of place, atmosphere of the meeting, how the space is organized in the office, time, etc.

Although all four of these elements interact, this section focuses on the first aspect, non-verbal communication, while recognizing that status, circumstances and the other aspects of context combine with it in bringing about culture-bound interpretations.

Communication through gestures

Body language is an infinite source of differences and misunderstandings. Condon and Youssef[19] give the following account. A professor who was of English origin and taught at the University of Cairo was sitting on his chair with his feet in front of him, the soles of his shoes facing toward his Egyptian students. A Muslim considers this to be an obvious insult. A student demonstration followed, and it was taken up by the newspapers, which denounced British arrogance and demanded the professor be sent back to his home country.

Website link 12.1

See some international business body language differences: **http://money.cnn.com/2000/05/03/career/q-body-language/**.

Ways of greeting people differ greatly between cultures. While the French have the custom of shaking hands the first time they meet a person each day, many cultures (e.g. Australia, the USA, the UK) use this custom much less extensively. They are surprised by what for them is an excessive use of the handshake by the French. In Japan, a bow is the appropriate manner of greeting. In certain large Japanese department stores there are hostesses whose sole job is to bow to each customer who comes into the store. Anyone who has observed bowing rituals in Japanese railway stations or airports cannot help but be struck by their complexity, where the number, depth and synchronization are accurately codified. As Ferraro (p. 73)[20] emphasizes: 'In fact it is possible to tell the relative social status of the two communicators by the depth of their bows (the deeper the bow, the lower the status) . . . The person of lower status is supposed to initiate the bow, and the person of higher status determines when the bow is completed'.

A challenge in intercultural communication is to understand what hand gestures mean in a particular culture. As Box 12.2 shows, a simple piece of advice would be to avoid gesturing with the hand for fear of being misunderstood. Yet there are circumstances and places where it may be acceptable.

The meaning of head gestures is also a point of great cultural difference. Moving the head up and down means 'yes' in most western European countries, but it means 'no' in Greece and Bulgaria, and moving the head from left to right is a sign of negation for some and affirmation for others. In many Western countries it is considered a gesture of affection to pat

BOX 12.2

Avoid gesturing with the hand, and yet . . .

In general, avoid gesturing with the hand. Many people take offence at being beckoned this way, or pointed at, even if only conversationally. In parts of Asia, gestures and even slight movements can make people nervous. If you jab your finger in the air or on a table to make a point, you might find that your movements have been so distracting that you have not made your point at all. Unintentionally, Americans come across as aggressive and pushy. Yet, in other parts of the world, particularly in Latin America or Italy, gesturing is important for self-expression, and the person who does not move a lot while talking comes across as bland or uninteresting. As always, watch what local people do. Or ask. While in England we once asked, 'How do you point out someone without pointing?' Our companion dropped a shoulder, raised his eyebrows and jerked his head to the side, as though tossing it in the direction he meant to point. Clear as day, he pointed without pointing.

(Source: Copeland and Griggs, p. 111.[21])

---

a child on the head, but in Malaysia and many Islamic countries the head is considered to be the source of spiritual and intellectual activity and is therefore sacred.[22]

> **Website link 12.2**
>
> Find a quick fact sheet on proxemics:
> http://www.cs.unm.edu/~sheppard/proxemics.htm.

Another area of non-verbal communication where the importance of cultural variations cannot be denied is that of physical contact and proxemics. Ferraro[20] offers a complete description of forms of non-verbal communication involving physical contact: various groups kiss (the cheek, lips, hand, foot), take a person by the arm, clasp the shoulders, pinch the cheek, shake hands, tickle, stroke, give a little pat, etc. These gestures, running over into the realm of familiarity and sexual conduct, are subject to extremely varied codes of use. The kiss, regarded as normal between Russian men or Arab men, who also hold hands in the streets, may appear shocking to Anglo-Saxons. Ferraro recounts his own experience while conducting anthropological field research in Kenya (pp. 85–6):

After several months of living and working with Kikuyu, I was walking through a village in Kiambu district with a local headman who had become a key informant and a close personal acquaintance. As we walked side by side my friend took my hand in his. Within less than 30 seconds my palm was perspiring all over his. Despite the fact that I knew cognitively that it was a perfectly legitimate Kikuyu gesture of friendship, my own cultural values (that is, that 'real men' don't hold hands) were so ingrained that it was impossible for me not to communicate to my friend that I was very uncomfortable.[20]

The significance of communication codes is complex, and it would be wrong to see as opposites peoples who are reserved in their physical contact (including Anglo-Saxons) and those who are more liberal. Nowhere does there exist true freedom from customs. The way in which American and European men and women show their feelings for each other by kissing in public may seem to be the shocking demonstration of something that should be kept private when seen by other peoples. Dancing, which is part of many cultures' social gatherings, may seem indecent to some and perfectly innocent to others.

Facial expressions and communication with the eyes

Laughing and smiling, frowning and knitting one's brow express communication. A smile can be a sign of satisfaction, of agreement, of embarrassment . . . or even not a sign at all. Certain cultures consider the spontaneous expression of attitudes and emotions by a facial expression to be normal. The reverse is true in other cultures, particularly in Asia where it is considered desirable not to show emotion. This has given rise to the impression of Asians as inscrutable and stoic. According to Morschbach (p. 308):

Self control, thought of as highly desirable in Japan, demands that a man of virtue will not show a negative emotion in his face when shocked or upset by sudden bad news; and, if successful, is lauded as *taizen jijaku to shite* (perfectly calm and collected) or *mayu hitotsu ugokasazu ni* (without even moving an eyebrow) . . . The idea of an expressionless face in situations of great anxiety was strongly emphasized in the *bushido* (way of the warrior) which was the guide-line for samurai and the ideal for many others.[23]

Visual contacts, such as looking someone straight in the eyes, or, conversely, looking away, or lowering the eyes, or turning them away when they meet someone else's eyes, are all given different meanings in different cultures. This is proof that the same conduct (innocent as it may be) can be arbitrarily given totally opposite meanings. As Harris and colleagues[24] remarked, Arabs often look each other straight in the eyes because they believe that the eyes are the windows of the soul and that it is important to know the heart and soul of those one is working with. By contrast, Japanese children are taught in school not to look their teacher in the eyes, but to look at the level of the neck. When they become adults, it is considered a gesture of respect to lower their eyes in front of their superiors. Europeans have a tendency to look people straight in the eyes; like the Americans and Australians, they tend to associate a lack of honesty with someone who looks away, and see it as potentially signalling an unfriendly, defiant, impersonal or inattentive attitude.

Dealing with unknown communication styles, especially non-verbal ones, is not an easy task. It is impossible to have an exhaustive knowledge of the full range of cultural interpretations of physical behaviour, gestures and contact. Although it is clear that one can avoid major behavioural mistakes, it is difficult to behave correctly without staying in a country long enough to have time to learn. However, it must be recognized that part of the locally 'adequate' behaviour was learned in childhood, through rearing and education practices, and it translates into a physical demeanour that is profoundly ingrained. Once again, knowledge falls short. Awareness begins with the capacity to *unlearn* or progressively discover the cultural relativity of one's own verbal and non-verbal communication behaviour. The *unlearning process* is a key point, it is a condition for the learning process to take place.

Common courtesy can not be ignored in international business. Politeness and courtesy are based on linguistic indirection used to show social consideration, by not being direct.[25] Thus, politeness is always a high-context communication in any culture. It has a certain core of universal rules, such as not spitting at a person or slapping another's face. However, the degree of contextuality varies according to language and culture. The word *courtesy* is derived from the word 'court', meaning the residence of a king or emperor. It emphasizes the kind of noble behaviour that enhances self-respect through the respect of others. Most languages have such a word. German, for instance, has the word *höflich* (polite), based on the German word for court, *Hof*. Much is forgiven of foreigners provided they are not arrogant and they show consideration for their hosts, even if ignorant of their customs. Modest, though firm, behaviour facilitates the acceptance of cultural mistakes by the other party.

12.3
Language shaping our world views

Language contains pre-shaped images of the real world that partly condition our experiences. In this section, we give examples that show how language shapes and reflects different assumptions in terms of time, emotions and feelings, attitude to action, social hierarchy, and how this is expressed in the colloquial phrases used in marketing communications. That language actually shapes culture, and therefore cultural behaviour is a major causal assumption that can be challenged, for often all that language does is simply reflect culture. That is why we set the limits of this assumption in the second part of this section.

Language influencing culture

The first proponent of the idea that language has a decisive influence on culture was the linguist Edward Sapir. Language creates categories in our minds, which in their turn directly influence the things we judge to be similar and those that *deserve* to be differentiated. It is our *Weltanschauung* that will be determined: our way of observing, of describing, of interacting and finally the way in which we construct our reality. Sapir (p. 214) writes:

The fact of the matter is that the real world is to a large extent unconsciously built up on the language habits of the group. No two languages are ever sufficiently similar as to be considered as representing the same social reality. The worlds in which different societies live are distinct worlds, not merely the same world with different labels attached.[26]

Website link 12.3

See the Sapir–Whorf hypothesis as used in George Orwell's *1984*: http://www.angelfire.com/journal/worldtour99/sapirwhorf.html.

The linguist and anthropologist Benjamin Lee Whorf developed and extended Sapir's hypothesis. The Sapir–Whorf hypothesis contends that the structure of language has a significant influence on perception and categorization. Whereas empirical testing of this hypothesis seems to have been fairly thorough,[27] it is not considered valid by many linguists. For example, the gender given to words is not necessarily indicative of a particular cultural meaning (e.g. the gender of the earth, the sun and the moon, or of vices and virtues); for most it often seems to reflect an arbitrary choice. It may be the case however that this attribution of gender had a certain meaning at the genesis of the language, but that the meaning has since been lost.

Spoken languages are not the only ones to evolve. For instance, Lanksheer and Knobel[28] discuss the 'new literacies' that are mediated by computing and communications technologies. These include the development of semiotic languages, such as emoticons in e-mail or online chat space, or instant messaging, using and constructing hyperlinks, identifying software that will 'read' files and the many other aspects of language developed to navigate the world of 'bits'. There are difficulties, for those not born to this culture, in understanding these new ways of thinking in a world that is not based on physical space (where value is related to scarcity), but rather on information space (where value is related to familiarity and attention to data).[29] They cite Barlow (the co-founder of the Electronic Frontier Foundation and a writer for the Grateful Dead) as follows:

Barlow's third distinction is between people who have been born into and have grown up in the context of cyberspace, on the one hand, and those who come to this new world from the standpoint of a life-long socialization in physical space, on the other. We will refer here to the former as 'insiders' and the latter as 'outsider-newcomers'. This distinction marks off those who 'understand the Internet, virtual concepts and the IT world generally' from those who do not . . . Newcomers to cyberspace don't have the experiences, history and resources available to draw on that insiders do. And so, to that extent, they cannot understand the space as insiders do. Barlow believes this distinction falls very much along age lines . . . people over the age of twenty-five (in 1995) are outsider-newcomers.[29]

Similarly, the language of marketing can be difficult for those 'not born to it'. The vast majority of marketing text is written in English and translated into other languages.[30] It rarely happens the other way around. Holden illustrates the difficulties in translating these largely *American* concepts into languages such as Russian, where the product life cycle cannot be easily illustrated and segmentation is literally translated into '*segmentatsiya*', which means little to Russians. On the positive side, Holden (p. 88)[30] points out that scholars from non-English-speaking countries 'acquire in effect two separate world-views about their academic discipline. But more than that . . . the experience of synthesising two professional world-views gives them, not necessarily a fully-fledged third world-view as such, but unquestionably new insights which would not have arisen without this experience-commingling process mediated through the knowledge of another foreign language.'

Box 12.3 illustrates how languages reflect different patterns of time. Levine and Norenzayan[31] investigated the pace of life in large cities in 31 countries by examining the average walking speed, the time in which postal clerks completed a request and the accuracy of public clocks. Overall, the speed was faster in stronger economies and individualist cultures. Specifically, they found that eight of the nine overall fastest countries were from western Europe: the top three, Switzerland, Ireland and Germany, were closely followed by Japan (p. 297):

Box 12.3

Time patterns revealed by language

Representations of time are conveyed through the medium of language, as a means of communication and therefore collective action. Whorf comments about the Hopi language in the following terms:

After long and careful study and analysis, the Hopi language is seen to contain no words, grammatical forms, constructions or expressions, that refer directly to what we call 'time', or to past, present, and future, or to motion as kinematic rather than dynamic (i.e. as a continuous translation in space and time rather than as an exhibition of a dynamic effort in a certain process), or that even refer to space in such a way as to exclude that element of extension or existence that we call 'time', and so by implication leave a residue that could be referred to as 'time'. Hence, the Hopi language contains no reference to 'time', either implicit or explicit. (Carroll, pp. 57–8.[27])

The vocabulary of time reveals much about the linkage between language and cultural representations. For those who have doubts about the existence of differences in cultural representations of time that are revealed, conveyed and reproduced by language, the example of the English/US word 'deadline' is illustrative. A quick translation into French would give 'échéance [temporelle]' or 'délai de rigueur'[5] but would not render the intensity of this word. Taken literally, it seems to suggest something like 'beyond this (temporal) line, you will (there is a danger of) die (dying)'. It therefore gives a genuine notion of urgency to what was originally a very abstract notion (a point which has been agreed upon on a line of time). The word deadline is used in French by many businesspeople as such (un deadline), even though it is not in the official dictionary, because it conveys a typically Anglo-American sense of urgency that French people do not find in their own language.

Language also reflects (and pre-shapes) how people envision the future. In some African languages (Kamba and Kikuyu), there are three future tenses which express (1) action in two to six months; (2) action that will take place immediately; and (3) action 'in the foreseeable future, after this or that event'. Commenting on the uses of these African tenses, M'biti (pp. 74–5) demonstrates how coherence and sophistication in the accurate use of the near future, are important to people.

You have these tenses before you: just try to imagine the tense into which you would translate passages of the New Testament concerning the Parousia of Our Lord Jesus Christ, or how you would teach eschatology . . . If you use tense no. 1, you are speaking about something that will take place in the next two to six months, or in any case within two years at most. If you use no. 2, you are referring to something that will take place in the immediate future, and if it does not take place you are exposed as a liar in people's eyes. Should you use no. 3 you are telling people that the event concerned will definitely take place, but when something else has happened first. In all these tenses, the event must be very near to the present moment: if, however, it lies in the far distant future – beyond the two-year limit – you are neither understood nor taken seriously.[32]

Levine (pp. 48–9), conducting research on Brazilian versus US time, highlights the way concepts of punctuality are reflected in the language. He takes the example of the translation from English to Portuguese of a questionnaire containing the verb 'to wait':

Several of our questions were concerned with how long the respondent would wait for someone to arrive versus when they hoped the person would arrive versus when they actually expected the person would come. Unfortunately for us, it turns out that the terms to wait, to hope and to expect are all typically translated as the single verb esperar in Portuguese. In many ways our translation difficulties taught us more about Brazilian–Anglo differences in time conception than did the subjects' answers to the questions.[33]

There is a sort of continuum across languages in the accuracy of description of the waiting phenomenon (a fundamental issue in time experience!). French language, which lies somewhere between English and Portuguese in terms of temporal accuracy, uses two words: attendre (to wait) and espérer (to hope). To expect has no direct equivalent in French and must be translated by a lengthy circumlocution ('compter sur l'arrivée de . . .').

the slowest speeds were in the nonindustrialized Third World. The very slowest were in three countries popularly associated with a relaxed pace of life: Brazil (where the stereotype of 'amanha' [literally, 'tomorrow'] holds that, whenever it is conceivably possible, people will put off the business of today until tomorrow); Indonesia (where the hour on the clock is often addressed as 'jam kerat' ['rubber time']); and, slowest of all, the archetypical land of a manana, Mexico.[31]

Languages in relation to actions, thoughts and emotions

Business vocabulary from Western contexts is often difficult to translate into other languages, if real equivalence of meaning is sought. Terms such as: *empirical evidence, feed-back, deadline, cognitive, emotional,* and *successful,* can be problematic. Even such an elementary word as *fact* contains a rather demanding content. In English a fact must be an *established* piece of reality. In French its equivalent, *fait,* is less demanding in terms of unanimously agreed-on reality (*les faits peuvent être discutés,* corresponding to a spirit of the facts being 'challenged' rather than just discussed). In German, a fact may be translated by *tatsache, wirklichkeit, wahrheit* or *tat* – it can mean equally a piece of *reality,* a piece of *truth* or a piece of *action.*

The following short passage caricatures the English way of acting:

This man is achievement and deadline oriented. He first reviews the issues at stake. Then he tries hard to gather data, to verify, measure. As much as possible he will bring hard facts, empirical evidence, not simple opinions. If and when his thoughts and his emotions are conflicting, he will choose to behave as a matter-of-fact and down-to-earth guy. Being individually rewarded, he is therefore eager to perform the task and complete the job. He (almost) always meets his schedule.

When trying to translate this short text into other languages, the difficulties extend far beyond the purely lexical and grammatical ones; there are *cultural translation* difficulties. These problems correspond to what is often called the *spirit* of a language (in French, *Le génie de la langue*): far from being merely a linking of a chain of words, a language contains a series of stands taken on the nature of our relationship to reality.

Let us compare, for instance, the respective *qualities* of the three most prolific western European languages. By *qualities* we mean that one of these languages may be better at expressing ideas, facts, or moods, than the others. A comparison between English, French and German suggests that German is stronger than English in the expression of abstractions. In German, word endings such as *-heit, -keit, -ung, -schaft, -tum* and *-nis* allow the 'abstractification' of concrete notions. English is not only less able to express pure concepts, it is also less prone to. English is more action and more outward oriented, and takes the view that data oriented and objective approaches to issues allow a separation between internal feelings and external actions. French expresses inner states more accurately, with an emphasis on emotions rather than pure thoughts, describing the self and others. This corresponds to a view that any action is related to affectivity. Stereotypically, we could say that English is a language of action, French a language of emotions and German a language of thoughts. Thus, while it is possible and very desirable to remove language barriers, it is still difficult to understand the emphasis on actions, thoughts and emotions.

Language and cultural skills are becoming increasingly important for multinational firms. Replacement costs for an employee who leaves an overseas post average US$1 million.[34] The most common reason for leaving is the inability to adjust to cultural and language differences.

Language as a reflection of status, hierarchy and a vision of appropriate social relationships

The way we address other people is another example of how language shapes or reflects a social hierarchy. There is only one word used in English for 'you', even when accompanying a first name. This reflects an emphasis on equality and informality between people. By contrast, the French often use the formal *vous* for people they do not know very well instead of the informal *tu,* which they reserve for family and friends. Thus, the French are reputed to be more formal. The Germans use *du* (second person singular) in informal and personal settings and *Sie* (third person plural) in formal address. The Germans, like the Spaniards, have three forms of address: while the second person plural (*ihr*) has been lost in practice in German, but remains in Spanish.

In fact, a closer look at these forms shows that the English 'you' was not originally a second person singular, which was 'thou' in old English (as in Shakespeare's plays), but the more polite second person plural. That means that the only address kept in English is based on an assumption of full respect and formality and not on the everyday and less formal form of 'thou'. In fact, the assumed informality of English address, advocated by many native English speakers, is difficult to grasp for a Latin. The addressing of people by their first name and the use of 'you' appears to the Latin as a different kind of formalism, rather than true informality.

Language reflects quite complex assumptions about equality between people. It is true that the French use of *vous* reflects the strong emphasis on hierarchical and status differences in French society. But it can be very diversely nuanced, with the addition for instance, of *Monsieur* (formal *vous*) or simply the first name (informal *vous*). Of course, it is not simply because they have used the polite form for so long that the French have a fairly hierarchical society. However, the language context contributes to a constant reframing of culture-bound assumptions about hierarchy in a society.

Language used in writing advertising messages

A common problem for advertisers worldwide is how to use language in order to describe consumer benefits, suggest product qualities and convince potential buyers. It must be done using words that represent local world views. That is why international advertising is very 'Whorfian', even if advertisers and their agencies are not conscious of it (see Box 12.4). The language input in marketing communications is much more significant than it may seem at first. It is directly useful for designing copy strategy, and indirectly useful for understanding consumer moods or viewers' emotions. For example, life insurance advertising implies the evocation of death, which may be taboo in certain cultures, or subject to the use of a particular vocabulary and subdued style. Advertising – especially when it comes to targets and strategies – is never as standardized as it appears to be at first sight.

In addition to vocabulary, accents can also affect perceptions of advertising. For instance, for Australia, Myanmar and Singapore Western-sounding English accents have the greatest positive influence on advertising effectiveness, followed by a familiar Asian accent, and finally by less familiar accents.[35]

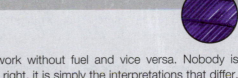

BOX 12.4

Global marketing communications?

The slogan 'Put a Tiger in your Tank', although often taken as the most perfect example of a standardized advertising campaign, is not as standardized as it might seem. It has been argued that it is standardized, because at first reading it looks as if it were fully equivalent across countries. However, studying the advertisements more closely, one sees that in some countries the power is located in the tank (northern Europeans: '*Pack den Tiger in den Tank*' in Germany, '*Stop'n Tiger in uw Tank*' in Holland). In other countries, the powerful tiger is located in the engine (in French, '*Mettez un Tigre dans votre moteur*', in Italian, '*Metti un Tigre Nel Motore*'). The interpretation as to where the power source is located differs. Note, however, that an engine can-

not work without fuel and vice versa. Nobody is really right, it is simply the interpretations that differ, the Anglo interpretation (tank) being more passive and the Latin interpretation (engine) more active. In Thailand and some neighbouring countries the tiger is experienced quite differently from how it is viewed in Europe, America or Japan. Until recently the tiger was a danger for the local population, especially in the countryside; therefore its image is that of jungle danger rather than of power. The image expressed by the word 'tiger' is not the same in a country where the tiger is experienced as a physical threat and sometimes as a source of terror for the local population as it is in countries where tigers have only been seen in books, films and zoos.

In Box 12.4 we illustrate the diverging cultural interpretations of a sign that prima facie seems universal (but is not so).

Languages and new international cultures

People have a great deal of leeway in using language. This is more clearly expressed in French than in English since two words correspond to 'language': *la langue* (in English, literally, 'tongue' – the same word serving in French to express both the physical organ and what it helps to create) and *le langage*. *La langue* is the language itself and *le langage* is largely how people use *la langue* in order to communicate.

The most obvious influence of culture on language is that of a vocabulary with its own particular capacities and limits. Specific examples of this are the new technological vocabularies from computer science, nuclear technology, audiovisual communication, aerospace technology, and so on, which are largely borrowed and exchanged between linguistic and national cultures: the benefit being the creation of a nearly universal technical culture.

There are also vocabularies that have been enriched because of physical occurrences that demand precise description, as in the huge number of terms for different types of snow that exist in the Eskimo languages and all peoples who live near the Arctic Circle. Another example is the rich culinary vocabulary in France, where a preoccupation with good food is an element of society that strongly influences daily life.

The language and culture causality debate, which is scientifically very complex, risks turning into a 'chicken and egg' argument. However, commonsense reveals limitations to the Whorfian hypothesis in relation to those who speak many languages, or those who were raised in various linguistic and cultural environments, or the Swiss who share a strong national culture in spite of language differences. In a static scenario where an individual or a certain group has been educated in a totally homogeneous cultural environment, language can influence world views and actions. But the theory is less valid in a dynamic scenario where language changes from generation to generation or where people travel abroad. Then they encounter opportunities to borrow language and culture. Interaction between language and culture is reciprocal, in particular in the light of cultural borrowing.

Choosing the correct vocabulary is one of the limitations with the automated translation technologies currently being developed. Translation software is now available that can automatically translate text, so that real-time chatting is possible over the Internet. However, there are still problems with accuracy: even error rates of 1 per cent can cause serious problems in international business. Take the example of homonyms or words with the same spelling that have multiple meanings. These are quite common in English, and many other languages. Lu[36] experimented with three of the currently available tools of translation on the web, which allow people to search the Internet in both English and Asian languages, and compose e-mail messages in your own language and send them in another. He found that homonyms still cause errors for machine translators (p. 39): 'EWSurf misunderstood the name of the Japanese electronics giant Sony as a term of endearment for a male child, and missed the true meaning of an MP3 player. So visitors to Sony's website are exhorted in Chinese to "enjoy your son's digital new music . . . using an MP3 contestant".'[36] Similarly, the word *dog* may mean a four-legged mammal in a strictly lexical definition, but it may also be used as verb meaning to persistently pursue, or a bad investment, or an ugly person, or ruin (as in 'going to the dogs').[37] Thus, all of these definitions need to be entered before *dog* can be associated with the foreign equivalents.

12.4

Ethnocentrism, stereotypes and misunderstandings in intercultural communication

Living according to one's culture in daily life is almost an unconscious action. The cost of adopting the cultural traits of the environment is minimal. But there are generally high costs associated with the identification and adoption of the traits of another culture. This is shown clearly by the difficulties encountered by immigrants in integrating, even those who have immigrated voluntarily.

Ethnocentrism

Owing to the high cost of changing cultures, few even consider doing so. This causes what James Lee[38] calls the SRC (Self-Reference Criterion): we all have an automatic and unconscious tendency to refer to our own thought framework, which is mainly tied to our national culture (which in general we did not choose), to interpret situations, evaluate people, communicate, negotiate or decide which attitude to take. This framework is generally modelled by ethnocentrism, which was discussed in Chapter 9 in relation to country-of-origin effects.

The concept of ethnocentrism was first introduced by G.A. Sumner[39] more than 80 years ago, to distinguish between *ingroups* (those groups with which an individual identifies) and *outgroups* (those regarded as antithetical to the *ingroup*). Ethnocentrism has been extended by psychologists at the level of the individual, where it relates to the natural tendency of people to refer themselves spontaneously to the symbols, values and ways of thinking of their own ethnic or national group (their ingroup). Ethnocentrism may lead to uninterest in and even contempt for the culture of other groups.[40] Lee (1966) suggests the following steps in order to try to eliminate the decisional bias related to the SRC when dealing with international operations:

1. Define the problem or the objectives, as would be done according to the customs, behavioural standards and ways of thinking of the decision maker's country.
2. Similarly, define the problem or the objectives as would be done according to the customs, behavioural standards and ways of thinking of the foreign country (where the decision will be implemented).
3. Isolate the influence of the self-reference criterion on the problem, and identify the extent to which it complicates the decision-making problem.
4. Redefine the problem (and often the objectives), without the bias related to the SRC and then find the solutions and make decisions that fit with the cultural context of the foreign market.

Take the following situation. People are standing in line at an amusement park, such as Disneyland, where there are some very popular attractions. In the original context in the US, discipline with respect to

queues is strong. They are usually well organized and there are even tangible indications for this (yellow line on the ground indicating to people where to stop to queue, visible corridors for queuing in line, etc.). In the foreign context of France, where there is a developed sense of 'free-for-all' and less of a habit of organized queues, combined with a reluctance towards anything that seems too socially structured, discipline with respect to queues cannot be assumed.

The SRC also comprises a degree of naivety and inadequacy. It assumes that a culture's mysteries can be easily understood. However, cultural expertise is a complex reality. Sometimes neither marketing experts from the home country (in total ignorance) nor foreigners (through lack of consciousness of their own culture) are capable of diagnosis in the second and third phases. The bias removal effect using the SRC approach does not result in immediate outcomes. For instance, Billikopf[41] describes his first trip to Russia. He was tutored on Russian culture, talking to interpreters about appropriate behaviour in various situations. On one of these occasions the interpreter explained that a gentleman must always be courteous to ladies, such as pouring her *limonad*. Later, he tried to use this reasoning when he offered his host's wife a banana. When she smiled and said yes without reaching for one, he picked one for her and peeled it half way before he handed it to her. His host's smile told him he had done the right thing. On a later trip he was informed that: 'In Russian, when a man peels a banana for a lady it means he has a romantic interest in her' (p. 1).[41] Billikopf cautions that generalizations about eye-contact, personal space, touch and interest in participation, especially based on faulty observation, can be dangerous.

Stereotypes

If the French perceive Americans as being arrogant and tough in business, and the British as insincere, it is for the most part due to stereotypes, which give a distorted view.[42] American arrogance is, in fact, related to a different hierarchy of values: professional relations are centred on the task at hand, the object of discussion, to the exclusion of personal relations with the other party.

Stereotypes, although sometimes representing a simplification that is intellectually useful, have the function of reducing and conserving our differences, which can make them dangerous. Soutar and colleagues[43] asked experienced Australian and Japanese international businesspeople to estimate the values of their own culture and those of others, finding the stereotypes of other cultures to be quite different from reality. For instance, relationships with others was the most important value for Japanese, but Australians felt this was much less important to the Japanese than other values such as being well respected, having a sense of belonging and security.[43] Even those who immerse themselves in another culture do not fully understand the nuances.

Gauthey (p. 63)[44] notes that: 'It seems a thousand times easier to stay attached to our own values and to transfer onto the foreigner the responsibility to change his point of view than to decenter ourselves, that is to leave our system of reference and put ourselves in the place of the other.' Stereotypes have a cognitive function as a simplified intellectual representation of other people and also an emotional function as self-defence against a difference that provokes anxiety. Michel Droit, in his book *Chez les Mangeurs d'hommes* (The Man Eaters), exposes the stereotype of the sorcerer in primitive societies. He describes the people of Papua New Guinea through the eyes of civilized observers who are necessarily their ideological enemies (Droit, p. 124, J.-C. Usunier translation):

Armed with tamed snakes which they use to execute their victims, with poisons, enchanted prayers and medicinal herbs known only to them, sorcerers, through well-organized propaganda and strong co-operative solidarity, let entire populations live in fear and sometimes in terror of their 'nepou', that is their evil powers.[45]

This does not necessarily mean that Michel Droit's description of the sorcerer is false. He reveals part of reality, but also ignores how the sorcerer is an integral part of Papuan communities. Stereotypes are often used to capture the salient traits of a 'foreign' national character. For instance, Yoshida (p. 1)[46] relates a very amusing anecdote of a European professor who assigned students from different nationalities to submit a report on elephants. Stereotypical submissions included: 'A philosophical analysis of the existence of the elephant' from a German student, 'How to raise an elephant in your backyard for money and fun without risk of litigation' from an

American student, 'A comparative analysis of elephant studies in foreign countries, particularly Europe and America: what the Elephant thinks of us Japanese' from a Japanese student, and a Chinese student simply submitted a recipe. Box 12.5 shows how French people are viewed (at least stereotypically) by people from other nations.

Website link 12.4

See a humorous look at stereotypes in Hollywood by comedian Jon Stewart of *The Daily Show*: http://www.thedailyshow.com/video.

Self-shock

Cultural encounters are more complex than simply 'getting to know the other'. When people from different cultures meet, such as expatriate managers meeting local executives or international sellers meeting local buyers, lacking knowledge of the other's culture makes for uncertainty. At first it may seem that the basic problem is 'getting to know the other'. But as Alder (p. 18)[47] describes, there is in fact a 'progressive unfolding of the self' in the intercultural encounter, which can be attributed to 'a set of intensive and evocative situations in which the individual perceives and experiences other people in a distinctly new manner and, as a consequence, experiences new facets and dimensions of existence'. Facing foreigners may disturb personal identities by challenging them through the 'mirror effect'.

Within the native cultural context, 'self-image' is built unconsciously. 'Self-image' is constructed from observations that are based on others' voiced opinions and behavioural responses. As Erikson (p. 13)[48] emphasises: 'Identity is the confidence gathered from the fact that our own ability to maintain interior resemblance and continuity equals the resemblance and continuity of the image and the sense that others have of us.' However, creating and maintaining personal identity has two main drawbacks that make it problematic in intercultural encounters: (1) it is primarily unconscious, and (2) it requires good interpersonal communication skills.

According to Zaharna[49] 'self-shock', unlike culture shock, which is considered to be a reaction to

BOX 12.5

Stereotypes of the French

How various nationalities perceive the French:

- The Germans: Pretentious and offhand. Fashionable, womanizing, frivolous, fickle, well-mannered, resourceful.
- The British: Nationalistic, chauvinistic, intransigent, centralist, dependent on the state, polite but not open-minded, humourless, short-tempered.
- The Dutch: Cultured, fond of good living, fidgety, talkative, not very serious, feelings of superiority.
- The Spanish: Pretentious, early sleepers, cold and distant, hypocritical, impolite, patronizing, hard working.
- The Swedish: In-built superiority complex, scornful, boastful, talkative, immoral, dirty, neo-colonialists, disorganized, cultured gastronomy, suffocating hierarchy.

- The Finns: Xenophobic, superficial, scornful, chauvinistic, courteous, romantic, enjoying life, patriotic, chaotic.
- The Americans: Chauvinistic, well-mannered. Combination of good food and good conversation, Paris. Curious about foreign people, pretentious, talkative, pleasant, intelligent.
- The Russians: Talkative, self-satisfied, lazy. Luxury, inequality, culture. Pleasant, intelligent, resourceful.
- The North Africans: Fairly racist, a little stingy, reasonably honest. Good education and good food. Selfish.
- The Asians: Exhibitionist, indiscreet. Reticent in making friends. Bureaucracy and red tape.
- The Black Africans: Racist, honest, lacking respect for elders and betters. At odds with themselves and nature. Not spontaneously hospitable.

(Source: Gruère and Morel, p. 51.[50])

---

difference, is a concept that extends to differences with and within the self. The root of 'self-shock' lies in the intimate workings of the relationship between the ego (that is, personal identity), personal behaviour, and the 'other' (as the 'other' actually is, and as the other is perceived by the ego). It also leads to self-reflection. Self-shock emerges as a deep imbalance between the need to confirm personal identity and personal ability to do so. In one way, this situation places the individual in a 'double-bind' position.[51] The self-shock situation increases the need for reinforcing personal identity, while at the same time resulting in a loss of ability to satisfy this need. Thus, certain stereotypes or abrupt judgements about foreigners result almost directly from individual attempts at self-defence by avoiding the painful double constraint of self-shock.

Gauthey (p. 64)[44] cites a general manager of a software company, a subsidiary of a French advertising and communications group, who says: 'I can't stand the English, and when I go to London, I never leave the airport.' This attitude is clearly defensive: in refusing to leave the airport, he remains on neutral international ground, refusing to run the risk of being confronted by the image that the English will have of him.

International empathy: a naive concept

Inherent in the concept of international empathy is a glimpse of the immense naivety of those who argue in favour of cultural empathy (being open-minded, sincerely interested in the other, ready to listen, etc.). This communication tactic, although well meant, may only last for a brief period; the time during which the personal identity of the 'empathizer' has not yet been revealed. There are a series of concrete issues at stake, which are important for people involved in intercultural business communication:

1. Which personality types and/or personal backgrounds are best suited to intercultural communication?
2. Are there particular countries and cultures that are easier to communicate with? How can individuals improve intercultural communication skills?

3. If an adjustment must be made during the intercultural encounter, who should be the one to adapt? Quite apart from personal capacity, empathy or the position of strength, can the intercultural learning situation be led other than bilaterally? In other words, why learn if the other does not learn too? Why not learn simultaneously, rather than in two parallel learning situations that may never meet?

12.5

How to improve communication effectiveness in international business

A 'reasonable' version of the use of the Whorfian hypothesis

The first consequence of the Sapir–Whorf hypothesis, in so far as one chooses to adhere to it, is that businesspeople from different cultures not only communicate in different ways, but also perceive, categorize and construct their realities differently. This supposes a 'state of alert' in communication, a readiness to accept that words, even those that are translated with no apparent difficulty, offer only an illusion of sharing in the same vision of reality. It is advisable to retain as many foreign words as possible in their original form, in the following ways:

1. By recognizing their unique nature and the need to keep culturally unique concepts in the native language form to signal their uniqueness.
2. By questioning the interpreters, or even one's foreign business partners, about the precise meaning of words or expressions in the context of a particular culture. See Sussman and Johnson[52] for a qualitative examination of the roles of interpreters.
3. By clearly identifying areas of shared meaning.

For instance, when examining contract clauses it is crucial to extricate the true meaning of each clause, starting from the perspective that they are never exactly equivalent. This is true even in the case of a dictionary seeming to indicate (falsely) that an English term is a strict equivalent of a French term, such as *act of God* and *force majeure*. A simple way of investigating the equivalence of terms is to take two language dictionaries and compare the translations in both directions.

Internet and language

It has already been observed in this chapter that languages other than English assume a highly prominent place on the Internet. Abas (pp. 1–2)[53] noted that 'about 146.2 million individuals access Web sites in the Asian languages (Arabic, Chinese, Hebrew, Japanese, Korean, Malay and Thai) . . . This was in contrast to only 25.5 million individuals doing the same three years ago, a jump of 5.73 times.' Such statistics seem to support Heppner and Farré's[54] assertion that English is no longer the Internet's *lingua franca*: translators have never had more work.

There are countless translation-related issues on the Internet, including making sure software can accept foreign language features, such as double-byte Asian characters,[55] and overcoming the subtleties involved in ever-expanding translation dictionaries[56] and cost.[57] Translation techniques are also evolving alongside dictionary size and hardware horsepower. As Bisby (p. 17)[56] notes, many translation software packages rely on example-based translation: 'If the program learns that French people write adjectives after nouns ("vin rouge" means "red wine" rather than "wine red"), it can use this knowledge to guess that "riviere rouge" means "red river", not "river red"'. Despite this, it can cost upwards of US$20,000 to translate a website consisting of 100 pages: software can only go so far, translation is still very much a human process.[57]

Website link 12.5

Find a free online translator for most languages: **http://www.online-translator.com/ text_translation.aspx**.

Linguistic ethnocentrism versus linguistic polycentrism

An unfortunate consequence of the Sapir–Whorf hypothesis is that linguistic ethnocentrism is largely inevitable. One might wonder whether it would be a more realistic approach to have only natives of a language and culture write about cultural topics for their fellow citizens. Anthropology, a discipline with a record of reporting on other cultures, would appear not to answer in the affirmative. Most famous anthropologists generally belonged to the cultures of their publishers and readers, not to the cultures they observed. The same holds true for area specialists. For instance, the two most well-known specialists of French culture are Harvard University's Theodore Zeldin and British journalist John Ardagh. Similarly, the most prominent specialist in Germany on French contemporary civilization is a German, Ulrich Wickert. It is often useful to be an outsider to make observations, and both a cultural and linguistic insider to report them. This evokes the issue of *cultural mediation* between ingroup and outgroup members.

However paradoxical and provocative it may seem, it is sometimes more important to be understood than to understand, inasmuch as the *understanding* depends on the mindset of the observer, as well as on the object to be understood. What is said by mere cultural insiders is often difficult to understand unless it has been in some way recalibrated in the linguistic background of the reader, which means more than simply translated.

For international businesspeople to be linguistically non-ethnocentric does not mean that they have to have a full command of several foreign languages. It is more important, and in fact much easier, to catch what is unique in the structure of the foreign language and some of its words than trying to become fluent in that language. Consulting a basic grammar book and paying careful attention to specific words can be a good start. Very often authors of books on Japanese business customs or management style keep Japanese words as they are originally pronounced when they want to signal a culturally specific meaning. Sometimes words that partly bridge the cultural divide are forged. For instance, Boye de Mente (p. 261)[58] cites the Japanese word *nomication*, which is made up of the first part of the Japanese word *nomimasu* (to drink) and the last half of 'communication': 'This Japlish word refers to business conversations and socializing that takes place in bars, cabarets, and other drinking establishments, and it is one of the institutionalized ways of "wisdom gathering" in Japan'.

Culturally unique life concepts have a major impact on decision-making processes inside companies and especially on the issue of labour – management relationships. They are signalled by words such as *Management by objectives* for the Americans, *ringi* for the Japanese, *mitbestimmung* for the Germans

and *concertation* for the French. The same holds for the managing institutions of a company: a German *Aufsichtsrat*, often translated into English as 'supervisory board', should be considered a specific institution, typical of German business culture, with particular consequences in the real life of real businesses.[59] Although linguistic ethnocentrism is largely inevitable, we must strive for linguistic polycentrism by trying to keep original words, understanding meaningful elements in the grammar (such as gender, tenses and sentence construction), and trying to behave as 'explorers' of the meanings and world views expressed by different languages.

Taking the true measure of language and communication abilities in international business

In assessing English as the *lingua franca* of international business, it is essential to consider two very distinct groups: native and non-native English speakers. For non-native English-speaking businesspeople, learning English and often one or two other languages is a must. For instance, the Swedes, Finns, Danes and Norwegians often speak three or four foreign languages: English, another Nordic language and French, German or Spanish. The situation is very different for native English speakers. Simon (p. 2)[60] observes: 'The US continues to be the only nation where you can graduate from college without having had one year of a foreign language'. Australia also falls into this category. Although regrettable, this may be explained and understood. The US and Australia are vast, linguistically homogeneous countries where nearly everyone speaks English. Australia is also geographically remote. For instance, the major city of Melbourne is around 3200 km from the nearest major non-English-speaking population centre (Port Moresby). In Australia, there is no real need to learn foreign languages, whereas in Europe most large cities are located less than 200 miles (330 km) from a foreign-speaking area and a foreign language is an asset. Although the US is now the fourth largest Spanish-speaking country in the world and more than half the population of Miami is of Spanish-speaking origin, this does not necessarily mean that Americans feel they have to learn Spanish. Rather, Hispanics have to learn English.

There are also differences in the amount of effort required to learn certain foreign languages. If an American or a European wants to really learn Japanese, the characters have to be learned, which implies a much greater effort than for the Japanese to learn the Roman alphabet: the *gai-jin* (non-Japanese) has to learn two syllabaries of about 100 characters each (*hiragana* and *katakana*, phonetic symbols) and about 1850 *kanjis* (ideographic symbols), whereas the Japanese have to learn the Roman alphabet's 26 phonetic characters, not a large addition given the skill needed to master Japanese writing.

English speakers can usually find other English speakers during their travels, and they can count on their foreign business partners having – at least superficially – a good command of English. Furthermore, most English speakers are tolerant and lenient towards the mistakes of their non-native counterparts: 'international English' sometimes has little to do with real English grammar and words.

These are good reasons for native English speakers to be somewhat lazy about foreign languages. Understandably, therefore, the impact of language differences has been systematically underestimated in international business literature because of an 'English-only' bias. Most international business textbooks do not include a single reference in a foreign language. Even a text devoted to the cultural dimension of international business such as Ferraro[20] does not have (among some 200 references) a single *truly* foreign reference, that is, from a foreign author in a foreign language, although some works by foreign authors are listed when they have been published in English. This may imply a substantial bias, since translated authors are not read in their own linguistic contexts and any foreign authors who have not been translated into English are not even considered. However, there are naturally good and practical reasons for maintaining language homogeneity in sources: the reader would not be able to find or to read these references, so this should not be considered only as a reflection of linguistic ethnocentrism.

What is unfortunate, however, is that native English speakers are at a disadvantage, although the opposite may appear to be true. The main disadvantage for them is that they cannot grasp the features of the foreign language in terms of world view and communication style. Furthermore, many native English speakers cannot imagine what it means or is like to express oneself in a language with little proficiency unless they themselves have tried to learn and speak a foreign language. Thus, native English speakers have to develop an awareness of their competitive disadvantage in terms of language.

The message is not to simply learn foreign languages. It is more important to understand the consequences of languages being different. Absolute proficiency in many languages is not needed. International businesspeople do not have to be multilingual. They do, however, need to have an awareness of what language differences imply.

Non-native English speakers may seem to have a good command of English, but they still have a world view that has been shaped by their native language and culture. Thus, proficient non-native English speakers may look quite the same, but they are quite different. This may be especially true for northern Europeans. They may seem quite similar as their English pronunciation is generally good, but in reality they have a different mindset and a much greater proficiency for oral than for written communication, which can cause problems when the written details of business contracts are discussed.

Some guidelines for effective communication in international business

Website link 12.6

Read about interpretation gone wrong, on a nuclear scale: **http://www.usatoday.com/news/world/ 2007-10-17-un-Syria_N.htm.**

The following are some guidelines for effective communication in international business:

1. Start by accurately assessing possible intercultural obstacles, such as language and communication issues. Businesspeople frequently underestimate or even completely overlook intercultural communication problems, since they often share a professional culture with their foreign partner. They are also deceived by a misleading international context. Glen Fisher (p. 8) points out:

   Obviously, the modern intensity of international interaction, especially in business and in technological, communication and educational fields, has produced something of an internationalized 'culture' which reduces the clash of cultural backgrounds and stereotyped images. Happily for us this *modus vivendi* is largely based on Western practices and even on the English language, so many otherwise 'foreign' counterparts are accommodating to the American style of negotiation.[61]

Unfortunately, businesspeople who feel no need to adapt, especially as far as language is concerned, may believe that their counterpart feels the same. Similarities are often illusions, especially when foreigners seemingly share an 'international culture'. Those who adapt are aware of differences, whereas those who must be adapted to remain unaware.

2. Be aware that what is explicitly said is not necessarily what is implicitly meant. Check, verify. Spend time on checking communication accuracy, especially when the stakes are high (orders, delivery dates, contractual involvement in general).

3. Learning other non-verbal communication styles may prove difficult. Deep cultural learning is hard for adults. It is better to aim for a state of alertness so that one does not decode non-verbal messages erroneously, rather than trying to gain full command of different types of non-verbal communication.

4. In many cases interpreters serve a crucial purpose; they are transposers of meaning. They do not work 'like a dictionary', translating literally. They may translate better from one language to another than in the reverse direction, depending on their language abilities and on their relationships with the parties. It is necessary to make sure that they are loyal to the party who has hired them. It may be advisable to hire several interpreters when the business at stake justifies it.

5. Parts of language simply cannot be translated as it conveys culture-specific meaning. Always keep in mind the Italian adage, cited above, *traduttore/traditore* (translator/traitor).

6. Develop a 'bomb squad' ability to defuse conflicts based on negative stereotypes. Misunderstanding in intercultural communication often snowballs and mixes with purely interest-based conflicts, resulting in lose–lose confrontations. Cultural misunderstanding may lead to breaking off negotiations.

7. Bear in mind that all this cannot be improvised. Helping others understand one's own culture is a prerequisite, often involving 'wine and dine'. When business negotiations start with one side lacking even minimal knowledge of the partner's culture, relations will often turn sour. Then, the only way to negotiate is to discuss on the substantive ground of 'business is business'. Skills in intercultural business communication are a long-term investment rather than a way of resolving urgent problems. In medical terms, cultural understanding in business appears as the prevention rather than the cure.

Questions

1. Comment on the following sentences from Fisher (1988, p. 172):

   It is the subjective meaning of words and expressions that needs to be captured. Time spent exploring why a given utterance does not translate well may be more productive for the one who is actually trying to communicate than concentrating on technical excellence.

2. Give examples of low-context versus high-context communication, explaining what is meant by low and high contexts.

3. Transform the following buyer's remark into low-context and high-context sentences: 'Your price is too high compared with that of the competitors.'

4. Discuss the following statements from Gannon (1994, pp. 5 and 68) on stereotyping:

   Many Germans, for instance, do not like to converse much during their meals. Germans will ordinarily begin their meals by taking a sip of beer or soda and then picking up and holding knives and forks throughout the meal, putting them down only when they are finished eating. For many Germans eating is a serious business that is not to be disturbed by trivial comments and animated conversation.

Germans also frequent the symphony on a regular basis; the former West Germany with its population of 62 millions boasts approximately 80 symphony orchestras . . . This societal and cultural love of music has produced some of the finest composers of classical symphonic music. In fact, many experts agree that the classical symphony reached its highest level of attainment and maturity in the works of Haydn and Mozart.

5. Why can the obvious showing of emotions be considered dangerous? Why do cultures vary in the degree of emotional restraint?

6. Consider the gender aspect of words in the following languages. In English almost everything is neutral except persons and some animals, and exceptionally an object such as a ship. French has feminine and masculine but no neutral. In German, persons, objects and concepts can be feminine, masculine or neutral. For instance 'sun', 'earth' and 'moon' are all neutral words in English; in French they are respectively masculine (*le soleil*) and feminine (*la terre, la lune*); in German the same words are feminine (*die Sonne, die Erde*) and masculine (*der Mond*). Elaborate on the possible cultural meanings of attributing gender to words. To what extent can we speak of more or less 'sexualized' languages (I mean here 'sexualized' and not simply 'gendered')? Outline the limitations of such an interpretive approach.

7. In Japanese there are no articles either definite or indefinite. *Hon*, for instance, means 'the book', 'a book', 'the books' or 'books'. What does this imply for the Japanese when they want to express their thoughts?

8. Consider gift-giving practices as an element of communication. What are the main dimensions of gift giving (consider the donor, the recipient, the size and nature of the gift, the circumstances and its meaning for either side)? How would cultural interpretations differ? Take into account the values involved. (You can base your discussion on elements found in articles about gift giving.)

9. Can you describe at least one circumstance when you had an ethnocentric attitude? If you find it hard, can you explain why?

References

1. Fisher, Glen (1988), *Mindsets*. Yarmouth, ME: Intercultural Press.
2. Bluedorn, Allen C. (1998), 'An Interview with Anthropologist Edward T. Hall', *Journal of Management Inquiry*, 7 (2), 109–15.
3. Hall, Edward T. (1976), *Beyond Culture*. New York: Doubleday.
4. Hemingway, Ernest (1976), *The Snows of Kilimanjaro and Other Stories*. New York: Charles Scribner's and Sons.
5. Langenscheidt (1989), *Compact Dictionary French–English/English–French*. New York: Kenneth Urwin Publishers.
6. Ueda, Keiko (1974), 'Sixteen Ways to Avoid Saying "No" in Japan', in *Intercultural Encounters in Japan*, J.C. Condon and M. Saito, Eds. Tokyo: Simul Press.
7. Woodward, Nancy Hatch (1999), 'Do You Speak Internet?', *HR Magazine*, 44 (4), 12–16.
8. Kim, Donghoon, Yigang Pan, and Heung Soo Park (1998), 'High Versus Low-Context Culture: A Comparison of Chinese, Korean, and American Cultures', *Psychology and Marketing*, 15 (6), 507–21.
9. MacLeod, Marcia (2000), 'Language Barriers', *Supply Management*, 5 (14), 37–8.
10. Axtell, Roger E. (1993), *Do's and Taboos around the World*. New York: Wiley.

11. Cutitta, Frank (2002), 'Language Matters', *Target Marketing*, 25 (2), 40–44.

12. Anon (2008), 'Top Internet Languages', *World Internet Usage Statistics*, 27 March 2008, www.internetworldstats.com/stats7.htm.

13. Luna, David, Laura A. Peracchio, and Maria D. de Juan (2002), 'Cross-Cultural and Cognitive Aspects of Web Site Navigation', *Journal of the Academy of Marketing Science*, 30 (4), 397–410.

14. Koslow, Scott, Prem Shamdasani, and Ellen Touchstone (1994), 'Exploring Language Effects in Ethic Advertising: A Sociolinguistic Perspective', *Journal of Consumer Research*, 20 (March), 575–85.

15. Mishima, Yukio (1969), *Le Tumulte des Flots [Shiosai]*, Translated from Japanese. Paris: Gallimard.

16. Hall, Edward T. (1960), 'The Silent Language in Overseas Business', *Harvard Business Review* (May–June), 87–96.

17. Sugimoto, Naomi (1998), 'Norms of Apology Depicted in U.S. American and Japanese Literature on Manners and Etiquette', *International Journal of Intercultural Relations*, 22 (3), 251–76.

18. Simintiras, Antonis C. (2000), 'The Role of Tautological Equivalence in Cross-Cultural Sales Negotiations', *Journal of International Consumer Marketing*, 12 (4), 33–53.

19. Condon, John C. and Fahti Youssef (1975), *Introduction to Intercultural Communication*. Indianapolis: Bobbs Merrill.

20. Ferraro, Gary P. (1990), *The Cultural Dimension of International Business*. Englewood Cliffs, NJ: Prentice Hall.

21. Copeland, Lennie and Lewis Griggs (1986), *Going International*. New York: Plume Books/New American Library.

22. Harris, Philip R. and Robert T. Moran (1987), *Managing Cultural Differences* (2nd edn). Houston, TX: Gulf Publishing Company.

23. Morschbach, Helmut (1982), 'Aspects of Non-Verbal Communication in Japan', in *Intercultural Communication: A Reader*, Larry Samovar and R.E. Porter, Eds. (3rd edn). Belmont, CA: Wadsworth.

24. Harris, Philip R., Robert T. Moran, and Sarah Moran (2004), *Managing Cultural Differences: Global Leadership Strategies for the 21st Century*. Oxford: Butterworth-Heinemann.

25. Morand, David A. (1996), 'Politeness as a Universal Variable in Cross-Cultural Managerial Communication', *International Journal of Organizational Analysis*, 4 (1), 52–74.

26. Sapir, Edward (1929), 'The Status of Linguistics as a Science', *Language*, 5, 207–14.

27. Carroll, John B. (1956), *Language, Thought and Reality: Selected Writings of Benjamin Lee Whorf*. Cambridge, MA: MIT.

28. Lankshear, Colin and Michele Knobel (2003), *New Literacies: Changing Knowledge and Classroom Learning*. Buckingham: Open University Press.

29. Lankshear, Colin and Michele Knobel (2001), 'New Technologies, Social Practices and the Challenge of Mindsets', AERA 2001 (available at www.geocities.com/c.lankshear/mindsets.html).

30. Holden, Nigel (1998), 'Viewpoint: International Marketing Studies – Time to Break the English-Language Strangle-Hold?', *International Marketing Review*, 15 (2), 86–100.

31. Levine, Robert A. and Ara Norenzayan (1999), 'The Pace of Life in 31 Countries', *Journal of Cross-Cultural Psychology*, 30 (2), 178–205.

32. M'biti, John (1968), 'African Concept of Time', *Africa Theological Journal*, 1, 8–20.

33. Levine, Robert V. (1988), 'The Pace of Life across Cultures', in *The Social Psychology of Time*, Joseph E. McGrath, Ed. Newbury Park, CA: Sage Publications.

34. Howard, David (2001), 'Lost in Translation', *Ziff Davis Smart Business*, 14 (11), 44.

35. Lwin, May and Chow-Hou Wee (1999), 'The Effect of an Audio-Stimulus: Accents in English Language on Cross-Cultural Consumer Response to Advertising', *Journal of International Consumer Marketing*, 11 (2), 5–37.

36. Lu, Caixia (2001), 'Chinese, or Just Chinglish?', *Far Eastern Economic Review*, 164 (15), 39.

37. Castellucio, Michael (1999), 'Hey, Can Anybody Read This?', *Strategic Finance*, 81 (1), 63–64.

38. Lee, James A. (1966), 'Cultural Analysis in Overseas Operations', *Harvard Business Review* (March–April), 106–11.

39. Sumner, G.A. (1906), *Folk Ways*. New York: Ginn Custom Publishing.

40. Levine, Robert A. and Donald T. Campbell (1972), *Ethnocentrism: Theories of Conflicts, Ethnic Attitudes, and Group Behavior*. New York: John Wiley.

41. Billikopf Encina, Gregorio (1999), 'Cultural Differences?', (available online at: www.cnr.berkeley.edu/ucce50/ag-labor/7article/article01.htm).

42. Gauthey, Franck and Dominique Xardel (1990), *Le Management Interculturel*. Paris: Collection 'Que Sais-Je?'

43. Soutar, Geoffrey N., Richard Grainger, and Pamela Hedges (1999), 'Australian and Japanese Value Stereotypes: A Two Country Study', *Journal of International Business Studies*, 30 (1), 203–16.

44. Gauthey, Franck (1989), 'Gérer les Différences dans L'entreprise Internationale', *Intercultures*, 6 (April), 59–66.

45. Droit, Michel (1952), *Chez les Mangeurs D'hommes*. Paris: La Table Ronde.

46. Yoshida, Susumu (2000), 'Can the West Understand the East? And Vice-Versa? Issues of Cross-Cultural Communication', *Management Japan*, 33, 1–13.

47. Adler, Peter S. (1975), 'The Transitional Experience: An Alternative View of Culture Shock', *Journal of Humanistic Psychology*, 15, 13–23.

48. Erikson, Erik (1950), *Childhood and Society*. New York: Norton.

49. Zaharna, R.S. (1989), 'Self Shock: The Double-Binding Challenge of Identity', *International Journal of Intercultural Relations*, 13 (4), 501–26.

50. Gruère, Jean-Pierre and Pierre Morel (1991), *Cadres Français Et Communications Interculturelles*. Paris: Eyrolles.

51. Bateson, Gregory (1971), 'Introduction to the Natural History of an Interview', in *University of Chicago Library Microfilm Collection of Manuscripts in Cultural Anthropology*, Series 15, Nos 95–98.

52. Sussman, Lyle and Denise Johnson (1996), 'Dynamics of the Interpreter's Role: Implications for International Executives', *Journal of Language for International Business*, 7 (2), 1–14.

53. Abas, Zoraini Wati (2002), 'Internet Growth Based on Languages', *Computimes Malaysia*, 16 (May), 1.

54. Heppner, Janet and Maria Eugenia Farré (2001), 'Of Two Minds: Is English the Lingua Franca for Global E-Business?', *Internet World*, 7 (12), 14.

55. Yunker, John (2000), 'Going Global', *Pharmaceutical Executive*, 20 (7), 138–46.

56. Bisby, Adam (1999), 'Translation Tools Speak Globally', *Computer Dealer News*, 15 (15), 17.

57. Heuberger, Andres (2001), 'Manage Your Global WWW Brand', *World Trade*, 14 (11), 56–60.

58. de Mente, Boye (1990), *How to Do Business with the Japanese*. Chicago, IL: NTC Books.

59. Schneider-Lenné, E. (1993), 'The Governance of Good Business', *Business Strategy Review*, 4 (1), 75–85.

60. Simon, Paul (1980), *The Tongue Tied American*. New York: Continuum Press.

61. Fisher, Glen (1980), *International Negotiation: A Cross-cultural Perspective*. Yarmouth, ME: Intercultural Press.

Appendix 12

Teaching materials

A12.1 Exercise

Multicultural class

Look at the person seated next to you in class, or anyone with whom you have frequent inter-action. Then select somebody originating from a foreign culture. List three examples of non-verbal communication that she or he uses, describe them accurately and decode their meaning. Now ask this person to look at you and do the same. Then work together and compare both interpretations and try to understand why meaning was shared or, possibly, not shared.

   (This exercise can be implemented only with a good degree of cultural diversity within the student group.)

A12.2 Exercise

I 'love' cake

Start from the English verb 'to like' and find its equivalents in French, German and Spanish. Do not hesitate to translate them back into English in order to detect differences in meaning. Include in your search some basic etymological grounds (e.g. *gusto* in Spanish is based on the word for 'taste'). What differences in terms of world views are suggested by the different conceptual dimensions of 'liking' (preference, affective, pleasure, love, enjoyment, eating/ingesting, etc.) and their attributions to people, things or situations? Suggest possible con-sequences for international marketing and advertising strategies.

A12.3 Case

Longcloud – languages in cyberspace

Language is a steed that carries one into a far country. (Arabic proverb.)

Brushing through green pastures in her rugged truck, Longcloud marketing director Sarah Elder mused over what she would say at this afternoon's meeting. Longcloud Lamb was a young company, specializing in chilled and frozen New Zealand lamb and goat products with a difference: it was organic and exceeded animal welfare stipulations in major export markets. With already five established export partners in the USA and Japan, and 32 regular customers in the area, Sarah and her colleagues were pleasantly surprised by the phenomenal demand growth in only seven years of operations. Accelerated global growth for Longcloud was now imperative to recoup costs of the recent acquisition of new lands, 42 per cent more stock, and an updated processing plant with EU and USDA certification and Halal capability.

Given that the company managed current wholesale customers in export markets using an e-commerce platform, it seemed obvious that a better website was the answer. In addition, the latest processing and shipping technology made it possible to send chilled cuts to smaller export customers on an individual basis. Most New Zealand exporters were beefing up their sites too, however, Canadian-born Sarah had been surprised that most were English-only. Longcloud aimed to capture certain European markets for organic chilled lamb and goat products, as well as niche markets around the world, such as organic restaurants, schools, and religious and non-profit organizations. The lamb meat cuts market was global, and interest in organic meats was a growing phenomenon. First in interest for organic lamb was the European Union, primarily Britain, France and Germany, followed by the USA. Then, there were smaller markets throughout North Africa, the Middle East, and India, many with a particular interest in Longcloud's Halal capacity. There was also a growing interest in organic goat meat in fragmented Latin American markets.

'Because we must differentiate ourselves from mainstream chilled lamb producers, we need to demonstrate our difference in our communications materials. What better way than to talk to customers and prospects in their own language?' Sarah would argue later that day in the meeting. Her colleagues then made a chorus of objections, such as 'The fact that Longcloud is organic is difference enough, we don't need to bother with languages', and: 'Translating is so costly, can't we just put one of those *Altavista Babelfish* translation icons on each page? How are you going to decide which languages to use anyways?' Jumping into the fray, general manager Linden Carmody stated, 'Fine, so we publish our multilingual site, but all we can speak is bad French . . . so what happens to our customer relationship beyond on-site ordering and payments? Right, and what about e-mails, how will we understand and answer them?' Each one had a point, Sarah conceded, however it was well established that customers appreciated the ease of conducting business in their own languages, at least for most of the transactions. Especially if Longcloud was to be dealing with niche markets, she opined, a more personalized approach would be necessary. She believed that was the case even if just two other languages were used, such as French for the 10 or more countries that speak the language and seek organic lamb, and Arabic for countries with a Halal market and some organic sensitivities. With potentially wider and more diverse business contacts around the world, Sarah argued further, Longcloud's medium-term goal to grow its own tanned organic lambskin and organic wool products businesses was more likely to be realized. In the website language debate, Longcloud was not alone: innumerable companies and organizations faced the same problem, and could find no easy solution.

According to *Maroto*, more than 63 per cent of people accessing the Internet do not do so in English. That figure should be up to 75 per cent by 2005, according to projections (Maroto, 2003). An online study by *Pastore* in 2000 found that 68.39 per cent of total web pages was in English, followed by Japanese (5.85 per cent), German (5.77 per cent), and Chinese (3.87 per cent).[1] There are manifold difficulties in estimating language use on web pages, however it is clear that English dominates the web although it does not dominate the world's languages, as Table 12.1 illustrates. English is spoken by approximately half the number of those who speak Chinese, yet Chinese is vastly underrepresented on web pages. China has one of the world's fastest-growing online populations. According to the Chinese Internet Network Information

Table 12.1 Ranking of languages according to number of speakers

Language	Principal countries or regions spoken	Estimated speakers in millions
Chinese	China, Taiwan, the diaspora	885
English	Australasia, North America, South Africa, British Isles	450
Hindi/Urdu	Indian Sub-continent, the diaspora	333
Spanish	Latin America, Spain	266
Portuguese	Angola, Brazil, Mozambique, Portugal	175
Bengali	Indian Sub-continent	162
Russian	Former Soviet Union	153
Arabic	Middle East, North Africa	150
Japanese	Japan	126
French	Belgium, Canada, France, North Africa, Sub-Saharan Africa, Switzerland	122

(Source: Ethnologue.[2])

Center, 68 million people have internet subscriptions, indicating a much higher number with online access – an increase of 6.8 million over six months. The number of Chinese internet users doubles every 12–18 months.[3] German, Japanese, and French appear to be relatively present on the Internet, however the languages themselves do not have a correspondingly large population of speakers, as is clear in Table 12.1.

According to *Nielsen/NetRatings*,[4] 580 million people worldwide had access to the Internet in the fourth quarter of 2002. This compares with 563 million online in the last quarter of 2001. The country experiencing the biggest year on year growth in terms of population was Spain, at 22 per cent, while the US experienced a corresponding increase of 3 per cent. The US still had the largest number online at 168.6 million, followed by Germany (41.8 million), the UK (30.4 million) and Italy (25.3 million). Spain also led in Internet use of e-mail, chat rooms, and instant messaging. In terms of online access populations, the USA remains the leader, although the margins are narrowing (see Table 12.2).

The role of e-commerce

In a best-case projection for 2006, e-commerce should comprise 18 per cent of the world's business-to-business and retail transactions.[5] This growth presupposes the participation of a diverse language base, and the adaptation of e-commerce platforms to linguistic and cultural conditions. Many multinational corporations have websites that are entirely in English, however, and the number of major global businesses who have adapted their sites is growing slowly.

How to adapt a website – more than just a translation

When adapting software to local contexts, the following elements need to be considered: language, literacy, and culture. For organizations looking to adapt their message locally around the globe, the same elements are pertinent in website and e-commerce platforms design. Apart from translations, which alone may account for half the localization costs for software, the choice of language or dialect may be critical. Should one select an 'Official language' to the detriment of a language spoken unofficially by large numbers of the target audience? Elements of website design that need to be adapted according to the culture of the target audience include colours used, text versus graphics, a 'busy' screen versus a minimalist one, animations, symbols, and icons.[6] Currently, there are software facilities for dealing with cultural

Table 12.2 Online access in terms of percentage of the total online population

Country or region	Share of world online population (%)
USA	29
Europe	23
Asia-Pacific	13
Latin America	2
Rest of world (countries not under *Nielsen/Netratings*)	33

(Source: *Nielsen/NetRatings*.[4])

variations in number formats, sort orders, and time and date formats. At this time, technology is not well prepared to implement non-Gregorian calendar types. The correct and locally adapted use of proper names is also problematic.[7]

Which language?

When deciding which languages to use in adapting a regionally targeted website, certain social and economic factors should be considered independently of the number of speakers of the languages under consideration. Predominant among these are literacy, language use, and access. Indian languages are a case in point. India, with 1 billion people, has two official languages: English and Hindi. There are 18 major languages and 418 other languages spoken by 10,000 or more people.[8] Firstly, there may be a large number of speakers for some languages, however the corresponding literacy rate may be quite low. Where this is the case the complexity of the language used and the share of online graphics may reflect this. In addition, it is now possible to integrate speech or speech recognition systems (currently only available for the world's 'main' languages) on the site's capabilities.[7]

Secondly, many people around the world are accustomed to using languages other than their own for business or general communication purposes. As in many developing countries, some Indians may feel uneasy conducting business in any other language than English, yet they may feel similar unease communicating at home in English. The user's website language of preference may depend on whether the Internet is accessed from home or from work. English may be more acceptable for work access, while a local language may be preferable for use from the home computer. For this reason, the company with international ambitions needs to determine the likely point of access for its target audiences.

Thirdly, access to the Internet may be uneven. For instance, raw Internet access numbers may be low in some rural areas, however one entrepreneur with a computer and Internet access may allow many others to access the net using the most basic equipment, in exchange for a user fee. Internet access may in this case be higher than initially assumed. Similarly, when looking at the size of the Internet audience in targeted nations, one should be wary of dismissing a small audience, such as the 0.1 per cent of Nigerians online. That small percentage represents 100,000 of the country's most affluent, and most likely the same people who make major decisions in government and its bureaucracies.[9]

Complicating the issue of adapting (or not) to a locally understood language are social factors that have imbued English with status as the language of preference for business in some countries. At the same time, there are fierce debates over the use and even the survival of some Indian languages.[10] One should not assume that English is generally a safe choice: it is vital to gauge the attitudes of the target audience towards the language because in some regions there may be historical or political reasons for polite hostility towards those who use English.

Those who decide to localize their websites should be aware of several software complexities involved in online publishing of non-Roman scripts, including Arabic, Bengali, Greek, Thai, and Hebrew, that have only recently been addressed. One of the problems caused by fonts online is the correct use of diacritics, the accents placed above and below letters – small symbols that can often change the meaning of a word depending on its orientation used in some Nordic languages, Greek, French, Turkish, and some eastern European languages, to name a few. The directionality of symbols is another issue. The fact that numerals are ordered from left to right in Arabic and Hebrew scripts which themselves are oriented from right to left, is another example of online font problems.[10] In addition, some non-Latin scripts require two bits in processing which complicates encoding and may considerably slow down an e-commerce site. The first program to address these problems was produced by the Unicode Consortium, with the goal of eventually codifying all characters produced by humans, anywhere and at any time in history. Currently in its fourth version, the Unicode Standard addresses issues like vertical script (as in East Asian languages) or the right–left orientation of Semitic scripts. Although there are other means of dealing with language representation, the Unicode Consortium has developed the only system to be accepted by the International Standards Organization, as well as the most widely used code within html format. The entire text of Unicode 4.0 is available at **www.unicode.com**, as well as useful guidance and information.

Questions

1. Assess how culture, religion and language may influence foreign marketing operations in the organic meat business. Does it differ whether maketing and sales are implemented through traditional marketing or by e-commerce?

2. Investigate the possibility of using automatic translation programmes for non-English-speaking visitors of a website. For this you can make your own trials on websites which offer free sample translation, such as www.freetranslation.com/, www.softissimo.com/ or www.linguatec.de/news.en.shtml.

3. Assess the approximate cost of developing a different language version of an English-based website.

4. Should Longcloud develop its website in languages other than English? If yes, which language(s)? Argue about the pros and cons of such decisions.

Saskia Faulk and Jean-Claude Usunier prepared this case solely to provide material for class discussion. The authors do not intend to illustrate either effective or ineffective handling of a business situation. The authors may have disguised certain names and other identifying information to protect confidentiality.

© IRM/HEC, 2006   Version: (A) 2006-04-12

A12.4 Case

Supreme Canning

The Supreme Canning Company (the true name of the company is disguised) is an independent US packer of tomato products (whole peeled tomatoes, chopped tomatoes, katsup, paste, pizza and other sauces, and tomatoes and zucchini). The company is located in California. Although it produces some cans with its own brand label, much of its output is canned for others and their brand names and labels put on the cans. It produces shelf-size cans for eventual sale at retail, gallon-size cans for use by restaurants and industrial users, and 55 gallon drums for use by others for repacking or further processing. Its annual processing capacity is in excess of 100,000 tons of tomatoes (processed during an operating season of approximately three months).

The California canning industry had suffered from heavy competition from abroad and inadequate local demand. A somewhat increasing domestic demand for speciality tomato products, especially pizza and other sauces, was not adequate to absorb increasing imports. The high value of the US dollar had made it difficult for US companies to sell abroad. Excess capacity and the resulting depressed prices had led to bankruptcy for a number of Californian canners. With the decline of the value of the dollar and the efforts of Japan to reduce its trade barriers and increase imports, it appeared that Supreme Canning Company might be able to get into the Japanese market. An inquiry received from a foodpacker and distributor in Japan indicated interest from that side. The Japanese firm produced and distributed a large number of products, was well known in Japan, and was much larger than the US company.

Since Supreme Canning Company did not have well-known brand names of its own, the company was interested in acting as a large-scale supplier of products made to customer specifications for use by the customer or distribution under the customer's label. Thus, the inquiry from Japan was most welcome.

The Japanese company invited senior executives of the American firm to visit its production facilities and offices in Japan. Both the president and chairman of the board of Supreme Canning Company had a four-day visit with the executives of the company in Japan. The president of the US company, who had some knowledge of Japanese business practice from studies at Stanford University and from his widespread reading, attempted to act as a guide to Japanese business practice. The chairman of the board had little knowledge of Japan, and viewed himself as a decisive man of action. Although there were a few minor misunderstandings, the visit was concluded successfully and the Americans invited the Japanese to visit their plant in California for four days.

The Japanese indicated their interest in the signing of a mutual letter of cooperation. The American chairman of the board was not interested in this, but rather wanted some specific agreements and contracts. As the time for the Japanese visit to the US drew near, the Japanese indicated that their president would not be able to come. Some senior executives would be able to meet, but they would only be able to spend two days instead of four. The vice-chairman of the board of the California company wrote asking why the Japanese were not going to send their president, and inquiring why they could not spend four days instead of two, 'as we did in Japan'. The letter was frank and direct. The tone was that of a person talking to an equal, but not with any great deal of politeness. The Japanese company decided to cancel the visit, and no further negotiations or serious contacts were made.

Some months later, a local businessman of Japanese extraction asked the president of Supreme Canning Company if some representatives of another (and even larger) Japanese food products producer and distributor could visit the plant. Four Japanese showed up along with the local businessman, who acted as interpreter and go-between. The three middle-aged Japanese produced their *meishi* (business cards) and introduced themselves. Each spoke some English. The older man did not present a card and was not introduced. When the president of the American company asked who he was, the go-between said, 'He's just one of the company's directors'. The visit concluded without discussion of any business possibilities, but this was to be expected in an initial visit from Japanese businessmen.

Supreme's president later found out the family name of the unknown visitor and immediately recognized it as being that of the president of the Japanese company. He assumed that the president of the Japanese company had come but had hidden the fact. He felt that he had been taken advantage of. He telephoned the go-between and told him that he never wanted anyone from that company in his plant again. From a description of the unknown visitor, a consultant to the company realized that the visitor was not the president of the Japanese company. Rather, it was the semi-retired father of the president. The father retained a position on the board of directors and maintained an active interest in company activities, but was not active in day-to-day affairs. Unlike his son who was fluent in English, he spoke only Japanese.

(Source: Duerr, pp. 85–7.[11])

Questions

1. Was the chairman of the American company wrong for not having found out in advance about Japanese business practices? Why did he not do so? (Answer the same questions in relation to the Japanese companies and US business practices.)

2. What are the principal cultural mistakes made (a) by the Americans from the Japanese perspective, and (b) by the Japanese from the American perspective?

3. What should the president of the American company do now?

A12.5   Critical incident

Scandinavian Tools Company

A major Swedish company that specialized in metal tools and factory equipment had created a French subsidiary a few years ago, based in Lyons, France. This plant was at first supplied with inputs (speciality steels, high-speed steels for blades and saws, etc.) from Sweden. It mostly produced and sold for the French markets and for exports to southern European markets, namely Italy, Spain and Portugal. The drive and energy for creating this new venture came from a young Swedish executive, Bo Svensson. Svensson had spent part of his time as a student, and then as a young engineer, in France. Thereafter he had been in a position to convince the top management of this large Swedish multinational company to launch a new subsidiary in France.

Svensson was very enthusiastic about France. He liked the country very much and had learnt the language, which he spoke fluently with a slight northern European accent. In the rush of starting the new company everything went smoothly. Svensson, who was chief executive officer of the French venture, knew how to secure customers and make them loyal; he also knew how to deal with the headquarters in Sweden. The market was growing quickly and competition was not particularly fierce. At the beginning, products were made in Sweden and then exported to France, where Svensson and the subsidiary dealt with marketing and distribution.

After a few years demand began to swell, so the parent company in Sweden decided to build a production plant in France. Machines and factory equipment for the new plant came from Sweden, and the factory was quickly operating at normal capacity. Svensson then hired a vice-president for administration, André Ribaud, an ambitious young executive, also in his thirties, with a law background. The two men got on well together, although their backgrounds and personal profiles were quite different. They shared the work and responsibilities: Svensson was in charge of relations with headquarters, marketing and the monitoring of financial performance; as plant manager, Ribaud was in charge of production operations, human resource management, cost accounting, monitoring cost prices and delivery delays.

After a few years it appeared that Svensson felt more and more relaxed in his job. Quite independent in his profitable subsidiary of (at that time) 200 employees located in a place remote from Sweden, he was able to have a very flexible timetable. He was also very free with personal expenses, which he was entitled to have reimbursed by the subsidiary: he simply had to sign his own expenses receipts. Svensson did not hesitate to use this facility: he did not make a clear distinction between his own money and the company's money. Svensson gradually got into the habit of abusing company-paid personal expenses. Ribaud was shocked. Svensson even went so far as to have the expenses of his mistress paid by the subsidiary.

Meanwhile, Ribaud was still working as efficiently as during the initial years. Growth had been impressive. Starting with a few employees in a two-room office in Lyons, the subsidiary had grown to a dynamic medium-sized company with more than 500 people on the payroll; Scandinavian Tools France had bought two plants from competitors. Following these changes, Ribaud's responsibilities quickly increased. He had involved himself completely and passionately with the company. He knew each member of staff personally and was respected by them.

Over time the relationship between the two men had considerably worsened. Svensson saw that Ribaud was winning more and more influence and power inside the company, and was well known by the customers. He felt jealous of him and tried his best to make Ribaud's life in the company difficult. Ribaud, on the other hand, increasingly resented the excessive expenses and the catty remarks of his boss, for whom he no longer felt any esteem. Svensson was a complex, energetic and whimsical character. His charisma and stamina had enabled him to seduce the French clients as well as the management staff at the headquarters in Sweden. The excellent financial performance of the French subsidiary had enabled him to retain the confidence of his superiors, who were also Swedish compatriots. They had trust in his management talents and therefore they allowed him a large degree of freedom. He had also established friendships with some of the senior directors at headquarters, especially with the director in charge of public relations. Svensson was well known at headquarters level, and he understood company 'politics' quite well.

After 15 years of almost steady growth, the market was reaching the stage of maturity. With the removal of borders within the EU, there were many acquisitions by large European and American competitors. The French subsidiary had lost some of its profitability. The middle managers were complaining to Ribaud about Svensson's lack of interest in the subsidiary and his mismanagement. Everybody believed that emergency decisions had to be taken before the situation got even worse. But Svensson turned a deaf ear to their complaints and remained unwilling to enter into discussion with either Ribaud or the other executives. The French were also amazed, and somewhat shocked, to see that there was no reaction from headquarters. It looked as if headquarters had little interest in the destiny of the French subsidiary. People at headquarters still seemed to have confidence in Svensson, who knew how to make them feel secure.

Ribaud did not feel comfortable in this situation. He felt that the financial balance of the subsidiary was threatened and that one factory would probably have to close in the near future. It also seemed to him that the interests of Swedish shareholders were not being adequately taken into account. Relations between Svensson and Ribaud were so damaged that Svensson was convinced that Ribaud was plotting against him. Svensson therefore systematically took a contradictory stance to Ribaud, at the risk of making inappropriate decisions that could possibly lead the subsidiary almost to the brink of bankruptcy.

Each time Ribaud brought up these problems during meetings with people from headquarters, Svensson abruptly interrupted him, shifting from English to Swedish in order to keep him out of the conversation. Under heavy pressure from some of the executives of the subsidiary who were about to resign and leave the company, Ribaud felt obliged to react. He had tried, during visits by members of the Swedish headquarters, to give them, indirectly, an idea of the situation. But he got the impression that he was not being heard. They had their own image of the chief executive officer which was clearly different.

In desperation, Ribaud decided to send an official note to the top management in Stockholm, in which he told them that he would be obliged to resign if nothing was done to put an end to the present disorder. He tried to write it as objectively as possible in a matter-of-fact style, citing evidence and hard facts. This was not an easy task since objectivity may prove difficult in such circumstances and, moreover, he was denouncing his boss, which is never very pleasant. He called one of the members of the top management in Stockholm whom he knew a little better than the others, explained about the letter and sent him a copy.

Question

What answer could he expect?

Appendix references

1. Pastore, Michael (2000), 'Web Pages by Language', Cyberatlas, 5 July, www.clickz.com/showPage.html?page=408521.
2. Ethnologue (1992), *Languages of the World*, Dallas, TX.
3. Anon (2003), 'China's Online Community Hits 68 Million', *CNET Asia*, 22 July, http://networks.silicon.com/broadband/0,39024661,10005249,00.htm.
4. Nilsen/Netratings (2003), 'Global Internet Population Grows an Average of Four Per Cent Year-over-Year', 20 February. www.netratings.com/pr/pr_030220_hk.pdf.
5. UNCTAD Secretariat (2002), *E-commerce and Development Report*, United Nations.
6. Kang, Kyeong Soon and Brian Corbett (2001), 'Effectiveness of Graphical Components in Web Site E-Commerce Application: A Cultural Perspective', *Electronic Journal of Information Systems in Developing Countries*, 7 (2), 1–6.
7. Hall, Patrick A.V. (2002), 'Bridging the Digital Divide', *Electronic Journal of Information Systems in Developing Countries*, 8 (1), 1–9.
8. Chowdhry, Amitav (2000), 'India Bursting at the Linguistic Seams', *The UNESCO Courrier*, April.
9. International Federation of Red Cross and Red Crescent Societies (IFRC) (2001), *Red Cross*. www.ifrc.org/.
10. Correll, Sharon (2003), 'Examples of Complex Rendering', *Non-Roman Scripts Initiative*, 21 April, www.scripts.sil.org/cms/scripts/page.php?site_id=nrsi&id=CmplxRndExamples.
11. Duerr, Mitsuko Saito (1989), 'Supreme Canning', in *International Marketing and Export Management*, Gerald Albaum and Jesper Strandskov and Edwin Duerr and Laurence Dowd, Eds. Reading, MA: Addison-Wesley.

13

Intercultural marketing communications 1: advertising

Advertising, which is based on language and communication, is the most culture-bound element of the marketing mix. When Polaroid introduced its cameras to Europe in the mid-1970s, it used the same advertising strategy as in the US, including TV commercials and print advertisements. These campaigns achieved little impact in raising awareness of instant photography and failed to pull customers into the stores. Later, the company developed very successful European campaigns on the basis of the strategy of Polaroid Switzerland, one of its smallest subsidiaries, located in a multicultural, central European country. The strategy of Polaroid Switzerland was to promote the functional uses of instant photography as a way to communicate with family and friends, which proved to be transferable in European countries.[1]

Even when companies try to adapt their advertising to suit a foreign culture there is still great scope for miscommunication. In 2004 Toyota introduced its Land Cruiser SUV to China, using an image of the Land Cruiser towing an unbranded truck, which happened to bear a very strong resemblance to the East-West brand Chinese-made military truck. Reports in local newspapers suggested an arrogant Toyota implied that the Chinese government was incompetent.[2]

This chapter could be subtitled 'national cultures, technological advances and the globalization of marketing communications'. As with previous chapters, it attempts to show that globalization is not the very simple process it is often believed to be. The first sections of this chapter describe cultural differences as they pertain to various aspects of advertising. Section 13.1 addresses general attitudes toward advertising (13.1). Sections 13.2 and 13.3 explore

how advertising strategy and creative standards are affected by local culture. Section 13.4 focuses on media selection, given differences in media availability and style. Finally, section 13.5 examines the globalization of advertising.

Advertising is strongly influenced by culture, as it is largely based on language and images. Cross-national differences continue to exist, for the simple reason that there are so many different languages. Moreover language, via words or images, is the strongest link between advertisers and their potential audiences in marketing communications.

The management process for marketing communication *per se* is not dependent on the particular country where the advertising campaign is launched. It should follow the six steps outlined in Figure 13.1. Logically, these steps should be taken in order, although feedback at any step is often necessary, especially after testing the campaign. The six basic steps are as follows:

1. Isolate the communication problem to be solved, such as increase brand awareness, change brand image, increase sales, differentiate from rival brands, take market share from the competition, etc.
2. Identify the relevant target population, including the consumer segments to be targeted and their sociodemographic characteristics, consumption habits, psychographic characteristics (consumer lifestyles and values), etc.
3. Define the marketing communication objective in terms of influencing the target population, at either the attitudinal or the behavioural level. Communication objectives include persuading consumers to like a product (improve product acceptance), encouraging people to try a product again (increase

sales by building consumer loyalty), enabling people to act, or educating the consumer, etc.

4. Select the advertising themes and a creative strategy, such as how the brand name will be portrayed and how the objective translates into copy.
5. Design a media plan, including which media to use, how to optimize the best media to reach the target audience, etc.
6. Implement and monitor the advertising campaign, including pre- and post-tests of advertisement effectiveness, research on different aspects (message recall, brand recall, aided brand recognition, actual influence on sales), etc.

The international dimension naturally has an influence on the implementation of each of these steps, but not an equal influence on each step. Many aspects of the local market need to be taken into consideration. For instance, before advertising life insurance in Tunisia, we need to take into account that this market is new, consumers have little knowledge about this type of financial service. For this reason,

the message might show a man and a woman watering a tree which grows by leaps and bounds. Finally, a large pine tree protects them with its branches, while they sit happily in its shade.

Certainly culture influences the objective, as the education of the consumer would be a basic objective in a country where life insurance is almost unknown. However, the changes caused by cultural differences are most obvious with respect to the creative strategy (step 4). There is a need to acknowledge and respect the values of Tunisian consumers, who belong to an Arab Muslim culture which is strongly linked to two European cultures (Italy and France). The complex mix of Muslim and Western culture has to be considered, since values that involve important matters (life and death, protecting one's family, betting on the future) are at stake.

The media plan will also be strongly influenced by local idiosyncrasies, including media availability, viewing habits and media regulations, which still differ greatly across countries. Conversely, the other steps in Figure 13.1 are not strongly affected by local

Figure 13.1 Main steps in the management of advertising communication

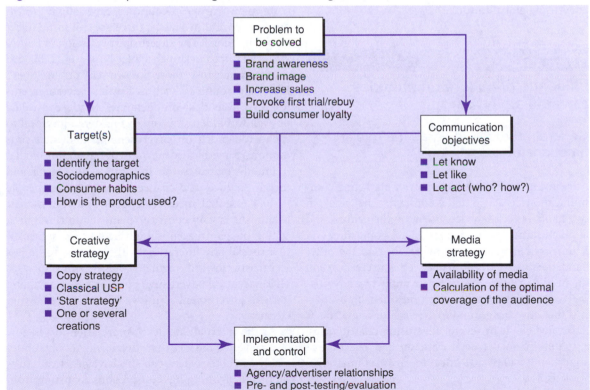

factors: defining a communication problem or a communication objective, or testing the effectiveness of a campaign, calls for a similar approach in each country.

Although the first three sections of this chapter favour customization of advertising, section 13.4 contrasts this. Technological advances such as satellite television and the global reach of the media have an undeniable impact on local attitudes and purchasing behaviour. The emergence of worldwide advertising media opens communication between cultures that previously were geographically and culturally separated, such as western and eastern Europe, or southern Europe and North Africa. Furthermore, it opens the way to new marketing communications in areas of the world which are culturally fragmented, for ethnic, linguistic or political reasons: Europe, South-East Asia, Central and Latin America. In this new style of international marketing communication, strictly national segments and audiences must be differentiated from cross-border regional segments and audiences. The choice of the appropriate media and language in which to advertise are therefore key success factors. The final section of this chapter deals with the issue of advertising globalization.

13.1

Influence of culture on attitudes towards advertising

General attitudes towards the role and functions of advertising

Advertising, which is a large part of marketing communications, is a field that is constantly changing. On one hand, it is closely dependent on the cultural and linguistic attitudes of the local target population and it mirrors changing social behaviour. On the other hand, the relative freedom of advertising creation and the need to capture the audience imply that advertising is sometimes challenging and often innovative. It is therefore the ground for societal debates. This is illustrated below by several advertising-related issues, e.g. 'publiphobia' (social criticism and rejection of advertising) and attitudes towards comparative advertising.

General attitudes towards publicity and 'publiphobia'

One view that has always existed is that advertising is nothing more than wasted money. This negative view of advertising is vaguely rooted in the ideas of the doctrine of St Simon, in which only production brings economic value to society. Retail sales and the service industry, including advertising, are considered to be parasitic activities. This view is often reinforced by the (misleading) argument that consumers pay for advertising costs, which are included in the price of the product they buy.

This social representation was a part of the Marxist doctrine, and its influence on real socialism often produced disastrous consequences, such as shortages of basic staple items. This was largely caused by the absence of any effective distribution system through which products would have been made available to consumers. The shortage was further reinforced by the absence of a marketing communication system to inform people which goods and services were available to them, when, where and at what price (traditional and useful functions!).

In many European countries, especially in northern Europe and in France, there are still some traces of 'publiphobia'. The advertising profession in France was even forced to launch a huge poster and billboard campaign against those known as 'publiphobes'. In certain countries such as Kuwait, advertisements for pharmaceutical products are strictly controlled or even forbidden. It is often considered immoral to spend too much on advertisements and sales promotions for ethical drugs, on the assumption that it unduly increases the final price of a drug and thereby reduces the chances of the poorest people to buy essential medical supplies and regain their health. As a consequence, many countries put a ceiling on pharmaceutical advertising, or subject it to a special tax. Interestingly, there seems to be less scepticism toward regulated advertising, such as pharmaceutical advertising, potentially due to a false sense of government scrutiny, at least in the US and Germany.[3]

At the international level, more attention is now being given to the idea that advertising, though undeniably useful to society, can also have negative results such as encouraging conspicuous consumption, harmful consumption, and the creation of wants that cannot be satisfied. An example of harmful consumption that has received considerable attention recently is the advertising of junk-food aimed at children, in light of the growing childhood obesity in many countries.[4] To combat these potential negative effects the economic and social committee of the UN (United Nations) has proposed a resolution that would protect consumers in developing nations.

Managers and consumers seem to differ in their attitudes towards advertising. For instance, across 14 countries, the majority of managers find advertising to be quite factual (75 per cent), to provide important information about products or services (71 per cent) and to be both entertaining and informative (78 per cent), whereas consumers rate it at a lower level on these dimensions (61, 48 and 50 per cent, respectively).[5] More than 50 per cent of consumers, on average across the 14 countries, tend to have a negative opinion about the information content of advertising.[5] This tends to differ across countries. For instance, young consumers from various countries (the United States, Denmark, Greece, India and New Zealand) differ in the perception of advertising in general: in the US they were more affective (with comments like entertaining and annoying) and less critical than the other countries.[6] Only 22 per cent of their statements indicated potentially negative effects, compared with 60 per cent for Greeks and 51 per cent for the Indians.[6] Similarly, young New Zealand consumers, who come from a country where advertising regulation is quite strict, had the most negative views of advertisements as 'meaningless repetition' or 'interrupt good programmes'.[6] Furthermore, people from developing countries are often more critical of advertising and more concerned with the impact of advertising on product costs than people from developed countries.[7]

Attitudes towards comparative advertising

Attitudes towards comparative advertising basically depend on the responses that are given in a particular society to the following questions:

1. What is the social function of comparative advertising?

2. What are the prevailing arguments concerning the legitimacy of comparative advertising?
3. How should competition between brands be facilitated?
4. Does comparative advertising result in fooling the consumer by using disputable information to praise one's own brand and put down others?

Website link 13.1

Find a quick checklist for using comparative advertising without getting sued:
http://www.findlaw.com.au/article/7864.htm.

Socially dominant responses to these questions directly influence comparative advertising regulations in a given country. In some countries, comparative advertising is held in low esteem. This is the case in France, where it has traditionally been considered a denigration of competing brands. It was forbidden under Article 1382 of the Civil Code. In order for the advertisement to be considered comparative, there needed only to be a comparison of two competing products, even if the terms are not inaccurate, tendentious or antagonistic. For instance, about 20 years ago Lip, the top French watchmaker, was under attack by Timex, the top company in the American watch industry. The main feature of Timex's Kelton brand was its distribution through tobacconists, whereas Lip was confined to the more traditional channel of watch and jewellery stores. With the purpose of counter-attacking in order to regain market share, Lip began an advertising campaign that showed a broken watch in an ashtray surrounded by a thick cloud of smoke, with a slogan that read: 'The watches sold in tobacconists are like cigarettes: they go up in smoke.' As a consequence, Lip was forced to pay heavy penalties to Timex.

While comparative advertising is allowed in many but not all countries, it invites scrupulous attention from competitors. For instance, Johnson and Johnson was awarded damages after Unilever's advertisements were found to be misleading and breach section 52 of the Trade Practices Act 1974. Unilever's advertisement claimed that '7 out of 10 Johnson's Holiday Skin users preferred new Dove Summer Glow', which was supported by a statement about marketing research: 'In use test of 105 women conducted in Australia by a leading research company in March 2006.' In this case, Unilever made several mistakes. First, the advertisements featured two tanning products, but the market research was only conducted on one product. Second, advertisements featured women of all ages, but the market research was only with women between 25 and 45. Third, the market research question asked participants a general question about 'Which product did you prefer?', for which the answers could have related to many aspects of the product, but the advertisement emphasized the tanning qualities of the product. Each of these mistakes cost them dearly.

Where legislation allows comparative advertising, it usually requires that advertising be based on features of the competing products or services that are material, relevant, verifiable and fairly chosen. Comparisons should be objective and should not discredit competitors or their brands. False or misleading comparative advertising is illegal under both United States and European legislation.[8] A recent report by Romano.[8] details many different examples and examined legal cases regarding comparative advertising in both the United States and France.

The basic arguments in favour of comparative advertising seem to make sense: it facilitates consumer information, choice and competition between brands. Hence automobile advertising frequently gives performance statistics of competing models, such as fuel consumption, speed and comfort. Opponents of comparative advertising argue that truly objective comparisons would need to be handled by completely independent testing organizations. As a consequence, comparative advertising would often end up giving either no information at all or partly misleading information to the consumer. Opponents of comparative advertising also implicitly support the idea that it is necessary to enforce moral business relationships between competitors. The role of marketing communications, by means of advertising, is to praise the virtues of their own product, not to put down the virtues of competing products (however indirectly).

James and Hensel (p. 55) emphasize the possibility that malicious comparative advertising can be negative. They take the example of a Kentucky Fried Chicken advertisement that made explicit reference to McDonald's:

The first ad, sponsored by Kentucky Fried Chicken, opens with a red-haired Ronald McDonald surrogate (sans clown outfit) being interrogated by a Senate 'subcommittee' rivalling the likes of that faced by Oliver North. Allegations are raised as to the defendant's lack of expertise and questionable ability to provide quality chicken (McNuggets) to the public. When pressed as to how he expects to be able to sell chicken given this lack of expertise, 'Ronald' responds, 'Toys, lots of toys!', while the man who appears to be his legal counsel buries his head in his hands.[9]

There is also evidence that the effectiveness of comparative advertising is likely to differ across countries. For instance, comparative advertising is perceived more favourably in the US than in South Korea.[10] Here, societal norms may be in play, as direct comparative ads have only been officially permitted in South Korea since 2001, while they are common in the US.

Website link 13.2

Find a top ten list of advertising mistakes:
http://www.mcmillan.ca/upload/publication.pdf.

13.2

Culture and advertising strategy

The function of an advertisement is to communicate a message to an audience based on two major elements: strategy and execution. While there is some overlap between these categories, advertising strategy comprises 'what is said' and execution concerns more 'how it is said'. Advertising strategy relates to the types of appeals used, the themes developed and the overall communication style, whether (1) direct or indirect, (2) explicit or implicit or (3) rational or emotional. Advertising style in communicating with the audiences of viewers, readers or listeners can be roughly divided into three basic categories: (1) persuasive, (2) informative and (3) oneiric, that is dream oriented.

Advertising appeals

A limited number of different advertising appeals can be identified based on common themes and concepts.

Although all of them are used worldwide, cultural sensitivity is portrayed through the varying usage of these same appeals.[11] For instance, the same ten basic appeals are used in the US and Japan, but the Japanese preference for implicit, indirect communication is reflected by a relative lack of hard-sell appeals.[12] Instead, there are four times as many soft-sell appeals in Japanese as in US advertisements.[12] Further, in accordance with Japanese values, there are also more advertisements that stress tradition and the veneration of the elderly.[12] The product-merit appeal, on the other hand, is dominant in US advertisements.[13] As stated by Lin (pp. 44–5), Japanese cultural values stress status symbols in advertising whereas Americans place emphasis on individual determinism:

Japanese advertisements reveal an indulgence with sensitive crafting of product image and appearance slated within a subtle frame of reference. This contrasts sharply with the American fixation on presenting facts and attributes to showcase product superiority . . . [In Japan] 'boasting' of product quality and 'bribing' consumers into submission are not in line with the custom of respectful treatment of consumers and respectable projection of company image. These same rationales explain why comparative and testimonial messages are not a desirable form of advertising in Japan.[14]

Similar patterns, in terms of soft-sell and traditional appeals, have been found across many Asian countries. For instance, Chinese advertising uses soft-sell appeals, elderly and tradition, oneness with nature and group consensus and status appeals more often than in the US, where there is more frequent use of the hard-sell appeal, time oriented and individualist appeals, as well as product merit appeals.[15] Taiwanese advertising is generally more effective when traditional (e.g. consensus, soft sell, veneration of elderly and traditional) and transformational appeals (e.g. user image, brand image, usage occasion) are used than relying on informational appeals (e.g. comparative, unique, pre-emptive) and Westernized appeals (e.g. independence, modernity, product merit).[16] However, there are also many differences in these countries. For instance, Chinese magazines are also likely to use product merit appeals and status appeals,[17] which is in contrast to Japanese advertisements.

Differences in the use of symbolic and informational appeals have been found in many countries.

For instance, in Japan there is little relationship between advertisement content and the advertised product, only brief dialogue in TV commercials with minimal explanatory content, priority placed on company trust rather than product quality, etc.[18,19] In Taiwan more informational and obligation related strategies are employed, in contrast to argument and imitation in the US and symbolic strategies in France.[20] Swedish ads also depend more on symbolic associations than US advertisements.[21]

Italian and French advertisements often appear as very dream oriented: viewers and readers are supposedly willing to escape from the real world. This oneiric style of advertisement enhances the fantasy of the consumer and emphasizes the image of satisfaction and enjoyment. It does so in a rather holistic way (the product and its benefits tend to be implied rather than actually shown). The oneiric style does not really concentrate on actual buying and consumption experiences. The dream-like dimension that surrounds the product is favoured at any price. Relying on the dream oriented part of the advertising audience is typical of the 'Séguéla' doctrine.

Germans, unlike the French or the Italians, are known to have a taste for highly informative advertising. A young German advertising specialist criticizes French advertising, and especially the most well-known publicist, Jacques Séguéla (co-founder of the RSCG agency, reputed for oneiric, dream-oriented copy strategies):

Certainly it [French advertising] is better than German advertising, but the French should take care not to sink in art for art's sake or in séguélomania. The message of the Citroen advertising campaign is horrible. What is the link between the Great Wall of China and Citroen? Are Citroen cars manufactured there now?[22]

A significant degree of similarity in advertising strategies only appears in culturally close countries like Australia, Canada, the US, and the UK. Overall, advertising agencies in all four use similar strategies in a number of cases. Problem solution is most popular, followed by USP (unique selling proposition), emotion, brand image and brand identity.[23,24]

At least some of the differences in emphasis across cultures may be due to a difference in the diagnosticity of information. For instance, there is evidence that the informational value or diagnosticity is greater for consensus information[25] and source expertise[26] in more collectivist cultures than it is in more individualist cultures.

The information content of advertising: cross-national differences

The information content of advertising is a key issue, since it shows whether the strategy focuses on information, persuasion or dream orientation. The information content will naturally be lower when the two last avenues are followed. Ever since the first systematic evaluation of information content by Resnik and Stern,[27] the informativeness of advertising has received considerable attention all over the world. Many researchers compared their country's advertising situation to that of the US. The most important findings of these studies are that information content varies by country – but also by broadcast time, product type and medium.[28]

Overall, it appears that US television advertising is less informative than most other television advertising worldwide. US television advertising contains less information than Australian.[29] French-Canadian,[30] Spanish,[31] Ecuadorian,[32] Irish,[33] French and German[34] and Japanese television advertising.[35] Only British TV advertisements seem to contain less information than US advertisements.[36] When other types of media are examined, a different pattern emerges. For instance, the US had higher levels of information cues than Japan, China and South Korea when television, radio and print advertising were considered.[37] In all countries, television and radio advertising were generally less informative than print advertising.[37]

In a meta-analysis of 59 studies about information content, an interesting result from a cross-cultural perspective is that advertising in developed countries is more informative than in developing countries.[38] Kaynak and Ghauri (p. 127)[39] explain that in developed countries advertising copy in general contains more writing and technical information, because most consumers have a high level of literacy and education: 'Unlike Canada and Sweden, most of the advertising copy used by the Turkish agencies is persuasive in nature rather than informative.' The Turkish word for advertising is *Reklam*: this corresponds to a more traditional vision of advertising, where persuasion and slogans are the key issues. Callow and Schiffman[40] investigated how students process visual images in print ads. Interestingly, consumers from the Philippines (a higher context culture) were more able to derive the implicit meaning from the visual images than consumers from the US.

A closer look at some of the many studies that compare advertising across countries offers additional valuable insights. Information content varies greatly from one country to another. Although product types and other environmental factors, such as the competitive environment and government regulation have an influence on information content, culture is the most important factor in explaining how much and what kind of information can be found in advertising. Both the types of information cues and the quantity of information are culture-bound. Whereas some targets, such as in the US, prefer rational, tangible cues, others expect emotional and more 'subjective' information. This is why many Japanese advertisements present 'company-sponsored research', an element that is much less important in Western countries. Even in neighbouring countries with a similar economic environment, such as France and Germany, information content varies fundamentally.[34] Because information reduces uncertainty, cultures known to avoid uncertainty such as the German culture.[41] will always have a tendency to ask for more information than cultures that have lower uncertainty avoidance. Furthermore, communication in Germany is based on explicit messages.

Assuming that consumers are rational information seekers (which is not true in most cultural contexts), advertising content should be related to information sought by consumers in order to improve the relevance of their choices. If for any reason consumers are not 'good' (motivated and educated) information seekers, they will be less sensitive to the information content of an advertisement. This is the case if they do not directly use advertising information in their brand evaluations in order to reduce perceived risks when purchasing. For instance, Mexicans generally display a much lower level of perceived risk related to their purchases than Americans, possibly due to the somewhat fatalistic tradition which exists in Mexican society versus the 'master-of-destiny' orientation in the US that implies a greater risk of being disappointed.[42] Thus Mexican consumers and, more generally, consumers belonging to fatalistic oriented societies react more easily to persuasive messages (the brand name repeated numerous times) and also oneiric messages (a dream that allows one to escape from a daily life that is not always bright).

Finally, it should be noted that the types of information cues vary by country. While Japanese advertisements, for example, have very few price, warranty and guarantee cues compared to US advertisements, they carry a much higher number of packaging cues.[12,14,35] Korean advertisements include the price 38 per cent of the time, whereas in other countries the average is between 8 per cent (India) and 16 per cent (France)[43] and the British prefer not to mention money at all.[44] French commercials present more quality information and new ideas, and in Taiwan information about product availability and special offers are significantly higher than average.[20]

As a general rule, advertising strategy must fit with the local orientation concerning information content and style of advertising. Advertising strategies that follow purely informative, oneiric or persuasive routes will have to be considered cautiously as applicants for cross-border transfer.

13.3

Culture and advertising execution

Once the advertising strategy is defined, execution remains a quite significant cross-cultural 'filter', since meaning transfer is fine-tuned through executional details, most of which are strongly culture-bound. This section reviews the empirical literature in the following domains of advertising execution: (1) language; (2) humour; (3) characters and roles represented; (4) the influence of mores and religion, and (5) visual elements of advertising.

Language

Advertisements usually have several text elements (catchphrase, product description, slogan) and use colloquial language, very subtle yet precise in meaning. The character and structure of these elements heavily influence the advertisement's effectiveness, while language differences are the strongest barrier to effective communication.

Duncan and Ramaprasad[45] show that companies which tend to favour standardized international advertising strategy (68 per cent) and standardized execution (54 per cent), standardize language much less (11 per cent) across all countries. In order to be effective in a French context, 50 per cent of all words in an advertisement should be nouns and verbs, the percentage of words exceeding three syllables should not be higher than 10 per cent, most of the long words should be familiar words, and sentences should have an average length of about 10–13 words.[46] Furthermore, advertising language often uses colloquial words or slang, which are particular to local people and as such are difficult to find in dictionaries. The viewer or the listener understands messages all the more readily when colloquial speech expresses the delicate messages of daily life – sentiments, sensations, family relations, friendships, love affairs – that are reflected in advertising. Translating colloquial speech is difficult since it uses idiomatic expressions, which change from one language to another.

Effective textual elements, including the use of foreign vocabulary in an advertisement, vary from one culture to another. English is the most frequently spoken second language.[47] The use of English in foreign advertising can convey cosmopolitan values,[48] or it can confuse the meaning, as English knowledge is only superficial in most countries.[47] As such, only certain elements, such as the brand and product class, are likely to be in English, whereas the body copy is more often in the local language.[49]

Nelson and Paek[49] found multinational products were more likely to advertise in English than local products in *Cosmopolitan* magazine, with the highest English-language use in the US and India (where English is one official language) and the lowest in France and Brazil. Somewhere in between lies Asian advertising, where South Korea had the most English followed by Thailand and then China, where English was often used by multinationals for the brand name, product class name, and slogan, but the local language was mostly used for body text.[49]

There may be some recognition of global brand names.[50] but when information is conveyed it is best to use the local language.

A very large percentage of Asian advertisements contain at least some English – and in some rare cases French – words.[51,52] Since the most important function of this foreign vocabulary ultimately is to achieve a positive 'cosmopolitan' or country-of-origin positioning, its use depends on product type and product origin. Those products consumers use in a similar manner, generally have more standardization in their advertising, such as high-tech goods,[53] personal care products,[54] and perfume.[55] However, it would be fundamentally wrong to conclude from the heavy use of foreign words in Asian countries that there is a trend towards a globalization of advertising language. The Japanese culture in particular uses English loanwords for their symbolic weight, however the symbolism is embedded in Japanese traditions.[52]

Since only a minority of persons worldwide can understand English, there are problems with the comprehension of foreign words. Multinational companies often translate directly from the origin copy, but there are many constraints, including local nuances and space. Differing language structures means that the textual part of advertisements grows by about 25 per cent when English is translated into Roman languages, and by 30 per cent when translated into Germanic languages.[56] This can alter the overall layout of the advertisement, and decrease the relative impact of visual elements.

As argued in the previous chapter, the slogan 'Put a tiger in your tank' is not as standardized as it might seem. At first reading, it seems as if it would be fully equivalent across countries, but the interpretation differs as to where the power source is located, engine or tank. Examples of translation and conceptual equivalence problems abound, especially for advertising campaigns in which message standardization has been attempted. A full rewrite is usually needed to transpose slogans from one language to another. This implies a thorough search for words that have the same intended meaning as in the source language, provided that these can be found (see section 6.2).

Even a 'good' translation of a message into each target country's language does not guarantee uniform comprehension. The meaning attributed to certain words depends on association norms that differ cross-culturally. When the English word 'quiet' is translated into German (*ruhig*) and French (*tranquille*), German consumers mostly think of a forest (41 per cent), sleep (35 per cent), church (20 per cent), but also of a cemetery (13 per cent) and a bed (8 per cent).[57] The pictorial associations of their French counterparts are fundamentally different and less homogeneous (countryside: 13 per cent; forest: 11 per cent; house: 9 per cent; library: 5 per cent, etc.). The congruency coefficient between both groups for the word 'quiet' is only 0.17.[57]

Where television advertisements must be easily transferable across countries, there should be a heavy emphasis on visual elements with voice-overs in the local language. For instance, television advertisements aimed at a European audience often use a script where the characters do not speak to the audience or to each other; a voice-over message is added to the image track. This avoids the drawbacks associated with dubbing. Most people lip-read unconsciously, at least in part. When watching a dubbed commercial, many people feel uneasy about the lag between lip movements and sounds.

Written communication should also be avoided in messages targeted at a multilingual audience. For instance, a commercial for a detergent where a housewife is handed a packet of '*Waschpulver*' will be identified by British, Italian or French viewers as foreign or German. A few years ago, IBM used the character of Charlie Chaplin and the mode of a silent film in a multinational campaign, the goal of which was to foster corporate image. This allowed the advertisement to be used in any country of the world. Written messages can also be reduced or avoided in magazine advertisements. Occasionally we see text in its original foreign language in ads for ethnic products. Here, the text must be short and strongly support an ethnic image (French for perfume, English for a large international newspaper, Italian for luxury leather shoes, etc.). If possible, some 'borrowed' words should be included, as the text must be universally understood, although not necessarily in full detail. The message should make sense with respect to the halo of meanings around the product proposal.

Several studies have focused on how bilinguals process information in advertising. Generally, bilinguals have been found to interpret information differently when they read in one or other language. The language tends to cue the salience of a self-concept related to one or other culture and their interpretation and behaviour changes. For instance, when bilinguals from Hong Kong were exposed to English advertisements and responded in English their reactions were more similar to the Canadian sample than when they reacted to the Chinese version.[58] Specifically, they perceived greater source honesty, less forcefulness on the part of the source and reported a more positive attitude toward the brand than those who were exposed to the Chinese advertisement and responded in Chinese.[58] Other effects found include a high level of congruity between picture and text increasing memory for second-language advertisements for Spanish–English bilinguals.[59]

Humour

Humour can be based on gestures, situations, or words. It is sometimes involuntary. For instance, when Charles De Gaulle decided to retire from public life, the British ambassador and his wife threw a gala dinner party in his honour. At the dinner table the ambassador's wife was talking with Madame De Gaulle: 'Your husband has been such a prominent public figure, such a presence on the French and International scene for so many years! How quiet retirement will seem in comparison. What are you most looking forward to in these retirement years?' 'A penis', replied Madame De Gaulle. A huge hush fell over the table. Everyone heard her answer . . . and no one knew what to say next. Le Grand Charles leaned over to his wife and said: 'Ma chérie, I believe ze English pronounce zat word, "appiness!"' (retrieved from www.gdargaud.net/Humor/French.html).

The basic concept of humour is universal since it can be found in every culture and in any country's advertising; however, preferences for types of humour vary cross-culturally.[60] Globally, most humour has an incongruity-resolution structure: people develop expectations based on category norms that are capable of being violated, sometimes in a humorous way;[61] a naked businessman or a clothed ape speaking to the audience are examples of incongruity-based humour. Some cross-cultural

support exists for a positive affect-based effect of humour in advertising, where the perceived funniness of an advertisement, liking the advertisement, and liking the product are all linked.[62] However, a closer look at the use of humour also reveals notable cultural differences.

> **Website link 13.3**
>
> A huge video collection of funny ads from all over the world: **http://www.veryfunnyads.com**.

First, the percentage of advertisements intending to be humorous varies across countries. For instance, there is generally a higher percentage of humorous advertisements in television commercials in the UK than in the US and France, and even less in Germany.[23,63]

Second, although the incongruity principle can be found in the advertising of different countries, the relative importance of such humour varies. For instance, more incongruent contrasts are found in German (92 per cent) and Thai (82 per cent) than in American (69 per cent) and Korean ads (57 per cent).[64]

Third, the kind of humour preferred by each target culture differs. Whereas English people are known for their black humour, Germans seem to prefer humour based on gloating.[65] Americans use more self-defeating and self-enhancing humour than Arabs, while both Arabs and Americans use about the same amount of affiliative (jokes and anecdotes) and aggressive (demeaning others) humour.[66] The latter would not be much appreciated in Japan, where slapstick or demeaning humour is seldom seen in advertising. Instead the Japanese make humorous dramatizations of situations involving family members, colleagues, neighbours, etc., to create a bond of mutual feelings between the advertiser and the viewer.[67] Additionally, black and earthy humour is also present in Japanese commercials. Subjects such as diseases, wars or funerals, which are taboo themes in the US, are treated with humour in some Japanese advertisements.[18]

Finally, in countries with high collectivism scores, significantly more characters are depicted in humorous advertisements than in more individualistic countries.[64] Similarly, in countries high on the power distance dimension (e.g. Korea, Thailand) characters portrayed in humorous advertisements are much more likely to have an unequal status than in low power distance countries (e.g. US and Germany).[64]

Thus, it appears that humour can be an element of standardization in cross-cultural advertising, especially when it is based on the incongruity principle, which has a fairly global appeal. Nevertheless, the creative presentation of humour in advertisements needs considerable adaptation to be effective.[64]

Characters and roles represented in advertisements

When depicting characters, advertising must be extremely careful. Whether it is the age, dress or situation of a character that is represented, nothing should be left to chance in advertising messages. In general, target audiences prefer characters with which they can identify.[68] Since the physique of a person – and even more so a hero-like person depicted in an advertisement – is a clear manifestation of a particular culture, the choice of characters needs particular attention in cross-cultural advertising.

Advertising is often accused of perpetuating traditional social roles, sometimes even acting as a vehicle for outdated ideas. However, the real situation is much more ambiguous: in most countries advertising acts as an agent of both social change and social maintenance. Advertising creation sometimes acts as an agent of change because social challenge is a method of capturing the attention of the audience, and because social innovators are also opinion leaders for new products and new ways of life. Advertising also reinforces traditional and sometimes old-fashioned social patterns, as it is the mirror of society as a whole. Potential dangers are brought home by Prendergast and colleagues,[69] who found that exposure to advertising was linked to eating disorders when they examined the relationship between the 'ideal woman' depicted in advertising and self-reports of eating disorders and body image dissatisfaction among females in Hong Kong.

Another important issue related to characters in advertising is the portrayal of gender roles. Several cross-cultural investigations have examined role portrayal in magazine and TV advertising. They all found that advertising reflects traditional stereotypes of male and female roles to varying degrees. In general, women are mostly shown in non-working roles, often in the home, and in decorative roles. When women appear in working roles, they are more likely than men to be depicted in clerical, blue-collar or secretarial roles. Although studies show that sex role stereotypes are found in all cultures, differences exist. Some of the factors we expect sex role stereotyping to differ by include masculinity, tradition and religion.

Several researchers have found that sex role stereotyping differs between countries classed as more masculine versus feminine. For instance, in web advertisements from South Korea (a more feminine culture) there was a greater proportion of female main characters and more depictions of relationships, compared to web advertisements from the more masculine US.[70] In masculine cultures, such as the US and Japan, women are less likely to appear in working situations.[71,72] This pattern is also depicted in the moderately masculine cultures of Malaysia and Singapore where men are more often depicted in working or leisure situations and woman as homemakers.[73] In Hong Kong and Singapore men are also more likely to be depicted as product authorities and women as product users.[74] In contrast, Swedish (more feminine) magazine advertisements are more likely to depict women in working and recreational roles, and far less likely to depict women in decorative roles than in US (more masculine) magazine advertisements.[75] In Swedish advertising, women were never depicted in housework and childcare activities, whereas they were shown twice as often as males in such situations in US advertisements.[76]

> ### Website link 13.4
>
> See how Kellogg's Special K successfully used a fitness ball promotion to target body shape conscious women in the UK: http://www.isp.org.uk/displaycs.php?cs=81&rs=1.

Sex role stereotyping also appears to be more prevalent in more traditional and religious cultures.

For instance, a Malaysian television channel oriented towards a mostly Muslim target audience typically depicts men in exciting and independent top executive roles and women as housewives who stay at home to look after the family.[77] In contrast, on Singapore television, men were more likely to be depicted in middle management roles, whereas women were depicted in white-collar and service occupations or in a more modern context: as young, attractive and concerned with beauty. Interestingly, the portrayal of women on a second Malaysian channel, targeted to both Malaysian and Singaporean audiences, shows a compromise between the stereotypes held by both audiences. However, this is not always the case. In a comparative study of three fairly masculine countries (Australia, Mexico, the US), we might expect tradition to play a role. That is, we might expect a more traditional image in Mexico and a more modern image in the US and Australia. Mary Gilly[78] analysed 12 hours of programmes for each country: 275 American, 204 Mexican and 138 Australian commercials were viewed. In both the US and Mexico (as opposed to Australia) men, more often than women, were shown in roles of authority or expertise with respect to the product, whereas women were more often shown in the role of the consumer. In addition, in the US a woman was more likely to be shown at home.

However, these generalizations do not always exist. For instance, no difference was found in gender stereotyping in advertising between the UK (masculine) and The Netherlands (feminine)[79] or between the US and the more traditional Arab world (comprising 12 Middle Eastern countries and 10 African countries).[80] The main difference, in the Arab world was that women were used mainly when their presence related to the advertised product.

We need to check our intuition with facts from the country. It seems that Australia and Sweden have a more balanced and non-traditional representation of men and women in their advertising than, for example, the US and Singapore. Malaysia, and to a lesser extent Mexico, where religious values and tradition are more important, display the biggest sex role differences in advertising. Whereas on Malaysian (Muslim) television the portrayal of the sexes lags behind changes in society (i.e. the number of housewives is grossly exaggerated; see Wee et al.[77])

marketers in countries like Sweden have a more proactive approach in defining sex roles, thus creating new trends. Even across countries with quite similar levels of development, stronger traditional values in the society, such as in Japan compared with the US, cause women's roles to be portrayed more traditionally.[12]

There is room for some standardization if both genders are depicted in recreational (men more than women) or decorative roles (women more than men). This is likely to be acceptable, for example, in the US, Sweden and The Netherlands.[81] Generally, in any country's advertising, women should ideally be young. However, the preference for beauty types presented in advertising differs across societies.[82] For instance, the Wash & Go shampoo advertising campaign by Procter & Gamble was standardized across Europe in terms of its core theme, but it was adapted locally using different beauty presenters appropriate for each country.

Similarly, a certain degree of standardization can be found regarding the use of Western models in Asian countries.[83] Such models can be found in more than one-third of magazine advertisements in Hong Kong, Taiwan, Japan and South Korea, and they are particularly frequent in advertisements for products from the West, notably personal care products.[54] At the same time however, many advertisements reviewed in those countries had a completely local character.

Cross-cultural differences are also observed with regard to the portrayal of the elderly in advertising. A country's degree of orientation towards traditional values has an impact on the portrayal of the elderly in advertising messages. For instance, Japanese magazine advertisements show more respect towards the elderly than their American counterparts.[12,13] However, common stereotypes are not always confirmed. For example, in Latin America the elderly are not presented more frequently in a family setting or as celebrity endorsers, nor is there a greater proportion of elderly males than in the US.[84]

Traditional roles that are not present in the source culture may unintentionally appear when they are interpreted by the target culture. A 'spurious' meaning may appear in the target culture which was not intended by the advertiser in the source culture. For instance, Douglas and Dubois[85] give the example of a brandy advertisement that was targeted at the South African Bantu market. It showed a couple seated at a table with a bottle superimposed over them. Many Bantus thought that the woman was carrying the bottle on her head, as many traditional African women do. This created an unintended and confusing contrast between the traditional, local aspect of the characters and situation and the modern, imported aspect of the product. It therefore prevented clear and effective marketing communication.[85]

As a consequence, one should study a representative sample of local advertising messages, whether commercials or magazine advertisements. This will give a better idea of the sex roles, age roles, typical everyday situations and social relations in a particular country. It can be achieved by conducting a systematic content analysis of newspaper, magazine and television advertisements (at least several dozen of each). An advertisement should always be created in cooperation with a native of the target culture, who acts as a test audience; in the case of internationally standardized advertisements, messages in the various linguistic/cultural contexts should be reviewed by natives of each target culture or subcultures.

In order to avoid creating spurious associations, the advertising script may go so far as to avoid presenting any characters at all, especially if the target audience is not clearly defined or too large, making the choice of characters a difficult one. For instance, in a Renault advertisement, a car without a driver was shown moving in the middle of a scale-model city. This avoided the choice of a specific character, whose age, sex or appearance would influence the product's positioning undesirably. However, a car without a driver may be negatively interpreted in countries where such a situation is associated with a safety issue (runaway car) or a distortion of reality (how can a car drive without a driver?). This may inhibit a positive response to the message.

The influence of mores and religion

It is crucial to choose the appropriate symbolic elements by which cultural meanings about products and services may be communicated to the audience. Mores and religion act as filters of advertising messages, transforming factual information into culturally interpreted meaning (e.g. a naked woman washing her hair in her bathroom) into elements of culture-based meaning (it incites people to sexual debauchery). If one focuses on information rather than meaning, it is difficult to become aware of the influence of mores and religion on advertising messages. This point is illustrated by the example of advertising in Saudi Arabia (Box 13.1).

Many of us are superstitious, even though we may deny it. Rarely will advertisements show people walking under ladders, unless, for the sake of humour, something happens to them. This is proof of the force of superstition. The social habits of daily life also play a role, particularly those that are related to what is (locally) considered polite, courteous or hospitable. In this way, a well-known brand of tea alienated the Saudi public when it showed a Saudi host using his left hand to serve tea to one of his guests. Moreover, the guest was wearing shoes, which is considered in Saudi Arabia to be inappropriate.

The influence of religion on advertising, exemplified by the Muslim religion, although strong, is not uniform across countries or individual viewers within a particular country (see Al-Makaty and colleagues,[86] for the case of Saudi Arabia). Many differences depend on the religious belief or zeal held by individuals and groups. For instance, strict Muslims are more interested in, and especially have a higher recall of, non-contentious advertisements whereas lenient Muslims show no difference between advertisement containing elements considered to be against the principles of Islam or not.[87] Furthermore, sensitive issues such as family planning can be treated successfully if creation adequately goes beyond traditional beliefs and taboos.[88]

Generally the relationship between men and women, depicted by advertising, is a ticklish problem. For instance, advertising for beer on the Turkish market portrays men and women drinking the beer in a social setting at home.[89] The emphasis on a family setting as the consumption situation overcomes the problems with showing men and women together in the predominantly male institutions of coffee houses and beer pubs, which would violate Turkish customs of courtship and social interaction.

Attitudes towards nudity differ from one country to another. French advertising is considered to have more nudity than most other countries. It is well

Box 13.1

The influence of religion on advertising in Saudi Arabia

The Saudi legal system is unique in the sense that it identifies law with the personal command of the 'one and only god, the Almighty'. The Islamic laws known as *Sharia* are the master framework to which all legislation, existing and proposed, is referred and with which it must be compatible. The *Sharia* is a comprehensive code governing the duties, morals and behaviour of all Muslims, individually and collectively in all areas of life, including commerce. *Sharia* is derived from two basic sources, the Quran or Holy Book, and the *Hadith*, based on the life, sayings, and practices of the Prophet Muhammed . . . At the very minimum, an understanding of fundamental *Sharia* laws as contained in Quranic injunctions is necessary in order to gain insights into advertising regulation and content . . .

Three sets of Quranic messages have special significance for advertising regulation. First there are strict taboos (*haraam*), such as alcohol, gambling, cheating, idol worship, usury, adultery and 'immodest' exposure . . . For example alcoholic products are banned. There are no local advertisements, and foreign print media are only allowed into the country after all advertisements of alcoholic beverages have been censored. Promotions involving games of chance are illegal . . .

Other dangers for advertisers include messages which may be considered as deceptive by religious standards. According to Islam, fraud may occur if the seller fails to deliver everything promised, and advertisers may need to use factual appeal, based on real rather than perceived product benefits. Statuary should not appear in advertising, since it may be perceived as a symbol of idol worship. Since religious norms require women to be covered, international print advertisements may have to be modified by superimposing long dresses on models or by shading their legs with black. Advertisers of cosmetics in Saudi Arabia refrain from picturing sensuous females; instead, in typical advertisements a pleasant-looking woman appears in a robe and headdress, with only her face showing . . . A second set of Quranic injunctions governs the duties a Muslim must perform, such as praying five times daily, fasting during the month of Ramadhan, giving *zakaat* (charity) to the poor, and respecting and caring for parents and the disadvantaged. Advertisers have to ensure that they do not hinder the performance of these obligations. For example, during the five prayer times, which last from 10 to 20 minutes, products cannot be promoted on radio or TV, retail shops close, and no commercial or official transactions are permitted. Advertisements should not depict, even humorously, children being disrespectful to parents and elders, whereas the image of a product could be enhanced by advertisements that stress parental advice or approval . . .

A third set of Quranic injunctions remind the faithful of God's bounties and enjoins them to thank Him for such blessings as good health, peace of mind, food, water and children. It is legal and sometimes recommended practice for advertisers to introduce their messages with Quranic words: 'In the Name of Allah, the Most Gracious, the Most Merciful'; 'By the Grace of God'; 'God is Great (Allah-o-Akbar)'; Al-Rabiah and Nasser, a manufacturer of water pumps, uses a Quranic verse: 'We made from water every living thing.' Such verses may also be used to legitimise operations or to assure that services are in accord with Islamic principles.

(Source: Luqmani *et al.*, pp. 61–4.[90] *International Marketing Review*, Musshtaq Luqmani, Ugur Yavas and Zahir Quraeshi, copyright 1989 by Emerald Group Publishing Limited in the format Textbook via Copyright Clearance Center.)

accepted in French society, since the meaning conveyed by nudity is very much related to beauty, excellence and nature. An example is the advertisement for the Guy Laroche perfume Drakkar Noir in France and Saudi Arabia.[91] The original French advertisement showed a man's bare forearm, held at the wrist by a woman's hand, with the man's hand holding a bottle of cologne. The Saudi advertisement showed the man's forearm covered by a suit jacket, with only the cuff of the shirt showing, while the woman lightly touched his hand with one of her fingers. Respect for the existing social conventions in the target society will long remain a prerequisite for the localization of advertising messages. Furthermore, the role of advertising has never been (at least officially) to change a society's mores, but rather to sell a product.

Visual elements

Advertising copy is complex and inevitably tends to reflect the cultural background of those who have created it. Some differences in colour perceptions and usage across cultures include:

- Blue being a masculine colour in the US, whereas red is masculine in France;[92]
- Black represents mourning in France and the US, whereas purple does in Venezuela;[92]
- Green is associated with money in the US; whereas in France it is associated with pharmacies;[92]
- Yellow is favoured in Taiwanese advertising (the colour of royalty), whereas brown was preferred in US advertisements;[93]
- Black and brown are common in France and the US, whereas red, orange and green are more common in Venezuelan advertisements.[92]

> **Website link 13.5**
>
> See advertising case studies from a global advertising agency: http://www.eurorscg.com/h/s/ow_cs_1.asp.

Background themes, the setting and roles depicted are also important aspects of the copy. For instance, Brazilian advertisements use significantly more urban and leisure themes than US advertisements.[94] Individualistic, as compared with collectivist, settings for product use have been shown to be significant elements of contrast between Chinese and US advertising[95–97] and Colombian and US advertising.[98]

Many visual elements commonly found in print advertisements (size of the visual, use of photographs, use of black and white advertisements, presentation of children) vary across countries. For instance, Cutler and colleagues[99] found that advertising content differs significantly:

- Indian advertisements use significantly more black and white and show more children than those in any other country;
- Korean advertisements show price two or three times as frequently as those in other countries, and represent more elderly persons whose wisdom is valued in Far Eastern cultures;
- French advertisements are by far the most oriented towards aesthetics: five times more than US, Korean or Indian advertisements, but only twice as much as British advertisements.
- US advertisements appear by far the most comparative (ten times more than in France).

Furthermore, US advertisements depict children in more idealistic settings – clean and smiling – than French advertisements, where they are more likely to appear quite realistic.[100] As such, standardization of magazine advertisements across the countries mentioned above will not be easy, since there are more differences than similarities for product types. Each country is unique on one or several visual characteristics. Overall, however, no systematic differences between industrialized and developing countries appear. Interestingly, the use of visual elements in the United Kingdom more closely resembles practice in the United States than in France. This means that there may be standardization barriers within the European Community.[99]

While pictures, as compared to language, are understood everywhere, the issue is not *whether* pictures are understood but rather *how* they are understood. As with language elements, pictures also present culture-specific association norms.[101] While rain evokes freshness for certain persons, it is associated with coldness by others. This is problematic for global advertising.[57]

People from different cultural origins do not evaluate information in the same way.[21] While concepts like product attributes are probably universal and the product function similar across nations, the exact form of attribute perception in each society might differ considerably.[102] After being exposed to a verbal briefing and photographs of a new car, British, German, French and Swedish respondents had different perceptions of the product.[103] The car's styling scored well in Germany and Sweden, but poorly in Britain and France. With regard to safety, the new car scored well only in Britain. At the same time it was perceived as particularly unreliable in Sweden.

Walle (p. 702) explains how the Marlboro man, a global promotional icon, is understood differently worldwide and re-invested with local meanings; it is, for instance, considered as a symbol of wealth and prosperity by Africans and was a symbol of freedom to East Germans in the time of communism:

To this East German woman, the Marlboro man was a seductive icon, but to her it did not represent the heritage of the American frontier. Juxtaposing the image of a man who lives without fences to the realities of her own life and the shadow of the Berlin wall, she viewed the Marlboro man as an alternative to the oppressive dictatorship in which she lived. We both saw the same ad; I interpreted it as an American while she processed it in ways which fit into her life. The product and promotion were homogeneous; the meaning and response were not.[104]

Advertising in societies experiencing rapid change

China has witnessed a dramatic change in the place of advertising in the overall business and social scene. In societies where people have been told for a long time that advertising is simply capitalist propaganda and as such evil and deceptive, advertisers today still face some degree of distrust and cannot just use the same approach as elsewhere. Many consumers still feel that good products sell themselves and that only bad products need advertising. Compared to the US, fewer Chinese respondents trusted the messages and believed in industry regulation.[105] In such a context, foreign companies have to target long-run acceptance, stressing product availability and building brand reputation.[106] They cannot just imitate what is done elsewhere.

Between 1982 and 1992, utilitarian values decreased and more symbolic values – with both Eastern and Western origins – increased.[107] Cultural values depicted by Chinese advertisements tend to reflect both Chinese culture and Western imports and have much to do with product categories and country of origin. The value of 'tradition', for instance, is more often used for food and drink whereas 'modernity' is found in a large number of Chinese advertisements that promote products for the new affluent society.[108] Over time, product availability as the main emphasis in Chinese advertisements decreased. Simultaneously, emphasis on brand superiority and comparative advertising has become more frequent.[109] Luxury goods evolved from hated symbols of decadent capitalism to consumption incentives for those who work hard.[110,111]

Since the Chinese advertising market opened to the outside world in late 2005, the industry has grown dramatically. All of the major global advertising agencies entered China in some form in the lead-up to the 2008 Olympic Games. However, advertising in China is still heavily regulated. The government attempts to control the negative effects of advertising through regulations, certification and censorship, but its regulations are vague and difficult to understand. Zhihong Gao[112] provides a detailed overview of advertising in China, for those interested.

Cross-national transferability of advertising copy

Multinationals frequently need to transfer promotional materials to other countries, where they are adapted as necessary.[113] When attempts are made to transfer advertising copy cross-culturally, the first issue is the grouping of countries within which cross-national transfers are easier. In broad terms, cultural similarity is likely to influence the success of standardization, as culturally similar people tend to consume similar goods and where the language is similar the transfer of copy is less problematic. However, other country-specific aspects should also be considered. For instance, Zandpour and Harich[114] grouped countries according to whether they value more rational (think) or more emotional (feel) advertising appeals.

The second issue deals with the precautions to be taken when transferring copy. Even between countries that look very similar, such as the US and the UK, there are very significant differences in the style of advertising copy. The first obvious difference is that broadcast television is more commercialized in the US than in the UK. The frequency of advertising also differs by product category: personal care, travel and cars are more frequently advertised in the US and services are more frequently advertised in the UK.[115] Further, cars and accessories, retail outlets and services are more frequently advertised in the UK, whereas household cleaning agents were more frequent in the Czech Republic.[116] Even within Europe there is no evidence that the content of advertising copy is converging. On the contrary, the cultural content specific to each country appears to be increasing over long periods of time.[117]

An interesting approach is to cluster countries according to cultural values – e.g. Hofstede's[41] dimensions or Schwartz's[118] values – in order to determine whether it is possible to transfer part or the whole of an advertising creation or even a full campaign. Since Hofstede's dimensions seem to be meaningful, Sriram and Gopalakrishna[119] combined these dimensions with economic and demographic as well as media availability indicators (televisions per 1000 people, radios per 1000 people, advertising spending per capita, etc.). They clustered countries into six groups: Japan is isolated in one group, and most other groups are fairly heterogeneous geographically, except northern Europe and a sort of central Asian area extending from Iran to the Philippines. The two Hofstede dimensions that discriminate significantly between these groups are power distance and individualism. As an example, status appeals are more often seen in advertisements in a high power distance society, such as South Korea than in a low power distance society such as the US.[43] Masculinity in Mexico (*Machismo*) is influential in the advertisements for traditional male oriented products such as automobiles.[120]

Similarly, Kale[121] gives the example of the promotion of India as a tourist destination for the US market. When trying to adapt, both the target (US) and the source (India) cultures have to be considered: they differ mostly on Hofstede's power distance (40 versus 77) and individualism (91 versus 48). Kale insists that the (Indian) message must be targeted to the (US) individual: the message must reflect friendliness and informality, and it must value autonomy, variety and pleasure, all positive values for highly individualistic cultures, such as that of the US. He further suggests that, since democracies are perceived as small power distance institutions, the message should emphasize that India has a democratic government, which would help bridge the gap of power distance between the source and the target country. Emphasizing cultural similarity is especially appropriate for tourism advertising, as tourists appear to seek elements of similarity, rather than difference. For example, Ng, Lee and Soutar (p. 1505) describe elements of cultural similarity that might be stressed in tourist destination advertising messages:

. . . religious similarity might be a strong marketing message for Muslims, as it facilitates their religious practices, which include eating 'Halal' food and praying at a mosque five times a day. In addition, stressing the presence of a 'multiethnic' culture might make potential international tourists feel more comfortable and secure, due to the presence of their ethnicity at the destination. . . . stressing 'food' similarity or availability might increase the level of comfort with a potential destination (e.g. Korean tourists prefer to include their ethnic accompaniments, such as 'kimchi' with their meals.[122]

Thus, it is not just the broad country-level similarities and differences that need to be considered. While country level information may guide strategy, more precise information should guide the executional details.

If advertising is to be transferred, the following elements should always be carefully checked to ensure the cultural adequacy of the final copy:

1. Comparative advertising or not;
2. Degree and type of informative content and style;
3. Adequacy of basic copy themes in relation to local mores and customs;
4. Execution: background themes, colour, use of words (puns, suggestive words), use of humour, use of symbols, type of characters and roles (age, sex, status), situations and types of relationship depicted; and
5. Implementation constraints, such as lack of a medium available locally.

Media worldwide: technological advances and cultural convergence

Worldwide differences in advertising expenditure

One cannot help but be struck by the difference in advertising expenses across countries, even though these countries may have comparable levels of economic development. This can be partially attributed to media availability (radio, television, newspapers, magazines, film, billboards). Where some media are non-existent or their availability is limited, expenses are automatically restricted by the lack of space for advertising. Despite the 11 September 2001 terrorist attacks and a recession, the US still spent the most on advertising in 2006 (US$163 billion), followed by China (US$48.5 billion), Japan (US$34.2 billion), the UK (US$25.8 billion), Germany (US$21.8 billion), Brazil (US$18.3 billion), Mexico (US$16.5 billion), France ($13.2 billion), Italy ($11.1 billion), and Canada (US$10.3 billion).[123] Per capita advertising expenditure is much lower in developing nations. For instance, while the US reached a per capita spend of over US$500 in 2006, China only reached a per capita spend of approximately US$40 despite its rank of second for total advertisement spending.[123]

Cross-cultural differences in media availability and use

The availability of advertising media is influenced by the level of a country's economic development and also by its view of the appropriate mix between business/commercial activities, on the one hand, and cultural/recreational activities on the other hand. For instance, there are no cinemas in Saudi Arabia, where traditional values do not permit the showing of films to public gatherings, although people are still able to watch films via satellite, DVD and video.[124,125] Ethical debates about whether certain products can be advertised have an influence on regulations, for instance about media space available for cigarettes and alcohol.

Prior to the European Union's ban on tobacco advertising and sponsorship, all member states prohibited television advertising of tobacco, but other restrictions varied by country. For instance, in Spain, tobacco advertising was only banned from the TV and in places where sales or consumption was prohibited. In Luxembourg advertising was allowed in sales outlets, in the press and on posters, although there were restrictions on advertising content and health warnings were compulsory. In France, Italy and Portugal there was a total ban on tobacco advertising, although some exceptions were permitted under strict conditions. In 2001, the EU outlawed tobacco advertising in the print media, on the radio and the Internet. In addition, it banned sponsorship of cross-border events, although national or local events are not covered by the directive.

Today, most developed and many developing countries are employing anti-smoking advertising, as these campaigns seem to be effective in curbing smoking. For instance, when US ninth graders' watched films with smokers in them, the result was enhanced perceptions of a smoker's stature and increased intent to smoke. When a similar audience watched the same film, but with anti-smoking advertisements in it, the result was negative thoughts about the movie characters who smoked.[126] Similar results have been found with other age groups in many countries (e.g. Australia and Malaysia): anti-smoking advertisements result in less favourable attitudes towards smoking.[127]

> ### Website link 13.6
>
> Find the Institute of Alcohol Studies fact sheet about alcohol advertising in Europe: **http://www.ias.org.uk/ resources/factsheets/advertising.pdf**.

In the lead-up to the Olympic Games, an anti-smoking campaign 'Toward a Smoke-free China' was launched in 2007. China is the world's largest tobacco producing and consuming country. In China, smoking is banned in many public gathering places, including cinemas, libraries and conference rooms, and there is a plan to ban all advertising of tobacco, including promotions and sponsorship by 2011.[128]

Advertising is largely based on the availability of news and entertainment media. The communication support systems, such as television and audiovisual equipment, printing presses, photographic equipment, etc. are costly and need to be balanced by sales, advertising or other sources of revenue. Financial support in countries where banks have limited lending capacity is often based on political influence (which may prove unstable). In many countries the press is even more dependent on politics than on advertisers.

Apart from purely economic factors, the availability of the media is also influenced by two social representations concerning the relationship between the media and its audience. First, what is considered a reasonable ratio between advertising and entertainment time (news and programmes) by the local audience and what is appropriate sequencing between advertising and entertainment, for instance in terms of television movies being sliced up by advertising? Second, is advertising considered an entertainment in itself? If entertaining the target audience is a necessary condition for capturing their interest, creative effort may have to be devoted to entertainment rather than communicating the core messages. This may reduce the effectiveness of the advertisement because the viewers' attention is attracted by the creative side of the message and diverted from the product that is being presented. Responses to the issue of how entertainment and advertising interrelate probably differ in the US and Europe.

Many countries have instituted rules that place limits on television advertising. For instance, many countries (e.g. Australia, New Zealand, Sweden, the UK) have national channels that prohibit advertising. Until recently Europe was notorious for the differences in regulations across countries. In December 2007, the Audiovisual Media Services Directive was adopted to align regulations across member countries. Some of the more important regulations include:

- Allowing product placement (previously illegal in most EU member states) provided the viewer is informed about it. Exceptions include news and current affairs programmes, children's TV, documentaries and advice programmes.

- Allowing up to 12 minutes per hour of advertising in television broadcasts, but for films more frequent breaks will be allowed (every 30 minutes, rather than the current 45 minutes).
- Limiting children's advertising with a code of conduct, which includes restrictions on junk food advertising.

Conversely, where little or even no advertising regulation exists, there can sometimes be such an invasion by advertising that viewing television programmes becomes little more than watching advertisements, a reproach frequently addressed by Europeans to US, Brazilian or Canadian television channels. The general contrast here seems to be between the Americas (the US, Mexico, Brazil and Canada), with liberal advertising regulations, and most other countries, where audiovisual media availability is more limited by regulation. For instance, while Saudi Arabia lifted the ban on commercial advertising on radio, all broadcasts are screened in order to ensure that they conform to Islamic moral and religious standards.

In many countries, radio stations have flourished with extensive advertising space, that is, up to 20 minutes of commercials per hour; programmes are constantly interrupted by advertising. This hectic schedule may be resented by listeners, who constantly change stations, obliging advertisers to buy media space for the same time blocks across several radio stations. The question of finding the acceptable proportion of advertising to total time is an important one. Studies have shown that in the US an increasing number of consumers consider television advertising as less than intelligent, leading to dissatisfaction.[21] The situation is fairly paradoxical: as the number of media channels increases, it becomes more difficult to reach and monitor a target audience since viewers' saturation with advertisements reduces their ability to listen to advertising and encourages zapping. It is surprising that the issue of whether the viewer/listener is entertained by advertising is rarely addressed, given its practical importance. Zapping has been widely studied, but most studies have only sought to demonstrate how an advertiser can avoid its unfortunate results. It is taken for granted that the audience has no saturation threshold, or at the very least an extremely high one. This assumption suggests the absolute legitimacy of mass advertising communication within a society that willingly portrays itself as being free-market oriented. In contrast, many European countries started from the opposite assumption, and advertising therefore took a long time to assert itself on television.

The emergence of global media

The previous sections placed emphasis upon differences in advertising across countries. These differences do not offset the similarities and convergence. Diverse media combine into a 'media landscape' which is primarily shaped by the freedom of choice of the audience. Some media have achieved almost worldwide recognition and a truly global audience. Among the international advertising media that have achieved the most impressive worldwide reach is the monthly *Reader's Digest*. *Readers Digest*'s 91 magazines (including 50 editions of *Reader's Digest* which

are sold in more than 70 countries), have a worldwide circulation of 41 million copies and readership of more than 100 million people.[129] It was founded in 1920 by DeWitt Wallace and his wife Lila Acheson. The first issue came out in February 1922 (see Box 13.2).

There are now some 'global' newspapers such as the *International Herald Tribune*, the *Wall Street Journal* and the *National Geographic* magazine. Their circulation covers almost the entire world. *Time* magazine's worldwide circulation is now well past the 4 million mark, with an estimated readership of 17 million in 150 countries. It publishes more than 400 geographic and demographic editions, which enables advertisers to reach precise target audiences in a large number of locations throughout the world. Many French magazines such as *L'Express*, *Le Point* and *Elle* and German magazines such as *Der Spiegel* and *Burda Moden* also publish international editions. The advertising clientele of these worldwide

---

Box 13.2

The internationalization of the *Reader's Digest*

'Since the formula of the Digest is so effective in the United States, why not attempt to repeat it elsewhere?' thought DeWitt Wallace. But exporting the formula of a magazine requires that the obstacle of language be overcome. The simplest solution was to begin in England, which could serve as a gateway into Europe. Accordingly, the first foreign edition of the *Reader's Digest* appeared in Great Britain in 1937. The second foreign edition, however, did not appear in Europe. In 1940, in the midst of the Second World War, the first issue of *Selecciones del Reader's Digest*, the Spanish-American edition, came out in Cuba. Why Cuba? The long-term objective was to attack the South American market, even if sales had to be made at a loss (as indeed occurred for many years). But for the time being, DeWitt Wallace's objective was more of a missionary one, for he sought to combat the Nazi advance. In 1942 a Portuguese edition in Brazil followed. This edition reached a print run of 300,000 copies. In 1943 there was a return to Europe with the publication of a Swedish edition.

The war was not yet over, but DeWitt Wallace was already contemplating market entry into Europe. He offered cut-price subscriptions of the *Digest* to families of young Americans who had been called up. Along with chewing gum and nylon stockings, the *Reader's Digest* was to arouse the interest of young Europeans. After the war, in 1947, *Sélection du Reader's Digest* finally appeared in France under the management of General Thompson. There was an initial print run of 275,397 copies, which almost doubled for the second issue. The global expansion of the *Reader's Digest* did not stop . . . Germany, Italy, Switzerland and Belgium, as well as India, South Africa, Australia and New Zealand, were all in turn to have their edition of the magazine. Today, 39 editions of the *Reader's Digest* are published, including one for schoolchildren, another in large type for those with sight problems and an edition in Braille. It can justifiably claim the distinction inscribed on every cover of being the most widely read magazine in the world.

(Source: Adapted from *Reader's Digest*.[130,131])

publications nevertheless remains fairly limited. It consists of 'global' advertisers who themselves are mostly targeting a global clientele, namely a segment of well-off consumers who travel internationally. Industries that use media with global reach are basically airlines, cars, banks and financial services, consumer electronics and telecommunications, tobacco and alcohol, pharmaceuticals, perfumes and luxury products. Such is the case in Asia, where pan-Asian advertising media reach an upper-scale audience composed of affluent business people and travellers.[132] However, advertisers should be cautious when using similar media globally since media perception, in terms of being enjoyable, informative, annoying and offensive, has been shown to vary cross-culturally.[133]

The global media landscape has two facets: while local media survive because language differences remain a pervasive reality, a globalized supply of media is emerging which greatly serves the globalization of advertising. The best example of such breakthroughs in international telecommunications is the growth of the World Wide Web as an advertising medium. The web is most attractive for reaching people under 35, called 'generation X', who have over US$200 billion purchasing power worldwide and comprise nearly 75 per cent of web users.[134] Industries such as telecommunications, computers, electronic entertainment equipment, publishing and financial services are the most intense users of the web as a global medium.[134]

The influence of television satellites

Television satellites now offer media with regional or global coverage. The US is a pioneer in this field, with programmes such as MTV, CNN, Discovery and BBC Worldwide reaching millions of homes on all continents through satellite television.

Daily newspapers are also becoming globalized as a result of information transmitted by satellites and computerized typesetting and the Internet; the core parts of the global newspaper are common to all local editions and are sent as digital information to local printing workshops, which add local news and advertising.

The problem of the satellite and cable network infrastructure is just as complex as the creation of new programmes to fill the screens of the new television channels. For the television industry the problem is acute: television channels cannot show just news from international news agencies and cheap talk shows, with the overall purpose of reducing the hourly cost of programmes. Television channels must set up some really entertaining programmes in order to attract viewers who then have a reason to watch the commercials. Europeans as well as Asians have difficulties creating and selling television series and soap operas internationally in comparison to the US.[135] It is estimated, for instance, that the changes in the European televisual industry necessitate over 50,000 hours of new programmes per year. Despite this, the American TV industry still has a leading edge on prices charged for broadcasting and rebroadcasting their shows.

Media giants have emerged which are likely to take control of large parts of the global media industry, such as Ted Turner, Berlusconi, Leo Kirsch, Springer, Bertelsmann, Hachette, the Luxemburg television company (RTL), Australian press magnate Rupert Murdoch and the Canadian ITC group. The bulk of these groups are multimedia interests and are equally engaged in the development of the press media covering regional areas.

In Europe, the 2007 Audiovisual without Frontiers Directive enables members to impose quotas that favour European productions. In effect, different countries in Europe have different quotas. The French, in particular, were somewhat disturbed by the invasion of American programmes, to the detriment of European culture and creation. Once again, self-contradiction is possible: some people may be both faithful viewers of American television series and opponents of imported television programmes as a whole. This implies an increasing influence of the English language, which the French and other Europeans fear could further damage the influence and reach of their own languages. Similarly, some Asian countries tend to protect their cultural identity often by prohibiting or discouraging the installation of satellite dishes, thus limiting the potential coverage of pan-Asian media.

Enlargement and overlapping of media

The influence on marketing communications of media globalization and potential media overlap is quite significant. There is a large increase in the available media space on television; the new channels are almost all private, and must finance their operations either by advertising or by subscription (cable and/or scrambler/decoder). Satellites such as Astra cover a significant number of countries in Europe. This produces great overlap zones where viewers are able to receive a large number of channels with a simple dish and decoder. This phenomenon can be observed worldwide, especially in Europe and Asia. However, it is questionable whether media overlapping has been a problem in Europe for advertisers. Some people tend to underrate the importance of media overlapping (see Dudley, pp. 287, 290):

Much is made of overlapping media particularly in classroom situations. Yet the impact of imported overlapping media has only a marginal beneficial effect on audiences. Evidence from Ireland, Austria and Switzerland indicates that where advertising comes in from adjacent countries it is largely ignored unless the product is also advertised locally, thus undermining the increased coverage potential. There is a need to harmonize creative presentation where overlaps occur to prevent confusion in the minds of potential customers.[136]

One has to address the issue of whether media overlapping in Europe may lead to a compulsory standardization of brands and of the creative themes and presentation of ads. For instance, Unilever's household cleanser is called Vif in Switzerland, Viss in Germany, Jif in the United Kingdom and Greece and Cif in France.[135] This adaptation carries the risk of being misunderstood by consumers.[137] Indeed, consumers would be disturbed if the same product were advertised under different brand names and had diversified packaging, and if different product uses and benefits were emphasized when they switched channels. However, not all viewers watch foreign channels, and not all products are marketed throughout Europe.

Technological and social changes open the door for more specific and segmented marketing

There are increasing numbers of standard brand names across Europe, especially within industries that are potential candidates for regional marketing globalization in Europe, such as banks and financial services for private clients, airlines, mass market consumer goods, as well as many consumer durables such as cars, household appliances, stereo and video systems and photographic equipment. Until now, domestic markets were considered to be the most likely units to be segmented; however, complex segments emerge where country is not necessarily the segmentable unit *par excellence* (see section 7.4 on intercultural marketing strategies based on cultural affinity zones and classes).

Some pan-European market segments include a homogeneous population across countries, for example, age groups. This is the case in relation to products for young people. Television stations such as MTV and Sky are well prepared for this. The rock radio image, supported by the emergence of European rock, is carefully cultivated by MTV. As pointed out by Tom Freston, the president of MTV: 'Music crosses borders very easily, and the lingua franca of rock'n'roll is English. Rock is an Anglo-American form.' Freston further indicates what he considers to be the mission of MTV: 'We want to be the global rock and roll village, where we can talk to youth world-wide'.[135]

Ethnicity plays an increasing role in Europe, and pan-European market segments may be fairly effective when cultural and linguistic minorities are targeted. At the national level, these minorities do not reach the critical numbers that could justify the creation of specific media, since they are scattered all over the countries of Europe. But minorities may be more significantly served at the European level. Mariet[138] cites the case of the development of Hispanic television in the US, including the two principal networks: Univision-SIN and Telemundo. Despite this, high levels of ethnic identification in advertising may not necessarily lead to positive responses from the targeted consumers, it depends on how the accommodation is interpreted.[139]

Cross-border segments may also be based on classes of cultural affinity (section 7.4). In these groupings, consumers share similar buying habits or a common language; segments may be further divided on the basis of traditional criteria such as sociodemographics (age, sex, income, etc.). For example, a relevant segment may consist of beer drinkers in the zone of cultural affinity of Mediterranean Europe, identified by several common sociodemographic characteristics and/or by criteria linked to their consumption habits and psychographics. MTV, TNT Cartoon and Eurosport are typical media for reaching classes of cultural affinity. Alden and colleagues (p. 77) give examples of global consumer positioning for the globally cosmopolitan segments including:

Sony ('My First Sony'), which positioned one of its products as appropriate for young people around the world; Phillips ('Let's Make Things Better'), whose advertisements explicitly feature people from different countries; and Benetton ('The United Colors of Benetton'), whose slogan emphasizes the unity of humankind.[140]

Some market segments and advertising audiences will remain mostly domestic ones. As a consequence, they will be only slightly influenced by market globalization in Europe. Ethnic food products such as the German Knödel would fall into this category. Regional and local marketing have developed alongside global marketing and are able to target very precise and quite small populations through local radio stations which have emerged over the past ten years. The marketing strategy of small segments of the service industry could be supported by emerging local media, for instance for local cultural products such as sports events, shows, private tutoring, etc. When marketing at the local level, cross-border geographical segments can be designed such as a county in northern France grouped with a neighbouring county in French-speaking Belgium (Walloon).

13.5

The globalization of advertising

Agencies internationalize

Advertising agencies are now largely internationalized. The largest agencies, including Euro-RSCG, WPP, Publicis, Dentsu, BBDO, McCann-Erickson, JWT, DDB, TBWA, Leo Burnett, and Hakuhodo, have built up a network of subsidiaries covering most countries over the last 20 or 30 years. The largest advertising agency in the world, Dentsu Inc., is Japanese, and the largest Japanese agencies are now present in a growing number of countries, mostly in Asia. The Japanese advertising market is a large one: it remains very attractive to Japanese agencies, which

then target South-East Asia and Australia in the first stages of their international expansion.

Large national agencies are compelled to follow the route towards the internationalization of marketing communications, media and audiences. As well as having to be able to organize cross-border campaigns for advertisers, they also try to remain knowledgeable experts on local idiosyncrasies in the implementation of marketing communication strategies. National agencies, because of limited financial resources, may acquire minority stakes in agencies in neighbouring foreign countries or may build international networks of national agencies through alliances or joint ventures. In 2006 the top five marketing organizations reported the following revenues: Omnicom Group (US$11.4 billion); WPP Group ($10.8 billion); IPG ($6.2 billion); the French Publicis group ($5.9 billion); and the Japanese Dentsu ($3.0 billion), according to *Advertising Age*'s 64th annual *Agency Report*.[141]

> ### Website link 13.7
>
> Find the *Advertising Age* 4th Annual Guide to Marketing: **http://adage.com/images/random/factpack06.pdf**.

Relationships between advertisers and agencies

Following the internationalization of advertisers, agencies have increased their foreign operations. In large multinational corporations with diversified product lines, this can lead to a complex advertiser/agency organization. The various organizational levels (national, regional and worldwide) within both the multinational agency and the multinational advertiser must be in constant contact with each other, increasing the usual communication problems within large international organizations. Different approaches may be chosen for the organization of international marketing communication with respect to the agency/advertiser relationship (see Case A13.1). One possibility is to use just one large international advertising agency, which allows for centralization of communication; this can be implemented for each product division separately, or for large brands or for the purpose of managing the corporate image worldwide. An opposite solution is to hire local agencies that are well acquainted with local constraints as they affect media and consumers. Intermediate solutions between these two extremes attempt to find an effective trade-off between worldwide coordination and the local tailoring of advertising campaigns. Ford has decided to regionalize its brand advertising in Europe with central coordination and five sub-regional teams which adapt advertising strategy to clusters of local European markets.[142]

Advertising standardization: feasibility and desirability

After a review of arguments for and against advertising standardization worldwide, a more meaningful question is whether standardized advertising should be used or not, even if it is feasible.[143] Harvey[144] considers the following arguments in favour of standardized advertising: (1) it provides consistent image across markets; (2) it avoids confusing mobile consumers; (3) it may decrease the cost of preparing campaign themes, copy and materials; and (4) it enables firmer control over the planning and execution of campaigns across markets. He gives a complete checklist of factors to be considered in order to assess whether the standardized approach is appropriate. These include product factors, competition, organization variables, media infrastructure, regulations and market/societal variables; some aspects of the advertising process may be standardized while others are not. The danger of this approach is that it does not distinguish desirability of standardization (which has to be assessed first) from its feasibility; he states initially that 'given the strong economic and administrative rationale it is assumed that, if possible, advertisers would prefer to standardize advertising' (p. 58).[144]

Interestingly, Norwegian exporters' knowledge of the local market led to more standardization: the more they learned about local conditions the more similarities they perceived and the more they felt able to standardize the marketing mix.[145] In the US and Japan multinational firms operating in Europe identified three overall factors that positively influenced the likelihood of using standardized advertising.[146] These included environmental factors (customer similarity, market similarity, similarity of advertising infrastructure, and the level of competition), strategic factors (seeking to emphasize global orientation, cost savings, and cross-border segmentation), and level of centralized control.[146] Evidence from companies concerning advertising standardization shows a mixed picture. Despite this, it seems that advertising standardization, as reported by major international agencies, has increased over the last 30 years under pressure from clients.[147] In order to determine the level of standardization, Mueller[148] analysed print and television campaigns for American consumer goods and services advertised in the US and either in Germany or Japan (for which market distance with the US is larger than for Germany). Between the US and Germany, the highest level of advertising standardization was exhibited by Mars Candy bars, followed by Marlboro cigarettes; the lowest levels were associated with Camel cigarettes and credit cards. In the case of Japan the level of adaptation was on average much greater, signalling the more important role of market distance compared with product type. Across Chinese-speaking countries standardization is feasible only for some strategic decisions (target segments, positioning, core themes) but cannot be used for tactical decisions such as executional style and media planning.[149] In a medium where we might expect more standardization, with advertising on the web, there were significant differences across the US, the UK and South Korea. All three nations use similar creative approaches and information cues, but they were distinctly different in their creative strategy and information content, even between the US and the UK.[150] This illustrates that standardization even between two relatively similar countries may not be easy. Interestingly, from the consumers' perspective the strongest influence on the perceived similarity of advertising was the picture used, followed by the general layout, advertising topic and language.[151]

The global campaign concept

One cannot underestimate the complexity of managing an international campaign.[152] especially in the realm of agency/advertiser relations, which are often difficult to manage even when both agency and advertiser are excellent companies. For instance,

Procter & Gamble has always had a reputation as a demanding advertiser for its agencies, but also for being very loyal to them. P & G, like many large companies, has had very stable relationships (sometimes for 40 years or more) with a group of agencies; some of them have worldwide responsibility for a product line and/or a major brand.[153] However, the creative work is sometimes a source of conflict between major advertisers and their agencies when their views diverge as to the strategy to be followed. Most advertisers then try to adopt a democratic style, by discussing opinions, facts, data and drafts of potential advertising campaigns. The final say always comes when campaigns are actually launched and their impact on various objectives may be monitored (brand awareness, brand image, sales increase, etc.).

Globalization of marketing communications may be less pervasive than it seems at first sight; therefore the necessary degree of adaptation should increase over a continuum of four levels: *mission* (long term identity and vision of the communicator), *proposition* (campaign themes), creative *concepts* (how themes are translated in the language and cultures of the target groups) and *execution*.[88] While mission can rather easily be globalized, execution will need much local tailoring. Kanso and Nelson[154] examined the role of American and non-American subsidiaries in designing and implementing campaigns for nondomestic markets. Their findings indicated '(1) the advertising theme should not be the same across countries; (2) even the use of similar appeals and symbols in advertising campaigns targeting foreign markets is ill advised; (3) the choice of illustrations and colours must tie well with consumers' aesthetic sense; and (4) the integration of local communication expertise is a necessity to overcome language and cultural barriers in worldwide markets' (p. 86).[154]

The objective of a global advertising campaign has to be clearly defined: it does not seek to save on creative costs. It aims to promote a global brand name and image. Accordingly, the creative director for McCann-Erickson worldwide, Marcio Moreira, emphasizes that an advertiser should not pursue a global advertising strategy as a way of saving money, trying to achieve in only one campaign what may in fact require 12. The correct implementation of a global campaign requires a great deal of effort and creative time, and ultimately its cost may prove higher than the sum total of individual campaigns.[155]

Dean M. Peebles[156], who was for many years the manager of international communications for Goodyear, the world's leading tyre manufacturer, recommends the following steps for the design and implementation of a global advertising campaign:

1. Choose a large advertising agency with subsidiaries all over the world; select in this agency an international account manager, who reports to the advertiser's headquarters.
2. Establish multinational planning meetings between the client and the agency, as well as a multinational creative team.
3. Brand managers and headquarters level should conduct and supervise consumer research and the pre-tests of the draft communication.
4. The resulting draft global campaign should be sufficiently finalized to facilitate discussion, but flexible enough to be transposed (rather than translated) into the various cultures and lifestyles of the target audiences.

Figure 13.2 presents a flowchart of headquarters–subsidiary relations for the planning and coordination of worldwide advertising at Goodyear. This flowchart indicates the tasks to be performed and the (tight) time schedule imposed.[157]

Practical implementation of global advertising campaigns is not an easy task. The organization must be completely interactive and use both bottom-up and top-down communication flows. Communication between headquarters and subsidiaries should not be a 'sham' dialogue in which decisions already taken at the very top level would have to be accepted by local executives as if they were their own. This issue is all the more complex because interaction problems between various levels within the multinational advertiser (international headquarters, regional headquarters, country subsidiaries) may snowball, leading to difficulties of communication and coordination with the international agency.

Global communication is primarily intended to establish the corporate image of a company or to foster recognition of one of its major brands across a large number of countries (e.g. McDonald's, Goodyear, Michelin, Nestlé). For instance, the Subtitles campaign of IBM was introduced globally in 1995 with the aim of promoting the universality of the brand imagery of IBM. The message was that IBM delivers simple and powerful solutions anywhere, at any time

Figure 13.2 Flowchart for the management of multinational advertising campaigns at Goodyear

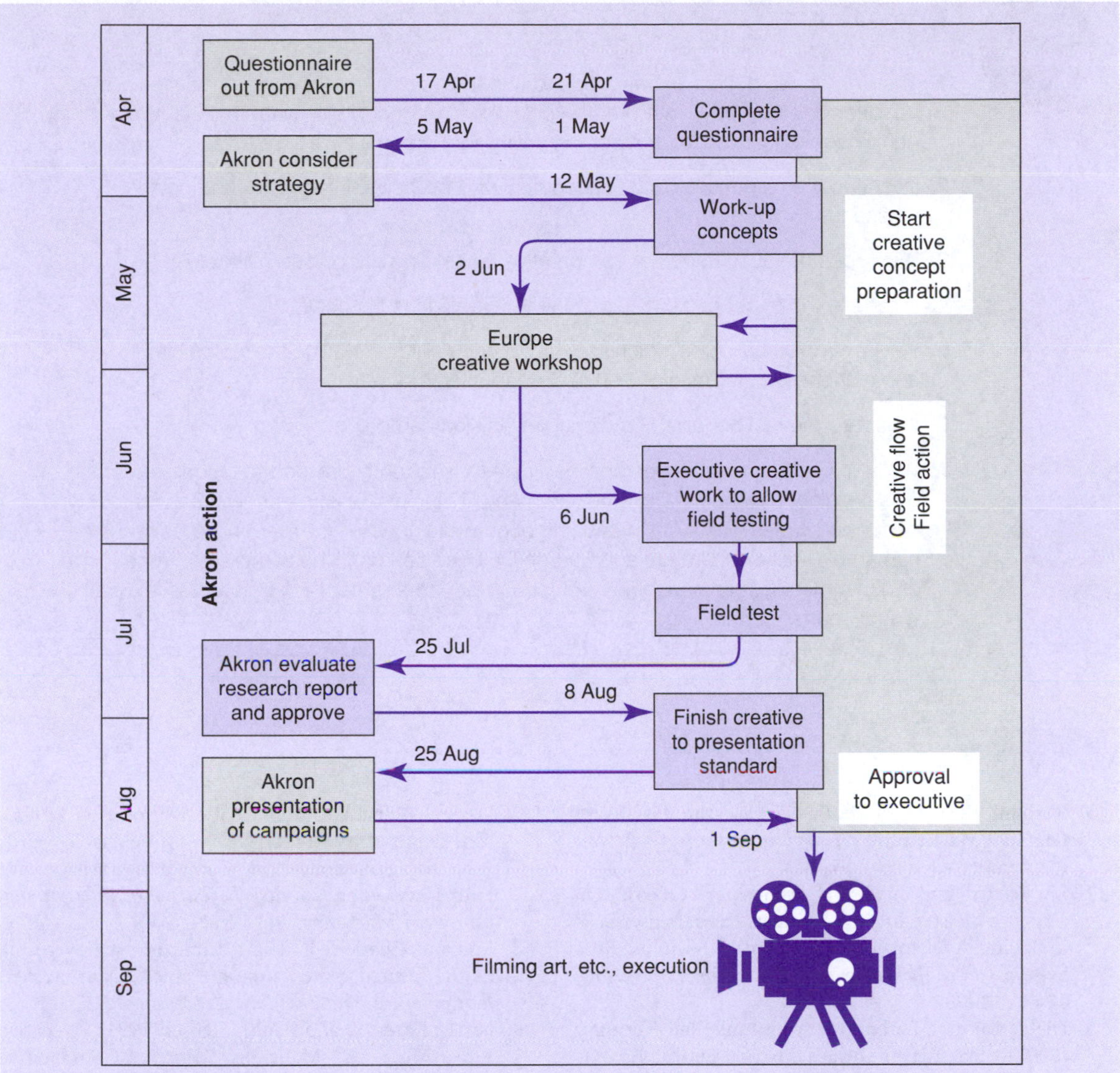

(Source: Peebles and Ryans, p. 83.[157])

and for anyone; the use of subtitles and voice-overs allowed for both a global message and a localized communication.[158] The next step is to advertise the products themselves, and at this point the creative input of local subsidiaries and regional headquarters, as well as their influence on the advertising strategy, is much more significant. But local campaigns, even if they advertise local products and local brand names must be carefully coordinated so that they make a positive contribution to the global message. The core values which are conveyed by the company's corporate image (e.g. high technology, robustness, innovativeness, style, social responsibility) should also be recognizable in its brand and product advertising at the local level. Finally, communication with market segments which remain specific to certain countries should be fully delegated to the local level. Not every piece of communication can be globalized.

Questions

1. The English word 'hair' corresponds to two totally different French words: *cheveux* (of head) or *poil* (on body). Interpret the difference in concepts of what 'hair' is. What might be the consequences in terms of marketing for personal care products?

2. Describe the respective cultural adequacy of persuasive, informative and oneiric messages.

3. Why does the acceptance of comparative advertising vary cross-culturally?

4. What are the target audiences of satellite television in Europe?

5. Give examples of mores which vary cross-culturally and outline their possible consequences in terms of advertising adaptation.

6. What are the real benefits of a global advertising campaign?

7. Wella, a German giant in personal hair care, has recently decided to globalize a brand of its subsidiary Mühlens in Cologne (Germany) 4711, which is the original Eau de Cologne perfumed water. The 4711 brand, although well known in the German-speaking area, has an old-fashioned image and Eau de Cologne seems to be associated in the minds of consumers in many countries with cheap perfume rather than tradition or luxury. How would you tackle this issue?

References

1. Kashani, Kamran (1989), 'Beware the Pitfalls of Global Marketing', *Harvard Business Review* (September–October), 91–8.
2. Li, Fengru and Nader H. Shooshtari (2006), 'On Toyota's Misstep in Advertising its Land Cruiser SUV in Beijing: A Distortion of Consumers' Sociolinguistic System', *Journal of International Consumer Marketing*, 18 (4), 61–78.
3. Diehl, Sandra, Barbara Mueller, and Ralf Terlutter (2007), 'Skepticism toward Pharmaceutical Advertising in the U.S. and Germany', in *Cross-Cultural Buyer Behavior*, Charles R. Taylor and Doo-Hee Lee, Eds. Vol. 18: JAI.
4. Hoek, Janet and Philip Gendall (2006), 'Advertising and Obesity: A Behavioral Perspective', *Journal of Health Communication*, 11 (4), 409–23.
5. Wills, James R. and John K. Ryans Jr (1982), 'Attitudes toward Advertising: A Multinational Study', *Journal of International Business Studies* (Winter), 121–41.
6. Andrews, J. Craig, Steven Lysonski, and Srinivas Durvasula (1991), 'Understanding Cross-Cultural Student Perceptions of Advertising in General: Implications for Advertising Educators and Practitioners', *Journal of Advertising*, 20 (2), 15–28.
7. Darley, William K. and Denise M. Johnson (1994), 'An Exploratory Investigation of Beliefs Towards Advertising in General: A Comparative Analysis of Four Developing Countries', *Journal of International Consumer Marketing*, 7 (1), 5–21.
8. Romano, Charlotte J. (2004), 'Comparative Advertising in the United States and in France', *Northwestern Journal of International Law and Business*, 25, 371.
9. James, Karen E. and Paul J. Hensel (1991), 'Negative Advertising: The Malicious Strain of Comparative Advertising', *Journal of Advertising*, 20 (2), 53–67.
10. Choi, Yung Kyun and Gordon E. Miracle (2004), 'The Effectiveness of Comparative Advertising in Korea and the United States', *Journal of Advertising*, 33 (4), 75–87.
11. Agrawal, Madhu (1995), 'Review of 40-Year Debate in International Advertising: Practitioner and Academician Perspectives to the Standardization/ Adaptation Issue', *International Marketing Review*, 12 (1), 26–48.
12. Javalgi, Rajshekhar, Bob D. Cutler, and Naresh K. Malhotra (1995), 'Print Advertising at the Component Level: A Cross-Cultural Comparison of the United States and Japan', *Journal of Business Research*, 34, 117–24.

13. Mueller, Barbara (1987), 'Reflections of Culture: An Analysis of Japanese and American Advertising Appeals', *Journal of Advertising Research*, 27 (3), 51–9.

14. Lin, Carolyn A. (1993), 'Cultural Differences in Message Strategies: A Comparison between American and Japanese TV Commercials', *Journal of Advertising Research*, 33 (4), 40–48.

15. Lin, Carolyn A. (2001), 'Cultural Values Reflected in Chinese and American Television Advertising', *Journal of Advertising*, 30 (4), 83–94.

16. Chiou, Jyh-shen (2002), 'The Effectiveness of Different Advertising Message Appeals in the Eastern Emerging Society: Using Taiwanese TV Commercials as an Example', *International Journal of Advertising*, 21 (2), 217–36.

17. Zheng, Lu, Joseph E. Phelps, Yorgo Pasadeos, and Shuhua Zhou (2007), 'Do the Little Emperors Rule? Comparing Informativeness and Appeal Types in Chinese, American, and French Magazine Advertising', in *Advances in International Marketing*, Charles R. Taylor and Doo-Hee Lee, Eds. Vol. 18: JAI.

18. Di Benedetto, C. Anthony, Mariko Tamate, and Rajan Chandran (1992), 'Developing Creative Advertising Strategy for the Japanese Marketplace', *Journal of Advertising Research*, 32 (January–February), 39–48.

19. Kishii, T. (1988), *Message vs. Mood: A Look at Some of the Differences between Japanese and Western Television Commercials*. Dentsu, Tokyo: Dentsu Japan Marketing/Advertising Yearbook.

20. Zandpour, Fred, Cypress Chang, and Joelle Catalano (1992), 'Stories, Symbols and Straight Talk: A Comparative Analysis of French, Taiwanese and U.S. TV Commercials', *Journal of Advertising Research*, 32 (January–February), 25–37.

21. Martenson, Rita (1987), 'Advertising Strategies and Information Content in American and Swedish Advertising: A Comparative Content Analysis in Cross-Cultural Copy Research', *International Journal of Advertising*, 6, 133–44.

22. Anon (1988), 'Numéro "Spécial Europe"', *Communication et Business*, 14 March, 18.

23. Appelbaum, Ullrich and Chris Halliburton (1993), 'How to Develop International Advertising Campaigns That Work: The Example of the European Food and Beverage Sector', *International Journal of Advertising*, 12, 223–41.

24. West, Douglas C. (1993), 'Cross-National Creative Personalities, Processes, and Agency Philosophies', *Journal of Advertising Research*, 33 (5, September–October), 53–62.

25. Aaker, Jennifer L. and Durairaj Maheswaran (1997), 'The Effect of Cultural Orientation on Persuasion', *Journal of Consumer Research*, 24 (December), 315–28.

26. Pornpitakpan, Chantikha and June N.P. Francis (2001), 'The Effect of Cultural Differences, Source Expertise, and Argument Strength on Persuasion: An Experiment with Canadians and Thais', *Journal of International Consumer Marketing*, 13 (1), 77–101.

27. Resnik, Alan J. and Bruce L. Stern (1977), 'An Analysis of Information Content in Television Advertising', *Journal of Marketing*, 44 (1), 50–53.

28. Stern, Bruce W. and Alan J. Resnik (1991), 'Information Content in Advertising: A Replication and Extension', *Journal of Advertising Research*, 31 (3), 36–46.

29. Dowling, G.R. (1980), 'Information Content in U.S. and Australian Television Advertising', *Journal of Marketing*, 44 (4), 34–37.

30. Johnstone, Harvey, Erdener Kaynak, and Richard M. Sparkman Jr (1987), 'A Cross-Cultural/Cross-National Study of the Information Content of Television Advertisements', *International Journal of Advertising*, 6, 223–36.

31. Bigne, Enrique, Marcelo Royo, and Antonio C. Cuenca (1993), 'Information Content Analysis of TV Advertising – the Spanish Case', in *Proceedings of the 6th World Marketing Congress*. Istanbul, 324–29.

32. Renforth, W. and S. Raveed (1983), 'Consumer Information Cues in Television Advertising: A Cross Country Analysis', *Journal of the Academy of Marketing Science*, 11 (3), 216–25.

33. Ward, James W. and Jim McQuirk (1987), 'Information Content in Television Advertising: Ireland, United States and Australia', in *Proceedings of the Second Symposium on Cross-Cultural Consumer and Business Studies*, C.F. Keown and A.G. Woodside, Eds. Honolulu, Hawaii, 37–40.

34. Schroeder, Michael (1991), 'France-Allemagne: La Publicité. L'existence de Deux Logiques de Communication', *Recherche et Applications en Marketing*, 6 (3), 97–109.

35. Lin, Carolyn A. and Michael B. Salwen (1995), 'Product Information Strategies of American and Japanese Television Advertisements', *International Journal of Advertising*, 14, 55–64.

36. Weinberger, Marc G. and Harlan E. Spotts (1989), 'A Situational View of Information Content in TV Advertising in the U.S. and U.K.', *Journal of Marketing*, 53 (1), 89–94.

37. Keown, Charles F., Lawrence W. Jacobs, Richard W. Schmidt, and Kyung-Il Ghymn (1992), 'Information Content in Advertising in the United States, Japan, South Korea, and the People's Republic of China', *International Journal of Advertising*, 11, 257–67.

38. Abernethy, Avery M. and George R. Franke (1996), 'The Information Content of Advertising: A Meta-Analysis', *Journal of Advertising*, 25 (2), 1–17.

39. Kaynak, Erdener and Pervez N. Ghauri (1986), 'A Comparative Analysis of Advertising Practices in Unlike Environments: A Study of Agency–Client Relationships', *International Journal of Advertising*, 5, 121–46.

40. Callow, Michael and Leon Schiffman (2002), 'Implicit Meaning in Visual Print Advertisements: A Cross-Cultural Examination of the Contextual Communication Effect', *International Journal of Advertising*, 21 (2), 259–77.

41. Hofstede, Geert (1991), *Culture and Organizations: Software of the Mind*. Maidenhead, Berkshire: McGraw-Hill.

42. Hoover, Robert J., Robert T. Green, and Joel Saegert (1978), 'A Cross-National Study of Perceived Risk', *Journal of Marketing* (July), 102–8.

43. Cutler, Bob D., Rajshekhar G. Javalgi, and Dongdae Lee (1995), 'The Visual Component of Print Advertising: A Five-Country Cross-Cultural Analysis', *Journal of International Consumer Marketing*, 8 (2), 45–58.

44. Reinhard, K. and W.E. Phillips (1985), 'Global Marketing: Experts Look at Both Sides', *Advertising Age*, 56 (15), 46.

45. Duncan, Tom and Jyotika Ramaprasad (1995), 'Standardized Multinational Advertising: The Influencing Factors', *Journal of Advertising*, 24 (3, Autumn), 55–68.

46. Tixier, Maud (1992), 'Comparison of the Linguistic Message in Advertisements According to the Criteria of Effective Writing', *International Journal of Advertising*, 11, 139–55.

47. De Mooij, Marieke (2005), *Global Marketing and Advertising: Understanding Cultural Paradoxes* (2nd edn). Thousand Oaks, CA: Sage.

48. Thurlow, Crispin and Adam Jaworski (2003), 'Communicating a Global Reach: In-Flight Magazines as a Globalizing Genre in Tourism', *Journal of Sociolinguistics*, 7 (4), 579–606.

49. Nelson, Michelle R. and Hye-JIn Paek (2007), 'A Content Analysis of Advertising in a Global Magazine across Seven Countries', *International Marketing Review*, 24 (1), 64–86.

50. Zhou, Nan and Russell W. Belk (2004), 'Chinese Consumer Readings of Global and Local Advertising Appeals', *Journal of Advertising*, 33 (3), 67–76.

51. Mueller, Barbara (1992), 'Standardization vs. Specialization: An Examination of Westernization in Japanese Advertising', *Journal of Advertising Research*, 32 (January–February), 15–23.

52. Sherry, John F. Jr and Eduardo G. Camargo (1987), '"May Your Life Be Marvelous": English Language Labelling and the Semiotics of Japanese Promotion', *Journal of Consumer Research*, 14 (September), 174–88.

53. Yip, George S. (1995), *Total Global Strategy: Managing for Worldwide Competitive Advantage*. Englewood Cliffs, NJ: Prentice-Hall.

54. Neelankavil, James P., Venkatapparao Mummalaneni, and David N. Sessions (1995), 'Use of Foreign Language and Models in Print Advertisements in East Asian Countries: A Logit Modelling Approach', *European Journal of Marketing*, 26 (4), 24–38.

55. Whitelock, Jeryl and Djamila Chung (1989), 'Cross-Cultural Advertising: An Empirical Study', *International Journal of Advertising*, 8 (3), 291–310.

56. Grüber, Ursula (1987), 'La Communication Internationale a sa Langue: L'adaptation', *Revue Française du Marketing*, 114 (1987/4), 89–96.

57. Kroeber-Riel, Werner (1992), 'Globalisierung der Euro-Werbung. Ein Konzeptioneller Ansatz der Konsumentenforschung', *Marketing ZFP*, 14 (4), 261–7.

58. Toffoli, Roy and Michel Laroche (2002), 'Cultural and Language Effects on Chinese Bilinguals' and Canadians' Responses to Advertising', *International Journal of Advertising*, 21, 505–34.

59. Luna, David and Laura A. Peracchio (2001), 'Moderators of Language Effects in Advertising to Bilinguals: A Psycholinguistic Approach', *Journal of Consumer Research*, 28 (September), 284–95.

60. McCullough, Lynette S. and Ronald E. Taylor (1993), 'Humor in American, British and German Ads', *Industrial Marketing Management*, 22, 17–28.

61. Suls, J. (1983), 'Cognitive Processes in Humour Appreciation', in *Handbook of Humour Research*, J. Goldstein, Ed. New York: Springer.

62. Unger, Lynette S. (1995), 'A Cross-Cultural Study on the Affect-Based Model of Humor in Advertising', *Journal of Advertising Research*, 35 (1, January–February), 66–71.

63. Weinberger, Marc G. and Harlan E. Spotts (1989), 'Humour in U.S. Versus U.K. TV Commercials: A Comparison', *Journal of Advertising*, 18 (2), 39–44.

64. Alden, Dana L., Wayne D. Hoyer, and Chol Lee (1993), 'Identifying Global and Culture-Specific Dimensions of Humor in Advertising: A Multinational Analysis', *Journal of Marketing*, 57 (April), 64–75.

65. Huth, Sabine and Fritz Unger (1988), 'Eine Vergleichende Untersuchung Zur Humorvollen Werbung: Brd vs. USA', *Planung und Analyse*, 5, 197–200.

66. Kalliny, Morris, Kevin W. Cruthirds, and Michael S. Minor (2006), 'Differences between American, Egyptian and Lebanese Humor Styles: Implications for International Management', *International Journal of Cross Cultural Management*, 6 (1), 121–34.

67. Hanna, Nessim, Geoffrey L. Gordon, and Rick E. Ridnour (1994), 'The Use of Humor in Japanese Advertising', *Journal of International Consumer Marketing*, 7 (1), 85–106.

68. Belch, George E. and Michael A. Belch (2003), *Advertising and Promotion: An Integrated Marketing Communications Perspective*. Columbus, OH: McGraw-Hill.

69. Prendergast, Gerard, Leung Kwok Yan, and Douglas C. West (2002), 'Role Portrayal in Advertising and Editorial Content, and Eating Disorders: An Asian

Perspective', *International Journal of Advertising*, 21 (2), 237–58.

70. An, Daechun and Sanghoon Kim (2007), 'Relating Hofstede's Masculinity Dimension to Gender Role Portrayals in Advertising', *International Marketing Review*, 24 (2), 181–207.

71. Huang, Jen-Hung (1995), 'National Character and Sex Roles in Advertising', *Journal of International Consumer Marketing*, 7 (4), 81–96.

72. Yeung, Kevin and K.F. Lau (1993), 'Gender Role Stereotyping in Print Advertisements: A Comparison of Hong Kong, Taiwan and Japan', in *Proceedings of the 4th Symposium on Cross-Cultural Consumer and Business Studies*, Gerald Albaum, Ed. University of Hawaii, 225–31.

73. Tan, Thomas Tsu Wee, Lee Boon Ling, and Eleanor Phua Cheay Thengh (2002), 'Gender-Role Portrayals in Malaysian and Singaporean Television Commercials: An International Advertising Perspective', *Journal of Business Research*, 55, 853–61.

74. Siu, Wai-Sum (1996), 'Gender Portrayal in Hong Kong and Singapore Television Advertisements', *Journal of Asian Business*, 12 (3), 47–61.

75. Wiles, Charles R. and Anders Tjernlund (1991), 'A Comparison of Role Portrayal of Men and Women in Magazine Advertising in the USA and Sweden', *International Journal of Advertising*, 10 (3), 259–67.

76. Wiles, Charles R., Judith A. Wiles, and Anders Tjernlund (1996), 'The Ideology of Advertising: The United States and Sweden', *Journal of Advertising Research*, 36 (3), 57–66.

77. Wee, Chow Hou, Mei-Lan Choong, and Siok-Kuan Tambyah (1995), 'Sex Role Portrayal in Television Advertising. A Comparative Study of Singapore and Malaysia', *International Marketing Review*, 12 (1), 49–64.

78. Gilly, Mary (1988), 'Sex Roles in Advertising: A Comparison of Television Advertisements in Australia, Mexico, and the United States', *Journal of Marketing*, 52 (April), 75–85.

79. Odekerken-Schröder, Gaby, Kristof De Wulf, and Natascha Hofstee (2002), 'Is Gender Stereotyping in Advertising More Prevalent in Masculine Countries? A Cross-National Analysis', *International Marketing Review*, 19 (4), 408–19.

80. Al-Olayan, Fahad S. and Kiran Karande (2000), 'A Content Analysis of Magazine Advertisements from the United States and the Arab World', *Journal of Advertising*, 29 (3), 69–82.

81. Wiles, Judith A., Charles R. Wiles, and Anders Tjernlund (1995), 'A Comparison of Gender Role Portrayals in Magazine Advertising: The Netherlands, Sweden and the USA', *European Journal of Marketing*, 29 (11), 35–49.

82. Bjerke, Rune (1995), 'An Experimental Study in Standardisation of Euro Advertising: A Beauty Type as Advertising Presenter', *University of Otago*, New Zealand.

83. Frith, Katherine Toland, Hong Cheng, and Ping Shaw (2004), 'Race and Beauty: A Comparison of Asian and Western Models in Women's Magazine Advertisments', *Sex Roles*, 50 (1/2), 53–61.

84. Bates, Constance and William Renforth (1987), 'The Elderly in Magazine Advertising: An Intercountry Comparison between the U.S. and Latin America', in *Proceedings of the Second Symposium on Cross-Cultural Consumer and Business Studies*, Charles F. Keown and Arch G. Woodside, Eds. Honolulu, Hawaii, 30–33.

85. Douglas, Susan and Bernard Dubois (1980), 'Looking at the Cultural Environment for International Marketing Opportunities', in *Marketing Management and Strategy: A Reader*, P. Kotler and K. Cox, Eds. Englewood Cliffs, NJ: Prentice Hall.

86. Al-Makaty, Safran S., G. Norman Van Tubergen, S. Scott Whitlow, and Douglas A. Boyd (1996), 'Attitudes Towards Advertising in Islam', *Journal of Advertising Research*, 36 (3), 16–26.

87. Al-Mossawi, Mohammed and Paul Michell (1992), 'The Impact of Cultural Factors on the Response of Viewers to TV Commercials in the Gulf Countries: An Empirical Study', in *Proceedings of the First Conference on the Cultural Dimension of International Marketing*. Odense, 443–69.

88. Van Raaij, W. Fred (1997), 'Globalisation of Marketing Communications', *Journal of Economic Psychology*, 18, 259–70.

89. Miller, Fred and A. Hamdi Demirel (1988), 'Efes Pilsen in the Turkish Beer Market: Marketing Consumer Goods in Developing Countries', *International Marketing Review*, 5 (Spring), 7–19.

90. Luqmani, Mushtag, Ugur Yavas, and Zahir Quraeshi (1988), 'Advertising in Saudi Arabia: Content and Regulation', *International Marketing Review*, 6 (1), 59–71.

91. Czinkota, Michael R. and Illka A. Ronkainen (1990), *International Marketing* (2nd edn). Hinsdale, IL: Dryden Press.

92. Clarke, Irvine III and Earl D. Honeycutt Jr (2000), 'Color Usage in International Business-to-Business Print Advertising', *Industrial Marketing Management*, 29, 255–61.

93. Huang, Jen-Hung (1993), 'Color in Us and Taiwanese Industrial Advertising', *Industrial Marketing Management*, 22, 195–98.

94. Tansey, Richard, Michael R. Hyman, and George M. Zinkhan (1990), 'Cultural Themes in Brazilian and U.S. Auto Ads: A Cross-Cultural Comparison', *Journal of Advertising*, 19 (2), 30–39.

95. Han, S-P. and S. Shavitt (1994), 'Persuasion and Culture: Advertising Appeals in Individualistic and Collectivistic Societies', *Journal of Experimental Social Psychology*, 30, 326–50.

96. Zhang, Yong and Betsy D. Gelb (1996), 'Matching Advertising Appeals to Culture: The Influence of Products' Use Conditions', *Journal of Advertising*, XXV (4, Winter), 29–40.

97. Zhang, Yong and James P. Neelankavil (1997), 'The Influence of Culture on Advertising Effectiveness in China and the USA: A Cross-Cultural Study', *European Journal of Marketing*, 31 (2), 134–49.

98. Gregory, Gary D., James M. Munch, and Mark Peterson (2002), 'Attitude Functions in Consumer Research: Comparing Value-Attitude Relations in Individualist and Collectivist Cultures', *Journal of Business Research*, 55, 933–42.

99. Cutler, Bob D., Rajshekhar G. Javalgi, and M. Krishna Erramilli (1992), 'The Visual Component of Print Advertising: A Five-Country Cross-Cultural Analysis', *European Journal of Marketing*, 26 (4), 7–20.

100. Hall, Edward T. and Mildred Reed Hall (1989), *Understanding Cultural Differences*. Yarmouth, ME: Intercultural Press.

101. Hung, Kineta and Marshall D. Rice (1995), 'A Comparative Examination of the Perception of Ad Meanings in Hong Kong and Canada', in *Proceedings of the 5th Symposium on Cross-Cultural Consumer and Business Studies*, Scott M. Smith, Ed. Provo, UT: Brigham Young University.

102. Hornik, Jacob (1980), 'Comparative Evaluation of International and National Advertising Strategies', *Columbia Journal of World Business*, 15 (1), 36–45.

103. Colvin, Michael, Roger Heeler, and Jim Thorpe (1980), 'Developing International Advertising Strategy', *Journal of Marketing*, 44 (Fall), 73–79.

104. Walle, A.H. (1997), 'Global Behaviour, Unique Responses: Consumption within Cultural Frameworks', *Management Decision*, 35 (10), 700–8.

105. Zhou, Dongsheng, Weijiong Zhang, and Ilan Vertinsky (2002), 'Advertising Trends in Urban China', *Journal of Advertising Research*, 42 (May–June), 73–81.

106. Liang, Kong and Lawrence Jacobs (1994), 'China's Advertising Agencies: Problems and Relations', *International Journal of Advertising*, 13, 205–15.

107. Cheng, Hong (1994), 'Reflections of Cultural Values: A Content Analysis of Chinese Magazine Advertisements from 1982 and 1992', *International Journal of Advertising*, 13, 167–83.

108. Cheng, Hong and John C. Schweitzer (1996), 'Cultural Values Reflected in Chinese and US Television Commercials', *Journal of Advertising Research*, 36 (3), 27–44.

109. Zhou, Nan and Russell W. Belk (1993), 'China's Advertising and the Export Marketing Learning Curve', *Journal of Advertising Research*, 33 (6), 50–66.

110. Swanson, Lauren A. (1996), 'People's Advertising in China: A Longitudinal Content Analysis of the *People's Daily* since 1949', *International Journal of Advertising*, 15, 222–38.

111. Tse, David K., Russell W. Belk, and Nan Zhou (1989), 'Becoming a Consumer Society: A Longitudinal and Cross-Cultural Content Analysis of Print Ads from Hong King, the People's Republic of China, and Taiwan', *Journal of Consumer Research*, 15 (March), 457–71.

112. Gao, Zhihong (2007), 'An in-Depth Examination of China's Advertising Regulation System', *Asia Pacific Journal of Marketing and Logistics*, 19 (3), 307–23.

113. Hill, John S. and William L. James (1991), 'Product and Promotion Transfers in Consumer Goods Multinationals', *International Marketing Review*, 8 (4), 6–17.

114. Zandpour, Fred and Katrin Harich (1996), 'Think and Feel Country Clusters: A New Approach to International Advertising Standardization', *International Journal of Advertising*, 15 (4), 325–44.

115. Katz, Helen and Wei-Na Lee (1992), 'Oceans Apart: An Initial Exploration of Social Communication Differences in US and UK Prime-Time Television Advertising', *International Journal of Advertising*, 11, 69–82.

116. Koudelova, Radka and Jeryl Whitelock (2001), 'A Cross-Cultural Analysis of Television Advertising in the UK and Czech Republic', *International Marketing Review*, 18 (3), 286–300.

117. Snyder, Leslie B., Bartjan Willenborg, and James Watt (1991), 'Advertising and Cross-Cultural Convergence in Europe, 1953–1989', *European Journal of Communication*, 6, 441–68.

118. Schwartz, S.H. (1992), 'Universals in the Content and Structure of Values: Theoretical Advances and Empirical Tests in 20 Countries', *Advances in Experimental Social Psychology*, 25, 1–65.

119. Sriram, Ven and Pradeep Gopalakrishna (1991), 'Can Advertising be Standardized among Similar Countries? A Cluster-Based Analysis', *International Journal of Advertising*, 10, 137–40.

120. Gregory, Gary D. and James M. Munch (1997), 'Cultural Values in International Advertising: An Examination of Familial Norms and Roles in Mexico', *Psychology and Marketing*, 14 (2), 99–119.

121. Kale, Sudhir H. (1991), 'Culture-Specific Marketing Communications: An Analytical Approach', *International Marketing Review*, 8 (2), 19–30.

122. Ng, Siew Imm, Julie Anne Lee, and Geoffrey N. Soutar (2007), 'Tourists' Intention to Visit a Country: The Impact of Cultural Distance', *Tourism Management*, 28 (6), 1497–506.

123. Anon (2007), *World Advertising Trends*, World Advertising Research Center.

124. Tunclap, Secil (1992), 'The Audio-Visual Media in Saudi Arabia: Problems and Prospects', *International Journal of Advertising*, 11, 119–30.

125. Tunclap, Secil (1994), 'Outdoor Media Planning in Saudi Arabia', *Marketing and Research Today*, 22 (2, May), 146–54.

126. Pechmann, Cornelia and Chuan-Fong Shih (1999), 'Smoking Scenes in Movies and Antismoking Advertisements before Movies: Effects on Youth', *Journal of Marketing*, 63 (3), 1–13.

127. Quester, Pascale (1999), 'A Cross-Cultural Study of Juvenile Response to Anti-Smoking Advertisements', *Journal of Euro-marketing*, 7 (2), 29–46.

128. Anon (2007), 'China to Ban All Tobacco Advertising by 2011', *CHINA Daily*, 28 August, www.chinadaily.com.cn/china/2007-08/28/content_6063029.htm.

129. Jackson, Sally (2008), 'Reader's Digest Chief Shakes up Empire', *The Australian*, 27 March, www.theaustralian.news.com.au/story/0,25197,23436991-13480,00.html.

130. *Reader's Digest* (1987), London: Reader's Digest Ltd.

131. *Reader's Digest* (1988), London: Reader's Digest Ltd.

132. Ha, Louise (1997), 'Limitations and Strengths of Panasian Advertising Media: A Review for International Advertisers', *International Journal of Advertising*, 16 (2), 148–63.

133. Somasundaram, T.N. and C. David Light (1994), 'Rethinking a Global Media Strategy: A Four Country Comparison of Young Adults' Perceptions of Media-Specific Advertising', *Journal of International Consumer Marketing*, 7 (1), 23–38.

134. Kassaye, W. Wossen (1997), 'Global Advertising and the World Wide Web', *Business Horizons*, 40 (3), 33–42.

135. Sarathy, Ravi (1991), 'European Integration and Global Strategy in the Media and Entertainment Industry', in *Global Competition and the European Community*, Alan M. Rugman and Alain Verbeke, Eds. Vol. 2. Greenwich, CT: JAI Press.

136. Dudley, James W. (1989), *Strategies for the Single Market*. London: Kogan Page.

137. Mourier, Pascal and Didier Burgaud (1989), Euromarketing. Paris: Editions d'Organisation.

138. Mariet, François (1990), *La Télévision Américaine*. Paris: Editions Economica.

139. Holland, Jonna and James W. Gentry (1999), 'Ethic Consumer Reaction to Targeted Marketing: A Theory of Intercultural Accommodation', *Journal of Advertising*, 28 (1), 65–77.

140. Alden, Dana L., Jan-Benedict E.M. Steenkamp, and Rajeev Batra (1999), 'Brand Positioning through Advertising in Asia, North America, and Europe: The Role of Global Consumer Culture', *Journal of Marketing*, 63, 75–87.

141. *Advertising Age* (2007), 'Agency Report'.

142. Advertising Age International (1997), 'Brand Management Goes Regional at Ford', October, 2.

143. Onkvisit, Sak and John J. Shaw (1987), 'Standardized International Advertising: A Review and Critical Evaluation of the Theoretical and Empirical Evidence', *Columbia Journal of World Business* (Fall), 43–55.

144. Harvey, Michael G. (1993), 'Point of View: A Model to Determine Standardization of the Advertising Process in International Markets', *Journal of Advertising Research*, 33 (4), 57–65.

145. Solberg, Carl Arthur (2002), 'The Perennial Issue of Adaptation or Standardization of International Marketing Communication: Organizational Contingencies and Performance', *Journal of International Marketing*, 10 (3), 1–21.

146. Okazaki, Shintaro, Charles R. Taylor, and Shaoming Zou (2006), 'Advertising Standardization's Positive Impact on the Bottom Line: A Model of When and How Standardization Improves Financial and Strategic Performance', *Journal of Advertising*, 35 (3), 17–33.

147. Rosenthal, Walter (1994), 'Standardized International Advertising: A View from the Agency Side', *Journal of International Consumer Marketing*, 7 (1), 39–62.

148. Mueller, Barbara (1991), 'Multinational Advertising: Factors Influencing the Standardised vs. Specialised Approach', *International Marketing Review*, 8 (1), 7–18.

149. Tai, Susan H.C. (1997), 'Advertising in Asia: Localize or Regionalize', *International Journal of Advertising*, 16 (1), 48–61.

150. Ju-Pak, Kuen-Hee (1999), 'Content Dimensions of Web Advertising: A Cross-National Comparison', *International Journal of Advertising*, 18 (2), 207–31.

151. Backhaus, Klaus, Katrin Mühlfeld, and Jenny Van Doorn (2001), 'Consumer Perspectives on Standardization in International Advertising: A Student Sample', *Journal of Advertising Research*, 31 (September/October), 53–61.

152. Clark, Harold F. Jr (1987), 'Consumer and Corporate Values: Yet Another View on Global Marketing', *International Journal of Advertising*, 6, 29–42.

153. *Advertising Age* (1987), 'The House that Built Ivory', 20 August, 26–27.

154. Kanso, Ali and Richard Alan Nelson (2002), 'Advertising Localisation Overshadows Standarization', *Journal of Advertising Research*, 42 (1), 79–89.

155. Hill, J.S. and J.M. Winski (1987), 'Goodbye, Global Ads', *Advertising Age*, 16 November.

156. Peebles, Dean M. (1988), 'Don't Write-Off Global Advertising: A Commentary', *International Marketing Review*, 6 (1), 73–78.

157. Peebles, Dean M. and John K. Ryans (1984), *Management of International Advertising*. Boston, MA: Allyn and Bacon.

158. McCullough, Wayne R. (1996), 'Global Advertising Which Acts Locally: The IBM Subtitles Campaign', *Journal of Advertising Research*, 36 (3), 11–15.

Appendix 13

Teaching materials

A13.1 Case

Brand USA – selling Uncle Sam like Uncle Ben's

'One does not need to destroy one's enemy, one need only destroy his willingness to engage', wrote the ancient Chinese strategist Sun Tzu, as quoted on the US Psychological Operations Veterans Association website (**www.psyop.com**). Using this rationale, nations throughout history have attempted to persuade potential adversaries of the justness of their cause, the certainty of their victory, or the reasons for war that do not justify the death and destruction it would cause. Although written more than 2500 years ago, Sun Tzu's thoughts are strikingly relevant in a world ever more dependent on the mass media for information.

It appears that the US government adopted Sun Tzu's rationale in the wake of the terrorist attacks of 11 September 2001, when it appointed Charlotte Beers as undersecretary of state for public diplomacy and public affairs (State Department). Charlotte Beers, the 'Queen of Branding', formerly chairperson of J. Walter Thompson Worldwide and executive at Ogilvy Mather, architect of brands ranging from IBM to top dog food and credit card brands.[1]

When facing criticism for filling the post with someone lacking diplomatic experience, Colin Powell personally defended Beers by crediting her advertising skills for his preference for Uncle Ben's brand rice. These were exactly the sales skills he thought useful in selling American policies worldwide, thereby lessening the well-documented hatred of the United States.[2] The US Congress apparently agreed, granting a congressional appropriation of US$520 million for Beers' projects.[3] Upon announcing her appointment, Colin Powell advocated that the United States must change from 'selling US . . . to really branding foreign policy'.[4]

Allen Rosenshine, Chairman-CEO of agency BBDO Worldwide, expressed his views about Charlotte Beers' appointment thus: branding precepts are just as appropriate for the American government as they are for commercial purposes because they may be effective in persuading people who 'hate' America to respect America's social, economic and political systems. The theory is that branding creates a psychological bond between user and product that enhances the value of that product. In the same manner, branding a country can create 'something people can value and aspire to with their minds and hearts'.[5] Naomi Klein[1] deconstructed the prevailing branding emphasis in government in her article 'Brand USA'.

Beers was to hinge her campaigns on the underlying belief that Americans and foreign Muslims share fundamental values – home, family and religion – and interests like pop music and sports.[6] The most public face of her work at the State Department was the US$15 million 'Shared values' campaign, designed by McCann-Erickson. According to a State Department official interviewed by the *New York Times*, the target audience for the advertising campaign was the 'non-elite', in 'disaffected countries', aged 15–59 years.[7] The ads were based on focus group research among Muslim Americans, resulting in a film of American Muslims, including a teacher, a broadcasting student, a paramedic and a banker, each speaking of the goodwill and respect for Islam they experienced from Americans (listen to video clips at: **www.opendialogue.org/english/bios.html**). The video was aired during Ramadan 2002 in several Arab countries, then pulled due to criticism and the reticence of the Lebanese government to allow the ad on government-owned television stations due to concern that the video constituted propaganda.[8]

The campaign was part of an effort to address the perceived misperception of the USA. Beers stated in a television interview that Muslims view the United States as 'anti-Islam' and not a fitting environment for Muslims to live and work in.[9] She told Congress members that 'a poor perception of the US leads to unrest, and unrest has proven to be a threat to our national and international security'.[10] Her job was publicly perceived as an effort to explain the foreign policy of the Bush administration, particularly the 'war on terrorism' to the world.[3] In a speech, Beers cited a February 2002 Gallup poll of nine predominantly Muslim countries, where less than 50 per cent of the population expressed a favourable view of the USA. In the case of Kuwait, Morocco and Saudi Arabia, the number expressing a favourable opinion was 28 per cent, 22 per cent, and 18 per cent respectively.[10] A number of misconceptions in the so-called 'Arab Street' were also to be addressed, such as the belief held by some that Israel planned the terrorist attacks of 11 September 2001.

In support of the 'Shared Values' campaign, a website was launched along the lines of the video (**www.opendialogue.org**), and video characters were made available for satellite interviews. Beers' team produced a booklet on the 9/11 terrorist attacks, replete with photos and Ossama Bin Laden's own admissions regarding the attacks in 1.3 million copies and 36 languages, distributed in predominantly Muslim countries, and notably as a supplement in Arab *Newsweek*.[10]

In December, 2002, Beers re-branded the US government-controlled Voice of America (VOA) Arabic radio station as Radio Sawa (**www.radiosawa.com**), broadcasting so-called '*pop*oganda', complete with Western and Arab pop music and zippy news bulletins instead of the usual VOA fare.[11] The initial success was such that the station's cross-cultural and news format were quickly copied by the army of Jordan, and other Arab countries.[11] The State Department also launched the similar Radio Farda, in the Farsi language. Radio Sawa was an attempt to win the ears and hearts of those who would otherwise get their news from Al-Jazeera (**www.english.aljazeera.net**) or, in the case of Iraq, from Iranian radio stations.[12] In a similar effort, on a more traditional bent, Beers expanded the almost defunct US educational and cultural exchanges. She also started a programme to disseminate pro-American films and programming materials to Arab countries, and provided American spokespeople to work with foreign television stations to produce programming that showcases US aid to their country. She was quick to locate speakers who could rebut foreign media attacks on the United States, most notably in the case of former US ambassador to Syria, Arabic-speaking Chris Ross, whom she sent frequently to speak on the pan-Arab network Al-Jazeera.

The US government is conscious that effective branding is also necessary in the military. According to Army Chief of Public Affairs, Major General Charles McClain, the perception of a military operation can be as important to its success as the execution itself.[13] Since the 1980s, military operations have been named self-consciously to please various audiences, in contrast with earlier names such as 'Operation Killer' in Korea or 'Operation Paperclip' in the Second World War (Table 13.1).

Table 13.1 Names of prominent US military operations and military/humanitarian operations conducted by the military that reflect a branding emphasis

Date and location	Name of operation reflecting branding emphasis
1987–1988 – Persian Gulf	Earnest Will
1989–1990 – Panama	Just Cause
1991 – Gulf War phases I and II	Desert Shield/Desert Storm
1991–1996 – Northern Iraq	Provide Comfort
1998 – Sudan and Afghanistan	Infinite Reach
2001 – Afghanistan 'War against Terrorism'	Infinite Justice (oops) name hastily changed after Muslim advisors warn that only Allah is 'infinite'
2001 – Afghanistan	Enduring Freedom

(Source: Seiminsky;[14] Solomon.[13])

During the past century, there were two government offices dedicated to swaying opinions on war at home and abroad. The first, the Committee on Public Information, was founded at the behest of President Woodrow Wilson during the First World War. J. Walter Thompson executives used pamphlets to convince German soldiers on the Western Front that their defeat was inevitable.[15] (To view leaflets used in the recent Iraq conflict, go to **www.centcom. mil/galleries/leaflets/showleaflets.asp**.) In the Second World War, the US Government called its wartime propaganda a 'strategy of truth' executed by the Office of Strategic Services for American allies and others. The war was portrayed in leaflets, press releases and short films as a battle between Good and Evil.[16] The Foreign Information Service broadcast news in Europe and Asia to counter the wartime propaganda run by other governments, a service called Voice of America, the precursor of today's service of the same name.[17] J. Walter Thompson continued to advise the government on the Marshall Plan, and was subsequently assigned to communications for NATO.[3] Throughout the Cold War the United States Information Agency and Radio Free Europe continued working towards the mission of understanding and influencing international public opinion – an effort culminating in the hiring of Charlotte Beers. The effort to influence the attitudes of the general public (as opposed to diplomats) in other countries is termed 'public diplomacy'. According to Harold Pachios, chair of the Advisory Commission on Public Diplomacy, public diplomacy is more important than the traditional type practised between diplomats because all governments (whether allies of the United States or not) are sensitive to domestic public opinion regarding their stance relative to American policies.[18] (For more on public diplomacy visit **www.publicdiplomacy.org**.)

Public diplomacy activities receive a budget of US$1 billion per year. Those who believe the USA faces a public relations problem in dealing with the world are advocating for more money. Richard Lugar, chair of the Senate Foreign Relations Committee stated that for each dollar spent on the US military, seven cents are spent on diplomacy and one-quarter of a cent is spent on public diplomacy.[18] Some believe that rising hostility towards the United States may be a consequence of the cuts to the US$70 million spent after the 11 September 2001 attacks on US-sponsored international news services.[19] Like a marketing-minded company, the State Department's International Information Programs monitors the reaction of foreign media to US-influenced international issues (**http://usinfo.state.gov/products/ medreac.htm**). The State Department then works to correct any perceived misconceptions or biases in the international media. Most other public relations efforts are carried out as in any commercial communications programme; however there is lack of coordination between the different functions within the State Department, according to former US Information Agency comptroller Stan Silverman. Silverman also stated his belief that advertising agency tactics, like those used by Charlotte Beers in her public diplomacy campaigns, are too 'simplistic' for other cultures.[19]

Since 11 September 2001, American politicians believe that hatred for the USA may come from envy, or perhaps ignorance of what their country represents. As a possible expression of that belief, 11 September is now known as 'Patriot Day' (go to **www.hallmark.com** and click on 'browse free e-cards' to view expressions of 'Patriot Day' sentiment). However, as Naomi Klein.[1] pointed out in her article 'Brand USA', children around the world are all too familiar with America's perceived high ground in terms of 'liberty and justice for all'. Hollywood has beamed American films and television programming all over the world, while CNN and other news sources disseminate the American perspective on reality. Therefore non-Americans are well versed in American values, however they are angry about the incompatibility of these stated values and United States' actual foreign policy on the Israel–Palestine conflict, Iraq and many others. Charlotte Beers resigned in March, 2003 due to health reasons.[20] As American popularity plummeted around the world and analysts and politicians argued over the best approach to public diplomacy, the department sought a new direction. Beers and her 'Shared Values' campaign may have clearly communicated that the USA is a good country for Muslims to live in. Her perception that the problems between the world and the USA are simply image or branding-related problems were probably too simplistic: as with any advertised product, the world is waiting for a foreign policy 'product' consistent with advertised American values like freedom, justice and equality. The search for a solution to the American public diplomacy problem has become urgent: a Pew Research Center study found that evaluations of the USA in 20 countries and the Palestinian Authority are markedly lower than a year previously. In only seven countries did a majority of people express a favourable opinion of the United States, of which the leader was Israel with 79 per cent approval ratings. In seven out of eight Muslim countries, the majority of people believe that the United States is a military threat to their nation.

Following the replacement of Charlotte Beers by Margaret Tutwiler towards the end of 2003, there was much speculation as to the future of 'Brand USA'. Tutwiler, a former ambassador and State Department Assistant Secretary for Public Affairs under the first President Bush, was widely thought to be less brand oriented than Beers. Public diplomacy continued, however, with Middle East Television Network (MTN) planned for launch in December 2003 to 'End the deafening silence from America'. Also continuing were other targeted communications efforts including *Hi* magazine, a glossy youth oriented magazine that attempts to focus on lifestyle and avoid politics altogether.[12] The magazine's Arabic-only website offers interactive boxes for readers to 'Ask America' questions, in the spirit of promoting dialogue (**www.himag.com**). MTN, a 24-hour news nemesis of Al-Jazeera is designed to work harder than Fox or CNN to 'discredit' the perceived anti-American stance of Arab news networks. The network has been outsourced to an independent media company by the State Department, with the mission to 'Sell America' in the crowded media markets of the Middle East.[12]

Questions

1. It is often said that marketing is about discovering what target audiences want and making it available. Consider what the United States could 'offer' to its 'target audiences', giving three examples of possible audiences.

2. Is it ethical for political leaders to use marketing strategies to persuade a nation to go to war, and to persuade others, including the enemy, that the war is going well?

3. Should a government market itself across cultures like Coca-Cola or Nike have done?

4. Is it likely that the Bush Administration, in constructing branded communications, may have increased loathing and distrust in the Arab world?

5. What is the difference between diplomacy and propaganda?

Saskia Faulk and Jean-Claude Usunier prepared this case solely to provide material for class discussion. The authors do not intend to illustrate either effective or ineffective handling of a business situation. The authors may have disguised certain names and other identifying information to protect confidentiality.

(©IRM, reprinted with kind permission.)

A13.2 Case

Excel and the Italian advertising campaign

Excel is a multinational company, based in northern Europe, which produces television sets, video recorders and other consumer electronics. In the 1980s it went through a phase of external growth by the takeover of the German and French subsidiaries of a large US-based company that had decided to divest itself of this industry. Within two years this Nordic company tripled in size. It changed from having a mainly Scandinavian base to having a complete European spread, with an 11 per cent share of the European market. The group, built in successive layers, inherited numerous local brands, namely those of the companies taken over. These brands are basically localized marketing assets, with only national coverage and brand recognition. Excel plans to have only one pan-European brand in the long run, with one local brand for each individual country.

The European headquarters were installed in Switzerland, near Lausanne. This location was chosen so that headquarters would be situated in central Europe but not in a country where Excel already had a plant, as this might imply some sort of 'national preference'. Over a period of two years an important reshaping of the industrial base was undertaken, with massive layoffs in some plants and industrial investment aimed at increasing productivity.

Excel wanted to minimize advertising expenses while simultaneously giving its brand a strong, similar image across Europe. In fact it inherited some very diverse brand names, which were those of the companies most recently acquired in their home markets. Excel was therefore willing to design a pan-European advertising campaign. The national subsidiaries were invited either to join this campaign or to design their own campaign. In the latter case, they would have to finance it with their own money. The campaign was scheduled for autumn 1990. Because of the World Cup which was taking place in Italy in June 1990, the Italian subsidiary decided that it could not wait until the autumn, as this type of sports event usually generates increased demand for television sets and video recorders. It managed to go ahead by itself: it made an advertisement which proved to be a real hit and generated a significant sales increase. A television commercial was created and a poster also. The same advertising theme was used for sales promotion. The advertisement showed a superb television set with a video recorder as an integral part, encircled by a red ribbon which largely hid the screen. The slogan was '*Venite a veder lo; dal vero*' (come and see it; for real).

This campaign was a success soon after it started, and was presented to the general managers of the subsidiaries, who met for a residential seminar in Switzerland with the people at European headquarters in Geneva. Reactions were very positive. They proposed the idea of using the same campaign, themes and creation in other European markets. At the beginning of March, Mr Makinen, in charge of marketing communications at the European headquarters, decided to send a memo to the marketing/advertising managers of each subsidiary. A poster and a video presenting the Italian campaign were also enclosed. This memo made a concrete suggestion to the subsidiaries that they should adopt the themes and creation of this campaign. It asked them for their opinions. Makinen invited them to study the feasibility of using such a campaign in their home market and to send their comments back quickly, so that a pan-European campaign could possibly be launched in August. The Italian advertising manager, Signor Ragoli, was available if the European headquarters or national subsidiaries wanted any additional information.

Responses from the subsidiaries (that is, the answers plus the course of action finally adopted) were as follows. It took quite a long time for answers to come back, which could be explained by the overload of work experienced by people in the subsidiaries during this period of reorganization. Some countries never answered the proposal. Otherwise reactions were quite positive, except for that of France. The Spanish answer came quickly. The advertising and public relations manager, Senor Gonzales, sent a copy of the letter to his Italian colleague at European headquarters. He wrote that Spain had decided to use the campaign created in Italy, in order to unify Excel marketing communication. The Spanish wanted to use five different television channels for a total of 22 slots. They supported this with a press campaign and sales promotion in distribution channels. They needed the original version of the Italian television commercial, with music on one track and speech on another (one image track plus two sound tracks). In Spain the final version of the Excel campaign was launched in May 1990. The image track remained unchanged, but the music had been modified and there were several other minor changes. What seemed, at first sight, to be a straight copy of the Italian concept, finally turned out to be a greatly modified version. Nevertheless Spain was the only country where the marketing team made the decision to use the experience of their Italian colleagues.

Sweden and Norway also responded quickly to the memo in similar terms. In neither of these two countries was advertising allowed on national television channels; furthermore, they traded under the Scandinavian brand name Scantel, rather than Excel. The Swedish response explained that the subsidiary did not advertise on television, since TV1 and TV2 did not offer any space; but with the growth of satellite television the Italian proposal might be interesting for the future. The Swedes thought that the Italian campaign was well designed and implemented. The model presented (Excel 7181) was usable with their brand name since they had the same make. The Norwegians' answer had also been very positive. They promised to keep in mind the concepts of the Italian campaign and further indicated that they would recommend its implementation for 1991.

In France the advertising and public relations manager, Monsieur Dubois, initially contacted by telephone, expressed a positive but rather cautious opinion. He said that he had first to discuss the themes and creation with his advertising agency. He called back to make it clear that even if he had any advertising funds left (in fact they were already entirely spent), he considered that the Italian campaign was not appropriate for Ariane (the brand name of the recently acquired French subsidiary). According to him, it did not fit in with the French criteria of what actually makes good advertising. In his opinion Ariane had a fairly traditional image in France, and French consumers would need more serious arguments to change their views. Consequently 'good' advertising for the Ariane brand had to emphasize, first of all, the high-technology image. Ultimately, he thought that the Italian campaign was not sophist-icated enough, and that French people prefer more in-depth, sophisticated and detailed campaigns.

Question

How can the failure of the European headquarters to have the Italian campaign adopted by the other European subsidiaries be explained? What is the right way to go about this in the future? What has to be changed?

A13.3 Exercise

Borovets – a Bulgarian ski resort

Compare the two short texts below (each dated the beginning of 1990). Both depict the Bulgarian ski resort Borovets. The first one is an extract from the magazine *Actuel* (no. 122), from an article entitled 'Guide des bons plans à l'Est' (A guide to travelling in Eastern countries), p. 69. The other is an extract from the trade brochure of the Bulgarian state tourist corporation, *Balkanturist*, entitled 'Bulgaria welcomes you', p. 10. This short exercise is not meant to serve any other purpose than as a pedagogical exercise; it does not aim to describe any real situation and should not prejudice readers concerning holidays in Bulgaria.

Text 1: a charter flight to Bulgaria

The phenomenon already exists, it never stops swelling. Bulgaria is a hospitable place for exhausted proletarians in quest of cheap snow and sun. For the time being, most of the troop comes from Britain: 75 per cent of the tourists are English, 20 per cent are German, the remaining 5 per cent are Dutch, Swedish or French.

The Bulgarian government rubs its hands. The blaze of freedom which blasts through the East has already brought hordes of capitalist tourists. Bulgaria is in urgent need of foreign cur-rencies. The country hopes to have its holiday resorts working at full capacity. Borovets is the most famous resort: in fact, it is a concrete boil encrusted on the mountains. The eight hotels, of luxurious appearance, offer limited comfort: water shortages, telephones out of order, ghost reception desks, bad-tempered staff and rooms where the cleanliness is somewhat dubious. Infrastructure, equipment and service do not meet minimum requirements.

Bulgarian tourism turns out dissatisfied customers. Like Franco's Spain of the 1970s, it is the same reinforced concrete everywhere. Varna and Burgas on the Black Sea coast look like Benidorm. The sea coast is built up with concrete rabbit hutches which swarm with Bulgarian city-dwellers, Greek spendthrifts or drunk Britons. Apocalypse! The rare night-clubs are inaccessible. Meals in the 300-seat restaurants have all the style and allure of gymnasium banquets.

Text 2: Borovets

In Bulgarian, Borovets literally means 'beautiful place'. Borovets during the winter has pure, ozone-rich air; it has 150 days of snow cover which provides exceptional ski slopes, from 1300 to 2500 metres high.

Each year Borovets is host to numerous international ski championships. Ingemar Stenmark, the Mahre brothers, Girardelli and many other famous skiers have spoken highly of this resort which welcomes everyone.

It is a very fashionable ski resort, with its numerous comfortable and cosy hotels, its enticing restaurants and various entertainment facilities for day and night. Borovets is located 50 miles from Sofia, and it has been enjoyed by children and adults since the end of the nineteenth century, when it was only a small holiday centre.

It is no exaggeration to say that Borovets can compete with the Swiss or the French ski resorts. Now why wait any longer to visit us? We wish only to welcome you.

Questions

1. Why is there such a difference between these two pictures? Do these two articles refer to the same reality?

2. How can one get an idea of the level of service in this resort?

3. How should the state company for Bulgarian tourism (which manages the resort) communicate? What prevents them from doing so?

 ## A13.4 Exercise

Slogans and colloquial speech

Marketing communications (advertising copy, slogans, promotional offers, text on coupons, etc.) are language based. The quality of reception of the marketing messages by the target audience is very sensitive to the accuracy of the wording. Marketing communication is based on everyday – colloquial – speech, often very idiomatic.

The basic purpose of this exercise is fairly simple: it may be implemented with a group of people who have different linguistic backgrounds, yet have a capacity to communicate with each other since some of them speak several languages. It does not imply that total fluency is necessary. Participants should simply take care to translate *into* the language(s) which they speak fluently (not *from*).

The exercise consists of the following:

1. Collecting slogans (and, more generally, short marketing communication texts) from magazines, billboards, posters, television commercials, sponsor announcements or short texts such as those found in greeting cards; translating them into other languages, with the objective of finding the equivalent meaning and local wording. The translation techniques explained in section 6.3 (back-translation, parallel translation and a combination of the two) should be used.
2. Collecting 'identical' slogans (again, generally any short marketing communication text) that are pushing the same international brand in different countries, then analysing and comparing how similar propositions and concepts are conveyed in the different languages. Bookshops that sell foreign newspapers and magazines will be useful places to find the basic data.

A13.5 Case

AIDS – designing a communication campaign for Mexico

It was late when Pilar Quiñones returned to her office after a meeting with Dr Perez-Bustamante, Director of the Centro Nacional Para la Prevención y Control de VIH/SIDA (CENSIDA), the Mexican Health Ministry's official HIV/AIDS organization. *Muy difícil*, she thought, looking at the mass of paperwork on her desk. UNAIDS reports and campaigns, Pan American Health Organization charts, internal CENSIDA statistics and scientific journal clippings occupied the space normally taken by glowing product reviews, colour-coded consumer research reports and shiny product samples.

Quiñones, Vice President of Mexico's largest advertising agency, had just agreed to design a national AIDS awareness campaign. At first, she had resisted the idea, arguing that the government should design its own AIDS programmes because an advertising agency does not have the specialized knowledge that is needed. Dr Perez-Bustamante of CENSIDA eventually persuaded her by saying that all governments that succeeded in their fight against AIDS have used advertising agencies.

As Quiñones worked on the project over the next few days, her interest deepened. She personally had never known anyone with AIDS, however she had heard of friends of friends who had it, and had read about several high-profile cases in the press. Mexico's AIDS infection rate among adults was relatively low at 0.3 per cent, the same as Canada's and much less than neighbouring Guatemala (1 per cent), Belize (2 per cent) and the USA (0.6 per cent).[21] HIV/AIDS cases were estimated at about 177,000, the 16th leading cause of death in Mexico and fourth leading cause of death among young men. The very poor, of whom 9 million are children living in absolute poverty, are unlikely to have access to anti-retroviral treatment for the disease.[22] Infection rates were not stabilizing and, more worrying, the raw data on infections were probably underrepresenting reality, reflecting a mobile population, highly dissuasive stigma, corruption and an inefficient health-recording system.

Why were the vast majority of drug-related AIDS cases in the north, close to the US border? Why were women taking up more and more of the AIDS burden? Why were homosexuals again starting to practise unsafe sex? Quiñones jotted down a list of 'barriers' to communication that appeared to be quite significant in Mexico, presented in Table 13.2.

Since stigma is such an important factor in AIDS prevention and treatment, what would be the best way to reduce it? Quiñones sat back in her leather and steel chair, pondering the realization that her campaign should create social norms for less risky behaviours and less stigma. *Aren't all campaigns like that, though, to create a social norm for product adoption and evaluation behaviours*, she mused, *to get people to value a particular brand is not so different from getting people to value safer sex practices. So, what is the need here?* The scientists and policy makers at CENSIDA had simply said her mandate was to raise awareness and reduce infections. She would need to quantify those goals so as to measure the success of the campaign later on. She started making another list, influenced by her discussions with HIV/AIDS experts, to be discussed later with the strategy people and the creative people within the agency. The list of 'needs' that should be satisfied by the country's HIV/AIDS programme is represented in Table 13.3.

Table 13.2 Informal notes on barriers to HIV/AIDS social marketing in Mexico

Literacy:	We need a message that sounds powerful when said on radio/TV, looks powerful when represented in image form, and can be expressed simply.
Language:	Campaign in Spanish and some major native languages, such as Mayan or Nahuatl? It appears that indigenous peoples not much affected by HIV . . . yet. Or is it not diagnosed/not reported? HIV/AIDS has tended to establish itself among the dispossessed, the poor, the marginalized in other countries.
Religion (Catholic):	The Pope has frequently condemned the use of condoms, and Mexican First Lady Marta Sahagun Fox was publicly attacked by bishops for exhorting Mexicans to use condoms (they stated that condom use was an invitation to depravity).
Demographic:	Massive undocumented flows of migrants (how to reach them?): ■ from south to north, some in transit from Central America *en route* to the USA; ■ Mexicans leaving for temporary, usually agricultural, work in the USA or manufacturing work on the northern border; ■ jobless/dispossessed farmers leaving the countryside to go to cities; ■ migrants returning from the USA, usually to homes in rural areas.
Cultural:	Male value of *machismo*, whereby men should be seen as invincible, not sick, not seeking help (how can we break through that?).

Table 13.3 Possible needs identified for HIV/AIDS infections reduction campaign

Simply to re-open public dialogue about HIV/AIDS:	A study in Peru (with some cultural similarities to Mexico) found that teachers and parents needed help to bring sexual issues out into the open. Doctors say that many rural Mexicans have never heard of the disease, partly because it is so difficult to talk openly about sex.
Reduce stigma:	There is anecdotal evidence that stigma is so strong in rural Mexican contexts that people refuse to be tested, and do not even tell their spouses if they suspect they have the disease for fear of reprisals by neighbours on their entire family.
Get Tested:	Pregnant women who visit clinics are tested for the disease, and there is some mandatory, but illegal testing in the private sector. Many young people believe that HIV/AIDS only happens to prostitutes, sexually promiscuous people and homosexuals.
Behaviour Change Communication (BCC):	Use condoms. Condom use is low; UNAIDS pinpointed condom use at about 59 per cent in a sample of Mexican men in 2001.

Quiñones wondered whether to segment the campaign geographically to reflect the large cultural differences between the northern states, the central cities and the south. On the other hand, it would be important to mirror the large differences in the urban and rural attitudes and access to testing, information and treatment. There were also specific groups common to different geographic areas, such as gay men. The affluent gay communities had often been profiled by the ad agency in the past as a favoured target market for travel and luxury goods. She opened a new page on her laptop to list the ever-growing questions posed by this HIV/AIDS campaign, one of the major ones being 'who are we trying to reach?' Targets are identified in Table 13.4.

Table 13.4 Potential target audiences identified in informal study

Residents of the big cities? e.g. in Mexico City 28 per cent of reported HIV/AIDS cases in 2001, other big cities smaller but still significant share.

Rural populations? Disease is spreading much faster in rural areas than in cities, yet there is less awareness, testing, and information about the disease, and more stigma related to it (AFAR, 2002). In rural areas, women comprise 21.3 per cent of those with HIV/AIDS, while in cities the percentage is closer to 14 (Country Profile, 2003). Rural populations may require a more conservative format.

Age segments? Street children used for prostitution and pornography, numbers estimated at 2 million by the government (MCL, 2003). Most danger for street children from sexual exploitation is in areas close to the US border. About 90 per cent of them are addicted to glue and solvents, also a low literacy level according to Casa Alianza, street children's charity.

Gender segments? Women comprised one-sixth of AIDS cases, whereas in the 1980s they comprised one-twentieth. In some southern states (with high concentrations of indigenous peoples), heterosexual transmission is the predominant mode, implying that women are increasingly victims of the disease (Country Profile, 2003).

Migrants in transit from neighbouring countries with high rates of the disease. An estimated 30 per cent of HIV/AIDS cases are temporary migrant workers returning home from the USA with the disease.[23]

Intravenous drug users make up a relatively small portion of HIV/AIDS cases. If targeted, geographic factors to be accounted for: vast majority in states bordering the United States.

Her assistant knocked at the door with his results of searching for ideas in other campaigns from around the world. He tabulated his preliminary findings in Table 13.5.

Quiñones was impressed by the range of social marketing strategies implemented in other countries, and particularly by the work in the area of international organizations and advocacy groups. The World Health Organization (WHO) provided a good example of this. Using a historical perspective in the publication 'Mobilizing for healthy behaviour', for instance, there was a comprehensive social marketing model named CAUSE. This model was inspired by the anti-apartheid movement in South Africa, the fight for civil rights in the USA, and the struggle for independence in India. The central idea is to roll out as many elements of CAUSE as possible, including[24]:

■ Celebrity (such as Princess Diana against landmines).
■ Activity (such as pacifist rallies and demonstrations).
■ Unexpected event/story (such as the media reports on contaminated blood).
■ Symbol (such as a flag, ribbon, or logo).
■ Event (such as World Aids Day).

Table 13.5 Non-inclusive survey of communications ideas implemented in other countries

Country/organization	Communications idea
UNAIDS 2002–03	'Live and let live' reducing AIDS-related stigma (mass media).
UNAIDS 2001–02	'I care . . . do you?' targeting men (mass media).
Several African countries	'A,B,C: Abstain, Be faithful, Condomise' simple reminder (billboard).
Several African countries	'Graze close to home' and cattle image: non-offensive allegory (billboard).
USA, France	Youth identification in 'slice of life' shots: public service announcements encouraging testing, condom use (television).
USA	Magic Johnson, ex-basketball player (spokesperson, events, press, public service announcements). Patti Labelle, singer: signature campaign 'Live long, sugar' (spokesperson, events, songs, public service announcements targeted at male homosexuals).
Brazil	Ronaldo, football player (spokesperson, events, press, public service announcements).
Many countries	'Myth breakers' mosaic of faces or photos, can you tell which one has AIDS? (Billboard, public service announcements).
South Africa	'Soul City', award-winning 'soap opera' type edutainment series based on television episodes, supported by radio shows, press discussions of issues, and high quality booklets.[25]
Brazil	Condom use promotion: condoms emblazoned with football team emblems.

From her experience with product launches and media campaigns, Quiñones knew that more research was needed. There was no need to reinvent the wheel, much effective work has already been done in other Latin American countries. For example, the output of groundbreaking activist communicators 'Calandria' in Peru included many ideas in media planning and products for social marketing of health and development programmes (see **www.accionensida.org.pe**).

The information she needed in order to design the campaign was of three types:

1. Profiles of targeted segments of the population. The advertising agency had many such profiles, however none that looked at sexual behaviour and attitudes. Quiñones would need a clear view of who these targeted audiences are, what they believe about HIV/AIDS, and what themes resonate with them that would help get the message across.

2. Literature review of AIDS-related behavioural change intervention research. There have been many critical analyses of AIDS behavioural change programmes. Ideally, each time such a programme is carried out, the results are monitored, results that could be useful to Quiñones in designing her campaign. Because much of this work is conducted by non-profit organizations and charities, it is easily accessible and will not bite too much out of the budget. A good resource to begin with is **www.comminit.com** (The Communication Initiative).

3. The final type of information that would be helpful in designing the campaign is a survey of current and past campaigns from around the world. *Why reinvent the wheel?* Surely Quiñones and her creative team could find some inspiring ideas, particularly ones that have proved their effectiveness in other settings. See Table 13.5 for her findings.

Table 13.6 Potential partners for the HIV/AIDS campaign

Potential partner	Quick summary of top advantages/disadvantages
Mexican film industry	Less reach over certain target audiences than television, possibly more impact on public relations; many possible spokespeople, although costly.
Family Health International (**www.fhi.org**)	As one of the primary female reproductive health providers, it is well entrenched at local/community levels around the country.
Casa Alianza (**www.casa-alianza.org**)	Prize-winning charity working with street children in Mexico and three other countries. Its 'Luna Project' focuses on HIV and AIDS. May be useful in sub-campaign targeted at street children and may give more credibility than a programme run by the Ministry of Health.
US Agency for International Development (**www.usaid.gov**)	USAID is a highly visible, credible and financially powerful organization. It is the largest donor on HIV and AIDS to Mexico, well known for social marketing of condoms. However, with Mexicans having such high levels of 'national pride' it would be better to keep the project as local as possible.
Radio stations	A multitude of radio stations, already well segmented in terms of audiences, listened to as background noise all day by many Mexicans. May lack the attention-getting power for a long message, however may be effective for 'edutainment' formats.
MTV	MTV has a well-established track record in AIDS activism.
Mexican passions	Football (everyone but mainly males), bullfighting (mainly older males) and *telenovelas*, soap operas or social dramas (mainly females of all ages, and some gay men). A spokesperson may be found from one of these areas, or sporting events may be used to educate the 'captive audience'.

Quiñones was aware that an isolated programme would get few results. It would be imperative to partner with a highly visible organization or company. She made a short list and handed it to her assistant to solicit ideas from other executives for cause-related marketing efforts (see Table 13.6).

In order to understand the best ways to reach the targeted audiences, Quiñones drew up a list of possible media and supporting vehicles to carry the message, and a quick note about the kind of information needed.

1. *Mass media*: readership of newspaper, magazines and frequency of exposure.
2. *Internet*: access to the Internet, frequency of use:
   - e-zines, weblogs, chat rooms, subscription material: type and frequency of use;
   - e-mail: access to and frequency of use;
   - Internet games: e.g. HIV/AIDS game by activists at **www.SuperShagLand.com**.
3. *Television*:
   - advertising spots/public service announcements;
   - edutainment show on the lines of Soul City (see Table 13.5);
   - insertion of AIDS issues into *telenovelas* (social dramas), comedies or talk shows.
4. *Radio*:
   - advertising spots/public service announcements;
   - programming including music/talk/interviews/*radionovela* (social dramas).

5. *Mobile and fixed line phones*:
   - new hotline for young people;
   - SMS and even MMS (short and media messages) to phone users, perhaps as a game.
6. *Minibus stickers*: minibus being the most common means of transport.
7. *Leaflets*, possibly to support television, radio and Internet efforts.
8. *Logo t-shirts, caps, pens, condoms, etc.*
9. *Youth mobilization programme*: festivals, street theatre, street football, popular song, video.

For an idea of the type of vehicle Quiñones might decide to use as one part of her campaign, go to the site of Media For Development International (MFDI) to watch a free 48-minute Ugandan AIDS prevention film using Real Player (**www.mfdi.org**).

Questions

1. How should sensitive messages about AIDS issues be conveyed to a Mexican audience given the cultural traits of Mexico? What is the best strategy: direct or indirect? Emotional or rational? Informative? Persuasive?

2. What should be the target audience(s) of the Mexican AIDS campaign?

3. Make propositions as concerns the copy strategy and media planning of the campaign.

4. Which potential partners would you approach for this campaign? Do you recommend that Quiñones uses sponsoring and other forms of marketing communication? If yes, how would you design an integrated marketing communications plan?

Saskia Faulk and Jean-Claude Usunier prepared this case solely to provide material for class discussion. The authors do not intend to illustrate either effective or ineffective handling of a business situation. The authors may have disguised certain names and other identifying information to protect confidentiality.

(©IRM, reprinted with kind permission.)

Appendix references

1. Klein, Naomi (2002), 'Brand USA', *Alternet.org*, 13 March, www.alternet.org/story/12617.
2. Sylvester, Rachel (2003), 'Brand USA Campaign Attempts to Win over UK', *The Age* (Australia), 25 January.
3. De Grazia, Voctoria (2002), 'Bush Team Enlists Madison Avenue in War on Terror', *International Herald Tribune* (online), 26 August, www.globalissues.org/Geopolitics/WarOnTerror/Madison.asp.
4. Teinowitz, Ira (2002), 'Charlotte Beers and the Selling of America', *Advertising Age*, 23 September.
5. Rosenshine, Allen (2002), 'Selling America to People Who Hate It', *Advertising Age*, 18 August.
6. Satloff, Robert (2003), 'How to Win Friends and Influence Arabs', *Weekly Standard*, 18 August.
7. Perlez, Jane (2002), 'Muslim as Apple Pie Video Greeted with Scepticism', *New York Times* (online), 30 October, http://query.nytimes.com/gst/fullpage.html?res=9E03E3DC133FF933A05753C1A9649C8B63.
8. Anon (2002), 'Lebanon Bans TV Spots Aimed at Improving U.S. Image', *Jordan Times*, 20 December.
9. Newshour Media Unit (2003), Undersecretary Charlotte Beers interviewed by Terence Smith, January.
10. Beers, Charlotte (2002), 'Funding for Public Diplomacy, Statement before the Subcommittee on Commerce, Justice, and State of the House Appropriations Committee', *US Department of State*, 24 April, www.state.gov/r/us/9778.htm.
11. Leonard, Mark (2002), 'Velvet Fist in an Iron Glove', *Observer*, 16 June, www.guardian.co.uk/world/2002/jun/16/2.
12. Harris, Shane (2003), 'Brand U.S.A.', *Government Executive Magazine*, 1 October.
13. Solomon, Norman (2002), 'Branding New and Improved Wars', *Fairness and Accuracy In Reporting (FAIR)*, 29 October.
14. Seiminski, Gregory C. (1995), 'The Art of Naming Operations', *Parameters*, 81–98.

15. Wells, Robert A. (2002), 'Mobilizing Public Support for War: An Analysis of American Propaganda During World War I', paper presented at the Annual Meeting of the International Studies Association.

16. Public Broadcasting Service (PBS) (2003), NOW with Bill Moyers, *Politics and Economics*, 31 January.

17. Gannett News Service (2002), *History of Public Diplomacy*, 14 July.

18. Weiser, Carl (2003), 'U.S. Losing Battle Worldwide on Public Relations Front', *Gannett News Service*, 31 March.

19. Orris, Michelle (2003), 'White House: Better PR Can Reverse Anti-American Sentiment', *Austin American Statesman*, 1 August.

20. Teinowitz, Ira (2003), 'Charlotte Beers to Resign from State Department', *Advertising Age* (March).

21. UNAIDS (2002), Global HIV/AIDS and STD Surveillance, Epidemological fact sheets, undated.

22. Bautista, Sergio Antonio, Tania Dmytraczenko, Gilbert Kombe, and Stefano M. Bertozzi (2003), 'Costing of HIV/AIDS Treatment in Mexico', *Partners for Health Reform Plus*, http://www.phrplus.org/Pubs/Tech020_fin.pdf.

23. American Foundation for Aids Research (AFAR) (2002), *Global Initiatives Mexico*, undated.

24. World Health Organization (WHO) (2002), *Infectious Diseases Report 2002*. www.who.int/infectious-disease-report/2002/.

25. Usdin, S. (2001), 'Soul City', *Urban Health and Development Bulletin* (June), Medical Research Council of South Africa, 3 (2).

Intercultural marketing communications 2: personal selling, networking and public relations

In Ghana there is a saying: 'Mouth smiles, money smiles better'. Money is always at the very centre of personal selling, but so are the intricacies of human relationships. This chapter deals with the last two of the four methods of marketing communications: 1. advertising examined the previous chapter; 2. sales promotion examined in section 11.5; 3. personal selling; and 4. public relations.

Cultural differences (time and space assumptions, interaction models and attitudes towards action, as described in Chapters 2 and 3) have a major impact on how relationships start and develop. It is argued in section 14.1 that people need to be *relationship and service* centred rather than purely *deal and product* centred. Section 14.2 develops this argument by comparing the Western view of business networks to the Chinese *guanxi*. We then discuss how culture impacts on buyer–seller interactions (section 14.3); naturally it involves personal contact which is culture bound. Personal selling issues are then examined from an organizational perspective focusing on how a sales force can be managed in a cross-cultural context (14.4). Section 14.5 deals with public relations, which, even though it does not directly contribute to sales, may be of prime concern for defending corporate image before various publics. In the last two sections we examine ethical issues related to selling, first by presenting facts about bribery (14.6) and second by suggesting some ways of appreciating the cultural relativity of ethical attitudes (14.7).

14.1

Intercultural commerce

Commerce as implementation of marketing programmes

Commerce is about personal selling and establishing continuity in the relationship with individual customers, organizational buyers and intermediaries. Commerce is defined by the Collins English Online Dictionary as follows: '1. the activity embracing all forms of the purchase and sale of goods and services; 2. social relationships and exchange, esp. of opinions, attitudes etc.' Commerce favours the social interaction between vendor (producer and/or distributor) and customer. The quality of this social interaction, including marketing strategies that respect cultural integrity, guarantees the effective implementation of global strategies.

This view is in line with the shift from a 'goods-dominant logic' (G-D) to a 'service-dominant logic' (S-D).[1] In this context, Vargo and Lusch (p. 2)[2] define a service as: 'the application of specialized competences (skills and knowledge), through deeds, processes, and performances for the benefit of another entity or the entity itself'. In this logic, the value creation moves from production in isolation from the customer, to a collaborative process of co-creation within the exchange. The focus is on the relationship and the exchange of services, with the knowledge and skills of the providers being the sources of value creation, not the goods which may be part of the exchange.[1] Many of the changes in focus from G-D to S-D suggested by Vargo and Lusch (p. 258)[1] are relevant to the sales force function:

1. From thinking about the purpose of firm activity as *making something* (goods or services) to a process of *assisting customers in their own value-creation processes.*
2. From thinking about value as something *produced* and sold to thinking about value as something *co-created* with the customer and other value-creation partners.
3. From thinking of *customers as isolated entities* to understanding them in the context of their own *networks.*
4. From thinking of *firm resources* primarily as *operand* (e.g., tangible resources such as natural resources) to *operant* (e.g., usually intangible resources such as knowledge and skills).
5. From thinking of *customers as targets* to thinking of *customers as resources.*
6. From making *efficiency primary* to increasing *efficiency through effectiveness.*

The implications for the sales force include both an increased use of technology to reduce some traditional sales force functions and an increased concentration on relationships with the most important customers.[3] (Sheth and Sharma, 2008). Sheth and Sharma (p. 264)[3] suggest that sales automation will reduce the sales function by allowing:

1. the exchange of detailed information instantaneously between employees, suppliers and customer 24/7 regardless of the time zones;
2. the identification of profitable customers through customer relationship management (CRM) software and activity-based accounting;
3. information on the entire set of offerings, rather than the products salespeople know most about;
4. customers the time to deliberate on decisions, especially in relation to customized products;
5. a reduction in error, as customers enter their own requirements directly; and
6. enhanced efficiency of ordering with electronic data interchange (EDI) between the customer and marketers' computers.

Thus, technology is able to bring customers and suppliers closer, despite distance, time and cultural separation in international business. In this manner, technology can serve the customer by enhancing the availability of information and allowing a higher level of service to the most important customers.[3] However, it is a support function, as cultures differ in the acceptability of initiating and managing relationships remotely: in South-East Asian countries the personal touch is still essential to build trust, while in other countries, such as Australia, people are more comfortable with remote relationships (Hulnick, 2000). Even in low context, more individualist cultures, such as the US, the majority of people still want contact with a live customer service representative.[4]

Continuity in commercial relationships: learning from consumers

Relationship marketing focuses on customer retention, customer commitment and share of the customer's business, rather than market share.[5] According to Sheth and Parvatiyar there are three unique aspects to relationship marketing: (1) it is a one-on-one relationship between the marketer and seller; (2) it is an interactive process, where boundaries of time, location and identity between the supplier and customers are blurring; and (3) it is a value-added activity, where there is collaboration and mutual interdependence.[5]

Relationship marketing has been made easier by the availability of customer relationship management software that helps track the records from each customer. The records of each customer provide detailed information about when and how customers buy products, what options they choose, and whether there are any differences between first time and repeat customers. This information can also be used to personalize marketing, by building a customer profile and adapting offerings to best suit the customer. Amazon online provides an example of this type of application: Once your profile is established the software identifies book suggestions based on prior purchases and tailors deals to specific customer preferences.

There are many reasons why the relationship and the lines of communication between a producer and the ultimate consumer may be broken. As Day (p. 14) explains, a company needs to activate sensors at the point of customer contact:

In most organizations front-line contact people – who handle the complaints, hear requests for new services, cope with lead users, or lose sales due to competitor initiative – are seldom motivated to inform management on a systematic basis. They may fear [to] have their job load increase, suspect the information won't be used, or not know where it should be sent . . . Channels for the upward flow of information need to be established and incentives need to be offered for useful insights.[6]

Distribution channels often act as a filter; consumers complain but there is no specific communication channel to the manufacturer and complaints are not taken seriously or are simply ignored (see Box 14.1). When the distributor is independent, located in a foreign country, and paid by commission on sales rather than rewarded for key consumer or competitor information, it is likely that the upward flow will be limited, unless specific action is taken. A product may, for instance, be refused by distribution for substantive reasons which remain ignored, such as store employees experiencing difficulties in opening cardboard boxes which are stapled in such a way that they are injured when trying to open them. Similarly, a class of potential consumers may be neglected by marketing communications, since only actual buyers are targeted and research has failed to examine alternative segments.

The example of Japanese *keiretsu*, presented in section 11.1, demonstrates the value of building communication channels which help in the design and implementation of marketing strategies. Where opportunities for the return of products are liberal, distributors may warn producers about defective products that consumers are simply not happy with. Conversely, when producers or retailers reject consumer complaints, they will often shift responsibility for the failure on to the consumers, telling them they have not read the instructions, or have misused the product, or fixed it incorrectly.

As indicated in Chapter 4, there may be cultural differences in people's willingness to complain. The five domains of attitude toward complaining outlined in Chapter 4 differ across cultures:

1. Beliefs about the effect experienced when one complains.
2. Perceptions of the objective cost or trouble involved in making a complaint.
3. Perception of retailer responsiveness to consumer complaints.

BOX 14.1

'Tubeless tyres', you said . . .

A consumer bought a leading European make of tyre for his car. He asked his garage to fit the tyres. In fact they fitted tubeless tyres since they were supposed to be cheaper (as they did not need air chambers). These tyres, however, kept deflating. When complaining for the first time, the consumer was told by the garage to be slightly more careful in inflating the tyres. They had to be reinflated roughly twice a week. The customer contacted his garage again but was merely told that it 'didn't usually happen'. The customer asked if the tyre manufacturer would take back the defective tyres but the garage told him that that was impossible and that in any case the tyres did at least stay inflated for a couple of days.

Finally, after going backwards and forwards several times, the customer had air chambers put into the tyres. The problem immediately ceased. When he spoke to his garage, they informed him that the wheel rims had warped slightly owing to the 30,000 miles (48,000 km) that the car had done. Other cars (the garage mentioned a German make) had rims made out of a thicker steel which was more resistant and therefore did not warp. Such a car could have tubeless tyres fitted successfully, whatever its age. The customer asked the garage to pass on this information to the tyre manufacturer so that it could inform tyre centres which cars were not suitable for tubeless tyres after a certain mileage had been covered. The garage said that this was impossible. The information was not passed on. Tubeless tyres continue to deflate in a fairly large number of cases. Customers either fit air chambers or buy a different car . . . or they change their make of tyre.

4. The extent to which consumer complaints are expected to benefit society at large.
5. The perceived social appropriateness of making consumer complaints.

In general, Asian consumers are less likely than non-Asian consumers to complain directly to management, but more likely to complain privately, such as negative word of mouth.[7-9] In many Western countries consumer rights are paramount, with external organizations, such as consumer protection, being able to intervene if a resolution between a business and purchaser cannot be reached. In many Eastern countries, this is not the case.

In addition, people from different cultural backgrounds may prefer different remedies to dissatisfaction. In many Western countries, consumers perceived compensation for damages as a fair and just response, whereas consumers from Eastern countries perceived a higher level of fairness when they are able to express dissatisfaction and someone listens.[10] Dissatisfied customers are less likely to receive monetary or material remedies in China than in Canada.[11]

A human resource emphasis

Both personnel *and* clients should be seen by a company as its human resources. The frontiers of the organization should be less clear-cut: most companies develop impermeable boundaries between their 'inside' and their 'outside'. Insiders are generally people listed on the payroll. It is often claimed in company slogans that 'the customer is king' (*le client est roi, der Kunde ist König*, etc.), but in reality they are treated as *outsiders* and there is little personal knowledge of who the consumers actually are. A customer will often have a hard time getting to see the manager, even to give positive feedback.

Very often distribution channels will be used as 'shock-absorbing mattresses'. As distribution channels are in direct contact with customers, if something goes wrong, it is *their* job to deal with it. The isolation of manufacturers is too often the rule for non-commerce-oriented organizations, though they claim to be marketing oriented. In fact, consumers must be viewed as one of the key human resources of the company. They are not kings, but they are an integral part of the buyer–seller relationship. The role of the salesperson is as a consultant for the buying firm.[3] Salespeople need to be customer experts, not just product experts, who provide solutions that may require sourcing outside of the organization. They have direct relationships and communications with the both the distribution network and final customers and must convey messages in both directions, from the manufacturer to the market *and* vice versa.

Making contacts

Making appropriate contacts and developing relationships is an essential part of commerce. The issue is, at what level of the organization and with which people must contacts be made to maximize the chances of a successful outcome. When making contacts in a cross-cultural setting people should be aware of the following: (1) status is not shown in the same way in all cultures; (2) influential persons are not the same and individual influence is not exerted in the same way; and (3) the decision-making process differs. Box 14.2 illustrates the first two points with an African example.

Trust and commitment encourage the preservation of relationships.[12] Trust, relating to the reliability and integrity of the partner, has two basic elements in Western societies: credibility and benevolence.[13] Credibility is related to the belief that the partner will effectively and reliably perform the exchange. Benevolence is related to the belief that the partner will act in the interests of the other party. Both of these constructs differ across cultures. First, there are clearly two levels where credibility has to be established depending on cultural codes: personal and organizational. For instance, in China the concept of credibility relies on an oral commitment (personal), which differs from the Western concept which relies on a written commitment (organizational).[14] As such, the personal rather than organizational relationship is more important in China. Second, the concept of benevolence is related to human nature orientation. In societies where a positive human nature orientation is predominant, people are viewed as capable of being trusted based on an assessment of personality

BOX 14.2

The little man in rags and tatters

The story takes place in the corridor to the office of the minister of industry of the Popular Republic of Guinea at the beginning of the 1980s. Whether you had an appointment or you came to solicit a meeting, you had to be let in by the door-keeper. Besides, the door was locked and he had the key. This little man looked tired and wore worn-out clothes; his appearance led foreign visitors to treat him as negligible and to pay little attention to him. When visitors had been waiting for a long time while seeing others being given quick access to the minister, they often spoke out unrestrainedly, voicing

their impatience to the old man, who seemed to have only limited language proficiency. In fact, the door-keeper spoke perfect French and was the uncle of the minister, which gave him power over his nephew according to the African tradition. It was notorious that the minister placed great confidence in his uncle's recommendations. Thus some foreign contractors never understood why they did not make deals although they had been developing winning arguments with the minister himself.

(Source: Gérard Verna, Laval University, Québec.)

traits and intentions. In societies where a negative human nature orientation is predominant, there is initial distrust. As such, benevolence is less relevant to trust in Chinese cultures, where *assurance* is built on the incentive structure (obligation and indebtedness) surrounding the relationship.[14]

Despite relationship marketing focusing on long-term relationships, there is necessarily a first contact. Here, the physical and behavioural attributes of people, as well as their social status, carry messages about their credibility (see section 3.1). It is important to become personally acquainted with key decision makers in potential target companies. There may be some problems in clearly identifying the key decision makers, and establishing one's credibility with them. They may resent dealing with 'mere salespeople', especially in countries where sales status is low and power distance is high, because it conflicts with their self-image and their organizational position. Complex codes of interpersonal relationships govern the establishment of credibility: it is therefore often necessary to use sales assistants or market researchers as 'door-openers', who will quickly be succeeded by higher-ranking sales executives or sales managers (Box 14.3).

Any 'detail' may be of importance in establishing credibility in the absence of more profound informational cues, which come only when the relationship is more established. Business cards are important because

they provide clear information on businesspersons: their family and first names, how to reach them, their status within the company, etc. A foreign-language card will also reflect sensitivity to the host culture[15] and when one is working mostly with a particular culture (e.g. a US businessperson exporting to Japan), it is advisable to have a card printed in English on the one side with the Japanese transliteration on the other side. Credibility is often based on first impressions: accent has been shown to influence the credibility and effectiveness of an international businessperson. In Guatemala, for instance, Guatemalan Spanish evokes more favourable judgements than the same sales pitch in foreign-accented Spanish.[16]

The decision-making process in the buyer's organization is a key issue for making adequate contact. Power distance (PD) plays an important role in the style of organizational decision making: the higher it is, the more centralized it is. In a French context, for instance, with high PD, individualism and uncertainty avoidance, decision making and budgetary power are located at the top of the organization. Most people cannot so much as buy a pencil without referring to the top. Thus, for personal selling, one has to target contacts at the top while keeping friendly contacts with people at intermediate levels because they could resent their lack of power being openly manifested by the seller's attitude and obstruct the deal. In

BOX 14.3

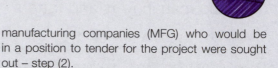

The Japanese 'message-boy'

During research into the key factors surrounding the success of Japanese engineering companies in world markets, I had the opportunity to interview several Japanese engineering specialists. One of them had worked for C. Itoh, a large Japanese trading company, on the sale and project follow-up of an oil refinery in Algeria. He explained by the use of a diagram (Figure 14.1) the Japanese 'method' for selling turnkey factories.

He stressed the central role of the *sogoshosha* (GTC: general trading company) as an *organizer*, a function that includes the responsibilities of information source, business intermediary and coordinator. An *organizer* is roughly equivalent to a 'sales prospection expert before, during and after the sale of a large and highly complex item'. One of C. Itoh's small offices in Algiers, which specialized in import–export, principally of textile products, learned of the existence of a new tender for an oil refinery which was shortly to be published. The Algiers office sent a fairly detailed fax to Tokyo – step (1) in Figure 14.1 – where the engineering company(ies) and the

manufacturing companies (MFG) who would be in a position to tender for the project were sought out – step (2).

Even at this early stage, a project team will begin to assemble from among the different companies involved (3). The trading company contacts the official bodies: first, the foreign insurance division of the Ministry of International Trade and Industry (GOV) to determine whether the project has a chance of being covered for political and commercial risk (4). The Japanese Exim-Bank, the public export-finance body (BKG), will also be contacted for a preliminary study into financing options. These bodies will not make any firm commitment, but they will give a preliminary response: if the project risks not being covered by official guarantees, or receiving only limited cover, the project team instituted by the trading company may decide to abandon the tender.

While all this is going on, and even before the bid documents are available, a preliminary team will be sent to the site to examine the possibilities of water and energy supply, transport facilities, etc. Already

Figure 14.1 The role of Japanese general trading companies as 'organizers' in the negotiation and implementation of international turnkey operations: a Japanese view

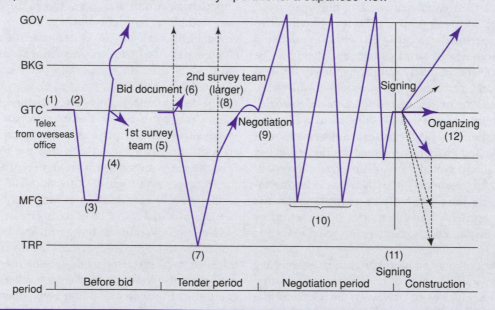

Box 14.3 *(continued)*

the Japanese are gaining time (5). Once the bid documents are available to companies (6), the trading company's local representative will go to collect them personally from the future owner and dispatch the documents to Tokyo after having summarized the main points in a long and detailed fax or e-mail. The representative will not hesitate to stay up most of the night to draft this text. By this stage, the Japanese have already gained 15 days on their international competitors (7).

Once the detailed fax or e-mail has been received, a larger team will go to examine the technical and economic conditions on-site. The results of this survey, and the consultation with various engineering partners, heavy equipment manufacturers (MFG) and carriers (TRP), will enable the formulation of a detailed bid, which very often has to be submitted within a fairly short time span (30 days) after the publication of the tender. The bid will not be sent, but handed over by a young executive, who will be 25 to 30 years old: a 'message-boy' (8). His task is an important one: thanks to him, there is no risk of the documents being blocked by customs; he also has the job of 'sizing up' the people being dealt with and of discerning the people who will really make the final decision. Once more the Japanese have gained time; they are never late in

submitting a tender, whereas a number of their foreign competitors submit theirs after the deadline. Although late delivery of a bid is usually accepted (bidding times are fairly short), it does not necessarily reflect favourably on the capacity to meet delivery dates.

Now the negotiation phase begins (9). This will easily last several months and in extreme cases will stretch, with long interruptions, over several years. Much shuttling back and forth between the various levels (10) will allow the finalizing of an offer. If successful, the offer will lead to the signature of the contract for a large-scale project (11), in which the trading company and the engineering company will generally be joint contractors. As a result, the trading company will adopt the role of coordinator between the various companies carrying out the project (12).

According to my Japanese informant, Nobuhiko Suto, now a professor at Tokai University, who had been personally involved in the deal, the 'message-boy' is typical of the Japanese way of doing business. He is even requested to scrutinize the faces of the people to whom he submits the offer to determine their reaction to the Japanese bid. In the West, it is difficult to conceive of such care being taken to assess subjective reactions objectively.

---

countries where power distance is small, such as Australia, decision making is more decentralized, and there are financial thresholds for decisions at each level of the hierarchy, especially when there is also an individualistic orientation in the culture. In this context the level of contact is roughly proportionate to the financial amount of the sales contract.

The Japanese style of reaching decisions by committee can disorientate people of other nationalities who are used to decisions being made by a boss, with a great deal of power being concentrated in one person's hands. There are many examples of companies that, after protracted negotiations with Japanese firms, heard nothing more for several months. They assumed that they had lost the deal, but to their surprise they ultimately received an agreement: the process of *ringi* had been at work in the Japanese

company, a procedure of written consultation that requires the input of various interested parties, meetings and careful consideration of objections and suggestions. Box 14.3 shows how the Japanese manage the process of preliminary contacts in a situation where both the seller's and the buyer's organization are complex.

14.2

Networks in business markets

Both suppliers and customers tend to develop networks. For instance, an airline builds regular relationships with an aircraft company over the lifetime of the aircraft, which is often 25 years; similarly the aircraft company is closely connected to the engine manufacturer because the design of the aircraft includes specific engines. Industrial companies also build alliances for developing common R & D projects or to manage common assets, such as jointly developed software or a joint distribution system. Thorelli (p. 38) describes a systematic *network* between two or more organizations involved in long-term relationships:

Generically, a network may be viewed as consisting of 'nodes' or positions (occupied by firms, households, strategic business units inside a diversified concern, trade associations and other types of organization) and *links* manifested by interaction between the positions . . . Networks may be tight or loose, depending on the quantity (number), quality (intensity), and type (closeness to the core activity of the partners involved) of interactions between the positions or members.[17]

The network approach to business was developed by the IMP group with the view that relationships between companies are as important as the exchanges they make.[18,19] According to Ford (p. 81),[19] personal contacts serve to reduce the uncertainty linked to complex deals: 'Mutual trust, respect and personal friendship between participants allows confidential information to be exchanged'. Social bonding (mutual personal friendship and liking) precedes the development of trust, face and cooperation.[20] Personal contacts enable partners in the network to assess each other's competence, to negotiate issues and go beyond the letter of the contract. If there is a critical problem, they offer a framework for the quick exchange of information and rapid decisions about corrective measures. However, in most Western 'doing' societies the relationship is focused at the organizational level of commercial goals. People are there to 'close the deal', not to enjoy the pleasures of social life. As Ford (p. 83)[19] points out 'some suppliers see the dangers of too close an involvement of their salesmen with customers, in that they may lose their objectivity and take actions in the interests of the social relationships, rather than in the wider interests of their company'.

While business networks are fairly universal, the relationships can be fundamentally different in other cultures. For instance, in China *guanxi* is a special type of relationship, which Wang (p. 82) describes as a mixed relationship, not as close as blood relations, but with an emotional attachment (*ganqing*) between the parties:

Guanxi marketing, however, goes beyond the commercial meaning as members in the *guanxi* network exchange both favor and *ganqing* (affection) and, at times, its affective value is more important than its monetary value in social interactions. *Guanxi* works at a personal level on the basis of friendship and *ganqing* is a measure of the level of emotional commitment and the closeness of the parties involved. It is not uncommon for a person to take his/her personal *guanxi* networks with him/her when leaving the organization. From the business perspective, people who have *ganqing* care about each other and treat each other more like friends than just business partners. *Ganqing* plays a key role in maintaining and enhancing a *guanxi* relationship and makes the impersonal business relationship more personal.[14]

Thus, in China business relationships are more personal than impersonal and more particularistic than universalistic.[14] This type of relationship cannot be easily imitated by competitors.

Chinese *guanxi* is similar to *Kankei* in Japan and *Kwankye* in Korea. In each of these concepts, after-hours socialization is important for meeting and convincing key decision makers in a more comfortable atmosphere.[15] The practice of *guanxi* translates into large sales forces for maintaining contacts and large accounts receivables (in a way similar to the liberal credit policy in Japan, see section 11.1). Firms engaged in a connected set of companies, called *guanxihu*, do their best to avoid embarrassing a business partner experiencing temporary financial problems. *Guanxi* enhances the performance of international joint ventures in China[21] as well as foreign-invested enterprises in China and Chinese domestic firms.[22,23]

According to Wang (p. 86)[14] Western firms entering China need to show they are 'considerate, patient, and willing to offer assistance whenever a need is detected. In addition, being empathetic also means giving a renqing without expecting an immediate payback'. As Luo and Chen (pp. 3–4)[23] caution: 'many Western business people are often in danger of overemphasizing the giftgiving and wining-and-dining components of *guanxi* relationships, thereby coming dangerously close to crass bribery or to [being] perceived as "meat and wine friends" which is a Chinese metaphor for mistrust'. The emphasis should be on the concept of enhancing face. Hutchings and Murray (p. 188)[24] found that Western managers in China feel that the concept of face was the greatest difference between guanxi and the Western concept of networking: 'to give face, to save face, and above all, to avoid causing loss of face. They highlighted the fact that in causing loss of face to another, then they automatically lost face themselves, and thus they viewed the saving and managing of face of others as essential to their own ongoing success in China'.

14.3

Buyer–seller interactions

Seller's status and the status of trade

In many countries, sales work has a low status. Selling is implicitly associated with persuasion techniques and taking money from people rather than usefully bringing products and services to them. Trade has some negative connotations in Latin countries, where it was traditionally associated with exploitation. In this view buying for resale (i.e. distribution) is seen as economically unproductive, whereas engineering and production are noble activities. This leads to a view that personal selling does not require formal training, rather it is based on an innate ability to communicate, a lack of scruples and a good deal of opportunism.

The value placed on money is also central to the status of trade. Cultures differ in their beliefs about money.[25] In fact, most cultures have a problem with money, which is often implicitly viewed as making people *bassement intéressés* (overly self-interested). This influences the preference for pricing solutions. For instance, price bargaining may be more common (section 10.2); with an explicit reference to price avoided, discussions about price entering the conversation later, or a supposedly 'favourable' price being ritually associated with friendship.

In many countries, it is an absolute necessity for the seller to be personally acquainted with the buyer, and common membership in the same ingroup may be required. In some cases, the buyer might find some personal characteristics of the seller difficult to accept, such as a European export saleswoman selling to a Saudi buyer.

In high power distance countries, the seller's role is often reduced to conveying the producer's conditions to the customer, with very limited leeway for negotiation. Jolibert and Tixier (p. 11), both French (high power distance), explain the distinction between sales (low power/low status) and marketing negotiations (high power/high status):

> During sale the business conditions are fixed by the vendor. The purchaser is not in a position to debate them . . . The job of the vendor therefore consists of convincing the purchaser of the worth of his offers, of the appropriateness of the product offered to meet the needs of the purchaser . . . Negotiation begins when there is a *possible discussion* about the terms of business between the purchaser and the vendor.[26]

In this definition the salesperson's role is persuasion; there is no consideration of the customer's needs or making these needs known to his or her company! More paradoxically, the purchaser is also in a subordinate situation to the supplying company.

Selling styles: arguments and presence

Consider the ethical position of a salesman who is asked to sell a poor quality product or who knows the customer believes the product is of poor quality. Should he inform the production department, or merely stick to the role of persuasion? When preparing arguments, a salesperson has two main concerns: one is for the customers and their needs; the other is for achieving the sale or 'closing the deal'. Adcock and colleagues (p. 306)[27] combine these as shown in Figure 14.2.

If sellers are purely there to sell products, then the role of salespeople is principally that of persuasion. Cultures vary considerably in their persuasive strategies. The following questions outline possible ways of differentiating the sales persuasion technique:

1. How far can one take persuasion without becoming insistent, and irritating?
2. Is one persuasive merely by listening, where clients appreciate salespeople to whom they can talk, or by talking?
3. What arguments will be the best and the quickest for persuading the prospective purchaser?

Figure 14.2 Selling orientations

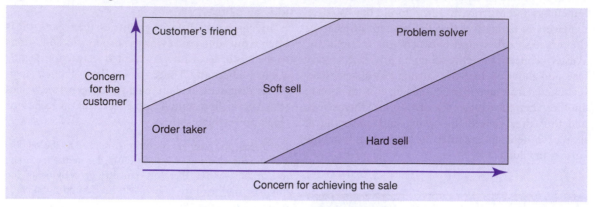

Cateora[28] proposes some stereotypes of selling styles:

1. In Asian countries, where people are modest and offended by arrogance and extreme self-confidence, vendors should make modest, rational, down-to-earth points; they should avoid winning arguments against the buyer, who could suffer a 'loss of face', and react quite negatively.
2. In Italy, a lack of self-confidence would be perceived as a lack of personal credibility and reliability; thus one needs to argue strongly in order to be considered a serious partner.
3. In Switzerland, precision is favoured; your words will be taken quite literally.
4. In the UK, people do not like pushy salespersons; it is advisable to use the *soft sell* approach. The favourable position of the 'soft sell' approach in Figure 14.2 (which is drawn from British authors) adds support to this.
5. In Germany, you should use the *hard sell* approach (make visits, offer trials, be very visible).
6. In Mexico, the *price* should be emphasized.
7. In Venezuela, the *quality* should be emphasized.

These stereotypes indicate cultural norms, but the style of selling also depends on the personality of the salesperson, the extent of the relationship, the size of the deal and the type of industry. However, culture dictates assumptions about the role adopted by the majority of sellers. For instance, if the view is that a good salesperson should be able to close the deal, then the focus will more than likely be on short-term persuasion at any price. The traditional seven-step process of selling may be followed: prospecting, pre-approach, approach, presentation, overcoming objections, close and follow-up. Conversely, if the seller is viewed as a client consultant within the company, salespeople will take a long-term approach toward problem identification, presentation of solutions and continued customer support.[3] They will work with the client to create value and even be willing to lose an order once in a while for the benefit of the customer. Selling styles also depend on which type of concrete results are expected and rewarded. Is the emphasis on winning new customers and reaching a sales target or more subjective achievements, such as building relationships and solving problems?

Equality in the buyer–seller relationship

Numerous empirical studies have been undertaken to determine which role, buyer or seller, holds the *ab initio* position of strength in intercultural marketing negotiations. Graham[29] suggests that one of the reasons for the American trade deficit with Japan was the difference regarding the position of strength in the representation of the buyer–seller relationship. The Japanese believe that strength lies with the purchaser, whom the salesperson must do the utmost to satisfy, whereas the Americans envisage a more egalitarian position, as Graham (p. 9) points out in his examination of which party adapts to the other in the relationship of intercultural business negotiation:

Table 14.1 A summary of the influence of culture on buyer–seller relationships

Cultural value	Influence on seller and buyer
Inferior status for trade	Poor status for sales; selling is reserved to a minority group
Being/doing	More personal relationship orientated; more impersonal deal orientated
Money	Price bargaining as friendship ritual
Ingroup orientation	Only people from a certain ingroup are considered as adequate for sales roles; transactions have to be made preferably across ingroup members
Family orientation	Buyer–seller relationships are viewed as an element of a larger family network
Short-term orientation	Achieving the sale is the paramount goal
Long-term orientation	Keeping the client is the paramount goal
Low/high power distance	Equality/inequality between buyer and seller
Listening versus talking	Soft sell versus hard sell

Anthropologists tell us that power relations usually determine who adopts and adapts behavior in a cross-cultural setting. Japanese executives in an American setting are likely to be the ones to modify their behavior . . . However, if an American seller takes his normative set of bargaining behavior to Japan, then negotiations are apt to end up abruptly. The American seller expects to be treated as an equal and acts accordingly. The Japanese buyer is likely to view this rather brash behavior in a lower status seller as inappropriate and lacking in respect. The Japanese buyer is made to feel uncomfortable, and he politely shuts the door to trade, without explanation. The American seller never makes the first sale, never gets an opportunity to learn the Japanese system.[29]

Table 14.1 gives a summary of the influence of culture on buyer–seller interactions.

14.4
Sales force management in a cross-cultural perspective

The idea that the promotion of sales personnel is based on merit and that decisions are made on an objective basis is very strong in Western societies. This is linked with the 'master of destiny' philosophy that underlies much of the US style of management thinking.[28] People are in control of their own destiny and therefore responsible for the effective use of their own resources. In many cultures which have a more fatalistic approach to life, controlling individual performance does not seem to make sense. Uncontrollable higher-order forces largely shape our acts and future. For instance, Saudi Arabian performance and evaluation control systems work informally, without systematic controls, established criteria or definite procedures.[30]

The influence of culture on sales force management is not considered exhaustively here, as it is based in the field of human resource management which is subject to significant cross-cultural variance. For instance, Western 'doing' societies which place value on 'affirmative action compliance programmes' ignore criteria that are considered essential to determine *who the person is* in many other societies. For instance, the birthplace of applicants, their marital status, age, citizenship or language competencies are standard, non-discriminatory enquiries in most cultures where there is still some *being* orientation. The 'affirmative action, equal opportunity' programme is derived from extremely strong *doing* and *outgroup* orientations, where it is seen as immoral to describe persons as they *are*.

This section relates to companies that have a local consumer base and local sales representatives in each country where they are established. These companies sell durable or non-durable consumer goods, equipment for small businesses or intermediate industrial goods. This section does not consider the question of whether to employ local or international sales representatives. The expatriation of highly qualified and often multilingual sales and marketing personnel is not discussed. Many problems arise when multinational companies try to unify the remuneration systems of local sales staff to apply a standardized incentive system linked to the parent company's culture. Several authors in the field of international marketing have stressed the influence of cultural differences on sales force remuneration systems.[28,31–34]

Incentives for sales representatives

Hofstede's[35,36] parameters can be used (section 3.2) as well as Hall's[37] theory of communication to clarify the incentives issue. The organization must encourage its sales representatives and/or the sales team to attain specific objectives (turnover target, profit target, promotion of certain products, gaining market share at the expense of competitors, etc.). There are therefore several steps, which are influenced by cultural differences:

1. Setting objectives.
2. Evaluation, i.e. setting up a system to calculate target-to-actual-sales deviation followed by feedback to the salespeople.
3. Remunerating the sales force achievements: designing the incentive system and attempting to standardize it across countries.
4. Implementing the sales force remuneration system.

Two incentive systems for monitoring the sales force (models 1 and 2 in Table 14.2) are described below. They are Weberian 'ideal types', not necessarily to be found in their pure form in the real world.

Table 14.2 Contrast models

Cultural traits	Model 1	Model 2
Power distance	Low	High
Individualism	High	Low
Uncertainty avoidance	Low	High
Context of communication	Low	High

Model 1 is appropriate for a firm belonging to an individualistic society where communication is fairly explicit (low context, see section 13.1), power distance is small and uncertainty avoidance is weak (e.g. the US). Model 2 is appropriate for a company originating from a society where communication is implicit (high context), power distance is high and uncertainty avoidance is strong (e.g. Japan). The masculinity/femininity dimension also influences the practical implementation of these two models of sales force remuneration: assertive (masculine) and nurturing (feminine) feedback to low-performing salespeople and corrective actions are carried out differently.

Attitudes towards the setting of objectives and their use in performance measurement

The first step is the setting of sales objectives. Differences in the precision and contextuality of communication style across societies influence the setting of objectives.[37] Where people communicate explicitly with a weak context, objectives will be precisely set, quantified and openly negotiated. In contrast, where people communicate with a high context, quantified objectives are less likely to seem accurate and, as such, do not serve the same purpose. 'Number crunching' is not a trait of high-context societies. Figures are not assumed to depict the complexities of the real world. In high-context societies, numbers are considered as efficient, but oversimplified. Despite that, some kind of quantified objectives are set, but not necessarily followed. Depending on which model (1 or 2) is appropriate, objectives may have different roles.

In model 1, formal *and realistic evaluation* is likely, where the sellers must earn their salary. In these societies relations are depersonalized and people can be evaluated by figures. Target levels of sales are negotiated with the salesperson. Any deviation of actual sales from target is measured precisely. Corrective actions, sanctions and rewards result from monitoring the salesperson's performance.

In model 2, *internal incentives* are likely, where the context is expected to influence the outcome. In these societies relations are personalized. The seller cannot easily be dismissed (e.g. lifetime employment and strong uncertainty avoidance, emphasizing a high level of job security), staff turnover is low and closer personal ties exist within a stable workforce. The objective is not openly and truly negotiated. In these higher power distance societies it is assumed that the boss knows what the sales staff should achieve, rather than the salespeople themselves. Therefore the objective cannot be as realistic as in model 1. The boss may set 'instrumental' excessively high target levels which serve as an ultimate goal. Although everybody knows (implicitly) that a lower performance level will be achieved, it is thought that the level of performance is influenced by the ambitious objective. The risk is that sellers may seek security and lack personal initiative and drive.

Accuracy of goal setting

After objectives have been set, deviation from the target must be measured. The accuracy of performance evaluation and incentive calculation is always higher in a situation of explicit communication. Model 1 rewards individual merits, as the individual is seen as the source of the performance (see the individualism assumptions detailed in section 3.1). Conversely, in high-context/implicit communication (model 2) the evaluation phase is neither precise nor formally implemented. There is no shame in failing to attain the set objectives, as it is significantly higher than a realistic target. Despite their best efforts, the sellers would be considered as underperforming if they were evaluated by model 1. However, there is unspoken awareness in the organization that sales objectives are not realistically set. No formal and quantified evaluation is implemented. Furthermore, what constitutes a good sales performance is implicitly clear within the company, making it relatively useless to precisely assess performance.

Individualism/collectivism, uncertainty avoidance and performance measurement

The individualist or collectivist orientation in a society is a meaningful axis of cultural differentiation.[35] In the US, where individualism is very strong, the cultural emphasis is on individual achievement.[38]

It implies precise and individualized sales targets, fostering competition within the sales force. Competition between the salespeople, within the sales team, is considered legitimate, even though it may undermine the coherence of collective action when this is needed (e.g. training other salespeople, transfer of experience from senior to junior salespeople, etc.).

More traditional societies tend not to engage in individual goal setting and variable commission rewarding. In Thailand, family background largely determines social position; money only confers limited status.[34] Fixed salaries demonstrate social status, stability and group belonging. As such, they are more desirable than a larger income with a variable commission component, as this emphasizes individualism and instability. This is similar to Japan, as indicated by Hill and colleagues (p. 23):

> Tradition is also an important determinant of Japanese compensation plans. Because their social system is based on hereditary and seniority criteria, salary raises, even for sales forces, are based on longevity with the company. Similarly commission systems are tied to the combined efforts of the entire sales force, fostering the Japanese team ethic and downplaying the economic aspirations of individuals.[32]

Precise measurement of salespeople's performance may be considered harmful in some countries. In South-East Asia, the ethics of non-confrontation clearly clash with an objective performance review, as this could cause the subordinate to 'lose face', infringing a societal norm.[39] The motivation theories, which underlie sales force compensation systems, are culturally bound. Because they were developed in one country (the US), they put a strong emphasis on individualism and rationalism as bases for human behaviour.[40]

In contrast to the US system of favouring individual performance, more collectivist societies, such as Japan, tend to favour team performance. Intrinsic rewards are preferred. In the US, job satisfaction is primarily driven by satisfaction with their pay, whereas in Japan it is also related to satisfaction with co-workers and happiness with work.[33,41] Similarly, in Spain (more collectivist), sales managers are more likely to give equal rewards for group effort, whereas those from more individualistic cultures (Anglo and Germanic regions, as well as France and Italy) are more likely to reward individual effort.[42]

The information used for intrinsic or extrinsic, individual or group-based reward systems will necessarily be different. In higher uncertainty avoidant countries, such as Germany, very detailed market information will be sought in an attempt to increase their certainty in decision making.[36] In lower uncertainty avoidant countries, especially those with high individualism and masculinity, such as the US, the same detailed information will be used for a different purpose; the precise tracking and control of salespeople.

Femininity/masculinity and ways of remedying underperformance

There are different methods to deal with the problem of sellers who are clearly underperforming. In masculine societies (e.g., Australia, Switzerland, the US), poor results will be called to attention in a fairly crude manner. Where an individual should be efficient and perform well, unsatisfactory achievements will first lead to a clear warning that performance must improve. Then, if the salesperson fails to justify his or her performance based on uncontrollable factors and continues to underperform, the employee will eventually be dismissed.

In feminine societies (Sweden, northern European countries, France), a higher value is placed on quality of life. There is a protective and maternal attitude on the part of the organization towards its members.

While these societies also strive for efficiency, a seller is entitled to more understanding. Checks are initially made to see if there are any external explanations for the weak performance (e.g. a sales territory with little potential or particularly strong competitors). When the reasons for their underperformance have been assessed with them (formally or informally), they receive assistance from colleagues and from the organization (e.g. additional training). Only after the organization has done everything within its power to help the salesperson to increase his or her performance is a final decision taken. On balance, the results from a hardline (masculine) method do not lead to better sales performance than the softer methods employed by companies based in feminine countries.

Compensation systems based on cultural values and industry characteristics

Table 14.3 describes some basic sales force remuneration systems that are related to the type of product or service being sold and the value systems in the society. In societies with high uncertainty avoidance, employees usually prefer job security with a fixed salary and only small variable commissions. Pure commission-based salaries will only be acceptable in model 1 (Table 14.2). Of course, sellers in all countries are rewarded in different ways, dependent on the type of product. Large individual sales (e.g. desalination or nuclear plants) requiring lengthy sales efforts from a team of experts tend to be rewarded with fixed salaries, in a way preferred by the cultural values of model 2.

Table 14.3 Basic sales force compensation systems, sectors and the cultural values involved

Objectives/type of goods	Compensation plans	Values involved
Long-term sales efforts; equipment, turnkey sales	Fixed salary and promotions	Lifetime employment; cooperation within the sales team; collective performance
Reach precise sales quotas; consumer goods	Pure (or quasi-pure) commission	Own business: no loyalty to the company; individualistic and competitive
Achieve more precise goals (sales of certain products, new territories or segments)	Fixed salary, plus monetary and non-monetary incentives	Mixed values: contract and long-term orientation; loyalty but not unlimited commitment

Smaller individual sales (e.g. consumer goods) requiring individually identifiable sales efforts, tend to be rewarded with salaries that have an element of commission and the cultural values of model 1.

So far, this discussion has been about extrinsic or material rewards, which are generally in cash or in kind in the form of bonuses and commissions. Extrinsic rewards can be linear (in direct proportion to sales exceeding the objective), progressive or retrospective, or can be triggered once a single objective has been attained. The criteria and formulae for calculating variable extrinsic rewards are very varied.[32,43] Purely extrinsic rewards, such as variable commissions on sales, are external motivators.

Intrinsic rewards are related to the satisfaction of inner needs. They are rewards which individuals give to themselves.[44] They involve no pecuniary element and have no influence on material life. People may be intrinsically motivated by a job well done, the esteem of their colleagues or even the securing of a contract per se.

Some rewards are on the fringe of intrinsic and extrinsic rewards. For example, medals or titles (best salesperson for the period). Rewards can be centred on the individual (e.g. gifts to seller or their family, payment of personal expenses), on the group (e.g. a leisure trip for the whole sales team) or on a mix of both (e.g. awards for the best sales teams). As is frequently the case in Japan, group rewards may take the form of a joint holiday for the sales team, which is both an individual and a group reward simultaneously and contributes to group bonding.

Whereas, models 1 and 2 (Table 14.2) depict extreme characteristics, real-world remuneration systems combine intrinsic and extrinsic, individual and collective rewards. Rewards such as promotion and salary increases combine recognition (intrinsic) and money (extrinsic). A large range of possibilities for remuneration exists, which can be used to design a sales force remuneration system adapted to the local culture. Using innovative designs, standardization of sales force remuneration is possible at the regional level where cultural variance is limited. It should be noted that neither model 1 nor 2 are universally 'good' or 'bad' in terms of people being treated fairly or levels of satisfaction. However, it is important that the reward structure is appropriate to the cultural values and the product category.

Public relations across cultures

Public relations (PR) consists of a set of coordinated communication programmes between an organization and its publics, designed to improve, maintain or protect a company product or image. The 'publics' can be internal, such as employees, or external to the firm, such as the general public, customers, suppliers, distributors or the media. Other PR targets include the government (e.g. lobbying for new or existing legislation), or stockholders and the financial community.

The functions of PR are twofold: (1) in normal situations, to create and enhance a favourable corporate image with the various publics concerned, with the view that a foreign firm is particularly susceptible to nationalistic criticism; (2) in crisis situations such as boycotts, accidents, strikes, product recalls, and so on, to maintain goodwill by responding to criticism, explaining remedial action to overcome the problem, and anticipating and countering messages that may damage the corporate image.

Cross-cultural differences have been noted in the way companies react to disasters such as plane crashes, major pollution, etc. They reflect the prevailing sense of responsibility vis-à-vis the community, but also the companies' sense of privacy and the view of what is culturally appropriate for dealing with these events. For instance, a company may choose to adopt a very low profile and wait for the storm to calm or conversely, adopt a high profile, pleading either guilty or not guilty. In some countries, such as Japan, formal apologies and explanations are expected. If the company does not step forward to do this, the government will. For instance, in 2004, when Mitsubishi Motors was found to have covered up truck defects, blamed for a series of accidents, the Japanese government made strong statements about how 'deplorable' their actions were and took steps against Mitsubishi Motors (banning purchases of vehicles for at least one year), as well as the executives involved. In other countries, where there is an emphasis on privacy and a dislike for public display (e.g. Switzerland), a company is likely to adopt an extremely low profile and engage in very little communication, even if it is clearly in the wrong.

PR is very different from advertising, in that it is focused on communications intended to build trust and relationships with key publics. PR people, whether employed by the firm or as outside consultants, have nothing to sell. They use publicity as a means of conveying messages to the public (whether by securing editorial space in the case of any kind of films, videotapes or slides), as well as the organization of events, meetings, conferences, sponsorship.

Cultural variance may occur in the following aspects of the PR process:

1. making contact;
2. managing relationships;
3. disclosing information, especially in the case of private, secret or sensitive information;
4. developing arguments, some of which cannot be understood locally; and
5. dealing with nationalistic feelings.

Thinking locally

People from Western countries do not naturally think in terms of who is a member of which group. However, the identification of key ethnic groups is important for good PR in many foreign contexts.

The model of a free press cannot be assumed. In many countries its freedom is curtailed by the government, such as is the case in China, and often in much more subtle ways than mere censorship.

The influence of local competition should not be underestimated. The lack of antitrust laws in many countries reflects the legitimacy agreements with competitors in regard to market-sharing or price agreements. Consequently, PR officers may be involved in talks with competing firms, a practice which would be considered unethical in most developed Western countries which have antitrust legislation. Such discussions are all the more important when the local competitors are technologically inferior to the foreign firm but are able to use their nationality as a weapon against a foreign intruder. When making agreements, PR officers should:

1. avoid disclosing information that local parties regard as secret since confidentiality is culturally relative;
2. avoid using arguments that clash with the logic of the host country, as they will not be understood; and
3. avoid conveying messages about local people and culture that are perceived as negative.

Foreign firms have to face nationalism: being foreign makes things slightly worse for a company when it is under attack. Multinational firms tend to have higher profiles and people recognize they can influence society's well-being either positively or negatively. As such, they are expected to do more for society than local firms. If the local employees of a multinational company receive better pay than the average worker in the country, this can be seen as beneficial to the recipients individually but detrimental to the community as a whole: it lures farmers to the industrial sector, or it causes merchants to raise their prices because of the purchasing power of a small affluent group. Emphasizing local citizenship is always necessary and it must be done with unambiguous arguments. As Holt and colleagues (p. 75) point out, the impact is greater if the social problems can be linked to what they sell and/or how they conduct their business:

> Over a billion people in the world use unsafe water every day, leading to more than 2 million deaths a year from diarrhea. P&G identified safe drinking water as a critical social problem that fell within its scope of expertise. It leveraged its knowledge of household sanitation to develop a water purification system that would be effective in poor countries. P&G found that people would try the product if it was easy to use and inexpensive and if they could see that the purified water was clean. Scaling down a technology used in water purification facilities, the company's engineers developed a satchel of particulate matter that consumers could stir into buckets. The particles would attract contaminants and dirt, and people could filter out the pollutants with a cloth. P&G's tests in Guatemala have demonstrated that the system can reduce the frequency of diarrhea episodes by around 25%. If the company markets the product globally, the social impact could be extraordinary. What's impressive is that P&G deployed its vast technological capabilities to tackle a problem that governments and NGOs have struggled with for decades.[45]

The case of product liability

Product liability is an area where PR is needed. As previously mentioned, there were dire consequences when Mitsubishi Motors was found to have covered up truck defects. The company was blamed for a series of accidents and its sales plummeted by 40 per cent.[46] Similarly, Nestlé, one of the largest food companies in the world, faced a boycott because its infant feeding formula had allegedly caused many deaths of babies in the Third World. In 1974, a report by a British journalist[47] and a pamphlet entitled 'Nestlé kills babies' started accusations that escalated during the mid-1970s. Nestlé withdrew its infant formula advertising and decided to participate in consumer education programmes. The key reasons for the 'problems experienced by Nestlé's Third World consumers' were cultural: the belief in the magic properties of Western products and the pressure to give what is the best, the most modern, as a sign of love for babies. A more down-to-earth reason was the poor use of the product, mixed with contaminated water. Nestlé should have anticipated the key reasons for misuses of its product: (1) high levels of illiteracy; (2) even when literate, people rarely rely on written materials, which have an abstract image; and (3) the inability to cope with ambiguous messages (the product is good, but can be bad). These problems are similar for pharmaceutical companies, in that most drugs have side effects. However, in many countries being explicit about the side effects may be harmful, as people may not believe in a drug whose manufacturer clearly acknowledges the potentially adverse consequences (most of which can be avoided by proper use!).

Website link 14.1

'How to spin an oil spill'. A satirical view of PR from Australian comedians Clarke and Dawe: **http://www.mrjohnclarke.com/html/**.

14.6

Bribery: facts

Bribery is associated with selling, obtaining favours, and making things work. It is a practice that can be found in almost all cultures, at some level. The Germans call it *Schmiergeld* ('grease money'), the French *pot-de-vin* (literally jug of wine), in the Middle East it is a *baksheesh*, in Italy a *Bastarella* (little envelope) and in Mexico a *mordida* (a bite). These practices know few borders and even the Japanese construction industry is heavily plagued by bribery. Naturally every country officially prohibits bribery, but laws are locally enforced (see Tables 3.6 and 3.7 on the types of rules). In some cases, judges may be open to accept a bribe.

Types of bribery

Information and data on illegal payments are very sparse and often fragmentary. Such issues are sensitive and companies remain very secretive. Factual data have, however, been collected, both through the investigations carried out by financial journalists[48] and academic researchers[49] and, more systematically in the US, as a consequence of prosecutions under the Foreign Corrupt Practices Act 1977.[50]

The practice is too widespread to be ignored. It takes various forms:

1. *Small and large gifts*. It could be as simple as a gift to the person or person's family. Alternatively, fully paid trips for influential foreign officials can quickly reach as much as $50,000, when it includes a prestigious hotel, a driver/guide for the duration of their stay, receptions, restaurants and potentially hostesses for the evenings.
2. *Percentages* paid based on the contract value. Here the illegal payments result in much larger sums being paid, in proportion to the size of the contract (whether it is for the sale of a squadron of fighter planes, or a turnkey plant, etc.).
3. *Tips*. When civil servants, who hold authority and responsibility (e.g. a police officer, a customs officer or a tax inspector) are poorly paid, it may be 'implicitly understood' that they will supplement their income. As such, a 'greasing' payment may be required to pass through customs or to obtain a tax form (for a mandatory declaration). The authorities are perfectly aware of the existence of such practices.

Website link 14.2

See the five major factors that lead to corruption or bribery: **http://www.worldbank.org/html/prddr/trans/dec03apr04/pgs4–5.htm**.

Methods

Whether illegal payments are made, and what sums are involved, varies widely from country to country. Payments are much more substantial, for example, in the construction industry or in Nigeria than in electronics or in Australia. An important caveat must be made: not everyone is corrupt. There is nothing worse than attempting to bribe someone who strongly disapproves of such immoral behaviour. This last point is clearly illustrated by Agpar,[51] who quotes the case of the managing director of a large multinational who offered 500 Saudi Riyals in cash to a Saudi police officer to ensure a favourable decision on a fairly minor offence against labour law. In a fury, the officer reported the attempted bribe to his superiors. After spending 20 days in prison, the businessman was fined 25,000 Riyals and was fortunate to escape a more serious penalty. Bribery, as with most gift exchange, follows a culturally coded etiquette that indicates who is willing to accept a bribe, where and when it can safely be given, and what to say and do when presenting the bribe to the recipient.[52] This case clearly demonstrates the danger and also the ineffectiveness of direct bribes. Accordingly, more indirect methods exist instead:

1. Slush funds are set up to effect small payments by cheque, nominally as payment for services rendered. Auditors have discovered systematically overstated expense reports where expense report copies are marked up an average of 1000 per cent from the actual expense.[53]
2. The transfer of what the English call 'brown paper packets' or 'plain brown envelopes' is often made by an intermediate consultancy company, who is involved right from the tender stage. These consultancy companies often have their head office in a tax haven, such as Luxemburg. For instance, a key decision maker may mention to the head of the negotiating team of a large engineering or construction company that it would be advantageous if his consultancy company were to carry out preliminary technical studies. These studies will in fact be largely fictitious. The fees paid for these studies will correspond to the commission. If these studies are further subcontracted to a nominee company in a tax haven, the *baksheesh* money will be transferred to a 'safe place'.
3. Nominee and local consultancy companies given 'phoney' consulting contracts may be used in different ways. For example, an adviser to the transport minister, who is well placed to influence the decision on an underground railway project, may be offered a part-time position in the Luxemburg-based nominee company. He will simply receive a

salary each month which, for reasons of discretion and convenience, will be paid into an account in Switzerland. When he goes skiing with his family, he takes money out of his bank account in Geneva to discreetly spend it in an exclusive ski resort. Money spent abroad is less compromising than money brought back home.

4. Finally, two other accounting solutions can be employed, (a) over-invoicing of expenditure or receipts, and (b) the recording of fictitious transactions. For example, a foreign Hospital Supply company pays a 10 per cent commission to help obtain the contract for the construction of a hospital in Saudi Arabia. The artificially inflated price of the contract allows the 10 per cent commission to become tax-deductible expenditure, which looks legitimate despite being illegal.[54] Vogl (p. 30)[55] gives the example of a European supplier of pharmaceuticals negotiating with the minister of health of a developing country that has received emergency funds from an aid agency to purchase urgently required medicines: 'Instead of agreeing on the purchase of new drugs, the minister and the supplier conspire to use the aid funds to purchase out-of-date drugs which are far cheaper. The supplier consequently makes a handsome profit and places a portion of it in an offshore bank account set up by the minister.'

14.7

Bribery: ethical aspects

Bribery is a key ethical issue in international marketing. More than one-third of a sample of US executives ranked bribery as the most serious of 10 possible ethical problems that may arise in international marketing operations.[56] Similarly, Australian and Canadian managers rank gifts, favours and entertainment, traditional small-scale bribery, and the confusing issue of whether gifts are intended as bribes or not in different cultures, as the three key ethical problems in international marketing out of a list of 10.[57] Approximately, 45 per cent of multinational firms (which answered the question) report that they pay bribes to public officials.[58] More than 50 per cent of firms did not answer the question in the survey.

The first ethical position is that of cultural relativism: whether it is right or wrong, good or bad, depends on one's culture. This is based on the view that rules are applicable locally in the ingroup territory: when in Rome, do as the Romans do. In relativistic terms, words such as 'right' or 'wrong', 'good' or 'bad' only have a meaning within a specific cultural context. The first part of this section gives a view of cultural relativism in the case of Africa where corrupt money is largely, but not completely, redistributed in society. However, one cannot ignore the negative consequences. According to Chen and colleagues (p. 232),[58] 'corruption tends to hamper economic growth, increase income inequality, lowers investments, and reduces the level of many other economic derivers of growth (i.e. human capital, urbanization, financial depth, and foreign trade). As an example, the property of late President Mobutu Sese Seko of Zaire is said to have been equivalent to the whole of the external debt of the country.[59] A second ethical position is cultural universalism, which is based on the view that there are core ethical principles which are universally applicable, independent of territory and group membership. The US Foreign Corrupt Practices Act of 1977, revised in 1988, is an example of such a universalist approach to ethics *and* rules. An alternative perspective is a pragmatic and respectful view of how ethical behaviour can be developed in a cross-cultural context.

Cultural relativism: the bribe as bonanza

There is a tendency to oversimplify the issue of international corruption to one of a face-to-face meeting between two people, a donor and a recipient. In reality the donor of the *baksheesh* often faces a group of recipients. An illegal payment rarely benefits one single person. As a result, bribery is intermingled with a dense network of social relationships. Bonds of fraternity and complicity develop between people of the same ethnic background or tribe. These people are necessary intermediaries to ensure that a *baksheesh* is effectively implemented. The bonds built on everyday cooperation call for redistribution of small parts of the bribe. For instance, the secretary who knows of the existence of the *baksheesh*, and the customs officer who intercepts a 'brown paper parcel', each take their

share in proportion to their level of influence and power in the society (see Box 14.4).

Most of Kinshasa's residents, who were abandoned by the corrupt regime of Mobutu Sese Seko, live by roadside trading in order to feed their families. Article 15, a fictional clause in the constitution, was a general licence to do whatever you liked, or 'Fend for Yourself' and almost nothing was outside its ambit. A clean-up campaign spearheaded by Kinshasa governor Theophile Memba, has attempted to transform Zaire. Tom Boland[60] reports that small traders were alarmed by measures that would deny them their living: 'With Article 15 still at the back of their minds, many of the traders who have been moved on in recent weeks, have bounced back and reappeared in nearby spaces.' One senior Kinshasa banker says 'It's only when the state has provided an alternative space for trading that this kind of operation has proved successful.'

Bonds may also be forged by the possibility of retaliation. Those who have not requested a *baksheesh*, but who have a strong suspicion as to its existence, may either inform the authorities, demand their 'cut', or take no action. If they take the risk of participating in illegal remuneration they may benefit personally, or they may risk offending those in power, ultimately leading to punishment. If they inform against the person who has accepted the bribe, they may also suffer adverse consequences.

Primitive hunter/gatherer societies, as described by ethnologists, can be used as an archetype for the redistribution of a bribe considered as plunder. While the men hunt (symbolically: those who hold power and go 'hunting' for large sums), the women, children and the elderly devote their efforts to gathering wild fruits and vegetables (symbolically: those who collaborate at a menial level, but who are still aware of what is happening). Ultimately the bribe/plunder is divided up according to fairly precise rules. Redistributing plunder and crops among the members of one's tribe is basic moral behaviour in many countries (see Box 14.5). However, the tendency to think that developing countries have 'lower' ethical standards should be resisted, even though the extent of bribery in some developing nations and evidence from research would suggest it. Many factors, including sellers' markets, high inflation, low wages and economic hardship explain questionable practices, although they do not excuse them. Very often, the bribery issue is not

BOX 14.4

'Article 15'

On the banks of the large Zaire river just as in the province of Shaba, no one in Zaire is surprised to see a civil servant demanding a 'matabiche' in return for a passport or some other official document. On the contrary, people would be worried if such a request was not made. No Zairian would take offence at having to pay for an official hearing, or to have a letter sent to a department head. Seals and headed note paper are bought and are even sometimes forged. In Zaire, civil servants are 'resourceful people' and know how to supplement their income. The police set up roadblocks when they need money: drivers never have the requisite paper and are therefore obliged to put their hands in their pockets.

At the main post office in 'Kin' (Kinshasa, the capital), letters and parcels may – like anywhere else in the world – be posted in a box, but it is less than certain that they will ever arrive at their destination. The 'citizen' (in Zaire, the 'Supreme Guide' has brought into fashion this revolutionary title) greatly increases the chances of this occurring if he greases the palm of the postman. Likewise, a citizen may make a telephone call to the other end of the planet for the price of a tip. All this comes under 'Article 15', a shameful way of designating the small-scale corruption practised by civil servants. This corruption is institutionalized and widespread; it also goes under the name of 'matabiche': bribe, backhander, a 'little something', brown paper packet.

The practice is so ingrained that President Mobutu did not shy away from encouraging it in a speech on 20 May 1976: 'If you are going to steal, steal a small amount and do it intelligently, in a nice way. If you are going to steal so much that you become rich in a single night, you will be arrested.'

(Source: Excerpt from Péan, pp. 139–40.[48] *L'argent Noir*, P. Péan, © Librairie Arthème Fayard 1988.)

BOX 14.5

A good minister in Senegal

For the man in the street, a good minister is a demagogue, someone who is adept at bypassing the law and its rulings to keep the voters from his region, his parents and his friends happy. If you try to behave like a minister acting objectively by treating your cousins, your allies, members of the branch of your party in the same way as all other citizens, even political opponents, the people will be totally confused. You will not be understood. You are not respecting the rules of the game. You will be the object of public contempt. You are not a minister for the purpose of serving the nation or carrying out the policies of a government which is in power for the good of all its citizens. You are first and foremost a minister for your own good, so that you may take advantage of your position, and enable your parents and allies, your friends and the members of your party to benefit too. No one will reproach you, everyone will understand. Those who are out of office are the only ones who will criticize this behaviour although if they were in office themselves they could not be sure of resisting the demands of their own tribe, family, or parents-in-law. There is nothing wrong in taking advantage of one's position to help out one's relatives; the ideal would be to consider all citizens as your own relatives.

(Source: Ndao, pp. 34–5.[61])

one of ethical standards, but a mere matter of survival. Arnould (p. 130)[62] gives the example of the consequences to West African traders who refuse to pay the bribes asked for by customs agents or policemen: 'A truck and its contents were burned at the border between Benin and Togo under mysterious circumstances when the driver working for one onion trader in Lomé refused to pay.'

Average citizens unfortunately get used to the behaviour of officials securing special privileges for themselves and their close friends. In Bulgaria, a survey showed that 57 per cent of the population believed that politicians were primarily interested in taking advantage of their power position.[63] Economic power is intermingled with political influence, such as in the tradition known as *coronelismo* in Brazilian politics, which corresponds to the case of wealthy landowners who can bribe, manipulate and pressurize the local electorate to vote for the candidates they choose. *Coronelismo* still flourishes in isolated and impoverished regions of the Brazilian countryside.[64]

It is sometimes difficult to distinguish between a gift and a bribe. Both obey the norms of reciprocity that are linked to the local context. As emphasized by Steidlmeier (p. 127),[65] 'phenomenologically, it is difficult to distinguish a bribe from a tip or a commission or consulting fee. In the end, moral judgment depends upon the social understanding of the meaning of the action as derived from the analysis of means and ends, consequences and intentions'.

Werner[52] also acknowledges the lack of clear boundary between gifts and bribes. She explains that in Kazakstan there are 10 words for different types of gifts and ritual payments according to the context and the nature of the gift; for instance *kiit* and *minit* are gifts to in-laws, the first in the form of clothing, the second in livestock or money. However, the word for bribe, *para*, is used consistently to refer to illegal exchanges: 'a traffic policeman may extort a relatively small amount of money, the local equivalent of a few dollars, from an innocent driver. In a different context, a young man who needs a job might voluntarily pay a bribe of $500 to $1,500 to a military official, who in return will forge a document specifying that the young man was exempt from military service for health reasons ($500) or a document specifying that the young man actually did complete military service ($1,500)' (p. 18).[52]

The OECD convention on the fight against bribery

Since the US adopted the Foreign Corrupt Practices Act in 1977, they have been constantly fighting at the international level to have such legislation adopted by the major industrialized countries.[66] Their efforts have been more successful since the implementation of the OECD Convention on Combating Bribery of Foreign Public Officials in International Business Transaction of 1997.[67] While all countries have laws against bribery, relatively few countries have laws against bribery abroad. This is important as laws against bribery become more effective when they are coordinated across multiple countries.[67]

The convention was adopted on 21 November 1997. It is has now been ratified by the 36 signatory countries (the 30 OECD countries as well as 6 non-OECD countries). The OECD requires the implementation of legal, regulatory and policy measures to prevent, detect, investigate, prosecute, and sanction bribery of foreign public officials. It also requires countries to impose sanctions such as fines and imprisonment for bribery of foreign public officials. These sanctions apply to both individuals and companies that commit foreign bribery. The convention also requires that countries seize the bribe or property of similar value and any profits from the bribery.[68]

The convention is not self-enforcing: countries have to modify their existing laws and enact new ones to comply with the provisions of the convention, which outlaws[69]:

1. kickbacks to obtain or retain government business;
2. the tax deductibility of bribes as business expenses;
3. off-the-books accounting practices;
4. loose public procurement procedures which facilitate bribes and collusion;
5. bribing through intermediaries, consultants and agents.

Most developed countries have now ratified the convention and modified their national legislation so as to make it locally enforceable. However, only some of the OECD countries have applied major sanctions against offenders. For instance, in 2006 the OECD recommended that Australia increase fines for foreign bribery to a maximum of A$300,000. In the same year, it recommended to Spain that liability and sanctions for companies engaging in foreign bribery and the prohibition of tax deductibility of foreign bribery be made explicit in the Spanish legal system.

Other efforts at combating bribery

The International Chamber of Commerce (ICC) has also been playing an active role by drafting a self-regulation code for companies. The ICC 'Rules of Conduct to Combat Extortion and Bribery' deal with ethical issues in international business negotiations such as payments to sales agents and other intermediaries, business entertainment and gifts, and political contributions. Contrary to the OECD convention, it covers bribery within the private sector as well as to public officials (Brademas and Heimann, 1998).

At the corporate level, the formulation of global corporate ethics codes involves 95 per cent of CEOs and 78 per cent of company boards of directors.[70] Bribery is a topic covered by a vast majority (92 per cent) of the ethics code. Many of them provide concrete operationalizations of what a bribe is and how to deal with it. Some, not all, target compliance by providing managers involved in foreign operations with precise procedures and guidelines. In relative terms, corruption tends to deter investors from negotiating foreign direct investment in countries with high levels of corruption.[71]

There are basically two sides in bribery: that of donors, which are principally concerned with the conventions and codes previously described, and that of the recipient countries, which are less directly concerned. Corruption in international deals will not cease by the simple virtue of donors becoming suddenly honest and drying up the supply of bribes. In most potential recipient countries no strong anti-bribery code exists or, if there is one, it is not actually enforced.

The level of corruption of particular countries can be measured, based on composite indicators of perception of corruption. They are published on a yearly basis by Transparency International (**www.transparency.org**), an NGO considered to be the most influential global anti-corruption organization.[72] Data is based on mean scores of seven to nine surveys

per country, rarely fewer. Highest scores correspond to the lowest levels of corruption. Some of the countries with lower levels of corruption based on the 2007 index are as follows[72]:

9.4 Denmark, Finland and New Zealand
9.3 Singapore and Sweden
8.6 Australia
7.8 Germany
7.3 France
7.2 US

Many developing countries and some eastern European countries are plagued by higher levels of corruption based on the 2007 index, including[72]:

4.1 Bulgaria, Turkey and Croatia
3.5 Brazil, China, India, Mexico, Morocco and Peru
<2 many African (e.g. Chad and Sudan), Middle Eastern (e.g. Iraq and Afghanistan) and Asian countries (e.g. Laos and Uzbekistan)
1.4 Somalia and Myanmar with the equal lowest scores

> ### Website link 14.3
>
> See Transparency International, the global coalition against corruption: **http://transparency.org**.

A number of countries where corruption is endemic show increased severity against offenders. China, for instance, is enforcing bribery sanctions, going as far as the execution of senior officials, like the Vice Governor of Southern Jiangxi province who was convicted of having accumulated about US$850,000 in bribes.[73] Similarly, a top banker was sentenced to 15 years' imprisonment on bribery charges in 2002. He had been found to have taken about US$500,000 in bribes from 1997 to 1999 when he was chairman of the group that controls one of China's largest banks.[74]

Comparison of ethical attitudes across industrial nations

Ethical attitudes within the major developed countries towards illegal payments are not uniform.[75] Until recently, in France, Germany and Switzerland bribery was simply seen as a cost of doing business abroad and could be claimed as a corporate tax deduction. US managers tend to adopt stronger ethical standpoints than their European and Japanese counterparts. Becker and Fritzsche.[76] suggested a scenario that posed a business ethics problem linked to an illegal payment. Three sample groups of businessmen were interviewed, from the US (124 respondents), West Germany (70 respondents) and France (72 respondents). The scenario was as follows (p. 89):

The Rollfast Bicycle company has been barred from entering the market in a large Asian country by collusive efforts of the local bicycle manufacturers. Rollfast could expect to net 5 million dollars per year from sales if it could penetrate the market. Last week a business man from the country contacted the management of Rollfast and stated that he could smooth the way for the company to sell in his country for a price of US$500,000. If you were responsible, what are the chances that you would pay the price?[76]

The Americans were less likely to pay the secret payment than the French or Germans. Nearly 50 per cent of the Americans explained that it was unethical, illegal and contrary to the corporate code of conduct, whereas the Germans and French were more likely to make statements about competition forcing acceptance and 'it's simply the price you have to pay for doing business'.

France and West Germany have legislation prohibiting the bribing of public civil servants, but these regulations do not apply extraterritorially. French and German businessmen cannot be prosecuted for bribes affected outside their national territory. Conversely, the FCPA as well as numerous other American regulations (antitrust, fiscal, and so on) do have extraterritorial application.

A pragmatic and respectful view of ethical behaviour in a cross-cultural context

As noted by Berenbeim (p. 26), host country conditions have to be taken into account:

You cannot say to a country manager, 'Don't do this, don't do that, now here are your goals for country X where all of your competitors do this and that. I don't want to hear any excuses if these objectives are not met.' Under those circumstances, either rules will have to be broken or ambitious goals will not be achieved. The way to avoid this kind of impossible situation is to build a consensus among practitioners for enforceable rules . . . The example of the FCPA is a case in point. Although it would be more satisfying to punish the person who demands the bribe than the company that pays it, obtaining legal prohibitions in the major industrial countries and targeting the companies that bribe rather than the local citizens who demand payment is likely to have greater impact.[77]

The first consideration is pragmatic: businesspeople who make illegal payments take (real) personal risks for (potential) organizational benefits, either through company loyalty or personal interest (sales commission or promotion). Doing this, they (1) involve their company in the risk of being involved in a scandal; and (2) themselves risk being implicated, indicted, and ultimately imprisoned.

The payment of a *baksheesh* always involves the individual responsibility of the donor, even if his or her company, or the consortium that he or she represents, also risks being drawn into the scandal. As Graham (p. 94)[78] states: 'From a legal standpoint, the recommendation is clear – avoid questionable deals. The loss of the few "questionable" contracts is not worth the risk of indictment, prosecution, conviction . . . Moreover, if you are indicted, will your company support you or opt to plead guilty and accept the fine?' A pragmatic view for an individual requires reference to a personal norm, not a corporate one.

Useful guidelines for those confronted with this issue are provided by the definition of a 'moral personality' proposed by John Rawls in his *A Theory of Justice*.[79] A moral personality is characterized by the capacity to conceive good and the capacity to develop a sense of justice. The first is realized through a rational project for one's life. The second implies a continuing desire to act in a just manner. Thus, for Rawls, a moral personality has chosen their own goals; and prefers conditions that enable full expression of their nature as rational, free and equal. The unity of the person is based on a higher order aspiration to follow the principles of rational choice in a manner that suits their sense of justice. If asked to do something that violates your sense of right and wrong, it is better not to do it, even if it means not behaving as a Roman in Rome. However, Rawls' definition of a 'moral personality' remains a rather Western one, in that it emphasizes rationality, individualism and the sense of equality with others. In many other cultural contexts, where moral personalities actually exist, these traits would not be emphasized in such a definition.

The final word may be given by Adam Smith, who describes some key aspects of the 'character of virtue' in the following terms (p. 214):

The prudent man is always sincere, and feels horror at the very thought of exposing himself to the disgrace which attends upon the detection of falsehood. But though always sincere, he is not always frank and open; and though he never tells any thing but the truth, he does not always think himself bound, when not properly called upon, to tell the whole truth. As he is cautious in his actions, so he is reserved in his speech; and never rashly or unnecessarily obtrudes his opinion concerning either things or persons.[80]

Questions

1. Indicate elements of variation in selling styles (including basic views of what is a buyer–seller interaction, the kind of arguments developed and the communication style).

2. Personal selling often plays a more important role in foreign than in domestic markets. Why?

3. Discuss the limitations to the standardization of a sales-force stimulation system.

4. Discuss how a strong emphasis on group belonging in a particular culture may influence the recruitment of salespeople.

5. Discuss the cultural relativity of the following statements about salespersons (excerpt from Hill *et al.*, pp. 68–9[81]):
   - Our salespersons are very achievement oriented.
   - Salespersons need patience to be successful.
   - Our salespersons consider the source of income, whether salary or commission, to be more important than the size of income.
   - Our sellers should have definite call schedules and planned routes.
   - Our salespersons are very time oriented.
   - Our salespersons need a lot of supervision.
   - Selling is a prestigious job in the country.
   - Salespersons are regarded as future managers.
   - A salesperson's social class can limit his/her contacts and effectiveness.
   - Family connections often help salespersons in their work.
   - A salesperson's religious beliefs can limit his/her contacts and effectiveness.

6. What is the borderline between a 'gift' and a 'bribe'? Outline possible criteria for defining such a border which allow for some cross-national flexibility.

7. How can bribery be related to space-related cultural assumptions?

8. WTD, a large US multinational chemical company, has recently been attacked in several large Latin American countries where it has plants. The company has been attacked by the local press for alleged pollution and poor safety conditions for employees. It has been argued that WTD has much lower standards in these areas than in the USA and that the company shows its Yankee and imperialist orientation in such choices. The company executive officers think these criticisms are largely wrong: inadequate local legislation and poor respect of safety rules by local employees have caused problems rather than a deliberate neglect on WTD's part. Advise the firm on a public relations programme.

9. Discuss the cultural relativity of the framework for a manager facing an ethical dilemma, who should ask the following questions:

- What are the **facts**; what are my alternatives?
- What parties will be affected?
- What do **I** owe to each of these parties?
- What would produce the greatest **benefits** for **all** parties?
- What **rights** does each party have, and how can these rights best be **respected**?
- Are all parties treated **fairly** and **justly**?
- On balance, what is the most **ethical** alternative?
- How do **I** best **implement** this alternative?

The words in bold are those which offer the best route for questioning about the cultural relativity of this framework.

References

1. Vargo, Stephen L. and Robert F. Lusch (2008), 'From Goods to Service(S): Divergences and Convergences of Logics', *Industrial Marketing Management*, 37 (3), 254–59.

2. Vargo, Stephen L. and Robert F. Lusch (2004), 'Evolving to a New Dominant Logic for Marketing', *Journal of Marketing*, 68 (1), 1–17.

3. Sheth, Jagdish N. and Arun Sharma (2008), 'The Impact of the Product to Service Shift in Industrial Markets and the Evolution of the Sales Organization', *Industrial Marketing Management*, 37 (3), 260–69.

4. Spiegelman, Paul (2000), 'Live Customer Interaction and the Internet Join in "Internation"', *Direct Marketing*, 63 (4), 38–41.

5. Sheth, Jagdish N. and Atul Parvatiyar (2002), 'Evolving Relationship Marketing into a Discipline', *Journal of Relationship Marketing*, 1 (1), 16–94.

6. Day, George S. (1994), 'Continuous Learning About Markets', *California Management Review*, 36 (4), 9–31.

7. Chan, Haksin and Lisa C. Wan (2008), 'Consumer Responses to Service Failures: A Resource Preference Model of Cultural Influences', *Journal of International Marketing*, 16 (1), 72–97.

8. Liu, Raymond R. and Peter McClure (2001), 'Recognizing Cross-Cultural Differences in Consumer Complaint Behavior and Intentions: An Empirical Examination', *The Journal of Consumer Marketing*, 18 (1), 54–75.

9. Ngai, Eric W. T., Vincent C. S. Heung, Y. H. Wong, and Fanny K. Y. Chan (2007), 'Consumer Complaint Behaviour of Asians and Non-Asians About Hotel Services an Empirical Analysis', *European Journal of Marketing*, 41 (11/12), 1375–91.

10. Hui, Michael K. and Kevin Au (2001), 'Justice Perceptions of Complaint Handling: A Cross-Cultural Comparison between PRC and Canadian Customers', *Journal of Business Research*, 52, 161–73.

11. Ho, Suk-ching (1997), 'The Emergence of Consumer Power in China', *Business Horizon* (September–October), 15–21.

12. Garbarino, Ellen and Mark S. Johnson (1999), 'The Different Roles of Satisfaction, Trust and Commitment in Customer Relationships', *Journal of Marketing*, 63 (2), 70–87.

13. Kumar, Nirmalya, Lisa K. Scheer, and Jan-Benedict E.M. Steenkamp (1995), 'The Effects of Perceived Interdependence on Dealer Attitudes', *Journal of Marketing Research*, 32 (3), 348–56.14.
   Freivalds, John (1991), 'Foreign-Language Business Cards', *Agri Marketing*, 29 (3), 48–9.

14. Wang, Cheng Lu (2007), 'Guanxi vs. Relationship Marketing: Exploring Underlying Differences', *Industrial Marketing Management*, 36 (1), 81–86.

15. Tung, Rosalie (1996), 'Negotiating with East Asians', in *International Business Negotiations*, P.N. Ghauri and J-C. Usunier, Eds. Oxford: Pergamon/Elsevier.

16. Tsalikis, John, Marta Ortiz-Buonafina, and Michael S. Latour (1992), 'The Role of Accent on the Credibility and Effectiveness of the International Business Person: The Case of Guatemala', *International Marketing Review*, 9 (4), 57–72.

17. Thorelli, Hans B. (1986), 'Networks: Between Markets and Hierarchies', *Strategic Management Journal*, 7, 37–51.

18. Ford, David (1990), *Understanding Business Markets*. London: Academic Press.

19. Johansson, Jan and Lars-Gunnar Mattsson (1988), 'Internationalization in Industrial Systems – a Network Approach', in *Strategies in Global Competition*, N. Hood and J.E. Vahlne, Eds. New York: Croom Helm.

20. Mavondo, Felix T. and Elaine Rodrigo (2001), 'The Effect of Relationship Dimensions on Interpersonal and Interorganizational Commitment in Organizations Conducting Business between Australia and China', *Journal of Business Research*, 52 (2), 111–21.

21. Luo, Yadong (1995), 'Business Strategy, Market Structure, and Performance of IJV', *Management International Review*, 35 (3), 249–64.

22. Luo, Yadong (1997), 'Guanxi and Performance of Foreign-Invested Enterprises in China', *Management International Review*, 37 (1), 51–70.

23. Luo, Yadong and Min Chen (1997), 'Does Guanxi Influence Firm Performance?', *Asia Pacific Journal of Management*, 14, 1–16.

24. Hutchings, Kate and Georgina Murray (2002), 'Working with Guanxi: An Assessment of the Implications of Globalisation on Business Networking in China', *Creativity and Innovation Management*, 11 (3), 184–90.

25. Ang, Swee Hoon (2000), 'The Power of Money: A Crosscultural Analysis of Business-Related Beliefs', *Journal of World Business*, 35 (1), 43–60.

26. Jolibert, Alain and Maud Tixier (1988), *La Négociation Commerciale*. Paris: Editions ESF.

27. Adcock, Dennis, Ray Bradfield, Al Halborg, and Caroline Ross (1993), *Marketing, Principles and Practice*. London: Pitman.

28. Cateora, Philip R. (1993), *International Marketing* (8th edn). Burr Ridge, IL: Richard D. Irwin.

29. Graham, John L. (1981), 'A Hidden Cause of America's Trade Deficit with Japan', *Columbia Journal of World Business* (Fall), 5–15.

30. Ali, Abbas and Paul M. Schwiercz (1985), 'The Relationship between Managerial Decision Styles and Work Satisfaction in Saudi Arabia', in *International Business in the Middle East*, Erdener Kaynak, Ed. New York: De Gruyter.

31. Hempel, Paul S. (1998), 'Designing Multinational Benefits Programs: The Role of National Culture', *Journal of World Business*, 33 (3), 277–94.

32. Hill, John S., Richard R. Still, and Ünal O. Boya (1991), 'Managing the Multinational Sales Force', *International Marketing Review*, 8 (1), 19–31.

33. Money, R. Bruce and John L. Graham (1999), 'Salesperson Performances, Pay, and Job Satisfaction: Tests of a Model Using Data Collected in the United States and Japan', *Journal of International Business Studies*, 30 (1), 149–72.

34. Still, Richard R. (1981), 'Cross-Cultural Aspects of Sales Force Management', *Journal of Personal Selling and Sales Force Management*, 1 (2), 6–9.

35. Hofstede, Geert (1991), *Culture and Organizations: Software of the Mind*. Maidenhead, Berkshire: McGraw-Hill.

36. Hofstede, Geert (2001), *Culture Consequences* (2nd edn). Thousand Oaks, CA: Sage Publications.

37. Hall, Edward T. (1976), *Beyond Culture*. New York: Doubleday.

38. Kotabe, Masaaki, Alan J. Dubinsky, and Chae Un Lim (1992), 'Perceptions of Organizational Fairness: A Cross-National Perspective', *International Marketing Review*, 9 (2), 41–58.

39. Redding, S. Gordon (1982), 'Cultural Effects of the Marketing Process in Southeast Asia', *Journal of the Market Research Society*, 24 (2), 98–114.

40. Adler, Nancy J. (1991), *International Dimensions of Organizational Behavior* (2nd edn). Boston: PWS-Kent.

41. Hanna, Nessim and Tanuja Srivastava (1998), 'Modeling the Motivational Antecedents of the Japanese Sales Force: How Relevant Are Western Models', *Journal of Global Marketing*, 11 (4), 49–74.

42. Segalla, Michael, Dominique Rouzies, Madeleine Besson, and Barton A. Weitz (2006), 'A Cross-National Investigation of Incentive Sales Compensation', *International Journal of Research in Marketing*, 23 (4), 419–33.

43. Chonko, Lawrence B., Ben M. Enis, and John F. Tanner (1992), *Managing Sales People*. Boston, MA: Allyn and Bacon.

44. Anderson, Paul F. and Terry M. Chambers (1985), 'A Reward/Measurement Model of Organizational Buying Behavior', *Journal of Marketing*, 49 (Spring), 7–23.

45. Holt, Douglas, John Quelch, and Earl Taylor (2004), 'How Global Brands Compete', *Harvard Business Review*, 82 (9), 68–75.

46. Treece, James B. and Yuzo Yamaguchi (2004), 'Mitsubishi's Japan Sales Collapse in May', *Automotive News*, 78 (6098), 44.

47. Sethi, S. Prakash (1979), 'A Conceptual Framework for Environmental Analysis of Social Issues and Evaluation of Business Response Patterns', *The Academy of Management Review*, 4 (1) 63–74.

48. Péan, Pierre (1988), *L'argent Noir*. Paris: Librairie Arthème Fayard.

49. Walter, Ingo (1989), *Secret Money* (2nd edn). London: Unwin-Hyman.

50. Gillespie, Kate (1987), 'Middle East Response to the US Foreign Corrupt Practices Ave', *California Management Review*, 24 (4, Summer), 9–30.

51. Agpar, M. (1977), 'Succeeding in Saudi Arabia', *Harvard Business Review* (January/February), 14–33.

52. Werner, Cynthia (2000), 'Gifts, Bribes, and Development in Post-Soviet Kazakstan', *Human Organization*, 59 (1, Spring), 11–22.

53. Thompson, Courtenay (2002), 'Below the Surface', *Internal Auditor*, 67–9.

54. Daniels, John D., Ernest W. Ogram, and Lee H. Radebaugh (1982), *International Business: Environments and Operations* (3rd edn). Reading, MA: Addison-Wesley.

55. Vogl, Frank (1998), 'The Supply Side of Global Bribery', *Finance and Development*, 35 (2), 30–33.

56. Mayo, Michel A., Lawrence J. Marks, and John K. Ryans Jr (1991), 'Perceptions of Ethical Problems in International Marketing', *International Marketing Review*, 8 (3), 61–75.

57. Chan, T.S. and Robert W. Armstrong (1999), 'Comparative Ethical Report Card: A Study of Australian and Canadian Manager's Perception of International Marketing Ethics Problems', *Journal of Business Ethics*, 12, 3–15.

58. Chen, Yanjing, Mahmut Yaçar, and Roderick M. Rejesus (2008), 'Factors Influencing the Incidence of Bribery Payouts by Firms: A Cross-Country Analysis', *Journal of Business Ethics*, 77 (2), 231–44.

59. Galtung, Frederick (1994), *Korruption*. Lamuv Verlag: Göttingen.

60. Boland, Tom (1998), 'Street Vendors: Congo War on Kinshasa's Informal Sector Fwd', *CNN* (online), http://hpn.asu.edu/archives/Jun98/0081.html.

61. Ndao, Cheikh Alioune (1985), *Excellences, Vos Épouses!* Dakar: Les Nouvelles Editions Africaines.

62. Arnould, Eric J. (1995), 'West African Marketing Channels', in *Contemporary Marketing and Consumer Behavior*, John F. Sherry, Ed. Sage Publications: Thousand Oaks, CA.

63. CIPE (1998), 'Corruption in Bulgaria Threatens Social Stability', *Economic Reform Today* (2), 18.

64. Gallant, Katheryn (1997), 'The Art of Stealing', *Brazzil* (online).

65. Steidlmeier, P. (1999), 'Gift-Giving, Bribery and Corruption: Ethical Management of Business Relationships in China', *Journal of Business Ethics*, 20, 121–32.

66. Lewis, Eleanor Roberts (1998), 'The OECD Anti-Corruption Treaty: Why Is It Needed? How Will It Work?', *Economic Perspectives*, 3 (5), 6–9.

67. Cuervo-Cazurra, Alvaro (2008), 'The Effectiveness of Laws against Bribery Abroad', *Journal of International Business Studies*, 39 (4), 634–51.

68. Organisation for Economic Co-Operation and Development (OECD) (2006), *OECD Working Group on Bribery: Annual Report*.

69. Hamra, Wayne (2000), 'Bribery in International Business Transactions and the OECD Convention: Benefits and Limitations', *Business Economics* (October), 33–46.

70. Brademas, John and Fritz Heimann (1998), 'Tackling International Corruption: No Longer Taboo', *Foreign Affairs*, 77 (5), 17–22.

71. Habib, Mohsin and Leon Zurawicki (2002), 'Corruption and Foreign Direct Investment', *Journal of International Business Studies*, 33 (2), 291–307.

72. Transparency International (TI) (2007), *Transparency International Corruption Perceptions Index 2007*. www.transparency.org.

73. ABC News (2002), 'Acting Tough as Part of Anti-corruption Stand, China Executes Official'. Available at: http://abcnews.go.com/sections/world/DailyNews/chinaexecute000308.html.

74. Xinhua News Agency (2002), 'Top Banker Sentenced on Bribery Charges (China through a lens)'. Available at: www.china.org.cn/english/2002/Oct/45463.htm.

75. Lee, K.H. (1981), 'Ethical Beliefs in Marketing Management: A Cross-Cultural Study', *European Journal of Marketing*, 15 (1), 58–67.

76. Becker, Helmut and David H. Fritzsche (1987), 'A Comparison of the Ethical Behavior of American, French and German Managers', *Columbia Journal of World Business* (Winter), 87–95.

77. Berenbeim, Ronald E. (1997), 'Can Multinational Business Agree on How to Act Ethically?', *Business and Society Review*, 98, 24–8.

78. Graham, John L. (1983), 'Foreign Corrupt Practices Act: A Manager's Guide', *Columbia Journal of World Business*, 18 (3), 89–94.

79. Rawls, John (1971), *A Theory of Justice*. Cambridge, MA: Belknap Press of Harvard University.

80. Smith, Adam (1759), *The Theory of Moral Sentiments*. London: A. Millar.

81. Hill, John S., Arthur Allaway, W., Colin Egan, and Ünal O. Boya (1993), 'Perceptions of Foreign Field Sales Forces: An Exploratory Factor Analysis of Their Characteristics, Behaviors and Sales', in *Proceedings of the 6th World Marketing Congress*. Istanbul, 67–70.

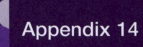

A14.1 Case

When international buyers and sellers disagree

No matter what line of business you're in, you can't escape sex. That may have been one conclusion drawn by an American exporter of meat products after a dispute with a German customer over a shipment of pork livers. Here's how the disagreement came about:

The American exporter was contracted to ship '30,000 lbs. of freshly frozen US pork livers, customary merchandisable quality, first rate brands'. As the shipment that was prepared met the exacting standards of the American market, the exporter expected the transaction to be completed without any problem. But when the livers arrived in Germany, the purchaser raised an objection: 'We ordered pork livers of customary merchantable quality – what you sent us consisted of 40 per cent sow livers.'

'Who cares about the sex of the pig the liver came from?' the exporter asked.

'We do', the German replied. 'Here in Germany we don't pass off spongy sow livers as the firmer livers of male pigs. This shipment wasn't merchantable at the price we expected to charge. The only way we were able to dispose of the meat without a total loss was to reduce the price. You owe us a price allowance of US$1000.'

The American refused to reduce the price. The determined resistance may have been partly in reaction to the implied insult to the taste of the American consumer: 'If pork livers, whatever the sex of the animal, are palatable to Americans, they ought to be good enough for anyone', the American thought.

It looked as if the buyer and seller could never agree on eating habits.

(Source: Dun and Bradstreet Corporation.)

Questions

1. What does 'customary merchandisable quality' mean? Where? In which language and cultural context?

2. Discuss how ethnocentrism and SRC (self-reference criterion) are at work in this case.

3. In this dispute, which country's law would apply, that of the United States or of Germany?

4. If the case were tried in US courts, who do you think would win? And if tried in German courts? Why?

5. Is formal litigation justified in such a case? How can one solve this problem? How can one avoid this type of conflict in the future?

A14.2 Case

Setco of Spain

Planning sales targets for the sales force is a universal practice. Nobody questions it. So it was when Mr Gonzales, a Spaniard, was recruited by Setco of Spain, the Spanish subsidiary of a large US multinational company. Soon after his job began, he was assigned a product line, of which he had some experience, in a new sales territory. The sales manager of Setco of Spain did not know precisely the market potential of this new area. Until then, potential customers in this area had never been regularly visited. Moreover few indicators were available in order to estimate the market potential of this new area in a quantified and precise manner.

When he first met the sales manager for Spain, Gonzales was amazed by his friendly tone; dialogue within the sales team and horizontal communication were the rule. Instead of being set an objective, he was invited to give his opinion on the matter. In fact, he could set his quarterly sales target himself, after visiting the area and making some preliminary contacts with prospects. Because of the newness of this area, the sales manager made no comment. Gonzales was confronted with a new freedom: in his previous positions as sales representative, he had never fixed his own sales targets by himself. He had always been given targets by his boss. His reaction was therefore to reduce significantly the objective relative to the sales he was reasonably expecting, in order to retain some leeway.

After four months, actual sales per area were released. Gonzales was used to this kind of report, since it provided basic data for computing possible bonuses. However, he was surprised to see that his actual sales figures were compared to target sales, and the difference between actual and target sales was explicitly presented. It looked flattering. The individual achievements of the other members of the sales team were mentioned in this memo as well. They did not match that of Gonzales.

At the meeting of the sales force, quarterly sales were examined, as well as the targets for the next quarter and the marketing programme. Gonzales was surprised to see how embarrassing his 'performance' appeared to the other sales representatives. Never had any sales representative at Setco of Spain so largely overshot the mark. He was teased by his colleagues, who made some bittersweet remarks and jokes. He felt bad about it, especially because he had been trying hard. He had used all his skills as a salesman, which were considerable and had been proved in his previous positions.

During the discussions, he acknowledged that his area's market potential had been largely underestimated. His sales target was therefore revised and increased by a large amount. This was done in full agreement with all the members (including him) of the sales team, who democratically discussed targets and achievements together during the quarterly sales meetings.

In the companies for which he had worked before, sales objectives were settled in a somewhat hierarchic way. The objectives were, fortunately, too high to be achieved. Being out of reach, the objectives worked as a sort of line of sight, an ideal level. It worked as a way of forcing lazy people to do more and of motivating the achievers to surpass themselves. Logically enough, actual sales were not carefully monitored, nor were individual achievements calculated by comparisons of target sales and actual sales.

At the end of the third quarter, Gonzales began to think that he had been set too high an objective. He had been working extremely hard for almost six months, pushed by enthusiasm for his new job. Moreover an unusually large order from a company in his sales area had swollen his first quarterly sales. This did not happen during the second and third quarters.

When the quarterly sales meeting took place, Gonzales once again appeared as the 'star' of the meeting: he had a record shortfall. No sales representative at Setco of Spain had ever experienced such a wide negative gap between target and actual sales. His colleagues made fun of him. They were slightly relieved to see him bite the dust. Some days later he received a personal memo from the marketing director, who made it clear that he had to adapt quickly or leave the company. 'You should know that in our company a salesman has to be able to settle his own objectives in a precise, realistic and dynamic way. Targets are the result of negotiations with the sales manager: they are based on market data. Individual sales targets are summed up, at every level in the corporation. They are the basis for the quarterly corporate sales figure forecast. The stocks of our company are registered on the New York Stock Exchange. Operators on the Stock Exchange are extremely sensitive to this kind of data. If every salesman in this company performed like you, our forecasts at the corporate level would be meaningless. Our headquarters simply cannot accept this.'

Question

What should Gonzales do?

 ## A14.3 Case

Union Carbide at Bhopal

In the 1970s, Union Carbide Corporation (UCC), one of America's largest chemical multinationals, had established production facilities in India. Its Indian subsidiary, Union Carbide India Limited (UCIL), under pressure from the Indian authorities, had built a new factory in 1978 to produce pesticides in Bhopal, the capital of Madhya Pradesh, a town situated 375 miles (600 km) south of New Delhi. It produced Sevin, a pesticide composed primarily of methyl isocyanate, extremely dangerous for humans and to be carefully kept in liquid form below 25 degrees Celsius. The project was plagued by problems of safety from the outset: in 1978, its year of construction, a huge fire broke out. Five major gas leaks in 1981 and 1983 left one dead and 47 injured. In 1982, a detailed inspection by American experts uncovered 10 serious faults in the factory's safety systems. In fact, the factory's alarm system was ringing so often that people living in the vicinity of the factory treated it almost as background noise.

The Indian government imposed restrictions on foreign companies, limiting their direct participation by requiring that they negotiate local partnerships. UCC was able to continue operating in India only by agreeing to the formation of a new company, Union Carbide India Limited (UCIL), in which UCC was reduced to a majority shareholder with 50.09 per cent of the share capital. A further 22 per cent went to the government and the remainder was divided amongst 23,500 private Indian investors. Bhopal's social and political environment developed rapidly as a result of the factory. Attracted by the availability of work and the water and electricity which were supplied to the site at reduced rates, people poured in to the surrounding area. As a consequence, the population grew from 385,000 in 1971 to 671,000 in 1981. By 1984, it stood at nearly 800,000. From its original position of isolation, the factory was soon totally enveloped by the town's growth. Creaking under the strain of this huge influx of population, the town struggled to accommodate everyone. In the absence of a better alternative, the poorest of the new arrivals congregated in 'Khasi Camp', a shanty town situated between the centre of Bhopal and the factory.

Links between UCIL and the local Indian political establishment were mutually rewarding in many ways. The factory's legal adviser, for instance, was a former local head of Indira Gandhi's Congress Party. The former local police chief magically won the contract to guard the factory. One of the nephews of the former state education minister was the head of public relations at the factory.

There were also financial difficulties. In 1982, a slump in sales of its products resulted in the factory suffering a dramatic reduction in profitability. UCC, the parent company of UCIL, even considered shutting the plant down completely, but the Indian government refused to countenance such a possibility for fear of frightening away potential foreign investors. To balance the books, UCIL determined to reduce the factory's overheads. They chose to make many of their most qualified personnel redundant. These vacant posts were then either filled by less experienced personnel or simply scrapped. The consequent loss of morale and expertise amongst the workforce adversely affected work at the factory. News of these unfortunate mishaps was carefully suppressed thanks to the close working relationship between UCIL and the local authorities. The Indian authorities even extended UCIL's operating licence for a further seven years despite objections from the press and opposition members in the state parliament.

The incident took place in the night of 2 December 1984. Water in substantial quantities was mixed by error with methylisocyanate, causing high pressure, the explosion of the vessel and massive leaks of lethal gas in the surroundings of the factory. The local population had no idea of what to do in the event of a serious incident at the factory: simply putting a wet cloth on the face would have protected a great many people. Even the local doctors were completely ignorant about the effects of the product being manufactured on their doorsteps. Warren Anderson, the chief executive officer of UCC, courageously decided to go to India.

Following the disaster, the state government of Madhya Pradesh carefully drew up an initial list of the human cost of this night of horror. The toll was a heavy one: they estimated that 3828 people had been killed and 358,712 injured. Of these, 22,955 were left with a permanent disability. A single night of tragedy in Bhopal had claimed 362,540 victims. Ten years later, the government believed that about 6600 people were killed in the incident. Bhopal pressure groups put the death toll at 16,000 and still rising by a few each week. They claimed that up to 600,000 people – more than half the city – suffered damage to their lungs, eyes and immune systems.

On 4 December 1984, Warren Anderson flew to Bhopal with a team of experts to try and discover the cause of the tragedy. His efforts were in vain. Anderson was arrested and imprisoned, then finally expelled. It was not until 20 December that the Indian authorities allowed a commission of inquiry to begin its work on site. They arrived to find that the factory had been closed since 6 December and was already being dismantled.

Public relations in such a context were extremely difficult to organize since most 'hard facts' arguments might have seemed insults to the Indian management, public authorities, doctors or even to the general Indian public. The solution was found in complex litigation: each party argued that the case should be heard in the jurisdiction of the other. Finally, UCC came out with the favourable decision that the final judgements be made in India where relevant jurisprudence was almost non-existent. On 14 February 1989, the Indian Supreme Court rendered its judgement: the American defendants were found liable and ordered to pay a total of US$470 million, US$50 million was to be paid in rupees by UCIL and US$415 million by UCC; the remaining US$5 million had been paid under the previous order of the American Federal Court as first aid to the victims. Many people found that the final award was rather low. For example, if this sum represented only those killed in the incident, it would be roughly equivalent to US$130,000 per victim. If it included those permanently disabled, the amount would represent only US$18,000 per person and if it was intended to compensate every injured person, it would represent an average of US$1350 per person.

Its reputation heavily tarnished by the Bhopal affair, UCC realized in 1986 that a great deal of time and effort would be needed to regain lost confidence. During a speech delivered to the Davos Economic Forum on 5 February 1991, the new Chief Executive Officer of UCC, Robert Kennedy, affirmed 'Care for the planet has become a critical business issue – central to our jobs as senior managers'. UCC prioritized respect for the environment and safety concerns and established a health, safety and environment committee staffed by independent outsiders and an executive vice-president was given specific responsibility for environmental issues. The global performance of UCC in tackling pollution and improving safety and respect for the environment is regularly checked by independent experts. The company now has drawn up a strategic environmental plan with specific verifiable goals.

Questions

1. What are the problems involved in facing social responsibility in a culturally alien context?

2. Was Warren Anderson's trip to Bhopal a 'good' decision? Why? On the basis of which behavioural standards, home or host country's, should a company react?

3. How would you describe Union Carbide's corporate responsibility in the Bhophal case?

 **A14.4 Case**

The *Brenzy nouveau* has arrived!

Legritte Company was founded just after the Second World War by a skilful engineer, Monsieur Legritte. Aided by the reconstruction boom which was followed by the rapid economic growth of the 1960s, the Legritte Company developed more by improving the quality of its products than by investing money in marketing and sales. The intrinsic quality of the products, namely electrical connections for industrial use, has been the strong point of the business from the very beginning.

The company is located near Lyons (France) and employs about 200 people, with an annual turnover of 80 million francs. Two years ago Legritte was taken over by a US-based multinational company, Brenzy. Monsieur Legritte, drawing near to retirement age and with no qualified successor, sold his property to the Brenzy Corporation, which now owns the full 100 per cent. Brenzy has progressively introduced more up-to-date management methods in this traditional family business. Inventory management, cost accounting and delivery systems have all been changed to fit with Brenzy's procedures.

Sales promotion in France, and Europe generally, is based on nicely printed catalogues, technical instructions and directions for use. Unit prices reduce according to the size of orders. Products are promoted through small gifts given to the purchasers. Thus the launch of a new pre-insulated line of products, recently certified by EDF (Electricité de France, the public utility for electricity), came with a free gift (electrical pliers) for any order higher than 10,000 francs. This offer was open for six months. In order to receive the gift, the buyer simply had to fill in the gift voucher and enclose it with the order, provided the amount was sufficient.

Brenzy-Legritte was a newcomer to advertising. Being a fairly traditional medium-sized industrial company, it had not up to now invested a lot of money in advertisements. When it decided for the first time to advertise its products it did so by promoting them along with what it called '*le Brenzy nouveau*', with a play on words between Brenzy and Beaujolais, a freshly harvested red wine and a fashionable drink.

An advertisement in a specialist journal showed a bottle of Beaujolais nouveau, with the following slogan above the image: 'The Brenzy nouveau has arrived!' Text in bold characters at the bottom stated: 'You are thirsty and craving a new line of effective products! Brenzy-Legritte is happy to join you in ordering Beaujolais nouveau!' It was indicated that a minimum order of €500 entitled buyers to receive three free bottles and a minimum order of €800 entitled them to receive six free bottles. The expiry date for this offer was stipulated. The new line of Brenzy-Legritte products was shown on the label of the bottle of Beaujolais.

EDF, which is a large customer of Brenzy-Legritte, was not very happy about this humorous advertisement. It seems that EDF experienced problems amongst its personnel when the boxes of Beaujolais arrived at its offices.

Brenzy-Legritte is now undergoing drastic changes in its organization. Computers have been linked to the European headquarters in Brussels. Strictly defined management procedures have been imposed by headquarters. Brenzy has issued a professional code of conduct, the implementation of which is compulsory for the French subsidiary as well as for all the other subsidiaries around the world. It is a complete code of business ethics, comprising precise and detailed prescriptions. Below are some extracts.

Suffice it to say that this code of conduct is perceived by most people at Brenzy-Legritte, especially the salespeople, as largely inappropriate to the French context and a mere interference in their business. They prefer to disregard it.

Excerpts from the code of conduct at Brenzy-Legritte

Correct use of company funds

1. Company funds will not be used in order to make payments, or concealed loans, with the purpose of dishonestly influencing a supplier, a client or a civil servant. This prohibition applies not only to direct use of company money, but also to any kind of indirect payments, by the means of consultants/intermediaries, or by reimbursing to employees, payments made by them.
2. No payment shall be made, for and in the name of the company or one of its subsidiaries, with the intent or knowledge that part of such a payment will serve other purposes than those described in the documents related to this payment.

Gifts, favours and entertainment

Small gifts of symbolic value, minor favours and modest receptions may be offered at the company's expense only when they meet all of the following conditions:

1. They must be compatible with the rules of the company and current business practices.
2. Their monetary worth must be limited; they must be presented in such a form as not to appear as a bribe or remuneration; they must not give rise to suspicions about the impartiality of the beneficiary.
3. They must be approved by the general manager of the subsidiary or by a vice-president at Brenzy Corporation; they must be compatible with the instructions previously approved by the direct superior, the managing director and a senior vice-president at Brenzy Corporation.

Gifts and entertainment for civil servants

As indicated above, gifts, other than symbolic ones or gifts of a very modest value, whatever their nature, or a sumptuous reception, whatever its motives, are not allowed.

Issues related to these procedures and their violations

1. Any employees who want to ask questions about this code and its implementation shall discuss it with the head of the department. If it entails legal or accounting matters, they shall refer to qualified personnel from the legal services and the accounting department, who shall be consulted.

2. The discovery of a case which is fraudulent, illegal, or which violates the rules of the company shall immediately be reported to the legal counsellor. If such cases are identified which implicate senior executives in the corporation, this case shall be reported to the executive vice-president for examination by the chairman of the board, the chief executive officer, and the chairman of the audit committee.

3. No derogation to this procedure will be accepted in these matters. There will probably be some 'business opportunities' in the future, when it would be necessary to make questionable payments in order to succeed against a competitor, for one reason or another. The duty of the employee, in this case, is to reject such 'opportunities'.

4. Any infringement of the above-mentioned principles will result in disciplinary sanctions, including dismissal, a suing of the employee and a detailed report to competent regulatory authorities.

5. Moreover, disciplinary sanctions will be directed against any executive who initiates or approves such actions, or knows about them, or may have known about them, and did not quickly act to rectify them in accordance with this code. Adequate disciplinary sanctions will also be directed against any executives who neglect their hierarchical responsibilities, by not ensuring that their subordinates have been properly informed about the rules established in this code.

Questions

1. Analyse cross-cultural differences in the perception of ethical behaviour as concerns sales promotion activities. Why is this code of conduct perceived by most people at Brenzy-Legritte as largely inappropriate?

2. Why was the American company legally obliged to introduce such a code of conduct in its subsidiary?

3. Analyse the border between gifts and bribes. How can they be clearly differentiated?

Author index

Subject index